Trademark Acknowledgments

All terms mentioned in this book that are known to be trademarks or service marks have been appropriately capitalized. Cisco Press or Cisco Systems, Inc., cannot attest to the accuracy of this information. Use of a term in this book should not be regarded as affecting the validity of any trademark or service mark.

Publisher: John Wait

Editor-in-Chief: John Kane

Executive Editor: Brett Bartow

Senior Development Editor: Christopher Cleveland

Copy Editor: Carlisle Communications

Editorial Assistant: Raina Han

Composition: Mark Shirar

Cisco Representative: Anthony Wolfenden

Cisco Press Program Manager: Jeff Brady

Production Manager: Patrick Kanouse

Senior Project Editor: San Dee Phillips

Technical Editors: David Chapman Jr., Kevin Hofstra, and Bill Thomas

Book and Cover Designer: Louisa Adair

Indexer: Eric Schroeder

CISCO SYSTEMS

Corporate Headquarters
Cisco Systems, Inc.
170 West Tasman Drive
San Jose, CA 95134-1706
USA
www.cisco.com
Tel: 408 526-4000
     800 553-NETS (6387)
Fax: 408 526-4100

European Headquarters
Cisco Systems International BV
Haarlerbergpark
Haarlerbergweg 13-19
1101 CH Amsterdam
The Netherlands
www-europe.cisco.com
Tel: 31 0 20 357 1000
Fax: 31 0 20 357 1100

Americas Headquarters
Cisco Systems, Inc.
170 West Tasman Drive
San Jose, CA 95134-1706
USA
www.cisco.com
Tel: 408 526-7660
Fax: 408 527-0883

Asia Pacific Headquarters
Cisco Systems, Inc.
Capital Tower
168 Robinson Road
#22-01 to #29-01
Singapore 068912
www.cisco.com
Tel: +65 6317 7777
Fax: +65 6317 7799

Cisco Systems has more than 200 offices in the following countries and regions. Addresses, phone numbers, and fax numbers are listed on the
Cisco.com Web site at www.cisco.com/go/offices.

Argentina • Australia • Austria • Belgium • Brazil • Bulgaria • Canada • Chile • China PRC • Colombia • Costa Rica • Croatia • Czech Republic Denmark • Dubai, UAE • Finland • France • Germany • Greece • Hong Kong SAR • Hungary • India • Indonesia • Ireland • Israel • Italy Japan • Korea • Luxembourg • Malaysia • Mexico • The Netherlands • New Zealand • Norway • Peru • Philippines • Poland • Portugal Puerto Rico • Romania • Russia • Saudi Arabia • Scotland • Singapore • Slovakia • Slovenia • South Africa • Spain • Sweden Switzerland • Taiwan • Thailand • Turkey • Ukraine • United Kingdom • United States • Venezuela • Vietnam • Zimbabwe

About the Authors

Michael Gibbs is the vice president of Consulting for Security Evolutions, Inc. (SEI), where he is responsible for the overall technical management of SEI's Cisco-centric IT security consulting services. Mr. Gibbs has more than 10 years of hands-on experience with Cisco Systems routers, switches, firewalls, IDSs, and other CPE equipment and IOS Software versions. He has been involved in IP network design, IP network engineering, and IT security engineering for large service provider backbone networks and broadband infrastructures. Mr. Gibbs is proficient in designing, implementing, and operating backbone IP and VoIP networks, implementing network operation centers, and designing and configuring server farms. Mr. Gibbs is also the author of multiple patents on IP data exchanges and QoS systems.

As SEI's technical leader for Cisco-centric IP network engineering and IT security consulting services, Mr. Gibbs provided technical program management, as well as technical support, for clients who utilize Cisco Systems CPE devices at the network ingress/egress. His hands-on, real-world experience designing and implementing Cisco-centric security countermeasures provided valuable experience in the authoring of this book.

Greg Bastien, CCNP, CCSP, CISSP, is the chief technical officer for Virtue Technologies, Inc. He provides consulting services to various federal agencies and commercial clients and holds a position as adjunct professor at Strayer University, teaching networking and network security classes. He completed his undergraduate and graduate degrees at Embry-Riddle Aeronautical University while on active duty as a helicopter flight instructor in the U.S. Army.

Earl Carter has been working in the field of computer security for approximately 11 years. He started learning about computer security while working at the Air Force Information Warfare Center. Earl's primary responsibility was securing Air Force networks against cyber attacks. In 1998, he accepted a job with Cisco to perform IDS research for NetRanger (currently Cisco IPS) and NetSonar (Cisco Secure Scanner). Currently, he is a member of the Security Technologies Assessment Team (STAT) that is part of Consulting Engineering (CE). His duties involve performing security evaluations on numerous Cisco products and consulting with other teams within Cisco to help enhance the security of Cisco products. He has examined various products from the PIX Firewall to the Cisco CallManager. Presently, Earl is working on earning his CCIE certification with a security emphasis. In his spare time, Earl is very active at church as a youth minister and lector. He also enjoys training in Taekwondo where he is currently a third-degree black belt and working on becoming a certified American Taekowndo Association (ATA) instructor.

Christian Abera Degu, CCNP, CCSP, CISSP, works as a senior network engineer for General Dynamics Network Systems Signal solutions, as consultant to the U.S. Federal Energy Regulatory commission. He holds a master's degree in computer information systems. Christian resides in Alexandria, Virginia.

About the Technical Reviewers

David W. Chapman Jr. CISSP-ISSAP, CCNP, CCDP, CSSP, is president and principal consultant for SecureNet Consulting, LLC, an information security consulting firm in Fort Worth, Texas, specializing in vulnerability assessments, penetration testing, and the design and implementation of secure network infrastructures. Mr. Chapman divides his time between teaching Cisco security courses and writing about network security issues. He is a senior member of the IEEE.

Kevin Hofstra, CCIE No. 14619, CCNP, CCDP, CCSP, CCVP, is a network optimization engineer within the Air Force Communications Agency of the U.S. Department of Defense. Mr. Hofstra has a computer science degree from Yale University and a master's of engineering in telecommunications from the University of Colorado.

Bill Thomas, CISSP, CCIE, CCSP, is a consulting engineer for Cisco Systems, within the Advanced Technology organization. Mr. Thomas currently focuses on design and implementation of security solutions for large, corporate customers of Cisco. He is a frequent public speaker in forums such as ISC2 and ISSA.

Dedication

This book is dedicated to Mustang Sallie.

Acknowledgments

I'd like thank David Kim and the SEI team for the opportunity to write this book.

Thanks to David Chapman, Kevin Hofstra, and Bill Thomas for keeping me straight when it came to deciphering the labyrinth of technical specifics.

A big thank you goes out to the production team for this book. Brett Bartow, Christopher Cleveland, and San Dee Phillips have been a pleasure to work with and incredibly professional. I couldn't have asked for a finer team.

Finally, I would like to thank my wife for putting up with me throughout the creation of this book. No woman is more understanding.

This Book Is Safari Enabled

The Safari® Enabled icon on the cover of your favorite technology book means the book is available through Safari Bookshelf. When you buy this book, you get free access to the online edition for 45 days.

Safari Bookshelf is an electronic reference library that lets you easily search thousands of technical books, find code samples, download chapters, and access technical information whenever and wherever you need it.

To gain 45-day Safari Enabled access to this book:

- Go to http://www.ciscopress.com/safarienabled
- Complete the brief registration form
- Enter the coupon code B7JC-2UFK-D1N1-LDK3-MKQ2

If you have difficulty registering on Safari Bookshelf or accessing the online edition, please e-mail customer-service@safaribooksonline.com.

Contents at a Glance

Contents

Icons Used in This Book

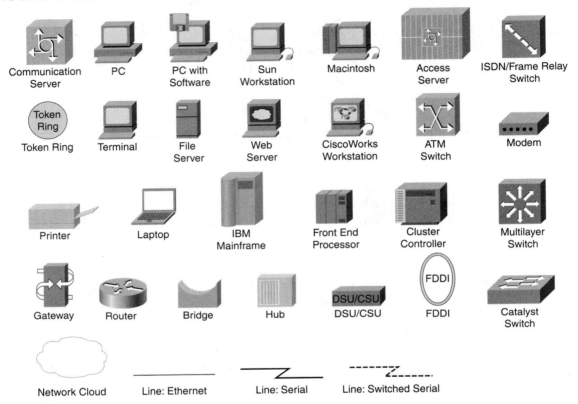

Command Syntax Conventions

The conventions used to present command syntax in this book are the same conventions used in the IOS Command Reference. The Command Reference describes these conventions as follows:

- **Boldface** indicates commands and keywords that are entered literally as shown. In actual configuration examples and output (not general command syntax), boldface indicates commands that are manually input by the user (such as a **show** command).
- *Italic* indicates arguments for which you supply actual values.
- Vertical bars (|) separate alternative, mutually exclusive elements.
- Square brackets [ ] indicate optional elements.
- Braces { } indicate a required choice.
- Braces within brackets [{ }] indicate a required choice within an optional element.

Foreword

CCSP SNPA Exam Certification Guide, Third Edition, is an excellent self-study resource for the CCSP SNPA exam. Passing the exam validates the knowledge and ability to configure, operate, and manage Cisco PIX 500 Series Security Appliances and Cisco ASA 5500 Series Adaptive Security Appliances. It is one of several exams required to attain the CCSP certification.

Cisco Press Exam Certification Guide titles are designed to help educate, develop, and grow the community of Cisco networking professionals. The guides are filled with helpful features that allow you to master key concepts and assess your readiness for the certification exam. Developed in conjunction with the Cisco certifications team, Cisco Press books are the only self-study books authorized by Cisco Systems.

Most networking professionals use a variety of learning methods to gain necessary skills. Cisco Press self-study titles are a prime source of content for some individuals, and they can also serve as an excellent supplement to other forms of learning. Training classes, whether delivered in a classroom or on the Internet, are a great way to quickly acquire new understanding. Hands-on practice is essential for anyone seeking to build, or hone, new skills. Authorized Cisco training classes, labs, and simulations are available exclusively from Cisco Learning Solutions Partners worldwide. Please visit http://www.cisco.com/go/training to learn more about Cisco Learning Solutions Partners.

I hope and expect that you'll find this guide to be an essential part of your exam preparation and a valuable addition to your personal library.

Don Field
Director, Certifications
Cisco System, Inc.
March 2006

Introduction

This book was created as a tool to assist you in preparing for the Cisco Securing Networks with PIX and ASA Certification Exam (SNPA 642-522).

Why the "Third Edition?"

Network security is *very* dynamic. New vulnerabilities are identified every day, and new technologies and products are released into the marketplace at nearly the same rate. The first edition of the *CCSP Cisco Secure PIX Firewall Advanced Exam Certification Guide* was on the shelves for approximately four months when Cisco Systems, Inc., completed the production release of PIX version 6.3(1) and, consequently, updated the certification exam to reflect the additional features available in the new release. The second edition was a rewrite to include the new additions and updates to the certification exam. With the creation of a new Security Appliance series, and release of Secure Firewall software version 7.0, the certification exam became obsolete. Cisco updated the certification exam to reflect the new operating system features and Security Appliances. This book is written to Secure Firewall software version 7.0(2), and we do not anticipate any major revisions to the Security Appliance operating system (OS) in the near future.

Who Should Read This Book?

Network security is a complex business. The PIX Firewall and ASA family of devices perform some very specific functions as part of the security process. It is very important that you be familiar with many networking and network security concepts before you undertake the SNPA certification. This book is designed for security professionals or networking professionals who are interested in beginning the security certification process.

How to Use This Book

The book consists of 20 chapters. Each chapter builds upon the chapter that precedes it. The chapters that cover specific commands and configurations include case studies or practice configurations. Chapter 20 includes additional case studies and configuration examples that might or might not work—it is up to you to determine if the configurations fulfill the requirement and why.

This book was written as a guide to help you prepare for the SNPA certification exam. It is a tool—not the entire toolbox. That is to say, you must use this book with other references (specifically Cisco TAC) to help you prepare for the exam. Remember that successfully completing the exam makes a great short-term goal. Being very proficient at what you do should always be your ultimate goal.

The chapters of this book cover the following topics:

- **Chapter 1, "Network Security"**—Chapter 1 provides an overview of network security, including the process and potential threats, and discusses how network security has become increasingly more important to business as companies become more intertwined and their network perimeters continue to fade. Chapter 1 discusses the network security policy and two Cisco programs that can assist companies with the design and implementation of sound security policies, processes, and architecture.

- **Chapter 2, "Firewall Technologies and the Cisco Security Appliance"**—Chapter 2 covers the different firewall technologies and the Cisco Security Appliance. It examines the design of the Security Appliance and discusses some security advantages of that design.

- **Chapter 3, "Cisco Security Appliance"**—Chapter 3 deals with the design of the Security Appliance in greater detail. This chapter lists the different models of the Security Appliance and their intended applications. It discusses the various features available with each model and how each model should be implemented.

- **Chapter 4, "System Management/Maintenance"**—Chapter 4 covers the installation and configuration of the Security Appliance IOS. This chapter covers the different configuration options that allow for remote management of the Security Appliance.

- **Chapter 5, "Understanding Cisco Security Appliance Translation and Connection"**—This chapter covers the different transport protocols and how they are handled by the Security Appliance. It also discusses network addressing and how the Security Appliance can alter node or network addresses to secure those elements.

- **Chapter 6, "Getting Started with the Cisco Security Appliance Family of Firewalls"**—This chapter is the meat of the Security Appliance: basic commands required to get the Security Appliance operational. It discusses the methods for connecting to the Security Appliance and some of the many configuration options available with the Security Appliance.

- **Chapter 7, "Configuring Access"**—Chapter 7 introduces the different configurations that enable you to control access to your network(s) using the Security Appliance. It also covers some of the specific configurations required to allow certain protocols to pass through the firewall.

- **Chapter 8, "Modular Policy Framework"**—Chapter 8 explains a new method of subdividing map-based policies to allow a more granular control over access to PIX-protected networks and systems.

- **Chapter 9, "Secure Contexts"**—Chapter 9 introduces the creation of virtual firewalls using separate security contexts. It also explains the benefits of multiple separate firewalls versus a single universal firewall.

- **Chapter 10, "Syslog and the Cisco Security Appliance"**—Chapter 10 covers the logging functions of the Security Appliance and the configuration required to allow the Security Appliance to log to a syslog server.

- **Chapter 11, "Routing and the Cisco Security Appliance"**—Chapter 11 discusses routing with the Security Appliance, the routing protocols supported by the Security Appliance, and how to implement them.

- **Chapter 12, "Cisco Security Appliance Failover"**—Chapter 12 details the advantages of a redundant firewall configuration and the steps required to configure two Security Appliances in the failover mode.

- **Chapter 13, "Virtual Private Networks"**—Many businesses have multiple locations that must be interconnected. Chapter 13 explains the different types of secure connections of virtual private networks (VPN) that can be configured between the Security Appliance and other VPN endpoints. It covers the technologies and protocols used for creating and maintaining VPNs across public networks.

- **Chapter 14, "Configuring Access VPNs"**—Chapter 14 discusses how the Security Appliance is used for creating remote-access VPNs.

- **Chapter 15, "Adaptive Security Device Manager"**—The PIX Firewall can now be managed using a variety of different tools. The Adaptive Security Device Manager is a web-based graphical user interface (GUI) that can be used to manage the Security Appliance.

- **Chapter 16, "Content Filtering on the Cisco Security Appliance"**—It is a common practice for hackers to embed attacks into the content of a web page. Certain types of program code are especially conducive to this type of attack because of their interactive nature. Chapter 16 discusses these types of code and identifies their dangers.

- **Chapter 17, "Overview of AAA and the Cisco Security Appliance"**—It is extremely important to ensure that only authorized users are accessing your network. Chapter 17 discusses the different methods for configuring the Security Appliance to interact with authentication, authorization, and accounting (AAA) services. This chapter also introduces the Cisco Secure Access Control Server (Cisco Secure ACS), which is the Cisco AAA server package.

- **Chapter 18, "Configuration of AAA on the Cisco Security Appliance"**—Chapter 18 discusses the specific configuration on the Security Appliance for communication with the AAA server, including the Cisco Secure ACS. It covers the implementation, functionality, and troubleshooting of AAA on the PIX Firewall.

- **Chapter 19, "IPS and Advanced Protocol Handling"**—Many different attacks can be launched against a network and its perimeter security devices. Chapter 19 explains some of the most common attacks and how the Security Appliance can be configured to repel such an attack.

- **Chapter 20, "Case Study and Sample Configuration"**—This chapter consists of two case studies that enable you to practice configuring the firewall to perform specific functions. One section includes configurations that may or may not work. You will be asked to determine if the configuration will work correctly and why or why not. The certification exam asks specific questions about configuration of the Security Appliance. It is very important to become intimately familiar with the different commands and components of the Security Appliance configuration.

Each chapter follows the same format and incorporates the following tools to assist you by assessing your current knowledge and emphasizing specific areas of interest within the chapter:

- **"Do I Know This Already?" Quiz**—Each chapter begins with a quiz to help you assess your current knowledge of the subject. The quiz is broken down into specific areas of emphasis that allow you to best determine where to focus your efforts when working through the chapter.

- **Foundation Topics**—The foundation topics are the core sections of each chapter. They focus on the specific protocol, concept, or skills you must master to prepare successfully for the examination.

- **Foundation Summary**—Near the end of each chapter, the foundation topics are summarized into important highlights from the chapter. In many cases, the foundation summaries are broken into charts, but in some cases the important portions from each chapter are simply restated to emphasize their importance within the subject matter. Remember that the foundation portions are in the book to assist you with your exam preparation. It is very unlikely that you will be able to complete the certification exam successfully by studying just the foundation topics and foundation summaries, although they are good tools for last-minute preparation just before taking the exam.

- **Q&A**—Each chapter ends with a series of review questions to test your understanding of the material covered. These questions are a great way not only to ensure that you understand the material but also to exercise your ability to recall facts.

- **Case Studies/Scenarios**—The chapters that deal more with configuration of the Security Appliance have brief scenarios included. These scenarios are there to help you understand the different configuration options and how each component can affect another component within the configuration of the firewall. The final chapter of this book is dedicated to case studies/scenarios.

- **CD-Based Practice Exam**—On the CD included with this book, you will find a practice test with more than 200 questions that cover the information central to the SNPA exam. With the customizable testing engine, you can take a sample exam that focuses on particular topic areas or randomizes the questions. Each test question includes a link that points to a related section in an electronic Portable Document Format (PDF) copy of the book, also included on the CD.

Figure I-1 depicts the best way to navigate through the book. If you feel that you already have a sufficient understanding of the subject matter in a chapter, you should test yourself with the "Do I Know This Already?" quiz. Based on your score, you should determine whether to complete the entire chapter or to move on to the "Foundation Summary" and "Q&A" sections. It is always recommended that you go through the entire book rather than skip around. It is not possible to know too much about a topic. Only you will know how well you really understand each topic—until you take the exam, and then it might be too late.

Figure I-1 *Completing the Chapter Material*

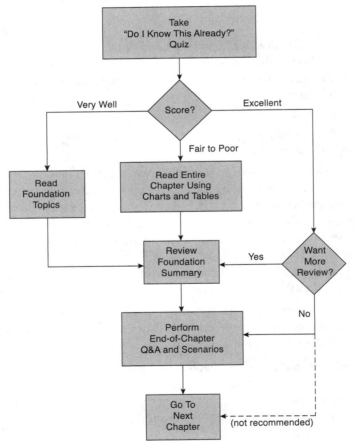

Certification Exam and This Preparation Guide

The questions for each certification exam are a closely guarded secret. The truth is that if you had the questions and could only pass the exam, you would be in for quite an embarrassing experience as soon as you arrived at your first job that required Security Appliance skills. The point is to know the material, not just to pass the exam successfully. We *do* know what topics you must know to complete this exam. These are, of course, the same topics required for you to be proficient with the Security Appliance. We have broken down these topics into foundation topics and have covered each topic in the book. Table I-1 lists each foundation topic and provides a brief description of each.

Table I-1 *SNPA Foundation Topics and Descriptions*

SNPA Exam Topic Area	Related Topic	Where It's Covered in the Book
Install and configure a Security Appliance for basic network connectivity.	Describe the Security Appliance hardware and software architecture.	Chapters 2 and 3
	Determine the Security Appliance hardware and software configuration and verify if it is correct.	Chapter 4
	Use setup or the CLI to configure basic network settings, including interface configurations.	Chapter 6
	Use appropriate **show** commands to verify initial configurations	Chapter 4
	Configure NAT and global addressing to meet user requirements.	Chapters 5 and 6
	Configure DHCP client option.	Chapter 6
	Set default route.	Chapters 6 and 11
	Configure logging options.	Chapter 10
	Describe the firewall technology.	Chapters 2 and 3
	Explain the information contained in syslog files.	Chapter 10
	Configure static address translations.	Chapters 5, 6, and 7
	Configure Network Address Translations: PAT.	Chapters 5, 6, and 7
	Configure static port redirection.	Chapter 5 and 7
	Configure a net static.	Chapter 5, 6, and 11
	Set embryonic and connection limits on the Security Appliance.	Chapter 7
	Verify NAT operation.	Chapter 6

continues

Table I-1 *SNPA Foundation Topics and Descriptions (Continued)*

SNPA Exam Topic Area	Related Topic	Where It's Covered in the Book
Configure a Security Appliance to restrict inbound traffic from untrusted sources.	Configure access lists to filter traffic based on address, time, and protocols.	Chapter 7
	Configure object-groups to optimize access-list processing.	Chapter 7
	Configure Network Address Translations: NAT0.	Chapters 5 and 7
	Configure Network Address Translations: Policy NAT.	Chapter 5 and 7
	Configure Java/ActiveX filtering.	Chapter 19
	Configure URL filtering.	Chapter 19
	Verify inbound traffic restrictions.	Chapters 7 and 19
Configure a Security Appliance to provide secure connectivity using site-to-site VPNs.	Explain certificates, certificate authorities, and how they are used.	Chapter 13
	Explain the basic functionality of IPSec.	Chapter 13
	Configure IKE with preshared keys.	Chapter 13
	Configure IKE to use certificates.	Chapter 13
	Differentiate the types of encryption.	Chapter 13
	Configure IPSec parameters.	Chapter 13
	Configure crypto-maps and ACLs.	Chapters 7 and 13
Configure a Security Appliance to provide secure connectivity using remote access VPNs.	Explain the functions of EasyVPN.	Chapter 14
	Configure IPSec using EasyVPN Server/ Client.	Chapter 14
	Configure the Cisco Secure VPN client.	Chapters 13 and 14
	Explain the purpose of WebVPN.	Chapter 13
	Configure WebVPN services: server/client.	Chapter 13
	Verify VPN operations.	Chapters 13 and 14

Table I-1 *SNPA Foundation Topics and Descriptions (Continued)*

SNPA Exam Topic Area	Related Topic	Where It's Covered in the Book
Configure transparent firewall, virtual firewall, and high availability firewall features on a Security Appliance.	Explain the differences between the L2 and L3 operating modes.	Chapters 3 and 6
	Configure the Security Appliance for transparent mode (L2).	Chapter 6
	Explain the purpose of virtual firewalls.	Chapters 3 and 9
	Configure the Security Appliance to support a virtual firewall.	Chapter 9
	Monitor and maintain a virtual firewall.	Chapter 9
	Explain the types, purpose, and operation of failover.	Chapters 3 and 12
	Install appropriate topology to support cable-based or LAN-based failover.	Chapter 12
	Explain the hardware, software, and licensing requirements for high-availability.	Chapter 12
	Configure the Security Appliance for active/standby failover.	Chapter 12
	Configure the Security Appliance for stateful failover.	Chapter 12
	Configure the Security Appliance for active-active failover.	Chapter 12
	Verify failover operation.	Chapter 12
	Recover from a failover.	Chapter 12
Configure AAA services for access through a Security Appliance.	Configure ACS for Security Appliance support.	Chapters 15 and 16
	Configure Security Appliance to use AAA feature.	Chapter 16
	Configure authentication using both local and external databases.	Chapters 15 and 16
	Configure authorization using an external database.	Chapter 16
	Configure the ACS server for downloadable ACLs.	Chapters 6 and 16
	Configure accounting of connection start/stop.	Chapters 15 and 16
	Verify AAA operation.	Chapters 15 and 16

continues

Table I-1 *SNPA Foundation Topics and Descriptions (Continued)*

SNPA Exam Topic Area	Related Topic	Where It's Covered in the Book
Configure routing and switching on a Security Appliance.	Enable DHCP server and relay functionality.	Chapters 6, 7, and 15
	Configure VLANs on a Security Appliance interface.	Chapters 6, 11, and 15
	Configure routing functionality of Security Appliance, including OSPF and RIP.	Chapters 11 and 15
	Configure Security Appliance to pass multicast traffic.	Chapters 7 and 11
	Configure ICMP on the Security Appliance.	Chapters 7 and 19
Configure a modular policy on a Security Appliance.	Configure a class map.	Chapter 8
	Configure a policy map.	Chapter 8
	Configure a service policy.	Chapter 8
	Configure an FTP map.	Chapters 7, 8 and 19
	Configure an HTTP map.	Chapters 7, 8 and 19
	Configure an inspection protocol.	Chapters 7 and 19
	Explain the function of protocol inspection.	Chapters 3, 7, and 19
	Explain the DNS guard feature.	Chapter 19
	Describe the AIP-SSM HW and SW.	Chapters 3 and 19
	Load IPS SW on the AIP-SSM.	Chapter 19
	Verify AIP-SSM.	Chapter 19
	Configure an IPS modular policy.	Chapter 7 and 19

Table I-1 *SNPA Foundation Topics and Descriptions (Continued)*

SNPA Exam Topic Area	Related Topic	Where It's Covered in the Book
Monitor and manage an installed Security Appliance	Obtain and apply OS updates.	Chapter 4
	Backup and restore configurations and software.	Chapters 4 and 6
	Explain the Security Appliance file management system.	Chapter 4
	Perform password/lockout recovery procedures.	Chapter 4
	Obtain and upgrade license keys.	Chapter 4
	Configure passwords for various access methods: Telnet, serial, enable, SSH.	Chapters 4 and 6
	Configure various access methods: Telnet, SSH, ASDM.	Chapters 4, 6, and 15
	Configure command authorization and privilege levels.	Chapters 4 and 15
	Configure local username database.	Chapters 4, 15, and 18
	Verify access control methods.	Chapters 6, 15, and 18
	Enable ASDM functionality.	Chapter 15
	Verify a Security Appliance configuration via ASDM.	Chapter 15
	Verify the licensing available on a Security Appliance.	Chapters 4 and 15

Overview of the Cisco Certification Process

In the network security market, demand for qualified engineers vastly outpaces the supply. For this reason, many engineers consider migrating from routing/networking to network security. Remember that network security is simply security applied to networks. This sounds like an obvious concept, and it is actually a very important one if you are pursuing your security certification. You must be very familiar with networking *before* you can begin to apply the security concepts. Although a previous Cisco certification is not required to begin the Cisco Security Certification process, it is a good idea to complete—at least—the Cisco Certified Networking Associate (CCNA) certification. The skill required to complete the CCNA certification will give you a solid foundation that you can expand into the network security field.

The security certification is called the Cisco Certified Security Professional (CCSP) certification and consists of the following exams:

- **SNPA**—Cisco Securing Networks with PIX and ASA (642-522)
- **SNRS**—Securing Networks with Cisco Routers and Switches (642-502)
- **IPS**—Securing Networks Using Intrusion Prevention Systems (642-532)
- **HIPS**—Securing Hosts Using Cisco Security Agent (642-513)
- **SND**—Securing Cisco Network Devices (642-551)

Taking the SNPA Certification Exam

As with any Cisco certification exam, it is best to be thoroughly prepared before taking the exam. There is no way to determine exactly which questions are on the exam, so the best way to prepare is to have a good working knowledge of all subjects covered on the exam. Schedule yourself for the exam and be sure to be rested and ready to focus when taking the exam.

Tracking CCSP Status

You can track your certification progress by checking https://www.certmanager.net/~cisco_s/login.html. You will have to create an account the first time you log on to the site.

How to Prepare for an Exam

The best way to prepare for any certification exam is to use a combination of the preparation resources, labs, and practice tests. This guide has integrated some practice questions and labs to help you better prepare. If possible, try to get some hands-on time with the PIX Firewall or ASA device. Experience has no substitute, and it is much easier to understand the commands and concepts when you can actually see the PIX in action. If you do not have access to a PIX Firewall or ASA device, a variety of simulation packages are available for a reasonable price. Last, but certainly not least, the Cisco website provides a wealth of information on the Security Appliance and all of the products with which it interacts. No single source can adequately prepare you for the SNPA exam unless you already have extensive experience with Cisco products and a background in networking or network security. At a minimum, you will want to use this book combined with http://www.cisco.com/public/support/tac/home.shtml to prepare for this exam.

Assessing Exam Readiness

After completing a number of certification exams, I have found that you do not really know if you are adequately prepared for the exam until you have completed about 30 percent of the questions. At this point, if you are not prepared, it is too late. Be sure that you are preparing for the correct exam. This certification exam is SNPA 3.3 and is a relatively new exam. The best way to determine your readiness is to work through this book's "Do I Know This Already?" quizzes, review questions, and case studies/scenarios. It is best to work your way through the entire book unless you can complete each subject without having to do any research or look up any answers.

Cisco Security Specialist in the Real World

Cisco is one of the most recognized names on the Internet. You cannot go into a data center or server room without seeing some Cisco equipment. Cisco-certified security specialists are able to bring quite a bit of knowledge to the table because of their deep understanding of the relationship between networking and network security. This is why the Cisco certification carries such clout. Cisco certifications demonstrate to potential employers and contract holders a certain professionalism and the dedication required to achieve a goal. Face it: If these certifications were easy to acquire, everyone would have them.

PIX and Cisco IOS Commands

A firewall or router is not normally something you fiddle with. That is to say, once you have it properly configured, you tend to leave it alone until there is a problem or you have to make some other configuration change. This is the reason that the question mark (?) is probably the most widely used Cisco IOS command. Unless you have constant exposure to this equipment, it can be difficult to remember the numerous commands required to configure devices and troubleshoot problems.

Most engineers remember enough to go in the right direction but use the (?) to help them use the correct syntax. This is life in the real world. Unfortunately, the question mark is not always available in the testing environment. Many questions on this exam require you to select the best command to perform a certain function. It is extremely important that you familiarize yourself with the different commands, the correct command syntax, and the functions of each command.

Rules of the Road

We have always found it very confusing when different addresses are used in the examples throughout a technical publication. For this reason, we use the address space depicted in Figure I-2 when assigning network segments in this book. Please note that the address space we have selected is all reserved space, per RFC 1918. We understand that these addresses are not routable across the Internet and are not normally used on outside interfaces. Even with the millions of IP addresses available on the Internet, there is a slight chance that we could have chosen to use an address that the owner did not want published in this book.

Figure I-2 *Addressing for Examples*

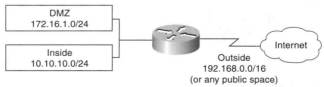

It is our hope that this book will assist you in understanding the examples and the syntax of the many commands required to configure and administer the Cisco Security Appliance.

Good luck!

This chapter covers the following subjects:

- Overview of Network Security

- Vulnerabilities, Threats, and Attacks

- Security Policies

- Network Security as a Process

- Network Security as a "Legal Issue"

- Defense in Depth

- Cisco Architecture for Voice, Video, and Integrated Data (AVVID)

- Cisco Security Architecture for Enterprises (SAFE)

CHAPTER 1

Network Security

Rather than jump directly into what you need to know for the Cisco Securing Networks with PIX and ASA (642-522) examination, this chapter presents some background information about network security and its integral role in business today. You need to understand this information because it is the basis for CCSP Certification and is a common theme throughout the five CCSP certification exams.

The term *network security* defines an extremely broad range of very complex subjects. To understand the individual subjects and how they relate to each other, it is important for you first to look at the "big picture" and get an understanding of the importance of the entire concept. Much of an organization's assets consist of data and computer resources that are interconnected and must be protected from unauthorized access. There are many different ways to ensure that network assets are adequately protected. The key is to correctly balance the business need with the requirement for security.

How to Best Use This Chapter

This chapter will give you an understanding of the general principles of network security. It will give you the foundation to understand the specifics of how the Cisco Security Appliance family of firewalls is incorporated into a network architecture.

"Do I Know This Already?" Quiz

The purpose of the "Do I Know This Already?" quiz is to help you decide if you really need to read the entire chapter. If you already intend to read the entire chapter, you do not necessarily need to answer these questions now.

The ten-question quiz, derived from the major sections in the "Foundation and Supplemental Topics" portion of the chapter, helps you determine how to spend your limited study time.

Table 1-1 outlines the major topics discussed in this chapter and the "Do I Know This Already?" quiz questions that correspond to those topics.

Table 1-1   *"Do I Know This Already?" Foundation Topics Section-to-Question Mapping*

Supplemental or Foundation Topics Section	Questions Covered in This Section	Score
Overview of Network Security	1	
Vulnerabilities, Threats, and Attacks	2 to 6	
Security Policies		
Network Security as a Process	7 to 8	
Network Security as a "Legal Issue"		
Defense in Depth		
Cisco AVVID	9	
Cisco SAFE	10	

CAUTION   The goal of self assessment is to gauge your mastery of the topics in this chapter. If you do not know the answer to a question or are only partially sure of the answer, you should mark this question wrong for purposes of the self assessment. Giving yourself credit for an answer you correctly guess skews your self-assessment results and might provide you with a false sense of security.

1.   Which single method is the best way to secure a network?

   a.   Allow dialup access only to the Internet

   b.   Install a personal firewall on every workstation

   c.   Use very complex passwords

   d.   Implement strong perimeter security

   e.   None of the above

2.   What are the three types of cyber attacks? (Choose three.)

   a.   Penetration attack

   b.   Access attack

   c.   Denial of service attack

   d.   Destruction of data attack

   e.   Reconnaissance attack

3. What type of threat is directed toward a specific target normally for a specific purpose?

   a. Structured threats

   b. Directed threats

   c. Unstructured threats

   d. Political threats

   e. None of the above

4. What type of threat normally scans networks looking for "targets of opportunity?"

   a. Structured threats

   b. Scanning threats

   c. Unstructured threats

   d. Script kiddies

   e. None of the above

5. What type of scan looks for all services running on a single host?

   a. Ping sweep

   b. Service scan

   c. Horizontal scan

   d. Vertical scan

   e. All of the above

6. What type of attack determines the address space assigned to an organization?

   a. Ping sweep

   b. DNS queries

   c. Vertical scan

   d. Horizontal scan

   e. None of the above

7. What are the steps of the security process?

    a. Secure, test, repair, retest

    b. Test, repair, monitor, evaluate

    c. Lather, rinse, repeat

    d. Evaluate, secure, test

    e. None of the above

8. What constant action sits between the individual steps of the security process?

    a. Test

    b. Retest

    c. Evaluate

    d. Repair

    e. Improve

9. True or false: Cisco AVVID uses only Cisco products.

10. Which of the following is *not* a component of Cisco SAFE?

    a. Perimeter security

    b. Policy implementation

    c. Identity

    d. Security management and monitoring

    e. Application security

The answers to the "Do I Know This Already?" quiz are found in Appendix A, "Answers to the 'Do I Know This Already?' Quizzes and Q&A Sections." The suggested choices for your next step are as follows:

- **8 or less overall score**—Read the entire chapter. This includes the "Foundation and Supplemental Topics," "Foundation Summary," and "Q&A" sections.

- **9 or 10 overall score**—If you want more review of these topics, skip to the "Foundation Summary" section and then go to the "Q&A" section. Otherwise, move to the next chapter.

Foundation and Supplemental Topics

This chapter does not contain any foundation topics. However, if you take a look at the foundation topics throughout the book, you will discover that understanding the foundation topics will be difficult if you do not already understand the supplemental topics.

Overview of Network Security

In the past, the term *information security* was used to describe the physical security measures used to keep vital government or business information from being accessed by the public and to protect it against alteration or destruction. These measures included storing valuable documents in locked filing cabinets or safes and restricting physical access to areas where those documents were kept. With the proliferation of computers and electronic media, the old way of accessing data changed. As technology continued to advance, computer systems were interconnected to form computer networks, allowing systems to share resources, including data.

The ultimate computer network, which interconnects almost every publicly accessible computer network, is the Internet. Although the methods of securing data have changed dramatically, the concept of network security remains the same as that of information security.

Because computers can warehouse, retrieve, and process tremendous amounts of data, they are used in nearly every facet of our lives. Computers, networks, and the Internet are integral parts of many businesses. Our dependence on computers continues to increase as businesses and individuals become more comfortable with technology and as technology advances make systems more user-friendly and easier to interconnect.

A single computer system requires automated tools to protect data on that system from users who have local system access. A computer system that is on a network (a *distributed system*) requires that the data on that system be protected not only from local access but also from unauthorized remote access and from interception or alteration of data during transmission between systems. Network security is not a single product, process, or policy, but rather a combination of products and processes that support a defined policy. Network security is the implementation of security devices, policies, and processes to prevent unauthorized access to network resources or alteration or destruction of resources or data.

Vulnerabilities, Threats, and Attacks

Attackers who attempt to access a system or network use various methods to find and exploit specific targets. This section discusses the basic concepts of a cyber attack.

Vulnerabilities

To understand cyber attacks, you must remember that computers, no matter how advanced, are still just machines that operate based on predetermined instruction sets. Operating systems and other software packages are simply compiled instruction sets that the computer uses to transform input into output. A computer cannot determine the difference between authorized input and unauthorized input unless this information is written into the instruction sets. Any point in a software package at which a user can alter the software or gain access to a system (that was not specifically designed into the software) is called a *vulnerability*. In most cases, a hacker gains access to a network or computer by exploiting a vulnerability. It is possible to remotely connect to a computer on any of 65,535 ports.

Different applications configure a system to *listen* on specific ports. It is possible to scan a computer to determine which ports are *listening,* and what applications are running on that system. By knowing what vulnerabilities are associated with which applications, you can determine what vulnerabilities exist and how to exploit them. As hardware and software technology continue to advance, the "other side" continues to search for and discover new vulnerabilities. For this reason, most software manufacturers continue to produce *patches* for their products as vulnerabilities are discovered.

Threats

Potential threats are broken into the following two categories:

- **Structured threats**—Threats that are preplanned and focus on a specific target. A structured threat is an organized effort to breach a specific network or organization.

- **Unstructured threats**—Threats that are random and tend to be the result of hackers looking for a target of opportunity. These threats are the most common because an abundance of script files are available on the Internet to users who want to scan unprotected networks for vulnerabilities. Because the scripts are free and run with minimal input from the user, they are widely used across the Internet. Many unstructured threats are not of a malicious nature or for any specific purpose. The people who carry them out are usually just novice hackers looking to see what they can do.

Types of Attacks

The types of cyber attackers and their motivations are too numerous and varied to list. They range from the novice hacker who is attracted by the challenge, to the highly skilled professional who targets an organization for a specific purpose (such as organized crime, industrial espionage, or state-sponsored intelligence gathering). Threats can originate from outside the organization or from inside. *External threats* originate outside an organization and attempt to breach a network either from the Internet or via dialup access. *Internal threats* originate from within an organization and are usually the result of employees or other personnel who have some authorized access to internal network resources. Studies indicate that internal attacks perpetrated by disgruntled employees or former employees are responsible for the majority of network security incidents within most organizations.

There are three major types of network attacks, each with its own specific goal:

- **Reconnaissance attack**—An attack designed not to gain access to a system or network but only to search for and track vulnerabilities that can be exploited later.

- **Access attack**—An attack designed to exploit vulnerability and to gain access to a system on a network. After gaining access, the goal of the user is to

    — Retrieve, alter, or destroy data.

    — Add, remove, or change network resources, including user access.

    — Install other exploits that can be used later to gain access to the network.

- **Denial of service (DoS) attack**—An attack designed solely to cause an interruption on a computer or network.

Reconnaissance Attacks

The goal of this type of attack is to perform reconnaissance on a computer or network. The goal of this reconnaissance is to determine the makeup of the targeted computer or network and to search for and map any vulnerability. A reconnaissance attack can indicate the potential for other, more-invasive attacks. Many reconnaissance attacks are written into scripts that allow novice hackers or script kiddies to launch attacks on networks with a few mouse clicks. Here are some of the more common reconnaissance attacks:

- **Domain Name Service (DNS) query**—Provides the unauthorized user with such information as what address space is assigned to a particular domain and who owns that domain.

- **Ping sweep**—Tells the unauthorized user how many hosts are active on the network. It is possible to drop ICMP packets at the perimeter devices, but this occurs at the expense of network troubleshooting.

- **Vertical scan**—Scans the service ports of a single host and requests different services at each port. This method enables the unauthorized user to determine what type of operating system and services are running on the computer.

- **Horizontal scan**—Scans an address range for a specific port or service. A very common horizontal scan is the FTP sweep. This is done by scanning a network segment to look for replies to connection attempts on port 21.

- **Block scan**—A combination of the vertical scan and the horizontal scan. In other words, it scans a network segment and attempts connections on multiple ports of each host on that segment.

Access Attacks

As the name implies, the goal of an access attack is to gain access to a computer or network. Having gained access, the user may be able to perform many different functions. These functions can be broken into three distinct categories:

- **Interception**—Gaining unauthorized access to a resource. This could be access to confidential data such as personnel records, payroll records, or research and development projects. As soon as the user gains access, he might be able to read, write to, copy, or move this data. If an intruder gains access, the only way to protect your sensitive data is to save it in an encrypted format (beforehand). This prevents the intruder from being able to read the data.

- **Modification**—Having gained access, the unauthorized user can alter the resource. This includes not only altering file content but also altering system configurations, changing the level of authorized system access, and escalating authorized privilege levels. Unauthorized system access is achieved by exploiting vulnerability in either the operating system or a software package running on that system. Unauthorized privilege escalation occurs when a user who has a low-level but authorized account attempts to gain higher-level or more-privileged user account information or to increase his or her own privilege level. This gives the user greater control over the target system or network.

- **Fabrication**—With access to the target system or network, the unauthorized user can create false objects and introduce them into the environment. This can include altering data or inserting packaged exploits such as a virus, worm, or Trojan horse, which can continue attacking the network from within:

  — **Virus**—Computer viruses range from annoying to destructive. They consist of computer code that attaches itself to other software running on the computer. This way, each time the attached software opens, the virus reproduces and can continue growing until it wreaks havoc on the infected computer.

  — **Worm**—A worm is a virus that exploits vulnerabilities on networked systems to replicate itself. A worm scans a network, looking for a computer with a specific vulnerability. When it finds a host, it copies itself to that system and begins scanning from there.

— **Trojan horse**—A Trojan horse is a program that usually claims to perform one function (such as a game) but also does something completely different (such as corrupting data on your hard disk). Many different types of Trojan horses get attached to systems. The effects of these programs range from minor user irritation to total destruction of the computer's file system. Trojan horses are sometimes used to exploit systems by creating user accounts on systems so that an unauthorized user can gain access or upgrade her privilege level. Trojans are also commonly used to enlist computers for a distributed denial of service (DDoS) attack without the knowledge of the system owner.

DoS Attacks

A DoS attack is designed to deny user access to computers or networks. These attacks usually target specific services and attempt to overwhelm them by making numerous requests concurrently. If a system is not protected and cannot react to a DoS attack, that system may be very easy to overwhelm by running scripts that generate multiple requests.

It is possible to greatly increase a DoS attack's magnitude by launching it from multiple systems against a single target. This practice is called a *distributed denial of service (DDoS) attack*. A common practice by hackers is to use a Trojan horse to take control of other systems and enlist them in a DDoS attack.

Security Policies

Security policies are created based upon the security philosophy of the organization. The policy should be a "top-down" policy that is consistent, understandable (nontechnical), widely disseminated within the organization, and fully supported by management. The technical team uses the security policy to design and implement the organization's security structure. The security policy is a formal statement that specifies a set of rules required for gaining access to network assets. The security policy is not a technical document; it is a business document that lays out the permitted and prohibited activities and the tasks and responsibilities regarding security. The network security policy is the core of the network security process. Every organization that maintains networked assets should have a written network security policy. At a minimum, that policy should fulfill the following objectives:

- Analyze the threat based on the type of business performed and type of network exposure
- Determine the organization's security requirements
- Document the network infrastructure and identify potential security breach points
- Identify specific resources that require protection and develop an implementation plan

> **NOTE** An effective network security policy must include physical security to prevent unauthorized users from gaining local access to equipment.

The *security process* is the implementation of the security policy. It is broken into four steps that run continuously, as shown in Figure 1-1. It is important to emphasize that this is a continuous process, that each step leads to the next, and that you should evaluate the results of each step and constantly improve your security posture.

Figure 1-1 *Security Process*

Step 1: Secure

Step 1 is to implement your network security design. This includes hardening your network systems by installing security devices such as firewalls, intrusion detection sensors, and authentication, authorization, and accounting (AAA) servers. Firewalls on the network perimeter prevent unwanted traffic from entering the network. Firewalls within the network verify that only authorized traffic moves from one network segment to another. Restrict access to resources to only authorized users, and implement a strong password convention. Implement data encryption to protect data that is passing from one network to another across an unsecured connection (via the Internet) or to protect sensitive data within your network. Cisco Security Appliance family of firewalls and Cisco Secure IDS are both industry-leading network security devices that are commonly used for securing the network perimeter and monitoring all traffic that traverses critical points on the network. The purpose of this step is to prevent unauthorized access to the network and to protect network resources.

Step 2: Monitor

After you secure your network, you should monitor the network to ensure that you can detect potential security incidents. By installing Cisco Secure IDS at key points of the network (as part of Step 1), you can monitor both internal and external traffic. It is important to monitor both internal and external traffic because you can check for violations of your network security policy from internal sources and attacks from external sources and determine if any external attacks have breached your network. All your perimeter devices, including firewalls and perimeter routers, provide log data that can be used to verify that your secure configuration is functioning properly and can be filtered to look for specific incidents.

Step 3: Test

Step 3 involves testing the effectiveness of your security design and is the completed by continuing to monitor the solution and generating traffic that should be mitigated by the solution that you implemented. Verify that the security equipment is properly configured and functioning correctly. Several excellent tools are available that you can use to verify the capabilities of your design and determine how effective your security devices will be as they are currently configured.

Step 4: Improve

Step 4 involves using the data from your intrusion detection sensors and your test data to improve the design. An effective security policy is always a work in progress. It continues to improve with every cycle of the process. This does not necessarily mean implementing new hardware with every cycle. The improvement cycle could involve changing certain organizational procedures or documenting new potential threats and vulnerabilities.

The security process is ongoing and constantly changing based on the results of evaluations that occur as part of each step of the process.

Network Security as a "Legal Issue"

Organizations are expected to exercise "reasonable care" to ensure that they protect assets on their networks and to ensure that their network resources are not used against others. Consider the following scenario: An employee of Company X uses his computer (without authorization) to scan the Internet and eventually finds a server that belongs to Company Y that he is able to take control of using a documented exploit. The employee then uses that server to break into the database server at Insurance Company Z and steal the medical records of a celebrity that contain very sensitive and potentially damaging personal information. The stolen information is later distributed to the public. Who is responsible? Of course, the employee is ultimately responsible but probably lacks the financial resources that make it worthwhile for the celebrity to seek legal recourse. However, companies X, Y, and Z will all likely become involved in legal action as a result of this theft.

Defense in Depth

Securing a network requires significantly more than implementing a strong network perimeter. The installation of a firewall is a part of the perimeter defense, but it cannot ensure that the entire network is secure. The concept of *defense in depth* refers to the military strategy of having multiple layers of defense. It is an architecture that includes a strong perimeter, intrusion detection/prevention at key points on the network, network monitoring and logging, and a design that allows administrators to dynamically alter the network in response to attacks.

Of course, the concept of defense in depth must always be balanced with the business need of the organization. It simply would not make sense to implement a complex and expensive security architecture for a home office with a couple of computers that do not contain any sensitive data.

Cisco AVVID and Cisco SAFE

Cisco has two programs in place—Cisco AVVID and Cisco SAFE—to help network architects design secure network solutions. Both programs are based on proven solutions that have been tested for full functionality and interoperability and both programs use the strategy of defense in depth.

Cisco AVVID?

AVVID is the Cisco Architecture for Voice, Video, and Integrated Data. Cisco AVVID is an open architecture that is used by Cisco partners to develop various solutions. Every Cisco partner solution is rigorously tested for interoperability with Cisco products. Cisco AVVID is designed for large enterprise networks that require an infrastructure that can support emerging applications such as IP telephone, content delivery, and storage. This *network of networks* concept allows the use of a single network infrastructure to support the concurrent operation of multiple solutions. The Cisco Enterprise Solutions Engineering team creates design guides for use when planning enterprise network infrastructure using Cisco products, software, and features. These solutions provide the following benefits:

- **Network performance**—This is measured by the following three metrics rather than just throughput:

  — **Application response time**— Measures how quickly an application responds to changes on a network and network congestion by changing its link speed.

  — **Device performance**—Measures the limitations in performance of individual network devices such as switches or routers. A poorly performing device can become a bottleneck to the network, so it is important to ensure that devices are not overtaxed. Device performance measures errors, drops, and CPU usage as well as packet-per-second throughput.

  — **Protocol performance**—Measures the ability of devices to operate dynamically by verifying that devices and the network can handle the use of routing protocols and the Spanning Tree Protocol (STP).

- **Scalability**— A scalable solution must allow a network to grow into the future. The network must be designed to allow growth in the following areas:

  — **Topology**—A topology must be selected so that changes do not require major reconfiguration of the entire network.

  — **Addressing**—The addressing scheme that you choose should be affected only minimally by changes to the network and should allow for route summarization.

  — **Routing protocols**—The design should be such that changes in the network are easily handled by the routing protocols.

- **Availability**—Availability is always a major concern to network managers. A network's ability to overcome outages and adapt to changes is paramount. Three availability issues are incorporated into the Cisco AVVID design model:

  — **Equipment and link redundancy**—This includes not only redundant components and high-availability configurations but also redundancy within the equipment, such as dual power supplies and other features designed into the modular products.

  — **Protocol resiliency**—The focus here is to use the most resilient protocol. Multiple redundant protocols do not necessarily provide the best solution.

  — **Network capacity design**—A network design should allow for significant expansion and support the capacity needs and redundancy to reduce the impact of a redundant link failure.

The Cisco AVVID network infrastructure design incorporates many different topologies and technologies to provide optimum efficiency and stability.

Cisco SAFE

SAFE is available for different sizes of networks. The Cisco white papers "SAFE: A Security Blueprint for Enterprise Networks and SAFE: Extending the Security Blueprint to Small, Midsize, and Remote-User Networks" are guides for network designers and focus on the implementation of secure network designs. Cisco SAFE is based on Cisco AVVID. SAFE uses best practices and the interoperability of various Cisco and Cisco partner products. Several SAFE white papers available on Cisco.com focus on the following design fundamentals (from the Cisco Systems white paper "SAFE: A Security Blueprint for Enterprise Networks," copyright 2000):

- Security and attack mitigation based on policy
- Security implementation throughout the infrastructure (not just specialized security devices)
- Secure management and reporting
- Authentication and authorization of users and administrators to critical network resources
- Intrusion detection for critical resources and subnets
- Support for emerging networked applications

The SAFE blueprint is composed of the critical areas of network security:

- **Perimeter security**—Protects access to the network by controlling access on the network's entry and exit points
- **Secure connectivity**—Provides secure communications via virtual private networks (VPNs)
- **Application security**—Ensures that critical servers and applications are protected
- **Identity**—Provides secure authentication and authorization services to ensure that access is restricted to only authorized users
- **Security management and monitoring**—Allows for centralized management of security resources and the detection of unauthorized activity on the network

NOTE Cisco SAFE Implementation (exam 642-541) is a requirement for CCSP Certification. For more information, see http://www.cisco.com/go/certifications.

Foundation Summary

The "Foundation Summary" is a collection of tables and figures that provide a convenient review of many key concepts in this chapter. If you are already comfortable with the topics in this chapter, this summary can help you recall a few details. If you just read this chapter, this review should help solidify some key facts. If you are doing your final preparation before the exam, these tables and figures are a convenient way to review the day before the exam.

Network Security

There is no single security solution for every network. Network security is a combination of products and processes that support the organization's security policy.

Vulnerabilities, Threats, and Attacks

Vulnerabilities, threats, and attacks are three components that create the environment for a cyber-attack.

Vulnerabilities

Vulnerabilities are unintentional weaknesses in an application, hardware component, or network design that can be exploited to gain entry to a computer system or network. Attackers generally target known vulnerabilities when looking for targets.

Threats

Threats are broken down into two categories based on the intent of the attacker:

- **Structured threats**—Threats that are preplanned and focus on a specific target. A structured threat is an organized effort to breach a specific network or organization.

- **Unstructured threats**—Threats that are random and usually the result of an attacker identifying the vulnerability by scanning the network looking for "targets of opportunity." This type of threat is by far the most common threat because it can be performed using automated tools (scripts) that are readily available on the Internet and can be performed by someone with very limited computer skills.

Attacks

There are three different types of attacks, which are named based on the attacker's intent:

- **Reconnaissance attack**—Designed to gain information about a specific target network or resource. Typical types of reconnaissance attacks include the following:

   — **DNS query**—Checks the DNS to see what address space is registered to a specific organization

   — **Ping sweep**—Directs ICMP packets at specific host addresses on a network, enabling the attacker to determine what addresses are being used based on the replies received

   — **Vertical scan**—Directs a scan against all the service ports of a specific host to determine which services are running on that host

   — **Horizontal scan**—Directs a scan for a single service port against a range of network addresses

   — **Block scan**—Directs a scan for multiple service ports against a range of network addresses

- **Access attack**—Designed to gain access to a network or resource. There are three main goals of an access attack:

   — **Interception**—Retrieve, alter, or destroy data

   — **Modification**—Add, move, or change network resources, including user access

   — **Fabrication**—Install exploits that can be used later to gain access to the network or resource

- **DoS attack**—Designed to deny authorized access to the target network or resource

Security Policies

A security policy is the written representation of an organization's security philosophy. The security policy is a guide that defines how the organization does business with respect to its network resources and defines, in general terms, how the network resources are to be secured. The security policy should fulfill the following objectives:

- Analyze the threat based on the type of business performed and type of network exposure

- Determine the organization's security requirements

- Document the network infrastructure and identify potential security breach points
- Identify specific resources that require protection and develop an implementation plan

Network Security as a Process

The security process is driven by the security policy. The *Security Wheel* demonstrates the four ongoing steps used to continuously improve the security of a network:

- **Secure**—Implement the necessary security hardware, management and operational processes, and secure your system configurations to reduce your network exposure.
- **Monitor**—Monitor the network to determine how changes have affected your network and look for additional threats.
- **Test**—Test the current network and system configurations to determine if any vulnerabilities exist.
- **Improve**—Make continuous improvements based on the results of your testing, based on vulnerabilities noted during the network monitoring, or based on normal component upgrades and improvements.

Defense in Depth

Defense in depth refers to implementing multiple layers of security to mitigate potential threats. Cisco has two specific programs to address defense in depth: Cisco AVVID and Cisco SAFE.

Cisco AVVID

AVVID is the Cisco Architecture for Voice, Video, and Integrated Data. Cisco AVVID is an open architecture that is used by Cisco partners to develop various solutions. Cisco AVVID solutions provide the following benefits:

- Network performance
    - Application response time
    - Device performance
    - Protocol performance
- Scalability
    - Topology
    - Addressing
    - Routing protocols

- Availability
    - Equipment and link redundancy
    - Protocol resiliency
    - Network capacity design

Cisco SAFE

The Cisco white papers "SAFE: A Security Blueprint for Enterprise Networks" and "SAFE: Extending the Security Blueprint to Small, Midsize, and Remote-User Networks" are guides for network designers and focus on the implementation of secure network designs. The SAFE blueprints comprise the following components:

- Perimeter security
- Secure connectivity
- Application security
- Identity
- Security management and monitoring

Key Terms

Table 1-2 lists the most important terms used in this chapter.

Table 1-2 *Chapter Key Terms*

Term	Definition
Network security	The implementation of security devices, policies, and processes to prevent the unauthorized access to network resources or the alteration or destruction of resources or data.
Security policy	A formal statement that specifies a set of rules that users must follow while gaining access to corporate network access.
Defense in depth	A network architecture that provides multiple layers of protection.
AVVID	Cisco Architecture for Voice, Video, and Integrated Data.
SAFE	The Cisco Secure Architecture for Enterprises.

Q&A

As mentioned in the Introduction, the questions in this book are more difficult than what you should experience on the exam. The questions are designed to ensure your understanding of the concepts discussed in this chapter and adequately prepare you to complete the exam. You should use the simulated exams on the CD to practice for the exam.

The answers to these questions can be found in Appendix A:

1. What is the difference between the network security policy and the network security process?

2. For unstructured threats, what is the normal anatomy of an attack?

3. What information can you gain from a ping sweep?

4. What is the single most important component when implementing defense in depth?

5. Why could an organization be legally responsible if its systems are compromised during an attack?

This chapter covers the following subjects:

- Firewalls

- Cisco Security Appliance Overview

CHAPTER 2

Firewall Technologies and the Cisco Security Appliance

Cisco Security Appliances, such as the Cisco PIX Firewall and Adaptive Security Appliances (ASA), are among the many firewalls currently on the market today. Different manufacturers employ different technologies in their designs. This chapter discusses the different technologies, which technology is employed by the Cisco Security Appliance, and how.

How to Best Use This Chapter

This chapter covers the basic concepts of firewall technology and discusses how they are applied to Cisco Security Appliances.

These concepts are the foundation of much of what you need to understand to pass the CCSP SNPA Certification Exam. Unless you do exceptionally well on the "Do I Know This Already?" quiz and are 100 percent confident in your knowledge of this area, you should read through the entire chapter.

"Do I Know This Already?" Quiz

The purpose of the "Do I Know This Already?" quiz is to help you decide if you really need to read the entire chapter. If you already intend to read the entire chapter, you do not necessarily need to answer these questions now.

The ten-question quiz, derived from the major sections in the "Foundation Topics" portion of the chapter, helps you determine how to spend your limited study time.

Table 2-1 outlines the major topics discussed in this chapter and the "Do I Know This Already?" quiz questions that correspond to those topics.

Table 2-1 *"Do I Know This Already?" Foundation Topics Section-to-Question Mapping*

Foundation Topics Section	Questions Covered in This Section	Score
Firewall Technologies	1, 5, 8 to 10	
Cisco Security Appliance Overview	2 to 4, 6, 7	

> **CAUTION** The goal of self assessment is to gauge your mastery of the topics in this chapter. If you do not know the answer to a question or are only partially sure of the answer, you should mark this question wrong for purposes of the self assessment. Giving yourself credit for an answer you correctly guess skews your self-assessment results and might provide you with a false sense of security.

1. True or false: Packet filtering on IOS routers provides security as good as that on the Cisco Security Appliances.

   a. True

   b. False

2. What design features enable Cisco Security Appliances, such as the PIX Firewall, to outperform conventional application firewalls?

   a. Adaptive Security Algorithm

   b. Super-packet filtering

   c. Purpose-built, real-time operating environment

   d. Hot standby proxy processing

   e. Cut-through proxy support

3. True or false: With AAA Authentication disabled, cut-through proxy technology allows users to do anything they want after authenticating at the firewall.

   a. True

   b. False

4. What steps are required to add an ARP entry to a Cisco PIX Firewall if the PIX failed to learn it through other means?

   a. Edit the /etc/interfaces/outside/arp.conf file.

   b. Use the **arp** command in global configuration mode.

    c. Add the ARP entry using the GUI.

    d. Use the **set arp** command in interface config mode.

5. True or false: There is no limit to the number of connections an application proxy firewall can handle.

    a. True

    b. False

6. True or false: The Adaptive Security Algorithm requires a tremendous amount of processing by the firewall. Although the PIX Firewall is not very efficient at processing the ASA, it can handle the task.

    a. True

    b. False

7. True or false: Redundancy allows you to configure two or more PIX Firewalls in a cluster to protect critical systems.

    a. True

    b. False

8. Of the three firewall technologies, which one generates a separate connection on behalf of the requestor and usually operates at the upper layers of the OSI reference model?

    a. Stateful inspection

    b. Packet filtering

    c. High-speed packet filtering

    d. Application proxy

    e. None of these answers are correct

9. Which of the following is *not* one of the three basic firewall technologies?

    a. Stateful inspection

    b. Packet filtering

    c. High-speed packet filtering

    d. Application proxy

    e. None of these answers are correct

10. Which firewall technology is commonly implemented on a router?

    a. Stateful inspection

    b. Packet filtering

    c. High-speed packet filtering

    d. Application proxy

    e. None of these answers are correct

The answers to the "Do I Know This Already?" quiz are found in Appendix A, "Answers to the 'Do I Know This Already?' Quizzes and Q&A Sections." The suggested choices for your next step are as follows:

- **8 or less overall score**—Read the entire chapter. This includes the "Foundation Topics," "Foundation Summary," and "Q&A" sections.

- **9 or 10 overall score**—If you want more review of these topics, skip to the "Foundation Summary" section and then go to the "Q&A" section. Otherwise, move to the next chapter.

Foundation Topics

Firewall Technologies

To understand the different firewall technologies, you first need to have a good understanding of the Open System Interconnection (OSI) reference model. The seven-layer OSI reference model is the standard for network communication and is the foundation upon which each firewall technology was built. The lower four layers of the OSI reference model are generally considered to be the layers that deal with networking, whereas the upper three layers deal more with application functions.

Firewalls are one of the primary components required to perform network perimeter security. The function of a firewall is to permit or to deny traffic that attempts to pass through it, based on specific predefined rules. All firewalls perform the function of examining network traffic and directing that traffic based on the rule set; however, the methods that the various firewalls use may differ. The following are the three different types of firewall technologies, each of which is discussed in more detail in the following sections:

- Packet filtering
- Proxy
- Stateful packet inspection

Packet Filtering

Packet-filtering firewalls are the oldest and most commonly used firewall technologies. A packet-filtering firewall simply inspects incoming traffic for items that occur at the network and transport layers of the OSI reference model. The packet-filtering firewall analyzes IP packets and compares them to a set of established rules called an *access control list (ACL)*. Packet filtering inspects the packet for only the following elements:

- Source IP address
- Source port
- Destination IP address
- Destination port
- Protocol (listed by name or IP protocol number)

NOTE In addition to the elements just listed, some packet-filtering firewalls check for header information to determine if the packet is from a new connection or an existing connection.

Figure 2-1 depicts how traffic passes through a packet-filtering firewall from the source to the destination as compared to the OSI reference model. Traffic is depicted as passing between the network and transport layers because some network layer items are checked (source and destination addresses) and some transport layer items are checked (the transport protocol, such as TCP or UDP). The items listed in the previous paragraph are verified against the ACL (rule set) to determine if the packets are permitted or denied.

Figure 2-1 *Packet-Filtering Firewall*

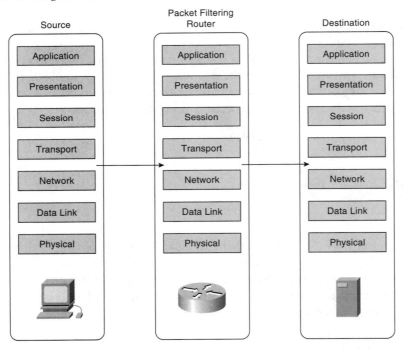

The advantage to using packet filters is that they tend to be very fast because they do not concern themselves with upper-layer data. Some of the disadvantages of packet filtering are as follows:

- ACLs may be very complex and difficult to manage.
- A packet-filtering firewall may be tricked into permitting access to an unauthorized user who is falsely representing himself (*spoofing*) with an IP address that is authorized by the ACL.

- Many new applications (such as multimedia applications) create multiple dynamically negotiated connections on random ports with no way to determine which ports will be used until the connection is established. Because access lists are manually configured, it is very difficult to provide support for these applications without reducing the security of the device.

Packet filtering is a feature that is commonly used on routers. Cisco Security Appliances also use ACLs for packet filtering. Chapter 7, "Configuring Access," discusses the unique context in which the Security Appliances employ ACLs.

Proxy

New Webster's Dictionary of the English Language defines *proxy* as "the agency of a person who acts as a substitute for another person; authority to act for another." Although this definition does not define a proxy firewall, the function is very similar.

A proxy firewall, commonly called a *proxy server,* acts on behalf of hosts on the protected network segments. The protected hosts never actually make any connections with the outside world. Hosts on the protected network send their requests to the proxy server, where they are compared to the rulebase. If the request matches a rule within the rulebase and is allowed, the proxy server sends a request on behalf of the requesting host to the external host and forwards the reply to the requesting host.

Proxies run at the upper layers of the OSI reference model. Once again, the connections are established between the network and transport layers; however, the application proxy then examines the request at the upper layers while verifying the request against the rule set. If the traffic meets the requirements of the upper-layer inspection and is verified against the rule set, the proxy firewall creates a new connection to the destination.

Using the OSI reference model, Figure 2-2 depicts how traffic passes through a proxy firewall from the source to the destination.

Most proxy firewalls are designed to cache commonly used information to expedite the response time to the requesting host. Application proxies tend to be very secure because the packets are inspected at all layers, but performance can suffer for the same reason. The processing workload required to perform proxy services is significant and increases with the number of requesting hosts.

Figure 2-2   *Proxy Firewall*

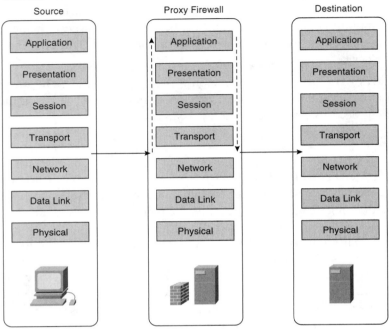

Large networks usually implement several proxy servers to avoid problems with throughput. The number of applications that a requesting host can access via a proxy is limited. This can be a key disadvantage when using a proxy server, because protocol traffic that the proxy server does not support passes through the proxy server untouched. By design, proxy firewalls support only specific applications and protocols. Another major disadvantage of proxy servers is that they are applications that run on top of operating systems. A device can be only as secure as the operating system it is running on. If the operating system is compromised, the unauthorized user may be able to take control of the proxy firewall and gain access to the entire protected network.

Stateful Packet Inspection

Stateful packet inspection, also called *stateful packet filtering,* provides the best combination of security and performance because connections are not only applied to an ACL but also logged in to a small database known as the *state table*. After a connection is established, all session data is compared to the state table. If the session data does not match the state table information for that connection, the connection is dropped.

Figure 2-3 depicts, using the OSI reference model, how traffic passes through a stateful packet inspection firewall from the source to the destination. Note that the traffic enters between the network and transport layers, and is verified against the state table and the rule set, while basic protocol compliance is checked at the upper layers.

Figure 2-3 *Stateful Packet Inspection Firewall*

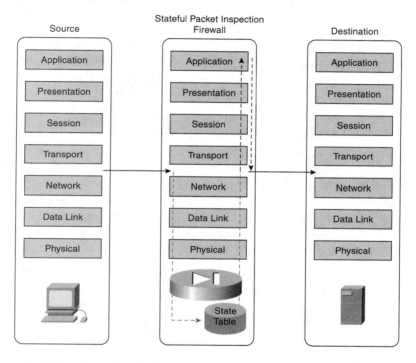

Chapter 3, "Cisco Security Appliance," covers stateful packet inspection in further detail. Stateful packet filtering is the method that is used by Cisco Security Appliance.

Cisco PIX Firewall

Five major characteristics of the Cisco Security Appliance design make it a leading-edge, high-performance security solution:

- Secure real-time embedded system
- Adaptive Security Algorithm
- Cut-through proxy
- Security Context
- Redundancy

Secure Real-Time Embedded System

Unlike most firewalls, Cisco Security Appliance using Software Version 7.0 or greater runs on a single, proprietary, embedded system. Whereas most firewalls run a firewall application over a general-purpose operating system, the Security Appliance has a single system that is responsible for operating the device. This single system is beneficial for the following reasons:

- **Better security**—A Cisco Security Appliance operating environment is a single system that was designed with functionality and security in mind. Because there is no separation between the operating system and the firewall application, there are no known vulnerabilities to exploit.

- **Better functionality**—The combined operating environment requires fewer steps when you configure the system. For example, if multiple IP addresses are bound to the external interface of an application firewall that runs over a general operating system, you must configure the networking portions (that is, Address Resolution Protocol [Proxy ARP] entries and routing) on the operating system and then apply the ACLs or rules in the firewall application. On the Cisco Security Appliance, all these functions are combined into a single system. As soon as an IP address is bound to an interface, the PIX Firewall automatically replies to ARP requests for that address without it having to be specifically configured.

- **Better performance**—Because the operating environment is a single unit, it allows for streamlined processing and much greater performance. The Cisco PIX 535 Firewall can handle 500,000 concurrent connections while maintaining stateful inspection of all connections.

Adaptive Security Algorithm

The *Adaptive Security Algorithm (ASA)* is the key to stateful connection control on the Cisco Security Appliance. The ASA creates a stateful session flow table (also called the *state table*). Source and destination addresses and other connection information are logged in to the state table. By using the ASA, the Cisco Security Appliance can perform stateful filtering on the connections in addition to filtering packets. Additionally, the ASA generates random TCP sequence numbers for outbound traffic by making it look like a response to an outbound request is unlikely to succeed.

Cut-Through Proxy

Cut-through proxy is a method of transparently performing authentication and authorization of inbound and outbound connections at the firewall. Cut-through proxy requires very little overhead because it occurs as the session is being established and provides a significant performance advantage over application proxy firewalls. Cut-through proxy is discussed in greater detail in Chapter 3.

Security Contexts (Virtual Firewall)

Before the introduction of Security Appliance Software Version 7.0, Cisco PIX Firewalls and ASA Security Appliances supported a universal firewall configuration to which all traffic flow must conform. With Version 7.0, the PIX Firewalls and ASA Security Appliances support multiple unique firewall configurations in a single device. This capability creates multiple virtual firewalls, each unique and independent of one another. Secure contexts are discussed in greater detail in Chapter 9, "Security Contexts."

Redundancy

The Cisco Secure PIX 515 series and above and the Cisco ASA Security Appliance can be configured in pairs with a primary system and a hot standby. This redundancy and stateful failover make the Cisco Security Appliance family of firewalls a high-availability solution for use in protecting critical network segments. If the primary firewall fails, the secondary automatically assumes the load, dramatically reducing the chances of a network outage. Failover is discussed in greater detail in Chapter 12, "Cisco Security Appliance Failover."

Foundation Summary

The "Foundation Summary" provides a convenient review of many key concepts in this chapter. If you are already comfortable with the topics in this chapter, this summary can help you recall a few details. If you just read this chapter, this review should help solidify some key facts. If you are doing your final preparation before the exam, this summary provides a convenient way to review the day before the exam.

Firewall Technologies

There are three firewall technologies:

- **Packet filtering**—Inspects the incoming and outgoing packets and allows/denies traffic based on source, destination, protocol, and service.

- **Proxy**—Connections are initiated by the firewall on behalf of the requestor. Traffic does not pass through a proxy-based firewall but rather is re-created by the firewall.

- **Stateful packet inspection**—Stateful packet inspection firewalls, also know as *stateful packet filters*, allow/deny traffic based on source, destination, and service while maintaining a state table to keep track of existing connections. This ensures that inbound connections are valid replies to outbound requests.

Cisco Security Appliance

Five major characteristics of the Cisco Security Appliance family of firewalls design make it a leading-edge, high-performance security solution:

- **Secure real-time embedded system**—A single proprietary embedded system designed for improved security, functionality, and performance.

- **Adaptive Security Algorithm**—The key to stateful session control in all Cisco Security Applicances. The ASA maintains state information in the state table and randomly generates TCP sequence numbers to prevent session hijacking.

- **Cut-through proxy**—A method for transparently performing authentication and authorization of inbound and outbound connections at the firewall.

- **Security contexts**—Provide a security professional with the ability to create multiple firewall configurations using a single PIX or ASA Firewall.

- **Redundancy**—The Cisco Secure PIX 515 series and above and all ASA Security Appliances can be configured in pairs with a primary system and a hot standby.

Q&A

As mentioned in the Introduction, the questions in this book are more difficult than what you should experience on the exam. The questions are designed to ensure your understanding of the concepts discussed in this chapter and to adequately prepare you to complete the exam. Use the simulated exams on the CD to practice for the exam.

The answers to these questions can be found in Appendix A:

1. What items does a packet filter look at to determine whether to allow the traffic?

2. What are the advantages of the Cisco Security Appliance family of firewalls over competing firewall products?

3. How many Security Appliances can you operate in a high-availability cluster?

4. What is the ASA, and how does Cisco Security Appliance use it?

5. Why is cut-through proxy more efficient than traditional proxy?

6. What are the advantages of a real-time embedded system?

This chapter covers the following subjects:

- PIX Firewall Models

- PIX Firewall Licensing

- ASA Firewall Models

- ASA Security Licensing

- ASA Security Levels

Cisco Security Appliance

This chapter discusses the Cisco PIX Firewall and ASA Security Appliance in greater detail than Chapter 2, "Firewall Technologies and the Cisco Security Appliance." It covers the many different models available, including their design and specifications.

How to Best Use This Chapter

Chapter 2 gave you insight into the different firewall technologies and the functionality designed into the Cisco PIX Firewall and ASA Security Appliance. This chapter gives you more specific information about this functionality and how this makes the PIX Firewall and ASA Security Appliance truly high-performance solutions. This chapter also covers all the PIX Firewall and ASA Security Appliance models that are available today and the possible configurations of each model. It is very important for you to understand in great detail the technology that powers Cisco Security Appliance. Test yourself with the "Do I Know This Already?" quiz, and see how familiar you are with the PIX Firewall and ASA Security Appliance in general and with the specifics of each available model.

"Do I Know This Already?" Quiz

The purpose of the "Do I Know This Already?" quiz is to help you decide if you really need to read the entire chapter. If you already intend to read the entire chapter, you do not necessarily need to answer these questions now.

The ten-question quiz, derived from the major sections in the "Foundation Topics" portion of the chapter, helps you determine how to spend your limited study time.

Table 3-1 outlines the major topics discussed in this chapter and the "Do I Know This Already?" quiz questions that correspond to those topics.

Table 3-1 *"Do I Know This Already?" Foundation Topics Section-to-Question Mapping*

Foundation Topics Section	Questions Covered in This Section	Score
PIX Firewall Models	2 to 6	
PIX Firewall Licensing	1, 10	
ASA Security Levels	7 to 9	

CAUTION The goal of self assessment is to gauge your mastery of the topics in this chapter. If you do not know the answer to a question or are only partially sure of the answer, you should mark this question wrong for purposes of the self assessment. Giving yourself credit for an answer you correctly guess skews your self-assessment results and might provide you with a false sense of security.

1. True or false: You do not need a license for any Cisco PIX Firewall. If you own the appliance, you can do anything you want with it.

   a. True

   b. False

2. How many physical interfaces does the PIX 525 support?

   a. Eight 10/100 interfaces or three Gigabit interfaces

   b. Eight 10/100 interfaces and three Gigabit interfaces

   c. Six 10/100 interfaces or three Gigabit interfaces

   d. Six 10/100 interfaces and three Gigabit interfaces

   e. None of the above

3. What are the three firewall technologies?

   a. Packet filtering, proxy, connection dropping

   b. Stateful inspection, packet filtering, proxy

   c. Stateful proxy, stateful filtering, packet inspection

   d. Cut-through proxy, ASA, proxy

4. How are optional component cards installed in the PIX Firewall?

   a. ISA slot

   b. USB port

   c. Serial connection

   d. PCI slot

   e. PCMCIA slot

5. What is the maximum firewall throughput of the ASA Security Appliance 5540?

    a. 1.0 Gbps

    b. 1.7 Gbps

    c. 100 Mbps

    d. 400 Mbps

6. How many physical interfaces does a PIX 501 have, and how many network segments does it support?

    a. Six interfaces, two network segments

    b. Six interface, six network segments

    c. Five interfaces, four network segments

    d. Two interfaces, two network segments

    e. None of these answers are correct

7. What happens to a reply that does not have the correct TCP sequence number?

    a. It generates an alert.

    b. The connection is dropped.

    c. The connection information is added to the state table.

    d. The session object is modified.

    e. None of these answers are correct.

8. Which of the following is the best way to remove the ASA from a PIX Firewall?

    a. Use the ASA removal tool, downloaded from Cisco.com.

    b. Use the **asa disable** command in the config mode.

    c. Configure all NATs to a single external address.

    d. Configure all NATs to a single internal address.

    e. You cannot remove the ASA from the PIX Firewall.

9. Which of the following four authentication methods is not supported by the PIX Firewall for performing cut-through proxy?

   a. Local Database

   b. TACACS+

   c. RADIUS

   d. Active Directory

   e. All of the above

10. What encryption algorithms does the PIX Firewall *not* support?

   a. Data Encryption Standard

   b. Triple Data Encryption Standard

   c. Diffie-Hellman

   d. Advanced Encryption Standard 128

   e. Advanced Encryption Standard 256

   f. Answers c, d, and e

The answers to the "Do I Know This Already?" quiz are found in Appendix A, "Answers to the 'Do I Know This Already?' Quizzes and Q&A Sections." The suggested choices for your next step are as follows:

- **8 or less overall score**—Read the entire chapter. This includes the "Foundation Topics," "Foundation Summary," and "Q&A" sections.

- **9 or 10 overall score**—You have a good understanding of the topic. If you want more review of these topics, skip to the "Foundation Summary" section and then go to the "Q&A" section. Otherwise, move to the next chapter.

Foundation Topics

Overview of the Cisco Security Appliance

As discussed in Chapter 2, the design of the Cisco PIX Firewall and ASA Security Appliance provides some significant advantages over application-based firewalls. The Cisco Security Appliances are designed to be "performance built, best of breed, all-in-one security appliances." The PIX Firewall appliance provides state-of-the-art stateful firewalling, protocol and application inspection, virtual private networking, inline intrusion prevention, and outstanding multimedia and voice security. Having a single operating environment allows the device to operate more efficiently. Also, because it was designed with security in mind, it is not vulnerable to any known exploits.

Two key components that facilitate the outstanding performance of the PIX Firewall are the Adaptive Security Algorithm (ASA) and cut-through proxy. Both are discussed in detail in the following sections.

ASA

A key part of the Cisco PIX operating environment is the ASA. The ASA is more secure and efficient than packet filtering and provides better performance than application-type proxy firewalls. The ASA segregates the network segments connected to the firewall, maintains secure perimeters, and can control traffic between those segments.

The firewall interfaces are assigned *security levels*. The PIX allows traffic to pass from an interface with a higher security level (inside) to an interface with a lower security level (outside) without an explicit rule for each resource on the higher-level segment. Traffic that is coming from an interface with a lower security level destined for an interface with a higher security level must meet the following two requirements:

- A static translation must exist for the destination.
- An access list or conduit must be in place to allow the traffic.

Access lists and conduits can be used to deny traffic from a higher security level to a lower security level just as they allow traffic from a lower level to a higher level.

> **NOTE** The use of conduits is not supported beyond PIX OS version 6.3.

The ASA is designed to function as a stateful, connection-oriented process that maintains session information in a *state table*. Applying the security policy and address translation to the state table controls all traffic passing through the firewall. A random TCP sequence number is generated, and the ASA writes the connection information to the state table as an outbound connection is initiated. If the connection is allowed by the security policy, the source address is translated to an external address and the request goes out. Return traffic is compared to the existing state information. If the information does not match, the firewall drops the connection. The security emphasis on the connection rather than on the packets makes it nearly impossible to gain access by hijacking a TCP session.

Figure 3-1 depicts the mechanics of the ASA and how it affects traffic flowing through a Cisco Security Appliance. The following numbered list explains the steps indicated in the figure. Notice that Steps 1 and 5 are performed by the requestor and responder. Steps 2, 3, 4, and 6 are all performed by the PIX Firewall.

1. The internal host initiates an IP connection to an external resource.

2. The Security Appliance writes the following connection information into the state table:

    — Source IP and port

    — Destination IP and port

    — TCP sequencing information

    — Additional TCP/UDP flags

    — A randomly generated TCP sequence number is applied (the state table entry is called a "session object")

3. The connection object is compared to the security policy. If the connection is not allowed, the session object is deleted, and the connection is dropped.

4. If the connection is approved by the security policy, the source address is translated and the request is forwarded to the external resource.

5. The external resource replies to the request.

6. The response arrives at the firewall and is compared to the session object. If the response matches the session object, the destination address is translated back to the original address and the traffic passes to the internal host. If it does not match, the connection is dropped.

Figure 3-1 *How ASA Works*

Cut-Through Proxy

The cut-through proxy feature on a Cisco Security Appliance provides significantly better performance than application proxy firewalls because it completes user authentication at the application layer, verifies authorization against the security policy, and then opens the connection as authorized by the security policy. Subsequent traffic for this connection is no longer handled at the application layer but is statefully inspected, providing significant performance benefits over proxy-based firewalls.

Figure 3-2 depicts the mechanics of cut-through proxy and the four steps that take place prior to the activation of the ASA. The following numbered list explains the steps indicated in the figure:

Step 1   Initiates an FTP, HTTP, or Telnet connection to the internal web server.

Step 2   The Cisco Security Appliance replies with a user logon and the user completes the logon.

Step 3   The Cisco Security Appliance uses TACACS+ or RADIUS to communicate the user account information to the authentication, authorization, and accounting (AAA) server, where it is authenticated.

Step 4   The connection to the web server is opened at the network layer, the session information is written to the connections table, and the ASA process begins.

Figure 3-2   *How Cut-Through Proxy Works*

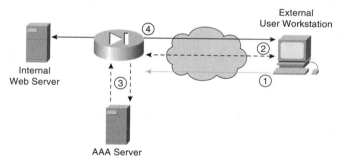

NOTE   Users can authenticate to a user database on Cisco Security Appliance, but it is more efficient to use an external authentication server with RADIUS or TACACS+ because the processing required by the PIX Firewall to maintain and query an internal database increases the firewall's workload.

Cisco PIX Firewall Models and Features

Cisco has named its family of security firewalls Security Appliances, encompassing both the PIX and ASA Security Appliances. Currently, six models of the Cisco PIX Firewall are available. Additionally, three models have been introduced in the new series of ASA Security Appliances. All these models provide services for users ranging from the small office/home office (SOHO) to the enterprise network and Internet service provider (ISP):

- **Cisco Secure PIX 501**—Intended for SOHO use and incorporates an integrated 10/100 Ethernet switch.

- **Cisco Secure PIX 506E**—Intended for remote office/branch office (ROBO) use and comes with two 10/100 Ethernet interfaces.

- **Cisco Secure PIX 515E**—Designed for small to medium-size businesses and branch office installations.

- **Cisco Secure PIX 525**—Intended for large enterprise networks and ISPs.

- **Cisco Secure PIX 535**—Intended for very large enterprise networks and ISPs. This model is the most robust of the PIX Firewall series.

- **Cisco ASA Security Appliance 5510**—Intended for small-to-medium businesses and enterprise installations.

- **Cisco ASA Security Appliance 5520**—Intended for small-to-medium-size business installations, as well as several large enterprise networks. The 5520 includes four gigabit Ethernet ports.

- **Cisco ASA Security Appliance 5540**—Intended for large enterprise networks and ISPs. This is the largest and most robust of the Cisco ASA models.

- **Cisco Firewall Service Module (FWSM)**—Designed for large enterprise networks and ISPs. The FWSM is a PIX Firewall blade for the Cisco Catalyst 6500 Series switches and 7600 Series routers.

NOTE The PIX 501 and 506/506E firewalls do not support 7.0 or more recent software and features.

All Cisco Security Appliances running software version 7.0 or later have the functionality described in the following sections incorporated into their design.

Intrusion Protection

Cisco Security Appliances were designed to detect a variety of attacks. They can also be integrated with the Cisco Secure Intrusion Detection Sensor to dynamically react to different threats. The ASA Security Appliances support a series of SSM modules that enable Intrusion

Prevention Services (IPS) in addition to those available in the software version 7.0 feature set. The SSM module supports unique capabilities, such as Anti-X, inline packet inspection, and failure modes.

AAA Support

Cisco Security Appliances work with RADIUS or TACACS+ and the Cisco Access Control Server (CSACS) or other AAA products to provide AAA functionality. It is also possible to configure a local user database on the Appliances rather than integrate with an external authentication server.

X.509 Certificate Support

Digital certificates are your digital identification that verifies you are who you claim to be and validates the integrity of your data. Digital certificates are most commonly combined with encryption to secure data in the following four ways:

- **Authentication**—Digital certificates are used to verify the identity of a user or server.

- **Integrity**—If data has been digitally signed and it is altered, the digital signature becomes invalid, indicating to the recipient that the data is no longer valid.

- **Token verification**—Digital tokens are a much more secure product that can be used to replace passwords. Passwords are less secure because several methods are available that can determine a password by using both dictionaries and number/letter/word combination generators to try every conceivable combination of characters until they discover the password. A digital certificate is an encrypted file that resides on your computer and can be decrypted only by your password. To compromise your certificate, a user would have to have *both* the encrypted file and your password.

- **Encryption**—Digital certificates verify the identity of both ends of an encrypted connection and dynamically negotiate the parameters of that connection. Using digital certificates to negotiate virtual private networks (VPN) is discussed in detail in Chapter 13, "Virtual Private Networks."

Cisco Security Appliances support the Simple Certificate Enrollment Protocol (SCEP) and can be integrated with the following X.509 digital identification solutions:

- **Entrust Technologies, Inc.**—Entrust/PKI 4.0

- **Microsoft Corp.**—Windows 2000 Certificate Server 5.0

- **VeriSign**—Onsite 4.5

- **Baltimore Technologies**—UniCERT 3.05

Modular Policy Framework

Cisco Security Appliances can control traffic flows in a more granular manner than traditional firewalls through the use of Modular Policies. Much like Cisco IOS Software QoS CLI, Modular Policy Framework (MPF) allows the security administrator flexibility when designing security policies. Individual traffic flows can be redirected to specific policies for rate limiting, IP Precedence, or deep packet inspection. MPFs are divided into three sections:

- **Class-map**—Identifies the type of traffic flow that the MPF will use. The flow type is packet specific and can be any packet type, such as a VPN tunnel, voice traffic, or basic IP traffic.

- **Policy-map**—Assigns one or more actions to traffic flows specified by a class-map. For example, all basic IP traffic entering the site would be packet inspected and rate limited through a policy-map.

- **Service policy**—Assigns one or more policy-maps to an interface.

The MPF feature is new to the Security Appliance with the introduction of Software Version 7.0. Chapter 8, "Modular Policy Framework," covers MPFs in more detail.

Network Address Translation/Port Address Translation

Cisco Security Appliances can statically or dynamically translate internal private (RFC 1918) addresses or any other address used internally to the assigned public addresses. They can also hide multiple hosts on the internal network behind a single public address. A one-for-one translation of addresses from internal to external, or from external to internal, is referred to as Network Address Translation (NAT). If multiple internal addresses are translated behind a single external address, each outgoing connection uses a different source port. This is called Port Address Translation (PAT).

Firewall Management

Cisco Security Appliances can be managed using one of three methods:

- **Cisco command-line interface (CLI)**—Uses commands consistent with other Cisco products. The PIX can be configured to allow access to the CLI via console, Telnet, and SSH. All system configurations can be saved as a text file for archive and recovery purposes.

- **Cisco Adaptive Security Device Manager (ASDM)**—A browser-based graphical user interface (GUI) that can be used to manage the PIX Firewall and ASA Security Appliance. The GUI connects to the device via a secure connection (SSL) and provides a simplified method of device management. The PDM and ASDM also provides real-time log data that can be used to track events and do limited troubleshooting.

> **NOTE** Until PIX Models 501/506E are supported in a future release of the Security Appliance OS, PASM alone is available to manage these devices.

■ **CiscoWorks Management Center for Firewalls (PIX MC)**—A component of the CiscoWorks Enterprise Management Center. The PIX MC allows you to manage as many as 1000 PIX Firewalls and can be used to manage the entire perimeter of your enterprise network. PIX MC support is forthcoming.

Simple Network Management Protocol

Cisco Security Appliances allow limited Simple Network Management Protocol (SNMP) support. Because SNMP was designed as a network management protocol and not a security protocol, it can be used to exploit a device. For this reason, Cisco Security Appliances allow only *read-only* access to remote connections. This enables the manager to remotely connect to the device and monitor SNMP traps but does not allow the manager to change any SNMP settings.

Syslog Support

Cisco Security Appliances log four different types of events onto syslog:

■ Security

■ Resource

■ System

■ Accounting

The Appliances can be configured to react differently to any of eight severity levels for each event type. Logs are stored in system memory and can be forwarded to a syslog server. It is a recommended practice to select the appropriate log level that generates the syslog details required to track session-specific data.

Security Contexts

Cisco Security Appliances support multiple standalone firewalls within a single firewall or appliance device. This functionality allows administrators greater flexibility when configuring policies for specific groups, sections, or departments by assigning each context its own independent policies. Each virtual firewall is completely contained and does not affect any other configuration on the device.

Transparent Firewalls

Beginning with software version 7.0, transparent firewalling allows you to drop in a firewall without having to consider the IP addressing structure and provides stealthy, high-speed traffic analysis and filtering at Layers 2 to 7. One need not consider routing protocols or providing special handling of multicast traffic.

NOTE   Security contexts and transparent firewalls are only supported on Cisco PIX Firewalls and ASA Security Appliances running Secure software version 7.0 or greater.

Virtual Private Networks

All Cisco Security Appliances are designed to function as a termination point, or *VPN gateway,* for VPNs. This functionality allows administrators to create encrypted connections with other networks over the Internet. The VPN performance of each PIX model is listed in its corresponding specifications section later in this chapter.

Optional Firewall Components

Cisco offers five optional components for use with the PIX 515E, 525, or 535 models. These components can increase the performance and functionality of the PIX Firewall. The five optional components include the following:

- **VPN Accelerator Card (VAC)**—The VAC is a card that fits into a PCI slot of the PIX 515E through 535 firewall appliances and increases VPN performance and security by segregating the processing required for the VPN from all other traffic traversing the firewall. The VAC supports both DES and 3DES encryption.

- **VPN Accelerator Card Plus (VAC+)**—The VAC+ is an improved version of the VAC. It also fits into a PCI slot of the PIX 515E through 535 appliances. The VAC+ supports DES, 3DES, and the Advanced Encryption Standard (AES). The VAC+ requires PIX OS version 6.3(1) or higher with a DES, 3DES/AES license.

NOTE   Only one VAC or VAC+ card can be installed in the PIX appliance.

- **Cisco PIX Firewall FastEthernet Interface Card (PIX-1FE)**—The PIX-1FE is a 10/100 Ethernet interface on a 33-MHz PCI card. This enables you to increase the number of interfaces on the 515E to 535 appliances.

- **Cisco PIX 64-bit/66-MHz Four-Port FastEthernet Interface Card (4FE-66)**—The 4FE-66 interface card is a single PCI card that combines four 10/100 Ethernet interfaces. This interface card works with the 515E, 525, and 535 firewall appliances and allows you to install four 10/100 interfaces per PCI slot up to the maximum number of interfaces per device model.

- **Cisco PIX Firewall 66-MHz Gigabit Ethernet Card (1GE-66)**—The 1GE-66 Gigabit interface fits into the PCI slot of the 525 and 535 firewall appliances. The 1GE-66 allows for full-duplex gigabit (1000BASE-SX) performance, compliant with the IEEE 802.2 and 802.3z Ethernet standards.

NOTE The type and number of interfaces that will function in the PIX Firewall appliance is normally determined by the license installed not the number of available PCI slots.

Cisco offers additional security services for the ASA Security Appliances using a Service Security Module (SSM). SSM adapters allow for an adaptable security architecture that allows a business or enterprise to deploy custom security solutions where they need them. Each SSM will enable new security inspection services and techniques that can be used by a Cisco ASA Security Appliance. The ATM Interface Processor-SSM (AIP-SSM) is the only SSM currently available. The AIP-SSM is a diskless module, based on a Pentium 4 processor, that adds additional security services, such as Intrusion Prevention Systems (IPS)and Anti-X protection. Two AIP-SSM modules currently are deployed by Cisco:

- **Cisco AIP-SSM-10**—The AIP-SSM-10 fits into the SSM module port on the ASA Security Appliance. The module enables Intrusion Prevention Services for the ASA models using inline or promiscuous operational modes. The AIP-SSM-10 supports a 2.0-GHz Celeron processor and 1.0 GB of RAM. An additional gigabit Ethernet management port is included with the module.

- **Cisco AIP-SSM-20**—The AIP-SSM-20 is an advanced version of the AIP-SSM-10. It supports a 2.6-GHz Pentium 4 processor and 2.0 GB of RAM. The AIP-SSM-20 is only supported by the ASA 5520 and ASA 5530 Security Appliances.

PIX Firewall Model Capabilities

The following sections describe the characteristics and capabilities of each of the PIX Firewall models. The *throughput* speeds mentioned for each model refer to the speeds at which the firewall can process the data. The actual throughput for the firewall is largely determined by the speed of the firewall interface, the speed of the connected link, or the packet (MTU) size.

Cisco PIX 501

The Cisco PIX 501 Firewall was designed for the SOHO environment. It has a 133-MHz processor, 16 MB of RAM, and 8 MB of Flash memory. It has an outside Ethernet interface and an integrated four-port Ethernet 10/100 switch on the internal side. It has a 9600-baud console port that is used for local device management. The PIX 501 does not support failover.

Connection capabilities for the PIX 501 are as follows:

- **Maximum clear-text throughput**—60 Mbps
- **Maximum throughput (DES)**—6 Mbps
- **Maximum throughput (AES-128)**—4.5 Mbps
- **Maximum throughput (3DES)**—3 Mbps
- **Maximum concurrent connections**—7500
- **Maximum concurrent VPN peers**—10

As shown in Figure 3-3, the front panel of the PIX 501 has a power indicator, a VPN tunnel indicator, and two rows of LEDs for link and network activity. These indicators are divided into two groups:

- The outside Ethernet interface
- The four inside Ethernet interfaces (switch)

Figure 3-3 *PIX 501 Front Panel*

There are several licenses available for the PIX 501 Firewall. Upgrades are available to increase the number of users or to implement VPN support. Table 3-2 describes the available licenses and their functions.

Table 3-2 *Cisco PIX 501 Licenses*

License	Function
10 User License	Support for up to ten concurrent connections from different source IP addresses on the internal network to traverse the firewall. Also provides DHCP server support for up to 32 leases.
50 User License	Support for up to 50 concurrent connections from different source IP addresses on the internal network to traverse the firewall. Also provides DHCP server support for up to 128 leases.
Unlimited User License	Support for an unlimited number of concurrent connections from different source IP addresses on the internal network to traverse the firewall. Also provides DHCP server support for up to 256 leases.
DES Encryption License	Support for 56-bit DES encryption.
3DES/AES Encryption License	Support for 168-bit 3DES and up to 256-bit AES encryption.

NOTE DES, 3DES, and AES encryption will be discussed in detail in Chapter 13.

Cisco PIX 506E

The Cisco PIX 506E Firewall was designed for the ROBO environment. It has a 300-MHz Celeron processor, 32 MB of RAM, and 8 MB of Flash memory. It has a fixed outside Ethernet interface and a fixed inside Ethernet interface. It has a 9600-baud console port that is used for local device management. The PIX 506 does not support failover.

Connection capabilities for the PIX 506 are as follows:

- **Maximum clear-text throughput**—100 Mbps
- **Maximum throughput (DES)**—20 Mbps
- **Maximum throughput (3DES)**—17 Mbps
- **Maximum throughput (AES-128)**—30 Mbps
- **Maximum concurrent connections**—25,000
- **Maximum concurrent VPN peers**—25

As shown in Figure 3-4, the PIX 506 has three status LEDs on the front panel that indicate power to the system, that the system is active (the OS is fully loaded), and that there is network activity on any interface.

Figure 3-4 *PIX 506 Front Panel*

As shown in Figure 3-5, the rear of the PIX 506 contains the Ethernet ports and the console port.

Figure 3-5 *PIX 506E Rear Panel*

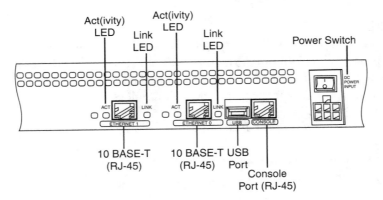

The console can be connected using an RJ-45 to a DB-9 or DB-25 serial adapter, as shown in Figure 3-6.

Figure 3-6 *PIX 506E Console Connection*

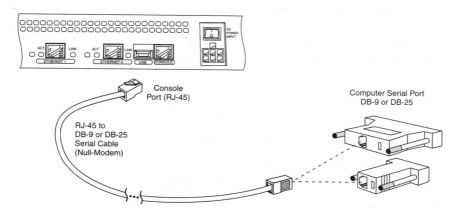

There are three licenses available for the PIX 506E Firewall. The basic license provides unlimited user access and the two upgrades allow for VPN support. Table 3-3 describes the available licenses and their function.

Table 3-3 *Cisco PIX 506E Licenses*

License	Function
Unlimited User License leases. This is the standard license that comes with the PIX 506E.	Support for an unlimited number of concurrent connections from source IP addresses on the internal network to traverse the firewall. Also provides DHCP server support for up to 256 leases. This is the standard license that comes with the PIX 506E.
DES Encryption License.	Support for 56-bit DES encryption.
3DES/AES Encryption License.	Support for 168-bit 3DES up to 256-bit AES encryption.

NOTE   With the introduction of software version 6.3, 3DES licenses add additional support for AES encryption.

Cisco PIX 515E

The Cisco PIX 515E Firewall was designed for small- to medium-size businesses. The PIX 515E is the smallest firewall of the PIX family that is designed to be rack-mountable and is a standard 1U (1.75-inch) configuration. It has a 433-MHz processor, 32 MB or 64 MB of RAM, and 16 MB of Flash memory. It has two fixed 10/100 Ethernet interfaces that have a default configuration of outside (Ethernet 0) and inside (Ethernet 1) and contains two PCI slots for the installation of up to four additional Ethernet interfaces.

The PIX 515E also supports the use of *virtual interfaces* for switched environments using 802.1q VLAN tagging. It has a 9600-baud console port that is used for local device management. The PIX 515E can be configured for failover using a failover cable connected to the 115-kbps serial connection. PIX Firewall OS version 6.2 provides the functionality for long-distance (LAN-based) failover. This is discussed in greater detail in Chapter 11, "Routing and the Cisco Security Appliance."

Connection capabilities for the PIX 515E are as follows:

- **Maximum clear-text throughput**—188 Mbps
- **Maximum throughput (3DES)**—63 Mbps with VAC
- **Maximum throughput (3DES)**—140 Mbps with VAC+
- **Maximum throughput (AES-128)**—135 Mbps with VAC+
- **Maximum throughput (AES-256)**—140 Mbps with VAC+
- **Maximum concurrent connections**—130,000
- **Maximum concurrent VPN peers**—2000

As shown in Figure 3-7, the PIX 515E has three status LEDs on the front panel that indicate power to the system, that the system is active (the OS is fully loaded and the system is operational), and that there is network activity on any interface. If you have two firewalls running in the failover mode, the active light indicates which firewall is active and which is standby.

Figure 3-7 *PIX 515E Front Panel*

The rear of the PIX 515E contains the Ethernet ports and the console port. The PIX 515E can handle up to four additional Ethernet interfaces. This could be a single four-port Ethernet card (see Figure 3-8) or two single-port cards (see Figure 3-9). The PIX 515E automatically recognizes and numbers any additional interfaces that are installed.

The PIX 515E also can be configured with a VAC or VAC+. The VAC and VAC+ handle much of the VPN traffic processing (encryption and decryption), thus improving the firewall's performance. The VAC and VAC+ are recommended for firewalls that connect multiple high-traffic VPNs.

Figure 3-8   *PIX 515E with Additional Four-Port Interface*

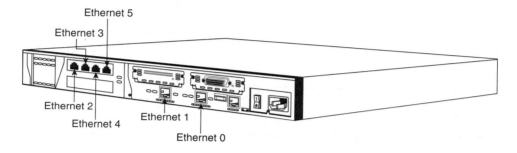

Figure 3-9   *PIX 515E with Two Additional Interfaces*

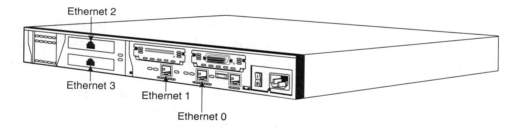

The installation of additional interfaces and failover requires that the software license be upgraded from the basic license (515-R) to the unrestricted license (515-UR). A maximum of three interfaces can be installed using the restricted license.

The console connection for the PIX 515E is the same as for the 506E.

There are three licenses available for the PIX 515E Firewall. Upgrades are available to implement VPN support. Table 3-4 describes the available licenses and their functions.

Table 3-4 *Cisco PIX 515E Licenses*

License	Function
Restricted Software License	Support for 32 MB of RAM and up to three 10/100 interfaces. The restricted license supports only limited VPN connectivity and does not support failover.
Unrestricted Software License	Support for 64 MB of RAM, up to six 10/100 interfaces, stateful failover, integrated VAC or VAC+, and 5 security contexts.
Failover Software License	Support for a "hot standby" system designed to operate in conjunction with an active system running the unrestricted license.

Cisco PIX 525

The Cisco PIX 525 Firewall is an enterprise firewall. It provides perimeter security for large enterprise networks. The PIX 525 is rack-mountable in a 2U (3.5-inch) configuration. It has a 600-MHz processor, up to 256 MB of RAM, and 16 MB of Flash memory. It has two fixed 10/100 Ethernet interfaces. The two fixed interfaces are Ethernet 0, which is the outside interface by default, and Ethernet 1, which is the inside interface by default.

The PIX 525 also includes three PCI slots for the installation of up to six additional Ethernet interfaces. It has a 9600-baud console port that is used for local device management. The PIX 525 can be configured for failover using a failover cable connected to the 115-kbps serial connection or can be configured for LAN-based failover. The PIX 525 also can be configured with a VAC. The VAC handles much of the processing of VPN traffic (encryption and decryption), thus improving the firewall's performance. The VAC is recommended for firewalls that will connect multiple high-traffic VPNs.

Connection capabilities for the PIX 525 are as follows:

- Maximum clear-text throughput—330 Mbps
- Maximum throughput (3DES)—72 Mbps with VAC
- Maximum throughput (3DES)—155 Mbps with VAC+
- Maximum throughput (AES-128)—165 Mbps with VAC+
- Maximum throughput (AES-256)—170 Mbps with VAC+
- Maximum concurrent connections—280,000
- Maximum concurrent VPN peers—2000

As shown in Figure 3-10, the PIX 525 has two LEDs on the front. These LEDs indicate that the firewall has power and that the system is active (the OS is loaded and the system is operational). The active light indicates which firewall is active in a failover pair.

Figure 3-10 *PIX 525 Front Panel*

The rear of the PIX 525, shown in Figure 3-11, is similar in design to the PIX 515E, with fixed interfaces and additional PCI slots. The PIX 525 can support 10/100 Mbps and Gbps Ethernet interface cards.

Figure 3-11 *PIX 525 Rear Panel*

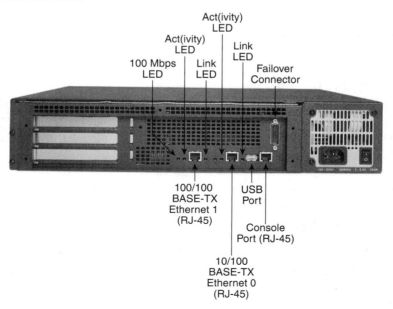

The console connection for the PIX 525 is the same as for the PIX 506E, 515E, and 535.

> **NOTE** The installation of additional physical interfaces and failover requires that the software license be upgraded from the Restricted Bundle.

The three licenses available for the PIX 525 Firewall are similar to those available for the PIX 515E but support a greater amount of RAM and more available physical interfaces. Upgrades are available to increase the number of supported physical interfaces or to implement VPN hardware (VAC/VAC+) support. Table 3-5 describes the available licenses and their functions.

Table 3-5 *Cisco PIX 525 Licenses*

License	Function
Restricted Software License	Support for 128 MB of RAM and up to six total 10/100 interfaces or three Gigabit interfaces (plus the two 10/100 onboard interfaces).
Unrestricted Software License	Support for 256 MB of RAM, a total of eight 10/100 interfaces or three Gigabit interfaces (plus the two onboard 10/100 interfaces), stateful failover, integrated VAC or VAC+, and 50 security contexts.
Failover Software License	Support for a "hot standby" system designed to operate in conjunction with an active system running the unrestricted license.

Cisco PIX 535

The Cisco PIX 535 Firewall is the ultimate enterprise firewall designed for enterprise networks and service providers. The PIX 535 is rack-mountable and fits a 3U configuration. It has a 1-GHz processor, up to 1 GB of RAM, and 16 MB of Flash memory. It has nine PCI slots for the installation of up to ten Ethernet interfaces. It has a 9600-baud console port that is used for local device management.

The PIX 535 can be configured for failover using a failover cable connected to the 115-kbps serial connection or configured for LAN-based failover. The PIX 535 is also available with redundant hot-swappable power supplies.

The PIX 535 can also be configured with a VAC or VAC+. The VAC and VAC+ handle much of the VPN traffic processing (encryption and decryption), thus improving the firewall's performance. The VAC and VAC+ are recommended for firewalls that connect multiple high-traffic VPNs.

Connection capabilities for the PIX 535 are as follows:

- **Maximum clear-text throughput**—1.7 GBps
- **Maximum throughput (3DES)**—100 Mbps with VAC
- **Maximum throughput (3DES)**—440 Mbps with VAC+
- **Maximum throughput (128 AES)**—535 Mbps with VAC+
- **Maximum throughput (256 AES)**—440 Mbps with VAC+
- **Maximum concurrent connections**—500,000
- **Maximum concurrent VPN peers**—2000

As shown in Figure 3-12, the PIX 535 has two LEDs on the front. These LEDs indicate that the firewall has power and that the system is active (the OS is loaded and passing traffic). The active light indicates which device of a failover pair is active and which is standby.

Figure 3-12   *PIX 535 Front Panel*

The PCI slots are divided into different bus speeds. The slots are numbered from right to left, and slots 0 through 3 run at 64-bit/66 MHz and can support Gigabit Ethernet interface cards (1GE-66). Slots 4 through 8 run at 32-bit/33 MHz and can support Fast Ethernet interface cards (PIX-1FE and PIX-4FE). Figure 3-13 depicts the rear panel of the PIX 535 Firewall.

Figure 3-13 *PIX 535 Rear Panel*

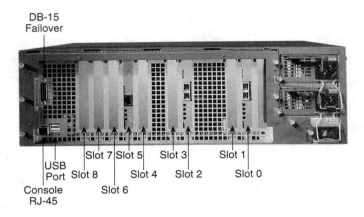

NOTE Do not mix 33-MHz and 66-MHz cards on the same bus. This causes the overall speed of the 66-MHz bus to be reduced to 33 MHz.

The PIX 535 also supports a VPN accelerator card (VAC and VAC+). It should be installed only on the 32-bit/33-MHz bus.

The console connection for the PIX 535 is the same as for the other PIX models.

The three licenses available for the PIX 535 Firewall are similar to those available for the PIX 515E and 525 but support a greater amount of RAM and more available physical interfaces. Upgrades are available to implement VPN hardware (VAC or VAC+) support. PIX OS version 6.3 supports logical interfaces and VLANs. Table 3-6 describes the available licenses and their functions.

Table 3-6 *Cisco PIX 535 Licenses*

License	Function
Restricted Software License	Support for 512 MB of RAM and up to eight 10/100 interfaces or eight Gigabit interfaces
Unrestricted Software License	Support for 1 GB of RAM, up to 10 10/100 interfaces or 9 Gigabit interfaces, stateful failover, integrated VAC or VAC+, and 50 security contexts
Failover Software License	Support for a "hot standby" system designed to operate in conjunction with an active system running the unrestricted license

NOTE The installation of additional interfaces and failover requires that the software license be upgraded from the Restricted Bundle.

NOTE The PIX 506E through 535 Firewall appliances all have an onboard USB port. At this time, the USB port is not used.

Cisco ASA Security Model Capabilities

The following sections describe the characteristics and capabilities of each firewall in the ASA Security Appliance family. The *throughput* speeds mentioned for each model refer to the speeds at which the firewall can process the data with most services enabled. The addition of an AIP-SSM module will reduce an interface's *throughput* speeds if enabled.

All the ASA Security Appliances feature the same chassis (see Figure 3-14).

Figure 3-14 *ASA Security Appliance 55X0 Front Panel*

The firewalls in the ASA Security Appliance family of firewalls are rack mountable and have a 1U footprint once installed. As shown in Figure 3-14, all ASA Security Appliances feature five LEDs on the front panel. The power LED illuminates if the ASA Security Appliance is powered on. The status LED indicates the boot state of the ASA Security Appliance. When the LED is green, the appliance booted successfully. If the LED displays a red light, it has failed to correctly boot up and should be examined. The active LED flashes as traffic flows through the appliance. If any active VPN tunnels terminate on the appliance, the VPN LED will light. The Flash LED will blink whenever the system flash is accessed.

As illustrated in Figure 3-15, the Adaptive Security Appliances include one expansion slot, a Compact Flash slot, fixed Ethernet interfaces, and two USB 2.0 ports (currently unused by the operating system), as well as a standard Cisco Console and AUX port.

Figure 3-15 *ASA Security Application 55X0 Rear Panel*

All ASA 55X0 Security Appliances support six physical interfaces. The 10/100/1000BASE-T Ethernet Management Port can be used for management access to the ASA Security Appliance. The ASA 5520 and ASA 5530 have the option of using this port as a normal Ethernet port, allowing standard traffic to flow through it. The ASA 5510 supports 10/100BASE-T Ethernet on this port.

Each ASA Security Appliance includes four 10/100/1000BASE-T Ethernet ports, excluding the management port. The ASA 5510 only supports 10/100BASE-T Ethernet.

The console connection for ASA Security Appliances is the same as for the PIX models.

Cisco ASA 5510 Security Appliance

The Cisco ASA 5510 Security Appliance is an advanced firewall and VPN solution designed for small to medium-size businesses, as well as remote offices. The ASA 5510 is a powerful security device, running on a 1.6-GHz Celeron processor, with up to 256 MB of RAM and 64 MB of Flash memory.

The ASA 5510 can be configured for failover only with the Cisco ASA 5510 Security Plus license upgrade.

The ASA 5510 does not support the Security Context feature. No VLAN support is available for the ASA 5510 without a Security Plus upgrade. The upgrade will enable support for ten VLANs. The ASA 5510 supports both IPSec VPNs and SSL VPNs (WebVPN).

Connection capabilities for the ASA 5510 Security Appliance are as follow:

- Maximum firewall throughput—300 Mbps
- Maximum throughput (with AIP-SSM-10)—150 Mbps

- Maximum VPN throughput—170 Mbps
- Maximum concurrent connections—32,000/64,000*
- Maximum concurrent IPSec VPN peers—50/150*
- Maximum concurrent WebVPN peers—50/150*

NOTE   * The larger number is only available with a Cisco ASA 5510 Security Plus License.

Two licenses are available for the ASA 5510. The Base software license enables the standard functions of the ASA Security Appliance, including 50 IPSec VPN peers. The Security Plus software license adds more VPN peers, enables VLAN support, and LAN-based failover support. Table 3-7 describes the available licenses and their functions.

Table 3-7   *Cisco ASA 5510 Licenses*

License	Function
Base Software License	Support for 256 MB of RAM, up to 3 10/100 interfaces, and 50 IPSec VPN peers
Security Plus Software License	Support for 256 MB of RAM, up to 5 10/100 interfaces, 10 VLANs, 150 IPSec VPN peers, and LAN-based failover

Cisco ASA 5520 Security Appliance

The Cisco ASA 5520 Security Appliance is a high-availability enterprise firewall and VPN. It is designed as a perimeter security device, as well as a VPN head point for all enterprise connectivity. The ASA 5520 supports a 2.0-GHz Celeron processor, with up to 512 MB of RAM and 64 MB of Flash memory.

The availability of security contexts allows the ASA 5520 to support more flexible firewall design than the ASA 5510. In addition, the ASA 5520 allows the use of SSL VPNs (WebVPN) to support up to 750 IPSec VPNs.

The ASA 5520 can be configured for LAN-based failover by default. Failover can be enabled as Active/Active or Active/Standby.

Connection capabilities for the ASA 5520 Security Appliance are as follows:

- Maximum firewall throughput—450 Mbps
- Maximum throughput (with AIP-SSM-10)—225 Mbps
- Maximum throughput (with AIP-SSM-20)—375 Mbps

- Maximum VPN throughput—225 Mbps
- Maximum concurrent connections—130,000
- Maximum concurrent IPSec VPN peers—300/750*
- Maximum concurrent WebVPN peers—300/750*

NOTE   * The larger number is only available with a Cisco ASA 5520 VPN Plus License.

Two licenses are available for the ASA 5520. The Base software license enables the standard functions of the ASA Security Appliance, 300 IPSec VPN peers, and 25 VLANs. With the ASA 5520, security contexts are enabled by default, and security contexts are installed with the Base License 2.

The Security Plus Software License supports all the Base Software License features. Security Plus upgrades the maximum VPN peers from 300 to 750. The ASA 5520 supports up to ten Security Contexts, with the purchase of the VPN Plus License. Table 3-8 describes the available licenses and their functions.

Table 3-8 *Cisco ASA 5520 Licenses*

License	Function
Base Software License	Support for 4 10/100/1000 MB interfaces, 1 10/100 MB interface, 25 VLANs, 2 security contexts, and 300 IPSec VPN peers
VPN + Software License	Support for 4 10/100/1000 MB interfaces, 1 10/100 MB interface, 25 VLANs, 2 security contexts, and 750 IPSec VPN peers

Cisco ASA 5540 Security Appliance

The Cisco ASA 5540 is the premiere Security Appliance for the large enterprise environment. The ASA 5540 can support up to 100 VLANs, allowing a security administrator greater flexibility when designing a corporate LAN. The ASA 5540 runs on a 2.0-GHz Pentium 4 processor, with up to 1,024 MB of RAM and 64 MB of Flash memory.

The ASA 5540, like the ASA 5520, supports LAN-based failover in either Active/Active or Active/Standby modes. The ASA 5540 supports up to 50 security contexts with purchase of the VPN Premiere License.

Connection capabilities for the ASA 5540 Security Appliance are as follows:

- **Maximum firewall throughput**—650 Mbps
- **Maximum throughput (with AIP-SSM-20)**—450 Mbps
- **Maximum VPN throughput**—325 Mbps
- **Maximum concurrent connections**—280,000
- **Maximum concurrent IPSec VPN peers**—500/2000*/5000**
- **Maximum concurrent WebVPN peers**—500/1250*/2500**

NOTE   * A Cisco ASA 5540 VPN Plus License is required for this upgrade.
** A Cisco ASA 5540 VPN Premiere License is required for this upgrade.

Three software licenses are available for the ASA 5540. The Base License enables the standard functions of the ASA Security Appliance, including 500 IPSec VPN peers. The VPN Plus License adds more VPN peers. The VPN Premiere License enables additional VPNS beyond the VPN Plus License. Table 3-9 describes the available licenses and their functions.

Table 3-9   *Cisco ASA 5540 Licenses*

License	Function
Base Software License	Support for 4 10/100/1000 MB interfaces, 1 10/100 MB interface, 100 VLANs, 2 security contexts, 500 IPSec VPN peers, and 500 WebVPNs
VPN + Software License	Support for 4 10/100/1000 MB interfaces, 1 10/100 MB interface, 100 VLANs, 2 security contexts, 2000 IPSec VPN peers, and 1250 WebVPNs
VPN Premiere License	Support for 4 10/100/1000 MB interfaces, 1 10/100 MB interface, 100 VLANs, 2 security contexts, 5000 IPSec VPN peers, and 2500 WebVPNs

Foundation Summary

The "Foundation Summary" provides a convenient review of many key concepts in this chapter. If you are already comfortable with the topics in this chapter, this summary can help you recall a few details. If you just read this chapter, this review should help solidify some key facts. If you are doing your final preparation before the exam, this summary provides a convenient way to review the day before the exam.

Adaptive Security Algorithm

The ASA is an algorithm used by the Cisco Security Appliance to provide better security than packet filters and better performance than application proxies. Each interface of the firewall is assigned a *security level*. Traffic flows through the firewall are managed by the security level combined with ACLs or conduits. TCP sequence numbers for outbound connections are randomly generated by the Cisco Security Appliance to greatly reduce the chances of an inbound TCP session being hijacked.

Cut-Through Proxy

Cut-through proxy is the method used by the Cisco Security Appliance to authorize users and then allow the connection to occur at the network level after completing the ASA process. This greatly improves firewall performance over application proxy firewalls because every packet traversing the firewall is not inspected.

Cisco PIX Firewall Models and Features

The following is a list of the Cisco PIX Firewall models. Table 3-10 lists the capabilities of each model except the FWSM, which is discussed in great detail in Chapter 19:

- PIX 501—Designed for SOHO use and has two effective interfaces, a single outside interface and a four-port inside switch.

- PIX 506E—Designed for ROBO use and has a single outside interface and a single inside interface.

- PIX 515E—Designed for small- to medium-size networks.

- PIX 525—Designed for large enterprise networks.

- PIX 535—Designed for large enterprise networks and ISPs.

- FWSM—A firewall blade designed for the Cisco Catalyst 6500 Series Switch and 7600 Series router.

Cisco ASA Security Appliance Models and Features

The following is a list of the Cisco ASA Security Appliance models. Table 3-11 lists the capabilities of each model:

- ASA 5510—Designed for small to medium-size networks.
- ASA 5520—Designed for medium-size to large networks and for enterprise environments.
- ASA 5540—Designed for large enterprise networks and ISPs.

Intrusion Protection

Cisco Security Appliances were designed to independently detect and react to a variety of attacks. They can also be integrated with the Cisco Secure Intrusion Detection System to dynamically react to different threats.

AAA Support

The Cisco Security Appliance supports the following AAA technologies:

- **Local database**—It is possible to configure a local AAA database on the PIX Firewall; however, it is not recommended because the additional processing required to utilize the local database can adversely effect the performance of the firewall.
- RADIUS—The Cisco Security Appliance supports RADIUS.
- TACACS+—The Cisco Security Appliance supports TACACS+.

X.509 Certificate Support

The Cisco Security Appliance supports X.509 certificates for digital identity verification. X.509 certificates are used in conjunction with encryption for the following:

- **Authentication**—Digital certificates are used to authenticate the identity of a user or server.
- **Integrity**—A digital certificate becomes invalid if the digitally signed data has been altered.
- **Token verification**—Digital certificates can be used as a replacement for passwords.
- **Encryption**—Digital certificates simplify the identity authentication process when negotiating a VPN connection.

The Cisco Security Appliance supports the Simple Certificate Enrollment Protocol (SCEP) and can be integrated with the following X.509 digital identification solutions:

- **Entrust Technologies, Inc.**—Entrust/PKI 4.0
- **Microsoft Corp.**—Windows 2000 Certificate Server 5.0
- **VeriSign**—Onsite 4.5
- **Baltimore Technologies**—UniCERT 3.05

Modular Policy Framework

Beginning with Firewall software version 7.0, Cisco Security Appliances can manage traffic flow at a more granular level. Security administrators can separate each type of traffic entering their networks and assign one or more actions to each flow per interface.

NAT/PAT

The Cisco Security Appliance can perform both NAT and PAT.

Firewall Management

Cisco Security Appliances can be managed using one of three methods:

- Cisco command-line interface (CLI)
- Cisco Adaptive Security Device Manager (ASDM)
- CiscoWorks Management Center for Firewalls (PIX MC)

SNMP

Cisco Security Appliances allow limited SNMP support. Because SNMP was designed as a network management protocol and not a security protocol, it can be used to exploit a device. For this reason, the Security Appliance allows only read-only access to remote connections. This allows the manager to remotely connect to the device and monitor SNMP traps but does not allow the manager to change any SNMP settings.

Syslog Support

Cisco Security Appliances log four different types of events onto syslog:

- Security
- Resource
- System
- Accounting

Virtual Private Networks

All Cisco Security Appliances are designed to function as a termination point, or *VPN gateway*, for VPNs. This functionality enables administrators to create encrypted connections with other networks over the Internet.

Security Context

Security context creates multiple virtual firewalls within a single Cisco Security Appliance. Each virtual firewall supports a unique policy configuration. A single administration context exists to control the main features of the Security Appliance not covered by each virtual firewall.

Cisco Security Appliance Models

Table 3-10 *PIX Models and Features*

Firewall Features	501	506E	515E	525	535
Intended Business Application	SOHO	ROBO	Small- to medium-size business	Enterprise	Enterprise/ISP
Intrusion Protection	Yes	Yes	Yes	Yes	Yes
AAA Support	Yes	Yes	Yes	Yes	Yes
X.509 Certificate Support	Yes	Yes	Yes	Yes	Yes
AVVID Partner Support	Yes	Yes	Yes	Yes	Yes
Maximum Installed Interfaces	One plus a four-port 10/100 switch	Two 10/100	Six 10/100	Eight 10/100 or Three Gigabit and two 10/100	Ten 10/100 or Nine Gigabit
Supports DHCP	Yes	Yes	Yes	Yes	Yes
NAT	Yes	Yes	Yes	Yes	Yes
PAT	Yes	Yes	Yes	Yes	Yes
PPP over Ethernet	Yes	Yes	Yes	Yes	Yes

continues

Table 3-10   *PIX Models and Features (Continued)*

Firewall Features	501	506E	515E	525	535
Cisco PIX Command Line	Yes	Yes	Yes	Yes	Yes
PIX Device Manager	Yes	Yes	Yes	Yes	Yes
Adaptive Security Device Manager	No	No	Yes	Yes	Yes
Cisco Secure Policy Manager	Yes	Yes	Yes	Yes	Yes
Cisco Modular Policy Framework	No	No	Yes	Yes	Yes
SNMP and Syslog Support	Yes	Yes	Yes	Yes	Yes
Failover Support	No	No	Yes	Yes	Yes
Maximum Throughput	60 Mbps	100 Mbps	188 Mbps	330 Mbps	1.7 GBps
Maximum Throughput (DES)	6 Mbps	20 Mbps	Not listed	Not listed	Not listed
Maximum Throughput (3DES)	3 Mbps	17 Mbps	63-Mbps VAC 140-Mbps VAC+	72-Mbps VAC 155-Mbps VAC+	100-Mbps VAC 440-Mbps VAC+
Maximum Throughput (AES)	4.5 Mbps (128 AES)	30 Mbps (128 AES)	135 Mbps (128 AES) 140 Mbps (256 AES)	165 Mbps (128 AES) 170 Mbps (256 AES)	535 Mbps (128 AES) 440 Mbps (256 AES)
Maximum Concurrent Connections	7500	25,000	130,000	280,000	500,000
Maximum Concurrent VPN Peers	10	25	2000	2000	2000
Maximum Number of Security Contexts	–	–	5	50	50

Table 3-10 *PIX Models and Features (Continued)*

Firewall Features	501	506E	515E	525	535
Processor	133 MHz	300 MHz	433 MHz	600 MHz	1.0 GHz
RAM	16 MB	32 MB	32/64 MB	Up to 256 MB	Up to 1 GB
Flash Memory	8 MB	8 MB	16 MB	16 MB	16 MB

Table 3-11 *ASA Models and Features*

ASA Features	5510	5520	5540
Intended Business Application	Small to medium-size businesses	Enterprise	Enterprise/ ISP
Intrusion Protection	Only with AIP-SSM-10	Only with AIP-SSM-10 or AIP-SSM-20	Only with AIP-SSM-10 or AIP-SSM-20
AAA Support	Yes	Yes	Yes
X.509 Certificate	Yes	Yes	Yes
Support AVVID Partner	Yes	Yes	Yes
Support Maximum Installed Interfaces	5 10/100	4 10.100.1000 1 10/100	4 10.100.1000 1 10/100
Supports DHCP	Yes	Yes	Yes
NAT	Yes	Yes	Yes
PAT	Yes	Yes	Yes
PPP Over Ethernet	Yes	Yes	Yes
Cisco Command Line	Yes	Yes	Yes
PIX Device Manager	No	No	No
Adaptive Security Device Manager	Yes	Yes	Yes
Cisco Secure Policy	Yes	Yes	Yes

continues

Table 3-11 *ASA Models and Features (Continued)*

ASA Features	5510	5520	5540
Cisco Modular Policy Framework	Yes	Yes	Yes
Manager SNMP and Syslog	Yes	Yes	Yes
Support Failover Support	Yes	Yes	Yes
Maximum Gbps Throughput (w/AIP-SSM) Maximum Mbps	300 Mbps	450 Mbps	650 Mbps
	150 Mbps	375 Mbps	450 Mbps
Throughput (3DES)	170 Mbps	225 Mbps	325 Mbps
Maximum Concurrent Connections	64,000	130,000	280,000
Maximum Number of Security Contexts	0	10	50
Maximum Concurrent VPN Peers	150	750	5000
Maximum Concurrent WebVPN Peers	150	750	2500
Processor	1.6-GHz Celeron	2.0-GHz Celeron	2.0-Ghz Pentium 4
RAM	256 MB	512 MB	1025 MB
Flash Memory	64 MB	64 MB	64 MB

Q&A

As mentioned in the Introduction, the questions in this book are more difficult than what you should experience on the exam. The questions are designed to ensure your understanding of the concepts discussed in this chapter and adequately prepare you to complete the exam. You should take the simulated exams on the CD to practice for the exam.

The answers to these questions can be found in Appendix A:

1. What is the ASA, and how does Cisco PIX Firewall use it?

2. Why does the ASA generate random TCP sequence numbers?

3. What components of a TCP session does the ASA write to the state table to create a session object?

4. What can cause a session object to be deleted from the state table?

5. What are the three ways to initiate a cut-through proxy session?

6. What X.509 certificates do SCEP and the Security Appliance support?

7. How many physical interfaces does the PIX 515E support?

8. What is the lowest model number of the PIX Firewall family to support failover?

9. What are two methods of managing a Cisco ASA Security Appliance?

10. List four advantages of the ASA.

This chapter covers the following topics:

- Accessing the Cisco Security Appliance

- Command-Level Authorization

- Installing a New Operating System

- Upgrading the Cisco Security Appliance

- Operating System

- Creating a Boothelper Disk Using a Windows PC

- Password Recovery

- Overview of Simple Network Management Protocol on the Cisco Security Appliance

- Configuring Simple Network Management Protocol on the Cisco Security Appliance

- Troubleshooting Commands

CHAPTER 4

System Management/ Maintenance

How to Best Use This Chapter

Chapter 3, "Cisco Security Appliance," provides insight into the different models of the Cisco Security Appliance as well as the features and available configurations. This chapter provides information about how to configure access for Cisco Security Appliance, how to access Cisco Security Appliance, and how to maintain the integrity of Cisco Security Appliance through upgrades. In addition, this chapter discusses password recovery and how to create a boothelper disk. It is very important for you to understand in great detail the technology that powers Cisco Security Appliance. Test yourself with the "Do I Know This Already?" quiz and see how familiar you are with these aspects of Cisco Security Appliance.

"Do I Know This Already?" Quiz

The purpose of the "Do I Know This Already?" quiz is to help you decide if you really need to read the entire chapter. If you already intend to read the entire chapter, you do not necessarily need to answer these questions now.

The ten-question quiz, derived from the major sections in the "Foundation Topics" portion of the chapter, helps you determine how to spend your limited study time.

Table 4-1 outlines the major topics discussed in this chapter and the "Do I Know This Already?" quiz questions that correspond to those topics.

Table 4-1 *"Do I Know This Already?" Foundation Topics Section-to-Question Mapping*

Foundation Topics Section	Questions Covered in This Section	Score
Accessing the Cisco Security Appliance	7, 8, 10	
Command-Level Authorization	5, 6	
Installing a New Operating System		
Upgrading the Cisco Security Appliance Operating System	1, 3	
Creating a Boothelper Disk Using a Windows PC		
Password Recovery	2, 4	
Overview of Simple Network Management Protocol on the PIX Firewall		
Configuring Simple Network Management Protocol on the Security Appliance	9	
Troubleshooting Commands		

CAUTION The goal of self assessment is to gauge your mastery of the topics in this chapter. If you do not know the answer to a question or are only partially sure of the answer, you should mark this question wrong for purposes of the self assessment. Giving yourself credit for an answer you correctly guess skews your self-assessment results and might provide you with a false sense of security.

1. Which command upgrades a PIX Firewall 525 device running a 6.3 OS version to 7.0?

   a. install

   b. setup

   c. copy 7.0

   d. copy tftp flash

2. Which binary file is required to perform a password recovery procedure on a PIX device running OS version 6.3?

   a. np63.bin

   b. pix52.bin

   c. bh52.bin

   d. pass52.bin

3. What circumstance(s) warrant(s) the use of a boothelper disk in the OS upgrade procedure?

    a. A corrupt binary image

    b. A PIX 520 device

    c. A PIX device running a 6.0 or later PIX OS

    d. No circumstance warrants the use of a boothelper disk

4. To what is the console password set after a successful password recovery procedure?

    a. password.

    b. cisco.

    c. secret.

    d. It is erased and set to blank.

5. How many privilege levels are there on the PIX Firewall?

    a. 2

    b. 16

    c. 32

    d. 4

6. Which of the following is the highest level of privilege to which a user account can be assigned?

    a. 32

    b. 16

    c. 8

    d. 15

7. Which command changes the SSH password for login?

    a. change ssh password

    b. secret

    c. password

    d. ssh pass

8. What is the default amount of time a Telnet session can be idle?

   a. 2 minutes

   b. 15 minutes

   c. 5 minutes

   d. 12 minutes

9. Which of the following pieces of information are sent to an SNMP management station by the PIX Firewall?

   a. Link up and link down

   b. Running configuration

   c. Show command outputs

   d. Authentication failure

10. Which version of SSH does the PIX Firewall support?

    a. 2.1

    b. 2.2

    c. 3.1

    d. 1

The answers to the "Do I Know This Already?" quiz are found in Appendix A, "Answers to the 'Do I Know This Already?' Quizzes and Q&A Sections." The suggested choices for your next step are as follows:

■ **8 or less overall score**—Read the entire chapter. This includes the "Foundation Topics," "Foundation Summary," and "Q&A" sections.

■ **9 or 10 overall score**—If you want more review of these topics, skip to the "Foundation Summary" section and then go to the "Q&A" section. Otherwise, move to the next chapter.

Foundation Topics

Accessing Cisco Security Appliance

A Security Appliance can be accessed by using the console port or remotely using the following methods:

- Telnet

- Secure Shell (SSH)

- A browser using Cisco Adaptive Security Device Manger (ASDM)

Console port access allows a single user to configure Security Appliance. A user connects a PC or portable computer to Security Appliance through the console access port using a rollover cable.

The following sections describe how to access Security Appliance remotely using Telnet and SSH. Chapter 15, "Adaptive Security Device Manager," covers using the ASDM to access the PIX Firewall and other aspects of the ASDM in greater detail.

Accessing a Cisco Security Appliance with Telnet

You can manage Security Appliance by using Telnet from hosts on any internal interface. With Internet Protocol Security (IPSec) configured, you can use Telnet to administer the console of a Cisco Security Appliance remotely from lower-security interfaces.

To access the Security Appliance using a Telnet connection, you have to first configure the PIX Firewall for Telnet access:

Step 1   Enter the PIX Firewall **telnet** command:

```
telnet local-ip [mask] [if-name]
```

You can identify a single host or a subnet that can have Telnet access to the Security Appliance. For example, to let a host on the internal network with an address of 10.1.1.24 access the PIX Firewall, enter the following:

```
telnet 10.1.1.24 255.255.255.255 inside
```

> **NOTE**   If you do not specify the interface name, the **telnet** command adds command statements to the configuration to let the host or network access the Telnet management session from all internal interfaces.

Step 2   Configure the Telnet password using the **password** command:

```
password telnetpassword
```

If you do not set a password, the default Telnet password is **cisco**.

> **NOTE**   The **passwd** command can be used interchangeably with the **password** command.

Step 3   If required, set the duration for how long a Telnet session can be idle before the Security Appliance disconnects the session. The default duration is 5 minutes. To configure the timeout for 15 minutes, you would enter the following:

```
telnet timeout 15
```

Step 4   (Optional) To protect access to the console with an authentication server, use the **aaa authentication telnet console** command. (Authentication, authorization, and accounting [AAA] authentication is optional.) This requires that you have a username and password on the authentication server or configured locally on the firewall. When you access the console, the Security Appliance prompts you for these login credentials. If the authentication server is offline, you can still access the console by using the username **pix** and the password set with the **enable password** command.

Step 5   Save the commands in the configuration using the **write memory** command.

As soon as you have Telnet configured on Cisco Security Appliance, you are ready to access the Security Appliance using a Telnet session. You can start a Telnet session to the Security Appliance from the Windows command-line interface (CLI).

Accessing the Cisco Security Appliance with Secure Shell

Secure Shell (SSH) is an application that runs over Transmission Control Protocol (TCP). SSH provides strong authentication and encryption capabilities. Cisco Security Appliances supports the SSH remote shell functionality provided in SSH version 1. SSH version 1 also works with Cisco IOS Software devices. Up to five SSH clients are allowed simultaneous access to the PIX Firewall console.

To gain access to Security Appliance console using SSH, at the SSH client, enter the username as **pix** and enter the Telnet password. You can set the Telnet password with the **password** command; the default Telnet password is **cisco**. To authenticate using the AAA server instead, configure the **aaa authenticate ssh console** command. SSH permits up to 100 characters in a username and up to 50 characters in a password.

> **NOTE**   SSH v1.*x* and v2 are entirely different protocols and are incompatible. Make sure that you download a client that supports SSH v1.*x*.

Like Telnet, SSH also first must be configured on Security Appliance. To configure SSH, follow these steps:

Step 1   Configure the firewall host name:

ROUTER (config)#*hostname* **PIXFW**

Step 2   Configure a domain for the Security Appliance:

PIXFW(config)#*domain-name* **cspa-example.com**

Step 3   Generate the firewall's RSA key pair:

PIXFW(config)#**ca generate rsa key 1024**

Step 4   Save the generated RSA key pair:

PIXFW(config)#**ca save all**

Step 5   Identify a host/network to be used to access the Security Appliance console using SSH. The syntax for the **ssh** command is as follows:

ssh ip_address [*netmask*] [*interface_name*]

For example, to let a host on the internal interface with an address of 10.1.1.25 access the Security Appliance using SSH, enter the following:

ssh 10.1.1.25 255.255.255.255 inside

Step 6   The password used to perform local authentication is the same as the one used for Telnet access. It is set using the **password** command:

password eXamP1e*pass*

Step 7   Specify in the number of minutes a session can be idle before being disconnected. The default duration is 5 minutes, although you can set this duration to be between 1 and 60 minutes. The command to configure this setting is as follows:

ssh timeout *number*

To gain access to Security Appliance console using SSH, you have to install an SSH client. After installing the SSH client, enter the username **pix** (the default), and then enter the password.

When you start an SSH session, a dot (.) appears on the Cisco Security Appliance console before the SSH user authentication prompt appears:

```
pix(config)# .
```

The display of the dot does not affect the functionality of SSH. The dot appears at the console when you generate a server key or decrypt a message using private keys during SSH key exchange before user authentication occurs. These tasks can take up to 2 minutes or longer. The dot is a progress indicator that verifies that the Security Appliance is busy and has not hung.

Command-Level Authorization

In some organizations, there may be more than one firewall administrator for the Security Appliances. In those instances, you can provide those other admins with full rights/privileges to the Security Appliances or curtail their ability to accomplish their assigned functions, thereby reducing the chance of unintended (or sometimes malicious) events from occurring on the firewall(s). The PIX operating system provides a mechanism of controlling what type of command a user can execute.

The Security Appliance software version 6.2 and higher supports up to 16 privilege levels. This is similar to what is available with IOS Software. With this feature, you can assign Security Appliance commands to one of 16 levels, 0 through 15.

When commands and users have privilege levels set, the two levels are compared to determine if a given user can execute a given command. If the user's privilege level is lower than the privilege level of the command, the user is prevented from executing the command. In the default configuration, each Security Appliance command is assigned to either privilege level 0 or privilege level 15.

The **privilege** command sets user-defined privilege levels for Security Appliance commands:

```
[no] privilege [show | clear | configure] level level
     [mode enable | configure] command command
```

Table 4-2 shows the description of the **privilege** command parameters.

Table 4-2 *Privilege Command Parameter Descriptions*

Parameter	Description
show	Sets the privilege level for the **show** command corresponding to the command specified.
clear	Sets the privilege level for the **clear** command corresponding to the command specified.
configure	Sets the privilege level for the **configure** command corresponding to the command specified.
level	Specifies the privilege level.
level	The privilege level, from 0 to 15. (Lower numbers are lower-privilege levels.)
mode	For commands that are available in multiple modes, use the **mode** parameter to specify the mode in which the privilege level applies.
enable	For commands with both enable and configure modes, this indicates that the level is for the enable mode of the command.
configure	For commands with both enable and configure modes, this indicates that the level is for the configure mode of the command.
command	The command to allow.
command	The command on which to set the privilege level.

For example, the following commands set the privilege of the different command modifiers of the **access-list** command:

```
Privilege show level 9 command access-list
Privilege configure level 11 command access-list
Privilege clear level 10 command access-list
```

The first line sets the privilege of **show access-list** (**show** modifier of **command access-list**) to 9. The second line sets the privilege level of the **configure** modifier to 11, and the last line sets the privilege level of the **clear** modifier to 10.

To set the privilege of all the modifiers of the **access-list** command to a single privilege level of 10, you would enter the following command:

```
Privilege level 10 command access-list
```

Once you have selected the commands for which you want to change the default privileges, you enable the command authorization feature to either LOCAL or TACACS+. The following command enables the command authorization feature to LOCAL:

```
aaa authorization command LOCAL
```

To define a user account in the LOCAL database, enter the following command:

```
Username username {nopassword|password password [encrypted]} [privilege level]
```

Table 4-3 shows the description of the parameters of the **username** command.

Table 4-3   *Parameters of the* **username** *Command*

Keyword/Parameter	Description
username	Name of the user (character string from 4 to 15 characters long).
password	Password (a character string from 3 to 16 characters long).
level	The privilege level you want to assign (0–15).
nopassword	Use this keyword to create a user account with no password.
encrypted	Use this keyword to encrypt your keyword.

When users log in to Security Appliance, they can enter any command assigned to their privilege level or to lower privilege levels. For example, a user account with a privilege level of 15 can access every command because this is the highest privilege level. A user account with a privilege level of 0 can access only the commands assigned to level 0.

For example, the following command assigns a privilege level of 10 to the user account Fwadmin2:

```
username Fwadmin2 password cspfa2ed privilege 10
```

If no privilege level is specified, the user account is created with a privilege level of 2. You can define as many user accounts as you need. If you are not sure what the privilege level assigned to commands is, use the **show running-config privilege all** command to view the assignments. To view the privilege level assignment of a specific command, enter the following command:

```
show running-config privilege command command
```

Replace *command* with the command for which you want to display the assigned privilege level. For example, the following command displays the command assignment for the **capture** command:

```
PXFW01# show running-config privilege command capture
privilege show level 15 command capture
privilege clear level 15 command capture
privilege configure level 15 command capture
```

Another useful command to see privilege level is the **show curpriv** command. This displays the current privilege level. The following examples show output from the **show curpriv** command for a user named noc_ops. Username indicates the name the user entered when he or she logged in, P_PRIV indicates that the user has entered the **enable** command, and P_CONF indicates the user has entered the **config terminal** command:

```
PIXFW01(config)# show curpriv
Username : noc_ops
Current privilege level : 15
Current Mode/s : P_PRIV P_CONF
pixfirewall(config)# exit
```

To change between privilege levels, use the **login** command to access another privilege level and the **disable** command to exit that level.

Installing a New Operating System

Installing a new operating system (OS) on a Cisco Security Appliance is similar in some respects to installing a new OS on your PC. You must consider fundamental questions such as whether you have enough memory and disk space (Flash size for Security Appliance) when deciding whether to upgrade the operating system. Table 4-4 shows the random-access memory (RAM) and Flash memory requirements for the different versions and releases of the Cisco Security Appliance OS prior to version 7.0.

Table 4-4 *Security Appliance Software RAM/Flash Minimum Memory Requirements for Software Versions pre-7.0*

Security Appliance Software Version	Memory
PIX Software Version 5.2(x)	16 MB Flash, 32 MB RAM
PIX Software Version 5.3(x)	16 MB Flash, 32 MB RAM
PIX Software Version 6.0(x)	16 MB Flash, 32 MB RAM
PIX Software Version 6.1(x)	16 MB Flash, 32 MB RAM
PIX Software Version 6.2(x)	16 MB Flash, 32 MB RAM
*PIX Software Version 6.3(x)	16 MB Flash, 32 MB RAM

* Except the Cisco PIX 501, 506, and 506E Security Appliance models, which require 8 MB of Flash, and Cisco PIX 501 Security Appliance, which requires 16 MB of RAM

Table 4-5 shows the RAM and Flash memory requirements for Cisco Security Appliance OS version 7.0.

Table 4-5 *Security Appliance Software RAM/Flash Minimum Memory Requirements for Software Version 7.0*

Security Appliance	Memory
PIX 515/515E (Restricted License)	16 MB Flash, 64 MB RAM
PIX 515/515E (Unrestricted License)	16 MB Flash, 128 MB RAM

continues

Table 4-5 *Security Appliance Software RAM/Flash Minimum Memory Requirements for Software Version 7.0 (Continued)*

Security Appliance	Memory
PIX 525 (Restricted License)	16 MB Flash, 128 MB RAM
PIX 525 (Unrestricted License)	16 MB Flash, 256 MB RAM
PIX 535 (Restricted License)	16 MB Flash, 512 MB RAM
PIX 535 (Unrestricted License)	16 MB Flash, 1024 MB RAM
ASA 5510	64 MB Flash, 256 MB RAM
ASA 5520	64 MB Flash, 512 MB RAM
ASA 5540	64 MB Flash, 1024 MB RAM

In addition to the memory and Flash requirements, you should consider the model of Cisco Security Appliance before installing an OS. If you are required to upgrade a PIX Firewall to software version 7.0, the firewall must currently be running software version 6.2 or 6.3. If your firewall is running an older software version, please upgrade to version 6.2 or 6.3 before upgrading to 7.0. Cisco ASA Security Appliance comes with a minimum of software version 7.0 installed.

To determine the RAM memory and Flash memory you have running on your Cisco Security Appliance, use the **show version** command. The output from this command also tells you which Security Appliance OS you are currently running, as shown in Example 4-1.

Example 4-1 *Sample Output from the* **show version** *Command*

```
pixfw(config)# show version
Cisco PIX Security Appliance Software Version 7.0(1)

Compiled on Thu 31-Mar-05 14:37 by builders
System image file is "flash:/pix-701.bin"
Config file at boot was "startup-config"

pixfw up 40328 mins 12 secs

Hardware: PIX-515, 128 MB RAM, CPU Pentium 200 MHz
Flash i28F640J5 @ 0x300, 16MB
BIOS Flash AT29C257 @ 0xfffd8000, 32KB

0: Ext: Ethernet0 : media index 0: irq 10
1: Ext: Ethernet1 : media index 1: irq 7
2: Ext: Ethernet2 : media index 2: irq 11

Licensed features for this platform:
Maximum Physical Interfaces : 3
```

Example 4-1 *Sample Output from the* show version *Command (Continued)*

```
Maximum VLANs : 25
Inside Hosts : Unlimited
Failover : Active/Active
VPN-DES : Enabled
VPN-3DES-AES : Enabled
Cut-through Proxy : Enabled
Guards : Enabled
URL Filtering : Enabled
Security Contexts : 5
GTP/GPRS : Disabled
VPN Peers : Unlimited

This platform has an Unrestricted (UR) license.

Serial Number: 480360257
Running Activation Key: 0x4431d243 0x54258b0f 0x90913408
0xb6bcd404 0x8f37eaac
Configuration has not been modified since last system restart.

In the preceding example, notice the following important bolded
parameters:
Nothing appears in bold. Fix?
Hardware: PIX-515, 128 MB RAM
Flash: 16MB
Licensed Features:
Failover: Active/Active
VPN-DES: Enabled
VPN-3DES-AES: Enabled
Security Contexts 5
This PIX 515 Security Appliance has an Unrestricted (UR) license.
Serial Number: 480360257
```

As you can see, the OS version is 7.0(1), and the Flash memory size is 16 MB.

In Example 4-1, the line that starts with **Running Activation Key** displays the activation key for the PIX Firewall. The activation key is the license key for the PIX Firewall OS. It is important to save your configuration and write down your activation key before upgrading to a newer version of the PIX Firewall OS.

> **NOTE** Starting with PIX Firewall Software and ASA Security Appliance software version 7.0, multiple OS images of different versions can be stored on the Flash. Cisco PIX 501, 506, and 506E do not support version 7.0 nor this option.
>
> PIX Firewalls that support software version 7.0 may not contain enough room on the Flash for additional OS images. The combination of the OS image for version 7.0 and the ASDM image are a little under 16 MBs in size. PIX Firewalls are deployed with 16 MB of Flash, leaving very little room for additional files or images.

Upgrading Your Activation Key

Three important reasons might prompt you to upgrade or change your activation key:

- Your Cisco Security Appliance does not have failover activated.

- Your Security Appliance does not currently have virtual private network Data Encryption Standard (VPN-DES) or virtual private network Triple DES (VPN-3DES) encryption enabled.

- You are upgrading from a connection-based license to a feature-based license.

Before the release of PIX Firewall version 6.2, the activation keys were changed in monitor mode. Cisco PIX Firewall version 6.2 introduced a method of upgrading or changing the license for your Cisco PIX Firewall remotely without entering monitor mode and without replacing the software image. With this feature, you could enter a new activation key for a different PIX Firewall license from the CLI. PIX Firewall and ASA Security Appliance software version 7.0(x) support this feature. To enter an activation key, use the following command:

```
activation-key license#
```

You replace *license#* with the key you get with your new license. For example:

```
activation-key 0x14355378 0xabcdef01 0x2645678ab 0xcdef0124
```

After changing the activation key, you must reboot the PIX Firewall to enable the new license. If you are upgrading to a newer version and you are changing the activation key, you must reboot the Cisco Appliance twice—once after the new image is installed, and again after the new activation key has been configured.

If you are downgrading to a lower Cisco Appliance or PIX Firewall software version, it is important to ensure that the activation key running on your system is not intended for a higher version before you install the lower-version software image. If this is the case, you must first change the activation key to one that is compatible with the lower version before installing and rebooting. Otherwise, your system might refuse to reload after you install the new software image.

The **show activation-key** command output indicates the status of the activation key:

- If the activation key in the PIX Firewall Flash memory is the same as the activation key running on the PIX Firewall, the **show activation-key** output reads as follows:

  ```
  The flash activation key is the SAME as the running key.
  ```

- If the activation key in the PIX Firewall Flash memory is different from the activation key running on the PIX Firewall, the **show activation-key** output reads as follows:

  ```
  The flash activation key is DIFFERENT from the running key.
  The flash activation key takes effect after the next reload.
  ```

- If the PIX Firewall Flash memory software image version is not the same as the running PIX Firewall software image, the **show activation-key** output reads as follows:

```
The flash image is DIFFERENT from the running image.
The two images must be the same in order to examine the flash activation key.
```

Example 4-2 shows sample output from the **show activation-key** command.

Example 4-2   show activation-key *Command Output*

```
pix(config)# show activation-key

Serial Number: 480221353 (0x1c9f98a9)
 Running Activation Key: 0x14355378 0xabcdef01 0x2645678ab 0xcdef0124

Licensed Features:
Failover:              Enabled
VPN-DES:               Enabled
VPN-3DES:              Enabled
Maximum Interfaces:  6
Cut-through Proxy:     Enabled
Guards:                Enabled
URL-filtering:         Enabled
Inside Hosts:          Unlimited
Throughput:            Unlimited
IKE peers:             Unlimited

The flash activation key is the SAME as the running key.
pix (config)#
```

Upgrading the Cisco Security Appliance Operating System

There are three procedures for upgrading a PIX Firewall OS. The use of these procedures is determined by which PIX Firewall OS is currently running on the PIX device and the model of the Cisco Security Appliance:

- You can use the **copy tftp flash** command with any Cisco Security Appliance model running PIX software version 5.1.1 or later, or ASA Software version 7.0.1 or later.

- PIX devices that do not have an internal floppy drive (501, 506(E), 515(E), 525, and 535) come with a read-only memory (ROM) boot monitor program that is used to upgrade the image of the Cisco PIX Firewall. For PIX devices that are running version 5.0 and earlier, a boothelper disk is required to create boothelper mode, similar to ROM monitor mode.

- PIX Firewall version 6.2 introduces a Hypertext Transfer Protocol (HTTP) client that lets you use the **copy http** command to retrieve PIX Firewall configurations, software images, or Cisco PDM software from any HTTP server.

Upgrading the Operating System Using the copy tftp flash Command

Step 1   Download the binary software image file pix*nnx*.bin, where *nn* is the version number and *x* is the release number (which you can find at Cisco.com in the document "Cisco PIX Firewall Upgrading Feature Licenses and System Software"). Place the image file in the root of your Trivial File Transfer Protocol (TFTP) server.

Step 2   Enter the **copy tftp flash** command.

Step 3   Enter the Internet Protocol (IP) address of the TFTP server.

Step 4   Enter the source filename (the image file you downloaded—*.bin).

Step 5   Enter **Yes** to continue.

Example 4-3 shows a sample upgrade.

Example 4-3 *Upgrading the OS Using the* **copy tftp flash** *Command*

```
PIX# copy tftp flash
Address or name of remote host [127.0.0.1]? 192.168.1.14
Source file name [cdisk]? pix-611.bin
copying tftp://192.168.1.14/pix-611.bin to flash
[yes¦no¦again]? yes
!!!!!!!!!!!!!!!!!!!!!!!!!!!!!!!!!!!!!!!!!!!!!!!!!!!!!!!!!!!!!!!!!!!!!!!!!!!!! !!
Received 2562048 bytes
Erasing current image
Writing 2469944 bytes of image
!!!!!!!!!!!!!!!!!!!!!!!!!!!!!!!!!!!!!!!!!!!!!!!!!!!!!!!!!!!!!!!!!!!!!!!!!!!!! !!
Image installed.
PIX#
```

> **NOTE** Under no circumstances must you ever download a Cisco PIX Firewall image earlier than version 4.4 with TFTP. Doing so corrupts the Cisco PIX Firewall Flash memory unit and requires special recovery methods that must be obtained from the Cisco Technical Assistance Center (TAC).

Upgrading the Operating System Using Monitor Mode

If you are upgrading your Cisco PIX Firewall from version 5.0.*x* or earlier to version 5.1.*x* or later, you will need to use the boothelper or monitor mode method for the upgrade because before version 5.1, the PIX Firewall software did not provide a way to TFTP an image directly into Flash. Starting with PIX Firewall software version 5.1, the **copy tftp flash** command was introduced to copy a new image directly into the PIX Firewall's Flash.

The following steps describe how to upgrade the PIX Firewall using monitor mode:

Step 1   Download the binary software image file pix*nnx*.bin, where *nn* is the version number and *x* is the release number (which you can find at Cisco.com in the document "Cisco PIX Firewall Upgrading Feature Licenses and System Software"). Place the image file in the root of your TFTP server.

Step 2   Reload the PIX Firewall, and press the **Esc** key (or enter a BREAK character) to enter monitor mode. For PIX devices running version 5.0 and earlier, a boothelper disk is required. (See the section "Creating a Boothelper Disk Using a Windows PC," later in this chapter.)

Step 3   Use the **interface** command to specify out of which PIX Firewall interface the TFTP server is connected. The default is **interface 1** (inside). The Cisco PIX Firewall cannot initialize a Gigabit Ethernet interface from monitor or boothelper mode. Use a Fast Ethernet or Token Ring interface instead.

Step 4   Use the **address** command followed by an IP address to specify the PIX Firewall interface IP address.

Step 5   Use the **server** command followed by an IP address to specify the TFTP server's IP address.

Step 6   Use the **file** command followed by the filename of the image on the TFTP server to specify the filename of the Cisco PIX Firewall image.

Step 7   Use the **ping** command followed by the IP address of the TFTP server to verify connectivity. (This is an optional, but recommended, command to test connectivity.)

Step 8   If needed, enter the **gateway** command to specify the IP address of a router gateway through which the server is accessible. (This is also an optional command.)

Step 9   Enter **tftp** to start downloading the image from the TFTP server.

Step 10   After the image downloads, you are prompted to install the new image. Enter **y** to install the image to Flash.

Step 11   When prompted to enter a new activation key, enter **y** if you want to enter a new activation key or **n** to keep your existing activation key.

Upgrading the OS Using an HTTP Client

You can also perform a PIX Firewall and ASA Security Appliance OS upgrade by connecting to an HTTP server on which the image is stored. The **copy http** command enables you to download a software image into the Flash memory of the firewall from an HTTP server. The syntax for the **copy http** command is as follows:

```
copy http[s]://[user:password@] location [:port ] / http_pathname flash [: [image
 | pdm] ]
```

Secure Sockets Layer (SSL) is used when the **copy https** command is specified. The *user* and *password* options are used for authentication when logging into the HTTP server. The *location* option is the IP address (or a name that resolves to an IP address) of the HTTP server. The *port* option specifies the port on which to contact the server. The value for port defaults to port 80 for HTTP and port 443 for HTTP through SSL. The *pathname* option is the name of the resource that contains the image or PIX Device Manager (PDM) file to copy.

The following example shows how to copy the PIX Firewall or ASA Security Appliance software image from an HTTP server into the Flash memory of your PIX Firewall:

```
copy http://192.168.1.22/software/download flash:image
```

The following example shows how to copy the PIX Firewall or ASA Security Appliance software image through HTTP over SSL (HTTPS), where the SSL authentication is provided by the username dan and the password example:

```
copy https://dan:example@192.168.1.22/software/download flash:image
```

Creating a Boothelper Disk Using a Windows PC

The boothelper disk, as described earlier in this chapter, provides assistance for Cisco PIX Firewall models 510 and 520 running PIX software version 5.0(*x*) or version 4.*x* to be upgraded to a newer version:

Step 1   Go to the Cisco website and download the rawrite.exe utility, which you use to write the PIX Firewall binary image to a floppy disk (you must have a Cisco.com account to do this).

Step 2   Download the PIX Firewall binary image (.bin file) that corresponds to the software version to which you are upgrading.

Step 3   Download the corresponding boothelper binary file that matches the version to which you are upgrading.

For example, if you are upgrading from PIX software version 5.0 to 6.1(1), you must download three files:

- rawrite.exe

- pix611.bin

- bh61.bin (boothelper file)

Step 4   Run the rawrite.exe program by entering **rawrite** at the DOS prompt. When prompted, enter the name of the boothelper file you want written to the floppy disk, as shown in Example 4-4.

Example 4-4   *Creating a Bootable Disk from Windows*

```
C:\>rawrite
RaWrite 1.2 - Write disk file to raw floppy diskette
Enter source file name: bh61.bin
Enter destination drive: a:
Please insert a formatted diskette into drive A: and press -ENTER- :
Number of sectors per track for this disk is 18.
Writing image to drive A:. Press ^C to abort.
Track: 11 Head: 1 Sector: 16
Done.
C:\>
```

Reboot the PIX Firewall with the disk you created. The PIX Firewall comes up in boothelper mode. Follow the procedure beginning with Step 3 of the earlier section "Upgrading the Operating System Using Monitor Mode," to continue with the upgrade process.

Password Recovery

If you ever find yourself in the unfortunate circumstance of having forgotten or lost the console and Telnet password to your Cisco PIX Firewall or ASA Security Appliance, do not panic. Like most Cisco products, Cisco Security Appliance devices have a procedure to recover lost passwords. Unlike the Cisco router password recovery process, which entails changing the configuration register number, PIX Firewall uses a different method. PIX Firewall uses a password lockout utility to regain access to the locked-out device. The password lockout utility is based on the PIX Firewall software release you are running. Table 4-6 shows the binary filename (that is included with the utility) and the corresponding PIX Firewall OS on which it is used. These files can be downloaded from the Cisco website.

Table 4-6   *PIX Firewall Password Lockout Utility Filenames*

Filename	PIX Firewall Software Version
nppix.bin	4.3 and earlier releases
np44.bin	4.4 release

continues

Table 4-6 *PIX Firewall Password Lockout Utility Filenames (Continued)*

Filename	PIX Firewall Software Version
np50.bin	5.0 release
np51.bin	5.1 release
np52.bin	5.2 release
np60.bin	6.0 release
np61.bin	6.1 release
np62.bin	6.2 release
np63.bin	6.3 release

When you boot the Cisco PIX Firewall with one of these binary files, the enable password is erased and the Telnet password is reset to **cisco**.

Cisco PIX Firewall Password Recovery: Getting Started

The procedure for password recovery on the Cisco PIX Firewall with a floppy drive is slightly different than with a diskless Cisco PIX Firewall. The difference is in how the Cisco PIX Firewall boots with the binary files listed in Table 4-6. Firewall models that have a floppy drive boot from a disk, and diskless firewall models boot from a TFTP server.

In addition to the binary files, you need the following items:

- Portable computer or PC
- Terminal-emulating software
- TFTP software (only for diskless PIX Firewall models)
- The rawrite.exe utility (needed only for firewall models that have floppy drives to create the boot disk)

Password Recovery Procedure for a PIX Firewall with a Floppy Drive (PIX 520)

Step 1 Create the boot disk by running the rawrite.exe file on your portable computer or PC and writing np*xn*.bin to the bootable floppy.

Step 2 Make sure that the terminal-emulating software is running on your PC and that you connected the console cable to the Cisco PIX Firewall.

NOTE Because you are locked out, you see only a password prompt.

Step 3   Insert the PIX Firewall password lockout utility disk into the PIX Firewall's floppy drive. Push the **Reset** button on the front of the PIX Firewall.

Step 4   The PIX Firewall boots from the floppy, and you see a message that says "Erasing Flash Password. Please eject diskette and reboot."

Step 5   Eject the disk, and press the **Reset** button. Now you can log in without a password.

Step 6   When you are prompted for a password, press **Enter**. The default Telnet password after this process is cisco. The enable password is also erased, and you have to enter a new one.

Password Recovery Procedure for a Diskless PIX Firewall (PIX 501, 506, 506E, 515E, 515, 525, and 535)

Step 1   Start the terminal-emulation software, and connect your portable computer or PC to the console port of the PIX Firewall.

Step 2   After you power on the Cisco PIX Firewall and the startup messages appear, send a BREAK character or press the **Esc** key. The **monitor>** prompt is displayed.

Step 3   At the **monitor>** prompt, use the **interface** command to specify which interface the PIX Firewall traffic should use.

Step 4   Use the **address** command to specify the IP address of the PIX Firewall interface.

Step 5   Use the **server** command to specify the IP address of the remote TFTP server containing the PIX Firewall password recovery file.

Step 6   Use the **gateway** command to specify the IP address of a router gateway through which the server is accessible.

Step 7   Use the **file** command to specify the filename of the PIX Firewall password recovery file, such as np62.bin.

Step 8   Use the **tftp** command to start the download. After the password recovery file loads, the following message is displayed:

```
Do you wish to erase the passwords? [yn] y
Passwords have been erased.
```

Password Recovery Procedure for the ASA Security Appliance

Unlike the PIX devices, the ASA Security Appliances use a method of changing the configuration register numbers to recover a lost password. This is similar to how you would recover a password on a Cisco router:

Step 1   Start the terminal-emulation software, and connect your portable or desktop computer to the console port of the PIX Firewall.

Step 2   After you power on the Cisco ASA Security Appliance and the start-up messages appear, press the **Esc** key. The **rommon #0>** prompt is displayed.

Step 3   Use the **confreg** command to view the current state of the configuration register. Enter **no** when you are prompted to make changes to the register.

Step 4   Use the **confreg 0x41** command if the configuration register has not already been set to 0x41. This will tell the ASA Security Appliance to ignore the start-up configuration on its next reboot.

Step 5   Use the **boot** command to reset the ASA Security Appliance. If all the commands have been successfully applied, the following should be displayed:

```
rommon #2> boot
Launching BootLoader...
Boot configuration file contains 1 entry.
Loading disk0:/PIX-7.0.bin... Booting...
##################
...
Ignoring startup configuration as instructed by configuration
register.
Type help or '?' for a list of available commands.
hostname>
```

Step 6   Use the **enable** command to gain privileged command access to the ASA Security Appliance. When prompted for a password, hit **Enter**. The password at this point is blank.

Step 7   Use the **copy startup-config running-config** command to reinstate the current configuration used before the password recovery process started. When you receive the following message, press **Enter** to accept:

```
Destination filename [running-config]?
```

This will not disable privileged access until you exit out or reboot the ASA Security Appliance.

Step 8   Use the **enable password NEWPASSWORD** command to set a new enable password for the ASA Security Appliance. The ASA should now have a new enable password for all future access attempts.

Step 9   Use the **config-register 0x01** to reset the configuration register to a normal boot mode. Once the ASA reboots, it will start using the current configuration with the new enable password.

Step 10   Use the **copy run start** command to save the current configuration. This will store the new password in the starting-config file if the Security Appliance resets.

Overview of Simple Network Management Protocol on the PIX Firewall

Using Simple Network Management Protocol (SNMP), you can monitor system events on the PIX Firewall. All SNMP values are read only (RO). SNMP events can be read, but information on Security Appliance cannot be changed by using SNMP.

The Cisco Security Appliance SNMP traps available to an SNMP management station are as follows:

Generic traps:

- Link up and link down
- Cold start
- Authentication failure

Security-related events sent by the Cisco syslog management information base (MIB):

- Global access denied
- Failover syslog messages
- Syslog messages

PIX Firewall Version 6.2 and later, as well as the ASA Security Appliance version 7.0, supports monitoring central processing unit (CPU) utilization through SNMP. Overall CPU busy percentage in the last 5-second period, 1-minute period, and 5-minute period are sent to the SNMP management server.

> **NOTE**   Similar information on CPU utilization can be displayed by typing **show cpu usage** on the Cisco Security Appliance.

This feature allows network administrators to monitor Security Appliance CPU usage using SNMP management software for capacity planning.

Configuring Simple Network Management Protocol on Security Appliance

The **snmp-server** command causes Security Appliance to send SNMP traps so that the Security Appliance can be monitored remotely. Use the **snmp-server host** command to specify which systems receive the SNMP traps. Example 4-5 shows a SNMP sample configuration on a PIX Firewall.

Example 4-5   *Sample SNMP Configuration on a PIX Firewall*

```
snmp-server host 10.10.1.22
snmp-server location DC-HQ
snmp-server contact Yung Park
snmp-server community SnMpKey
snmp-server enable traps
```

The **location** and **contact** commands identify where the host is and who administers it. The **community** command specifies the password in use at the PIX Firewall SNMP agent and the SNMP management station for verifying network access between the two systems.

Troubleshooting Commands

The two most important troubleshooting commands on Security Appliance are the following:

- debug
- show

The **debug** command provides real-time information that helps you troubleshoot protocols operating with and through a Security Appliance. There are more than three dozen debug commands that are available on Security Appliance.

Like the **debug** command, the **show** command also has many options available on Security Appliance. One helpful **show** command is the **show tech-support** command.

The **debug packet** command sends its output to the Trace Channel. All other **debug** commands do not. Use of Trace Channel changes the way you can view output on your screen during a Security Appliance console or Telnet session. If a **debug** command does not use Trace Channel, each session operates independently, which means any commands started in the session appear only in the session. By default, a session not using Trace Channel has output disabled by default. The location of the Trace Channel depends on whether you have a simultaneous Telnet console session running at the same time as the console session or you are using only the Security Appliance serial console:

- If you are only using the Security Appliance serial console, all **debug** commands display on the serial console.

- If you have both a serial console session and a Telnet console session accessing the console, no matter where you enter the **debug** commands, the output displays on the Telnet console session.

- If you have two or more Telnet console sessions, the first session is the Trace Channel. If that session closes, the serial console session becomes the Trace Channel. The next Telnet console session that accesses the console will then become the Trace Channel.

The **debug** commands, except the **debug crypto** commands, are shared between all Telnet and serial console sessions.

The following is sample output from the **show debug** command output:

```
Pixfw#show debug
debug crypto ipsec 1
debug crypto isakmp 1
debug crypto ca 1
debug icmp trace
```

The **show tech-support** command lists information that technical support analysts need to help you diagnose Security Appliance problems. Using this command is very similar to running half a dozen **show** commands at once. The syntax for the command is as follows:

```
show tech-support [no-config]
```

The **no-config** option excludes the output of the running configuration. Example 4-6 shows a sample output of the **show tech-support** command with the **no-config** option.

Example 4-6 *Sample Output of the* **show tech-support no config** *Command*

```
Pix_fw# show tech-support no-config

Cisco PIX Firewall Version 6.3(1)
Cisco PIX Device Manager Version 2.1(1)

Compiled on Tue 16-Sept-03 17:49 by morlee

PIXFW01 up 17 days 5 hours

Hardware:   PIX-525, 256 MB RAM, CPU Pentium III 600 MHz
Flash E28F128J3 @ 0x300, 16MB
BIOS Flash AM29F400B @ 0xfffd8000, 32KB
```

continues

Example 4-6   *Sample Output of the* show tech-support no config *Command (Continued)*

```
Encryption hardware device : IRE2141 with 2048KB, HW:1.0, CGXROM:1.9, FW:6.5
0: ethernet0: address is 0008.a3db.87ea, irq 10
1: ethernet1: address is 0008.a3db.87eb, irq 11
2: ethernet2: address is 00e0.b605.5817, irq 11
3: ethernet3: address is 00e0.b605.5816, irq 10
4: ethernet4: address is 00e0.b605.5815, irq 9
5: ethernet5: address is 00e0.b605.5814, irq 5
6: ethernet6: address is 0003.47ac.5edd, irq 5
Licensed Features:
Failover:          Enabled
VPN-DES:           Enabled
VPN-3DES:          Enabled

Maximum Interfaces: 8
Cut-through Proxy:  Enabled
Guards:             Enabled
URL-filtering:      Enabled
Inside Hosts:       Unlimited
Throughput:         Unlimited
IKE peers:          Unlimited

Serial Number: 406044528 (0x1833bf0c)
Running Activation Key: 0xb974f13e 0x3253edba 0x0d0365e4 0xbae9e768
Configuration last modified by enable_15 at 13:36:25.580 EST Sat Jan 10 2004

----------------- show clock -----------------
14:26:55.403 EST Sat Jan 10 2004

----------------- show memory -----------------
Free memory:        197058560 bytes
Used memory:         71376896 bytes
------------        ----------------
Total memory:       268435456 bytes

----------------- show conn count -----------------
134 in use, 5168 most used

----------------- show xlate count -----------------
93 in use, 3279 most used

----------------- show blocks -----------------

  SIZE    MAX    LOW    CNT
     4   1600   1581   1600
    80    400    344    400
   256    500      0    500
```

Example 4-6 *Sample Output of the* **show tech-support no config** *Command (Continued)*

```
    1550    2724    1472    1824
    2560       1       0       1
    4096       1       0       1


----------------- show interface -----------------

 interface ethernet0 "outside" is up, line protocol is up
  Hardware is i82559 ethernet, address is 0008.a3db.87ea
  IP address 192.168.100.2, subnet mask 255.255.255.0
  MTU 1500 bytes, BW 100000 Kbit full duplex
    383875955 packets input, 1546242085 bytes, 0 no buffer
    Received 1958243 broadcasts, 0 runts, 0 giants
    22 input errors, 0 CRC, 0 frame, 22 overrun, 0 ignored, 0 abort
    362851238 packets output, 2335666853 bytes, 0 underruns
    0 output errors, 0 collisions, 0 interface resets
    0 babbles, 0 late collisions, 0 deferred
    0 lost carrier, 0 no carrier
    input queue (curr/max blocks): hardware (128/128) software (0/134)
    output queue (curr/max blocks): hardware (0/102) software (0/63)
 interface ethernet1 "inside" is up, line protocol is up
  Hardware is i82559 ethernet, address is 0008.a3db.87eb
  IP address 10.20.29.187, subnet mask 255.255.255.0
  MTU 1500 bytes, BW 100000 Kbit full duplex
    328261488 packets input, 1334827221 bytes, 0 no buffer
    Received 16099319 broadcasts, 0 runts, 0 giants
    0 input errors, 0 CRC, 0 frame, 0 overrun, 0 ignored, 0 abort
    428793671 packets output, 3583318676 bytes, 0 underruns
    0 output errors, 0 collisions, 0 interface resets
    0 babbles, 0 late collisions, 0 deferred
    0 lost carrier, 0 no carrier
     input queue (curr/max blocks): hardware (128/128) software (0/128)
    output queue (curr/max blocks): hardware (2/128) software (0/472)
                     .
                     .
                     .

----------------- show cpu usage -----------------

CPU utilization for 5 seconds = 0%; 1 minute: 0%; 5 minutes: 0%

----------------- show process -----------------

    PC       SP       STATE      Runtime    SBASE    Stack Process

Hsi 800b0e09 807d3938 8052ddd8        0 807d29b0 3716/4096 arp_timer
Lsi 800b5271 80846a48 8052ddd8        0 80845ad0 3788/4096 FragDBGC
Cwe 8000a945 80bd5e48 80375d90        0 80bd4ee0 3944/4096 CryptIC PDR poll
```

continues

Example 4-6 *Sample Output of the* **show tech-support no config** *Command (Continued)*

```
Lwe 8000f9fe 80bd6de8 80531508        0 80bd5f70 3704/4096 dbgtrace
Lwe 8020685d 80bd8f48 80507300  4655470 80bd7000 6352/8192 Logger
Hsi 8020a4ed 80bdc010 8052ddd8        0 80bda098 7700/8192 tcp_fast.
                       .
                      .
----------------- show failover ------------------

Failover On

Cable status: Normal
Reconnect timeout 0:00:00
Poll frequency 8 seconds
failover replication http
    This host: Primary - Active
         Active time: 1499048 (sec)
         Interface failover (192.168.10.3): Normal
         Interface intf5 (127.0.0.1): Link Down (Shutdown)
         Interface EXTRA-NET (10.2.0.1): Normal
         Interface Dialindmz (10.2.28.1): Normal
         Interface Serverdmz (10.10.43.2): Normal
         Interface outside (192.168.100.2): Normal
         Interface inside (10.20.29.187): Normal
    Other host: Secondary - Standby
         Active time: 0 (sec)
         Interface failover (192.168.10.2): Normal
         Interface intf5 (0.0.0.0): Link Down (Shutdown)
         Interface EXTRA-NET (10.2.0.2): Normal
         Interface Dialindmz (10.2.28.2): Normal
         Interface Serverdmz (10.10.43.3): Normal
         Interface outside (192.168.100.4): Normal
         Interface inside (10.20.29.24): Normal

Stateful Failover Logical Update Statistics


    Link : failover
    Stateful Obj     xmit      xerr      rcv       rerr
    General       65534709     0       198872      0
    sys cmd        198871      0       198872      0
    up time        2           0       0           0
    xlate          7312548     0       0           0
    tcp conn       58023288    0       0           0
    udp conn       0           0       0           0
    ARP tbl        0           0       0           0
    RIP Tbl        0           0       0           0
```

Example 4-6 *Sample Output of the* **show tech-support no config** *Command (Continued)*

```
      Logical Update Queue Information
                Cur     Max      Total
      Recv Q:    0       1      198872
      Xmit Q:    0       1     9861326
---------------- show traffic ----------------
outside:
      received (in 1501994.020 secs):
          384156904 packets    1628831642 bytes
          1 pkts/sec    1001 bytes/sec
      transmitted (in 1501994.020 secs):
          363147896 packets    2525315383 bytes
          1 pkts/sec    1000 bytes/sec
inside:
      received (in 1501994.020 secs):
          328515373 packets    1453897436 bytes
          1 pkts/sec    1 bytes/sec
      transmitted (in 1501994.020 secs):
          429046804 packets    3666788039 bytes
          2 pkts/sec    2000 bytes/sec
          .
          .
          .

---------------- show perfmon ----------------

PERFMON STATS:     Current      Average
Xlates              0/s          0/s
Connections         4/s          0/s
TCP Conns           1/s          0/s
UDP Conns           3/s          0/s
URL Access          0/s          0/s
URL Server Req      0/s          0/s
TCP Fixup         146/s          0/s
TCPIntercept        0/s          0/s
HTTP Fixup         87/s          0/s
FTP Fixup           0/s          0/s
AAA Authen          0/s          0/s
AAA Author          0/s          0/s
AAA Account         0/s          0/s
```

Foundation Summary

The "Foundation Summary" provides a convenient review of many key concepts in this chapter. If you are already comfortable with the topics in this chapter, this summary can help you recall a few details. If you just read this chapter, this review should help solidify some key facts. If you are doing your final preparation before the exam, this summary provides a convenient way to review the day before the exam.

- Cisco Security Appliance can be accessed for management purposes in several different ways. It can be accessed through the console port, remotely through Telnet, through SSH, and through the ASDM.

- Before upgrading the Cisco Security Appliance OS, it is important to determine your current hardware settings—namely, the RAM and Flash memory size.

- PIX Firewall version 6.2 and later, as well as ASA Security Appliance version 7.0 and later, supports up to 16 privilege levels. This is similar to what is available with IOS software. With this feature, you can assign Security Appliance commands to one of 16 levels, 0 through 15.

- The **privilege** command sets user-defined privilege levels for Security Appliance commands.

- The activation key is the license for Security Appliance OS. Before the release of PIX Firewall version 6.2, the activation keys were changed in monitor mode. Cisco PIX Firewall version 6.2 introduces a method of upgrading or changing the license for your PIX Firewall remotely without entering monitor mode and without replacing the software image using the **activation-key** command.

- There are three ways to perform a Security Appliance OS upgrade:
    - Using **copy tftp flash**
    - Using monitor mode with a boothelper disk for PIX Firewalls with an OS version earlier than 5.0
    - Using an HTTP client (available only with version 6.2)

- It is possible to recover from a lockout on a Cisco PIX Firewall caused by forgotten or lost passwords. You can download the corresponding file and boot the PIX Firewall through monitor mode.

■ It is possible to recover from a lost password on an ASA Security Appliance. You can reset a lost password through a process requiring a reset of the configuration register, which is similar to the method of password recovery used on Cisco routers.

■ Using SNMP, you can monitor system events on Security Appliance. All SNMP values are read only (RO). SNMP events can be read, but information on the PIX Firewall cannot be changed with SNMP.

Q&A

As mentioned in the Introduction, the questions in this book are more difficult than what you should experience on the exam. The questions do not attempt to cover more breadth or depth than the exam; however, they are designed to make sure that you know the answer. Hopefully, these questions will help limit the number of exam questions on which you narrow your choices to two options and then guess. Be sure to use the CD and to take the simulated exams.

The answers to these questions can be found in Appendix A:

1. How many ways can you access the PIX Firewall?

2. What is the command to change the Telnet password?

3. Which command would you use to view the privilege level assigned to the **access-list** command?

4. Which version of SSH does ASA Security Appliance support?

5. What is the activation key?

6. Give one reason why you would need to change the activation key on your Security Appliance.

7. How many privilege levels are available on the PIX Firewall?

8. How do you determine which version of Security Appliance operating system is installed?

9. Which command would you use to create locally a user called mason with a password of Fr33 on the PIX Firewall?

10. How do you find out what your activation key is?

This chapter covers the following subjects:

- ASA Security Levels

- Transport Protocols

- Network Address Translation

- Port Address Translation

- Configuring DNS Support

Understanding Cisco Security Appliance Translation and Connection

This chapter presents an overview of the different network transport protocols and how they are processed by the Cisco Security Appliance family of firewalls.

How to Best Use This Chapter

Reconsider the comment in the Introduction about how important it is to *know* the Cisco Security Appliance commands, not just have an idea of what they are and what they do. It is very important to fully understand the concepts discussed in this chapter because they are the basis for the topics discussed in Chapter 6, "Getting Started with the Cisco Security Appliance Family of Firewalls." To completely understand how the many different Security Appliance commands work, you must first have a good understanding of how the Cisco Security Appliance processes network traffic.

"Do I Know This Already?" Quiz

The purpose of the "Do I Know This Already?" quiz is to help you decide if you really need to read the entire chapter. If you already intend to read the entire chapter, you do not necessarily need to answer these questions now.

The ten-question quiz, derived from the major sections in the "Foundation Topics" portion of the chapter, helps you determine how to spend your limited study time.

Table 5-1 outlines the major topics discussed in this chapter and the "Do I Know This Already?" quiz questions that correspond to those topics.

Table 5-1 *"Do I Know This Already?" Foundation Topics Section-to-Question Mapping*

Foundation Topics Section	Questions Covered in This Section	Score
ASA Security Levels	2, 4	
Transport Protocols	8	
Network Address Translation	1, 3, 5, 6	
Port Address Translation	7, 10	
Configuring DNS Support	9	

CAUTION   The goal of self assessment is to gauge your mastery of the topics in this chapter. If you do not know the answer to a question or are only partially sure of the answer, you should mark this question wrong for purposes of the self assessment. Giving yourself credit for an answer you correctly guess skews your self-assessment results and might provide you with a false sense of security.

1. By default, how long will an embryonic connection remain open?

   a. 2 minutes

   b. 3600 seconds

   c. 1800 seconds

   d. Unlimited

   e. 30 minutes

2. You have configured two additional DMZ interfaces on your ASA Security Appliance. How do you prevent nodes on DMZ1 from accessing nodes on DMZ2 without adding rules to the security policy?

   a. Route all traffic for DMZ2 out the outside interface.

   b. Dynamically NAT all DMZ2 nodes to a multicast address.

   c. Assign a higher security level to DMZ2.

   d. All of the above.

3. Which of the following is not a method of address translation supported by the PIX Firewall?

   a. Network Address Translation

   b. Socket Address Translation

   c. Port Address Translation

   d. Static Address Translation

4. What happens if you configure two interfaces with the same security level?

   a. Traffic will pass freely between those connected networks.

   b. Traffic will not pass between those interfaces.

   c. Specific ACLs must allow traffic between those interfaces.

   d. The two interfaces will not apply the **nat** or **global** commands.

5. When should you run the command **clear xlate**?

   a. When updating a conduit on the firewall

   b. When editing the NAT for the inside segment

   c. When adding addresses to the global pool

   d. All of the above

6. How do you define the global addresses used when configuring NAT?

   a. Define a subnet.

   b. Define an address range.

   c. Define individual IP addresses.

   d. You can define only /24 address segments for global addresses.

   e. None of the above.

7. How many external IP addresses are required to configure PAT?

   a. A single address

   b. A /24 subnet

   c. A defined address range

   d. Any of the above

   e. None of the above

8. What command shows all active TCP connections on the PIX Firewall?

   a. show conn

   b. show xlate

   c. show connection status

   d. show tcp active

   e. None of the above

9. Why is it difficult to penetrate the Security Appliance over UDP port 53?

   a. The Security Appliance allows multiple outbound queries but randomizes the UDP sequence numbers.

   b. The Security Appliance allows queries to go out to multiple DNS servers but drops all but the first response.

   c. The Security Appliance allows responses only to outbound DNS queries.

   d. All of the above

10. How many connections can you hide behind a single global address?

    a. 65,536

    b. 255

    c. 17,200

    d. An unlimited number

    e. None of the above

The answers to the "Do I Know This Already?" quiz are found in Appendix A, "Answers to the 'Do I Know This Already?' Quizzes and Q&A Sections." The suggested choices for your next step are as follows:

■ **8 or less overall score**—Read the entire chapter. This includes the "Foundation Topics," "Foundation Summary," and "Q&A" sections.

■ **9 or 10 overall score**—If you want more review of these topics, skip to the "Foundation Summary" section and then go to the "Q&A" section. Otherwise, move to the next chapter.

Foundation Topics

How the Cisco Security Appliance Handles Traffic

The term *network security* simply refers to the application of security principles to a computer network. To apply security to a network, you must first understand how networks function. It stands to reason that to secure how traffic flows across a network, you must first understand how that traffic flows. This chapter discusses end-to-end traffic flow and how that traffic is handled by the Cisco Security Appliance.

Interface Security Levels and the Default Security Policy

By default, a Cisco Security Appliance applies security levels to each interface. The more secure the network segment, the higher the security number. Security levels range from 0 to 100. By default, 0 is applied to Ethernet 0 and is given the default name *outside*; 100 is applied to Ethernet 1 and is given the default name *inside*. Any additional interfaces are configured using the **nameif** command. The security level for these additional interfaces can be from 1 to 99.

The Adaptive Security Algorithm (ASA) allows traffic from a higher security level to pass to a lower security level without a specific rule in the security policy that allows the connection as long as a **nat/global** or **static** command is configured for those interfaces. Any traffic that passes from a lower security level to a higher security level must be allowed by the security policy (that is, access lists or conduits). If two interfaces are assigned the same security level, traffic cannot pass between those interfaces (this configuration is not recommended).

Transport Protocols

Traffic that traverses a network always has a source and destination address. This communication is based on the seven layers of the OSI reference model. Layers 5 through 7 (the upper layers) handle the application data, and Layers 1 through 4 (lower layers) are responsible for moving the data from the source to the destination. The data is created at the application layer (Layer 7) on the source machine. Transport information is added to the upper-layer data, and then network information is added, followed by data-link information. At this point, the information is transmitted across the physical medium as electronic signals.

The upper-layer data combined with the transport information is called a *segment*. As soon as the network information is added to the segment, it is called a *packet*. The packet is encapsulated at the data link layer (Layer 2) with the addition of the source and destination

MAC address, at which point it is called a *frame*. Figure 5-1 shows how the data is encapsulated at each layer of the OSI reference model.

Figure 5-1 *Encapsulation of Upper-Layer Data*

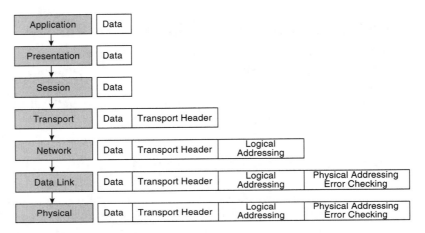

The two transport protocols most commonly used by TCP/IP are Transmission Control Protocol (TCP) and User Datagram Protocol (UDP). These protocols are very different. Each has its strengths and weaknesses. For this reason, they are used in different ways to play on their strengths:

■ TCP—A connection-oriented transport protocol that is responsible for reliability and efficiency of communication between nodes. TCP completes these tasks by creating connections as *virtual circuits* that act as two-way communications between the source and destination. TCP is very reliable and guarantees the delivery of data between nodes. TCP also can dynamically modify a connection's transmission variables based on changing network conditions. TCP sequence numbers and TCP acknowledgment numbers are included in the TCP header. These features allow the source and destination to verify the correct, orderly delivery of data. Unfortunately, the overhead required for TCP can make it slow and keeps it from being the optimum transport protocol for some connections.

■ UDP—A connectionless transport protocol that is used to get the data to the destination. UDP provides no error checking, no error correction, and no verification of delivery. UDP defers the reliability issues to the upper-layer protocols and simply sends the data without verifying delivery. UDP is a very simple and very fast protocol.

The upper layers determine which of the transport protocols is used when data is encapsulated at the source node.

Figure 5-2 illustrates the TCP communication between nodes that do not have a firewall between them. The TCP "three-way handshake" is a four-step process that requires three different transmissions to negotiate the connection:

1. The source sends a segment to the destination, asking to open a TCP session. A TCP flag is set to SYN, indicating that the source wants to initiate synchronization or a handshake. The source generates a random TCP sequence number. In this example, we will use 125.

2. The destination receives the request and sends back a reply with the TCP flags ACK and SYN set, indicating an acknowledgment of the SYN bit (receive flow) and initiation of the transmit flow. It generates and sends its own random TCP sequence number, 388, and replies to the original TCP sequence number by adding 1, sending back a sequence number of 126. The source receives the SYN/ACK and sends back an ACK to indicate the acknowledgment of the SYN for the setup of the receive flow. It adds 1 to the value of the TCP sequence number generated by the destination and sends back the number 389.

3. The acknowledgment is received, the handshake is complete, and the connection is established. Note in Figure 5-2 that the source begins to send data to the destination as soon as the connection is established.

Figure 5-2   *TCP Communication Between Nodes Without a PIX Firewall*

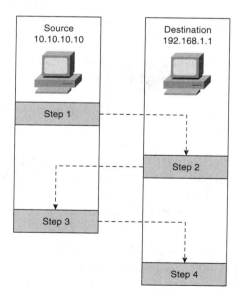

Now look at how this communication is handled by the Cisco PIX Firewall (see Figure 5-3). You first notice that the number of steps required for the same transaction has changed from four to eight and the number of transmissions has increased from three to six, although everything appears to be the same to both the source and destination.

Figure 5-3 *TCP Communication Between Nodes with a PIX Firewall*

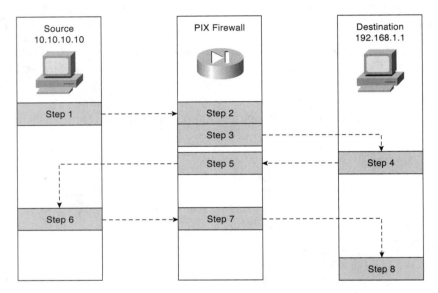

The following is a list of actions taken by the Cisco PIX Firewall when processing a TCP handshake and opening a TCP session (refer to Figure 5-3):

1. The source machine initiates the connection by sending a packet with the SYN flag set. It is a Cisco Security Appliance en route to the destination. The Security Appliance verifies the connection against the running configuration to determine if translation is to be completed. The running configuration is stored in memory, so this process occurs very quickly. The Security Appliance checks whether the inside address, 10.10.10.10, is to be translated to an outside address—in this case, 192.168.1.10. If the translation is to be completed, the Security Appliance creates a *translation slot* if one does not already exist for this connection.

2. All the session information is written to the state table, and the Cisco Security Appliance randomly generates a new TCP sequence number. This connection slot is marked in the state table as an *embryonic* (half-open) connection.

3. After the connection is verified against the security policy, the Security Appliance allows the connection outside using the translated source address and the newly generated TCP sequence number.

4. The destination receives the connection request (SYN) and replies with an SYN ACK.

5. The Security Appliance verifies the SYN ACK from the destination and matches the acknowledgment number against the randomly generated sequence number. It verifies the connection slot and forwards the connection back to the source using the original source address and original sequence number plus 1.

6. Any packets that do not match the session object exactly are dropped and logged.

7. The source completes the connection by responding with an ACK. The acknowledgment number is not randomized as it passes through the Security Appliance, and the connection slot is marked as *active-established*.

8. The embryonic counter is reset, and data is transmitted between the nodes.

The process used by the Security Appliance to handle UDP traffic is completely different from the process that it uses for TCP traffic. This is due to UDP's characteristics. UDP is a connectionless protocol that does not negotiate a connection. Without any setup or termination, it is very difficult to determine the state of a UDP session. Because of the inability to determine session state, it is very easy to spoof UDP packets and hijack a UDP session. Some applications use UDP rather than TCP for data transfer. Many of these are real-time applications or applications that either have no reliability requirements or have their reliability requirements handled by the application rather than by the transport protocol. These applications include network video, Common Internet File System (CIFS), NetBIOS, Domain Name System (DNS), and remote-procedure call (RPC) applications.

The default security policy allows UDP packets to pass from a higher security level to a lower security level. For UDP packets to pass in the other direction, they must be allowed by the security policy. It is very important to restrict inbound UDP access as much as possible. Due to UDP's limitations, many applications that operate over UDP are targets for exploitation by hackers.

A Cisco Security Appliance handles UDP traffic in the following manner:

1. The source machine initiates the UDP connection. It is received by the Security Appliance en route to the destination. The Security Appliance applies the default rule and any necessary translation, creates a session object in the state table, and allows the connection to pass to the outside interface.

2. Any return traffic is matched with the session object, and the session timeout is applied. The session timeout is 2 minutes by default. If the response does not match the session object or is not within the timeout, the packet is dropped. If everything matches, the response is allowed through to the requesting source.

3. Any inbound UDP sessions from a lower security level to a higher security level must be allowed by the security policy, or the connection is dropped.

Address Translation

The current Internet Protocol standard being used is version 4 (IPv4). IPv4 addresses consist of 32 bits, which represents approximately 4 billion individual IP addresses. This seems like a tremendous number of addresses, but the Internet continues to grow at an incredible rate, and with the current standard, available addresses will run out. Two solutions are being implemented to help conserve the public address space or increase the number of available public addresses. The first is Internet Protocol version 6 (IPv6), a total redesign of the Internet Protocol that is still in development. The second solution is the use of RFC 1918 addressing combined with Port Address Translation (PAT). RFC 1918 sets aside network space to be used for private networks, and PAT provides a method for hiding literally thousands of private addresses behind a single public address. This private address space is not accessible via the public Internet. Static Network Address Translation (NAT) is used to create a one-to-one relationship between public addresses and RFC 1918 addresses and allows external users to access internal resources.

The Internet Assigned Numbers Authority (IANA) reserved the following address space for private networks:

> 10.0.0.0 through 10.255.255.255: 16,777,214 hosts
> 172.16.0.0 through 172.31.255.255: 1,048,574 hosts
> 192.168.0.0 through 192.168.255.255: 65,534 hosts

RFC 1918 has had a tremendous impact on Internet addressing and the design of public and private networks. The challenge to RFC 1918 addressing is that private addresses cannot be publicly routed. Hence, address translation is implemented. Address translation provides not only a method of conserving public address space, but also an additional level of protection for internal nodes because there is no way to route to a private address from the Internet.

Address translation is the method used by the Cisco PIX Firewall to give internal nodes with private IP addresses access to the Internet. The internal node addresses that are translated are called *local addresses,* and the addresses that are translated as well are called *global addresses.* **nat** and **global** commands are applied to specific interfaces. Most commonly, NAT takes place, translating internal addresses to external addresses, although the PIX Firewall is not limited to this configuration. It is possible to translate any address at one interface to another address at any other interface. Two types of NAT can be implemented on a Cisco Security Appliance:

- **Dynamic address translation**—Translates multiple local addresses into a limited number of global public addresses or possibly a single global address. This is called *dynamic address translation* because the firewall selects the first available global address and assigns it when creating an outbound connection. The internal source retains the global address for the duration of the connection. Dynamic address translation is broken into two types:

  - **Network Address Translation (NAT)**—Translating multiple local addresses to a pool of global addresses.

  - **Port Address Translation (PAT)**—Translating multiple local addresses to a single global address. This method is called *Port Address Translation* because the firewall uses a single translated source address but changes the source port to allow multiple connections via a single global address. The limitation for PAT is approximately 64,000 hosts because of the limited number of available ports (65,535) and the number of ports already assigned to specific services. Some applications do not work through PAT because they require specific source and destination ports.

- **Static translation**—Allows for a one-to-one translation of local to global addresses. Static translation is commonly used when the internal node must be accessed from the Internet. Web servers and mail servers must have static addresses so that users on the Internet can connect to them via their global address.

Translation Commands

Table 5-2 describes the commands and arguments used to configure NAT, PAT, and static translation on a Cisco Security Appliance. All the Security Appliance commands are covered in much greater detail in Chapter 6. Table 5-2 helps you understand the syntax of the commands given in the following examples.

Table 5-2 *Translation Commands*

Command	Description
nat	Associates a network with a pool of global addresses.
global	Identifies the global addresses to be used for translation.
static	Maps the one-to-one relationship between local addresses and global addresses.

continues

Table 5-2 *Translation Commands (Continued)*

Command	Description
netmask	A reserved word that is required to identify the network mask.
dns	Specifies that DNS replies that match the **xlate** command should be translated.
outside	Allows you to enable or disable address translation for the external addresses.
timeout	Sets the idle timeout for the translation slot.
id	Also called the *nat_id*. The number that matches the **nat** statement with the **global** statement. This is how the Security Appliance determines which local addresses translate to which global address pool.
internal_if-name	The interface name for the network with the higher security level.
external_if-name	The interface name for the network with the lower security level.
local-ip	The IP addresses or network addresses that are to be translated. This can be a specific network segment (10.10.10.0) or can include all addresses (0.0.0.0).
global_ip	The IP address or range of IP addresses to which the local addresses translate.
network_mask	The network mask for a specific network segment. This applies to both local and global addresses.
max-cons	The maximum number of concurrent connections allowed through a static translation.
em_limit	The maximum number of allowed embryonic connections. The default is 0, which allows unlimited connections. You can limit the number of embryonic connections to reduce an attack's effectiveness by flooding embryonic connections.
norandomseq	Stops the ASA from randomizing the TCP sequence numbers. This normally is used if the firewall is located inside another firewall and data is being scrambled, with both firewalls randomizing the sequence number.

NAT

NAT allows you to translate a large number of local addresses behind a limited number of global addresses. This lets you keep your internal network addressing scheme hidden from external networks. To configure NAT on a Cisco Security Appliance, you simply need to define the local and global addresses. In Figure 5-4, all nodes on the internal network are being translated to a pool of addresses on the external network.

Figure 5-4 *Network Address Translation*

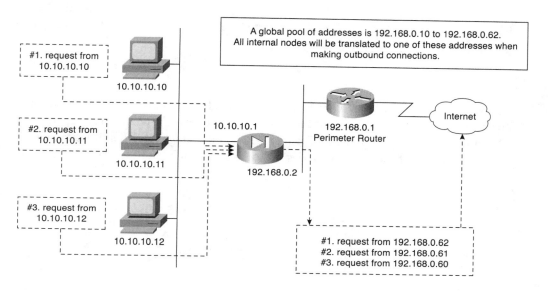

Two commands are required to complete this configuration:

- **nat**—Defines the addresses to be translated:

  ```
  LabPIX(config)# nat [(internal_if_name)] id local_ip [network_mask]
  ```

  Here is an example:

  ```
  LabPIX(config)# nat (inside) 1 0.0.0.0 0.0.0.0
  ```

- **global**—Defines the pool of addresses to translate to:

  ```
  LabPIX(config)# global [(external_if_name)] id {global_ip[-global_ip] [netmask
  network_mask] | interface}
  ```

  Here is an example:

  ```
  LabPIX(config)# global (outside) 1 192.168.0.10-192.168.0.62 netmask   255.255.255.192
  ```

Notice the *id* in both the **nat** and **global** commands. It enables you to assign specific addresses to translate. The addresses in the **nat** command translate to the addresses in the global command that contains the same ID. The only ID that cannot be used here is 0. The command **nat 0** is used on the Security Appliance to identify addresses that are *not* to be translated. The **nat 0** command is commonly called the "no nat" command.

PIX Firewall OS Version 6.3(2) incorporated the ability to configure a *policy NAT*. This provides the functionality to enable translations to occur on a specific source and destination basis. The policy NAT is configured with the access control lists and will be discussed in greater detail in Chapter 7, "Configuring Access."

PAT

PAT enables you to translate your local addresses behind a single global address. The commands required to perform PAT are exactly the same as the commands to perform NAT. The only difference in defining PAT is that you define a single global address rather than a range. Figure 5-5 shows all local nodes behind a single global address being translated.

Figure 5-5 *PAT*

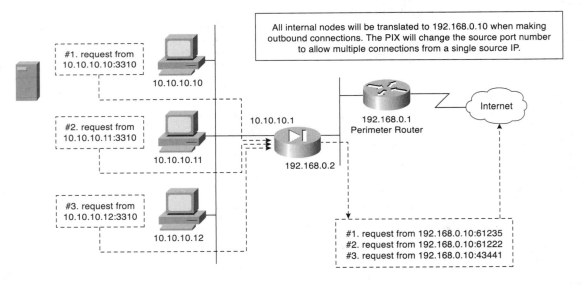

The correct syntax for configuring PAT uses the **nat** and **global** commands and is depicted here:

```
LabPIX(config)# nat [(internal_if_name)] id local_ip network_mask
```

The following is an example of the correct syntax for configuring the **nat** portion of PAT for an internal network consisting of 10.0.0.0 addresses:

```
LabPIX(config)# nat (inside) 4 10.0.0.0 0.0.0.0
```

Here is the **global** command syntax:

```
LabPIX(config)# global [(external_if_name)] id global_ip netmask  network_mask
```

The following is an example of the correct syntax for configuring the **global** portion of PAT for the external address 192.168.0.10:

```
LabPIX(config)# global (outside) 1 192.168.0.10 netmask 255.255.255.255
```

Static Translation

Although static translation is not specifically defined as an exam topic, it is very important for you to know the commands and to understand how static translation works. Static translation maps a single local address to a single global address. It is most commonly used when the local node must be accessed from the public space (Internet):

```
LabPIX(config)# [static] (local_if_name, global_if_name) {global_ip/interface} local_ip
```

In the following command, the local node 10.10.10.9 is configured to have a global address of 192.168.0.9. Remember that the **static** command configures only the address translation. To allow access to the local node from a lower security level interface, you need to configure either a conduit or an access list:

```
LabPIX(config)# static (inside, outside) 192.168.0.9 10.10.10.9
LabPIX(config)# conduit permit tcp host 192.168.0.9 eq www any
```

or

```
LabPIX(config)# access-list 101 permit tcp any host 192.168.0.9 eq www
```

If you are using an access list, you need to create an access group to apply the access list to the correct interface:

```
LabPIX(config)# access-group 101 in interface outside
```

NOTE   Chapter 7 discusses conduits and access lists in greater detail.

This is the configuration used in Figure 5-6. Note that the node is now accessible from the Internet.

Figure 5-6 *Static Translation*

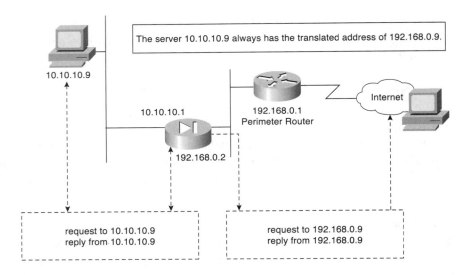

Using the static Command for Port Redirection

One of the improvements of PIX OS Version 6.0 is that the **static** command can be used to redirect services to specific ports and to translate the host's address. This command enables the outside user to connect to a specific address/port and have a Security Appliance redirect the traffic to the appropriate inside/DMZ server. The syntax for this command is as follows:

```
LabPIX(config)# [static] (local_if_name, global_if_name) {tcp | udp} {global_ip/
   interface} local_ip local port netmask mask [norandomseq] [max connections[emb_limit]]
```

For example:

```
LabPIX(config)# static (inside, outside) tcp 192.168.0.9 ftp
   10.10.10.9 2100 netmask 255.255.255.255 0 0
```

The configuration in the preceding example would redirect all traffic that hits the outside interface of the Security Appliance for IP address 192.168.0.9 on TCP port 21 to 10.10.10.9 on TCP port 2100.

Configuring Multiple Translation Types on the Cisco Security Appliance

It is a good practice to use a combination of NAT and PAT. If you have more internal hosts than external IP addresses, you can configure both NAT and PAT. Your first group of hosts translates to the global addresses that are listed and the remaining hosts use PAT and translate to the single global address. PAT is configured separately from NAT. If NAT is configured without PAT, once the available global IP address range is depleted, additional translation attempts will be refused. If the location has any servers that need to be accessed from the Internet (web servers, mail servers, and so on), they must be configured for static translation.

In the following examples, the internal network consisting of 254 hosts translates to 52 external addresses (192.168.0.10 to 192.168.0.62). This means that the remaining 202 hosts translate to 192.168.0.63:

```
LabPIX(config)# nat [(local_interface)] id local_ip network_mask
LabPIX(config)# nat (inside) 1 10.10.10.0 255.255.255.0
LabPIX(config)# [global] [(global_interface)] id global_ip [netmask]  network_mask
LabPIX(config)# global (outside) 1 192.168.0.10-192.168.0.62 netmask
  255.255.255.192
LabPIX(config)# [global] [(global_interface)] id global_ip [netmask]  network_mask
LabPIX(config)# global (outside) 1 192.168.0.63 netmask 255.255.255.255
```

NOTE   It is recommended that you segregate from the rest of the internal network any devices that have a static translation and are accessed from the Internet. These devices should be on a separate network segment that connects to an additional interface on a Cisco Security Appliance. This is normally called a *demilitarized zone (DMZ) segment.*

NOTE   The addresses assigned for static translation cannot be part of the global IP pool. This is a one-to-one relationship between the outside address and the address being translated.

Example 5-1 shows the commands for this type of configuration.

Example 5-1   *Configuring Multiple Translation Types*

```
LabPIX(config)# nat (inside) 1 0.0.0.0 0.0.0.0
LabPIX(config)# global (outside) 1 192.168.0.10-192.168.0.61 netmask
  255.255.255.192
LabPIX(config)# global (outside) 1 192.168.0.62 netmask 255.255.255.255
LabPIX(config)# static (DMZ, outside) 192.168.0.2 172.16.1.2
LabPIX(config)# static (DMZ, outside) 192.168.0.3 172.16.1.3
LabPIX(config)# static (DMZ, outside) 192.168.0.4 172.16.1.4
LabPIX(config)# access-list 101 permit tcp [any] host 192.168.0.2 eq
  smtp
LabPIX(config)# access-list 101 permit tcp any host 192.168.0.3 eq www
LabPIX(config)# access-list 101 permit udp [any] host 192.168.0.4 eq
  domain
LabPIX(config)# access-group 101 in interface outside
```

Figure 5-7 depicts the configuration shown in Example 5-1. Note that the traffic that is allowed inbound is routed to the DMZ rather than going to the internal network. Remember that static translation provides the mechanism for external hosts to connect to internal nodes, but because the connection is from a lower security level to a higher security level, there must be a rule in the security policy allowing the connection.

Figure 5-7 *Combined NAT, PAT, and Static Translation*

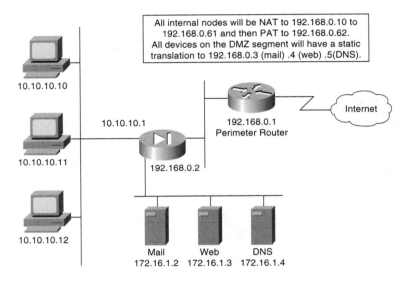

Bidirectional NAT

Cisco PIX Firewall software version 6.2, as well as ASA Security Appliance software version 7.0, allows NAT of external source IP addresses for packets traveling from the outside interface to an inside interface. All the functionality available with traditional **nat**, **pat**, and **static** commands is available bidirectionally.

Translation Versus Connection

Consider this scenario: A single user on a workstation located on the internal network is connecting to his web-based e-mail account, making an online stock purchase, researching a new software package that he intends to buy, and backing up a database at a remote branch office. How many connections does he have going from his workstation? It is difficult to tell because many of these tasks require multiple connections between the source and destination. How many translated sessions does he have going? One.

Most configurations create a single translated session, and from that session, the user can create multiple connections. It is possible to create multiple translated sessions. This normally occurs when the internal node is accessing resources via different network segments all attached to the firewall (such as outside, DMZ1, DMZ2, and so on).

Translation occurs at the network layer (Layer 3) of the OSI reference model and deals only with packets. Connections, however, deal with the transport layer (Layer 4). Therefore, connections can be considered a subset of a single translation. It is possible to troubleshoot both translation and connection issues. It is recommended that you verify translation before attempting to troubleshoot a connection problem because the connection cannot be established if the translation has not occurred.

The argument or keyword used to troubleshoot translations is **xlate**. You can see the translation table by using the command **show xlate**, or you can clear the table with **clear xlate**. Any time you make a change to the translation table, it is a good idea to use **clear xlate**. This forces the translation slots to drop, and the Cisco Security Appliance rebuilds the translation table. If you do not run the **clear xlate** command, the system does not drop the translation slots until they time out, which is 3 hours by default. The following commands can make a change to the translation table:

- **nat**—Identifies the internal address that should be translated.

- **global**—Identifies the external address or addresses to which internal addresses translate.

- **static**—Allows external users to connect to specific addresses and have the Security Appliance redirect that connection specific internal/DMZ address. The **static** command also can be used for port redirection.

- **route**—Provides routing functionality for traffic that is traversing the PIX Firewall.

- **alias**—Was used to translate addresses between overlapping networks but now is used infrequently because of the recent improvements in the functionality of the **nat** and **static** commands.

- **conduit**—Configures the firewall to apply specific rules based on conduits to the traffic. Conduits are not commonly used because of the increased performance and functionality of ACLs.

Table 5-3 documents the options and arguments that are available with the **show xlate** and **clear xlate** commands. Table 5-4 lists the translation flags.

Table 5-3   show/clear xlate *Command Options*

Command Option	Description
detail	If specified, displays the translation type and interface information
[global | local *ip1*[-*ip2*] [netmask *mask*]	Displays active translations by global IP address or local IP address using the network mask to qualify the IP address
interface *if1* [,*if2*] [,*ifn*]	Displays active translations by interface
lport | gport *port* [-*port*]	Displays active translations by local and global ports
state	Displays active translations by state (use the translation flags listed in Table 5-4)

Table 5-4   *Translation Flags*

Flag	Description
s	Static translation slot
d	Dumps the translation slot on the next cleaning cycle
r	Port map translation (PAT)
n	No randomization of TCP sequence number
o	Outside address translations
i	Inside address translations
D	DNS A Resource Record rewrite
I	Identity translation from nat0

If you cannot clear **xlate**, it is possible (but not preferred) to clear the translation table by doing a reload or by rebooting the PIX Firewall.

The command used to troubleshoot connections is **show conn**. This command displays the number and status of all active TCP connections for the specific options selected. Table 5-5 lists the many options for the **show conn** command. Table 5-6 lists the connection flags.

Table 5-5 show conn *Command Options*

Command Option	Description
count	Displays the number of used connections (its accuracy depends on the volume and type of traffic)
detail	Displays the specified translation type and interface information
foreign	local *ip* [*-ip2*] netmask *mask*	Displays active connections by foreign or local IP address and qualifies connections by network mask
fport	lport *port1* [*-port2*]	Displays foreign or local active connections by port
protocol tcp	udp	*protocol*	Displays active connections by protocol type
state	Displays active connections by their current state (see Table 5-6)

Table 5-6 *Connection Flags*

Flag	Description
U	Up
f	Inside FIN
F	Outside FIN
r	Inside acknowledged FIN
R	Outside acknowledged FIN
s	Awaiting outside SYN
S	Awaiting inside SYN
M	SMTP data
T	TCP SIP connection
I	Inbound data
O	Outbound data
q	SQL*Net data
d	Dump

continues

Table 5-6   *Connection Flags (Continued)*

Flag	Description
P	Inside back connection
E	Outside back connection
G	Group
a	Awaiting outside ACK to SYN
A	Awaiting inside ACK to SYN
B	Initial SYN from outside
R	RPC
H	H.323
T	UDP SIP connection
m	SIP media connection
t	SIP transient connection
D	DNS

Configuring DNS Support

It is not necessary to configure DNS support on Cisco Security Appliance. By default, the Security Appliance identifies each outbound DNS request and allows only a single response to that request. The internal host can query several DNS servers for a response, and the Security Appliance allows the outbound queries. However, the Security Appliance allows only the first response to pass through the firewall. All subsequent responses to the original query are dropped.

PIX Version 6.3(2) includes a DNS fixup protocol that enables you to configure a maximum packet length for connections to UDP port 53. The default value is 512 bytes. If you configure the DNS fixup protocol, the Security Appliance drops all connections to UDP port 53 that exceed the configured maximum length. The command for this configuration is

```
fixup protocol dns [maximum length <512-65535>]
```

Foundation Summary

The "Foundation Summary" provides a convenient review of many key concepts in this chapter. If you are already comfortable with the topics in this chapter, this summary can help you recall a few details. If you just read this chapter, this review should help solidify some key facts. If you are doing your final preparation before the exam, this summary provides a convenient way to review the day before the exam.

All interfaces on Cisco Security Appliance are assigned security levels. The higher the number, the more secure the interface. Traffic is allowed to pass from an interface with a higher security level to an interface with a lower security level without a specific rule in the security policy. By default, the outside interface (Ethernet 0) is assigned a security level of 0, and the inside interface (Ethernet 1) is assigned a security level of 100. All other interfaces must be manually assigned a security level using the **nameif** command. Traffic does not pass through two interfaces if they have the same security level.

The Security Appliance handles transport protocols completely differently. TCP is a connection-oriented protocol that creates a session and is relatively simple traffic for the Security Appliance to handle. The TCP sequence number that is generated by the source machine is replaced by a randomly generated number as it passes through the Security Appliance on its way to the destination. It becomes very difficult to hijack a TCP session because the initial TCP sequence numbers are randomly generated by the firewall and you cannot simply select the next sequence number in a series. Figure 5-8 shows how a PIX Firewall would handle a TCP handshake.

Because UDP is a connectionless protocol, determining a connection's state can be very difficult. When outbound UDP traffic is generated, the Security Appliance completes the necessary address translation and saves the session object in the state. If the response does not arrive within the timeout period (the default is 2 minutes), the connection is closed. If the response arrives within the timeout, the Security Appliance verifies the connection information. If it matches the session object in the state table, the Security Appliance allows the traffic. Figure 5-9 shows how a PIX Firewall would typically handle UDP traffic.

Figure 5-8 *PIX Firewall Handling TCP Traffic*

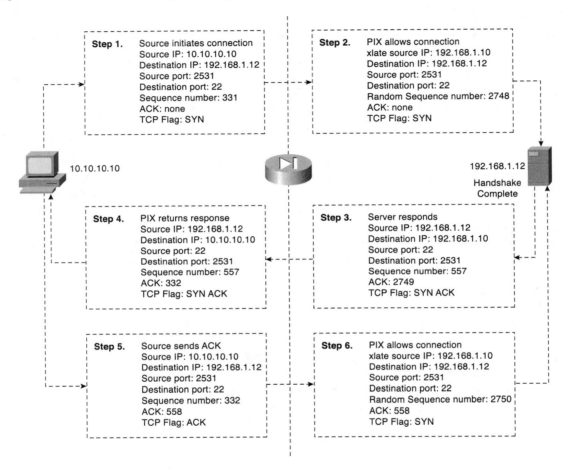

There are two types of address translation:

■ **Dynamic address translation**—Is broken into two categories:

— **Network Address Translation (NAT)**—Multiple local hosts translate to a pool of global addresses.

— **Port Address Translation (PAT)**—Multiple local hosts translate to a single global address.

■ **Static translation**—A single local address translates to a single global address. Static rules provide the translation to allow connection from a lower security level to a higher security level, but this connection must be allowed in the security policy. This connection can be allowed using either the **conduit** or **access-list** command. Access lists must be part of an access group and must be configured to a specific interface.

Figure 5-9 *PIX Firewall Handling UDP Traffic*

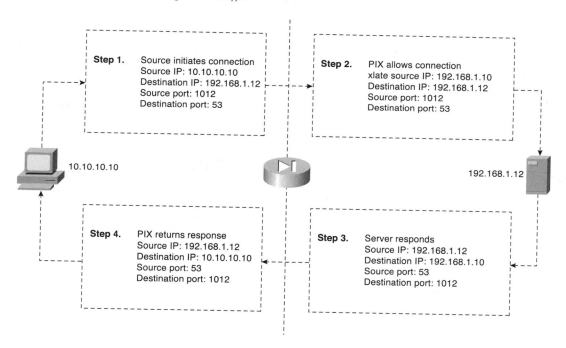

Multiple connections can take place through a single translation. Translations take place at the network layer, and connections occur at the transport layer. Therefore, connections are a subset of translations. Two specific commands are used to troubleshoot translation:

■ **show xlate**—Displays translation slot information. Many options are available to display specific information about the address translations.

■ **clear xlate**—Clears the translation table. Again, many options enable you to clear specific portions of the translation table.

A single command with numerous options is used to troubleshoot connections:

■ **show conn**—Displays the number of and information about the active connections for the options specified.

Q&A

As mentioned in the Introduction, the questions in this book are more difficult than what you should experience on the exam. The questions are designed to ensure your understanding of the concepts discussed in this chapter and adequately prepare you to complete the exam. You should use the simulated exams on the CD to practice for the exam.

The answers to these questions can be found in Appendix A:

1. What is the difference between TCP and UDP?

2. What is the default security for traffic origination on the inside network segment going to the outside network?

3. True or false: You can have multiple translations in a single connection.

4. What commands are required to configure NAT on a Cisco Security Appliance?

5. How many nodes can you hide behind a single IP address when configuring PAT?

6. What is an embryonic connection?

7. What is the best type of translation to use to allow connections to web servers from the Internet?

8. How does a Cisco Security Appliance handle outbound DNS requests?

9. True or false: The quickest way to clear the translation table is to reboot the Security Appliance.

10. True or false: If you configure a static translation for your web server, everyone can connect to it.

11. What does a Security Appliance, such as PIX Firewall, normally change when allowing a TCP handshake between nodes on different interfaces and performing NAT?

12. What does the Cisco Security Appliance normally change when allowing a TCP handshake between nodes on different interfaces and performing PAT?

13. True or false: TCP is a much better protocol than UDP because it does handshakes and randomly generates TCP sequence numbers.

14. What are the two commands (syntax) to perform NAT of all internal addresses?

15. When would you want to configure NAT and PAT for the same inside segment?

16. What is RFC 1918?

17. Why is there an *id* field in the **nat** command?

This chapter covers the following subjects:

- User Interface

- Configuring the Cisco Security Appliance

- Time Settings and NTP Support

Getting Started with the Cisco Security Appliance Family of Firewalls

This chapter describes the basic preparation and configuration required to use the network firewall features of the Cisco Security Appliance family of firewalls. It focuses on how to establish basic connectivity from the internal network to the public Internet.

How to Best Use This Chapter

This chapter provides an overview of the initial configuration steps required to get a Cisco Security Appliance operational. Besides explaining the basic configuration steps, it also explains the operation of the Security Appliance user interface. If you are at all familiar with the Security Appliance, you will probably find the topics in this chapter easy to understand. Test yourself with the "Do I Know This Already?" quiz.

"Do I Know This Already?" Quiz

The purpose of the "Do I Know This Already?" quiz is to help you decide if you really need to read the entire chapter. If you already intend to read the entire chapter, you do not necessarily need to answer these questions now.

The ten-question quiz, derived from the major sections in the "Foundation Topics" portion of the chapter, helps you determine how to spend your limited study time. Table 6-1 outlines the major topics discussed in this chapter and the "Do I Know This Already?" quiz questions that correspond to those topics.

Table 6-1 *"Do I Know This Already?" Foundation Topics Section-to-Question Mapping*

Foundations Topics Section	Questions Covered in This Section	Score
User Interface	5, 7	
Configuring the Security Appliance	1 to 4	
Configuring Transparent Mode	8	
Time Settings and NTP Support	6	
DHCP Server Configuration	9	

CAUTION The goal of self assessment is to gauge your mastery of the topics in this chapter. If you do not know the answer to a question or are only partially sure of the answer, you should mark this question wrong for purposes of the self assessment. Giving yourself credit for an answer you correctly guess skews your self-assessment results and might provide you with a false sense of security.

1. Which command tests connectivity?

   a. ping

   b. nameif

   c. ip address

   d. write terminal

2. Which command saves the configuration you made on the Cisco PIX Firewall?

   a. write terminal

   b. show start-running config

   c. write memory

   d. save config

3. Which command assigns security levels to interfaces on the PIX Firewall?

   a. ip address

   b. route

   c. security-level

   d. secureif

4. Which command flushes the ARP cache of the PIX Firewall?

   a. flush arp cache

   b. no arp cache

   c. clear arp

   d. You cannot flush the ARP cache

5. Which of following configures a message when a firewall administrator enters the **enable** command?

   a. banner motd enter the enable password

   b. banner enable enter the enable password

    c. banner exec enter the enable password

    d. banner login enter the enable password

6. Why would you want authentication enabled between the PIX and the NTP server?

    a. To ensure that the PIX does synchronize with an unauthorized NTP server

    b. To maintain the integrity of the communication

    c. To increase the speed of communication

    d. To reduce latency

7. How do you access the enable mode?

    a. Enter the **enable** command and the enable password.

    b. Enter the **privilege** command and the privilege password.

    c. Enter the super-secret password.

    d. Enter only the command **privilege**.

8. How do you view the current configuration on your PIX Firewall?

    a. show running-config

    b. show current

    c. write memory

    d. save config

9. What command enables transparent mode?

    a. firewall mode transparent

    b. firewall transparent

    c. transparent enable

    d. no ip firewall standard

10. In a DHCP client configuration, what is the command to release and renew the IP address on the outside interface?

    a. ipconfig release

    b. ip address dhcp outside

    c. outside ip renew

    d. ip address renew outside

The answers to the "Do I Know This Already?" quiz are found in Appendix A, "Answers to the 'Do I Know This Already?' Quizzes and Q&A Sections." The suggested choices for your next step are as follows:

- **8 or less overall score**—Read the entire chapter. This includes the "Foundation Topics," "Foundation Summary," and "Q&A" sections.

- **9 or 10 overall score**—If you want more review on these topics, skip to the "Foundation Summary" section and then go to the "Q&A" section. Otherwise, move to the next chapter.

Foundation Topics

Access Modes

The Cisco Security Appliance family of firewalls contains a command set based on Cisco IOS Software technologies that provides three administrative access modes:

- Unprivileged mode is available when you first access the Security Appliance through console or Telnet. It displays the > prompt. This mode lets you view only restricted settings.

- You access privileged mode by entering the **enable** command and the enable password. The prompt then changes from > to #. In this mode, you can change a few of the current settings and view the existing Cisco Security Appliance configuration. Any unprivileged command also works in privileged mode. To exit privileged mode, enter the **disable** or **exit** command.

- You access configuration mode by entering the **configure terminal** command. This changes the prompt from # to (config)#. In this mode, you can change system configurations. All privileged, unprivileged, and configuration commands work in this mode. Use the **exit** or **^z** command to exit configuration mode.

> **NOTE** PIX version 6.2 and later, as well as ASA Security Appliance version 7.0 and later, supports 16 privilege levels. This feature enables you to assign Cisco Security Appliance commands to one of the 16 levels. These privilege levels can also be assigned to users. This is discussed in detail in Chapter 4, "System Management/ Maintenance."

Configuring a Cisco Security Appliance

Eight important commands are used to produce a basic working configuration for a Security Appliance:

- interface
- security-level
- nameif
- ip address
- nat
- nat-control

- global
- route

Before you use these commands, it can prove very useful to draw a diagram of your Cisco Security Appliance with the different security levels, interfaces, and Internet Protocol (IP) addresses. Figure 6-1 shows one such diagram that is used for the discussion in this chapter.

Figure 6-1 *Documenting Cisco Security Appliance Security Levels, Interfaces, and IP Addresses*

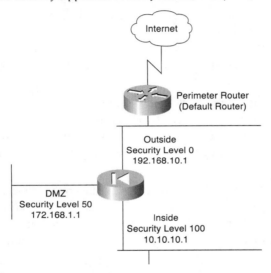

interface Command

The **interface** command identifies the interface hardware card and enables the interface all-in-one command. All interfaces on a Cisco Security Appliance are shut down by default and are explicitly enabled by the **interface** command. The basic syntax of the **interface** command is as follows:

```
interface physical_interface[.subinterface] | mapped_name[shutdown]*
```

> **NOTE** The **interface** command and the configuration of interfaces changed with software version 7.0. The method used to configure an interface is now similar to how you would configure an interface on Cisco IOS routers.

Table 6-2 describes the command parameters for the **interface** command.

Table 6-2 *interface Command Parameters*

Command Parameter	Description
physical_interface	Indicates the interface's physical location on the Cisco Security Appliance. Based on your Security Appliance, the choices would be • **ethernet** • **gigabitethernet** • **management**
subinterface	(Optional) An integer between 1 and 4,294,967,293 designating a logical subinterface. This can be used with VLANs to create multiple VLAN segments on a single physical interface.
mapped_name	In multiple context mode, enter the mapped name if it was assigned using the **allocate-interface** command. This is described in more detail in Chapter 9, "Security Contexts."
shutdown	Administratively shuts down the interface. This parameter performs a very similar function in Cisco IOS Software. However, unlike with Cisco IOS, the command **no shutdown** cannot be used here. To place an interface in an administratively up mode, you reenter the **interface** command without the **shutdown** parameter.

Example 6-1 shows some examples of the **interface** command.

Example 6-1 *Sample Configuration for the* **interface** *Command*

```
Pix(config)# interface ethernet0
Pix(config-if)# speed 100
Pix(config-if)# duplex full
```

You can only set the speed through two commands that must be used in the interface configuration mode. Use the **speed** command to set the speed of the interface, and use the **duplex** command to set the duplex of the interface.

security-level Command

The *security-level* value controls how hosts/devices on the different interfaces interact with each other. By default, hosts/devices connected to interfaces with higher-security levels can access hosts/devices connected to interfaces with lower-security interfaces. Hosts/devices connected to interfaces with lower-security interfaces cannot access hosts/devices connected to interfaces with higher-security interfaces without the assistance of access lists. The **security-level** command is new to version 7.0 and replaces the older **nameif** command feature that assigned the security level for an interface. Two interfaces, the **inside** and **outside** interfaces, have set security levels but can be overridden using this command. The **inside** interface has a default security level of 100; the **outside** interface has a default security level of 0. Newly added interfaces receive a default security level of 0. To assign a new security level to an interface, use the **security-level** command in the interface command mode. The syntax of the **security-level** command is as follows:

```
security-level number
```

where *number* can be a numerical value from 1 to 99 indicating the security level.

nameif Command

As the name intuitively indicates, the **nameif** command is used to name an interface. The outside and inside interfaces are named by default and have default security values of 0 and 100, respectively. By default, the interfaces have their hardware ID. Ethernet 0 is the outside interface, and Ethernet 1 is the inside interface. The names that are configured by the **nameif** command are user-friendly and are easier to use for advanced configuration later.

> **NOTE** The **nameif** command can also be used to assign security values of 0 and 100. The names "inside" and "outside" are merely reserved for security levels 100 and 0, respectively, and are assigned by default, but they can be changed.

To assign a name for an interface, use the command in interface configuration mode. The syntax of the **nameif** command is as follows:

```
nameif hardware-id if-name
```

Table 6-3 describes the command parameters for the **nameif** command.

Table 6-3 nameif *Command Parameters*

Command Parameter	Description
hardware-id	Indicates the interface's physical location on the Cisco Security Appliance.
if-name	Specifies the name by which you refer to this interface. The name cannot have any spaces and must not exceed 48 characters.

Example 6-2 shows some examples of the **nameif** command.

Example 6-2 *Sample Configuration for the* **nameif** *Command*

```
nameif ethernet0 outside
nameif ethernet1 inside
nameif ethernet2 dmz
```

You can verify your configuration by using the **show nameif** command.

ip address Command

All the interfaces on a Security Appliance that will be used must be configured with an IP address. The IP address can be configured manually or through Dynamic Host Configuration Protocol (DHCP). The DHCP feature is usually used on Cisco Security Appliance small office/home office (SOHO) models. DHCP is discussed later in this chapter.

The **ip address** command, while in interface configuration mode, is used to configure IP addresses on the Security Appliance interfaces. The **ip address** command binds a logical address (IP address) to the hardware ID. Additionally, you can use the **ip address** command to assign a standby IP address for a Security Appliance that will be used during a failover situation. Table 6-4 describes the parameters for the **ip address** command, the syntax of which is as follows:

```
ip address ip-address [netmask] [standby ip_address]
```

Table 6-4 ip address *Command Parameters*

Command Parameter	Description
ip-address	Specifies the IP address of the interface.
netmask	Specifies the appropriate network mask. If the mask value is not entered, the firewall assigns a classful network mask.
standby *ip_address*	Specifies the IP address for the standby unit for failover.

Example 6-3 shows configuration of the inside interface with an IP address of 10.10.10.14/24.

Example 6-3 *Sample Configuration for the* ip address *Command*

```
Pix(config)# interface ethernet0
Pix(config-if)# ip address 10.10.10.14  255.255.255.0
```

In addition to manually assigned IP addresses, the Security Appliance can act as a DHCP client. With version 7.0, the **ip address** command can use **dhcp** as an entry instead of an IP address.

This will allow a DHCP server to assign an IP address and netmask to the interface. A default gateway will also be assigned to the Security Appliance if it is required. You can flush and renew the IP address assignment through the DHCP server by reentering the **ip address dhcp** command.

Use the **show ip** command to view the configured IP address on a Security Appliance interface.

nat Command

The **nat** (Network Address Translation) command lets you dynamically translate a set of IP addresses (usually on the inside) to a global set of IP addresses.

> **NOTE** PIX version 6.2 and later support bidirectional translation of inside network IP addresses to global IP addresses and translation of outside IP addresses to inside network IP addresses.

The **nat** command is always paired with a **global** command, with the exception of the **nat 0** command. Table 6-5 describes the command parameters for the **nat** command, the syntax of which is as follows:

```
nat (if-name) nat-id local-ip [netmask] [dns] [[tcp] tcp_max_conns [emb_limit]
[norandomseq]]] [udp udp_max_conns]
```

Table 6-5 nat *Command Parameters*

Command Parameter	Description
(if-name)	Specifies the internal network interface name.
nat-id	Specifies the ID number to match with the global address pool.
local-ip	Specifies the IP address that is translated. This is usually the inside network IP address. It is possible to assign all of the inside network for the local-ip through **nat** (**inside**) **1 0 0**.
netmask	Specifies the network mask for the local IP address.
dns	Informs NAT[1] to use an existing translation to rewrite the DNS[2] address records.
tcp	Specifies that the maximum TCP connections and embryonic limit are set for the TCP protocol. This is optional.
tcp_max_conns	The maximum number of simultaneous TCP connections that the local_ip hosts allow. Idle connections are closed after the time that is specified. This is optional and used in conjunction with **tcp**.
emb_limit	The maximum number of embryonic connections per host. (An embryonic connection is a connection request that has not finished the necessary handshake between source and destination.) Set a small value for slower systems and a higher value for faster systems. The default is 0, which allows unlimited embryonic connections.
udp	Specifies a maximum number of UDP[3] connection parameters that can be configured. This is optional.
udp_max_conns	Sets the maximum number of simultaneous UDP connections that the local_IP hosts are each allowed to use. Idle connections are closed. This is optional and used in conjunction with **udp**.

[1] NAT = Network Address Translation

[2] DNS = Domain Name System

[3] UDP = User Datagram Protocol

Example 6-4 shows an example of the **nat** command.

Example 6-4 *Sample Configuration for the* nat *Command*

```
nat (inside) 1 10.10.10.0 255.255.255.0 0 0
nat (inside) 2 172.16.1.0 255.255.255.0 0 0
```

Chapter 5, "Understanding Cisco Security Appliance Translation and Connection," discusses NAT in greater detail.

Configuring Port Address Translation

Port Address Translation (PAT) can be configured using the same command as NAT. PAT maps a single global IP address to many local addresses. PAT extends the range of available outside addresses at your site by dynamically assigning unique port numbers to the outside address as a connection is requested. A single IP address has up to 65,535 ports available for making connections. For PAT, the port number uniquely identifies each connection.

PAT translates a group of local addresses to a single global IP address with a unique source port (above 1024). When a local host accesses the destination network, the Firewall services module assigns it the global IP address and then a unique port number. Each host receives the same IP address, but because the source port numbers are unique, the responding traffic, which includes the IP address and port number as the destination, can be assigned to the correct host. It is highly unlikely that you would run out of addresses in PAT configuration because there are more than 64,000 ports available.

PAT enables you to use a single global address, thus conserving routable addresses. You can even use the destination actual interface IP address as the PAT IP address (this type of configuration is used, but not limited to, the outside interface). PAT does not work with multimedia applications that have an inbound data stream different from the outgoing control path.

In large enterprise environments, to use NAT, you must have a large number of routable addresses in the global pool. If the destination network requires registered addresses, such as the Internet, you might encounter a shortage of usable addresses. This can be a disadvantage.

PAT does not work with applications that have an inbound data stream on one port and the outgoing control path on another, such as multimedia applications. For those situations, it is more advantageous to use NAT. Example 6-5 shows a sample configuration for PAT.

Example 6-5 *Sample Configuration for Configuring PAT on the Inside Interface*

```
nat (inside)  1  10.10.30.0  255.255.255.0
global (outside)  1  interface
```

speed Command

The **speed** command is used to set the communication speed of the interface. The speed setting is only used on copper Ethernet interfaces (RJ-45), with the fiber Gigabit Ethernet interfaces set to a speed of 1000 Mbps by default using the nonegotiate syntax. You can use the **speed** command to set the speed on the interface to 10 Mbps or 100 Mbps. Additionally, you can set the **speed** command to autodetect the speed of the interface from the line connected to the interface using the **auto** syntax. Table 6-6 describes the command parameters for the **speed** command, which must be used in the interface configuration mode. The syntax for the speed command is as follows:

```
speed {auto | 10 | 100 | nonegotiate}
```

Table 6-6   speed *Command Parameters*

Command Parameter	Description
auto	Autodetects the speed of the interface.
10	Sets the speed to 10BASE-T (10 Mbps)
100	Sets the speed to 100BASE-T (100 Mbps)
nonegotiate	For SFP[1] media type, sets the speed to 1000 Mbps. SFP does not allow any other setting.

[1] SFP = Small Form-factor Pluggable

duplex Command

The **duplex** command is used to set an interfaces duplex mode. The duplex for an interface can be set manually by defining if the interface should be in half-duplex or full-duplex mode. Additionally, you can set the interface to autodetect the duplex from the line connected to the interface.

Table 6-7 describes the command parameters for the **duplex** command, which must be used in the interface configuration mode. The syntax for the **duplex** command is as follows:

```
duplex {auto | full | half}
```

Table 6-7   duplex *Command Parameters*

Command Parameter	Description
auto	Auto detects the duplex of the interface.
full	Sets the duplex to full duplex.
half	Sets the duplex to half duplex.

nat-control Command

The **nat-control** command is used to enforce address hinding on the inside and outside interfaces of a Security Appliance. With **nat-control** enabled, all packets that flow through the Security Appliance require a NAT rule, or the packets will be denied access through the appliance. If an inside NAT policy is enabled on an interface, each inside address must have an inside NAT rule configured or communication will not be permitted through the Security Appliance. Additionally, if an outside NAT policy is enabled on an interface, all outside addresses must have an outside NAT rule configured or communication will not be permitted through the Security Appliance.

The **nat-control** command is not enabled by default, requiring that only hosts that undergo NAT need a NAT rule.

global Command

The **global** command is used to define the address or range of addresses into which the addresses defined by the **nat** command are translated. It is important that the *nat-id* be identical to the *nat-id* used in the **nat** command. The *nat-id* pairs the IP address defined by the **global** and **nat** commands so that network translation can take place. The syntax of the **global** command is as follows:

```
global  (if-name) nat-id global-ip | global-ip-global-ip [netmask  netmask]
```

Table 6-8 describes the parameters and options for the **global** command.

Table 6-8 global *Command Parameters*

Command Parameter	Description
(if-name)	Specifies the external network where you use these global addresses.
nat-id	Identifies the global address and matches it with the **nat** command with which it is pairing.
global-ip	Specifies a single IP address. When a single IP address is specified, the Security Appliance automatically performs PAT. A warning message indicating that the Security Appliance will use PAT for all addresses is displayed on the console.
global-ip-global-ip	Defines a range of global IP addresses to be used by the PIX to NAT.
netmask	Specifies the network mask for the global IP address(es).

There should be enough global IP addresses to match the local IP addresses specified by the **nat** command. If there are not, you can leverage the shortage of global addresses by PAT entry, which permits more than 64,000 hosts to use a single IP address. PAT divides the available ports per global IP address into three ranges:

- 0 to 511

- 512 to 1023

- 1024 to 65,535

PAT assigns a unique source port for each User Datagram Protocol (UDP) or Transmission Control Protocol (TCP) session. It attempts to assign the same port value of the original request, but if the original source port has already been used, PAT starts scanning from the beginning of the particular port range to find the first available port and then assigns it to the conversation. PAT has some restrictions in its use. For example, it cannot support H.323. Example 6-6 shows a configuration using a range of global IP addresses and a single IP address for PAT.

Example 6-6   *Sample Configuration for NAT and PAT*

```
nat (inside) 1 10.0.0.0 255.0.0.0
global (outside) 1 192.168.100.20-192.168.100.50 netmask 255.255.255.0
global (outside) 1 192.168.100.55 netmask 255.255.255.0
```

When a host or device tries to start a connection, the Security Appliance checks the translation table to see whether there is an entry for that particular IP address. If there is no existing translation, a new *translation slot* is created. The default time that a translated IP address is kept in the translation table is 3 hours. You can change this with the **timeout xlate** *hh:mm:ss* command. To view the translated addresses, use the **show xlate** command.

route Command

The **route** command tells the Cisco Security Appliance where to send information that is forwarded on a specific interface and that is destined for a particular network address. You add static routes to the Security Appliance using the **route** command.

Table 6-9 describes the **route** command parameters, the syntax of which is as follows:

> route *if-name ip-address netmask gateway-ip* [*metric* | **tunneled**]

Table 6-9   route *Command Parameters*

Command Parameter	Description
if-name	Specifies the name of the interface from which the data leaves.
ip-address	Specifies the IP address to be routed.
netmask	Specifies the network mask of the IP address to be routed.
gateway-ip	Specifies the IP address of the next-hop address. Usually, this is the IP address of the perimeter router.

Table 6-9 route *Command Parameters (Continued)*

metric	The administrative distance of this route. This can be used to create floating static routes.
tunneled	Specifies the route as the default tunnel gateway for VPN[1] traffic.

[1] VPN = virtual private network

Example 6-7 shows a default route configuration on a Cisco Security Appliance.

Example 6-7 *Default Route of 192.168.1.3*

```
route outside 0.0.0.0 0.0.0.0 192.168.1.3 1
```

NOTE   On a Security Appliance, such as the PIX Firewall, several default routes are permitted. To allow more then a single default route, each additional default route must be set up as a floating static route.

The **1** at the end of the route indicates that the gateway router is only one hop away. If a metric is not specified in the **route** command, the default is 1. You can configure only one default route on a Security Appliance. It is good practice to use the **clear arp** command to clear the Address Resolutions Protocol (ARP) cache of a Security Appliance before testing your new route configuration.

Routing Information Protocol

The Routing Information Protocol (RIP) can be enabled to build the Cisco Security Appliance routing table. RIP configuration specifies whether the Security Appliance updates its routing tables by passively listening to RIP traffic and whether the interface broadcasts itself as a default route for network traffic on that interface. When using RIP version 2 with Security Appliance software versions earlier than 5.3, it is important to configure the router providing the RIP updates with the network address of the Security Appliance interface. The default version is 1 if not explicitly specified. The syntax to enable RIP is as follows:

```
rip if-name default | passive [version [1 | 2]] [authentication [text | md5
key (key-id)]]
```

Table 6-10 describes the **rip** command parameters.

Table 6-10 rip *Command Parameters*

Command Parameter	Description
if-name	Specifies the interface name.
default	Broadcasts a default route on the interface.
passive	Enables passive RIP on the interface. The Cisco Security Appliance listens for RIP routing broadcasts and uses that information to populate its routing tables.
version	Specifies the RIP version number. Use version 2 for RIP update encryption. Use version 1 to provide backward compatibility with the earlier versions.
authentication	Enables authentication for RIP version 2.
text	Sends RIP updates in clear text.
md5	Encrypts RIP updates using MD5 encryption.
key	Specifies the key to encrypt RIP updates. This value must be the same on the routers and on any other device that provides RIP version 2 updates. The key is a text string up to 16 characters in length.
key-id	Specifies the key identification value. The *key-id* can be a number from 1 to 255. Use the same *key-id* that is used on the routers and any other device that provides RIP version 2 updates.

NOTE   RIP is not supported in transparent mode. This is due to transparent mode relying on Layer 2 bridging instead of Layer 3 routing to pass packets.

Testing Your Configuration

Making sure that the configuration you entered works is an important part of the configuration process. At this point, you test basic connectivity from the inside interface out to the other interfaces. Use the **ping** and **debug** commands to test your connectivity.

The **ping** command sends an Internet Control Message Protocol (ICMP) echo request message to the target IP address and expects an ICMP echo reply. By default, the Security Appliance denies all inbound traffic through the outside interface. Based on your network security policy, you should consider configuring the Security Appliance to deny all ICMP traffic to the outside interface, or any other interface you deem necessary, by entering the **icmp** command. The **icmp** command controls ICMP traffic that terminates on the Security Appliance. If no ICMP control list is configured, the Security Appliance accepts all ICMP traffic that terminates at any interface (including the outside interface). For example, when you first configure a PIX Firewall, it is a good idea to be able to ping an interface and get a response. The following makes that possible for the outside interface:

```
icmp permit any any outside
```

The **icmp permit any any outside** command is used during the testing/debugging phase of your configuration process. Make sure that you change it so it does not respond to ping requests after you complete testing. It is a security risk to leave it set to accept and respond to ICMP packets.

After the **icmp permit** command has been configured, you can ping the outside interface on your Cisco Security Appliance and ping from hosts on each firewall interface. For example:

```
ping outside 192.168.1.1
```

You also can monitor ping results by starting **debug icmp trace**. The **debug** command will display messages that contain **icmp** type values. Table 6-11 describes the **icmp**-type values supported in version 7.0.

Table 6-11   icmp *Type Values*

Type Values	Description
0	Echo-reply
3	Unreachable
4	Source-quench
5	Redirect
6	Alternate-address
8	Echo
9	Router-advertisement
10	Router-solicitation
11	Time-exceeded
12	Parameter-problem
13	Timestamp-request
14	Timestamp-reply
15	Information-request
16	Information-reply
17	Mask-request
18	Mask-reply
31	Conversion-error
32	Mobile-redirect

Saving Your Configuration

Configuration changes that you have made stay in the random access memory (RAM) of the Security Appliance unless you save them to Flash memory. If for any reason the Security Appliance must be rebooted, the configuration changes you made are lost. So, when you finish entering commands in the configuration, save the changes to Flash memory by using the **write memory** command, as follows:

```
Pix# write memory
```

NOTE There is one obvious advantage of not having configuration changes committed to Flash memory immediately. For example, if you make a configuration change that you cannot back out from, you simply reboot and return to the settings you had before you made the changes.

You are now finished configuring the Cisco Security Appliance. This basic configuration lets protected network users start connections and prevents users on unprotected networks from accessing (or attacking) protected hosts.

Use the **write terminal** or **show running-config** command to view your current configuration.

Support for Domain Name System Messages

Security Appliance fully supports NAT and PAT Domain Name System (DNS) messages originating from either a more secure interface or less secure interfaces. This means that if a client on an inside network requests DNS resolution of an inside address from a DNS server on an outside interface, the DNS record is translated correctly. To illustrate this point, Figure 6-2 shows a user from inside obtaining DNS resolution from the outside (maybe from an Internet service provider) for a web server on the inside. This process is called *DNS reply modification* or *DNS doctoring*.

Figure 6-2 *User Obtaining DNS Resolution from the Outside*

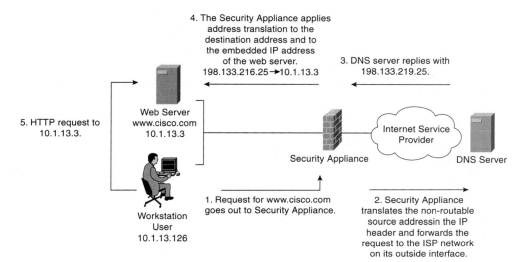

Before the release of version 7.0, you would use the **alias** command to modify DNS server replies. As for version 7.0, this feature has been integrated into the translation commands, such as the **static** command. Using the example shown in Figure 6-2, you would use the following command to create the DNS reply modification:

```
Pix(config)# static (inside,outside) 198.133.219.25 10.1.33.3 netmask 255.255.255.255
```

You can use DNS doctoring to manipulate the DNS replies for servers that exist outside your network, with **Outside NAT** enabled. Using this process will allow you to restrict your users to only destination IP addresses that reside on the Inside subnet, shielding them from the possibility of relying on outside DNS problems. Using the example shown in Figure 6-3, you would use the following command to create the DNS reply modification:

```
Pix(config)# static (outside,inside) 10.1.33.3 198.133.219.25 netmask
    255.255.255.255
```

Figure 6-3 *DNS Reply Modification Using Outside NAT*

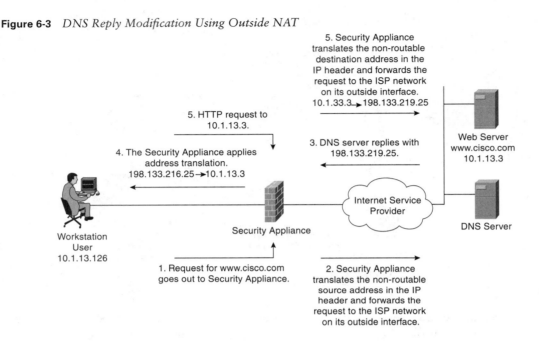

Configuring Dynamic Host Configuration Protocol on the Cisco Security Appliance

The Cisco Security Appliance can be configured as either of the following:

- DHCP server
- DHCP client

Using the Cisco Security Appliance DHCP Server

The DHCP server is usually used in, but not limited to, SOHO environments. The address pool of a Cisco Security Appliance DHCP server must be within the same subnet of the Security Appliance interface that is enabled, and you must specify the associated Security Appliance interface with *if- name*. In other words, the client must be physically connected to the subnet of a Security Appliance interface. The size of the pool is limited to 32 addresses with a 10-user license and 128 addresses with a 50-user license on the PIX 501. The unlimited user license on the PIX 501 and all other Security Appliance platforms supports 256 addresses. To configure DHCP on a Security Appliance, use the **dhcpd** command. The following is the syntax for the **dhcpd** command:

```
dhcpd address ip1[-ip2] if-name
dhcpd auto-config [outside]
dhcpd dns dns1 [dns2]
```

```
dhcpd wins wins1 [wins2]
dhcpd lease lease-length
dhcpd domain domain-name
dhcpd enable if-name
dhcpd option 66 ascii {server-name | server-ip-str}
dhcpd option 150 ip server-ip1 [ server-ip2]
dhcpd ping-timeout timeout
debug dhcpd event
debug dhcpd packet
```

Table 6-12 describes the different **dhcpd** command parameters.

Table 6-12 **dhcpd** *Command Parameters*

Parameter	Description
address *ip1*- [*ip2*]	Specifies the IP pool address range.
auto-config	Enables the Security Appliance to configure DNS, Windows Internet Naming Service (WINS), and domain name values automatically from the DHCP client to the DHCP server. If the user also specifies DNS, WINS, and domain parameters, the command-line interface (CLI) parameters overwrite the **auto-config** parameters.
binding	Specifies the binding information for a given server IP address and its associated client hardware address and lease length.
code	Specifies the DHCP option code, either 66 or 150.
dns *dns1* [*dns2*]	Specifies the IP addresses of the DNS servers for the DHCP client.
domain *domain-name*	Specifies the DNS domain name; for example, cspfa2.com.
if-name	Specifies the interface on which to enable the DHCP server.
lease *lease-length*	Specifies the length of the lease, in seconds, granted to the DHCP client from the DHCP server. The lease indicates how long the client can use the assigned IP address. The default is 3600 seconds. The minimum lease length is 300 seconds, and the maximum lease length is 2,147,483,647 seconds.
option 150	Specifies the Trivial File Transfer Protocol (TFTP) server IP address(es) designated for Cisco IP Phones in dotted-decimal format. DHCP **option 150** is site-specific; it gives the IP addresses of a list of TFTP servers.
option 66	Specifies the TFTP server IP address designated for Cisco IP Phones and gives the IP address or the host name of a single TFTP server.
outside	Specifies the outside interface of the firewall.
ping-timeout	Specifies the timeout value of a ping, in milliseconds, before an IP address is assigned to a DHCP client.
server-ip(1,2)	Specifies the IP address(es) of a TFTP server.

continues

Table 6-12 dhcpd *Command Parameters (Continued)*

Parameter	Description
server-ip-str	Specifies the TFTP server in dotted-decimal format, such as 1.1.1.1, which is treated as a character string by the Security Appliance DHCP server.
server-name	Specifies an American Standard Code for Information Interchange (ASCII) character string representing the TFTP server.
statistics	Provides statistical information, such as address pool, number of bindings, malformed messages, sent messages, and received messages.
wins *wins1 [wins2]*	Specifies the IP addresses of the Microsoft NetBIOS name servers (Windows Internet Naming Service servers). The second server address is optional.

In addition to supporting a DHCP client and DHCP server configuration, the Security Appliance also supports a DHCP relay configuration. The DHCP relay configuration enables the Security Appliance to assist in dynamic configuration of IP device hosts on any Ethernet interface. When the Cisco Security Appliance receives a request from a host on an interface, it forwards the request to a user-configured DHCP server on another interface. The DHCP relay agent is a feature that is provided by security software version 6.3.

A Security Appliance allows any number of integrated DHCP servers to be configured, and on any interface. The DHCP client can be configured only on the outside interface, and the DHCP relay agent can be configured on any interface. The DHCP server and DHCP relay agent cannot be configured concurrently on the same Security Appliance, but the DHCP client and DHCP relay agent can be configured concurrently.

As with all other DHCP servers, DNS, Windows Internet Naming Service (WINS), IP address lease time, and domain information on the Security Appliance can be configured. The following six steps are required to enable the DHCP server feature on the Security Appliance:

Step 1   Enable the DHCP daemon on the Cisco Security Appliance to listen to DHCP requests from clients:

```
pix(config)#dhcpd enable inside
```

Step 2   Specify the IP address range that the Security Appliance DHCP server assigns:

```
pix(config)#dhcpd address 10.10.10.15-10.10.10.100 inside
```

Step 3   Specify the lease length to grant to the client (the default is 3600 seconds):

```
pix(config)#dhcpd lease 2700
```

Step 4   Specify a DNS server (optional):

`pix(config)#dhcpd dns 192.168.10.68 192.168.10.73`

Step 5   Specify a WINS server (optional):

`pix(config)#dhcpd wins 192.168.10.66`

Step 6   Configure the domain name the client will use (optional):

`pix(config)#dhcpd domain axum.com`

Configuring the Security Appliance DHCP Client

DHCP client support on the Cisco Security appliance is designed for use in SOHO environments in which digital subscriber line (DSL) and cable modems are used. The DHCP client can be enabled only on the outside interface of the Security Appliance. When the DHCP client is enabled, DHCP servers on the outside provide the outside interface with an IP address.

> **NOTE**   The DHCP client does not support failover configuration.

The DHCP client feature on a Security Appliance is enabled by the **ip address dhcp** command:

`ip address dhcp [setroute] [retry retry-cnt]`

The **setroute** option tells the Cisco Security Appliance to set its default route using the default gateway parameter that the DHCP server returns. Do not configure a default route when using the **setroute** option.

> **NOTE**   **ip address dhcp** is used to release and renew the outside interface's IP address.

To view current information about the DHCP lease, enter the following command:

`show ip address outside dhcp`

The partial configuration in Example 6-8 demonstrates how to use three new features that are associated with each other: DHCP server, DHCP client, and PAT using the interface IP address to configure a Security Appliance in a SOHO environment with the inside interface as the DHCP server.

Example 6-8 *Sample Configuration for the* dhcpd *Command*

```
ip address dhcp setroute
ip address 10.100.1.1 255.255.255.0
dhcpd address 10.100.1.50-10.100.1.60 inside
dhcpd dns 192.168.1.106 192.168.1.107
dhcpd wins 192.168.1.106
dhcpd lease 1200
dhcpd domain cspfa.com
dhcpd enable inside
nat (inside) 1 0 0
global (outside) 1 interface
```

> **NOTE** To configure DHCP client features for a VPN connection, you must use **dhcp-server** command in a tunnel-group. This will assign an IP address from an outside DHCP server. The **ip address dhcp** command cannot be used in this way.

Configuring Time Settings on the Cisco Security Appliance

The Security Appliance obtains its time setting information in two ways:

- By Network Time Protocol (NTP) server
- By system clock

NTP

The NTP is used to implement a hierarchical system of servers that provide a source for a precise synchronized time among network systems. It is important to maintain a consistent time throughout all network devices, such as servers, routers, and switches. When analyzing network events, logs are an important source of information. Analyzing and troubleshooting network events can be difficult if there is a time inconsistency between network devices on the network. Furthermore, some time-sensitive operations, such as validating certificates and certificate revocation lists (CRLs), require precise time stamps.

Cisco PIX Firewall version 6.2 and later, as well as ASA Security version 7.0, enable you obtain the system time from NTP version 3 servers.

The syntax to enable an NTP client on the Security Appliance is as follows:

    ntp server *ip-address* [**key** *number*] **source** *if-name* [**prefer**]

Table 6-13 describes the parameters of the **ntp** command.

Table 6-13 ntp *Command Parameters*

Command Parameter	Description
ip-address	Specifies the IP address of the time server with which the Security Appliance synchronizes.
key	This keyword indicates that you are configuring the NTP client to use the specified authentication key (identified by number) when sending packets to the NTP server.
number	Specifies the authentication key. This value is useful when you use multiple keys and multiple servers for identification purposes.
source	Specifies the interface. If the **source** keyword is not specified, the routing table is used to determine the interface.
if-name	Specifies the interface name used to send packets to the NTP server.
prefer	Specifies the preferred time server. This option reduces switching back and forth between servers by making the specified server the preferred time server.

Communication of messages between the Security Appliance and the NTP servers can be authenticated to prevent the Security Appliance from synchronizing time with rogue NTP servers. The three commands used to enable NTP authentication are as follows:

```
ntp authenticate
ntp authentication-key number md5 value
ntp trusted-key number
```

NOTE   NTP uses port 123 for communication.

The **ntp authenticate** command enables NTP authentication and refuses synchronization with an NTP server unless the server is configured with one of the authentication keys specified using the **ntp trusted-key** command.

The **ntp authentication-key** command is used to define authentication keys for use with other NTP commands to provide a higher degree of security. The *number* parameter is the key number (1 to 4,294,967,295). The **md5** option is the encryption algorithm. The *value* parameter is the key value (an arbitrary string of up to 32 characters).

The **ntp trusted-key** command is used to define one or more key numbers that the NTP server is required to provide in its NTP packets for the Security Appliance to accept synchronization with that NTP server. The Cisco Security Appliance requires the NTP server to provide this key number in its NTP packets, which provides protection against synchronizing the Security Appliance system clock with an NTP server that is not trusted.

NTP configuration on the Security Appliance can be verified and viewed by using the following **show** commands:

- The **show ntp** command displays the current NTP configuration.
- The **show ntp associations** [**detail**] command displays the configured network time server associations.
- The **show ntp status** command displays the NTP clock information.

To remove the NTP configuration, use the **clear ntp** command.

Cisco Security Appliance System Clock

The second method of configuring the time setting on the Security Appliance is by using the system clock. The system clock is usually set when you answer the initial setup interview question when you are configuring a new Cisco Security Appliance. You can change it later using the **clock set** command:

```
clock  set  hh:mm:ss month day year
```

Three characters are used for the *month* parameter. The *year* is a four-digit number. For example, to set the time and date to 17:51 and 20 seconds on April 9, 2003, you would enter the following:

```
clock  set  17:51:20  apr  9  2003
```

> **NOTE**   The system clock, unlike NTP, is not synchronized with other network devices.

Cisco PIX Firewall version 6.2 included improvements to the **clock** command. The **clock** command now supports daylight saving (summer) time and time zones. To configure daylight saving time, enter the following command:

```
clock summer-time zone recurring [week weekday month hh:mm week weekday
   month hh:mm [offset]]
```

Table 6-14 describes the parameters for the **clock** command.

Table 6-14   clock *Command Parameters*

Command Parameter	Description
summer-time	Automatically switches to summer time (for display purposes only).
zone	Specifies the name of the time zone.
recurring	Indicates that summer time should start and end on the days specified by the values that follow this keyword. The summer time rule defaults to the United States rule.

Table 6-14 clock *Command Parameters (Continued)*

CommandParameter	Description
week	Specifies the week of the month. The week is 1 through 4.
week day	Sets the day of the week (Sunday, Monday).
month	Specifies the full name of the month, such as April.
hh:mm	Specifies the time in 24-hour clock format.
offset	Specifies the number of minutes to add during summer. The default is 60 minutes.

Time zones are set only for display. Setting a time zone does not change the internal Security Appliance time, which is kept according to Coordinated Universal Time (UTC). To set the time zone, use the **clock timezone** command. The syntax for the command is as follows:

```
clock timezone zone hours [minutes]
```

The following **clock summer-time** command specifies that summer time starts on the first Sunday in April at 2 A.M. and ends on the last Sunday in October at 2 A.M.:

```
pix(config)# clock summer-time PDT recurring 1 Sunday April 2:00 last Sunday
October 2:00
```

You can check your clock configuration by simply entering the **show clock** command as shown in Example 6-9.

Example 6-9 show clock *Sample Output*

```
PIXFW# show clock
10:04:06.334 PDI Thu Feb 13 2004
```

> **NOTE** In 2007, the United States will be extending Daylight Savings Time (DST) by a month. Starting in 2007, DST will start on the second Sunday in March and will end on the first Sunday in November. The following **clock** command will set the Security Appliance to the new DST setting (to be precise, summer begins on June 21, or thereabouts):
>
> ```
> pix(config)# clock summer-time PDT recurring 2 Sunday March 2:00 1 Sunday
> November 2:00
> ```

Configuring Login Banners on the Cisco Security Appliance

PIX Firewall version 6.3 introduced support for message-of-the-day (MOTD), EXEC, and login banners, similar to the feature included in Cisco IOS Software. Banner size is limited only by available system memory or Flash memory.

You can create a message as a warning for unauthorized use of the firewall. In some jurisdictions, civil and/or criminal prosecution of crackers who break into your system are made easier if you have incorporated a warning banner that informs unauthorized users that their attempts to access the system are in fact unauthorized. In other jurisdictions, you may be forbidden to monitor the activities of even unauthorized users unless you have taken steps to notify them of your intent to do so. One way of providing this notification is to put the information into a banner message configured with the Security Appliance **banner** command.

Legal notification requirements are complex and vary in each jurisdiction and situation. Even within jurisdictions, legal opinions vary, and this issue should be discussed with your own legal counsel. In cooperation with counsel, you should consider which of the following information should be put into your banner:

- A notice that the system can be logged in to or used only by specifically authorized personnel, and perhaps information about who may authorize use
- A notice that any unauthorized use of the system is unlawful and may be subject to civil and/or criminal penalties
- A notice that any use of the system may be logged or monitored without further notice and that the resulting logs may be used as evidence in court
- Specific notices required by specific local laws

From a security, rather than a legal, point of view, your login banner usually should not contain any specific information about your router, its name, its model, what software it is running, or who owns it; such information may be abused by crackers.

The banner messages can be displayed when a user enters privileged EXEC mode, upon line activation, on an incoming connection to a virtual terminal, or as a MOTD. To create a banner message, use the following command:

```
banner {exec | login | motd} text
```

Table 6-15 describes the parameters of the **banner** command.

Table 6-15 banner *Command Parameters*

Parameter	Description
exec	Configures the system to display a banner before displaying the enable prompt.
Login	Configures the system to display a banner before the password login prompt when accessing the firewall using Telnet.
motd	Configures the system to display a MOTD banner.
text	Specifies the line of message text to be displayed in the firewall command-line interface. Subsequent *text* entries are added to the end of an existing banner unless the banner is cleared first. The tokens $(domain) and $(hostname) are replaced with the host name and domain name of the firewall.

Spaces are allowed, but tabs cannot be entered using the CLI. You can dynamically add the host name or domain name of the Security Appliance by including $(hostname) and $(domain) in the string. Example 6-10 shows a sample configuration using the **banner** command.

Example 6-10 *A Sample Configuration of the **banner** Command*

```
pixfw(config)# banner login Warning Notice
This is a U.S. Government computer system, which may be accessed and used only
for authorized Government business by authorized personnel. Unauthorized access
or use of this computer system may subject violators to criminal, civil, and/or
administrative action.
All information on this computer system may be intercepted, recorded, read, copied,
and disclosed by and to authorized personnel for official purposes, including criminal
investigations. Such information includes sensitive data encrypted to comply with
confidentiality and privacy requirements. Access or use of this computer system
by any person, whether authorized or unauthorized, constitutes consent to these
terms. There is no right of privacy in this system.    ^d
```

To replace a banner, use the **no banner** command before adding the new lines. The **no banner** {**exec** | **login** | **motd**} command removes all the lines for the banner option specified. The **no banner** command removes all the lines for the banner option specified and does not selectively delete text strings. The **clear banner** command removes all the banners.

Configuring Transparent Mode

With the release of Security software version 7.0, a Security Appliance can run as a Layer 2 firewall. Standard firewalls act in a similar fashion as a router, routing packets through the firewall instead of switching them. This creates an extra hop in the IP path that a user can detect. With transparent firewall enabled, the Security Appliance will act as a Layer 2 filtering bridge, switching the packets instead of routing them, and the user will not see an additional hop within the IP path. This allows the Security Appliance to bridge packets from one interface to another, instead of routing them. These interfaces are usually on the same VLAN or IP subnet.

Because transparent firewalls perform MAC address lookup instead of routing, a Security Appliance with this feature enabled can be placed in a network without a need to reconfigure any part of the network, including NAT or IP readdressing. With the change from routing to switching, enabling transparent firewalling removes or restricts support for several Security Appliance features:

- **Interface limits**—A Security Appliance with transparent firewalls enabled can only use two interfaces. Each interface must be on a different VLAN to support transparent firewalls. This restriction is based on a single context. If multiple contexts have been enabled, each context created can use only two interfaces. These interfaces can only be used by one context and cannot be shared between multiple contexts in transparent mode.

- **NAT**—NAT does not apply when the Security Appliance is running in a Layer 2 mode. NAT would be done by a Layer 3 device in this design.

- **Dynamic routing protocols**—Because the Security Appliance is set to be a bridge, dynamic routing protocols are not needed, as they are used in an environment to assist in routing packets. Static routes can be configured for traffic that may originate from the Security Appliance.

- **IPv6**—IPv6 is not supported due to transparent mode working at Layer 2 and not Layer 3.

- **DHCP relay**—The Security Appliance cannot act as a DHCP relay, although it can act as a DHCP server.

- **Quality of service (QoS)**—Most QoS options rely on the TCP header, which is not used in transparent mode.

- **Multicast**—Multicast traffic is not supported by default in transparent mode. To pass multicast traffic through the Security Appliance in transparent mode, you must use extended access lists.

- **VPN termination for through traffic**—The Security Appliance with transparent firewalls enabled can only support site-to-site VPN tunnels for the management connections.

A Security Appliance in transparent mode can still run virtual firewalls. Each context must be configured with an IP address to use for management access. This IP address assigned to the port must be part of the connecting network, since the Security Appliance cannot route a subnet that is not directly connected. Additionally, each connecting network must reside in the same subnet to be supported in transparent mode.

> **NOTE**   A Security Appliance can be set to either transparent or router mode. If multiple contexts are enabled, all contexts must be set to the same mode.

The bridging of traffic by the Security Appliance does not work like a normal switch by default. A Security Appliance in transparent mode will only pass ARP traffic between the two interfaces until an extended access list or EtherType access list is configured. With either of these access lists configured, you can allow Layer 3 traffic to pass through the Security Appliance.

Enabling Transparent Mode

When you decide to enable transparent mode, ensure that your configuration has been backed up. When this feature is enabled, it will clear the current configuration to avoid any command conflicts that may exist with the currently deployed configuration. To enable transparent mode, use the **firewall transparent** command in the global configuration mode. If you are using multiple contexts, you must execute this command in the system configuration mode, which will affect all configured contexts. Use the **show firewall** command in privileged mode to verify that the firewall has accepted the new transparent mode, as shown in Example 6-11.

Example 6-11 *Enabling Transparent Mode Output*

```
Pix(config)# firewall transparent
Pix(config)# exit
Pix# show firewall
Firewall mode: Transparent
```

The last configuration required to enable transparent mode is to assign an IP address to an interface for management access to the Security Context:

> **ip address** *ip_address* [*netmask*]

This will allow you to manage the Security Appliance remotely. The IP address will also be used as the source address for any traffic that originates from the Security Appliance, or for syslog and Simple Network Management Protocol (SNMP) alarm messages. If you are using multiple contexts, you must assign an IP address for each context configured. To configure an IP address, use the **ip address** command in global-configuration mode. The IP address used must be in the same subnet as a network directly connected to the Security Appliance. You can display the current management-port configuration using the **show ip address** command in privileged mode, as shown in Example 6-12. Example 6-13 uses the same process but in multicontext mode.

Example 6-12 *Assigning an IP Address to Management Port in Single-Context Mode*

```
Pix(config)# ip address 10.10.10.1 255.255.255.0
Pix(config)# exit
Pix# show ip address
    Management System IP Address:
    ip address 10.10.10.1 255.255.255.0
Management Current IP Address:
    ip address 10.10.10.1 255.255.255.0
```

Example 6-13 *Assigning an IP Address to Management Ports in Multiple-Context Mode*

```
Pix/admin(config)# ip address 10.10.10.1 255.255.255.0
Pix/admin(config)# changeto context1
Pix/context1(config)# ip address 10.10.11.1 255.255.255.0
Pix/context1(config)# changeto context2
Pix/context2(config)# ip address 10.10.12.1 255.255.255.0
```

Traffic Management in Transparent Mode

Now that you have transparent mode enabled on the Security Appliance, you must allow more than just ARP traffic through the firewall. Extended access lists must be configured for each traffic type you wish to allow through the firewall. For non-IP traffic, you must configure EtherType access lists. Both types of access lists, once configured, must be assigned to one of the two interfaces, or both, to be enabled. The syntax for extended access lists is the same as those used in nontransparent mode, and detailed configuration of these access lists can be found in Chapter 7, "Configuring Access." EtherType access lists are used when non-IP traffic is required to pass through the firewall. EtherType access lists are connectionless and must be applied to both interfaces to operate correctly. To create an EtherType access list, use the **ethertype** attribute with the **access-list** command:

```
access-list id ethertype {deny | permit}{ipx | bpdu | mpls-unicast | mpls-multicast | any
| hex_number}
```

Table 6-16 describes the parameters for the **access-list ethertype** command.

Table 6-16 access-list ethertype *Command Parameters*

Parameter	Description
id	Name or number of an access list.
deny	Denies access if the conditions are matched.
permit	Permits access if the conditions are matched.
ipx	Specifies access to IPX.
npdu	Specifies access to bridge protocol data units.
mpls-unicast	Specifies access to MPLS unicast.
mpls-multicast	Specifies access to MPLS multicast.
any	Specifies access to anyone.
hex_number	A 16-bit hexadecimal number greater than or equal to 0x600 by which an EtherType can be identified.

NOTE In transparent mode, the Security Appliance relies on EtherTypes to determine traffic selection. This forces the Security Appliance to only pass Ethernet II frames, due to 802.3 frames requiring a length field instead of EtherType.

Remember that the Security Appliance defaults do not allow any non-ARP traffic through the firewall.

You can manage the ARP traffic through inspection on the Security Appliance. Inspection can help restrict malicious users from attempting ARP floods on or through the firewall or connected networks. Using the **arp-inspection** command in global-configuration mode, you can check each request to flood ARP requests through an interface for mismatched IP addresses, MAC addresses, or fake interfaces, and you can drop the request packets before they can cause problems. The full command syntax for the **arp-inspection** command is as follows:

```
arp-inspection interface_name enable [flood | no-flood]
```

Table 6-17 describes the parameters for the **arp-inspection ethertype** command.

Table 6-17   arp-inspection ethertype *Command Parameters*

Parameter	Description
interface_name	The interface on which you want ARP inspection.
enable	Enables ARP inspection.
flood	(Default) Specifies that packets not matching any element of a static ARP entry are flooded out of all interfaces except the originating interface. If a mismatch occurs between the MAC address, IP address, or interface, the Security Appliance drops the packet.
no-flood	(Optional) Specifies that packets not exactly matching a static ARP entry are dropped.

Monitoring in Transparent Mode

All traffic flows based on MAC address lookup via bridging. MAC addresses are either statically assigned by the administrator or dynamically learned through traffic over an interface. The Security Appliance lists all known MAC addresses in the MAC address table. This table is used by the Security Appliance to switch traffic that passes through it, based on any filters applied to each interface. To display the current MAC address table, you can use the **show mac-address-table** command in privileged mode, as shown in Example 6-14.

Example 6-14   show mac-address-table *Command Output*

```
pix# show mac-address-table
interface mac  address        type      Age(min)
inside   0010.7cbe.6101       static
inside   0008.e3bc.5ee0       dynamic   5
outside  0050.8DFB.19C2       dynamic   5
```

The Security Appliance will learn MAC addresses from the interface by default. This can be a dangerous setting to allow on a secured network. If a malicious user spoofed (faked) the MAC address of a network device already connected to the network, or just used a random MAC address, that user could gain access to the secured network. The Security Appliance would see the new MAC address and add it to the MAC table, giving the user access to that part of the network. You can disable the Security Appliance's ability to learn new MAC addresses using the **mac-learn** command in global-configuration mode:

```
mac-learn interface_name disable
```

This will allow only static MAC addresses into the MAC address table. If the same malicious user attempted to spoof the MAC address of an entry in the static table but on the wrong interface, or tried to use a random MAC address not in the table, the MAC address and all packets from that user would be dropped. An administrator can assign static MAC addresses through the following command:

```
mac-address-table static interface_name mac_address
```

Sample Security Appliance Configuration

Examples 6-15 and 6-16 show sample output for a Security Appliance configuration in routed and transparent mode. Included are some of the commands discussed in this chapter.

Example 6-15 *Sample PIX Configuration in Routed Mode*

```
pix# show config
: Saved
: Written by deguc at 11:29:39.859 EDT Fri Aug 8 2005
PIX Version 7.0(4)
interface Ethernet 0
 nameif outside
 security-level 0
 speed 100
 duplex full
 ip address 192.168.1.1 255.255.255.224
interface Ethernet 1
 nameif inside
 security-level 100
 speed 100
 duplex full
 interface Ethernet 2
 nameif dmz
 security-level 20
 speed 100
 duplex full
enable password GgtfiV2tiXAndr3w encrypted
passwd kP3Eex5gnkza7.lan encrypted
```

Example 6-15 *Sample PIX Configuration in Routed Mode (Continued)*

```
hostname pix
domain-name axum.com clock timezone EST -5
clock summer-time EDT recurring
class-map ips_class
    match access-list IPS
class-map inspection_default
    match default-inspection-traffic
policy-map global_policy
    class inspection_default
        inspect dns maximum length 512
        inspect ftp
        inspect h323 h225
        inspect h323 ras
        inspect netbios
        inspect sunrpc
        inspect rsh
        inspect rtsp
        inspect sip
        inspect skinny
        inspect esmtp
        inspect sqlnet
        inspect tftp
        inspect xdmcp
        inspect icmp
    class ips-class
        ips promiscuous fail-close
service-policy global_policy global
Hyphenate in command, as for "service-policy"?
access-list IPS permit ip any any
pager lines 24
no logging on
ip audit info action alarm
ip audit attack action alarm no failover

route outside 0.0.0.0 0.0.0.0 192.168.1.3 1
timeout xlate 3:00:00
timeout conn 1:00:00 half-closed 0:10:00 udp 0:02:00 rpc 0:10:00 h323 0:05:00
  sip 0:30:00 sip-media 0:02:00
timeout uauth 0:05:00 absolute
aaa-server TACACS+ protocol tacacs+
aaa-server RADIUS protocol radius
aaa-server LOCAL protocol local
http server enable
http 10.10.10.14 255.255.255.255 inside
no snmp-server location
no snmp-server contact
snmp-server community public
```

continues

Example 6-15 *Sample PIX Configuration in Routed Mode (Continued)*

```
no snmp-server enable traps
telnet 10.10.10.14  255.255.255.255 inside
telnet timeout 5
 terminal width 80
Cryptochecksum:62a73076955b1060644fdba1da64b15f
```

Example 6-16 *Sample PIX Configuration in Transparent Mode*

```
pix# show config
: Saved
: Written by deguc at 11:49:39.859 EDT Fri Aug 8 2005
PIX Version 7.0(4)
interface Ethernet 0
 nameif outside
 security-level 0
 speed 100
 duplex full
interface Ethernet 1
 nameif inside
 security-level 100
 speed 100
 duplex full
interface Ethernet 2
 speed 100
 duplex full
 shutdown
enable password GgtfiV2tiXAndr3w encrypted
passwd kP3Eex5gnkza7.lan encrypted
firewall transparent
hostname pix
domain-name axum.com clock timezone EST -5
clock summer-time EDT recurring
ip address 192.168.1.1 255.255.255.0
route outside 0.0.0.0 0.0.0.0 192.168.1.3 1
telnet 10.10.10.14  255.255.255.255 inside
arp outside 198.168.1.1 0009.7cbe.2100
arp-inspection outside enable
access-list ACLIN permit icmp 192.168.1.0 255.255.255.0 192.168.1.0 255.255.255.0
access-list ETHER ethertype permit ipx
access-group ETHER in interface inside
access-group ETHER in interface outside
access-group ACLIN in interface inside
access-group ACLIN in interface outside
pager lines 24
no logging on
timeout xlate 3:00:00
         timeout conn 1:00:00 half-closed 0:10:00 udp 0:02:00 rpc 0:10:00 h323 0:05:00
```

Example 6-16 *Sample PIX Configuration in Transparent Mode (Continued)*

```
        sip 0:30:00 sip-media 0:02:00
        timeout uauth 0:05:00 absolute
        aaa-server TACACS+ protocol tacacs+
        aaa-server RADIUS protocol radius
        aaa-server LOCAL protocol local
        no snmp-server location
        no snmp-server contact
        snmp-server community public
        no snmp-server enable traps
        telnet timeout 5
        terminal width 80
Cryptochecksum:62a73076955b1060644fdba1da64b15f
```

Foundation Summary

The "Foundation Summary" provides a convenient review of many key concepts in this chapter. If you are already comfortable with the topics in this chapter, this summary can help you recall a few details. If you just read this chapter, this review should help solidify some key facts. If you are doing your final preparation before the exam, this summary provides a convenient way to review the day before the exam.

Table 6-18 provides a quick reference to the commands needed to configure the Cisco Security Appliance, time server support, and the DHCP server.

Table 6-18 *Command Reference*

Command	Description
enable	Specifies to activate a process, mode, or privilege level.
interface	Identifies the speed and duplex settings of the network interface boards.
security-level	Assigns a security level to an interface.
nameif	Enables you to name interfaces.
ip address	Identifies addresses for network interfaces and enables you to set how many times the PIX Firewall polls for DHCP information.
nat	Enables you to associate a network with a pool of global IP addresses.
global	Defines a pool of global addresses. The global addresses in the pool provide an IP address for each outbound connection and for inbound connections resulting from outbound connections. Ensure that associated **nat** and **global** command statements have the same *nat-id*.
route	Specifies a default or static route for an interface.
write terminal	Displays the current configuration on the terminal.
rip	Enables IP routing table updates from received RIP broadcasts.
dhcpd	Controls the DHCP server feature.
ntp server	Synchronizes the Security Appliance with the network time server that is specified and authenticates according to the authentication options that are set.
clock	Lets you specify the time, month, day, and year for use with time-stamped syslog messages.

With software version 7.0, Cisco Security Appliances can now support transparent firewalls. You can configure the Security Appliance to bridge traffic at Layer 2 instead of route traffic to allow for seamless integration into an existing network. Layer 3 traffic can pass through a transparent firewall through access lists and connection tables, the same as in routed mode.

Q&A

As mentioned in the Introduction, the questions in this book are more difficult than what you should experience on the exam. The questions are designed to ensure your understanding of the concepts discussed in this chapter and adequately prepare you to complete the exam. You should use the simulated exams on the CD to practice for the exam.

The answers to these questions can be found in Appendix A:

1. How do you access privileged mode?

2. What is the function of the **nameif** command?

3. Which seven commands produce a basic working configuration for a Cisco Security Appliance?

4. Why is the **route** command important?

5. What is the command to flush out the ARP cache on a Cisco PIX Firewall?

6. What is the syntax to configure a MOTD banner that says, "System shall not be available on 18:00 Monday January 19th for 2 hours due to system maintenance?"

7. What is the command used to configure PAT on a Cisco Security Appliance?

8. Which command releases and renews an IP address on the PIX?

9. Give at least one reason why it is beneficial to use NTP on the Cisco PIX Firewall.

10. Why would you want to secure the NTP messages between the Cisco PIX Firewall and the NTP server?

11. What is the difference between a Security Appliance in transparent mode and a Security Appliance in routed mode?

This chapter covers the following subjects:

- ACLs

- Using ACLs

- Overview of Object Grouping

- Getting Started with Group Objects

- Configuring Group Objects

- Nested Object Groups

- Advanced Protocols

- Multimedia Support

CHAPTER 7

Configuring Access

Managing controlled access to network resources from an untrusted (Internet) network is a very important function of the Cisco Security Appliance. Access lists, network address translations, authentication, and authorization are ways to provide access through a Security Appliance in a controlled fashion. In addition, PIX software version 6.2 and later, as well as ASA software version 7.0, have new features such as object grouping and TurboACL, which make managing and implementing a complex security policy much easier and more scalable.

How Best to Use This Chapter

Limiting access to systems and services on your network is one of the primary responsibilities of the Cisco Security Appliance that you deploy on a network. This chapter provides the information on how to restrict network traffic using access lists, hide internal addresses using Network Address Translation (NAT) (both static and dynamic), as well as configuring fixup protocols that monitor common protocols to dynamically open up access through the Security Appliance. Understanding these concepts is vital to successfully securing your network using a Security Appliance such as a PIX Firewall. Test yourself with the "Do I Know This Already?" quiz and see how familiar you are configuring access restrictions on Cisco Security Appliances.

"Do I Know This Already?" Quiz

The purpose of the "Do I Know This Already?" quiz is to help you decide if you really need to read the entire chapter. If you already intend to read the entire chapter, you do not necessarily need to answer these questions now.

The seven-question quiz, derived from the major sections in the "Foundation Topics" portion of the chapter, helps you determine how to spend your limited study time.

Table 7-1 outlines the major topics discussed in this chapter and the "Do I Know This Already?" quiz questions that correspond to those topics.

Table 7-1 *"Do I Know This Already?" Foundation Topics Section-to-Question Mapping*

Foundation Topics Section	Questions Covered in This Section	Score
ACLs	1, 5, 6	
Using ACLs	4, 8	
Getting Started With Object Groups	2	
Configuring Object Groups	3	
Advanced Protocols	6, 7	

CAUTION   The goal of self assessment is to gauge your mastery of the topics in this chapter. If you do not know the answer to a question or are only partially sure of the answer, you should mark this question wrong for purposes of the self assessment. Giving yourself credit for an answer you correctly guess skews your self-assessment results and might provide you with a false sense of security.

1. Which of the following are constraints when configuring policy NAT?

   a. A global address *can* be used concurrently for NAT and PAT.

   b. An access list must be used *only twice* with the **nat** command.

   c. Access lists for policy NAT *cannot* contain deny statements.

   d. An access list must be used only once with the **nat** command.

2. Which of the following is *not* one of four options for object types when you create an object group?

   a. Network

   b. Protocol

   c. Application

   d. Services

3. Which command lets you create a network object group?

   a. **object-group network** *group-id*

   b. **enable object-group network** *group-id*

   c. **create network object-group**

   d. **network object-group enable**

4. What command can you configure the Security Appliance to allow access to higher-security subnets?

   a. nat (outside) 0

   b. nat (inside) 0

   c. global

   d. static

   e. None of these answers are correct.

5. How many SMTP commands are made by the ASA application inspection function?

   a. 3

   b. 2

   c. 7

   d. 5

6. How do you change the port of an FTP inspection?

   a. Using a class-map to create a traffic class

   b. fixup protocol ftp port

   c. inspect ftp port

   d. redirect ftp port

7. Which of the following is the correct syntax for mapping an internal web server with an IP address of 10.10.10.15 to an outside IP address of 192.168.100.15 for HTTP traffic?

   a. static (inside, outside) 192.168.100.15 80 10.10.10.15 netmask 255.255.255.255 eq www

   b. static (inside, outside) 192.168.100.15 80 10.10.10.15 netmask 255.255.255.255

   c. static (inside, outside) tcp 192.168.100.15 80 10.10.10.15 www netmask 255.255.255.255

   d. static (inside, outside) 192.168.100.15 80 10.10.10.15 netmask 255.255.255.255

The answers to the "Do I Know This Already?" quiz are found in Appendix A, "Answers to the 'Do I Know This Already?' Quizzes and Q&A Sections." The suggested choices for your next step are as follows:

■ 5 or less overall score—Read the entire chapter. This includes the "Foundation Topics," "Foundation Summary," and "Q&A" sections.

■ 6 or 7 overall score—If you want more review on these topics, skip to the "Foundation Summary" section and then go to the "Q&A" section. Otherwise, move to the next chapter.

Foundation Topics

Configuring Inbound Access Through a Cisco Security Appliance

A two-step approach lets connections initiated from lower-security interfaces access higher-security interfaces:

Step 1 Network Address Translation

Step 2 Access lists

Static NAT

Static NAT creates a permanent, one-to-one mapping between an address on an internal network (a higher-security-level interface) and an external network (a lower-security-level interface) in all Security Appliance versions. For an external host to initiate traffic to an inside host, a static translation rule needs to exist for the inside host. Without the persistent translation rule, the translation cannot occur.

> **NOTE** Access from a lower-security level to a higher-security level can also be configured using a **nat 0 access-list** address rule.

> **NOTE** Unlike NAT and Port Address Translation (PAT), static NAT requires a dedicated address on the outside network for each host, so it does not save registered Internet Protocol (IP) addresses.

The syntax for the **static** command is as follows:

```
static [(prenat-interface, postnat-interface)] {mapped-address | interface}
    real-address [dns] [netmask mask] [max-conns [emb-limit]] [norandomseq]
```

Table 7-2 describes the **static** command parameters.

Table 7-2   static *Command Parameters*

Command Parameter	Description
prenat-interface	Usually the inside interface, in which case the translation is applied to the inside address.
postnat-interface	The outside interface when *prenat-interface* is the inside interface. However, if the outside interface is used for *prenat-interface,* the translation is applied to the outside address, and the *postnat-interface* is the inside interface.
mapped-address	The address into which *real-address* is translated.
interface	Specifies to overload the global address from **interface**.
real-address	The address to be mapped.
dns	Specifies that DNS replies that match the xlate are translated.
netmask	A reserved word that is required before you specify the network mask.
mask or *network-mask*	Pertains to both *global-ip* and *local-ip*. For host addresses, always use 255.255.255.255. For network addresses, use the appropriate class mask or subnet mask. For example, for Class A networks, use 255.0.0.0. A sample subnet mask is 255.255.255.224.
norandomseq	Does not randomize the TCP/IP packet's sequence number. Use this option only if another inline firewall is also randomizing sequence numbers and the result is scrambling the data. Using this option opens a security hole in the PIX Firewall.
max-conns	The maximum number of connections permitted through the static IP address at the same time.
emb-limit	The embryonic connection limit. An embryonic connection is one that has started but has not yet completed. Set this limit to prevent an attack by a flood of embryonic connections. The default is 0, which means unlimited connections.

The following example maps a server with an internal IP address of 10.1.100.10 to the IP address 192.168.100.10:

```
PIXFIREWALL(conf)#static (inside, outside) 192.168.100.10 10.1.100.10 netmask
  255.255.255.255
```

The static command can also be used to translate an IP subnet:

```
PIXFIREWALL(conf)#static (inside, outside) 192.168.100.0 10.1.100.0 netmask
  255.255.255.0
```

The following syntax shows a server with an internal IP address of 10.1.100.10 translated to IP address 192.168.100.10:

```
PIXFIREWALL(conf)#static (inside, outside) 192.168.100.10 10.1.100.10 255.255.255.255
```

Static PAT

The port redirection feature allows outside users the ability to connect to a particular IP address/port and have the Security Appliance redirect the traffic to the appropriate inside server. The shared address can be a unique address or a shared outbound PAT address, or it can be shared with the external interface. For example, static PAT lets you redirect inbound Transmission Control Protocol (TCP) and User Datagram Protocol (UDP) services. Using the **interface** option of the **static** command, you can use static PAT to permit external hosts to access TCP or UDP services residing on an internal host. (As always, though, an access list should also be in place to control access to the internal host.) The command to configure static PAT is as follows:

```
static [(internal-if-name, external-if-name)] {tcp | udp}{global-ip | interface}
   global-port local-ip local-port [netmask mask][max-conns [emb-limit
   [norandomseq]]]
```

Static PAT supports all applications that are supported by (regular) PAT, including the same application constraints. Like PAT, static PAT does not support H.323 or multimedia application traffic. The following example enables static PAT for File Transfer Protocol (FTP) traffic:

```
static (inside, outside) tcp 192.168.1.14 ftp 10.1.2.8 ftp
```

The next example shows the following:

- The Security Appliance redirects external users' Telnet requests to 192.168.1.24 to IP address 10.1.2.19.

- The Security Appliance redirects external users' Hypertext Transfer Protocol (HTTP) port 8080 requests to 192.168.1.24 to PAT address 10.1.2.20 port 80:

```
static (inside,outside) tcp 192.168.1.24 telnet 10.1.2.19 telnet netmask
   255.255.255.255
static (inside,outside) tcp 192.168.1.24 8080 10.1.2.20 www netmask
   255.255.255.255
access-list 101 permit tcp any host 192.168.1.24 eq 8080
access-list 101 permit tcp any host 192.168.1.24 eq telnet
```

Notice that the outside IP address 192.168.1.24 is the same for both mappings, but the internal IP address is different. Also notice that external users directed to 192.168.1.24:8080 are sent as HTTP requests to 10.1.2.20, which is listening on port 80.

TCP Intercept Feature

Before version 5.2, the Cisco PIX Firewall Security Appliance offered no mechanism to protect systems that could be reached using a static and TCP conduit from TCP SYN attacks. When the embryonic connection limit was configured in a **static** command statement, the earlier PIX versions simply dropped new connection attempts as soon as the embryonic threshold was reached. A mild TCP SYN attack could potentially create service disruption to the server in question. For **static** command statements without an embryonic connection limit, PIX Firewall passes all traffic. If the affected system does not have TCP SYN attack protection (most operating systems do not offer sufficient protection), the affected system's embryonic connection table overloads, and all traffic stops.

With the TCP intercept feature, as soon as the optional embryonic connection limit is reached, and until the embryonic connection count falls below this threshold, every SYN bound for the affected server is intercepted. For each SYN, a Security Appliance, such as the PIX Firewall, responds on behalf of the server with an empty SYN/ACK segment. The Security Appliance retains pertinent state information, drops the packet, and waits for the client's acknowledgment. If the ACK is received, a copy of the client's SYN segment is sent to the server, and a TCP three-way handshake is performed between the Security Appliance and the server. If this three-way handshake completes, the connection resumes as normal. If the client does not respond during any part of the connection phase, Security Appliance retransmits the necessary segment.

In addition to the TCP intercept feature, software version 6.3 and later introduced SYN cookies as a means to stop a SYN flood from filling the SYN queue and causing dropped connections. SYN cookies use a cryptographic method to create the initial TCP sequence numbers for a TCP flow. This new method helps the Security Appliance manage the TCP queue by responding to TCP connections with a SYN+ACK when the SYN queue fills up. The Security Appliance will wait for an ACK from the remote device, and verifies the ACK with the assigned 24-bit secret. The Security Appliance will then rebuild the SYN queue based on this information. This allows the SYN queue to become larger, but never to a size that will cause dropped backs, and removes the biggest effect of a SYN flood attack, which is to disable large windows.

nat 0 Command

As mentioned earlier in the text, one can configure access to higher-security subnets by using the **nat 0** command. For instance, if you have a host with a public address on the inside network and the outside network needs access to this host, you can use **nat 0**, which disables address translation so that inside IP addresses are visible to the outside. The following short example demonstrates the use of the **nat 0** command:

```
nat (inside) 0 192.168.1.10 255.255.255.255
```

This can also be configured as follows:

```
access-list 121 permit 192.168.1.10 255.255.255.255 any
nat (inside) 0 access-list 121
```

Policy NAT

Policy NAT provides additional capabilities in configuring address translation. The Policy NAT feature lets you identify local traffic for address translation by specifying the source and destination addresses (or ports), whereas regular NAT uses only ports/source addresses. In other words, the same local traffic for address translation can have multiple "global" translations depending on the destination IP address or port. This is aptly demonstrated in Figure 7-1.

Figure 7-1 *Identifying Multiple External Addresses Using Policy NAT*

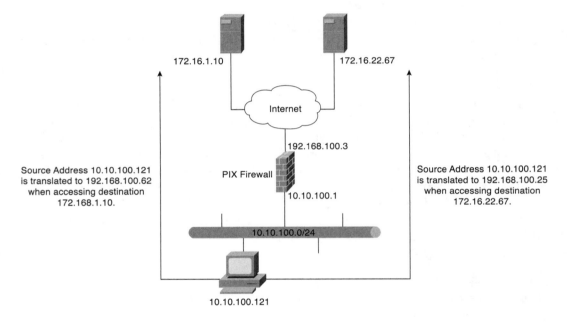

The translation configuration for Figure 7-1 is as follows:

```
pixfw(config)#access-list 120 permit ip 10.10.100.0
  255.255.255.0 172.16.1.10 255.255.255.255
pixfw(config)#access-list 130 permit ip 10.10.100.0
  255.255.255.0 172.16.22.67 255.255.255.255
pixfw(config)#nat (inside) 1 access-list 120
pixfw(config)#global (outside) 1 192.168.100.62 255.255.255.255
pixfw(config)#nat (inside) 2 access-list 130
pixfw(config)#global (outside) 2 192.168.100.25 255.255.255.255
```

There are constraints of which you have to be aware when configuring Policy NAT:

■ A global address cannot be used concurrently for NAT and PAT.

■ Access lists for Policy NAT cannot contain deny statements. Access lists must contain only permit statements.

- Use an access list between the **nat** and **static** commands.

- **static** commands are matched and executed before **nat** commands.

NOTE   Policy NAT does not support SQL*Net, which is supported by regular NAT.

Access Lists

An access list typically consists of multiple access control entries (ACE) organized internally by Security Appliance as a linked list. When a packet is subjected to access list control, the Cisco Security Appliance searches this linked list linearly to find a matching element. The matching element is then examined to determine if the packet is to be transmitted or dropped. By default, all **access-list** commands have an implicit deny unless you explicitly specify permit. In other words, by default, all access in an access list is denied unless you explicitly grant access using a permit statement.

The general syntax of the **access-list** command is as follows:

```
access-list id [line line-num] deny¦permit {protocol |
object-group prot-obj-grp-id} {source-addr source-mask} |
object-group netw-grp-grp-id [operator port [port] | interface if-name
| object-group service-obj-grp-id ]
{destination-addr destination-mask} | object-group new-obj-grp-id |
[operator port [port] | object-group service-obj-grp-id]}
[log [disable ¦default] | [level]]
```

Table 7-3 describes the parameters for the **access-list** command.

Table 7-3   **access-list** *Command Parameters*

Parameter	Description
id	Name of an access list. You can use either a name or number.
line-num	The line number at which to insert a remark or an ACE.
deny	The **deny** option does not allow a packet to traverse the PIX Firewall.
permit	The **permit** option selects a packet to traverse the PIX Firewall.
protocol	Name or number of an IP protocol. It can be one of the keywords **icmp, ip, tcp,** or **udp,** or an integer in the range of 1 to 254 representing an IP protocol number. To match any Internet protocol, including ICMP, TCP, and UDP, use the keyword **ip.**
object-group	Specifies an object group.
source-addr	Address of the network or host from which the packet is being sent.
source-mask	Netmask bits (mask) to be applied to *source-addr*, if the source address is for a network mask.

continues

Table 7-3 access-list *Command Parameters (Continued)*

Parameter	Description
port	Specifies services to which you permit or deny access. Specify services by the port that handles it, such as **smtp** for port 25, **www** for port 80, and so on. You can specify ports by either a literal name or a number in the range of 0 to 65,535.
interface *if-name*	The name of the firewall interface.
obj-grp-id	An existing object group.
destination-addr	IP address of the network or host to which the packet is being sent.
destination-mask	Netmask bits (mask) to be applied to *destination-addr*, if the destination address is a network mask.
log disable | default | *level*	When the **log** option is specified, it generates syslog message 106100 for the ACE to which it is applied. An optional syslog *level* (0–7) may be specified for the generated syslog messages (106100). If no *level* is specified, the default level is 6 (informational) for a new ACE. If the **log disable** option is specified, access list logging is completely disabled. No syslog message, including message 106023, will be generated.
interval *secs*	The time interval in seconds, from 1 to 600, at which to generate an 106100 syslog message. The default interval is 300 seconds for a new ACE.

The **access-list** command creates the rule you want. The created rule is applied by using the **access-group** command to the desired Security Appliance interface. It is also important to note that unlike Cisco IOS software access lists, which use wildcards (that is, 0.0.0.255 for a Class C address) to identify their network masks, PIX software uses a regular subnet mask (that is, 255.255.255.0 for a Class C address) when defining the network mask.

NOTE Specify only one **access-group** command for each interface. Security Appliance allows you to configure only one access group per interface.

The syntax for the **access-group** command is as follows:

```
access-group id in interface interface-name
```

The *id* is the same identifier that was specified in the **access-list** command. The *interface-name* parameter is the name of the interface.

Example 7-1 illustrates the use of the **static** and **access-list** commands to permit connections from lower-security interfaces to higher-security interfaces on the Security Appliance.

Example 7-1 *Permitting Connections from Lower-Security Interfaces to Higher-Security Interfaces on the Security Appliance*

```
asafirewall(config)# static (inside, outside) 192.168.1.10 10.1.100.10
netmask 255.255.255.255
asafirewall(config)# access-list acl-out permit tcp any host 192.168.1.10 eq www
asafirewall(config)# access-group acl-out in interface outside
```

The **static** command statically translates 10.1.100.10 to 192.168.1.10. The **access-list** command permits HTTP access only to host 10.1.100.10 (translated into 192.168.1.10). The **access-group** command applies the access list acl-out to the outside interface.

To view the created access list, use the **show access-list** *id* command, where *id* is the access list name or number.

Access lists also can be used to control outbound access on the PIX Firewall. An outbound access list restricts users from starting connections from a trusted network to a less trusted network; for example, users from an inside interface accessing hosts or networks on the outside interface. By default, outbound access is permitted, so you use the **deny** action to restrict access when using an outbound access list.

For example, if you want to restrict users on the inside interface from accessing a website at address 172.16.68.20 on the outside interface, you would use the commands shown in Example 7-2.

Example 7-2 *Restricting Inside Users' Access to an External Web Server on Port 80*

```
pixfirewall(config)# access-list acl-in deny tcp any host 172.16.68.20 eq www
pixfirewall(config)# access-list acl-in permit ip any any
pixfirewall(config)# access-group acl-in in interface inside
```

This access list configuration lets any user start World Wide Web (WWW) connections to any destination, with the exception of 172.16.68.20.

> **NOTE** Access lists are implemented by using the **access-list** and **access-group** commands. These commands are used instead of the **conduit** and **outbound** commands, which were used in earlier versions of PIX Firewall software. Pix Firewall software version 6.3 does support the **conduit** and **outbound** commands. To convert PIX the configuration file that contains **conduit** and **outbound** commands to a supported configuration file that contains the equivalent **access-list** commands, Cisco Systems has created a tool. This tool can be found at http://www.cisco.com/cgi-bin/tablebuild.pl/pix (the link requires a Cisco.com account).

Organizing and Managing ACE

It is quite common to have several access lists with several access-list elements in them on a Cisco Security Appliance. To deal with this sometimes becomes arduous, especially in the following situations:

■ When attempting to identify the reason for each ACE in the access list because no descriptions or comments are included for software releases earlier than version 6.3

■ When removing a single ACE from an access list at the command line on software earlier than version 6.3, which becomes a several-step process

Configuring a remark or comment allows you and other administrators to understand and identify access-list entries. Cisco Security Appliances lets you include comments about entries in any access control list (ACL). A remark can be up to 100 characters and can precede or follow an **access-list** command. The following is the syntax for configuring an access-list remark:

```
access-list acl-id remark text
```

The ACL remark can be placed before or after an **access-list** command statement, but it should be placed in a consistent position so that it is clear which remark describes which **access-list** command. For example, it would be confusing to have some remarks before the associated **access-list** commands and some remarks after the associated **access-list** commands. Example 7-3 shows a sample configuration on how to create comments for ACEs.

Example 7-3 *Configuring Comments for ACEs*

```
Pixfw(config)#access-list 115 remark Allow network engineering group to telnet
PixfW(config)#access-list 115 permit tcp 192.168.1.0 255.255.255.224 host
   10.10.100.20 telnet
PixfW(config)#access-list 115 remark Allowsales group to login
PixfW(config)#access-list 115 permit tcp 192.168.3.0 255.255.255.224 host
   10.10.100.12
```

In addition to adding remarks to access lists, version 6.3 and later add numbering to access-list elements. Each ACE and remark has an associated line number. Line numbers can then be used to insert or delete elements at any position in an access list. These numbers are maintained internally in increasing order starting from 1. The line numbers are always maintained in increasing order, with an individual line number for each ACE.

> **NOTE**   All ACEs resulting from a single object group **access-list** command statement have a single line number. Consequently, you cannot insert an ACE in the middle of object-group ACEs.

The **show access-list** command displays the line numbers. The line numbers, however, are not shown in the configuration. Example 7-4 shows a sample output from a **show access-list** command.

Example 7-4   *Sample Output from the* **show access-list** *Command*

```
pixfw(config)#show access-list 115
access-list 115 ; 4 elements
access-list 115 line 1 remark-Allow network engineering group
    to telnet (hitcnt=0)
access-list 115 line 2 permit tcp 192.168.1.0 255.255.255.224 host 10.10.100.20
    telnet (hitcnt=0)
access-list 115 line 3 remark-Allow sales group to login (hitcnt=0)
access-list 115 line 4 permit tcp 192.168.3.0 255.255.255.224 host
    10.10.100.12 (hitcnt=0)
```

To remove remarks from an access list, simply use the following command:

> **no access-list** *id* **line** *line-num* **remark** *text*

or

> **no access-list** *id* **line** *line-num*

Both remove the remark at the specified line number.

Object Grouping

Object grouping allows you to group objects such as hosts (servers and clients), services, and networks and apply security policies and rules to the group. Object grouping lets you apply access rules to logical groups of objects. When you apply an access list to an object group, the command affects all objects defined in the group. Object grouping provides a way to reduce the number of access rules required to describe complex security policies. This in turn reduces the time spent configuring and troubleshooting access rules in large or complex networks.

The syntax for creating object groups is as follows:

> [no] **object-group** *object-type grp-id*

Use the first parameter, *object-type,* to identify the type of object group you want to configure. There are four options:

- **network**
- **protocol**
- **service**
- **icmp-type**

Replace *grp-id* with a descriptive name for the group.

network Object Type

The **network** object type is used to group hosts and subnets. Server and client hosts can be grouped by functions. For example, mail servers, web servers, or a group of client hosts that have special privileges on the network can be grouped accordingly.

Example 7-5 shows a web servers object group.

Example 7-5 *Configuring an Object Group*

```
pixfirewall(config)#object-group  network  web-servers
pixfirewall(config-network)#description  Public  web  servers
pixfirewall(config-network)#network-object  host  192.168.1.12
pixfirewall(config-network)#network-object  host  192.168.1.14
pixfirewall(config-network)#  exit
pixfirewall(config)#access-list  102  permit  tcp  any  object-group  web-servers  eq  www
pixfirewall(config)#access-group  102  in  interface  outside
```

Notice that when you enter the **object-group** command, the system enters the appropriate subcommand mode for the type of object you are configuring. In this case, you see the config-network subcommand prompt. The **network-object host** subcommand adds the host to the network object group. The description is optional, but it is helpful to include it.

NOTE It is also possible to use a name instead of an IP address when defining the network host. For example:

```
pixfw(config)#  object-group  network  mis-ftp-servers
pixfw(config-network)#network-object  host  10.10.100.154
pixfw(config-network)#network-object  host  10.10.100.155
pixfw(config-network)#network-object  host  10.10.100.156
pixfw(config-network)#exit
```

To display the configured object group, use the **show object-group** command, as shown in Example 7-6.

Example 7-6 *Displaying Configured Object Groups*

```
pix(config)# show object-group
object-group network web-servers
  description: Public web servers
  network-object host 192.168.1.12
  network-object host 192.168.1.14
```

protocol Object Type

The **protocol** object type identifies a group of IP protocols using keywords such as **icmp, tcp, udp,** or an integer in the range of 1 to 254 representing an IP protocol number. The syntax for the command is **object-group protocol** *grp-id*. To add a single protocol to the current protocol object group, use the **protocol-object** *protocol* command. Example 7-7 shows how to use object-group protocol subcommand mode to create a new protocol object group.

Example 7-7 *Creating a New Protocol Object Group*

```
pixfw(config)#object-group  protocol  grp-citrix
pixfw(config-protocol)#protocol-object  tcp
pixfw(config-protocol)#protocol-object  1494
pixfw(config-protocol)#exit
```

service Object Type

The **service** object type identifies port numbers that can be grouped. This is particularly useful when you are managing an application. The syntax for **service** *object-type* is

[no] object-group *service obj-grp-id* tcp | udp | tcp-udp

As soon as you are in the **service** subcommand, the command **port-object eq** *service* adds a single TCP or UDP port number to the service object group. The **port-object range** *begin-service end-service* command adds a range of TCP or UDP port numbers to the service object group. Example 7-8 shows how to use object-group service subcommand mode to create a new port (service) object group.

Example 7-8 *Creating a New Port (Service) Object Group*

```
pixfw(config)#object-group  service  mis-service  tcp
pixfw(config-service)#port-object  eq  ftp
pixfw(config-service)#port-object  range  5200  6000
pixfw(config-service)#exit
```

icmp-type Object Type

Internet Control Message Protocol (ICMP) object groups can be created to group certain types of ICMP messages. For example, ICMP messages of ECHO-REQUEST, ECHO-REPLY, and DESTINATION-UNREACHABLE with numerical type values of 8, 0, and 3, respectively, can be grouped as shown in Example 7-9.

Example 7-9 *Grouping ICMP Messages*

```
pix(config)#  object-group  icmp-type  icmp-test
pix(config-icmp-type)#  icmp-object  0
pix(config-icmp-type)#  icmp-object  3
pix(config-icmp-type)#  icmp-object  8
```

Nesting Object Groups

You can add an object group within an object group. The **object-group** command allows logical grouping of the same type of objects and construction of hierarchical object groups for structured configuration. To nest an object group within another object group, use the **group-object** command. Example 7-10 illustrates the use of nested object groups.

Example 7-10 *Configuring Nested Object Groups*

```
pixfirewall(config)#  object-group  network  web-servers
pixfirewall(config-network)#  description  web  servers
pixfirewall(config-network)#  network-object  host  192.168.1.12
pixfirewall(config-network)#  network-object  host  192.168.1.14
pixfirewall(config-network)#  exit
pixfirewall(config)#  object-group  network  Public-servers
pixfirewall(config-network)#  description  Public  servers
pixfirewall(config-network)#  network-object  host  192.168.1.18
pixfirewall(config-network)#  group-object  web-servers
pixfirewall(config-network)#  exit
```

ACL Logging

The ACL logging feature lets you log the number of permits or denies of a flow during a specific period of time. A flow is defined by protocol, source IP address, source port, destination IP address, and destination port. When a flow is permitted or denied, the system checks to see if the flow already exists in the system. If not, an initial syslog message with a hit count of 1 for the flow is generated. The flow entry is then created and the hit count for the flow is incremented every time the flow is permitted or denied. The command syntax to enable logging of the number of permits or denies of a flow by an ACL entry is as follows:

> **access-list** *acl-id* [**log** [*level*] [**interval** *seconds*] | [**disable**|**default**]]

For an existing flow, a syslog message is generated at the end of each configurable interval to report the nonzero hit count for the flow in the current interval. After the syslog message is generated, the hit count for the flow is reset to 0 for the next interval. If there is no hit recorded during the interval, the flow is deleted and no syslog message is generated. Large numbers of flows may concurrently exist at any point in time. To prevent unlimited consumption of memory and central processing unit (CPU) resources, a limit is placed on the number of concurrent deny flows. When the limit is reached, no new deny flow will be created until the existing deny flows expire. To specify the maximum number of concurrent deny flows that can be created, enter the following command:

> **access-list deny-flow-max** *num-of-flows*

The **deny-flow-max** keyword specifies the maximum number of concurrent deny flows that can be created. New values for this option go into effect immediately. The default is set for 4096 flows allowed.

When the maximum number of flows has been reached, a syslog message (106101) is generated. By default, this message is repeated once every 300 seconds.

The syslog message generated for the ACL entry has the following format:

```
106101: access-list <acl-id> <grant> <prot> <intf/src-ip(src-port)> ->
        <intf/dst-ip(dest-port)> hit-cnt <nnn> (first hit|n-second interval)
```

Table 7-4 *syslog Format Description*

Field	Description
<grant>	Displays whether the flow is permitted or denied.
<prot>	Displays the protocol type: tcp, udp, icmp, or an IP protocol number.
<intf>	Displays the interface name (as configured by the **nameif** command) for the source or destination of the logged flow. This can include logical (virtual LAN) interfaces.
<src-ip>	Displays the source IP address of the logged flow.
<dst-ip>	Displays the destination IP address of the logged flow.
<src-port>	Displays the source port of the logged flow (TCP or UDP). For ICMP, this field is 0.
<dst-port>	Displays the destination port of the logged flow (TCP or UDP). For ICMP, this field is icmp-type.
<nnn>	Displays the number of times this flow was permitted or denied by the ACL entry in the configured time interval. The value is 1 when the first syslog message is generated for the flow.
first hit	Displays the first message generated for this flow.
n-second interval	Displays the interval over which the hit count is accumulated.

Advanced Protocol Handling

Some applications require special handling by the Cisco Security Appliance application inspection function. These types of applications typically embed IP addressing information in the user data packet or open secondary channels on dynamically assigned ports. The application inspection function works with NAT to help identify the location of embedded addressing information.

In addition to identifying embedded addressing information, the application inspection function monitors sessions to determine the port numbers for secondary channels. Many protocols open secondary TCP or UDP ports to improve performance. The initial session on a well-known port is used to negotiate dynamically assigned port numbers. The application inspection function monitors these sessions, identifies the dynamic port assignments, and permits data exchange on these ports for the duration of the specific session. Multimedia applications and FTP applications exhibit this kind of behavior.

FTP

The FTP application inspection inspects FTP sessions and performs four tasks:

- Prepares a dynamic secondary data connection
- Tracks the **ftp** command-response sequence
- Generates an audit trail
- Translates the embedded IP address using NAT

FTP application inspection prepares secondary channels for FTP data transfer. The channels are allocated in response to a file upload, a file download, or a directory listing event, and they must be prenegotiated. The port is negotiated through the PORT or PASV (227) commands.

You can use the **inspect ftp** command in a policy map to inspect the default port assignment for FTP. The command syntax is as follows:

```
I [no] inspect ftp [strict]
```

The **strict** option prevents web browsers from sending embedded commands in FTP requests. Each **ftp** command must be acknowledged before a new command is allowed. Connections sending embedded commands are dropped. The **strict** option lets only the server generate the PASV reply command (227) and lets only the client generate the PORT command. The PASV reply and PORT commands are checked to ensure that they do not appear in an error string.

If you disable FTP fixups with the **no inspect ftp** command, inbound FTP is disabled. If you have FTP servers using ports other than port 20 and 21, you need to use the **class-map** command to identify these other traffic flows with their different FTP port numbers.

DNS

DNS uses a UDP connection. This makes DNS queries subject to generic UDP handling based on activity timeouts. DNS, therefore, requires application inspection. As soon as the first response is received for a DNS query, the UDP connection is terminated. This is known as DNS guard and is discussed further in Chapter 19, "IPS and Advanced Protocol Handling." The DNS inspection task includes the following:

- Compares the ID of the DNS reply to the ID of the DNS query.
- Translates the DNS A record.
- Confirms the length of the DNS packet is less than the maximum length specified by the user. Otherwise, the packet is dropped.

Simple Mail Transfer Protocol

Simple Mail Transfer Protocol (SMTP) packets are closely monitored. An SMTP server responds to client requests with numeric reply codes and optional human-readable strings. SMTP application inspection controls and restricts the commands that the user can use as well as the messages that the server returns. SMTP inspection performs these primary tasks:

- Monitors the SMTP command-response sequence.

- Permits only 7 of the 14 SMTP commands (HELO, MAIL, RCPT, DATA, RSET, NOOP, and QUIT).

- With ESMTP inspection, an additional eight commands are supported (AUTH, DATA, EHLO, ETRN, SAML, SEND, SOML, and VRFY).

- Generates an audit trail. Audit record 108002 is generated when an invalid character embedded in the mail address is replaced.

Foundation Summary

The "Foundation Summary" provides a convenient review of many key concepts in this chapter. If you are already comfortable with the topics in this chapter, this summary can help you recall a few details. If you just read this chapter, this review should help solidify some key facts. If you are doing your final preparation before the exam, this summary provides a convenient way to review the day before the exam.

Rules or translations have to be put in place to allow data traffic to and from hosts in a network. Rules are usually made up of a static **nat** command and access list. The static **nat** command identifies the subnet or host to which connections will be permitted to go. Access lists are then configured to identify and permit the type of traffic to the subnet or host identified by the **static** command.

The object grouping feature enables you to group objects such as hosts (servers and clients), services, and networks and apply security policies and rules to the group. The four types of object groups are these:

- network
- protocol
- service
- icmp-type

The Cisco Security Appliance supports several popular multimedia applications. Its application inspection function dynamically opens and closes UDP ports for secure multimedia connections. Popular multimedia applications such as RealPlayer and Microsoft NetMeeting are supported by Cisco Security Appliance.

Q&A

As mentioned in the Introduction, the questions in this book are more difficult than what you should experience on the exam. The questions are designed to ensure your understanding of the concepts discussed in this chapter and adequately prepare you to complete the exam. You should use the simulated exams on the CD to practice for the exam.

The answers to these questions can be found in Appendix A:

1. What do static NAT settings do?

2. What is the difference between regular NAT and policy-based network translation?

3. True or false: The following commands constitute the correct way to set up NAT on a ASA 5520?

```
pixfw(config)#access-list 120 permit ip 10.10.100.0 255.255.255.0
    172.16.1.10 255.255.255.255
pixfw(config)#access-list 130 deny ip 10.10.100.0255.255.255.0
    172.16.22.67 255.255.255.255
pixfw(config)#nat (inside) 1 access-list 120
pixfw(config)#global (outside) 1 192.168.100.62 255.255.255.255
pixfw(config)#nat (inside) 2 access-list 130
pixfw(config)#global (outside) 2 192.168.100.25 255.255.255.255
```

4. Which command would you use to create a description/remark "Linda's group extranet server access" for access list 112?

5. How would you change the default port assignment for FTP?

6. What is the function of object groups?

7. What are the four object type options available when you are creating object groups?

8. How would you specify the maximum number of concurrent deny flows that can be created with an access list?

9. What are the seven SMTP commands allowed by SMTP inspection?

This chapter covers the following subjects:

- Modular Policy Framework Overview

- Defining Traffic Classes

- Creating Policies for Traffic Classes

- Using Policies on Interfaces

CHAPTER 8

Modular Policy Framework

The primary function of the Cisco Security Appliance is to prevent and to protect internal hosts from malicious attacks from an outside network. Some hackers try to gain access to an internal network, but others attack network resources to disrupt network services. This chapter describes some of the features of the Cisco Security Appliance that are used to mitigate known attacks against specific traffic classes.

How to Best Use This Chapter

The Security Appliance provides a more granular way to control and inspect traffic flows using Modular Policy Framework (MPF). Besides identifying attacks against certain protocols, protocol inspection on the traffic can enable the Security Appliance to dynamically open up the ports necessary for the communicating systems to transfer data. The Security Appliance also provides some intrusion detection capability along with the ability to dynamically shun intrusive traffic when combined with an Advanced Inspection and Protection Security Services Module (AIP-SSM). Test yourself with the "Do I Know This Already?" quiz and see how familiar you are with the intrusion prevention and attack guards supported by the Security Appliance.

"Do I Know This Already?" Quiz

The purpose of the "Do I Know This Already?" quiz is to help you decide if you really need to read the entire chapter. If you already intend to read the entire chapter, you do not necessarily need to answer these questions now.

The eight-question quiz, derived from the major sections in the "Foundation Topics" portion of this chapter, helps you determine how to spend your limited study time.

Table 8-1 outlines the major topics discussed in this chapter and the "Do I Know This Already?" quiz questions that correspond to those topics.

Table 8-1 *"Do I Know This Already?" Foundation Topics Section-to-Question Mapping*

Foundations Topics Section	Questions Covered in This Section	Score
Modular Policy Framework	1, 8	
Configure a Class Map	2	
Configure a Policy Map	3, 4, 6	
Configure a Service Map	5	
Intrusion Prevention	7	

CAUTION The goal of selfassessment is to gauge your mastery of the topics in this chapter. If you do not know the answer to a question or are only partially sure of the answer, you should mark this question wrong for purposes of the selfassessment. Giving yourself credit for an answer you correctly guess skews your selfassessment results and might provide you with a false sense of security.

1. What part of the Modular Policy Framework assigns a Traffic Class?

   a. Service map

   b. Priority map

   c. Class map

   d. Policy map

2. Which **match** command will match a specific TCP port?

   a. **match flow**

   b. **match rtp**

   c. **match tunnel-group**

   d. **match dscp**

   e. None of these answers are correct

3. Which are the five feature domains on a policy map? (Choose four.)

   a. set-connection

   b. inspect

   c. TCP normalization

   d. priority

   e. policy

   f. IPS

   g. Police

4. What is the name of the global policy map?

   a. world_policy

   b. default_policy

   c. asa_global_fw_policy

   d. Base_policy

   e. None of these answers are correct

5. How many policies can be assigned to an interface?

   a. 3

   b. 6

   c. 2

   d. 4

   e. 1

6. Which feature action works with bidirectional traffic flows on a single interface?

   a. IPS

   b. QoS policing

   c. Global interface

   d. QoS priority queuing

7. If an AIP-SSM module fails while using an IPS policy, what command allows traffic to continue to transmit during the failure?

   a. pass-thru

   b. fail-close

   c. cross-connect

   d. fail-open

8. The global policy affects which specific interface or interfaces on a Security Appliance?

   a. Inside

   b. Outside

   c. Global

   d. DMZ

   e. None of these answers are correct

   f. All these answers are correct

The answers to the "Do I Know This Already?" quiz are found in Appendix A, "Answers to the 'Do I Know This Already?' Quizzes and Q&A Sections." The suggested choices for your next step follow:

- **6 or less overall score**—Read the entire chapter. This includes the "Foundation Topics," "Foundation Summary," and "Q&A" sections.

- **7 or 8 overall score**—If you want more review on these topics, skip to the "Foundation Summary" section and then go to the "Q&A" section. Otherwise, move to the next chapter.

Foundation Topics

Modular Policy Framework Overview

Today, more and more corporations are becoming active on the Internet, resulting in an ever-increasing need for a more granular means to configure network security policies. Therefore, a security administrator needs to manipulate and control the flow of traffic in pieces and with more flexibility. Rate limiting and prioritizing voice traffic, and deep packet inspecting of untrusted traffic flows, are just some of the responsibilities of today's security administrator. With Security Appliance software version 7.0, this functionality has been enabled through Modular Policy Framework (MPF). An MPF gives the security administrator the tools to segment traffic flows into traffic classes and to assign one or more actions to each traffic class. Traditional policy maps only allowed actions to be assigned to the total traffic flow on the Security Appliance, whereas with an MPF, HTTP traffic can have a policy separate from H.323 or ICMP.

Traffic Flow Matching

One of the essential features of an MPF is the granularity in which a security administrator can inspect traffic flow. Class maps allow a security administrator to segregate the network traffic flow within the network at the packet level. Each packet is identified for its content and matched to attributes listed in the class map using the **match** command. The matched traffic becomes a new traffic class. The class map representing the traffic class will then be assigned to a policy map, which will apply actions (policies) to matched traffic. Creating a class map requires two steps:

Step 1   Create a class map.

Step 2   Define class map matches.

Figure 8-1 illustrates how you can use class maps to inspect traffic flow.

Figure 8-1 *Modular Policy Example Flow*

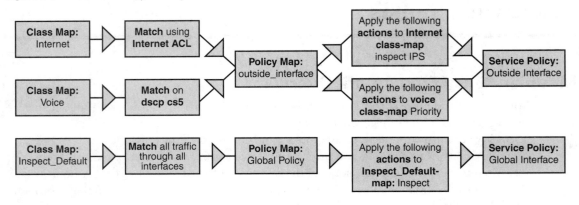

Step 1: Create a Class Map

You must assign a name to the class map. This name must be unique and should be intuitive to the content it will be matching. Use the **class-map** command to create and assign a name to a class map. To disable the command, use the **no** form of this command:

    class-map *class-map_name*

When this command has been executed, it will enter the class map configuration mode. Setting the different match criteria, as well as creating a description of the class map, can be done in this mode. Table 8-2 provides a list of available commands.

Table 8-2 match *Command Syntax*

Command	Description
description	Specifies a description for the class-map command.
match any	Specifies that all traffic is to be matched. This can be used to catch all traffic flowing through an interface, regardless of the content, type, or destination.
match access-list	Specifies the name of an access list to be used as match criteria. This can be used when a specific destination or source requires special attention, as well as a unique set of policy actions. Using access to the Internet falls under this category.
match port	Specifies to match traffic using a TCP/UDP destination port. Use this to assign a traffic class to a port not already specified by the default port lists. Additionally, you can use this match type to reassign matching for a known port, such as FTP, to a new port location, such as 10234 instead of 21.

Table 8-2 match *Command Syntax (Continued)*

Command	Description
match precedence	Specifies to match the precedence value represented by the ToS[1] byte in the IP header. Use this match when you are creating a set of policy actions that affect priority and queuing, such as voice and video. Make sure that the ToS byte has been assigned at the source for this to function correctly.
match dscp	Specifies to match the IETF[2]-defined DSCP[3] value in the IP header. Like the precedence match criteria cited previously, this should be used when assigning actions that will affect priority and queuing.
match rtp	Specifies to match an RTP[4] UDP[5] port. This matching criterion will allow you to set priority and queue settings for video in a priority map.
match tunnel-group	Specifies to match security-related tunnel groups. Use this if you would like to match a VPN[6] group of remote uses and force its traffic into a priority map for inspection, IPS[7], and so on.
match flow	Specifies to match every flow based on a unique IP destination address. This augments the **match tunnel-group** command, and must be used with the **tunnel-group** command.
match default-inspection-traffic	Specifies to match default traffic for the inspect commands. This is used on the global interface and through the default policies. You can also use it to match the default match criteria, so that you can add additional actions via a policy map. It would be easier to just modify the default policy map instead of creating a new one.

[1]   ToS = Type of Service
[2]   IETF = Internet Engineering Task Force
[3]   DSCP = Differentiated Services Code Point
[4]   RTP = Real-Time Transport Protocol
[5]   UDP = User Datagram Protocol
[6]   VPN = virtual private network
[7]   IPS = Intrusion Protection Services

NOTE   You cannot assign the class map **class-default**, as it is a default catch-all class map assigned to the global policy map. You can remove the default class map, although it is not recommended. To do so, use the following commands in sequence:

```
pix(config)# no service-policy asa_global_fw_policy global
pix(config)# no policy-map asa_global_fw_policy
pix(config)# no class-map inspection_default
```

Step 2: Define Class Map Matches

With a class map defined and given a name, you must assign a match parameter to the class map. This parameter will match traffic using the packet content, Layers 3 to 7. Examples of content would be voice, video, or HTTP. When assigning a match criterion, you can assign one **match** command to a class map, with the exception of the **tunnel-group** and **default-inspection-traffic** criteria. Use the **match** command to assign match criteria to a class map.

A class map can match to nine criteria. The **match** commands for each are as follows:

- **access-list** *{access-list name}* —Match using a predefined access list. If a packet fails to match an entry in the access list or matches a **deny** statement in the access list, the match will result in a no-match. Otherwise, if the packet matches a **permit** statement in the access list, the match results in a match.

- **any**—Match on any traffic flow or content. The **class-map class-default** command uses this match criterion as its default.

- **dscp** *{DSCP value}*—Match on the IETF-defined Differential Service Code Point (DSCP) field in the IP header defined in the ToS byte.

- **flow ip destination-address**—Keyword pair specifies to match the destination address within a tunnel group. This match criterion must be used with the tunnel group criteria.

- **port tcp | udp** *{eq n | range n1 n2}*—Match using a TCP or UDP destination port.

- **precedent** *{precedent value}*—Matches the precedence value in the TOS byte in the IP header.

- **RTP** — Match using RTP destination ports. This allows matching using a range of destination UDP ports.

- **tunnel-group** *{tunnel-group name}*—Matches tunnel traffic. This match criterion can only be used with quality of service (QoS) configurations.

- **default-inspection-traffic**—Matches default traffic for the **inspect** command in a policy map.

The **tunnel-group** command, an exception to the single **match** statement rule, matches a previously configured tunnel group as its first match criteria. An additional match criterion can be added to the class map already configured to match tunnel groups. This second match criteria will apply to traffic within that specific tunnel group.

Additionally, the **default-inspection-traffic** command can also be assigned a second match criterion. In a class map with a **default-inspection-traffic** command and a second **match** command, the class map will logically combine the two matches for use in an **inspect** command assigned in a policy map. Example 8-1 provides several examples of class map configurations.

Example 8-1 *Class Map Configuration Examples*

```
ASAfirewall(config)# class-map http1
ASAfirewall(config-cmap)# match port tcp eq 80
ASAfirewall(config)# class-map internet
ASAfirewall(config-cmap)# match access-list cleaninet
ASAfirewall(config)# class-map vpn1
ASAfirewall(config-cmap)# match tunnel-group vpn-group1
ASAfirewall(config-cmap)# match flow ip destination-address
```

Viewing the Class Map Configuration

A security administrator can view the class map configuration using the **show run class-map** command. The output from this command will display each class map and its match criteria, as illustrated in Example 8-2.

Example 8-2 **show run class-map** *Command Output*

```
ASAfirewall(config)# show run class-map
class-map http1
match port tcp eq 80
class-map internet
match access-list cleaninet
class-map vpn1
match flow ip destination-address
match tunnel-group vpn-group1
ASAfirewall(config)#
```

Assigning Actions to a Traffic Class

For purposes of managing, controlling, and manipulating the traffic classes, actions should be assigned to these traffic classes. A security administrator might want to rate-limit only the HTTP traffic that crosses the network, and use deep inspection on all TCP traffic entering the network. This can be done by assigning one or more traffic classes, through class maps, to policy maps. Policy maps assign one or more actions to one or more class maps assigned to it. Each action is called a *domain,* and the sets are known as *feature domains.* Similar to creating a class map, three steps are required to create a policy map:

Step 1   Create a policy map.

Step 2   Assign traffic classes to the policy map.

Step 3   Assign policies for each class.

Step 1: Create a Policy Map

A policy map can be created in the same way as a class map. Using the **policy-map** command, a policy map is created with a unique name. To disable the command, use the **no** form of this command:

```
policy-map class-map_name
```

Like a class map, the execution of a **policy-map** command will place you in the policy map configuration mode. The policy map configuration mode supports two commands:

- **description** *{description}*—Specifies a description for the **policy-map** command.
- **class** *{class-map name}*—Specifies the class map that will be associated with the policy map. You can associate multiple class maps with a single policy map.

> **NOTE**   Like class maps, there is a default policy map called global_policy. This is a policy map that cannot be removed or turned off and is defaulted to protocol inspection.

Step 2: Assign Traffic Classes to the Policy Map

With the policy map created, traffic classes must be assigned to the policy map. To do this, use the **class** command while in the policy map configuration mode. This will access the class configuration mode for that specific class map assigned to the policy map, as illustrated in Example 8-3.

Example 8-3   *Adding a Traffic Class to a Policy Map*

```
ASAfirewall(config)# class-map http1
ASAfirewall(config-cmap)# match port tcp eq 80
ASAfirewall(config-cmap)# exit
ASAfirewall(config)# policy-map outside1
ASAfirewall(config-pmap)# class-map http1
ASAfirewall(config-pmap-c)#
```

Each class map added to the policy map will have its own class configuration mode. All actions assigned in these modes will only affect traffic matched using that specific class map.

Step 3: Assign Policies for Each Class

You can assign five policies, or domains, to traffic classes within a policy map. The five policies are as follows:

- **police**—Allows rate limiting of matched traffic flows.
- **inspect**—Allows protocol inspection services on the matched traffic flows.

- **priority**—Allows strict scheduling priority for matched traffic flows.

- **Intrusion Protection Services (IPS)**—Allows IPS for all traffic flows that have been matched.

- **TCP normalization**—Allows the limiting of TCP and UDP connections, as well as embryonic connections.

You can assign more than one domain to a traffic class, allowing inspection, policing, or any of the other three policy types on a single traffic flow.

Police Policy Overview

The **police** command creates bandwidth restrictions on traffic flows. Table 8-3 describes the parameters for the **police** command, the syntax for which is as follows:

```
police conform-rate conform-burst | conform-action {drop | transmit} | exceed-action
  {drop | transmit}
```

Table 8-3 police *Command Parameters*

Syntax	Description
conform-action	The action to take when the traffic rate is below the *conform-burst* value.
conform-rate	Sets the maximum speed (rate limit) for the traffic flow. This value can be between 8000 and 2,000,000,000.
conform-burst	Sets the maximum number of bytes allowed in a sustained burst at any one instance. This value can be between 1000 and 512,000,000.
exceed-action	The action to take when the traffic rate exceeds the *conform-burst* value.
drop	Drop the packet.
transmit	Transmit the packet.

This **police** command allows a security administrator to set maximum transmit limits, or caps, on egress traffic through a specific interface or the global interface. The rate limit is compared to the sustained traffic rate of the associated traffic flow. In Figure 8-2, Client A has a VPN connection to Headquarters through an ASA 5520 Security Appliance. A policy map has been applied to Client A's traffic flow, and the rate has been limited to 64 kbps using the following **police** command:

```
ASAfirewall(config-pmap-c)# police 64000 1000 conform-action transmit exceed-action
  drop
```

Figure 8-2 *Rate-Limited Connection to Headquarters*

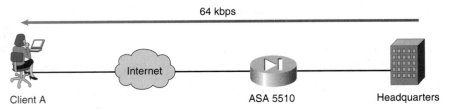

As long as the traffic flow does not exceed 64,000 bytes per second, the police policy will transmit the data. The *conform-rate* syntax sets the maximum rate of traffic in bits per second. The traffic that never exceeds the rate limit can be either transmitted or dropped. This is assigned by the **conform-action** attribute within the **police** command. If the traffic flow exceeds the rate limit, that traffic would normally be dropped. The problem with this is that IP traffic is inherently bursty, and dropping the bursty traffic might not be the correct action. It is common for a traffic flow to burst beyond its average sustained rate for a very short time. To allow for bursty traffic, you can configure the **police** command with a burst size set in the *conform-burst* syntax. This new burst rate specifies the maximum amount of bytes that can exceed the set rate limit during any one instance. Traffic might still exceed the burst rate, and the security administrator must determine what action should apply to the excess traffic. Using the **exceed-action** command within the **police** command allows the traffic either to continue to be transmitted or to be dropped.

NOTE   When deciding the burst size for a police policy, you should use the following formula:

(conform-rate/8) * 1.5

For example, if you use a conform rate of 80 kbps, use the formula to get the following as your burst size:

(80/8) * 1.5 = 15 kbps

Priority Policy Overview

With video and audio streaming, as well as voice over IP (VoIP) services becoming more mainstream, the need for high-quality bandwidth connections is critical due to jitter and latency restrictions. Many national and international companies rely on VoIP traffic to communicate between offices that run over the Internet. VPNs over the Internet between offices are becoming more prevalent, requiring QoS features. The Security Appliance can use low-latency queuing (LLQ) to prioritize egress packet transmission, enabling a form of QoS for the prioritized packets. This can be done within a policy map using the **priority** command. The **priority** command assigns the class map to the low-latency queue, while all egress traffic not assigned the **priority** command will be sent into the default, best-effort queue. The **priority** command will only queue traffic from a single direction, and it is considered a unidirectional policy. The **priority** command has no parameters and simply is applied to the class configuration mode within the policy map configuration mode, as follows:

```
ASAfirewall(config-pmap)#class video1
ASAfirewall(config-pmap-c)#priority
ASAfirewall(config-pmap-c)#
```

Remember that the **priority** command gives absolute priority to the LLQ. If configured incorrectly, this can easily cause starvation of the best-effort traffic flows on the Security Appliance.

Inspect Policy Overview

Today, many services and applications are run on the Internet. With corporations and small businesses using the Internet more and more, it is crucial to restrict and control the applications and services accessed through the Internet. Many applications use static ports, making inspection by classic firewalls quick and simple. More recently, applications such as FTP, multimedia, and SQL require dynamic port assignments, which can confuse classic firewalls to the point of breaking these applications. Security administrators have to decide if the applications can be allowed to access the network, and if so, they will have to create a security hole in the firewall for all the dynamic port assignments to work properly. Creating any hole, permanent or not, in a security system makes it vulnerable to attack and breach. Cisco has found a way around this issue on the Security Appliance by enabling the **inspect** command in policy maps. As of version 7.0, the **inspect** command replaces the **fixup** comment for all inspection features.

The **inspect** command allows the firewall to inspect bidirectional packets at Layers 3 to 7 on an interface, and it permits them to transverse the network using dynamic, stateful adjustments to the security policy. By default, protocol inspection is enabled in the global policy map and inspects the following protocols:

```
policy-map global_policy
 class inspection_default
  inspect dns maximum length 512
  inspect ftp
  inspect h323 h225
  inspect h323 ras
  inspect netbios
  inspect sunrpc
  inspect rsh
  inspect rtsp
  inspect sip
  inspect skinny
  inspect esmtp
  inspect sqlnet
  inspect tftp
  inspect xdmcp
```

Unlike a normal interface, the global interface will only support ingress packet inspection using the **inspect** command. The **inspect** command used in the class configuration mode uses the same configuration rules and syntax as described in Chapter 19 "IPS and Advanced Protocol Handling."

IPS Policy Overview

With the optional AIP-SSM module installed in the Security Appliance, detailed deep packet inspection is available for traffic flows assigned to the IPS policy. The Security Appliance will take a subset of the traffic flow on the firewall and send it to the AIP-SSM module for inspection. This grants the Security Appliance greater efficiency with packet inspections and will cause fewer false-positives due to only having to inspect a subset of the total traffic flow in the Security Appliance. Like the **inspect** command, the AIP-SSM module will inspect both the ingress and egress traffic flows assigned to it from a normal interface, but it is restricted to the ingress traffic flows from the global interface. Use the **ips** command to assign the IPS policy to a class map:

```
ips {inline | promiscuous} {fail-close | fail-open}
```

NOTE The SSM is only supported on the ASA series of Cisco Security Appliances.

Table 8-4 describes the options available with the **ips** command.

Table 8-4 ips *Command Syntax*

Syntax	Description
Inline	Redirects packets to the AIP-SSM module for inspection
promiscuous	Duplicates packets for the AIP-SSM module for inspection
fail-close	Blocks traffic if the AIP-SSM module fails
fail-open	Permits traffic if the AIP-SSM module fails

The IPS policy works in one of two modes:

- **Inline mode**—The Security Appliance will redirect live traffic flow assigned to the IPS policy to the AIP-SSM for inspection. The module inspects the live packets envelope, as well as Layers 3 to 7, for malicious or dangerous content and drops the packet if needed. An inline AIP-SSM module sits in the forwarding path, allowing the IPS process to stop attacks by dropping malicious traffic before it reaches its final destination. Any traffic found to be clean is released and transmitted to its final destination. This can affect the flow of traffic and reduces the maximum throughput of the Security Appliance.

■ **Promiscuous mode**—The Security Appliance can send copies of live traffic assigned to the IPS policy to the AIP-SSM for inspection. Using promiscuous mode avoids direct manipulation of the live traffic flow, allowing higher throughput and less latency that may be caused during inline mode. What is lost is the ability to stop an attack as it is happening. Without direct access to the live traffic flow, the AIP-SSM is working in a reactive security state, rarely responding during the fact and potentially causing a need for manual intervention by a security administrator to stop the attack.

Redirecting traffic to a secondary module can cause an additional point of failure. If the AIP-SSM module fails for any reason, the traffic that has been redirected there would be dropped altogether. This could be a problem if the security policy for a site is to be always online. Two options are supported in the **ips** command to resolve this issue:

■ **fail-close**—Enabling this **ips** command option will cause all traffic flows assigned to the IPS policy to be dropped if for any reason the AIP-SSM fails. This is the recommended setting, as it is the most secure of the two options.

■ **fail-open**—Enabling this **ips** command option will allow all traffic flows assigned to the IPS policy to be transmitted without inspection to its destination, pending any other policy assigned to the traffic flow.

Policy Map TCP Connection Policy Overview

Policy maps have four basic actions that can be assigned to traffic flow. In addition to these four actions, policy maps offer a general connection policy that can manage the actual traffic flow's connection state. This is useful if a security administrator needs to restrict the number of HTTP connects allowed through parts of the network or needs to restrict the time a connection is allowed to stay up. To assign a connection policy, the **set connection** command must be applied to a class map in class configuration mode like the other four policy map actions:

```
set connection {[conn-max number] [embryonic-conn-max number] [random-sequence-number
   {enable | disable}}
```

Table 8-5 describes the options of the **set connection** command.

Table 8-5 set connection *Command Options*

Command Parameter	Description
conn-max	The maximum number of simultaneous TCP and UDP connections that are allowed.
embryonic-conn-max	The maximum number of half-open TCP connections associated with a policy map.
random-sequence-number	Enables or disables TCP sequence number randomization. This option should be used when multiple Security Appliances are placed inline with each other, with one appliance performing the sequence number randomization.

Using the **set connection** command, you can control the timeout for TCP connections. The connection types that a timeout can be set for are connections, embryonic (half-opened) connections, and half-closed connections. The **set connection** command uses a different syntax for timeouts:

```
set connection {[embryonic hh[:mm[:ss]]] [half-closed hh[:mm[:ss]]] [tcp hh[:mm[:ss]]]}
```

Viewing the Policy Map Configuration

To display all policy map configurations, a security administrator can use the **show run policy-map** command. The output from this command will display all policy maps, the class maps assigned to them, and each action applied to the class maps, as illustrated in Example 8-4.

Example 8-4 show run policy-map *Command Output*

```
ASAfirewall(config)# show run policy-map
    policy-map outside1
      class http1
        police 64000 1000
      class internet
        IPS inline fail-close
      class vpn1
        set connection conn-max 256
        embryonic-conn-max 25
ASAfirewall(config)#
```

Assigning Policies to an Interface

For interfaces to be activated, you need to assign policies to them. An interface is defined as any physical interface or as a logical interface that can be defined by the **nameif** command. Additionally, you can apply a policy to the global interface. To assign a policy to an interface, use the **service-policy** command. The **service-policy** command assigns a policy map to a specific interface. Only one service-policy command can be made on any one interface. To disable the command, use the **no** form of this command:

```
service-policy policy-map_name [global | interface intf]
```

Table 8-6 describes the parameters of the **service-policy command.**

Table 8-6   service-policy *Command Syntax*

Syntax	Description
policy-map_name	The name of a configured policy map-map.
global	Assign the policy map to all interfaces. By default, the Global_policy is already assigned to this setting.
interface	Assigns the policy map to a specific interface.
intf	The interface name defined in the **nameif** command.

Service policies use several parameters that govern the traffic direction based on the classification that is performed. Some policies will affect inbound traffic flows for specific classifications, while others may affect bidirectional traffic flows. The three types of policies follow:

- **Input**—Input or ingress refers to all traffic flow entering the Security Appliance through the assigned interface.

- **Output**—Output or egress refers to all traffic flow leaving the Security Appliance through the assigned interface.

- **Bidirectional**—Bidirectional, both ingress and egress, affects both directions of all traffic that accesses the assigned interface.

Each action has an implicit direction policy assigned to it by the Security Appliance, including the global policy, as shown in Table 8-7. The global policy treats inspection-type actions as input-only actions. These actions handle only traffic flow that *enters* the security appliance and ignores traffic *leaving* the Security Appliance. This would include **inspect, ips,** and **set-connection** policies. The QoS-type of actions are treated by the global policy as output-only actions. This would include the police and priority actions.

Table 8-7   *Service Policy Directional Use Table*

Policy Type	Single Interface Direction	Global Direction
IPS	Bidirectional	Ingress
TCP normalization; connection limits and timeouts (**set-connection**)	Bidirectional	Ingress

continues

Table 8-7   *Service Policy Directional Use Table (Continued)*

Policy Type	Single Interface Direction	Global Direction
QoS policing	Egress	Egress
QoS priority queue	Egress	Egress
Application inspection	Bidirectional	Ingress

Interface-specific service policies treat some actions differently from the global policy. The inspection-type actions are considered bidirectional actions. These actions can affect ingress and egress traffic on the specified interface. The interface-specific service policies treat QoS-type actions in the same way as the global policy.

Service Policy Matching Logic

When the Security Appliance applies a service policy to an interface, it must sort the matching criteria. In a traditional policy map or access list, the Security Appliance would use a first-match rule; as soon as a packet matched a criteria in the policy map or access list, the action was handled and the service appliance went on to the next packet. Using an MPF, it is possible to require a packet to match multiple criteria, each with separate actions that should be applied to the packet. The first-match rule is used, as it only supports a single action per packet. To allow for multiple matches and allow multiple actions to apply to a packet, two policies dictate how the service policy handles matching criteria.

Multimatch Classification Policy

The multimatch classification policy applies to any service policy containing a policy map that applies multiple domains to traffic classes. For example, a policy map that assigns an inspect action to class map A and a police action to class map B would qualify as a multimatch classification. Each domain is allowed an attempt to match its criteria to the packet. Once all matches have been verified, all actions assigned by these matches are applied to the packet. For example, an H.323 traffic class could be assigned an inspection domain, while all TCP traffic could be assigned a **set-connections** domain and all voice traffic could be set a priority domain. If a VoIP traffic flow enters the Security Appliance, all three domains would affect and match this traffic flow, causing it to be inspected, have TCP connection limits applied to the flow, and be prioritized in the LLQ.

The Security Appliance will apply these actions in a specific order that does not reflect the order in which the actions have been configured:

1. IPS

2. TCP Flow Control

3. Inspection

4.   Policing

5.   Priority

First-Match Classification Policy

If a service policy contains only a single domain throughout all assigned class maps, the service policy will use the first-match classification policy. Like an access list, each packet will enter the service policy and have the match criteria compared to it. If it fits a match criterion, the action applied to that match criteria takes effect and the service policy stops attempting to match the packet. The order in which the service policy compares the match criteria is based on how the service policy is configured, with the first match in the configuration taking effect first.

Viewing the Service Policy Configuration

To display all service policy configurations, a security administrator can use the **show running-config service-policy** command in the global configuration mode. The output from this command displays each service policy, the policy map assigned to them, and the interface to which it is assigned, as illustrated in Example 8-5.

Example 8-5   show running-config service-policy *Command Output*

```
ASAfirewall(config)# show running-config service-policy
service-policy global_policy global
service-policy outside1 interface outside
ASAfirewall(config)#
```

Viewing the Service Policy Statistics

Security administrators like to have as much information as possible in front of them about their networks' health. To help with this, the Security Appliance gathers statistics on each service policy, including details such as the number of hits to a policy and how much traffic uses a policy. The **show service-policy** command displays the service policy statistics per interface:

```
show service-policy [global | interface intf] [ action | flow flow_description]
```

Table 8-8 describes the parameters for this command.

Table 8-8   show service-policy *Command Syntax*

Syntax	Description
global	Refers to the global policy map (that is, all interfaces).
interface	Refers to a specific interface to which the policy map is applied.

continues

Table 8-8 show service-policy *Command Syntax (Continued)*

Syntax	Description
intf	Specifies the interface name.
action	Specifies an action for which the statistics data are to be shown.
flow *flow_description*	Specifies a data flow on which policies that are enacted will be displayed, including the following: Protocol host source_ip | source_ip source_mask source_ip source_mask eq source_port destination_ip destination_mask destination_port icmp icmp_type

Example 8-6 demonstrates the information displayed by executing the **show service-policy** command.

Example 8-6 show service-policy *Command Output*

```
ASAfirewall(config)# show service-policy
Interface outside
  Service-policy: outside1
    Class-map:  http1
 police:
    cir 64000 bps, bc 1000 bytes
  conformed 0 packets, 0 bytes; actions:
    transmit
  exceeded 0 packets, 0 bytes; actions:
    drop
  conformed 0 bps, exceed 0 bps
    Class-map:  internet
IPS: mode inline, packet 0
```

Foundation Summary

This "Foundation Summary" provides a convenient review of many key concepts in this chapter. If you are already comfortable with the topics in this chapter, this summary can help you recall a few details. If you just read this chapter, this review should help solidify some key facts. If you are doing your final preparation before the exam, this summary provides a convenient way to review on the day before the exam.

Cisco Service Appliance software version 7.0 and later introduced a new way to dynamically manipulate traffic flows. With the introduction of Modular Policy Framework, a security administrator could manage, inspect, and set priorities on specific traffic flows instead of applying these settings to the total traffic on the Security Appliance. A Modular Framework Policy consists of three parts:

- **Class maps**—Class maps define the traffic flow that will be managed.
- **Policy maps**—Policy maps define one or more actions that will be applied to the traffic flow.
- **Service maps**—Service maps assign the policies to specific interfaces or globally to all interfaces.

Policy maps assign actions, or domains, to traffic classes assigned by the class map. These five actions, called *feature domains,* control the inspection and QoS actions that a policy map can apply. The featured actions are as follows:

- **inspect**—Inspects a traffic flow assigned to it at Layer 3 to Layer 7.
- **ips**—Sends traffic to the AIP-SSM module for deep packet inspection.
- **priority**—Assigns traffic flows to the low-latency queue for prioritization.
- **police**—Sets a rate limit and burst limit on assigned traffic flows.
- **set-connection**—Allows the limiting of TCP and UDP connections, as well as embryonic connections.

Q&A

As mentioned in this text's Introduction, the questions in this book are more difficult than what you are likely to experience on the exam. The questions are designed to ensure your understanding of the concepts discussed in this chapter and to adequately prepare you to complete the exam. You should use the simulated exams on the CD to practice for the exam.

The answers to these questions can be found in Appendix A:

1. What differentiates Modular Policy Framework from classic policy maps?

2. What are the three parts to an MPF and what do they do?

3. How many matches are allowed in a class map?

4. What is an embryonic connection?

5. Which actions are available in the IPS policy configuration?

6. What are the feature domains and what do they do?

7. How does the IPS policy handle hardware failure?

8. How many policy maps can be assigned to an interface?

9. Are policy maps directional, and if so, what feature groups access which directions?

10. What does the default policy map do, and how is it applied?

This chapter covers the following subjects:

- Security Context Overview

- Configuring Security Contexts

- Managing Security Contexts

CHAPTER 9

Security Contexts

A new function of the Security Appliance is the capability to segment the appliance and its resources into multiple virtual firewalls though contexts. Virtual firewalls make it possible for a security administrator to restrict and control parts of a managed network. This chapter describes some of the features of the Cisco Security Appliance that are used to create virtual firewalls.

How to Best Use This Chapter

With the release of Secure Firewall software version 7.0, the Cisco Security Appliances allow a security administrator the use of virtual firewalls. These virtual firewalls, called *security contexts,* are independent firewalls with their own security policies, interfaces, and administrators. Configuring multiple security contexts is similar to deploying multiple firewall units. Test yourself with the "Do I Know This Already?" quiz and see how familiar you are with the security contexts and their uses on the Security Appliance.

"Do I Know This Already?" Quiz

The purpose of the "Do I Know This Already?" quiz is to help you decide if you really must read the entire chapter. If you already intend to read the entire chapter, you do not necessarily need to answer these questions now.

The eight-question quiz, derived from the major sections in the "Foundation Topics" portion of the chapter, helps you determine how to spend your limited study time.

Table 9-1 outlines the major topics presented in this chapter and the "Do I Know This Already?" quiz questions that correspond to those topics.

Table 9-1 *"Do I Know This Already?" Foundation Topics Section-to-Question Mapping*

Foundations Topics Section	Questions Covered in This Section	Score
Security Context Overview	1, 2, 3, 5	
Configuring Security Contexts	4, 6, 7	
Managing Security Contexts	8	

> **CAUTION** The goal of selfassessment is to gauge your mastery of the topics in this chapter. If you do not know or are unsure of the answer to a question, you should mark this question wrong for purposes of the selfassessment. Giving yourself credit for an answer you correctly guess skews your selfassessment results and might provide you with a false sense of security.

1. What are the benefits of using security context over multiple firewall units?

   a. It reduces the overall cost of the security platform.

   b. Management of the firewalls becomes a much easier task.

   c. It uses less physical space.

   d. All of these answers are correct.

2. What determines the amount of security contexts a Security Appliance can have?

   a. Hardware model.

   b. OS software version.

   c. License purchased.

   d. There is no limit.

   e. The hardware model and license purchased.

3. What is the name used for the default administrative context?

   a. default

   b. context1

   c. admin

   d. cisco

4. Where can you store context configuration files?

   a. FTP server

   b. Flash memory DIMM

   c. TFTP server

   d. HTTP server

   e. All of these answers are correct

5. The Security Appliance classifies traffic flows by using which of the following characteristics of the packet?

    a. VLAN

    b. Destination address

    c. Source address

    d. Port type

    e. Both VLAN and destination address

6. Which command enables multiple security context mode?

    a. **multiple-context enable**

    b. **context-mode multiple**

    c. **mode multiple**

    d. **enable multimode**

    e. None of these answers are correct

7. Which of the following does the invisible parameter in the **allocate-interface** command do?

    a. Disables an interface for the whole system

    b. Hides physical interface properties from non-administrative users of a context

    c. Enables transparent firewall support in a context

    d. Hides a list of privileged commands from users of a context

8. Which command identifies the location from which the system downloads the context configuration file?

    a. **context-config**

    b. **config-url**

    c. **remote-config context**

    d. **copy tftp flash**

The answers to the "Do I Know This Already?" quiz are found in Appendix A, "Answers to the 'Do I Know This Already?' Quizzes and Q&A Sections." The suggested choices for your next step are as follow:

■ **6 or less overall score**—Read the entire chapter. This includes the "Foundation Topics," "Foundation Summary," and "Q&A" sections.

■ **7 or 8 overall score**—If you want to review these topics further, skip to the "Foundation Summary" section and then go to the "Q&A" section. Otherwise, move to the next chapter.

Foundation Topics

In the ever-expanding workplace, companies are requiring more and more security on sensitive material. In addition, the need to control and manage the network activities of employees has become a paramount duty for security administrators. Traditionally, when a security administrator required unique security configurations for different departments, multiple firewalls would be deployed, one for each department. As companies and campuses have grown, this practice has become complex and difficult to manage. With Secure Firewall software version 7.0, a security administrator can create multiple virtual firewalls within a single Security Appliance.

Security Context Overview

Within a single Security Appliance, a security administrator can create more then one security context (see Figure 9-1). Each context uses a separate configuration that describes the security policy, assigned interfaces, and options that the security context manages. This reduces the amount of equipment, cost, rack space, and administrative duties that a security department would normally incur if each department required a separate firewall unit.

Figure 9-1 *Multiple Security Contexts*

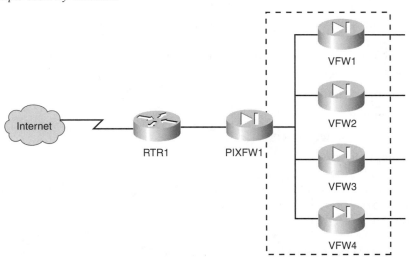

Each security context configuration is stored in a separate file that can be saved on the local Flash RAM drive or accessed from a remote location using TFTP, FTP, or HTTP(S).

Multiple security contexts should be used in the following scenarios:

- A large enterprise company or campus with a requirement to completely separate each department.

- An enterprise that requires unique security policies for each department.

- An Internet service provider (ISP) that wishes to sell security and firewall services to multiple companies.

- A network that requires more than one firewall.

Although security contexts give a security administrator more flexibility when designing a security platform, a few features are not supported within a security context when enabled in multiple context mode:

- Dynamic routing protocols such as OSPF or RIP. Only static routes are supported.

- VPNs.

- Multicasts.

For the Security Appliance to route traffic flows through the appropriate security context, the Security Appliance must first classify the traffic flow based on the contents of the flow packets. Using two characteristics of the packets within the flow, the Security Appliance classifies the packets based on which characteristic is unique to the Security Appliance contexts and is not shared across them. The two characteristics that the Security Appliance checks for are these:

- Source interface (VLAN)

- Destination address

Multiple Context Modes

A Security Appliance can support either a single or multiple context mode. In a single-mode configuration, the Security Appliance does not separate the firewall options from the system resources. When the multiple-contexts mode is enabled, the Security Appliance creates a new configuration scheme. The Security Appliance separates the context options from the current start-up configuration and places these configurations in an administrative context called the *admin context*. The remaining system configurations are stored in the start-up configuration file. The administration configuration uses the *admin.cfg* file. The original running configuration is saved as old_running.cfg on the local Flash disk when the security context mode is changed. If the running configuration differs from the start-up configuration, the start-up configuration should also be saved manually. If you are copying a configuration from a Security Appliance in multiple-context mode to a device configured for single-context mode, the context mode must be manually changed, or scripted with the [**noconfirm**] switch.

This is needed because the security context mode is not saved in the configuration file. All mode changes must be made from the command-line interface (CLI) and cannot be done through the Cisco Adaptive Security Device Manager (ASDM). To enable the multiple-context mode, use the **mode** command:

```
mode {single | multiple} [noconfirm]
```

With the **noconfirm** command syntax, the mode of the Security Appliance can be changed without confirmation. This can be done when managing the appliance through scripts through the CLI, but it will cause the Security Appliance to reboot without a warning.

If the security administrator chooses to return the Security Appliance to single mode, the Security Appliance will inherit most of the necessary configuration options from the multiple contexts to create a nonfunctioning configuration for a single-mode firewall. It is recommended that a full start-up configuration be applied to the Security Appliance before converting to single mode. After the Security Appliance resets to single-context mode, all the interfaces will be offline. To enable the interfaces, as well as to copy any additional configuration settings back onto the Security Appliance, access to the CLI will be required.

A security administrator can verify the security-context mode that the Security Appliance has enabled by using the **show mode** command in EXEC mode. Example 9-1 shows sample output from the **show mode** command.

Example 9-1 show mode *Output*

```
pixfw1# show mode
Firewall mode: multiple
The flash mode is the same as the running mode.
```

Administration Context

Security Appliances with multiple security contexts enabled use a special context to manage the system interfaces, as well as all other contexts contained on the firewall. As described previously, the admin context is created by the Security Appliance when enabled in multiple security context and uses the *admin.cfg* file to store the admin context configuration.

Unlike in single mode, where the system configuration controls the network resources, in multiple-security context mode, the admin context handles all the system network resources for the Security Appliance. This is required because the system execution space does not contain any traffic-passing interfaces. All policies and interfaces that have been configured on the admin context will be used by the system to communicate with other devices.

The authentication, authorization, and accounting (AAA) feature commands are not accepted in the admin context. This will require local database credentials for individual logins. It is recommended that restrictions be placed on logins created in the local database to limit system execution space.

The admin context is also used to acquire a configuration file from a remote location for another security context. Additionally, these network settings configure appropriate system-level syslog options to send syslog data for remote capture.

The admin context is designed to allow a security administrator control over other security contexts. To create new security contexts or change the admin context, a security administrator must log into the admin context.

At times, a department or division head requires control over department or division firewall configurations. This can be accommodated through the assignment of context administrators. These administrators can only configure and manage the specific context to which they are assigned and cannot configure or view system resources or the administration context. To stop different contexts from inadvertently affecting each other, system resources and VLAN management are done outside the multiple security contexts and within the system configuration.

An admin context can also be used as a regular security context. This can be a bit tricky, as all policies applied to the admin context affect the system as well as the assigned interfaces for the context. If the first new security context is created before an admin context has been created, the new security context is labeled as the admin context. An already configured security context can be assigned to act as the admin context. This will convert the current admin context to a regular security context and will install the newly assigned context as the admin context. To do this, use the **admin-context** command in global configuration mode:

```
admin-context name
```

> **NOTE**   You can only use a context as an admin context if its configuration file resides on the internal Flash memory.

Configuring Security Contexts

In multiple-context mode, a security administrator can create new security contexts up to the Security Appliances license limit. These contexts will have policies that apply only to the interfaces that are assigned to that context. A security context contains two parts:

- **System configuration of the context**—Defines the context name, VLAN, interfaces and configuration file URL that the context will use.

- **Context configuration file**—Contains all the firewall policies and interface configurations that will be used on the context.

Creating a New Context

Each security context will have a unique case-sensitive name, using alphanumeric characters no longer than 32 characters. The context names are case sensitive, and a context cannot be assigned either "System" or "Null" as names, as these are reserved by the system. To create a context, use the **context** command in global configuration mode:

```
context [name]
```

The **context** command, when executed, will enter into a context configuration submode. In this configuration mode, interface assignments and the location of the context firewall configuration file are input.

Assigning Interfaces to a Context

Each context can be allocated a number of interfaces that have been enabled in the system configuration mode. Assigned interfaces will be given a mapped name that the contexts configuration file will reference for policies and network settings specific to the context. The interfaces can be physical or logical, including subinterfaces. To assign one or more interfaces to a security context, use the **allocate-interface** command:

```
allocate-interface physical_interface[map_name][visible ¦ invisible]
allocate-interface physical_interface.subinterface[=physical_interface.subinterface]
    [map_name[-name_name]][visible | invisible]
```

Table 9-2 describes the parameters for the **allocate-interface** command.

Table 9-2 allocate-interface *Command Parameters*

Parameter	Description
map_name	(Optional) Sets a mapped name. The **map_name** is an alphanumeric alias for the interface that can be used within the context instead of the interface ID. If a mapped name is not specified, the interface ID is used within the context
	A mapped name must start with a letter, end with a letter or digit, and have as interior characters only letters, digits, or an underscore. For example, you can use the following names: • Int0 • Inta • Int_a For subinterfaces, you can specify a range of mapped named such as int0-int100.
physical_interface	Assigns the interface ID.

Table 9-2   allocate-interface *Command Parameters (Continued)*

Parameter	Description
subinterface	Assigns the subinterface number. You can specify a range of subinterfaces such as ethernet1.0–ethernet0.100
visible	(Optional) Allows context users to see the physical interface properties in the **show interface** command even if a mapped name is assigned.
invisible	(Default) Allows context users to only see the mapped name (if configured) in the **show interface** command.

The **allocate-interface** command can assign multiple interfaces at once, as long as they are the same interface type or they are all subinterfaces of the same physical interface.

Each interface or group of interfaces is assigned mapped names that must adhere to the following guidelines:

- The mapped name must consist of an alphabetic portion followed by a numeric portion. The alphabetic portion must be consistent throughout an assigned range of interfaces.

- The numeric portion of the mapped name must include the same quantity of numbers as the subinterface range.

Example 9-2 illustrates how to assign a range of interfaces to a context. Interfaces assigned to a context are seen as the mapped name by default when a **show interface** command is executed. This restricts administrators of specific security contexts from being able to see the physical interface names. This can be changed by adding the **visible** attribute to the **allocate-interface** command on a context. An administrator in the admin context can always see the physical interface named.

Example 9-2   *Allocating Interfaces to a Context*

```
pixfw1(config)# context sciencelab1
pixfw1(config-ctx)# allocate-interface gigabitethernet0/1 int0
pixfw1(config-ctx)# allocate-interface gigabitethernet1/1.1-gigabitethernet1/1.100 int1-
  int100
pixfw1(config-ctx)#
```

NOTE   If a context is configured as a transparent firewall, the context can only be assigned two interfaces, with the exception of the management port, which can be assigned as the third interface.

The Security Appliance allows interfaces to be shared between contexts. This is allowed only with adherence to the following guidelines:

■ The Security Appliance must be in routed mode.

■ The shared interface must have either a unique IP address for each context or a unique VLAN for each context that will be using it.

After you have decided to enable shared interfaces on a Security Appliance, you must consider several issues. To allow traffic through shared interfaces, Network Address translation (NAT) must be enabled on that interface. The classifier used by the Security Appliance requires an address translation configuration that classifies the packet within a context. Using NAT translation commands, the destination address of the traffic must be translated to comply with this restriction. This can also be achieved through the use of the **global** command if NAT translation is not performed.

A restriction arises when considering where traffic flows will originate from the shared interfaces on the Security Appliance. When dynamic NAT is used for the destination addresses, a connection through those addresses cannot be initiated. This restricts the interfaces in such a way that they can only respond to existing connections, and a new connection can never be initiated. To get around this issue, static NAT must be used for the destination addresses, allowing the interface to initiate as well as to respond to connections.

Configuring an inside shared interface might pose another potential problem when using shared interfaces and NAT. This problem arises when communication between a shared interface and an external network, such as the Internet, is desired and the destination addresses are unlimited. The Security Appliance requires Static NAT translation to support this configuration, which will limit the kind of Internet access that can be provided to users on the inside shared interface. As previously stated, many issues must be considered before configuring shared interfaces, especially when NAT is also deployed on the Security Appliance. Take time to work out the design so that these issues do not hinder your network's stability.

Uploading a Configuration Using the config-url Command

To enable a security context, you must specify a configuration file. The **config-url** command is used in context-configuration mode to specify where to find the configuration file for the context:

```
config-url url
```

The *url* argument assigns the context configuration URL. All remote URLs must be accessible from the admin context:

- **disk0:/**[path/]filename—This option is only available for the ASA platform and indicates the Flash memory DIMM.

- **disk1:/**[path/]filename—This option is only available for the ASA platform and indicates the Flash memory card.

- **flash:/**[path/]—This option indicates the Flash memory DIMM.

- **http[s]://**[user[:password]@]server[:port]/[path/]filename — This option indicates the HTTP or HTTPS server from which to download.

- **tftp://**[user[:password]@]server[:port]/[path/]filename—This option indicates the TFTP server from which to download.

- **ftp://**[user[:password]@]server[:port]/[path/]filename[;**type**=xx]—This option indicates the FTP server from which to download.

    type can be one of the following:

    — **Ap**—ASCII passive mode

    — **An**—ASCII normal mode

    — **Ip**—(Default) Binary passive mode

    — **In**—Binary normal mode

The configuration file can be stored in several locations:

- **Disk0/flash**—Security Appliance's Flash filesystem
- **disk1**—Security Appliance's compact Flash
- **tftp**—TFTP server
- **ftp**—FTP server
- **http(s)**—WebServer (read only)

The admin context must reside on the local Flash memory DIMM. Configuring a **config-url** on a context will cause the context to immediately attempt to retrieve the configuration file. Make sure all interfaces have been allocated to a context with mapped names before the **config-url** command is executed. If a **config-url** has been configured on a security context before any interfaces for that context have been assigned mapped names, the newly acquired context configuration may fail commands referencing the missing interfaces. If the context cannot retrieve the requested context configuration, the system will create an empty context configuration file that can be manually configured from the Security Appliance command-line interface (CLI).

After a context configuration file has been assigned and loaded into the context, a security administrator might need to move the remote configuration file to a different location. Changing the **config-url** to take the move into consideration can be done by reentering the

config-url command. By reentering the **config-url**, the context will immediately attempt to download the new configuration file and merge it with the current running configuration for that context. The merge will only add new configurations to the running configuration. To avoid this, a security administrator can clear the running configuration, though doing so will disrupt any communications through the context until the new configuration file is acquired.

Managing Security Contexts

Security contexts can be accessed on two levels. A security administrator can log into the admin context or system execution space. This will allow the security administrator access to the configuration of all configured contexts, as well as the ability to create new contexts. Additionally, users can be set up as security administrators for specific contexts. When users logs into the Security Appliance, they will be able to see only the security context to which they have been assigned. Within that context, they can change the configuration file information and can monitor the context.

Deleting Contexts

There are two aspects to deleting contexts. To delete a single context, use the **no context** command in global configuration mode:

    no context name

This will remove the named context from the running configuration. Remember to save the running configuration to the start-up configuration to make the change permanent.

To remove all currently configured context on a Security Appliance, use the **clear configure context** command in the global configuration mode. Both the **clear configure context** and **no context** commands will remove contexts immediately. Also note that the admin context cannot be removed with the **no context** command until all other contexts have been deleted.

Navigating Multiple Contexts

When you log into the admin context or the system execution space, you might need to switch between multiple contexts. This will enable you to perform configuration changes and monitor separate contexts while logged on. Each context has reserved system execution space that is limited to that context's running configuration. This will require you to swap between contexts to show the configuration of each context. This will also require you to do a **write memory** command in each context to save the running configuration, as this cannot be done from a separate context. To change between contexts, you must use a special command, which is unlike how you can change between interfaces. Use the following command to change between contexts:

— **changeto** {system | **context** *name*}

This command will also allow you to change from a context to the system execution space, and back if the need arises.

Viewing Context Information

You can use several methods to display the current configuration and status of the different aspects of the security contexts. As described previously, to see the current of the context mode, use the **show mode** command. This will show you if the Security Appliance is in single- or multiple-security context mode.

To see a list of all the currently configured security contexts, and a brief description of the interfaces and configuration file location, use the **show context** command in global configuration mode. Example 9-3 shows a sample of the output when this command is executed.

Example 9-3 show context *Command Output*

```
Pixfw1(config)# show context
Context Name       Interfaces                                  URL
*admin             GigabitEthernet0/0,GigabitEthernet0/1 disk0:/admin.cfg
 context1          GigabitEthernet0/0,GigabitEthernet0/1,GigabitEthernet0/3 disk0:/
   context1.cfg
 sciencelab1       GigabitEthernet0/0,GigabitEthernet0/1,GigabitEthernet0/3 disk0:/
   sciencelab1.cfg
Total active Security Contexts:  3…
```

You can display a more detailed view of each security context, including running state and information for internal use, by using the **show context detail** command in global configuration mode, as illustrated in Example 9-4.

Example 9-4 show context detail *Command Output*

```
Pixfw1(config)# show context detail
Context "admin", has been created, but inital ACL rules not complete
 Config URL: disk0:/admin.cfg
 Real Interfaces: GigabitEthernet0/0, GigabitEthernet0/1
 Mapped Interfaces: GigabitEthernet0/0, GigabitEthernet0/1
 Flags" 0x00000013. ID: 1
```

The **show context count** command lists the number of contexts currently configured on the Security Appliance.

Step-by-Step Configuration of a Security Context

To help with the initial configuration of multiple contexts, this section runs through a step-by-step configuration of a Cisco ASA 5510. This configuration will feature three contexts for the executive staff, sales staff, and IT staff on an enterprise site. This is a new firewall and does not contain a configuration. The Security Appliance will require basic configurations in addition to context-specific settings:

Step 1 Enable multiple context mode on the ASA 5510:

```
hostname(config)# mode multiple
```

Step 2 Configure the basic system setting for the firewall through system configuration mode:

```
hostname(config)# hostname ASAfirewall1
ASAfirewall1(config)# password m#p0(U-j3df
ASAfirewall1(config)# enable password F8ru3#49fjwC%1
```

Step 3 The enterprise LAN uses six different VLANS to segment the network. These virtual interfaces must be created and enabled before creating and configuring a context:

```
ASAfirewall1(config)# interface gigabitethernet 0/0.3
ASAfirewall1(config-if)# vlan 3
ASAfirewall1(config-if)# no shutdown
ASAfirewall1(config-if)# interface gigabitethernet 0/1
ASAfirewall1(config-if)# no shutdown
ASAfirewall1(config-if)# interface gigabitethernet 0/1.4
ASAfirewall1(config-if)# vlan 4
ASAfirewall1(config-if)# no shutdown
ASAfirewall1(config-if)# interface gigabitethernet 0/1.5
ASAfirewall1(config-if)# vlan 5
ASAfirewall1(config-if)# no shutdown
ASAfirewall1(config-if)# interface gigabitethernet 0/1.6
ASAfirewall1(config-if)# vlan 6
ASAfirewall1(config-if)# no shutdown
ASAfirewall1(config-if)# interface gigabitethernet 0/1.7
ASAfirewall1(config-if)# vlan 7
ASAfirewall1(config-if)# no shutdown
ASAfirewall1(config-if)# interface gigabitethernet 0/1.8
ASAfirewall1(config-if)# vlan 8
ASAfirewall1(config-if)# no shutdown
ASAfirewall1(config-if)# exit
ASAfirewall1(config)#
```

Step 4 Configure an administration context for the Security Appliance:

```
ASAfirewall1(config)# admin-context admin
```

Step 5 With the administration context created, assign interfaces to the context and configure a location to find the context configuration file. This requires the use of the context-configuration mode in the system area. This is different from the configuration mode within a context you changed to:

```
ASAfirewall1(config)# context admin
```

Step 6   Now that you are in the context configuration mode for the admin
context, assign the interfaces this context will be able to access:

```
ASAfirewall1(config-ctx)# allocate-interface gigabitethernet 0/0.3
ASAfirewall1(config-ctx)# allocate-interface gigabitethernet 0/1.4
```

Step 7   To complete the setup configuration of this context, specify the location
of the configuration file:

```
ASAfirewall1(config-ctx)# config-url disk0://admin.cfg
ASAfirewall1(config-ctx)# exit
ASAfirewall1(config)#
```

Step 8   The system configuration for the administration context is now
complete. You must create the other three contexts using the same
process:

```
ASAfirewall1(config)# context exec
ASAfirewall1(config-ctx)# allocate-interface gigabitethernet 0/0.3
ASAfirewall1(config-ctx)# allocate-interface gigabitethernet 0/1.4
ASAfirewall1(config-ctx)# config-url disk0://Exec.cfg
ASAfirewall1(config-ctx)# exit
ASAfirewall1(config)#
ASAfirewall1(config)# context sales
ASAfirewall1(config-ctx)# description This is the context for the Sales
  Offices
ASAfirewall1(config-ctx)# allocate-interface gigabitethernet 0/0.3
ASAfirewall1(config-ctx)# allocate-interface gigabitethernet 0/1.5
ASAfirewall1(config-ctx)# config-url disk0://Sales.cfg
ASAfirewall1(config-ctx)# exit
ASAfirewall1(config)#
ASAfirewall1(config)# context IT
ASAfirewall1(config-ctx)# description This is the context for the IT Offices
ASAfirewall1(config-ctx)# allocate-interface gigabitethernet 0/0.3
ASAfirewall1(config-ctx)# allocate-interface gigabitethernet 0/1.7-
  gigabitethernet 0/1.8
ASAfirewall1(config-ctx)# config-url disk0://IT.cfg
ASAfirewall1(config-ctx)# exit
ASAfirewall1(config)# exit
```

Step 9   All the contexts are now created, and interfaces are assigned to each
context. At this point, each context must be configured as a firewall.
Each context creates a separate execution space for routing, switching,
and so on. To configure these functions on a context, you must change
to the context. Start with the administration context:

```
ASAfirewall1# changeto admin
ASAfirewall1/admin#
```

Step 10 Now configure the admin context with the configurations used by
default throughout each context. Each context can override these
setting through commands in each separate context, if required:

```
ASAfirewall1/admin# configure terminal
ASAfirewall1/admin(config)# hostname Admin
ASAfirewall1/admin(config)# domain isp
ASAfirewall1/admin(config)# interface gigabitethernet 0/0.3
ASAfirewall1/admin(config-if)# nameif outside
ASAfirewall1/admin(config-if)# security-level 0
ASAfirewall1/admin(config-if)# ip address 209.165.201.2 255.255.255.224
ASAfirewall1/admin(config-if)# no shutdown
ASAfirewall1/admin(config-if)# exit
ASAfirewall1/admin(config)# interface gigabitethernet 0/1.4
ASAfirewall1/admin(config-if)# nameif inside
ASAfirewall1/admin(config-if)# security-level 100
ASAfirewall1/admin(config-if)# ip address 10.1.1.1 255.255.255.0
ASAfirewall1/admin(config-if)# no shutdown
ASAfirewall1/admin(config-if)# exit
ASAfirewall1/admin(config)# enable password 9Ij97^%fyc@4syCI
ASAfirewall1/admin(config)# route outside 0 0 209.165.201.1 1
ASAfirewall1/admin(config)# ssh 10.1.1.75 255.255.255.255 inside
ASAfirewall1/admin(config)# nat (inside) 1 10.1.1.0 255.255.255.0
ASAfirewall1/admin(config)# global (outside) 1 209.165.201.10-209.165.201.29
ASAfirewall1/admin(config)# static (inside,outside) 209.165.201.30 10.1.1.75
  netmask 255.255.255.255
ASAfirewall1/admin(config)# exit
```

Step 11 Now configure the executive context. First, change to the exec context:

```
ASAfirewall1/admin# changeto exec
ASAfirewall1/exec#
```

Step 12 Now you can enter all the firewall settings for the exec context. This is
identical to the commands you would use if this were a single-context
firewall:

```
ASAfirewall1/exec# configure terminal
ASAfirewall1/exec(config)# interface gigabitethernet 0/0.3
ASAfirewall1/exec(config-if)# nameif outside
ASAfirewall1/exec(config-if)# security-level 0
ASAfirewall1/exec(config-if)# ip address 209.165.201.3 255.255.255.224
ASAfirewall1/exec(config-if)# no shutdown
ASAfirewall1/exec(config-if)# exit
ASAfirewall1/exec(config)# interface gigabitethernet 0/1.5
ASAfirewall1/exec(config-if)# nameif inside
ASAfirewall1/exec(config-if)# security-level 100
```

```
ASAfirewall1/exec(config-if)# ip address 10.1.2.1 255.255.255.0
ASAfirewall1/exec(config-if)# no shutdown
ASAfirewall1/exec(config-if)# exit
ASAfirewall1/exec(config)# passwd j)Y765fuf$3SD45
ASAfirewall1/exec(config)# enable password *7hoh^r5fd$s543
ASAfirewall1/exec(config)# route outside 0 0 209.165.201.1 1
ASAfirewall1/exec(config)# route inside 192.168.1.0 255.255.255.0 10.1.2.2 1
ASAfirewall1/exec(config)# nat (inside) 1 10.1.2.0 255.255.255.0
ASAfirewall1/exec(config)# global (outside) 1 interface
ASAfirewall1/exec(config)# exit
```

Step 13 The sales context must be configured next. First, change to the sales context:

```
ASAfirewall1/exec# changeto sales
ASAfirewall1/sales#
```

Step 14 Now add the configuration for the sales context:

```
ASAfirewall1/sales# configure terminal
ASAfirewall1/sales(config)# interface gigabitethernet 0/0.3
ASAfirewall1/sales(config-if)# nameif outside
ASAfirewall1/sales(config-if)# security-level 0
ASAfirewall1/sales(config-if)# ip address 209.165.201.4 255.255.255.224
ASAfirewall1/sales(config-if)# no shutdown
ASAfirewall1/sales(config-if)# exit
ASAfirewall1/sales(config)# interface gigabitethernet 0/1.6
ASAfirewall1/sales(config-if)# nameif inside
ASAfirewall1/sales(config-if)# security-level 100
ASAfirewall1/sales(config-if)# ip address 10.1.3.1 255.255.255.0
ASAfirewall1/sales(config-if)# no shutdown
ASAfirewall1/sales(config-if)# exit
ASAfirewall1/sales(config)# passwd %&R7fi68)h08ji
ASAfirewall1/sales(config)# enable password #d)uj;1M987tFG
ASAfirewall1/sales(config)# route outside 0 0 209.165.201.1 1
ASAfirewall1/sales(config)# nat (inside) 1 10.1.3.0 255.255.255.0
ASAfirewall1/sales(config)# global (outside) 1 209.165.201.9 netmask
  255.255.255.255
ASAfirewall1/sales(config)# access-list INTERNET extended permit tcp any any
  eq http
ASAfirewall1/sales(config)# access-list INTERNET extended permit tcp any any
  eq https
ASAfirewall1/sales(config)# exit
```

Step 15 Last, configure the IT context. First, change to the IT context:

```
ASAfirewall1/sales# changeto IT
ASAfirewall1/IT#
```

Step 16   Now input all the configurations for the IT context to complete the
Security Appliance configuration:

```
ASAfirewall1/IT# configure terminal
ASAfirewall1/IT(config)# interface gigabitethernet 0/0.3
ASAfirewall1/IT(config-if)# nameif outside
ASAfirewall1/IT(config-if)# security-level 0
ASAfirewall1/IT(config-if)# ip address 209.165.201.5 255.255.255.224
ASAfirewall1/IT(config-if)# no shutdown
ASAfirewall1/IT(config-if)# exit
ASAfirewall1/IT(config)# interface gigabitethernet 0/1.7
ASAfirewall1/IT(config-if)# nameif inside
ASAfirewall1/IT(config-if)# security-level 100
ASAfirewall1/IT(config-if)# ip address 10.1.4.1 255.255.255.0
ASAfirewall1/IT(config-if)# no shutdown
ASAfirewall1/IT(config-if)# exit
ASAfirewall1/IT(config)# interface gigabitethernet 0/1.8
ASAfirewall1/IT(config-if)# nameif dmz
ASAfirewall1/IT(config-if)# security-level 50
ASAfirewall1/IT(config-if)# ip address 192.168.2.1 255.255.255.0
ASAfirewall1/IT(config-if)# no shutdown
ASAfirewall1/IT(config-if)# exit
ASAfirewall1/IT(config)# passwd h&58ouf%$e6H&T
ASAfirewall1/IT(config)# enable password h79g7G7f^$8-0ji
ASAfirewall1/IT(config)# route outside 0 0 209.165.201.1 1
ASAfirewall1/IT(config)# url-server (dmz) vendor websense host 192.168.2.2
  url-block block 50
ASAfirewall1/IT(config)# url-cache dst 128
ASAfirewall1/IT(config)# filter url http 10.1.4.0 255.255.255.0 0 0
ASAfirewall1/IT(config)# nat (inside) 1 10.1.4.0 255.255.255.0
ASAfirewall1/IT(config)# global (outside) 1 209.165.201.9 netmask
  255.255.255.255
ASAfirewall1/IT(config)# static (dmz,outside) 209.165.201.6 192.168.2.2
  netmask 255.255.255.255
ASAfirewall1/IT(config)# access-list MANAGE extended permit tcp host
  209.165.201.30 host 209.165.201.6 eq pcanywhere-data
ASAfirewall1/IT(config)# access-list MANAGE extended permit udp host
  209.165.201.30 host 209.165.201.6 eq pcanywhere-status
ASAfirewall1/IT(config)# access-group MANAGE in interface outside
ASAfirewall1/IT(config)# exit
```

Step 17   At this point, the Security Appliance should be fully configured for
multiple contexts, with each context configured to support each virtual
firewall's needs.

Foundation Summary

The "Foundation Summary" provides a convenient review of many key concepts in this chapter. If you are already comfortable with the topics in this chapter, this summary can help you recall a few details. If you have just read this chapter, this review should help solidify some key facts. If you are doing your final preparation before the exam, this summary provides a convenient way to review the day before the exam.

Secure Firewall software version 7.0 and later support the use of multiple contexts within a single Security Appliance. This allows a security administrator access to security contexts that act like individual virtual firewalls, with their own policies, interfaces, and user access. To enable multiple security contexts, use the **mode multiple** command in global configuration mode.

Security contexts are commonly used in the following scenarios:

■ A large enterprise company or campus with a requirement to completely separate each department.

■ An enterprise requires unique security policies for each department.

■ An ISP wishes to sell security and firewall services to multiple companies.

■ A network requires more then one firewall.

Traffic is routed to each context based on how the packets within the traffic flow are classified. The two characteristics that the Security Appliance checks for are these:

■ Source interface (VLAN)

■ Destination address

Each context must be created in the global configuration mode using the **context** command. The Security Appliance uses an administrative context that handles the system's network interfaces and settings. This context is called the *admin context*, and it can be any regular context.

The configuration of a context has two parts:

■ The system configuration of the context

■ The context configuration file that holds the firewall options for the context, such as policies and access control lists(ACL)

The system configuration of a context defines the interfaces that will be assigned to the context, including any mapped name aliases assigned to these interfaces. To allocate one or more interfaces to a context, use the **allocate-interface** command. This command can include a single interface ID or a range of IDs.

Additionally, the system configuration of the context defines the location of the configuration file, which can be located locally or on a remote system.

The configuration file can be stored in several locations:

- **Disk0/flash**—Security Appliance's Flash filesystem
- **disk1**—Security Appliance's compact Flash
- **tftp**—TFTP server
- **ftp**—FTP server
- **http(s)**—WebServer (read only)

The admin context must be stored in the local Flash memory.

Q&A

As mentioned in the Introduction, the questions in this book are more difficult than what you should experience on the exam. The questions are designed to ensure your understanding of the concepts discussed in this chapter and to adequately prepare you to complete the exam. You should use the simulated exams on the CD to practice for the exam.

The answers to these questions can be found in Appendix A:

1. What are the two methods used to direct traffic flows to a security context?

2. Using Figure 9-2, configure the security contexts for PIXFW1. Assume that Context1 to Context3 store their configuration files on the web server configs.cisco.com in the directory /configlets using the username PIXCONFIG and password CISCO123. Context2 stores its configuration on the Flash drive. All nonadministrative contexts use the naming scheme context[x].cfg.

Figure 9-2 *Sample Security Context Network*

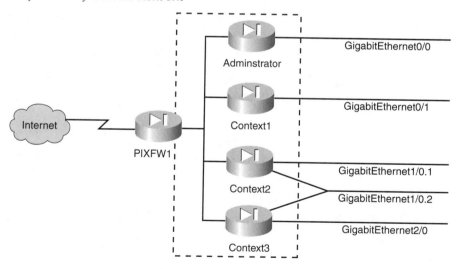

3. How do you enable multiple security contexts?

4. What are the interface limitations of a security context when the firewall is in transparent mode?

5. What happens to the configuration files when multiple context mode is enabled?

6. What are the potential problems when you change the **config-url** setting for a context that is live?

7. What are the limitations of the **allocate-interface** command?

8. What does clear configure context do?

This chapter covers the following subjects:

- Understanding How Syslog Works

- Configuring Syslog on the Cisco Security Appliance

- Configuring the Adaptive Security Device Manager to View Logging

Syslog and the Cisco Security Appliance

System logging, otherwise known as *syslog*, on the Cisco Security Appliance makes it possible for you as an administrator to gather information about the Security Appliance unit's traffic and performance. You can use syslog messages generated by a Security Appliance to troubleshoot and analyze suspicious activity on the network.

This chapter describes how to configure syslog on the Cisco Security Appliance and interpret the messages it generates.

How to Best Use This Chapter

Monitoring and logging the traffic on your network is an important step in monitoring the health of your network and identifying attacks against your network. Syslog messages provide valuable information concerning the health of your Security Appliance. These messages can also indicate attacks that are being launched against your network. Understanding the meaning and severity of various syslog messages is the first step toward using these messages to actively monitor the operation of your network. Test yourself with the "Do I Know This Already?" quiz and see how familiar you are with the syslog functionality available on Cisco Security Appliances.

"Do I Know This Already?" Quiz

The purpose of the "Do I Know This Already?" quiz is to help you decide if you really need to read the entire chapter. If you already intend to read the entire chapter, you do not necessarily need to answer these questions now.

The nine-question quiz, derived from the major sections in the "Foundation Topics" portion of the chapter, helps you determine how to spend your limited study time.

Table 10-1 outlines the major topics discussed in this chapter and the "Do I Know This Already?" quiz questions that correspond to those topics.

Table 10-1 *"Do I Know This Already?" Foundation Topics Section-to-Question Mapping*

Foundation Topics Section	Questions Covered in This Section	Score
How Syslog Works	2 to 5, 7, 8	
Configuring Syslog on the Cisco Security Appliance	6	
Configuring the Adaptive Security Device Manager to View Logging	1, 9	

CAUTION The goal of self assessment is to gauge your mastery of the topics in this chapter. If you do not know the answer to a question or are only partially sure of the answer, you should mark this question wrong for purposes of the self assessment. Giving yourself credit for an answer you correctly guess skews your self-assessment results and might provide you with a false sense of security.

1. What is the command for sending syslog messages to the Telnet session?

    a. logging console

    b. logging monitor

    c. telnet logging

    d. send log telnet

2. Which of the following is the correct command syntax to set the logging level to 5 for syslog message 403503?

    a. logging message 403503 level 5

    b. logging 403503 5

    c. logging message 403503 5

    d. logging 403503 level 5

3. A Cisco Security Appliance can be configured to send syslog messages to all of the following except which one?

    a. Console

    b. Telnet session

    c. Serial port

    d. Syslog server

4. Which of the following is *not* an example of a severity level for syslog configuration?

    a. Emergency

    b. Alert

    c. Prepare

    d. Warning

5. What is syslogd?

    a. A message type that forms the syslog services

    b. A service that runs on UNIX machines

    c. A hardware subcomponent that is required for syslog configuration on a PIX

    d. Cisco application software

6. Which port does syslogd use by default?

    a. UDP 512

    b. TCP 514

    c. TCP 512

    d. UDP 514

7. Which of the following logging severity levels are matched up correctly?

    a. Error → 4

    b. Alert → 2

    c. Warning → 4

    d. Notification → 1

8. Which of the following is the highest-importance logging level?

    a. 9

    b. 7

    c. 0

    d. 3

9. By using which command could you view the logging setting from the command line?

    a. show log setting

    b. show logging

    c. show syslog

    d. view log

The answers to the "Do I Know This Already?" quiz are found in Appendix A, "Answers to the 'Do I Know This Already?' Quizzes and Q&A Sections." The suggested choices for your next step are as follows:

- **7 or less overall score**—Read the entire chapter. This includes the "Foundation Topics," "Foundation Summary," and "Q&A" sections.

- **8 or 9 overall score**—If you want more review of these topics, skip to the "Foundation Summary" section and then go to the "Q&A" section. Otherwise, move to the next chapter.

Foundation Topics

How Syslog Works

The syslog message facility in a Cisco Security Appliance is a useful means to view troubleshooting messages and to watch for network events such as attacks and denials of service. The Cisco Security Appliance reports on events and activities using syslog messages, which report on the following:

- **System status**—When the Cisco Security Appliance reboots or a connection by Telnet or the console is made or disconnected

- **Accounting**—The number of bytes transferred per connection

- **Security**—Dropped User Datagram Protocol (UDP) packets and denied Transmission Control Protocol (TCP) connections

- **Resources**—Notification of connection and translation slot depletion

It is important to become familiar with the logging process and logging command parameters on a Security Appliance before you dive in and start configuring the Cisco Security Appliance for logging. Syslog messages can be sent to several different output destinations on or off the Security Appliance unit:

- **ASDM logging**—Logging messages can be sent to the Adaptive Security Device Manager (ASDM).

- **Console**—Syslog messages can be configured to be sent to the console interface, where the security administrator (you) can view the messages in real time as they happen when you are connected to the console interface.

- **Internal memory buffer**—Syslog messages can be sent to the buffer.

- **Telnet console**—Syslog messages also can be configured to be sent to Telnet sessions. This configuration helps you remotely administer and troubleshoot Security Appliance units without being physically present at the location of the firewall.

- **Syslog servers**—This type of configuration is particularly useful for storing syslog messages for analysis on performance, trends, and packet activities on the Security Appliance unit. Syslog messages are sent to UNIX servers/workstations running a syslog daemon or to Windows servers running PIX Firewall Syslog Server (PFSS).

- **SNMP management station**—Syslog traps can be configured to be sent to an SNMP management station.

After you decide where to send the syslog messages, you have to decide what type of messages you want to see at the output destination.

All syslog messages have a severity level; however, not all syslog messages are required to have a facility.

Logging Facilities

When syslog messages are sent to a server, it is important to indicate through which *pipe* the Security Appliance will send the messages. The single syslog service, syslogd, can be thought of as having multiple pipes. It uses the pipes to decide where to send incoming information based on the pipe through which the information arrives. Syslogd is a daemon/service that runs on UNIX machines. In this analogy, the *logging facilities* are the pipes by which syslogd decides *where* to send information it receives—that is, to which file to write.

Eight logging facilities (16 through 23) are commonly used for syslog on the Cisco Security Appliance. On the syslog server, the facility numbers have a corresponding identification—local0 to local7. The following are the facility numbers and their corresponding syslog identification:

- local0 (16)
- local1 (17)
- local2 (18)
- local3 (19)
- local4 (20)
- local5 (21)
- local6 (22)
- local7 (23)

The default facility is local4 (20). To change the default logging facility on the Security Appliance, you use the **logging facility** *facility* command. The following command shows the logging facility changed to 21:

```
Pix(config)# logging facility 21
```

Logging Levels

Different *severity levels* are attached to incoming messages. You can think of these levels as indicating the type of message. A Security Appliance can be configured to send messages at different levels. Table 10-2 lists these levels from highest to lowest importance.

Table 10-2 *Logging Severity Levels*

Level/Keyword	Numeric Code	System Condition
Emergency	0	System unusable message
Alert	1	Take immediate action
Critical	2	Critical condition
Error	3	Error message
Warning	4	Warning message
Notification	5	Normal but significant condition
Informational	6	Information message
Debug	7	Debug message, log FTP commands, and WWW URLs

Many of the **logging** commands require that you specify a severity level threshold to indicate which syslog messages can be sent to the output locations. The lower the level number, the more severe the syslog message. The default severity level is 3 (error). During configuration, you can specify the severity level as either a number or a keyword, as described in Table 10-2. The level you specify causes the Cisco Security Appliance Firewall to send the messages of that level and below to the output location. For example, if you specify severity level 3 (error), a Security Appliance, such as the PIX, sends severity level 0 (emergency), 1 (alert), 2 (critical), and 3 (error) messages to the output location.

Changing Syslog Message Levels

PIX Firewall version 6.3 gives you the option to modify the level at which a specific syslog message is issued and to disable specific syslog messages. This feature provides you with more flexibility because you can specify which message you are logging and at what level. To change the logging level for all syslog servers, enter the following command syntax:

```
logging message syslog_id [level levelid]
```

To change the level of a specific syslog message, enter the following command syntax:

```
logging message syslog_id level levelid
```

The variables *syslog_id* and *levelid* represent the numeric identifier and severity level assigned to the syslog message, respectively, as shown in Table 10-2.

Example 10-1 shows how you can view the level of a syslog message and display its current and default levels:

Example 10-1   *Changing the Level of a Syslog Message*

```
pixfirewall(config)#n
syslog 403503: default-level errors (enabled)
rpixfirewall(config)#logging message 403503 level 6
pixfirewall(config)#show logging message 403503
syslog 403503: default-level errors, current-level informational (enabled)
```

To disable a particular syslog message, enter the following command:

```
no logging message messageid
```

How Log Messages Are Organized

Syslog messages are listed numerically by message code. Each message is followed by a brief explanation and a recommended action. If several messages share the same explanation and recommended action, the messages are presented together, followed by the common explanation and recommended action.

The explanation of each message indicates what kind of event generated the message. Possible events include the following:

- Authentication, authorization, and accounting (AAA) events
- Connection events (for example, connections denied by the PIX configuration or address translation errors)
- Failover events reported by one or both units of a failover pair
- File Transfer Protocol (FTP)/Uniform Resource Locator (URL) events (for example, successful file transfers or blocked Java applets)
- Mail Guard/SNMP events
- Security Appliance management events (for example, configuration events or Telnet connections to the Security Appliance console port)
- Routing errors

How to Read System Log Messages

System log messages received at a syslog server begin with a percent sign (%) and are structured as follows:

```
%PIX-level-message-number: message-text
```

- **PIX** identifies the message facility code for messages generated by the Cisco Security Appliance.

- *level* reflects the severity of the condition described by the message. The lower the number, the more serious the condition.

- *message-number* is the numeric code that uniquely identifies the message.

- *message-text* is a text string describing the condition. This portion of the message sometimes includes IP addresses, port numbers, or usernames.

You can find more information on syslog messages at http://www.cisco.com/en/US/products/sw/secursw/ps2120/products_system_message_guide_book09186a00801582a9.html.

Configuring Syslog on a Cisco Security Appliance

The **logging** command is used to configure logging on the PIX Firewall. Logging is disabled by default. Table 10-3 describes the parameters of the **logging** command.

Table 10-3   **logging** *Command Parameters*

Command	Description
logging on	Enables the transmission of syslog messages to all output locations. You can disable sending syslog messages with the **no logging on** command.
no logging message *n*	Allows you to disable specific syslog messages. Use the **logging message** *message_number* command to resume logging of specific disabled messages.
logging buffered *n*	Stores syslog messages in the Cisco Security Appliance so that you can view them with the **show logging** command. Cisco Systems recommends that you use this command to view syslog messages when the PIX Seecurity Appliance is in use on a network.
clear logging	Clears the message buffer created with the **logging buffered** command.
clear logging message	Reenables all disabled syslog messages.
logging console *n*	Displays syslog messages on a Security Appliance console as they occur. Use this command when you are debugging problems or when there is minimal load on the network. Do not use this command when the network is busy because it can reduce the Security Appliance performance.
logging monitor *n*	Displays syslog messages when you access the Security Appliance console with Telnet.

continues

Table 10-3 logging *Command Parameters (Continued)*

Command	Description
loggin device -id *n*	Sets the device ID that will be logged with a syslog message.
logging host [*interface*] *ip_address*	Specifies the host that receives the syslog messages.
[*protocol/ port*]	A Cisco Security Appliance can send messages across UDP or TCP (which you specify by setting the *protocol* variable). The default UDP port is 514. The default TCP port is 1470.
logging history *severity_level*	Sets the logging level for SNMP traps.
logging queue *msg_count*	Specifies how many syslog messages can appear in the message queue while waiting for processing. The default is 512 messages. Use the **show logging queue** command to view queue statistics.
logging timestamp	Specifies that each message sent to the syslog server should include a timestamp to indicate when the event occurred.
logging trap *n*	Sets the logging level for syslog messages.
show logging disabled	Displays a complete list of disabled syslog messages.
show logging	Lists the current syslog messages and which **logging** command options are enabled.
logging standby	Lets the failover standby unit send syslog messages.

Configuring the ASDM to View Logging

The ASDM Log panel, shown in Figure 10-1, allows you to view syslog messages that are captured in the ASDM Log buffer in the Security Appliance memory. You may select the level of syslog messages you want to view. When you view the ASDM Log, all the buffered syslog messages at and below the logging level you choose are displayed.

Figure 10-1 *ASDM Log Viewer Screen*

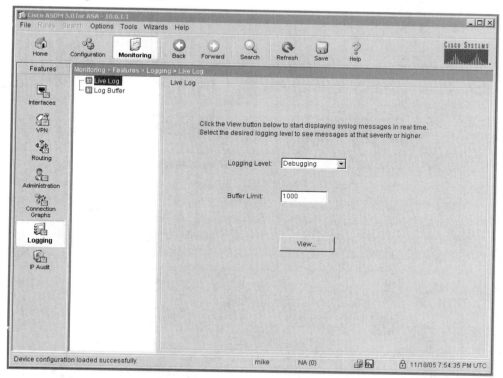

The ASDM logging panel has the following fields:

■ **Logging Level**—Enables you to choose the level of syslog messages to view.

To view the logs using the PDM interface, click the **View** button shown in Figure 10-1. Figure 10-2 shows a sample output of logs viewed from the PDM logging panel.

■ **Buffer Limit**—Sets the maximum number of log messages that will display. The default for this value is 1000.

Figure 10-2 *Sample ASDM Logging Output*

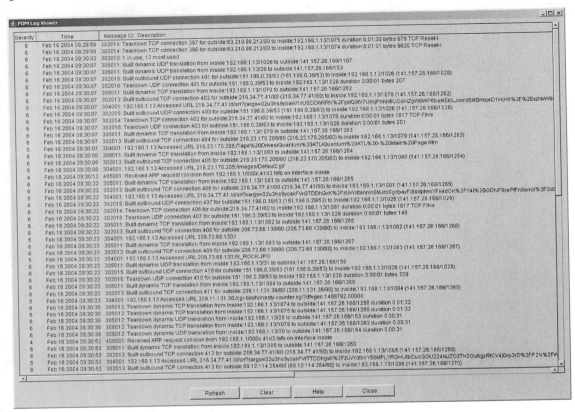

ASDM is discussed in further detail in Chapter 15, "Adaptive Security Device Manager."

Configuring Syslog Messages at the Console

Configuring logging on the console interface is useful when you are troubleshooting or observing traffic patterns directly from a Security Appliance. This gives you real-time information about what is happening on the Security Appliance. To configure logging at the Security Appliance console interface, use the **logging console** command as follows. After logging into configuration mode, enter the following:

```
Pixfw(config)#logging on
Pixfw(config)#logging console 5
```

The 5 indicates the logging level. In this case, it is logging notification. From the console, you can see the logs in real time.

Sending Syslog Messages to a Telnet Session

Remotely troubleshooting or viewing real-time Security Appliance traffic patterns can be done by configuring the PIX to send logging information to a Telnet session. The **logging monitor** command configures the Security Appliance to send syslog messages to Telnet sessions. For example, after logging into configuration mode, enter the following:

```
Pixfirewall (config)#logging monitor 6
Pixfirewall(config)#terminal monitor
```

In this example, syslog messages 0 to 6, or emergency to informational, are sent to a Telnet session. To disable logging to Telnet, you use the **no logging monitor** command.

The *terminal monitor* displays messages directly to the Telnet session. You can disable the direct display of messages by entering the **terminal no monitor** command. A Telnet session sometimes is lost in busy networks when the **logging monitor** command is used.

Configuring the Cisco Security Appliance to Send Syslog Messages to a Log Server

Configuring a Security Appliance to send logging information to a server helps you collect and maintain data that can later be used for forensic and data traffic analysis. The Security Appliance syslog messages are usually sent to a syslog server or servers. The Security Appliance uses UDP port 514 by default to send syslog messages to a syslog server. The syntax for configuring the Security Appliance Firewall to send syslog messages to a syslog server is as follows:

```
Pixfirewall(config)#Logging host [interface] ip_address [tcp[/port] |udp[/port]]
   [format emblem]
```

The variables *[interface]* and *ip-address* are replaced with the name of the interface on which the syslog resides and the Internet Protocol (IP) address of the syslog server, respectively. The Cisco Security Appliance supports the EMBLEM format. EMBLEM syslog format is designed to be consistent with the Cisco IOS Software format and is more compatible with CiscoWorks management applications, such as Resource Manager Essentials (RME) syslog analyzer. Use the option **format emblem** to send messages to the specified server in EMBLEM format.

> **NOTE**   This option is available only for UDP syslog messages, used by the RME syslog analyzer.

The following steps show you how to configure a Security Appliance to send syslog messages:

Step 1   Designate a host to receive the messages with the **logging host** command:

```
Pixfirewall(config)#logging host inside  10.1.1.10
```

You can specify additional servers so that if one goes offline, another is available to receive messages.

Step 2   Set the logging level with the **logging trap** command:

```
Pixfirewall(config)#logging trap informational
```

If needed, set the **logging facility** command to a value other than its default of 20. Most UNIX systems expect the messages to arrive at facility 20.

> **NOTE**   In the event that all syslog servers are offline, the Cisco Security Appliance stores up to 100 messages in its memory. Subsequent messages that arrive overwrite the buffer starting from the first line. PIX buffer logging is enabled by the command **logging buffered** *level*.

Step 3   Start sending messages with the **logging on** command. To disable sending messages, use the **no logging** command.

Step 4   To view your logging setting, enter **show logging**.

Centrally managing several Cisco Security Appliances can be challenging if you cannot identify the origin of a particular message that is sent to the central log server. The Security Appliance supports defining a unique device ID for log messages sent to a syslog server. If several Security Appliances are configured to send their syslog messages to a single syslog server, a unique identification can be configured so the message source can be identified. To enable this option, use the following command:

```
logging device-id {hostname | ipaddress if_name | string text}
```

Table 10-4 gives a description of the parameters of the **logging device-id** command.

Table 10-4 logging device-id *Command Parameters*

Parameter	Description
hostname	The name of the Security Appliance
ipaddress	Specifies to use the IP address of the specified Security Appliance interface to uniquely identify the syslog messages from the PIX Firewall
if-name	The name of the interface with the IP address that is used to uniquely identify the syslog messages from the Security Appliance
string text	Specifies the text string to uniquely identify the syslog messages from the Security Appliance

When this feature is enabled, the message will include the specified device ID (either the hostname or IP address of the specified interface—even if the message comes from another interface—or a string) in messages sent to a syslog server. The Cisco Security Appliance will insert the specified device ID into all non-EMBLEM-format syslog messages.

> **NOTE**   The device ID does not appear in EMBLEM-formatted messages, Simple Network Management Protocol (SNMP) traps, or on the firewall console, management session, or buffer. This command does not affect the syslog message text in EMBLEM format or its display on the Security Appliance console or in the log file.

To disable this feature, use the following command:

```
no logging device-id
```

Configuring SNMP Traps and SNMP Requests

SNMP requests can be used to query the Security Appliance on its system status information. If you want to send only the cold start, link up, and link down generic traps, no further configuration is required. SNMP traps send information about a particular event only when the configured threshold is reached.

To configure a Security Appliance to receive SNMP requests from a management station, you must do the following:

- Configure the IP address of the SNMP management station with the **snmp-server host** command.
- Set the **snmp-server** options for **location, contact,** and the **community** password as required.

To configure SNMP traps on the PIX, you must do the following:

- Configure the IP address of the SNMP management station with the **snmp-server host** command.
- Set the **snmp-server** options for **location, contact,** and the **community** password as required.
- Set the trap with the **snmp-server enable traps** command.
- Set the logging level with the **logging history** command.

Configuring a Syslogd Server

Because syslogd was originally a UNIX concept, the features available in the syslogd products on non-UNIX systems depend on the vendor implementation. Features might include dividing incoming messages by facility or debug level or both, resolving the names of the sending devices, and reporting facilities. For information on configuring the non-UNIX syslog server, refer to the vendor's documentation.

NOTE   Configuring the syslog server is not covered on the PIX CSPFA 642-522 exam.

To configure syslog on UNIX, follow these steps:

Step 1   On SunOS, AIX, HPUX, or Solaris, as root, make a backup of the /etc/syslog.conf file before modifying it.

Step 2   Modify /etc/syslog.conf to tell the UNIX system how to sort out the syslog messages coming in from the sending devices—that is, which *logging-facility.level* goes in which file. Make sure there is a tab between the *logging-facility.level* and *file-name*.

Step 3   Make sure the destination file exists and is writable.

Step 4   The **#Comment** section at the beginning of syslog.conf usually explains the syntax for the UNIX system.

Step 5   Do not put file information in the **ifdef** section.

Step 6   As root, restart syslogd to pick up changes.

For example, if /etc/syslog.conf is set for

```
local7.warn      /var/log/local7.warn
```

warning, error, critical, alert, and emergency messages coming in on the local7 logging facility are logged in the local7.warn file. Notification, informational, and debug messages coming in on the local7 facility are not logged anywhere.

If /etc/syslog.conf is set for

```
*.debug          /var/log/all.debug
```

all message levels from all logging facilities go to this file.

PIX Firewall Syslog Server

PIX Firewall Syslog Server (PFSS) lets you view PIX Firewall event information from a Windows NT system. It includes special features not found on other syslog servers:

- The ability to receive syslog messages by TCP or UDP
- Full reliability, because messages can be sent using TCP

PFSS can receive syslog messages from up to ten PIX units. You can install this product for use with any model of Cisco PIX Firewall. If you have specified that the PIX send syslog messages using TCP, the Windows NT disk might become full and the PIX unit stops its traffic. If the Windows NT file system is full, the Windows system beeps, and the PFSS disables all TCP connections from the PIX unit(s) by closing its TCP listen socket. The PIX tries to reconnect to the PFSS five times, and during the retry it stops all new connections through the PIX.

NOTE PFSS does not support the ASA Security Appliance.

Foundation Summary

The "Foundation Summary" provides a convenient review of many key concepts in this chapter. If you are already comfortable with the topics in this chapter, this summary can help you recall a few details. If you just read this chapter, this review should help solidify some key facts. If you are doing your final preparation before the exam, this summary provides a convenient way to review the day before the exam.

The syslog message facility in the Cisco Security Appliance is a useful means to view troubleshooting messages and to watch for network events such as attacks and service denials. Syslog messages can be configured to be sent to the following:

- ASDM log
- Console
- Telnet console
- Internal memory/buffer
- Syslog server
- SNMP management station

Common to all ways of viewing syslog messages is the message level, or severity. The level specifies the types of messages sent to the syslog host, as shown in Table 10-5.

Table 10-5 *Logging Severity Levels*

Level	Numeric Code	System Condition
Emergency	0	System unusable message
Alert	1	Take immediate action
Critical	2	Critical condition
Error	3	Error message
Warning	4	Warning message
Notification	5	Normal but significant condition
Informational	6	Information message
Debug	7	Debug message, log FTP commands, and WWW URLs

System log messages received at a syslog server begin with a percent sign (%) and are structured as follows:

```
%PIX-level-message_number: message_text
```

You can set the *level* with the **logging** command so that you can view syslog messages on the Security Appliance console, from a syslog server, or with SNMP.

Q&A

As mentioned in the Introduction, the questions in this book are more difficult than what you should experience on the exam. The questions are designed to ensure your understanding of the concepts discussed in this chapter and adequately prepare you to complete the exam. You should use the simulated exams on the CD to practice for the exam.

The answers to these questions can be found in Appendix A:

1. What command would you use to view logs that are in memory?

2. On which port does syslogd listen by default?

3. What is the total number of logging facilities available for Cisco Security Appliance syslog configuration?

4. What is the command for sending syslog messages to Telnet sessions?

5. For what is the **logging trap** command used?

6. What is the command used to enable logging on the failover Cisco Security Appliance unit?

7. Why would you use the *timestamp* command parameter?

8. What is PFSS?

This chapter covers the following subjects:

- Overview of General Routing Principles

- Overview of Cisco Security Appliance Routing Functionality

- Configuring Static Routes

- Configuring Dynamic Routes

- Configuring VLANs and VLAN Tagging

- Permitting Multicast Traffic

CHAPTER 11

Routing and the Cisco Security Appliance

Configuring your Cisco Security Appliance to forward traffic to other networks is crucial for the correct operation of your Security Appliance. Forwarding traffic to the next hop on its path toward its final destination is known as *routing*. Although the Security Appliance is not a router, it does provide sufficient routing features to effectively pass traffic through its interfaces. This functionality covers Ethernet VLAN tagging, static routes, dynamic routes, and even multicast traffic.

How to Best Use This Chapter

Protecting your network with a Cisco Security Appliance provides a strong perimeter defense, but for valid traffic to reach your protected network, you must understand how to configure routing on your Security Appliance. This can be as simple as defining a single static default route or as complex as configuring your Security Appliance to use the Open Shortest Path First (OSPF) routing protocol. The concepts in this chapter explain how to configure your Cisco Security Appliance to forward network traffic across your network. Test yourself with the "Do I Know This Already?" quiz, and see how familiar you are with the routing functionality available on Security Appliance.

"Do I Know This Already?" Quiz

The purpose of the "Do I Know This Already?" quiz is to help you decide if you really need to read the entire chapter. If you already intend to read the entire chapter, you do not necessarily need to answer these questions now.

The ten-question quiz, derived from the major sections in the "Foundation and Supplemental Topics" portion of the chapter, helps you determine how to spend your limited study time.

Table 11-1 outlines the major topics discussed in this chapter and the "Do I Know This Already?" quiz questions that correspond to those topics.

Table 11-1 *"Do I Know This Already?" Foundation Topics Section-to-Question Mapping*

Foundation Topics Section	Questions Covered in This Section	Score
Overview of Cisco Security Appliance Routing Functionality	1	
Configuring Static Routes	2	
Configuring Dynamic Routes	6, 9, 10	
Configuring VLANs and VLAN Tagging	4, 7, 8	
Permitting Multicast Traffic	3, 5	

CAUTION   The goal of self assessment is to gauge your mastery of the topics in this chapter. If you do not know the answer to a question or are only partially sure of the answer, you should mark this question wrong for purposes of the self assessment. Giving yourself credit for an answer you correctly guess skews your self-assessment results and might provide you with a false sense of security.

1. Which dynamic routing protocols are supported by the Cisco Security Appliance?

    a. RIP

    b. OSPF

    c. BGP

    d. EIGRP

2. Which command do you use to configure static routes?

    a. interface

    b. mroute

    c. route

    d. static

    e. None of these answers are correct

3. Which command do you use to configure the PIX Firewall to statically receive a multicast session?

    a. igmp forward

    b. igmp static

    c. multicast static

    d. igmp join-group

    e. None of these answers are correct

4. What type of Ethernet VLAN tagging does the PIX Firewall support?

   a. ISL

   b. 802.1x

   c. 802.1q

   d. 802.3

   e. None of these answers are correct

5. IP multicasting is a technique that

   a. Consumes more network bandwidth by sending IP traffic to multiple hosts on the network.

   b. Enables the PIX Firewall to communicate with multiple hosts on the network.

   c. Sends traffic to specific Class C IP addresses.

   d. Sends traffic to specific Class D IP addresses, thus enabling multiple recipients to receive the same traffic stream.

   e. None of these answers are correct.

6. Which of the following is true with respect to Cisco Security Appliance RIP support?

   a. RIP routing updates cannot be propagated by a Security Appliance.

   b. A Security Appliance can advertise a default route.

   c. Authentication is supported only for RIP version 2.

   d. RIP version 1 supports classless addressing on a Security Appliance.

   e. None of these answers are correct.

7. Which Cisco Security Appliance command do you use to create logical interfaces?

   a. interface

   b. nameif

   c. logical

   d. static

   e. None of these answers are correct

8. Which Security Appliance command enables you to configure the security level for logical interfaces?

    a. static

    b. interface

    c. nameif

    d. logical

    e. None of these answers are correct

9. Which OSPF subcommand defines which Type 3 LSA traffic to filter?

    a. network

    b. area

    c. router ospf

    d. prefix-list

    e. access-list

10. PIX Firewall can propagate which types of routes?

    a. BGP

    b. OSPF

    c. RIP

    d. Static

    e. None of these answers are correct

The answers to the "Do I Know This Already?" quiz are found in Appendix A, "Answers to the 'Do I Know This Already?' Quizzes and Q&A Sections." The suggested choices for your next step are as follows:

- **8 or less overall score**—Read the entire chapter. This includes the "Foundation and Supplemental Topics," "Foundation Summary," and "Q&A" sections.

- **9 or 10 overall score**—If you want more review on these topics, skip to the "Foundation Summary" section and then go to the "Q&A" section. Otherwise, move to the next chapter.

Foundation and Supplemental Topics

General Routing Principles

Although your Cisco Security Appliance is not a router, it does need to provide certain routing and switching functionality. Whenever your Security Appliance processes valid traffic, it must determine which interface provides the correct path for the destination network. It may also have to tag the traffic for the appropriate Virtual LAN (VLAN). Not only can your Security Appliance route valid traffic, you can also configure it to forward multicast traffic. Sending multicast traffic to a multicast broadcast address enables multiple systems to receive a data stream that otherwise would have to be sent to each individual system.

This chapter focuses on the following three features that enable your Cisco Security Appliance to effectively route and switch traffic:

- Ethernet VLAN tagging
- IP routing
- Multicast routing

Ethernet VLAN Tagging

To pass traffic between the different VLANs on your switched network, Ethernet packets can be tagged with a VLAN identifier that indicates the VLAN to which the traffic belongs. Ethernet tagging enables you to pass traffic for different VLANs across the same Layer 2 interface. The following sections explain how to use Ethernet VLAN tagging with your Cisco Security Appliance.

Understanding VLANs

At the Ethernet layer, you can partition your network using VLANs. These VLANs limit the scope of broadcast traffic on your network because each VLAN represents an individual broadcast domain. By dividing your switched network using VLANs, you improve the security of your network by limiting the scope of broadcast traffic that is vital for the operation of your network, such as Address Resolution Protocol (ARP) traffic and Dynamic Host Configuration Protocol (DHCP) traffic.

Understanding Trunk Ports

Usually, you configure a switch as a member of a specific VLAN. This automatically associates all of the regular Ethernet traffic received on that port with that VLAN. Sometimes, however, you may want a single port to receive traffic from multiple VLANs. A switch port that accepts traffic from multiple VLANs is known as a *trunk port*.

To differentiate between the different VLANs, each packet is tagged with a specific VLAN identifier. This identifier informs the switch to which VLAN the traffic needs to be forwarded. By using trunk lines on your switch, your Security Appliance can send and receive traffic from multiple VLANs using only a single physical interface.

Understanding Logical Interfaces

Your Security Appliance has a limited number of physical interfaces. This limits the number of Layer 3 networks to which the Security Appliance can be directly connected. If you use VLANs to segment your network into smaller broadcast domains, each of these VLANs represents a different Layer 3 network. By using logical interfaces, you can accommodate multiple VLANs by using trunk lines on your switch ports and configuring multiple logical interfaces on a single physical interface on your Security Appliance. Logical interfaces overcome the physical interface limitation by enabling a single physical interface to handle multiple logical interfaces.

Table 11-2 shows the maximum number of interfaces allowed using a PIX Firewall restricted license, while Table 11-3 shows the maximum number of interfaces allowed for a PIX Firewall unrestricted license.

Table 11-4 shows the maximum number of interfaces allowed using an ASA Security Appliance base license, while Table 11-5 shows the maximum number of interfaces allowed for an ASA Security Appliance Security Plus license.

Table 11-2 *Maximum Interfaces for Restricted License*

Cisco Secure PIX Model	Total Interfaces	Physical Interfaces	Logical Interfaces
515E	5	3	10
525	8	6	25
535	10	8	50

NOTE VLANs are not supported on the PIX 501. The PIX 506/506E support 802.1q trunking with the introduction of PIX OS 6.3.4.

Table 11-3 *Maximum Interfaces for Unrestricted License*

Cisco Secure PIX Model	Total Interfaces	Physical Interfaces	Logical Interfaces
501	2	2	Not supported
506E	2	2	Not supported
515E	10	6	25
525	12	8	100
535	24	10	150

Table 11-4 *Maximum Interfaces for ASA Security Appliances Base License*

Cisco ASA Security Model	Physical Interfaces	Logical Interfaces
5510	5	0
5520	5	25
5540	5	100

Table 11-5 *Maximum Interfaces for ASA Security Appliances Security Plus*

Cisco ASA Security Model	Physical Interfaces	Logical Interfaces
5510	5	10
5520	5	25
5540	5	100

NOTE The maximum number of logical interfaces that you can use is equal to the total number of interfaces available minus the total number of physical interfaces that you currently have configured on your PIX Firewall.

Unique VLAN tags differentiate the traffic to each logical interface. Currently, a Cisco Security Appliance supports configuring multiple 802.1Q VLANs on a physical port and the ability to send and receive 802.1Q tagged packets. The Security Appliance does not perform any trunk negotiations or participate in bridging protocols.

To create a logical interface on the Security Appliance, you use the subinterface argument of the **interface** command, the syntax for which is as follows:

```
interface {hardware-id [.suninterface-num] | mapped-name} [shutdown]
```

The parameters for the **interface** command are shown in Table 11-6.

Table 11-6 interface *Command Parameters*

Parameter	Description
hardware-id	Specifies the network interface on which the command will be applied (such as Ethernet0).
subinterface-num	The subinterface identifier that will be assigned for this logical interface, which can be between 1 and 4,294,967,293.
mapped-name	In multiple-context mode, enter the mapped name if it was assigned using the **allocate-interface** command.
shutdown	Keyword indicating that the interface should be administratively shut down.

After you have created a subinterface on the physical interface, the subinterface must be assigned to a VLAN. Use the VLAN command while in the subinterface to assign that subinterface to a specific VLAN, the syntax for which is as follows:

```
vlan [vlan-id]
```

The *vlan-id* parameter for the **vlan** command specifies the VLAN identifier to be associated with either the network or the logical interface.

Suppose that interface Ethernet0 on your Security Appliance, such as an ASA 5520, is connected to an enterprise LAN and that you want to configure three logical interfaces on that same physical interface for VLAN 40 through VLAN 42. The commands to accomplish this are as follow:

```
pix515a(config)# interface  Ethernet0.1
pix515a(config-subif)# vlan 40
pix515a(config)# interface Ethernet0.2
pix515a(config-subif)# vlan 41
pix515a(config)# interface Ethernet0.3
pix515a(config-subif)# vlan 42
```

NOTE You do not need to assign a VLAN to the physical interface to assign logical interfaces to an interface.

Managing VLANs

After you create your logical interfaces, you also need to assign the following parameters to each logical interface:

- Interface name
- Security level
- IP address

Using the **nameif** interface command, you can assign an interface name to a logical interface. The syntax for the **nameif** command is as follows:

```
nameif    interface-name
```

The *interface-name* parameter for the **nameif** command is the name to be assigned to the specified interface.

Using the **security-level** interface command, you can assign a security level to a logical interface. The syntax for the security-level command is as follows:

```
security-level security-level
```

The *security-level* parameter is the security level for the specified interface in the range from 0 to 100, with 0 being the least trusted interface and 100 being the most trusted interface.

Finally, you need to complete your logical interface configuration by assigning an IP address to the logical interface. To assign an IP address to an interface, you use the **ip address** command. The syntax for this command is as follows:

```
ip address ip-address
```

IP Routing

At the IP layer, your Cisco Security Appliance routes traffic based on the IP addresses in the network traffic. It does not provide all the functionality of a router, but it does enable you to define the following two types of routes:

- Static routes
- Dynamic routes

Static Routes

Static routes are manually configured routes that do not frequently change. They essentially direct your Security Appliance to send traffic destined for a specific network to a specific router that has connectivity to the destination network. Static routes are perhaps best explained by using a network example. Figure 11-1 illustrates a simple network configuration with hosts on both the 10.10.10.0 and 10.10.20.0 networks.

Figure 11-1 *Static Routes*

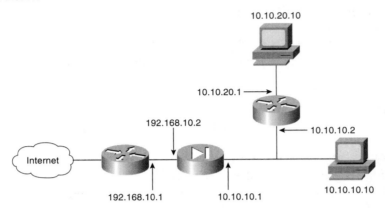

When you configure the inside interface on the Security Appliance with a Class C address of 10.10.10.1, the Security Appliance automatically creates a route that enables it to send traffic for the 10.10.10.0 network to the inside interface (identified by the keyword CONNECT when viewing the routes). The Security Appliance may also receive traffic for the host whose IP address is 10.10.20.10. By default, if the Security Appliance receives traffic for 10.10.20.10, it will not know where to send it. To enable the Security Appliance to know where to send traffic for 10.10.20.10, you can configure a static route using the **route** command. The syntax for the **route** command is as follows:

```
route interface-name ip-netmask gateway [metric]
```

The parameters for the **route** command are explained in Table 11-7. Using the network in Figure 11-1, you can define a static route for the 10.10.20.0 network using the following command:

```
pix515a(config)# route inside 10.10.20.0 255.255.255.0 10.10.10.2 1
```

Table 11-7 **route** *Command Parameters*

Parameter	Description
interface-name	The name of the interface on the Security Appliance through which the traffic will travel to reach the destination network (the name assigned in the **nameif** command).
ip-address	The IP address(es) of the traffic to which the route pertains.
netmask	The network mask of the route, which indicates the number of addresses covered by the route. (For example, a Class C network pertains to 256 different addresses and is specified as 255.255.255.0.)

Table 11-7 route *Command Parameters (Continued)*

Parameter	Description
gateway	The IP address of the gateway to which the routed traffic will be sent.
metric	The administrative distance of the route. Normally, this indicates the number of hops to the destination network. When routing, this value is used to choose the best route when multiple routes exist.

There might be times where you will want a secondary, or redundant, path for a specific route on the network. This can be achieved though dynamic routing protocols such as OSPF or Routing Information Protocol (RIP). The routes learned through these means will cause the Security Appliance to load balance the route paths for all traffic flows by default. If you are not using dynamic routing protocols, you can still achieve redundancy through the use of static routes. Static routes are considered highly preferred routes in the routing table, and they will usually be preferred over dynamically learned routes. A redundant static route must be seen as a less preferred route in the routing table. This can be achieved through the use of administrative distance. Static routes, by default, have an administrative distance of 1. By applying the correct administrative distance, you can create a route that exists in the routing table, but it will not be used by the Security Appliance unless the more preferred routes have failed. Static routes with a greater administrative distance than the administrative distance of other routes are called *floating routes*.

Default Route

Configuring multiple routes can be a time-consuming task, especially for the traffic bound for the Internet. Therefore, you can create a special route known as a default route. This route is automatically used for any traffic that does not match any other routes on the system. When configuring the default route, you use a destination IP address of 0.0.0.0 and a netmask of 0.0.0.0.

Instead of using the address of a gateway router when you are configuring a static route, you can specify the IP address of one of the Security Appliance's own interfaces. When you create a route in this manner, the Security Appliance does not have a destination IP address to which to send the traffic. Therefore, the Security Appliance broadcasts an ARP request on the specified interface to determine the address to which to send the traffic. Any router that has a route to the destination address can generate a proxy ARP (using its own interface's Ethernet address), enabling the Security Appliance to update its ARP cache with an entry for the IP address of the traffic. The Security Appliance uses this proxy ARP to then send the traffic to the router that has a route to the destination IP address.

> **NOTE** Although you can configure the Security Appliance to generate an ARP request to determine the destination address to which to send traffic, this configuration is not recommended. ARP is an unauthenticated protocol and this configuration can pose a security risk.

Static routes are stored in your Security Appliance configuration and restored when your Security Appliance is reloaded. To view the routes on your Security Appliance, you use the **show route** command. This command displays all the routes in the Security Appliance's routing table, such as shown in Example 11-1.

Example 11-1 *Output of the* **show route** *Command*

```
pix515a# show route
   intf5 0.0.0.0 0.0.0.0 10.89.141.1 1 OTHER static
   inside 10.10.10.0 255.255.255.0 10.10.10.1 1 CONNECT static
   inside 10.10.20.0 255.255.255.0 10.10.10.2 2 OTHER static
   intf5 10.89.141.0 255.255.255.0 10.89.141.80 1 CONNECT static
   intf4 172.16.1.0 255.255.255.0 172.16.1.1 1 CONNECT static
   outside 192.168.10.0 255.255.255.0 192.168.10.80 1 CONNECT static
pix515a#
```

The static routes with the keyword CONNECT indicate routes that are automatically created when you define the IP address for an interface. The routes with the OTHER keyword indicate static routes that have been manually entered.

Sometimes, you may want to remove the static routes that you have already configured. You can do this using the **clear route** command.

> **NOTE** You can also remove individual routes by placing the **no** keyword in front of the original command used to create the static route.

Dynamic Routes

Besides creating static routes manually, the Cisco Security Appliance also supports some dynamic routing functionality. Dynamic routes are created based on routing protocols that automatically add entries into the Security Appliance's routing table. The Security Appliance supports the following two different routing protocols, but only one can be active on a single Security Appliance:

- RIP
- OSPF

The Security Appliance can learn new routes based on the RIP routing broadcasts, but the Security Appliance does not have the functionality to propagate these learned routes to other devices. With OSPF, the Security Appliance learns new routes, and it can also propagate that information to other devices.

> **NOTE**   Authentication should be used with all routing protocols whenever possible. Route redistribution between OSPF and other protocols (such as RIP) is a prime target for attackers. By subverting the routing information, an attacker can potentially bypass your defined security configuration.

Configuring RIP

To enable the Security Appliance to learn new routes based on RIP routing updates, you use the **rip** command. The syntax for the **rip** command is as follows:

```
rip if-name default | passive [version {1 | 2}] [authentication {text | md5} key key_id]
```

Table 11-8 describes the various parameters for the **rip** command.

Table 11-8   rip *Command Parameters*

Parameter	Description
if-name	The name of the interface to which the RIP configuration will apply (the name assigned in the **nameif** command).
default	Keyword indicating that you want to broadcast the address of the specified interface as a default route.
passive	Enables passive RIP on the interface. The Security Appliance listens for RIP routing updates and uses the information received to populate its routing table.
version	Keyword used to specify the version of RIP to use. This keyword must be followed by either **1** or **2** to indicate the RIP version to use.
authentication	Keyword to enable RIP version 2 authentication.
text	Keyword indicating that RIP updates should be sent in the clear.
md5	Keyword indicating that RIP updates should use MD5 authentication.
key	The key to encrypt routing updates. This key is a text string of up to 16 characters.
key_id	The key identification value in the range between 1 and 255. The same key ID must be used on all of your RIP-enabled devices that communicate with one another.

By configuring RIP on a specific Security Appliance interface, your firewall watches for RIP routing updates. It then uses this information to update its routing table. The information cannot be distributed by the Security Appliance to other devices. The Security Appliance can, however, broadcast the address of one of its interfaces as a default route.

To turn off RIP on a specific interface, you use the **no** keyword in front of the original RIP configuration command. You can also remove all the RIP configuration commands from your configuration by using the **clear rip** command.

Suppose that you want to enable RIP on the outside interface by using MD5 authentication, using MYKEY as the key and a key ID of 2. The command to accomplish this is as follows:

```
Pix515a(config)# rip outside passive version 2 authentication md5 MYKEY 2
```

NOTE   Because authentication is supported only with RIP version 2, you must specify version 2 in the command. The default is RIP version 1.

OSPF Overview

Route propagation and greatly reduced route convergence times are two of the many benefits that occur by using OSPF. OSPF is widely deployed in large internetworks because of its efficient use of network bandwidth and its rapid convergence after changes in topology. The Cisco Security Appliance implementation supports intra-area, interarea, and external routes. The distribution of static routes to OSPF processes and route redistribution between OSPF processes are also included.

NOTE   The PIX 501 does not support OSPF functionality.

An OSPF router that has interfaces in multiple areas is called an Area Border Router (ABR). A router that redistributes traffic or imports external routes (Type 1 or Type 2) between routing domains is called an Autonomous System Boundary Router (ASBR). An ABR uses link-state advertisements (LSA) to send information about available routes to other OSPF routers. Using ABR Type 3 LSA filtering, you can have separate private and public areas, with the Security Appliance acting as an ABR. Type 3 LSAs (interarea routes) can be filtered from one area to another. This lets you use NAT and OSPF together without advertising private networks.

The Security Appliance OSPF supported features are as follows:

- Support for intra-area, interarea, and external routes
- Support for virtual links

- Authentication for OSPF packets
- The capability to configure the Security Appliance as a designated router, ABR, and limited ASBR
- ABR Type 3 LSA filtering
- Support for stub and not so stubby areas (NSSA)
- Route redistribution

NOTE   Your Cisco Security Appliance can filter only Type 3 LSAs. If you configure your Security Appliance to function as an ASBR in a private network, then information about your private networks will be sent to the public interfaces, because Type 5 LSAs describing private networks will be flooded to the entire autonomous system (including the public areas) unless you configure two separate OSPF processes.

OSPF Commands

To configure OSPF on your Security Appliance, you use various commands. To enable OSPF on your PIX Firewall, you use the **router ospf** command. The syntax is as follows:

```
router ospf pid
```

The *pid* represents a unique identification for the OSPF routing process in the range from 1 to 65,535. Each OSPF routing process on a single Security Appliance must be unique, and Security Appliance Version 6.3 supports a maximum of two different OSPF routing processes.

After you issue the **router ospf** command, the Security Appliance command prompt enters a subcommand mode indicated by a command prompt similar to the following:

```
pix515a(config-router)#
```

In subcommand mode, you can configure various OSPF parameters (see Table 11-9).

Table 11-9   router ospf *Subcommand Options*

Parameter	Description
area	Configures OSPF areas
compatible	Runs OSPF in RFC 1583 compatible mode
default-information	Distributes a default route
distance	Configures administrative distances for OSPF process
ignore	Suppresses syslog for receipt of Type 6 (MOSPF) LSAs
log-adj-changes	Logs OSPF adjacency changes

continues

Table 11-9 router ospf *Subcommand Options (Continued)*

Parameter	Description
network	Adds/removes interfaces to/from OSPF routing process
redistribute	Configures route redistribution between OSPF processes
router-id	Configures router ID for an OSPF process
summary-address	Configures summary address for OSPF redistribution
timers	Configures timers for an OSPF process

Using the **network** command, you can define which interfaces will be running OSPF. Using the **network** command also enables you to add networks to or remove networks from the OSPF routing process and define OSPF area information for each network. The syntax for the **network** command is as follows:

```
network prefix-ip-address netmask area area-id
```

The parameters for the **network** command are shown in Table 11-10.

Table 11-10 network *Command Parameters*

Parameter	Description
prefix-ip-address	IP address of the network being configured.
netmask	The network mask, which indicates the number of addresses covered by the area (for example, a Class C network pertains to 256 different addresses and is specified as 255.255.255.0).
area	Keyword indicating that the area information will follow.
area-id	The ID of the area to be associated with this OSPF address range.

OSPF advertises routes to networks. To prevent information about your private network from being advertised, you need to filter LSAs. The **prefix-list** and **area** commands enable you to filter Type 3 LSA advertisements. This filtering is based on the prefix list defined by the **prefix-list** command. Once configured, only the specified prefixes are sent from one area to another, and all other prefixes are restricted to their OSPF area. The syntax for the **prefix-list** command is as follows:

```
prefix-list list-name [seq seq-number] {permit | deny prefix/len}
```

NOTE Unlike the other OSPF configuration commands, the **prefix-list** command is executed from normal configuration mode instead of the OSPF subcommand mode.

Table 11-11 shows the parameters for the **prefix-list** command.

Table 11-11 prefix-list *Command Parameters*

Parameter	Description
list-name	The name of the prefix list.
seq	Keyword indicating that you want to provide a sequence number.
seq-number	Specifies the sequence number for the prefix list entry in the range from 1 to 4,294,967,295.
permit	Keyword indicating that the specified prefix list should be allowed.
deny	Keyword indicating that the specified prefix list should be disallowed.
prefix	Prefix address that is being identified.
len	A network mask indicator that identifies the number of valid bits in the prefix. (For instance, to specify a Class C address, the *len* value is 24.)

After configuring a prefix list, you apply that prefix list to an area by using the **area** command. Filtering can be applied to traffic going into or coming out of an OSPF area or to both the incoming and outgoing traffic for an area. The syntax for the **area** command is as follows:

```
area area-id filter-list prefix {prefix-list-name in | out}
```

The parameters for the **area** command are shown in Table 11-12.

Table 11-12 area *Command Parameters*

Parameter	Description
area-id	The identifier of the area on which filtering is being configured
filter-list	Keyword indicating that you are configuring LSA filtering
prefix	Keyword indicating that you are specifying a configured prefix list to use for filtering
prefix-list-name	The name of the prefix list that you created using the **prefix-list** command
in	Keyword that applies the configured prefix to prefixes advertised inbound to the specified area
out	Keyword that applies the configured prefix to prefixes advertised outbound from the specified area

Running two separate OSPF processes on your Security Appliance enables you to perform address filtering when your Security Appliance is configured as an ASBR. LSA Type 5 advertisements pass between areas on the same OSPF process (and cannot be filtered like LSA Type 3 advertisements), but they do not pass between separate OSPF processes. Using two OSPF processes can be advantageous in various situations, such as the following:

- NAT is being used.
- OSPF is operating on the public and private interfaces.
- LSA Type 5 advertisement filtering is required.

ASBR
An ASBR is located on the edge of your OSPF autonomous system and is responsible for advertising external routes for the entire OSPF autonomous system.

When using two OSPF processes, one process is usually configured for the external interface while the other process handles the private interfaces. Each OSPF process is configured by using a separate **router ospf** command with a different process identification (PID) number for each process.

In some situations, it may be advantageous to distribute route advertisements between separate OSPF processes, such as to enable routes received on the public interface to pass to the OSPF process running on the private interfaces. To redistribute routes between different OSPF processes or domains, you use the **redistribute ospf** subcommand, the syntax for which is as follows:

```
redistribute ospf pid
```

Because the **redistribute ospf** command is executed from the OSPF subcommand mode, *pid* identifies the OSPF process identification (PID) whose LSA Type 3 advertisements you want forwarded to the current OSPF process.

Configuring OSPF

Figure 11-2 shows a typical OSPF deployment configuration. In this configuration, a PIX Firewall is operating as an ABR. Because you do not want the information about private networks sent out on the public interface, LSA filtering is applied to the Internet interface. NAT is applied only to the inside interface (for the private networks).

In this configuration, the inside interface learns routes from both the DMZ and the outside interface, but you do not want private routes to be propagated to either the DMZ or the public interfaces.

Figure 11-2 *PIX OSPF Network*

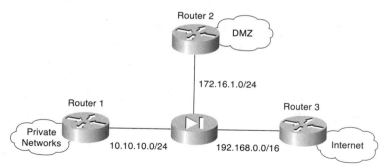

Configuring OSPF on your Security Appliance requires you to perform the following steps:

Step 1   Enable OSPF.

Step 2   Define the Security Appliance interfaces that need to run OSPF.

Step 3   Define OSPF areas.

Step 4   Configure LSA filtering to protect private addresses.

Using the configuration shown in Figure 11-2, the following commands configure OSPF based on the scenario described:

```
pix515a(config)# router ospf 1
pix515a(config-router)# area 0 filter-list prefix ten in
pix515a(config-router)# network 192.168.0.0 255.255.0.0 area 0
pix515a(config-router)# network 172.16.1.0 255.255.255.0 area 172.16.1.0
pix515a(config-router)# network 10.10.10.0 255.255.255.0 area 10.10.10.0
pix515a(config-router)# prefix-list ten deny 10.10.10.0/24
pix515a(config)#
pix515a(config)# router ospf 1
pix515a(config-router)# prefix-list ten permit 172.16.1.0/24
pix515a(config)#
```

NOTE   If you configure your Security Appliance as an ASBR, then you need to configure multiple OSPF processes on the firewall if you want to perform address filtering.

When configuring OSPF, you should also enable one of the following authentication mechanisms:

- Password
- MD5 (message digest algorithm 5)

You enable authentication for each area individually by using the following command:

```
area area-id authentication [message-digest]
```

Next, you need to define the authentication to be used for communication with the specific routers with which each area will be communicating. You do so by defining a *virtual-link* using the **area** command. Continuing with the example shown in Figure 11-2, to enable MD5 authentication with a key ID of 4 and a key of Ab1&05K! for **area 172.16.1.0** when communicating with router 172.16.1.250, you would use the following commands:

```
pix515a(config)#  router  ospf  1
pix515a(config-router)#  area  172.16.1.0  authentication  message-digest
pix515a(config-router)#  area  172.16.1.0  virtual-link
    172.16.1.250 authentication message-digest message-digest-key  4  md5  Ab1&05K!
```

> **NOTE**   To enable password authentication (using a password of R5!s4&Px*) for the same router (instead of using MD5), you would use the following commands:
>
> ```
> pix515a(config)#  router ospf 1
> pix515a(config-router)#  area 172.16.1.0 authentication
> pix515a(config-router)#  area 172.16.1.0 virtual-link 172.16.1.250 authentication
>    authentication-key
> R5!s4&Px*
> ```

Viewing the OSPF Configuration

After setting up OSPF on your Security Appliance, it helps to view parts of the configuration. Using the **show ospf** command, you can view the general information about the OSPF routing processes. When you enter this command, you see output similar to Example 11-2, depending on the OSPF features that you have configured.

Example 11-2   *Output from the* **show ospf** *Command*

```
pix515a#  show  ospf
Routing Process "ospf 1" with ID 192.168.10.80 and Domain ID 0.0.0.1
 Supports only single TOS(TOS0) routes
 Supports opaque LSA
SPF schedule delay 5 secs, Hold time between two SPFs 10 secs
 Minimum LSA interval 5 secs. Minimum LSA arrival 1 secs
 Number of external LSA 0. Checksum Sum 0x      0
 Number of opaque AS LSA 0. Checksum Sum 0x     0
 Number of DCbitless external and opaque AS LSA 0
 Number of DoNotAge external and opaque AS LSA 0
 Number of areas in this router is 3. 3 normal 0 stub 0 nssa
 External flood list length 0

pix515a(config)#
```

Multicast Routing

IP multicasting is a mechanism that conserves network bandwidth by delivering a stream of information simultaneously to multiple recipients. Some common applications that take advantage of IP multicasting include the following:

- Video conferencing
- Distance learning
- News feeds

IP multicasting actually involves sending an IP packet to a single multicast IP address. Routers send Internet Group Management Protocol (IGMP) query messages to locate hosts that belong to any multicast groups (wishing to receive specific multicast traffic). Any host that wishes to receive multicast traffic must join the multicast group by using an IGMP report message that indicates all the multicast groups to which it belongs. When a host no longer wishes to receive a multicast data stream, it sends an IGMP Leave message to the multicast router.

With the introduction of software version 7.0, the Security Appliances can now support PIM sparse-mode. Sparse-mode PIM defines a rendezvous point (RP) for the Security Appliance that keeps track of multicast groups. Instead of flooding the network to determine the status of the multicast member, a receiver that wants to send data can register with the RP. Sparse-mode PIM assumes that hosts do not want to participate in multicast traffic unless they specifically request it.

If several Security Appliances are participating in multicast traffic on a network segment, PIM requires that a designated router (DR) be assigned. A DR is responsible for sending PIM register, join, and prune messages to the RP. This reduces the amount of noise that can be created if each multicast Security Appliance sends duplicate requests to the RP.

You can configure your Security Appliance to act as a Stub Multicast Router (SMR) because it forwards requests only between end hosts and multicast routers. Instead of supporting the functionality of a fully operational multicast router, the Security Appliance functions only as an IGMP proxy agent. To illustrate the configuration tasks associated with configuring your Security Appliance as an SMR, you need to understand the following topics:

- Multicast commands
- Inbound multicast traffic
- Outbound multicast traffic
- Debugging multicast

Multicast Commands

Configuring multicast functionality on your Security Appliance requires you to understand various multicast configuration commands. The major multicast configuration commands are as follows:

- multicast routing
- mroute command
- igmp
- igmp forward
- igmp join-group
- igmp access-group
- igmp version
- igmp query-interval
- igmp query-max-response-time
- pim
- pim rp-address

multicast interface Command

The **multicast-routing** command enables PIM and IGMP on all interfaces. The syntax for this command is

```
[no] multicast-routing
```

mroute Command

To configure your Security Appliance to forward multicast traffic when the multicast router is on the inside interface, you need to use the **mroute** command. The syntax for this command is as follows:

```
mroute source source-mask in-interface dest dest-mask out-interface
```

The parameters for the **mroute** command are shown in Table 11-13.

Table 11-13   mroute *Command Parameters*

Parameter	Description
source	The source address of the multicast transmission device
source-mask	The network mask associated with the multicast source address
in-interface	The interface on which the multicast traffic enters the Security Appliance

Table 11-13 mroute *Command Parameters (Continued)*

Parameter	Description
dest	The Class D address of the multicast group
dest-mask	The network mask associated with the destination multicast address
out-interface	The interface on which the multicast traffic leaves the Security Appliance

NOTE   To clear static multicast routes created with the **mroute** command, you use the **clear mroute** command. To actually stop a Security Appliance from forwarding multicast traffic, use the **no** keyword in front of your original **mroute** command.

igmp Command

IGMP processing will be enabled on all interfaces by default if the **multicast-routing** command has been used. If IGMP processing has been disabled on an interface, you can reinstate IGMP processing by using the **igmp** command in interface-configuration mode. To disable IGMP processing on an interface, use the **no igmp** command.

igmp forward Command

To join a multicast group, the host IGMP message must reach the multicast router. The **igmp forward** command enables you to cause one Security Appliance interface to pass IGMP messages to another interface. The syntax for this command is as follows:

```
igmp forward interface interface-name
```

The parameters for the **igmp forward** command are shown in Table 11-14.

Table 11-14 igmp forward *Command Parameters*

Parameter	Description
interface	Keyword indicating that the next parameter will be an interface name
interface-name	The name of the interface to forward the IGMP messages that are received on the current interface being configured

igmp join-group Command

To statically configure the Security Appliance to join a multicast group, you can use the **igmp join-group** command. This command is useful if you have clients who are unable to send the IGMP messages on their own. The syntax for this command is as follows:

```
igmp join-group group
```

The only parameter for the **igmp join-group** command is the multicast group (multicast address) that is statically being joined. Multicast addresses use the entire range of 224.0.0.0 through 239.255.255.255 (Class D addresses); however, you can configure a value only in the range of 224.0.0.2 through 239.255.255.255 for the **igmp join-group** command.

> **NOTE**   The multicast address 224.0.0.0 is the base address for IP multicasting, and 224.0.0.1 is permanently assigned to a group that includes all IP hosts.

igmp access-group Command

To limit which multicast groups (addresses) are allowed on a specific interface, you use the **igmp access-group** command. To use this command, you must first create an access list (using the **access-list** command) that defines the allowed multicast addresses. The syntax for this command is as follows:

```
igmp access-group access-list-id
```

igmp version Command

To define the IGMP version, you use the **igmp version** command. The syntax for this command is as follows:

```
igmp version 1 | 2
```

> **NOTE**   The default version for IP multicasting is 2.

igmp query-interval Command

To configure the frequency, in seconds, at which IGMP query messages are sent by an interface, you use the **igmp query-interval** command. The default value is 60, but you can specify a value from 1 to 65,535. The syntax for this command is as follows:

```
igmp query-interval seconds
```

> **NOTE**   To set the query interval back to the default value, you use the **no igmp query-interval** command.

pim Command

PIM support will be enabled on all interfaces by default if the **multicast-routing** command has been used. If PIM support has been disabled on an interface, you can re-enable it by using the **pim** command in interface-configuration mode. To disable PIM support on an interface, use the **no pim** command.

pim rp-address Command

With PIM sparse mode, you are required to assign at least one rendezvous point for the Security Appliance. Using the **pim rp-address** command in global-configuration mode, you can assign a RP, which can be restricted to specific multicast groups using an optional access control list (ACL). The complete syntax for this command is as follows:

```
pim rp-address ip-address [acl][bidir]
```

Table 11-15 describes the parameters for this command.

Table 11-15 pim rp-address *Command Parameters*

Parameter	Description
ip-address	IP address of a router to be the PIM RP
acl	(Optional) The name or number of a standard IP access list that defines with which multicast groups the RP should be used
bidir	(Optional) Indicates that the specified multicast groups are to operate in bidirectional mode instead of PIM sparse mode

pim dr-priority Command

Using the **pim dr-priority** command will allow you to change default DR priority assigned to the Security Appliance. If multiple Security Appliances have the same DR priority, the Security Appliance with the highest IP address will become the new DR. The complete syntax for this command is as follows:

```
pim dr-priority number
```

where *number* is used to determine the priority of the device when determining which device will be the DR. The number can be from 0 to 4,294,967,294. Using 0 will prevent the Security Appliance from becoming the DR.

igmp query-max-response-time Command

When using IGMP version 2, you can specify the maximum query response time, in seconds, using **igmp query-max-response-time.** The default value is 10, but you can configure a value in the range from 1 to 65,535.

> **NOTE** To set the query interval back to the default value, you use the **no igmp query-max-response-time** command.

Inbound Multicast Traffic

Allowing inbound multicast traffic involves the configuration shown in Figure 11-3. In this configuration, the multicast router is located outside the Security Appliance and the hosts that want to receive multicast traffic are being protected by the Security Appliance.

Figure 11-3 *Inbound Multicast Configuration*

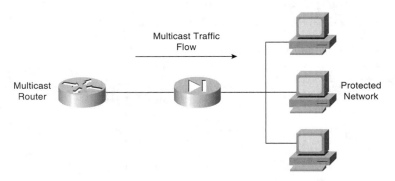

Because the hosts that need to receive the multicast traffic are separated from the multicast router by your Security Appliance, you need to configure the Security Appliance to forward IGMP reports from the hosts protected by the firewall to the multicast router. You also need to forward multicast transmissions from the multicast router. The following configuration steps enable this multicast configuration:

Step 1   Use the **multicast routing** command to enable multicast processing on a specific interface and place the interface in multicast promiscuous mode. This also places the command line in multicast subcommand mode, designated by the *(config-multicast)*# prompt.

Step 2   Use the **igmp forward** command to enable IGMP forwarding on the interfaces connected to hosts that will receive multicast transmissions. This also enables the interface to forward all IGMP Host Report and Leave messages.

Step 3   (Optional) If your network contains clients that cannot respond to IGMP messages but still require the reception of multicast traffic, you use the **igmp join-group** command to statically join the Security Appliance to the specific multicast group.

Step 4   (Optional) Define an access list to define which Class D addresses
(multicast addresses) are allowed to traverse the Security Appliance.
Then, use the **igmp access-group** command to apply the access list to a
specific interface.

Assume that you want to allow protected hosts to join the multicast group 224.0.1.100 from
a multicast router that is located outside the protected network. To accomplish this, you
would use the following commands:

```
pix515a(config)#  access-list  120  permit  udp  any  host  224.0.1.100
pix515a(config)#  multicast  interface  outside
pix515a(config-multicast)#  igmp  access-group  120
pix515a(config-multicast)#  exit
pix515a(config)#  multicast  interface  inside
pix515a(config-multicast)#  igmp  forward  interface  outside

pix515a(config-multicast)#  exit
```

Outbound Multicast Traffic

Allowing outbound multicast traffic involves the configuration shown in Figure 11-4. In this
configuration, the multicast transmission source is located inside the Security Appliance and
the hosts that want to receive multicast traffic are not protected by the Security Appliance.

Figure 11-4   *Outbound Multicast Configuration*

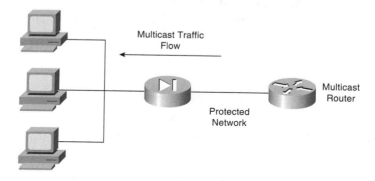

When the multicast transmission source is on the protected or secure interface of a Security
Appliance, you must specifically configure the Security Appliance to forward the multicast
transmissions. The following configuration steps enable this multicast configuration:

Step 1   Use the **multicast interface** command to enable multicast forwarding on
each Security Appliance interface.

Step 2   Use the **mroute** command to create a static route from the multicast
transmission source to the next-hop router interface.

Suppose that your multicast router is located at 10.10.10.100 and broadcasting to the multicast group 230.0.1.100. To get the Security Appliance to forward multicast transmissions from this multicast router to the outside interface, you would use the following commands:

```
pix515a(config)# multicast interface outside
pix515a(config-multicast)# exit
pix515a(config)# multicast interface inside
pix515a(config-multicast)# mroute 10.10.10.100 255.255.255.255
    inside 230.0.1.100 255.255.255.255 outside

pix515a(config-multicast)# exit

pix515a(config)#
```

Debugging Multicast

Not only can you configure IP multicasting, you can also debug the operation of your IP multicasting configuration. The commands that you use to do so fall into the following two categories:

■ Commands to view the multicast configuration

■ Commands to debug multicast traffic

Commands to View the Multicast Configuration

You can use the following commands to view your multicast configuration:

■ **show multicast**

■ **show igmp**

■ **show mroute**

The **show multicast** command displays the multicast settings for either a specific interface or all the interfaces. The syntax for this command is as follows:

```
show multicast [interface interface-name]
```

If you do not specify an interface, then the information for all the Security Appliance interfaces is displayed.

The **show igmp** command displays information about either a specific IGMP group or all the IGMP groups for a specific interface. The syntax for this command is as follows:

```
show igmp [group | interface interface-name] [detail]
```

The final command that you can use to view your multicast configuration is **show mroute,** which displays the current multicast routes. Its syntax is as follows:

```
show mroute [destination [source]]
```

Commands to Debug Multicast Traffic

After you configure IP multicasting on your Security Appliance, you may need to debug multicast traffic to identify configuration problems. Two commands are useful for debugging multicast traffic:

- **debug igmp**—Enables debugging for IGMP events
- **debug mfwd**—Enables debugging for multicast forwarding events

NOTE   To disable either of these debugging commands, simply place a **no** in front of the command (for instance, **no debug igmp**).

Foundation Summary

The "Foundation Summary" provides a convenient review of many key concepts in this chapter. If you are already comfortable with the topics in this chapter, this summary can help you recall a few details. If you just read this chapter, this review should help solidify some key facts. If you are doing your final preparation before the exam, this summary provides a convenient way to review the day before the exam.

The Security Appliance needs to support some basic routing and switching functionality. This functionality falls into the following three areas:

- Ethernet VLAN tagging
- IP routing
- Multicast routing

To support traffic from multiple VLANs, the Security Appliance supports 802.1Q tagging and the configuration of multiple logical interfaces on a single physical interface. For each logical interface that you establish, you must configure the following parameters:

- Interface name
- Security level
- IP address

For IP routing, the Security Appliance supports both static and dynamic routes. Using the **route** command, you can configure static routing information on the Security Appliance. The Security Appliance also supports dynamic updates from the following two routing protocols:

- RIP
- OSPF

With RIP, the Security Appliance can only *receive* RIP routing updates. It does not support the capability to propagate those updates to other devices. It can, however, advertise one of its interfaces as a default route.

Using OSPF, the Security Appliance can actually propagate route information and actively participate in the OSPF routing protocol. Some of the OSPF functionality supported by the Security Appliance includes the following:

- Support for intra-area, interarea, and external routes
- Support for virtual links

- Authentication for OSPF packets
- The capability to configure the Security Appliance as a DR, ABR, and limited ASBR
- ABR Type 3 LSA filtering
- Route redistribution

Configuring OSPF on your Security Appliance requires you to perform the following steps:

Step 1   Enable OSPF.

Step 2   Define the Security Appliance interfaces that need to run OSPF.

Step 3   Define OSPF areas.

Step 4   Configure LSA filtering to protect private addresses.

You enable OSPF using the **router ospf** command. The **network** command enables you to define which IP addresses fall into which areas, and which interfaces use OSPF. The **prefix-list** and **area** commands enable you to filter Type 3 LSAs to prevent the Security Appliance from advertising information about private networks. If you configure your Security Appliance as an ASBR OSPF router, then using multiple OSPF processes enables you to perform address filtering.

Finally, you can configure the Security Appliance to operate as a Stub Multicast Router (SMR). This enables you to support various applications such as remote learning and video conferencing. The multicast transmission source can be either inside or outside the Security Appliance. Some of the important multicast configuration commands include the following:

- **multicast interface**
- **igmp forward**
- **igmp join-group**
- **igmp access-group**
- **igmp version**
- **igmp query-interval**
- **igmp query-max-response-time**

Q&A

As mentioned in the Introduction, the questions in this book are more difficult than what you should experience on the exam. The questions are designed to ensure your understanding of the concepts discussed in this chapter and adequately prepare you to complete the exam. You should use the simulated exams on the CD to practice for the exam.

The answers to these questions can be found in Appendix A:

1. What type of Ethernet tagging does the Cisco Security Appliance support?

2. Which command do you use to configure logical interfaces?

3. What three basic configuration parameters do you need to define for each logical interface?

4. What command do you use to define static routes on a PIX Firewall?

5. What is the default route and what values do you use for the IP address and netmask when creating the default route?

6. The ASA Security Appliance provides functionality for which two routing protocols?

7. Can a Security Appliance propagate RIP routes?

8. Which LSAs can the Security Appliance filter, and why is this important?

9. Which two commands enable you to configure LSA filtering?

10. What are the steps involved in setting up OSPF on your Security Appliance?

11. Can a Security Appliance operate as a fully functional multicast router?

12. If you have clients that cannot send IGMP messages, which command do you use to statically configure the Security Appliance to receive messages from a multicast group?

13. What is the range of addresses for multicast traffic?

14. If the multicast transmission source is protected by the Security Appliance, which command do you use to configure the Security Appliance to allow clients to access it?

15. Which two commands can you use to view the multicast configuration on a PIX 535 Firewall?

16. Which command enables you to view the routes currently in use on the Security Appliance?

17. Which command enables you to pass OSPF routing information between multiple OSPF domains or processes?

18. Why would you run multiple OSPF processes on your Security Appliance?

This chapter covers the following subjects:

- Understanding Failover

- Failover Configuration

- LAN-Based Failover Configuration

CHAPTER 12

Cisco Security Appliance Failover

Today, most businesses rely heavily on critical application servers that support the business process. The interruption of these servers due to network device failures or other causes has a great financial cost, not to mention the irritation such an interruption causes in the user community. With this in mind, Cisco has designed most of its devices, including the Security Appliance products (models 515 and up), such that they can be configured in a redundant or highly available configuration.

The failover feature makes the Cisco Security Appliance a highly available firewall solution. The purpose of this feature is to ensure continuity of service in case of a failure on the primary unit.

The failover process requires two Security Appliances—one primary (active mode) and one secondary (active or standby mode). The idea is to have the primary Security Appliance handle all traffic from the network and to have the secondary Security Appliance wait in standby mode in case the primary fails, at which point, it takes over the process of handling all network traffic. With version 7.0 of the Security Appliance software, the second Security Appliance can stay in an active mode, allowing both appliances to act as separate firewalls, while serving as a failover for the other. If a primary (active) unit fails, the secondary Security Appliance changes its state from standby mode to active, unless the appliance is in active-active mode, assumes the IP address and MAC address of the previously active unit, and begins accepting traffic for it. The new standby unit assumes the IP address and MAC address of the unit that was previously the standby unit, thus completing the failover process.

How to Best Use This Chapter

Computer networks are a vital component to the operation of most businesses. Protecting these networks from attacks using firewalls is also vital. Many businesses deploy some type of power backup (on critical systems) to insure that these important components continue to operate in the case of a temporary power failure. Similarly, depending on a single device to protect important networks is not acceptable in many environments. Using multiple Security Appliances operating in a failover configuration enables your network to remain operational (and protected from attack) even if a single

Security Appliance fails. Test yourself with the "Do I Know This Already?" quiz and see how familiar you are with the failover functionality available on Security Appliance.

"Do I Know This Already?" Quiz

The purpose of the "Do I Know This Already?" quiz is to help you decide if you really need to read the entire chapter. If you already intend to read the entire chapter, you do not necessarily need to answer these questions now.

The eleven-question quiz, derived from the major sections in the "Foundation Topics" portion of the chapter, helps you determine how to spend your limited study time. Table 12-1 outlines the major topics discussed in this chapter and the "Do I Know This Already?" quiz questions that correspond to those topics.

Table 12-1 *"Do I Know This Already?" Foundation Topics Section-to-Question Mapping*

Foundation Topics Section	Questions Covered in This Section	Score
Understanding Failover	1 to 3, 5, 6, 8 to 10	
LAN-Based Failover Configuration	4, 7	
Serial Failover Configuration	11	

CAUTION The goal of selfassessment is to gauge your mastery of the topics in this chapter. If you do not know the answer to a question or are only partially sure of the answer, you should mark this question wrong for purposes of the selfassessment. Giving yourself credit for an answer you correctly guess skews your selfassessment results and might provide you with a false sense of security.

1. Which of the following causes a failover event?

   a. A reboot or power interruption on an active PIX Firewall

   b. Low HTTP traffic on the outside interface

   c. Issuance of the **failover active** command on a standby PIX Firewall

   d. Low memory utilization for several consecutive seconds

2. What is the command to view failover configuration?

   a. **show failover**

   b. **failover**

   c. **view failover**

   d. **show me failover**

3. Which of the following is/are replicated in stateful failover operation?

    a. Configuration

    b. TCP connection table, including timeout information for each connection

    c. Translation (xlate) table

    d. Negotiated H.323 UDP protocols

    e. All of these answers are correct

4. Which of the following is *not* replicated in stateful failover operation?

    a. User authentication (uauth) table

    b. ISAKMP and IPSec SA table

    c. ARP table

    d. Routing information

    e. All of these answers are correct

5. What is the command to force configuration replication to the standby unit?

    a. **write standby**

    b. **copy to secondary**

    c. **force secondary**

    d. **force conf**

6. Which of the following is a stateful failover hardware restriction?

    a. The stateful failover configuration is supported only by PIX Firewall 535 models.

    b. Only fiber connections can be used in a stateful failover hardware configuration.

    c. A PIX Firewall with two FDDI cards cannot use stateful failover, because an additional FDDI interface is not supported.

    d. There is no hardware restriction for stateful failover configuration.

7. What command assigns an IP address to the standby Cisco Security Appliance?

    a. **secondary ip address** *ip address*

    b. **ip address** *ip-address* **standby** *ip-address*

    c. **ip address** *ip address* **secondary**

    d. **ip address** *ip address* **failover**

8. What is the command to configure a LAN-based failover?

a. conf lan failover

b. failover ip LAN

c. failover lan interface if-name

d. lan interface failover

9. What is an advantage of a LAN-based failover?

a. It quickly fails over to a peer when a power failure on the active unit takes place.

b. It does not have the 6-foot-cable distance limitation for failover communication.

c. It is preconfigured on the PIX Firewall.

d. All of these answers are correct.

10. What is the default failover poll, in seconds?

a. 10 seconds

b. 15 seconds

c. 30 seconds

d. 25 seconds

11. Which of the following is true about the serial link cable connection in a PIX Firewall failover configuration?

a. Serial link cable can transfer data at 100 Mbps.

b. The two units maintain the heartbeat network over the cable.

c. Network link status is not communicated over the serial link.

d. Keepalive packets and configuration replication are communicated over the serial link.

The answers to the "Do I Know This Already?" quiz are found in Appendix A, "Answers to the 'Do I Know This Already?' Quizzes and Q&A Sections." The suggested choices for your next step are as follows:

■ **8 or less overall score**—Read the entire chapter. This includes the "Foundation Topics," "Foundation Summary," and "Q&A" sections.

■ **9 to 11 overall score**—If you want more review on these topics, skip to the "Foundation Summary" section and then go to the "Q&A" section. Otherwise, move to the next chapter.

Foundation Topics

What Causes a Failover Event?

In a Security Appliance failover configuration, one of the Security Appliances is considered the *active* unit, and the other is the *standby* unit. As their names imply, the active unit performs normal network functions and the standby unit monitors and is ready to take control should the active unit fail to perform its functionality. A failover event occurs after a series of tests determines that the primary (active) unit can no longer continue providing its services, at which time the standby Security Appliance assumes the role of the primary. The main causes of failover are shown in Table 12-2.

> **NOTE** If multiple contexts are enabled on a Security Appliance, the Security Appliance can act as a standby unit for another Security Appliance while acting as an active unit for traffic flowing through it.

Table 12-2 *Possible Failover Event Situations*

Failure Condition	Reasons That Standby Becomes Active
No Failure	Failover active—An administrator can force the standby unit to change state by using the **failover active** command, which causes failover to occur. This is the only situation in which failover occurs without the primary (active) unit having any problems. A **no failover active** command will return the active unit back to the standby unit.
Power loss or reload	Cable errors—The cable is wired so that each unit can distinguish between a power failure in the other unit and an unplugged cable. If the standby unit detects that the active unit is turned off (or resets), it takes active control. Loss of power—When the primary (active) unit loses power or is turned off, the standby unit assumes the active role.
PIX Firewall hardware failure	Memory exhaustion—If block memory exhaustion occurs for 15 straight seconds on the active unit the standby unit becomes the active unit.
Network failure	Failover communication loss—If the standby unit does not hear from the active unit for more than twice the configured poll time (or a maximum of 30 seconds), and the cable status is OK, a series of tests is conducted before the standby unit takes over as active.

What Is Required for a Failover Configuration?

The hardware and software for the primary and secondary Security Appliance must match in the following respects for failover configuration to work properly:

- Firewall model
- Software version (which should be the version with unrestricted [UR] licensing)
- Flash memory size
- RAM size
- Activation key
- Number and type of interfaces

> **NOTE**   Failover for 501 and 506E models is not supported.

> **NOTE**   With Security Appliance software version 7.0, the requirement for the same software versions on both the primary and secondary Security Appliances has been relaxed. Different maintenance levels are permitted for the purpose of hit-less updates.

The only additional hardware that is needed to support failover is the failover cable. Both units in a failover pair communicate through the failover cable. The failover cable is a modified RS-232 serial link cable that transfers data at 115 kbps. It is through this cable that the two units maintain the heartbeat network. This cable is not required for LAN-based failover. Some of the messages communicated over failover cable are

- Hello (keepalive packets)
- Configuration replication
- Network link status
- State of the unit (active/standby)
- MAC address exchange

> **NOTE**   With Security Appliance software version 7.0, serial cable failover supports message encryption.

It is also important to examine the labels on each end of the failover cable. One end of the cable is labeled "primary," and the other end is labeled "secondary." To have a successful failover configuration, the end labeled "primary" should be connected to the primary unit, and the end labeled "secondary" should be connected to the secondary unit. Changes made to the standby unit are never replicated to the active unit.

In addition to the hardware and software requirements, it is also important to correctly configure the switches where the Security Appliances directly connect. *Port Fast* should be enabled on all the ports where the Security Appliance interface directly connects, and trunking and channeling should be turned off. This way, if the Security Appliance's interface goes down during failover, the switch does not have to wait 30 seconds while the port is transitioned from a listening state to a learning state to a forwarding state.

NOTE   The ASA 55x0 Security Appliance family of firewalls does not support the serial cable for failover.

Port Fast

Many Cisco switches provide a Port Fast option for switch ports. Configuring this option on a switch port enables a simplified version of the Spanning Tree Protocol that eliminates several of the normal spanning-tree states. The preforwarding states are bypassed to more quickly transition ports into the forwarding states. Port Fast is an option that you can enable on a per-port basis. It is recommended only for end-station attachments.

Failover Monitoring

The failover feature in the Cisco Security Appliance monitors failover communication, the power status of the other unit, and hello packets received at each interface. If two consecutive hello packets are not received within an amount of time determined by the failover feature, failover starts testing the interfaces to determine which unit has failed and transfers active control to the standby unit. At this point, the "active" LED on the front of the standby Security Appliance lights up and the "active" LED on the failed Security Appliance unit dims.

NOTE   The **failover poll** *seconds* command enables you to determine how long failover waits before sending special failover hello packets between the primary and standby units over all network interfaces and the failover cable. The default is 15 seconds. The minimum value is 3 seconds, and the maximum is 15 seconds.

Failover uses the following tests to check the status of the units for failure:

- **Link up/down test**—If an interface card has a bad network cable or a bad port, is administratively shut down, or is connected to a failed switch, it is considered failed.

- **Network activity test**—The unit counts all received packets for up to 5 seconds. If any packets are received at any time during this interval, the interface is considered operational and testing stops. If no traffic is received, the ARP test begins.

- **Address Resolution Protocol (ARP) test**—The unit's ARP cache is evaluated for the ten most recently acquired entries. One at a time, the Security Appliance sends ARP requests to these machines, attempting to stimulate network traffic. After each request, the unit counts all received traffic for up to 5 seconds. If traffic is received, the interface is considered operational. If no traffic is received, an ARP request is sent to the next machine. If, at the end of the list, no traffic has been received, the ping test begins.

- **Ping test**—A broadcast ping request is sent out on all interfaces. The unit then counts all received echo-reply packets for up to 5 seconds. If any packets are received at any time during this interval on an interface, the interface is considered operational and testing stops. If no traffic is received, failover takes place.

Configuration Replication

Configuration changes, including initial failover configurations to the Cisco Security Appliance, are done on the primary unit. The standby unit keeps the current configuration through the process of configuration replication. For configuration replication to occur, the two Security Appliance units should be running the same software release. Configuration replication usually occurs when

- The standby unit completes its initial bootup and the active unit replicates its entire configuration to the standby unit.

- Configurations are made (commands) on the active unit and the commands/changes are sent across the failover cable to the standby unit.

- Issuing the **write standby** command on the active unit forces the entire configuration in memory to be sent to the standby unit.

When the replication starts, the Security Appliance console displays the message Sync Started. When the replication is complete, the Security Appliance console displays the message Sync Completed. During the replication, information cannot be entered on the Security Appliance console.

The **write memory** command is important, especially when failover is being configured for the first time. During the configuration replication process, the configuration is replicated from the active unit's running configuration to the running configuration of the standby unit. Because the running configuration is saved in RAM (which is unstable), you should issue the **write memory** command on the primary unit to save the configuration to Flash memory.

In addition to configuration replication, operating system (OS) upgrades are required from time to time as maintenance releases are deployed by Cisco. Beginning with software version 7.0(1), the zero-downtime software upgrade feature has been added to give an administrator the ability to perform software upgrades of failover pairs without impacting network uptime or connections flowing through the units. Security Appliances have the ability to do inter-version state sharing between failover pairs, as long as both pairs use software version 7.0 or later. Inter-version state sharing makes it possible for an administrator to perform software upgrades to new maintenance releases without impacting the traffic flow over either Security Appliance.

Stateful Failover

In stateful failover mode, more information is shared about the connections that have been established with the standby unit by the active unit. The active unit shares per-connection state information with the standby unit. If and when an active unit fails over to the standby unit, an application does not reinitiate its connection because stateful information from the active unit updates the standby unit.

> **NOTE**   Some applications are latency-sensitive. In some cases, the application times out before the failover sequence is completed. In these cases, the application must reestablish the session.

Replicated state information includes the following:

- TCP connection table, including timeout information for each connection
- Translation (xlate) table and status
- Negotiated H.323 UDP ports, SIP, and MGCP UDP media connections
- Port allocation table bitmap for PAT
- HTTP replication

Because failover cannot be prescheduled, the state update for the connection is packet-based. This means that every packet passes through the Security Appliance and changes a connection's state and triggers a state update.

However, some state information does not get updated to the standby unit in a stateful failover:

- User authentication (uauth) table
- ISAKMP and the IPSec SA table
- ARP table
- Routing information

Most UDP state tables are not transferred, with the exception of dynamically opened ports that correspond to multichannel protocols such as H.323.

In addition to the failover cable, stateful failover setup requires a 100-Mbps or Gigabit Ethernet interface to be used exclusively for passing state information between the active and standby units. IP 105 is used to pass data over this interface.

The stateful failover interface can be connected to any of the following:

- Category 5 crossover cable directly connecting the primary unit to the secondary unit
- 100BASE-TX full duplex on a dedicated switch or a switch's dedicated VLAN
- 1000BASE-SX full duplex on a switch's dedicated VLAN

> **NOTE** Cisco does not recommend using a crossover cable for stateful failover. Using a crossover cable might cause a Security Appliance to incorrectly determine if a failover event has occurred.

A Cisco Security Appliance with two FDDI cards cannot use stateful failover because an additional Ethernet interface with FDDI is not supported in stateful failover.

LAN-Based Failover

The distance restriction of 6 feet of serial cable between two PIX Firewall devices in a failover configuration is no longer a limitation starting with Security Appliance software version 6.2. LAN-based failover is a feature (available only on Security Appliance software version 6.2 or higher) that extends Security Appliance failover functionality to operate through a dedicated LAN interface without the serial failover cable. This feature provides a choice of failover configuration on the Security Appliance.

The obvious benefit of LAN-based failover is that it removes the 6-foot distance limitation from the Security Appliance devices in a failover configuration. If the LAN-based failover command interface link goes down, the Security Appliance notifies the peer through "other" interfaces, and then the standby unit takes over. If all connectivity between the two Security Appliance units is lost, both Security Appliance could become active. Therefore, it is best to use a separate switch for the LAN-based failover command interface, so that a failed switch will not cause all connectivity to be lost between the two Security Appliance units.

The weakness of LAN-based failover is the delayed detection of its peer power loss, consequently causing a relatively longer period for failover to occur.

> **NOTE**   Crossover Ethernet cables cannot be used to connect the LAN-based failover interface on Security Appliances running software versions before version 7.0. Additionally, it is recommended that you dedicate a LAN interface for LAN- based failover, but the interface can be shared with stateful failover under lightly loaded configurations.

The standby unit in a Security Appliance failover pair can be configured to use a virtual MAC address. This eliminates potential "stale" ARP entry issues for devices connected to the Security Appliance failover pair in the unlikely event that both firewalls in a failover pair fail at the same time.

Active-Active Failover

Prior to version 7.0, a security administrator could only have one Security Appliance actively passing user traffic, while keeping a second Security Appliance in standby mode, only to be activated during a failure. With active-active failover, both Security Appliances are active and passing user traffic, while still acting as standby Security Appliances for each other. This feature can only be using in conjunction with virtual firewall contexts.

To enable active-active failover, create two virtual contexts in the primary and secondary Security Appliances participating in active-active failover. In the primary Security Appliance, virtual context 1 is designated as the active context. Virtual context 2 will be designated as the standby context. Each context will peer with a context on the secondary Security Appliance. In Figure 12-1, context 1 on the primary Security Appliance peers with context 2 on the secondary Security Appliance. Context 2 on the secondary Security Appliance is designated as a standby context for the primary Security Appliance's context 1.

Figure 12-1 *Active-Active Failover Setup*

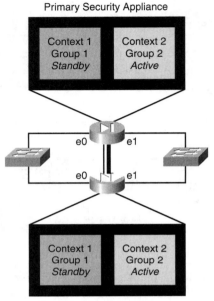

Active-active failover is done at a context basis, compared to active-standby in which failover is handled on a unit basis. Each Security Appliance monitors any failover peers for failure. With active-active failover logic, a failure can be unit based or virtual context-based. If a Security Appliance detects a failure state in a peer, the Security Appliance will gradually transition the standby context to active. The Security Appliance will then have two active contexts passing traffic. Failover groups must be active, and the contexts participating in active-active failover must be grouped together to function properly.

> **NOTE** Serial cable-based failover can support active-active failover mode.

Failover Group

Failover groups are designed to combine one or more contexts into a failover group. A security appliance uses failover groups to manage virtual contexts as explained in Chapter 9, "Security Contexts." A Security Appliance can only support up to two failover groups. Each failover group in a Security Appliance contains separate state machines that keep track of a failover group's contexts failover state.

In Figure 12-2, Context 1 on the primary and secondary Security Appliances are grouped together into failover Group 1. Context 2 of each Security Appliance is grouped into failover Group 2.

Figure 12-2   *Active-Active Failover Group Assignment*

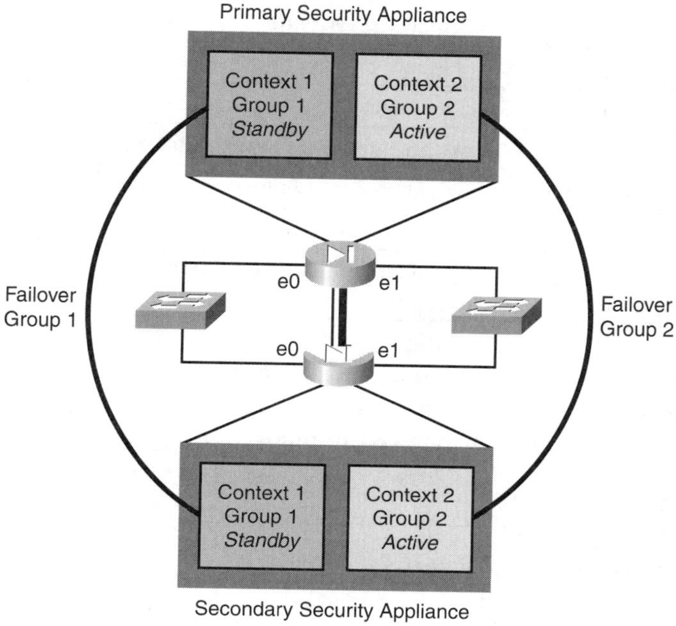

To configure a failover group, use the following command:

```
failover group nn
```

The security administrator must be in multiple-context mode system configuration, with failover disabled, to access this command. When this command is used, you will be placed in a failover group subcommand mode, similar to an **interface** command. With two failover groups, one must be assigned a higher priority, as shown in Example 12-1. This should be assigned to the active context on the Security Appliance.

Example 12-1   *Assigning Failover Groups and Priorities*

```
primary-pix (config)# failover group 1
primary-pix (config-fover-group)# primary
primary-pix (config)# failover group 2
primary-pix (config-fover-group)# secondary
```

Table 12-3 shows the command used to configure a failover group in failover subcommand mode.

Table 12-3 *Failover Sub-Command Mode Commands*

Primary	Gives higher priority to the primary unit.
secondary	Gives higher priority to the secondary unit.
Polltime Interface	Specifies interface polling time.
preempt	Allows preemption of lower priority active units.
replication http	Enables an assigned failover group the ability to replicate over HTTP.
mac address	Assigns a virtual MAC address for a physical interface.
show failover	This popular command displays the status of the failover configuration.

After you have created failover groups on a Security Appliance, you must assign virtual context to each group. Using the **join-failure-group** command within the virtual context sub-command mode, you can join context 1 to failover group 1, as shown in Example 12-2.

Example 12-2 *Assigning a Context to a Failover Group*

```
primary-pix (config)# context ctx1
primary-pix (config-ctx)# join-failover-group 1
```

NOTE All context changes in active-active mode must be done on the active context of the failover group only.

Configuring Failover

To configure failover, you need to become familiar with a few key commands. Table 12-4 shows the commands used to configure and verify failover.

Table 12-4 *Security Appliance Failover Commands*

failover lan enable	Enables LAN-based failover.
failover	Enables the failover function on the PIX Firewall. Use this command after you connect the failover cable between the primary and secondary unit. Use the **no failover** command to disable the failover feature.
failover lan key *key-secret*	Specifies the shared secret key.

Table 12-4 *Security Appliance Failover Commands (Continued)*

failover active	Makes the Security Appliance unit it is issued on the active unit. This command is usually used to make the primary unit active again after repairs have been made to it.
ip address *ip-address* [*mask*][standby *ip_address*]	Issued on the primary unit to configure the standby unit's IP address. This is the IP address that the standby interface uses to communicate with the active unit. Therefore, it has the same subnet as the system address.* The first *ip-address* is the interface name's IP address. The second *ip-address* parameter is the standby unit's IP address.
failover link *stateful-if-name*	Enables stateful failover on the specified.
show failover	This popular command displays the status of the failover configuration.
failover poll *seconds*	Specifies how long failover waits before sending special hello packets between the primary and secondary units. The default is 15 seconds. The minimum is 3 seconds, and the maximum is 15 seconds.
failover reset	Can be entered from either unit (active or standby), preferably the active unit. This forces the units back to an unfailed state and is used after repairs have been made.
write standby	Enter the write standby command from the active unit to synchronize the current configuration from RAM-to-RAM memory to the standby unit.
failover lan interface *interface-name*	Configures LAN-based failover.
failover lan unit primary | secondary	Specifies the primary or secondary Security Appliance to use for LAN-based failover.
failover replicate http	Allows the stateful replication of HTTP sessions in a stateful failover environment.

*The system address is the same address as the active unit IP address. When the active unit fails, the standby assumes the system address so that there is no need for the network devices to be reconfigured for a different firewall address.

Figure 12-3 shows two PIX Firewall units in a failover configuration. Example 12-3 shows a sample configuration for a PIX Firewall failover configuration.

Figure 12-3 *Network Diagram of Failover Configuration*

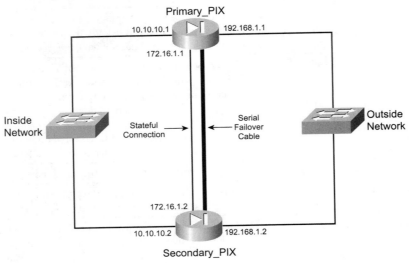

Primary_PIX

Example 12-3 *Sample Configuration for primary-PIX*

```
hostname primary-PIX
interface Ethernet0
  speed 100
  duplex full
  nameif outside
  security-level 0
  ip address 192.168.1.1 255.255.255.0 standby 192.168.1.2
interface Ethernet1
  speed 100
  duplex full
  nameif inside
  security-level 2
  ip address 10.10.10.1 255.255.255.0 standby 10.10.10.2
interface Ethernet2
  description LAN/STATE failover
  shutdown
failover lan unit primary
failover lan interface failover Ethernet4
failover lan enable
failover link failover Ethernet4
failover interface ip failover 172.16.10.1 255.255.255.0 standby 172.16.10.2
global (outside) 1 192.168.1.15-192.168.1.40 netmask 255.255.255.224
nat (inside) 1 0.0.0.0 0.0.0.0 0 0
```

Configuring failover involves defining your configuration on the primary Security Appliance or virtual context. This configuration is then replicated to the standby Security Appliance or virtual context. The following steps illustrate the tasks needed to define a basic PIX Firewall configuration utilizing a serial failover deployment.

> **NOTE** Before you begin the failover configuration, be sure that you connect the failover cable to the units correctly. Also be sure that the standby unit is not powered on.

Step 1   Enable LAN-based failover:

```
Primary-pix (config)#  failover lan enable
```

Step 2   Enable the Security Appliance as the designated primary unit:

```
Primary-pix (config)#  failvoer lan unit primary
```

Step 3   Define the failover interface:

```
Primary-pix (config)#  failover lan interface failover ethernet3
```

Step 4   Assign an IP address and standby IP address to the failover interface:

```
Primary-pix (config)#  failover interface ip failover 172.16.10.1
255.255.255.240 standby 172.16.10.2
```

Step 5   Verify your failover configuration:

```
Primary-pix (config)#  show failover
```

Step 6   Configure the secondary unit IP address from the primary unit by using the **ip address** command. Add the **ip address** command for *all* interfaces, including the one for the dedicated failover interface and any unused interfaces:

```
Primary-pix (config)#  interface ethernet0
Primary-pix (config-if)#  ip address  192.168.1.1 255.255.255.0 standby
192.168.1.2
Primary-pix (config)#  interface etherenet1
Primary-pix (config-if)#   ip address 10.10.10.1 255.255.255.0 standby
10.10.10.2
```

Step 7   Enable the failover interface:

```
Primary-pix (config)#  interface ethernet3
Primary-pix (config)#  no shutdown
```

Step 8   Save your configuration:

```
Primary-pix (config)#  write memory
```

Step 9   Use the **show ip address** command to view the addresses you specified:

```
Primary-pix (config)#  show  ip  address
System IP Addresses:
     ip address outside 192.168.1.1 255.255.255.0
     ip address inside 10.10.10.1 255.255.255.0
     ip address failover 172.16.10.1 255.255.255.240
```

```
Current IP Addresses:
    ip address outside 192.168.1.1 255.255.255.0
    ip address inside 10.10.10.1 255.255.255.0
    ip address failover 172.16.10.1 255.255.255.244
```

The current IP addresses are the same as the system IP addresses on the failover active unit. When the primary unit fails, the current IP addresses become those of the standby unit.

Step 10   Enable stateful failover:

```
Primary-pix (config)# failover link failover
```

Step 11   Power up the secondary unit. At this point, the primary unit starts replicating the configuration to the secondary.

Step 12   Verify your failover configuration:

```
Primary-pix (config)# show failover
Failover On
Cable status: N/A - LAN-based failover enabled
Failover unit Primary
Failover LAN Interface: failover Ethernet3 (up)
Unit Poll frequency 15 seconds
Interface Policy 1
Monitored Interfaced 3 of 250 maximium
Last Failover at: 22:19:11 UTC Mon Jan 19 2005
        This host: Primary - Active
              Active time: 345 (sec)

                    Interface outside (192.168.1.1):  Normal
                    Interface inside (10.10.10.1):  Normal
        Other host: Secondary - Standby
              Active time: 0 (sec)
                    Interface outside (192.168.1.1):  Normal
                    Interface inside (10.10.10.1):  Normal
Stateful Failover Logical Update Statistics
        Link : fover Ethernet3 (up)
        Stateful Obj    xmit        xerr        rcv         rerr
        General         0           0           0           0
        sys cmd         0           0           0           0
        up time         0           0           0           0
        RPC services    0           0           0           0
        TCP conn        6           0           0           0
        UDP conn        0           0           0           0
        ARP tbl         106         0           0           0
        Xlate_Timeout   0           0           0           0
        VPN IKE upd     15          0           0           0
        VPN IPSEC upd   90          0           0           0
        VPN CTCP upd    0           0           0           0
        VPN SDI upd     0           0           0           0
        VPN DHCP upd    0           0           0           0
```

```
        Logical Update Queue Information
                         Cur       Max       Total
            Recv Q:       0         0          0
            Xmit Q:       0         0          0
```

The **show failover** command displays the last occurrence of a failover. The first part of the **show failover** command output describes the cable status. Each interface on the PIX Firewall unit has one of the following values:

- **Normal**—The active unit is working, and the standby unit is ready.

- **Waiting**—Monitoring of the other unit's network interfaces has not yet started.

- **Failed**—The PIX Firewall has failed.

- **Shutdown**—The interface is turned off.

The second part of the **show failover** command describes the status of the stateful failover configuration. Each row is for a particular static object count:

- **General**—The sum of all stateful objects.

- **Sys cmd**—Refers to logical update system commands, such as **login** and **stay alive**.

- **Up time**—The value for PIX up time that the active PIX Firewall unit passes on to the standby unit.

- **Xlate**—The PIX Firewall translation information.

- **Tcp conn**—The PIX Firewall dynamic TCP connection information.

- **Udp conn**—The PIX Firewall dynamic UDP connection information.

- **ARP tbl**—The PIX Firewall dynamic ARP table information.

- **RIF tbl**—The dynamic router table information. The **Stateful Obj** has these values:

  — **Xmit**—Indicates the number of packets transmitted.

  — **Xerr**—Indicates the number of transmit errors.

  — **Rcv**—Indicates the number of packets received.

  — **rerr**—Indicates the number of receive errors.

Step 13   Enter the **write memory** command from the active unit to synchronize the current configuration to the Flash memory on the standby unit.

Foundation Summary

The "Foundation Summary" provides a convenient review of many key concepts in this chapter. If you are already comfortable with the topics in this chapter, this summary can help you recall a few details. If you just read this chapter, this review should help solidify some key facts. If you are doing your final preparation before the exam, this summary provides a convenient way to review the day before the exam.

Failover enables you to connect a second Security Appliance unit to your network to protect your network should the first unit go offline. If you use stateful failover, you can maintain operating state for TCP connections during the failover from the primary unit to the standby unit. If you use active-active failover, you can maintain two active firewalls, each acting as standby for the other.

Failover is triggered by some of the following events:

- Loss of power
- Standby unit is forced by an administrator to be active
- Cable errors
- Memory exhaustion
- Failover communication loss

Failover requires you to purchase a second Security Appliance unit, sold as a failover unit, that works only as a failover unit. Active-active failover mode removes this restriction and allows both the primary and secondary Security Appliance to act as active and standby failover units. You need to ensure that both units have the same software version (which should be the version with unrestricted licensing), activation key type, Flash memory, and the same RAM. After you configure the primary unit and attach the necessary cabling, the primary unit or context automatically copies the configuration over to the standby unit or context.

> **NOTE** With Security Appliance software version 7.0, the requirement for the same software versions on both the primary and secondary Security Appliances has been relaxed. Different maintenance levels are permitted for the purpose of hit-less updates.

If a failure is due to a condition other than a loss of power on the other unit, failover begins a series of tests to determine which unit failed. This series of tests begins when hello messages are not heard for two consecutive 15-second intervals. (The interval length depends on how you set the **failover poll** command.) Hello messages are sent over both network interfaces and the failover cable. Failover uses the following tests to determine the other unit's availability:

- Link up/down
- Network activity
- ARP
- Ping

The stateful failover feature passes per-connection stateful information to the standby unit. After a failover occurs, the same connection information is available at the new active unit. Most end-user applications do not have to reconnect to maintain the communication session.

Q&A

As mentioned in the Introduction, the questions in this book are more difficult than what you should experience on the exam. The questions are designed to ensure your understanding of the concepts discussed in this chapter and adequately prepare you to complete the exam. You should use the simulated exams on the CD to practice for the exam.

The answers to these questions can be found in Appendix A:

1. What are some things that trigger a failover event?

2. What command assigns an IP address to the standby Security Appliance?

3. How many PIX Firewall devices can be configured in a failover configuration?

4. What are the disadvantages of LAN-based failover?

5. What is some of the information that is updated to the standby unit in a stateful failover configuration?

6. What command forces replication to the standby unit?

7. What command configures a LAN-based failover?

8. What is the default failover poll, in seconds?

9. Does configuration replication save the running configuration to Flash memory on the standby unit during normal operations?

10. How long does it take to detect a failure?

11. How many failover groups are allowed per Security Appliance?

This chapter covers the following subjects:

- Examining the Security Appliance Status

- PIX Firewall Enables a Secure VPN

- Prepare to Configure VPN Support

- Configure IKE Parameters

- Configure IPSec Parameters

- Test and Verify VPN Configuration

- Scale Security Appliance VPNs

CHAPTER 13

Virtual Private Networks

Virtual private networks (VPN) have become crucial components of nearly all enterprise networks. The ability of VPN technologies to create a secure link interconnecting offices over the Internet saves companies the expense of dedicated connections. Additionally, VPN connections enable remote users to connect to their headquarters securely.

How to Best Use This Chapter

This chapter provides an overview of the different VPN technologies available and discusses where the Cisco Security Appliance can be used as an endpoint for VPNs. You must become very familiar with the methodology used to implement VPNs and how that methodology is applied to the Security Appliance. As you read through this chapter, consider how encryption technology is applied in general, and then focus on the configuration steps required to configure the Security Appliance. If you are at all familiar with configuring VPNs on any Cisco Systems product, you will probably find this chapter very easy.

"Do I Know This Already?" Quiz

The purpose of the "Do I Know This Already?" quiz is to help you decide if you really need to read the entire chapter. If you already intend to read the entire chapter, you do not necessarily need to answer these questions now.

The eleven-question quiz, derived from the major sections in the "Foundation Topics" portion of the chapter, helps you determine how to spend your limited study time. Table 13-1 outlines the major topics discussed in this chapter and the "Do I Know This Already?" quiz questions that correspond to those topics.

Table 13-1 *"Do I Know This Already?" Foundation Topics Section-to-Question Mapping*

Foundations Topics Section	QuestionsCoveredinThisSection	Score
Examining the Security Appliance Status	10	
Security Appliance Enables a Secure VPN	9	
Prepare to Configure VPN Support	6, 7	
Configure IKE Parameters	2, 3	
Configure IPSec Parameters	1, 4	
Test and Verify VPN Configuration	10	
Scale Security Appliance VPNs	5, 8	
Explain the Purpose of WebVPN	11	
Configure WebVPN Parameters	11	

CAUTION   The goal of self assessment is to gauge your mastery of the topics in this chapter. If you do not know the answer to a question or are only partially sure of the answer, you should mark this question wrong for purposes of the self assessment. Giving yourself credit for an answer you correctly guess skews your self-assessment results and might provide you with a false sense of security.

1. Which type of encryption is stronger?

    a. Group 2 Diffie-Hellman

    b. AES-128

    c. 3DES

    d. AES-192

    e. DES

2. Which service uses UDP port 500?

    a. IPSec

    b. OAKLEY

    c. IKE

    d. None of these answers are correct

3. Which service uses TCP port 50?

    a. aIKE

    b. AH

    c. OAKLEY

    d. ESP

    e. None of these answers are correct

4. What is the size of the output for a MD5 hash?

    a. There is no fixed size.

    b. 256 bits

    c. 255 bits

    d. 128 bits

    e. None of these answers are correct

5. What is the most scalable VPN solution?

    a. Manual-IPSec with CAs

    b. IKE using OAKLEY

    c. IKE using CAs

    d. CAs using preshared keys

    e. None of these answers are correct

6. What is the function of the access list with regard to VPNs?

    a. It tells the Security Appliance what traffic should be allowed.

    b. It tells the Security Appliance what traffic should be encrypted.

    c. It tells the Security Appliance what traffic should be denied.

    d. None of these answers are correct.

7. What is the configuration value for the unlimited ISAKMP phase 1 lifetime?

    a. Unlim

    b. 99999

    c. 86400

    d. 19200

    e. 0

8. The X509v3 standard applies to which standard or protocol?

    a. Authentication Header format

    b. ESP header format

    c. Digital certificates

    d. Diffie-Hellman negotiation

    e. AES encryption

9. What are three types of VPNs?

    a. Hardware, software, and concentrator

    b. Manual, dynamic, and very secure

    c. Dialup, cable, and LAN

    d. Access, intranet, and extranet

    e. Internet, extranet, and dialup

10. What command will allow you to watch the IKE negotiations?

    a. debug isakmp sa

    b. debug crypto isakmp

    c. view isakmp neg

    d. view crypto isakmp

    e. debug isakmp crypto

11. What features of WebVPNs differ from IPSec VPNs?

    a. WebVPNs are clientless.

    b. WebVPNs allow port forwarding.

    c. WebVPNs securely accesses e-mail systems.

    d. WebVPNs are supported only by ASA 55X0 firewalls.

    e. None of these answers are correct.

The answers to the "Do I Know This Already?" quiz are found in Appendix A, "Answers to the 'Do I Know This Already?' Quizzes and Q&A Sections." The suggested choices for your next step are as follows:

- **8 or less overall score**—Read the entire chapter. This includes the "Foundation Topics," "Foundation Summary," and "Q&A" sections.

- **9 to 11 overall score**—If you want more review of these topics, skip to the "Foundation Summary" section and then go to the "Q&A" section. Otherwise, move to the next chapter.

Foundation Topics

Overview of Virtual Private Network Technologies

Before the creation of VPN technologies, the only way for companies to secure network communications between different locations was to purchase or lease costly dedicated connections. VPNs allow companies to create secure encrypted tunnels between locations over a shared network infrastructure such as the Internet. A VPN is a service that offers secure, reliable connectivity over a shared public network infrastructure. VPNs are broken into three types based on the business component accessing the VPN and the assets available by using the VPN:

- **Access VPNs**—An access VPN, as shown in Figure 13-1, provides secure communications with remote users. Access VPNs are used by users who connect using dialup or other mobile connections. A user working from home would most likely use an access VPN to connect to the company network. Access VPNs usually require some type of client software running on the user's computer. This type of VPN is commonly called a *remote-access VPN*.

Figure 13-1   *Access VPN*

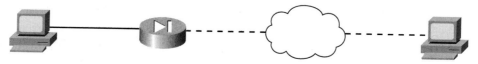

- **Intranet VPNs**—An intranet VPN is used to interconnect a company's different locations securely. This allows all locations to have access to the resources available on the enterprise network. Intranet VPNs link headquarters, offices, and branch offices over a shared infrastructure using connections that are always encrypted. This type of VPN is normally configured as a *site-to-site VPN*.

- **Extranet VPNs**—Extranet VPNs provide a secure tunnel between customers, suppliers, and partners over a shared infrastructure using connections that are always encrypted. This type of VPN is also normally configured as a site-to-site VPN. The difference between an intranet VPN and an extranet VPN is the network access that is granted at either end of the VPN. Figure 13-2 shows a site-to-site VPN, the configuration commonly used for both intranet and extranet VPNs.

Figure 13-2 *Site-to-Site VPN*

Internet Protocol Security

Internet Protocol Security (IPSec) is not a protocol. It is a framework of open-standard protocol suites designed to provide data authentication, data integrity, and data confidentiality. IPSec runs at the Internet Protocol (IP) layer and uses Internet Key Exchange (IKE) to negotiate the security association (SA) between the peers. There are actually two *phases* of negotiation that must take place. The *phase 1* negotiation establishes the IKE SA. The IKE SA must be established to begin the *phase 2* negotiations to establish the IPSec SA. The following items must be negotiated as phase 1 of IKE SA negotiation:

- Encryption algorithm

- Hash algorithm

- Authentication method

- Diffie-Hellman group

As soon as the IKE SA negotiation is complete, the established SA is bidirectional.

The phase 2 negotiations establish unidirectional SAs between two IPSec peers. The SAs determine the keying, protocols, and algorithms to be used between the peers. Two primary security protocols are included as part of the IPSec standard supported by the Cisco Security Appliance:

- **Encapsulating Security Payload (ESP)**—ESP provides data authentication, encryption, and antireplay services. ESP is protocol number 50 assigned by the Internet Assigned Numbers Authority (IANA). ESP is primarily responsible for getting the data from the source to the destination in a secure manner, verifying that the data has not been altered, and ensuring that the session cannot be hijacked. ESP also can be used to authenticate the sender, either by itself or in conjunction with Authentication Header (AH). ESP can be configured to encrypt the entire data packet or only the packet's payload. Figure 13-3 shows how ESP encapsulates the Internet Protocol version 4 (IPv4) packet, which portions are encrypted, and which are authenticated.

- **Authentication Header (AH)**—AH provides data authentication and antireplay services. AH is protocol number 51 assigned by the IANA. The primary function of AH is origin authentication. AH does not provide any data encryption. It provides only origin authentication or verifies that the data is from the sender. This functionality also prevents session hijacking. AH does not work with Network Address Translation (NAT) because the address translation occurs prior to the IPSec SA being established. NAT will change the IP address of the original IP header, creating a mismatch with the AH and causing the hash to fail. Figure 11-4 shows how AH is inserted into the IPv4 packet.

It is important to note that ESP authenticates only the payload, and AH authenticates the entire packet including the IP header.

Figure 13-3 *ESP Encapsulation*

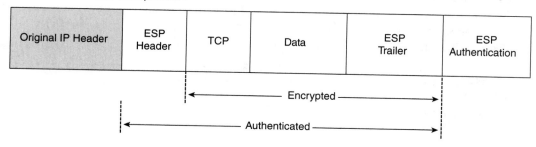

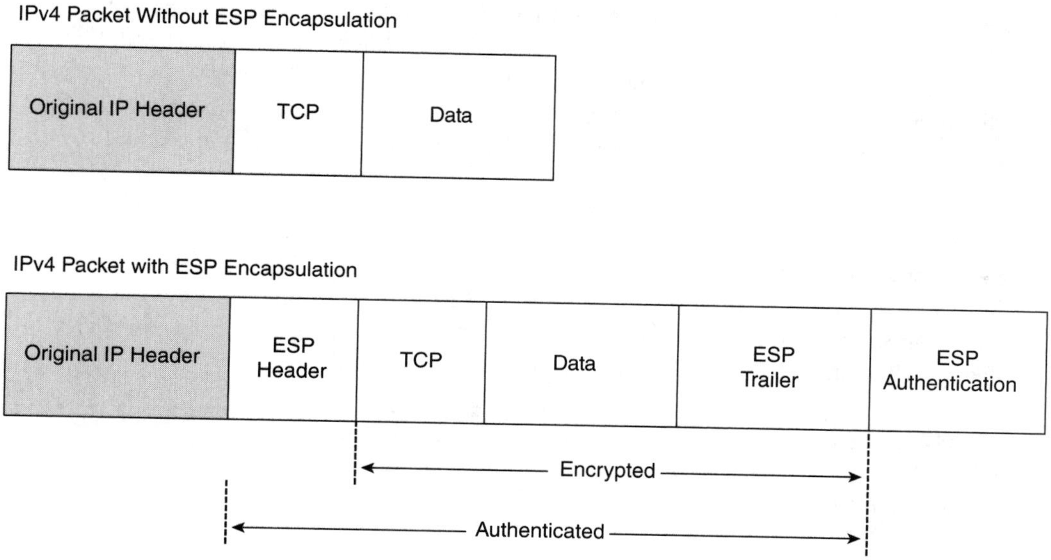

Figure 13-4 *AH Insertion into the IPv4 Packet*

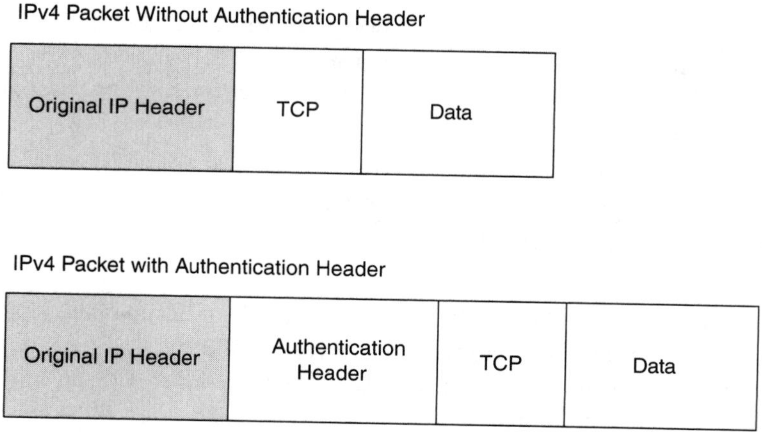

IPv4 Packet Without Authentication Header

Original IP Header	TCP	Data

IPv4 Packet with Authentication Header

Original IP Header	Authentication Header	TCP	Data

Support for NAT and Port Address Translation

The Cisco Security Appliance supports ESP with NAT using a *fixup* protocol that allows for application inspection of ESP. The Security Appliance also supports ESP with Port Address

Translation (PAT) by restricting ESP to a single port (port 0) but with only a single ESP tunnel. The Cisco Security Appliance performs ESP tunnel serialization and the matching and recording of Security Parameter Indexes (SPI) for each ESP connection. The SPI is a number that combines with the destination IP address and security protocol to uniquely identify the SA. AH does not support either a NAT or PAT device between the two AH peers.

Another feature supported by the Security Appliance is NAT Traversal. NAT Traversal allows ESP packets to pass through one or more NAT devices. The command for NAT Traversal is **isakmp nat-traversal** [*natkeepalives*]. The values for *natkeepalives* is between 10 and 3600 seconds.

Supported Encryption Algorithms

Both ESP and AH can be configured to use a specific encryption algorithm and hash algorithms. An encryption algorithm is the mathematical algorithm used to encrypt and decrypt the data. The hash algorithm is used to ensure data integrity.

NOTE   The Cisco Security Appliance requires an activation key (license) to implement the IPSec features. Refer to Chapter 3, "Cisco Security Appliance" for the specific licenses available for each firewall model.

The Security Appliance supports the following encryption algorithms:

- **Data Encryption Standard (DES)**—DES is a 56-bit symmetric encryption algorithm. Although it is still widely used, DES is somewhat outdated and should not be used if your data is highly sensitive. It is commonly used for VPN connections to locations outside the United States that cannot purchase higher levels of encryption because of U.S. technology export policies.

- **Triple Data Encryption Standard (3DES)**—3DES is a 168-bit symmetric key cipher derived by encrypting the data three consecutive times using DES. The data is encrypted using a 56-bit key, decrypted using a second 56-bit key, and then reencrypted using a third 56-bit key.

- **Advanced Encryption Standard (AES)**—AES is a symmetric block cipher based on the Rijndael algorithm that encrypts and decrypts data using cryptographic keys of 128, 192, or 256 bit lengths. The encrypted data is placed into 128-bit blocks that are combined into *cipher block chains*.

A hash algorithm takes a message as input and creates a fixed-length output called the *message digest*. The message digest is put into the digital signature algorithm, which generates or verifies the signature for the message. Signing the message digest rather than the actual message usually improves the processing of the message, because the message digest is smaller than the message. The same hash algorithm must be used by the originator and verifier of the message. The Cisco Security Appliance supports the Keyed-Hash Message Authentication Code (HMAC) variant of the following hash algorithms:

- **Secure Hash Algorithm 1 (SHA-1)**— The output of SHA-1 is 160 bit. Because the output is larger than Message Digest 5 (MD5), SHA-1 is considered more secure.

- **Message Digest 5 (MD5)**—The output of MD5 is 128 bit. MD5 is slightly faster to process because of its smaller message digest.

Internet Key Exchange

Internet Key Exchange is the protocol that is responsible for negotiation. IKE is the short name for ISAKMP/Oakley, which stands for Internet Security Association and Key Management Protocol (with Oakley distribution). The terms *IKE* and *ISAKMP* are used interchangeably throughout this chapter. IKE operates over User Datagram Protocol (UDP) port 500 and negotiates the key exchange between the ISAKMP peers to establish a bidirectional SA. This process requires that the IPSec systems first authenticate themselves to each other and establish ISAKMP (IKE) shared keys. This negotiation is called *phase 1* negotiation, and it is during this phase that the Diffie-Hellman key agreement is performed. During phase 1, IKE creates the IKE SA, which is a secure channel between the two IKE peers. IKE authenticates the peer and the IKE messages between the peers during IKE phase 1. Phase 1 consists of *main mode* or *aggressive mode*.

A main mode negotiation consists of six message exchanges:

- The first two messages simply negotiate the exchange policy.

- The second two messages exchange Diffie-Hellman public-key values and an 8- to 256-bit *nonce* (a random number generated by a peer).

- The last two messages authenticate the key exchange.

Figure 13-5 shows main mode key exchanges.

Figure 13-5 *Main Mode Key Exchanges*

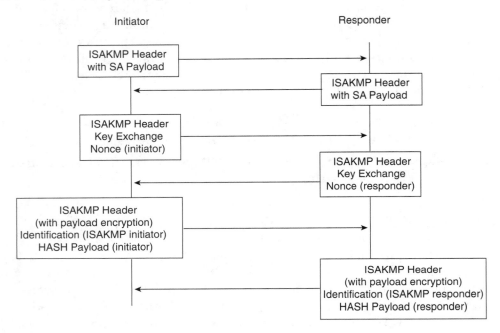

> **NOTE** There are three message exchanges in an aggressive mode exchange:
>
> - The first two messages negotiate policy, exchange public-key values, and authenticate the responder.
>
> - The third message authenticates the initiator and is normally postponed until the negotiation is complete and is not sent as clear text.

Figure 13-6 shows aggressive mode key exchanges.

> **NOTE** Diffie-Hellman is a public-key cryptography protocol that is used between two IPSec peers to derive a shared secret over an unsecured channel without transmitting it to each peer. The Security Appliance supports three Diffie-Hellman groups: Group 1 is 768-bit, group 2 is 1024-bit, and group 5 is 1536-bit.

Figure 13-6 *Aggressive Mode Key Exchanges*

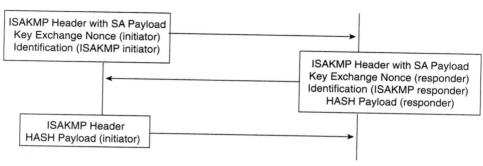

Peers that want to participate in the IPSec session *must* authenticate themselves to each other before IKE can proceed. Peer authentication occurs during the main mode/aggressive mode exchange during IKE phase 1. The IKE protocol is very flexible and supports multiple authentication methods as part of the phase 1 exchange. The two entities must agree on a common authentication protocol through a negotiation process. IKE phase 1 has three methods to authenticate IPSec peers in Cisco products:

- **Preshared keys**—Case-sensitive key values entered into each peer manually and used to authenticate the peer.

- **RSA signatures**—A public-key cryptographic system that uses a digital certificate authenticated by an RSA signature.

- **RSA encrypted nonces**—Use Rivest-Shamir-Adleman (RSA) encryption to encrypt a nonce value (a random number generated by the peer) and other values. The Security Appliance does not support this authentication type.

Having completed the phase 1 negotiation, IKE provides a secure channel for the completion of phase 2. The phase 2 exchange occurs only after the IKE SA negotiation is complete. It is used to derive keying material and negotiate policies for non-ISAKMP SAs (such as the IPSec SA). IKE performs the following functions and provides the following benefits:

- It automatically negotiates the security parameters for SAs between peers, removing the requirement of manually configuring each peer.

- It provides the capability to configure an SA's lifetime.

- It allows the encryption key to change dynamically while the IPSec session is open.

- It provides antireplay (hijacking) protection to IPSec services.

- It provides dynamic authentication of SA peers.

- It provides support for certification authorities.

- It allows for the scalable implementation of IPSec.

Perfect Forward Secrecy

Perfect Forward Secrecy (PFS) is the function of two parties agreeing on a temporary session key that is different for each message. This provides confidence that the compromise of the long-term private key does not compromise previous session keys. PFS prevents an eavesdropper from being able to decrypt traffic even if the eavesdropper has the private keys from both parties because the parties negotiate the temporary session key.

Certification Authorities

IKE interoperates with X.509v3 certificates for authentication that requires public keys. Certification authorities (CA) manage certificate requests, issue digital certificates, and publish certificate revocation lists (CRL) to list certificates that are no longer valid. A digital certificate contains information about the user or device and includes a copy of its public key. This technology enables IPSec-protected networks to scale, because the peers simply exchange digital certificates that have been authenticated by a CA, removing the requirement to configure the preshared key manually for each IPSec peer. The PIX interoperates with CA server products from the following vendors:

- Baltimore Technologies
- Entrust Corporation
- Microsoft Corporation
- VeriSign

After ensuring that you have correctly configured the firewall host name, domain name, and the system date/time, you can initiate enrollment with a CA server. It is important that your date and time are correctly configured so that you can verify the validity of the certificate when received. The process that a PIX uses to enroll with a CA server is as follows:

Step 1   The firewall generates an RSA key pair.

Step 2   The firewall contacts the CA server and obtains the CA server's certificate, which contains the public key.

Step 3   The firewall requests a signed certificate from the CA server using the generated key and the public key from the CA.

Step 4   The CA administrator verifies the request and returns the signed certificate.

Overview of WebVPN

WebVPNs are a new form of VPN access introduced with the ASA 55X0 family of firewalls. A WebVPN is a clientless remote-access VPN that uses a web browser to access an enterprise information technology (IT) network. Unlike a standard IPSec VPN, which requires a specific VPN client software, a WebVPN client can use any web browser that supports Java Runtime Environment (JRE) 1.4.1 or later. This allows more mobility for an end user, access from home or extranet computers, and use by employees who may only need infrequent access.

WebVPN uses secure Secure Sockets Layer (SSL) and Secure Sockets Layer/Transport Layer Security (SSL/TLS) protocols to create secure connections to an internal IT resource from an end user's system. Through the WebVPN, a client will have access to many of the IT resources normally accesses through a traditional IPSec VPN. The services that can be enabled through a WebVPN connection are as follows:

- **E-mail Proxy**—Allows proxy access to many common mail servers and software, including POP3S, IMAP4S, Post Office, and SMTPS
- **MAPI Access**—Allows **proxy access to a** Microsoft Exchange Server
- **HTTPS**—Allows secure (SSL) access to internal websites, **Microsoft Web Outlook Access,** and **other web-based** resources
- **Windows File Access**—Allows access to file browsing on the IT network, **NT/Active Director (AD), and other preconfigured file servers**
- **Port Forwarding**—Allows access through port forwarding of several TCP-based applications

Although WebVPN has some advantages over an IPSec VPN, as previously described, enabling WebVPN on a Security Appliance will also have a few disadvantages. One major disadvantage in that enabling WebVPN on a Security Appliance causes a reduction in performance. Essentially, all WebVPN connections are proxied through the Security Appliance. Another major disadvantage in enabling WebVPN is that several features are disabled for WebVPN connections. This is due to the way the Security Appliance handles the WebVPN SSL and SSL/TLS connections. These features are only unavailable to WebVPN users and do not effect any other traffic flows or VPN users on the Security Appliance. The following features are not supported with a WebVPN connection:

- NAT
- PAT
- Active-active or active-standby stateful failover
- The Modular Policy Framework inspection feature

- Filter configuration commands
- Rate limiting using the **police** command and **priority-queue** command
- Connection limits
- The **established** command

Additionally, if WebVPN has been configured on the outside interface of the Security Appliance, management of the outside interface by the Cisc Adaptive Security Device Manager (ASDM) will be lost. Additional security concerns arise when implementing WebVPNs for remote users. Key loggers can be used on public terminals to capture username and password sets for future access. Web browsers could capture in their caching mechanisms username and password sets that could be used by a malicious user to gain access. Make sure a vulnerabilities assessment has been done before enabling WebVPN for public Internet access.

> **NOTE**   WebVPN can only be used on the ASA 55X0 Security Appliances and is not supported by the PIX 500 series firewalls.

WebVPN Portal Interface

WebVPN uses a front-end portal interface to authenticate and give access to end users. To access the WebVPN portal, an end user will first authenticate using the authentication, authorization, and authorization (AAA) method configured on the ASA that has the WebVPN enabled. The end user will connect to a domain name or IP address, such as 192.168.11.103, which represents the interface that WebVPN in enabled on using https://. Port 80 access to WebVPN is not allowed. The end user will be greeted with an authentication screen, as shown in Figure 13-7.

The portal interface uses SSL/TLS encryption during access and runs on a local https server. Through the portal interface, the end user gains access to authorized parts of the internal network and accesses e-mail and file servers via click-through links. The https server that controls the portal interface shown in Figure 13-8 resides on the ASA 55x0 Security Appliance and is fully customizable by the security administrator.

Figure 13-7   *WebVPN Login Authentication Window*

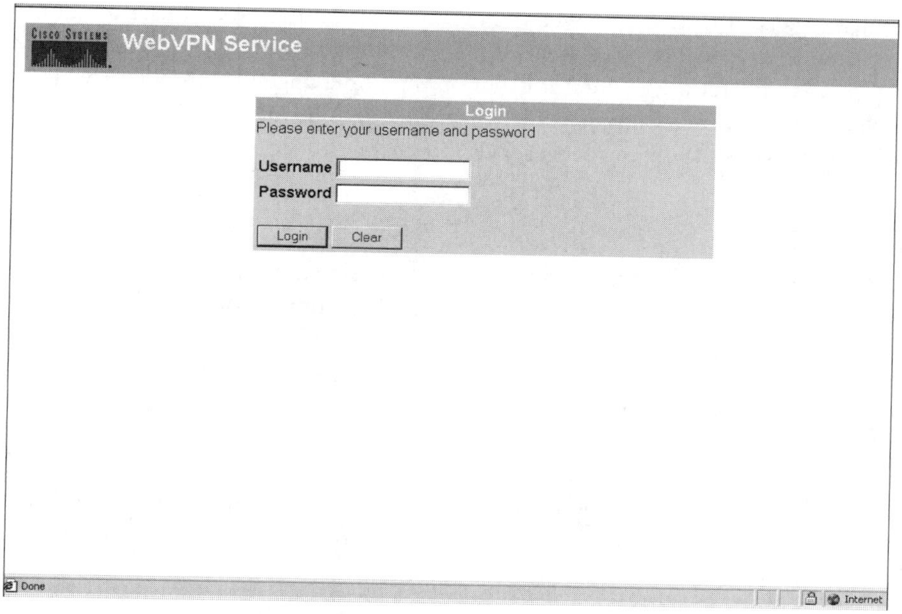

Figure 13-8   *Default Portal Homepage*

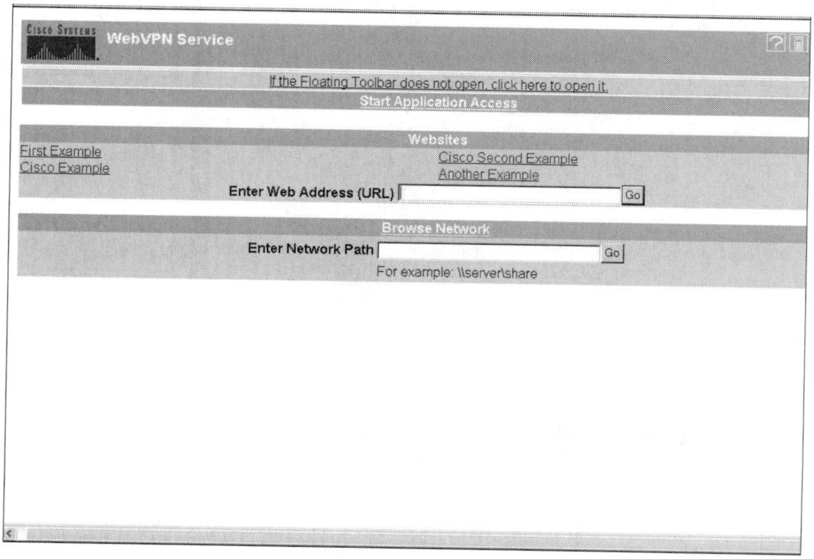

After WebVPN has authenticated an end user, the portal home page will be displayed on the end user's web browser. The WebVPN home page allows an end user direct access to preconfigured websites, such as "Cisco Example" in Figure 13-7. In addition, an end user can manually enter a website not listed on the home page into the Enter web address (URL) field, can access a preconfigured file server through the Enter Network Path field, or browse an internal NetBIOS Name Server (NBNS) network through the Browse Network link.

Port Forwarding

WebVPN supports TCP-based port forwarding through a Java-based applet located on the portal home page. The Java-based applet maps an application-specific port on the end user's computer to the same port on a server located behind the ASA Security Appliance. An example of this would be mapping port 22 for SSH access from the end user's computer to a UNIX server inside the enterprise network.

A list of applications preconfigured for port forwarding can be found through the Start TCP application access link on the Portal home page. Once clicked, a new window, shown in Figure 13-9, is opened with a list of applications. All of these listed applications are available until the window is closed.

Figure 13-9 *Application Access Window*

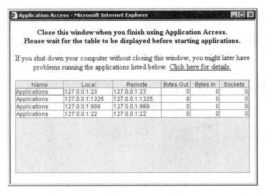

NOTE Due to program limitations in the Java Applet, end users using Microsoft Windows may have access and connection problems to port forwarded applications if the end user shuts down their computer before closing the Application Access window.

Configuring the Security Appliance as a VPN Gateway

Configuring the Cisco Security Appliance as a VPN gateway or VPN termination point is a process that requires four specific tasks:

- Selecting the configuration
- Configuring IKE
- Configuring IPSec
- Testing and troubleshooting the connection

Selecting the Configuration

Selecting a standardized configuration is perhaps the most important step in creating a VPN. You need to follow these steps when selecting your configuration:

Step 1   Determine which hosts will participate in this connection and which devices to use as VPN gateways. The Cisco Security Appliance can create a VPN connection to another PIX, VPN appliances, routers, other third- party firewalls that support IPSec, and so on.

Step 2   Gather information about the peers and all hosts and networks that will participate in this VPN.

Step 3   Select which phase 1 and phase 2 IKE policies to use based on the number and location of the peers.

Step 4   Verify the current configuration of your Cisco Security Appliance to ensure that you do not select any policies (such as access control lists [ACL], ISAKMP policies, or crypto maps) that conflict with the current configuration:

- Ensure that you have connectivity with your peers. If you are unable to connect with a peer in the clear, you will be unable to create an encrypted connection.

- Ensure that perimeter devices, such as routers, are allowing the traffic required to create and maintain the VPN connection. Most notable are UDP port 500 (used for IKE negotiation), protocol 50 (ESP), and protocol 51 (AH).

It is extremely important to ensure that VPN peers have configurations with matching elements. If both peers are not configured to have compatible VPN components, they will be unable to create the encrypted connection.

Configuring IKE

Remember that IKE is the method used by the peers to negotiate and establish the SA. Determining which IKE configuration to use is not difficult. Most companies have a standard configuration that they employ when creating any VPN connection. If you do not have a preestablished policy, you should select a policy that allows your minimum amount of security to be not less than that required for the most sensitive data to travel across the connection. The following steps are required to configure IKE on a Cisco Security Appliance:

Step 1   Enable IKE—This is a simple command on the PIX. You turn on IKE by enabling it on a specific interface. The syntax for the command is **isakmp enable** *if_name*. For example:

```
tgpix(config)#  isakmp enable outside
```

Step 2   Create your IKE policies (phase 1)—To create the IKE policies, you select certain options and configure them as policies. Again, it is extremely important that both peers are configured in the same manner. Any undefined policies use the current default values. You must make the following choices when creating the policy:

• **Authentication method**—Preshared secret or RSA signature

> **NOTE**   You need to configure your SA peer's preshared secret for each IP address.

• **Message encryption algorithm**—DES, 3DES, AES, AES-192, or AES-256

• **Message integrity algorithm**—SHA-1 or MD5

• **Key exchange parameters**—Diffie-Hellman group 1, group 2, or group 5

• **IKE established SA lifetime**—The default is 86,400 seconds. Security Appliance supports an unlimited ISAKMP SA (phase 1) lifetime by using a value of 0. This allows for VPN connectivity with third-party VPN products that do not support rekeying the ISAKMP SA. An unlimited ISAKMP SA lifetime will be much less secure than a constantly rekeyed SA and should be used only if required to support connections to third-party gateways.

The **isakmp policy** command is a simple command with several options. In the event that you do not select a specific option, the Security Appliance will automatically choose a default value. Table 13-1 describes the **isakmp policy** command parameters.

Table 13-2   **isakmp policy** *Command Parameters*

Parameter	Description
priority	Allows you to prioritize your ISAKMP policies. Policy priorities range from 1 to 65,534, with 1 being the highest priority.
authentication pre-share	Specifies that the peer authentication method is the preshared key. This requires that the preshared key be manually configured on both peers.
authentication rsa-sig	Specifies that the peer authentication method is RSA signatures. This method allows peer authentication to be completed automatically and is a more scalable solution. This is the default setting.
encryption des	Specifies that the encryption algorithm is DES. This is the default setting.
encryption 3des	Specifies that the encryption algorithm is 3DES.
encryption aes	Specifies that the encryption algorithm is AES-128.
encryption aes-192	Specifies that the encryption algorithm is AES-192.
encryption aes-256	Specifies that the encryption algorithm is AES-256.
group 1	Specifies that Diffie-Hellman group 1 (768-bit) is used. This is the default setting.
group 2	Specifies that Diffie-Hellman group 2 (1024-bit) is used.
group 5	Specifies the Diffie-Hellman group 5 (1536-bit) is used.
hash md5	Specifies that the MD5 hash algorithm is used.
hash sha	Specifies that the SHA-1 hash algorithm is used. This is the default setting.
lifetime	Specifies the SA's lifetime. The range is from 60 seconds to unlimited. The default setting is 86,400 seconds.

For example, to configure ISAKMP policies configured for VPN peers, you would have a configuration similar to this:

```
LOCAL PIX FIREWALL>>>>>>>>>>>
tgpix(config)# isakmp policy 10 authentication pre-share tgpix(config)#
isakmp policy 10 encryption 3des tgpix(config)# isakmp policy 10 group
2
tgpix(config)# isakmp policy 10 hash md5 tgpix(config)# isakmp policy
10 lifetime 86400 tgpix(config)# isakmp enable outside
```

```
REMOTE PIX FIREWALL>>>>>>>>>>

gonderpix (config)# isakmp policy 10 authentication pre-share gonderpix
(config)# isakmp policy 10 encryption 3des gonderpix (config)# isakmp
policy 10 group 2
gonderpix (config)# isakmp policy 10 hash md5 gonderpix (config)# isakmp
policy 10 lifetime 86400 gonderpix (config)# isakmp enable outside
```

Note that the policies are the same on both peers; however, it is not a
requirement for the policy number to match on each peer.

Step 3   **Configure the preshared key**—You can configure the same preshared key for all
your SAs. This method is not recommended, however, because it is more secure
to specify a different key for each SA. To configure the preshared key, you need
to determine how the peers identify themselves. SA peers can identify themselves
by IP address or host name. It is recommended that you use the same method of
identification for all SAs. If you choose to identify the peers by host name, the
negotiations could fail if a Domain Name System (DNS) issue prevents the host
name from resolving correctly. Here is the command for configuring
identification:

```
isakmp identity (address | hostname)
```

Here is the command for configuring the preshared key:

```
isakmp key string address | peer-address [netmask mask]
```

NOTE   You can configure your preshared key with a wildcard IP address and
netmask, but this is not recommended and could be considered a security risk.

To configure ISAKMP policies for both Cisco Security Appliances with
the ISAKMP identities and **isakmp key** commands added, use a
configuration similar to this:

```
LOCAL PIX FIREWALL>>>>>>>>>>>
tgpix(config)#  isakmp  policy  10  authentication  pre-share
tgpix(config)#  isakmp  policy  10  encryption  3des
tgpix(config)#  isakmp  policy  10  group  2
tgpix(config)#  isakmp  policy  10  hash  md5
tgpix(config)#  isakmp  policy  10  lifetime  86400
tgpix(config)#  isakmp  enable  outside
tgpix(config)#  isakmp  identity  address
tgpix(config)#  isakmp  key  abc123  address  192.168.2.1  netmask
  255.255.255.255

REMOTE PIX FIREWALL>>>>>>>>>>
gonderpix (config)#  isakmp  policy  10  authentication  pre-share
gonderpix (config)#  isakmp  policy  10  encryption  3des
```

```
gonderpix (config)#  isakmp  policy  10  group  2
gonderpix (config)#  isakmp  policy  10  hash  md5
gonderpix (config)#  isakmp  policy  10  lifetime  86400
gonderpix (config)#  isakmp  enable  outside
gonderpix (config)#  isakmp  identity  address
gonderpix (config)#  isakmp key abc123 address 192.168.1.1 netmask
     255.255.255.255
```

Step 4   **Verify your configuration**—Because of the complexity of the configurations, it is a good idea to verify your configuration. Remember that both peers must have an exactly matched phase 1 policy for the key exchange to occur, which is the first step in establishing the VPN connection. As always, the **show** command is a very effective tool for checking your configuration. You can get extended output with **show isakmp policy**, or you can see the commands that were input with **show isakmp.** You get the same output with **write terminal** as with **show isakmp.** Here is some sample output from **show isakmp:**

```
tgpix#  show  isakmp
isakmp policy 10 authentication pre-share isakmp policy 10 encryption 3des
isakmp policy 10 group 2
isakmp policy 10 hash md5
isakmp policy 10 lifetime 86400
isakmp enable outside

isakmp key ***** 192.168.2.1 netmask 255.255.255.255
```

You can see that policy 10 uses preshared secrets for authentication, 3DES encryption, the group 2 (1024-bit) Diffie-Hellman key exchange, MD5 hash, and a connection lifetime of 86,400 seconds (24 hours), and it is enabled on the outside interface.

Here is some sample output from **show isakmp policy:**

```
tgpix#  show  isakmp  policy
Protection suite or priority  10
    encryption algorithm:    Three key triple DES
    hash algorithm:          Message Digest 5
    authentication method:    Pre-Shared Key
    Diffie-Hellman group:    #2 (1024 bit)
    lifetime:         86400 seconds, no volume limit
Default protection suite
    encryption algorithm:    DES - Data Encryption Standard (56-bit keys)
hash algorithm:          Secure Hash Standard
    authentication method:    Rivest-Shamir-Adleman Signature
    Diffie-Hellman group:    #1 (768 bit)
    lifetime:         86400 seconds, no volume limit
```

In this output, you can see the two ISAKMP policies that are configured on the firewall (policy 10 and default). If you do not configure a specific ISAKMP policy, the default values are used.

Configuring IPSec

Now that you have successfully configured IKE on your firewall, you are ready to configure IPSec. Follow these steps:

Step 1   Create a crypto access list to define the traffic to protect.

Step 2   Configure a transform set that defines how the traffic is protected.

Step 3   Create a crypto map entry.

Step 4   Apply the crypto map set to an interface.

Step 1: Creating a Crypto Access List

Crypto access lists are used to identify which IP traffic is to be protected by encryption and which traffic is not. After the access list is defined, the crypto maps reference it to identify the type of traffic that IPSec protects. The **permit** keyword in the access list causes IPSec to protect all IP traffic that matches the access list criteria. If the **deny** keyword is used in the access list, the traffic is not encrypted. The crypto access lists specified at the remote peer should be mirror images of the access lists specified at the local peer. This ensures that traffic that has IPSec protection applied locally can be processed correctly at the remote peer. The crypto map entries should also support common transforms and should refer to the other system as a peer.

It is not recommended that you use the **permit ip any any** command, because it causes all outbound traffic to be encrypted (and all encrypted traffic to be sent to the peer specified in the corresponding crypto map entry), and it requires encryption of all inbound traffic. With this type of access list, the firewall drops all inbound packets that are not encrypted.

The syntax for the **access-list** command is as follows:

```
access-list  acl_name  permit | deny  protocol  src_addr src_mask
   [operator  port[port]]  dest_addr dest_mask [operator  port[port]]
```

Table 13-3 lists and describes the command arguments and options for the **access-list** command.

Table 13-3 *access-list Command Parameters*

Parameter	Description
acl-name	Specifies the access list name or number.
permit	Encrypts the packet.
deny	Does not encrypt the packet.
protocol	Specifies the protocol by name or IP protocol number. Protocols include **icmp**, **tcp**, **udp**, and **ip**. (**ip** is the keyword for any.)
src_addr, dest-addr	Specifies the IP address of the network or host for the source and destination. The term **any** is the wildcard for 0.0.0.0 0.0.0.0. It is also possible to use the word **host** to indicate a 32-bit mask.
src_mask, dest-mask	Specifies the subnet masks of the source or destination network.
operator	An optional field. It includes the following options: **lt** = Less than **gt** = Greater than **eq** = Equal to **neq** = Not equal to **range** = Inclusive range
port	Specifies the TCP or UDP port used for the IP service.

NOTE The configuration examples in this chapter build on each other (they include the previous portion). The specific items that are being addressed as part of the current configuration are highlighted.

Example 13-1 shows the current ISAKMP policy configuration with the access list added.

Example 13-1 *Crypto Access List*

```
tgpix(config)# isakmp policy 10 authentication pre-share
tgpix(config)# isakmp policy 10 encryption 3des
tgpix(config)# isakmp policy 10 group 2
tgpix(config)# isakmp policy 10 hash md5
tgpix(config)# isakmp policy 10 lifetime 86400
tgpix(config)# isakmp enable outside
tgpix(config)# isakmp identity address
tgpix(config)# isakmp key abc123 address 192.168.2.1 netmask 255.255.255.255
tgpix(config)# access-list 90 permit ip 10.10.10.0 255.255.255.0 10.10.20.0 255.255.255.0
```

Step 2: Configuring a Transform Set

A transform set defines the combination of encryption algorithms and message integrity algorithms to be used for the IPSec tunnel. Transforms are combined to make *transform sets*. Both peers agree on the transform set during the IPSec negotiation. You can define multiple transform sets because both peers search for a common transform set during the IKE negotiation. If a common transform set is found, it is selected and applied to the protected traffic. Table 13-4 shows the transform sets supported on the Cisco PIX Firewall.

Table 13-4 *PIX-Supported IPSec Transforms*

Transform	Description
ah-md5-hmac	AH-MD5-HMAC transform used for authentication
ah-sha-hmac	AH-SHA-HMAC transform used for authentication
esp-null	ESP transform that does not provide any encryption
esp-des	ESP transform using DES encryption (56-bit)
esp-3des	ESP transform using 3DES encryption (168-bit)
esp-aes	ESP transform using AES encryption (128-bit)
esp-aes-192	ESP transform using AES-192 encryption (192-bit)
esp-aes-256	ESP transform using AES-256 encryption (256-bit)
esp-md5-hmac	ESP transform with HMAC-MD5 authentication, used with either ESP-DES or ESP-3DES to provide additional integrity of ESP packets
esp-sha-hmac	ESP transform with HMAC-SHA authentication, used with either ESP-DES or ESP-3DES to provide additional integrity of ESP packets

> **NOTE** hmac represents Keyed-Hashing for Message Authentication and is outlined in RFC 2104.

The syntax for the **transform-set** command is as follows:

```
crypto ipsec transform-set transform-set-name transform1 [transform2 [transform3]]
```

Example 13-2 shows the current ISAKMP policy configuration with the access list and transform set defined.

Example 13-2 *Crypto Transform Set*

```
tgpix(config)#  isakmp  policy  10  authentication  pre-share
tgpix(config)#  isakmp  policy  10  encryption  3des
tgpix(config)#  isakmp  policy  10  group  2
tgpix(config)#  isakmp  policy  10  hash  md5
tgpix(config)#  isakmp  policy  10  lifetime  86400
tgpix(config)#  isakmp  enable  outside
```

Example 13-2   *Crypto Transform Set (Continued)*

```
tgpix(config)# isakmp identity address
tgpix(config)# isakmp key abc123 address 192.168.2.1 netmask 255.255.255.255
tgpix(config)# access-list 90 permit ip 10.10.10.0 255.255.255.0 10.10.20.0
255.255.255.0
tgpix(config)# crypto ipsec transform-set strong esp-3des esp-md5-hmac
```

Step 3: Configuring IPSec Security Association Lifetimes

To preclude any opportunity to gather sufficient network traffic using a single encryption key, it is important to limit the key lifetime. This forces a key exchange, changing the encryption scheme and greatly reducing the possibility of cracking the key. Technology continues to advance, producing computers that can break code at faster rates. However, these systems require a certain amount of traffic encrypted under a single key. The idea is to change encryption keys before any system can feasibly crack your encryption. The PIX enables you to configure your SA lifetimes, forcing a key exchange. It is possible to limit the SA lifetime either by the amount of traffic passing through the connection or by how long the encrypted connection remains open. The command for configuring SA lifetimes is as follows:

```
crypto ipsec security-association lifetime [kilobytes | seconds]
```

Example 13-3 shows the current configuration, including an SA lifetime of 15 minutes (900 seconds).

Example 13-3   *Crypto IPSec SA Lifetime*

```
tgpix(config)# isakmp policy 10 authentication pre-share
tgpix(config)# isakmp policy 10 encryption 3des
tgpix(config)# isakmp policy 10 group 2
tgpix(config)# isakmp policy 10 hash md5
tgpix(config)# isakmp policy 10 lifetime 86400
tgpix(config)# isakmp enable outside
tgpix(config)# isakmp identity address
tgpix(config)# isakmp key abc123 address 192.168.2.1 netmask 255.255.255.255
tgpix(config)# access-list 90 permit ip 10.10.10.0 255.255.255.0 10.10.20.0
 255.255.255.0
tgpix(config)# crypto ipsec transform-set strong esp-3des esp-md5-hmac
tgpix(config)# crypto ipsec security-association lifetime seconds 900
```

Step 4: Configuring Crypto Maps

Just as the **isakmp policy** command configures the parameters for the IKE negotiations, **crypto map** tells the PIX Firewall how to negotiate the IPSec SA. The **crypto map** command is the final piece of the puzzle that is used on both peers to establish the SA. Again, it is extremely important that the settings are compatible on both ends. If both peers do not have a compatible configuration, they cannot establish the VPN connection. This does not mean that the configuration must be an exact match (like the ISAKMP configurations), but the peers must have matching elements within the crypto map. Many different components are covered by the **crypto map** command. The following parameters are set using this command:

- **What traffic is to be encrypted and what traffic is not**—Earlier in this chapter, the **access-list** command was said to designate which traffic the PIX should encrypt. This is correct; however, the access list is applied by the **crypto map**.

- **What type of IPSec to apply to the connection**—**crypto map** tells the firewall which transform set to use.

- **How the SA is to be initially established**—This tells the firewall if the SA is manually established or established using IKE.

- **Who the peer is for this SA**—This can be one or more peers. You can configure a primary peer and backup peers. In the event that the firewall cannot establish the connection with the primary peer, it will attempt to connect to the secondary, and so on. These additional peers are called *backup gateways*.

- **What the SA's local address is**—The crypto map is applied to a specific interface on the PIX.

- **Any additional options that should be configured for this SA**—This can include setting a specific timeout in kilobytes or adding an AAA server.

Three steps are required for configuring crypto maps:

Step 1   Creating a crypto map entry

Step 2   Applying the crypto map set to an interface

Step 3   Specifying that IPSec traffic be permitted

It is important that you ensure that all three steps are completed. Although each line of the crypto map is considered "creating the crypto map," specific lines apply the crypto map and specify the IPSec traffic. These lines are discussed next.

Normally, you have at least five **crypto map** entries with the same name. These entries combine to list your IPSec SA configuration. Each line of the configuration has its own purpose. The following text shows and explains the syntax of each line.

```
crypto map map-name seq-num ipsec-isakmp
```

This line establishes the crypto map by name and sequence number and specifies that IKE negotiates the SA.

```
crypto map map-name seq-num match address acl_name
```

This line binds the access list to the crypto map. It establishes which traffic is encrypted and which is not. This line specifies which IPSec traffic is permitted. It defines the traffic as "interesting."

```
crypto  map  map-name seq-num  set  transform-set  transform-set-name
```

This line identifies which transform set is to be used. The *transform-set-name* is assigned to the transform set using the **crypto ipsec transform-set** command.

```
crypto  map  map-name seq-num  set  peer  ip-address
```

This line identifies the SA peer by IP address.

```
crypto  map  map-name  interface  if_name
```

This line applies the crypto map to a specific interface. In much the same way that the **access-group** command is used to bind the access lists to an interface for standard ACLs, this command binds the entire crypto map process (including the crypto access list) to the interface. This line applies the crypto map set to a specific interface on the firewall.

Additional **crypto map** entries can include **set pfs**, **set security-association lifetime**, and **client authentication** settings.

Example 13-4 shows the current configuration, including the crypto map entries. Note that the access list is numbered 90 and the **match address** command references **90**. The **ipsec transform-set** is named **strong**, and the **set transform-set** references the name **strong**.

Example 13-4 *Crypto Map Entries*

```
tgpix(config)#  isakmp  policy  10  authentication  pre-share
tgpix(config)#  isakmp  policy  10  encryption  3des
tgpix(config)#  isakmp  policy  10  group  2
tgpix(config)#  isakmp  policy  10  hash  md5
tgpix(config)#  isakmp  policy  10  lifetime  86400
tgpix(config)#  isakmp  enable  outside
tgpix(config)#  isakmp  identity  address
tgpix(config)#  isakmp  key  abc123  address  192.168.2.1  netmask  255.255.255.255
tgpix(config)#  access-list  90  permit  ip  10.10.10.0  255.255.255.0  10.10.20.0
  255.255.255.0
tgpix(config)#  crypto  ipsec  transform-set  strong  esp-3des  esp-md5-hmac
tgpix(config)#  crypto  ipsec  security-association  lifetime  seconds  900
tgpix(config)#  crypto  map  gonder  10  ipsec-isakmp
tgpix(config)#  crypto  map  gonder  10  match  address  90
tgpix(config)#  crypto  map  gonder  10  set  transform-set  strong
tgpix(config)#  crypto  map  gonder  10  set  peer  192.168.2.1
tgpix(config)#  crypto  map  gonder  interface  outside
```

Table 13-5 describes the different **crypto map command arguments** and options that are available when you are configuring crypto maps.

Table 13-5 crypto map *Arguments and Options*

Argument/Option	Description
map-name	You can apply multiple crypto maps on a single Security Appliance. It is a good idea to assign a name that allows you to keep track of which crypto map goes with which access list. The easiest way to do this is to use the same name or number for both components.
seq-num	Because you can add multiple crypto maps to the Security Appliance, you must give each a sequence number so that the system can process each in the correct order. The lower the number, the higher the priority.
ipsec-isakmp	Indicates that the Security Appliance uses IKE to negotiate the SA. This is the recommended configuration.
ipsec-manual	Indicates that the SA is configured manually and that IKE is not used to negotiate it. This is not the recommended configuration because it is difficult to ensure that both peers are configured correctly and because a manual session does not expire (no renegotiation of the keys).
set session-key	Manually specifies the session keys within the crypto map entry.
inbound	Manual IPSec requires that session keys be configured directionally. You must specify both inbound and outbound session keys.
outbound	Manual IPSec requires that session keys be configured directionally. You must specify both inbound and outbound session keys.
match address	Identifies the access list for the IPSec SA.
acl-name	The name of the access list that indicates that the traffic should be encrypted.
set peer	Specifies the SA peer using either of the following two arguments.
hostname	Identifies the SA peer's host name and any backup gateways.
ip-address	Identifies the SA peer's IP address(es) and any backup gateways.
interface	Identifies the interface that is to be used for the local SA peer address.
if-name	The interface name.
set pfs	Initiates PFS, which provides an additional layer of security to the SA negotiation and renegotiation. It requires that a new Diffie-Hellman exchange occur every time a key negotiation takes place. This causes the key exchange to use a new key for every negotiation rather than renegotiating based on a key that is currently being used. This process increases the processor load on both peers.

Table 13-5   **crypto map** *Arguments and Options (Continued)*

Argument/Option	Description
group 1	Indicates that the Diffie-Hellman group 1 (768-bit) modulus should be used when the key exchange for the **esp-des** and **esp-3des** transforms is performed.
group 2	Indicates that the Diffie-Hellman group 2 (1024-bit) modulus should be used when the key exchange for the **esp-des** and **esp-3des** transforms is performed.
group 5	Indicates that the Diffie-Hellman group 5 (1536-bit) modulus should be used. This group should always be used with **aes**, **aes-192**, and **aes-256** due to the large key sizes used by AES.
set transform-set	Specifies the transform to be used for the crypto map entry. You can list up to six transform sets by priority. The Security Appliance automatically selects the most secure transform that is listed on both peers.
transform-set-name	Specifies the transform set by name.
set security-association lifetime	A second location for configuring the SA lifetime. This setting will override the global SA lifetime for a specific crypto map.
seconds *seconds*	The SA lifetime in seconds.
kilobytes *kilobytes*	The SA lifetime in kilobytes.
dynamic	Specifies that the crypto map entry must reference a preexisting dynamic crypto map.
dynamic-map-name	Specifies the dynamic crypto map.
aaa-server-name	Specifies the AAA server that authenticates the user during IKE authentication. The Security Appliance supports Terminal Access Controller Access Control System (TACACS+) and Remote Authentication Dial-In User Service (RADIUS) for this function.

sysopt connection permit-ipsec Command

The **sysopt** command reconfigures the system options. The command **sysopt connection permit-ipsec** implicitly permits all packets that arrive from the IPSec tunnel to bypass any checking of access lists, conduits, or **access-group** command statements for IPSec connections. If the **sysopt connection permit-ipsec** command is not specified, an explicit rule (conduit or ACL) must be coded to allow the traffic arriving from the IPSec tunnel through the firewall.

Example 13-5 shows the current configuration with this command included.

Example 13-5   sysopt connection permit-ipsec

```
tgpix(config)#  isakmp  policy  10  authentication  pre-share
tgpix(config)#  isakmp  policy  10  encryption  3des
tgpix(config)#  isakmp  policy  10  group  2
tgpix(config)#  isakmp  policy  10  hash  md5
tgpix(config)#  isakmp  policy  10  lifetime  86400
tgpix(config)#  isakmp  enable  outside
tgpix(config)#  isakmp  identity  address
tgpix(config)#  isakmp  key  abc123  address  192.168.2.1  netmask  255.255.255.255
tgpix(config)#  nat  (inside)  0  access  list  90
tgpix(config)#  access-list  90  permit  ip  10.10.10.0  255.255.255.0  10.10.20.0
  255.255.255.0
tgpix(config)#  crypto  ipsec  transform-set  strong  esp-3des  esp-md5-hmac
tgpix(config)#  crypto  ipsec  security-association  lifetime  seconds  900
tgpix(config)#  crypto  map  gonder  10  ipsec-isakmp
tgpix(config)#  crypto  map  gonder  10  match  address  90
tgpix(config)#  crypto  map  gonder  10  set  transform-set  strong
tgpix(config)#  crypto  map  gonder  10  set  peer  192.168.2.1
tgpix(config)#  crypto  map  gonder  interface  outside
tgpix(config)#  sysopt  connection  permit-ipsec
```

Troubleshooting the VPN Connection

Configuring an SA peer can be extremely complicated and must be exact. If both peers are not configured correctly, they cannot successfully establish the VPN connection. The most common VPN issue is an incorrect configuration of either of the SA peers. The first step of troubleshooting a VPN should always be to compare the configurations of both peers and verify that they match. Three commands and a variety of command options are available to help you troubleshoot VPN issues:

- show
- clear
- debug

show Command

The **show** command lets you view different portions of the configuration and see the condition of ISAKMP and IPSec SAs. Table 13-6 explains the different **show** commands.

Table 13-6 show *Commands*

Command	Description
show isakmp	Displays all ISAKMP configurations.
show isakmp policy	Displays only configured ISAKMP policies.
show access-list	Displays configured access lists.
show crypto map	Displays all configured crypto map entries.
show crypto ipsec transform-set	Displays all configured IPSec transform sets.
show crypto ipsec security-association lifetime	Displays the global SA lifetime. If not defined specifically by a **crypto ipsec security-association lifetime** command, it displays the default lifetime values.
show crypto isakmp sa	Displays the status of current IKE SAs.
show crypto ipsec sa	Displays the status of current IPSec SAs.

Example 13-6 displays the output from the **show crypto isakmp sa** command on the PIX Firewall in 192.168.1.2 that is configured for a VPN connection to 192.168.2.1.

Example 13-6 show crypto isakmp sa *Command Output*

```
tgpix#  show  crypto  isakmp  sa
dst            src            state      conn-id     slot
192.168.2.1  192.168.1.1    QM_IDLE    1              0
```

Example 13-7 displays the output from **show crypto ipsec sa for the same firewall.**

Example 13-7 show crypto ipsec sa *Command Output*

```
tgpix#  show  crypto  ipsec  sa interface: outside
 Crypto map tag: 10, local addr. 192.168.1.1
 local  ident (addr/mask/port/port): (10.10.10.0/255.255.255.0/0/0)
 remote ident (addr/mask/prot/port): (192.168.2.1/255.255.255.255/0/0)
 current_peer: 192.128.1.1
 dynamic allocated peer ip: 192.168.2.1
 PERMIT, flags={}
#pkts encaps: 345, #pkts encrypt: 345, #pkts digest 0
 #pkts decaps: 366, #pkts decrypt: 366, #pkts verify 0
 #pkts compressed: 0, #pkts decompressed: 0
 #pkts not compressed: 0, #pkts compr. failed: 0, #pkts decompress failed: 0
 #send errors 0, #recv errors 0
  local crypto endpt.: 192.168.1.1, remote crypto endpt.: 192.168.2.1
  path mtu 1500, ipsec overhead 56, media mtu 1500
  current outbound spi: 9a46ecae
  inbound esp sas:
```

continues

Example 13-7   *show* **crypto ipsec sa** *Command Output (Continued)*

```
     spi: 0x50b98b5(84646069)
       transform: esp-3des esp-md5-hmac ,
       in use settings ={Tunnel, }
       slot: 0, conn id: 1, crypto map: Chapter11
       sa timing: remaining key lifetime (k/sec): (460800/21)
       IV size: 8 bytes
       replay detection support: Y
   inbound ah sas:
   inbound pcp sas:
   outbound esp sas:
     spi: 0x9a46ecae(2588339374)
       transform: esp-3des esp-md5-hmac ,
       in use settings ={Tunnel, }
       slot: 0, conn id: 2, crypto map: Chapter11
       sa timing: remaining key lifetime (k/sec): (460800/21)
       IV size: 8 bytes
       replay detection support: Y
     outbound ah sas:
```

clear Command

The **clear** command allows you to remove current settings. You must be very careful when using the **clear** command to ensure that you do not remove portions of your configuration that are needed. The most common use of the clear command for troubleshooting VPN connectivity is to clear current sessions and force them to regenerate. Table 13-7 explains the two **clear** commands used to troubleshoot VPN connectivity.

Table 13-7   **clear** *Commands*

Command	Description
clear isakmp sa	Removes all ISAKMP statements from the configuration
clear [crypto] isakmp sa	Clears all active ISAKMP SAs
clear [crypto] ipsec sa	Clears all active IPSec SAs

debug Command

The **debug** command lets you watch the VPN negotiation take place. This command is available only from configuration mode on the PIX and will not display any output in a Telnet session. Table 13-8 explains the two **debug** commands most commonly used to troubleshoot VPN connectivity.

Table 13-8 debug *Commands*

Command	Description
debug crypto isakmp	Displays IKE communication between the PIX and its IPSec peers
debug crypto ipsec	Displays IPSec communication between the PIX and its IPSec peers

Example 13-8 displays the output from the **debug crypto isakmp** command on the PIX Firewall in 192.168.1.1 that is configured for a VPN connection to 192.168.2.1. Note the highlighted comments "atts are not acceptable" and "atts are acceptable" that are generated during the negotiation as address transforms attempt to find a match.

Example 13-8 debug crypto isakmp *Command Output*

```
crypto_isakmp_process_block: src 192.168.1.1, dest 192.168.2.1
OAK_AG exchange
ISAKMP (0): processing SA payload. message ID = 0
ISAKMP (0): Checking ISAKMP transform 1 against priority 1 policy
ISAKMP:       encryption DES-CBC ISAKMP:       hash MD5
ISAKMP:       default group 1
ISAKMP:       auth pre-share
ISAKMP (0): atts are not acceptable. Next payload is 3
ISAKMP (0): Checking ISAKMP transform 3 against priority 1 policy
ISAKMP:       encryption ESP_3DES ISAKMP:       hash HMAC-MD5
ISAKMP:       default group 2
ISAKMP:       auth pre-share
ISAKMP (0): atts are acceptable. Next payload is 3
ISAKMP (0): processing KE payload. message ID = 0
ISAKMP: Created a peer node for 192.168.2.1
OAK_QM exchange
ISAKMP (0:0): Need config/address
ISAKMP (0:0): initiating peer config to 192.168.2.1. ID = 2607270170 (0x9b67c91a)
return status is IKMP_NO_ERROR
crypto_isakmp_process_block: src 192.168.2.1, dest 192.168.1.1
ISAKMP_TRANSACTION exchange
ISAKMP (0:0): processing transaction payload from 192.168.2.1. message ID =
  2156506360
ISAKMP: Config payload CFG_ACK
ISAKMP (0:0): peer accepted the address!
ISAKMP (0:0): processing saved QM. oakley_process_quick_mode: OAK_QM_IDLE
ISAKMP (0): processing SA payload. message ID = 448324052
ISAKMP : Checking IPSec proposal 1
ISAKMP: transform 1, ESP_DES ISAKMP:   attributes in transform:
ISAKMP:       authenticator is HMAC-MD5
ISAKMP:       encaps is 1
IPSec(validate_proposal): transform proposal (prot 3, trans 2, hmac_alg 1) not
  supported
ISAKMP (0): atts not acceptable. Next payload is 0
```

continues

Example 13-8 debug crypto isakmp *Command Output (Continued)*

```
ISAKMP : Checking IPSec proposal 2
ISAKMP: transform 1, ESP_3DES ISAKMP:    attributes in transform:
ISAKMP:        authenticator is HMAC-MD5
ISAKMP:        encaps is 1
ISAKMP (0): atts are acceptable.
ISAKMP (0): processing NONCE payload. message ID = 448324052
ISAKMP (0): processing ID payload. message ID = 44
ISAKMP (0): processing ID payload. message ID = 44
INITIAL_CONTACTIPSec(key_engine): got a queue event...
```

Example 13-9 displays the output from **debug crypto ipsec** for the same firewall. Notice that this **debug** command actually depicts the real address of the node behind the firewall that is initiating the VPN connection.

Example 13-9 debug crypto ipsec *Command Output*

```
IPSec(key_engine): got a queue event...
IPSec(spi_response): getting spi 0xd532efbd(3576885181) for SA
       from  192.168.2.1  to  192.168.1.1  for prot 3
return status is IKMP_NO_ERROR
crypto_isakmp_process_block: src 192.168.2.1, dest 192.168.1.1
OAK_QM exchange oakley_process_quick_mode: OAK_QM_AUTH_AWAIT
ISAKMP (0): Creating IPSec SAs
       inbound SA from  192.168.2.1  to  192.168.1.1  (proxy 10.10.10.3 to 192.168.1.1.)
       has spi 3576885181 and conn_id 2 and flags 4
       outbound SA from  192.168.1.1  to  192.168.2.1  (proxy 192.168.1.1 to 10.10.10.3)
       has spi 2749108168 and conn_id 1 and flags 4IPSec(key_engine): got a queue
         event... IPSec(initialize_sas): ,
(key eng. msg.) dest= 192.168.1.1, src= 192.168.2.1,
   dest_proxy= 192.168.1.1/0.0.0.0/0/0 (type=1),
   src_proxy= 10.10.10.3/0.0.0.0/0/0 (type=1),
   protocol= ESP, transform= esp-3des esp-md5-hmac ,
   lifedur= 0s and 0kb,
   spi= 0xd532efbd(3576885181), conn_id= 2,        keysize= 0, flags= 0x4
IPSec(initialize_sas): ,
  (key eng. msg.) src= 192.168.1.1, dest= 192.168.2.1,
   src_proxy= 192.168.1.1/0.0.0.0/0/0 (type=1),
   dest_proxy= 10.10.10.3/0.0.0.0/0/0 (type=1),
   protocol= ESP, transform= esp-3des esp-md5-hmac ,
   lifedur= 0s and 0kb,
   spi= 0xa3dc0fc8(2749108168), conn_id= 1, keysize= 0, flags= 0x4
return status is IKMP_NO_ERROR
```

Configuring the Security Appliance as a WebVPN Gateway

Configuring the Cisco Security Appliance as a WebVPN gateway is a process that requires five specific tasks:

- WebVPN global configuration
- Configuring URL and file server access
- Configuring port forwarding
- Configuring e-mail proxies
- Setting up filters and ACLs

WebVPN Global Configuration

WebVPN requires five steps to initialize the WebVPN service. Each of these steps requires some basic configurations in global configuration mode. You need to follow these steps to configure the global attributes for WebVPN:

Step 1   Enable the WebVPN HTTPS server.

Step 2   Access WebVPN configuration mode.

Step 3   Assign an interface to WebVPN.

Step 4   Assign authentication for WebVPN.

Step 5   Assign a NetBIOS name server.

The sections that follow cover these steps in greater detail.

Step 1: Enable the WebVPN HTTPS Server

As stated previously, WebVPN uses an internal HTTPS server on an ASA 55X0 Security Appliance. This HTTPS server acts as the portal home page for WebVPN. To enable the HTTPS server, the **http server enable** command is used.

> **NOTE** WebVPN requires cookies to be enabled on the end user's browser. If cookies are disabled, the end user will be forced to open a new window each time a link from the home page is accessed. This will cause the end user to log in each time a new window is open.

Step 2: Access WebVPN Configuration Mode

To make changes to the WebVPN global configuration, the WebVPN subcommand mode (WebVPN mode) must be accessed. Configuration of proxy services, AAA authentication servers, policies, and the portal home page are all done through the WebVPN mode.

Configuration for e-mail proxies through WebVPN are done in a similar fashion, using the **pop3s, imap4s,** or **smtps** commands to access their specific subcommand modes. The commands are used as follows:

```
tgasa(config)# webvpn
tgasa(config-webvpn)#
tgasa(config)# pop3s
tgasa(config-pop3s)#
```

Table 13-9 describes the available WebVPN global commands that are available in WebVPN mode.

Table 13-9 *WebVPN Global Commands*

Command	Description
accounting-server-group	Assigns a preconfigured accounting server group to use with WebVPN.
authentication	Assigns an authentication mode for WebVPN users.
authentication-server-group	Assigns a preconfigured authentication server group to use with WebVPN.
authorization-server-group	Assigns a preconfigured authorization server group to use with WebVPN.
authorization-required	Requires users to successfully authorize to connect.
authorization-dn-attributes	Identifies the DN of the peer certificate to use as a username for authorization.
default-group-policy	Assigns the name of the group policy.
default-idle-timeout	Sets the default idle timeout.
enable	Assigns WebVPN to a specific interface.
http-proxy	Sets the proxy server for HTTP requests.
https-proxy	Sets the proxy server for HTTPS requests.
login message	Sets the HTML text that prompts a user to log in.
logo	Sets the logo image displayed on the WebVPN login and home page.
logout message	Sets the HTML text that prompts a user logging out.
nbns-server	Sets a NetBIOS server for CIFS resolution.
username-prompt	Sets the prompt for a username at the login page for WebVPN.
password-prompt	Sets the prompt for a password at the login page for WebVPN.
title	Sets the title HTML string for the WebVPN home page.
title-color	Sets the color of the title bars on the login, home, and file access pages.

Table 13-9 *WebVPN Global Commands (Continued)*

Command	Description
text-color	Sets the color of the text bars on the login, home, and file access pages.
secondary-colors	Sets the color of the secondary title bars on the login, home, and file access pages.
secondary-text-colors	Sets the color of the secondary text bars on the login, home, and file access pages.

Step 3: Assign an Interface to WebVPN

With the HTTPS server enabled, WebVPN must be assigned an interface. WebVPN must be enabled on all interfaces from which the end user will access the WebVPN service. This can be accomplished by using the **enable** command while in the WebVPN mode:

```
enable if-name
tgasa(config)# webvpn
tgasa(config-webvpn)# enable outside
```

NOTE   Because both WebVPN and ASDM use HTTPS, they cannot be assigned the same interface. If this is done, an error message will display, informing the end user of the problem.

Step 4: Assign Authentication for WebVPN

Assignment of an authentication server group to WebVPN is the final step to enable basic WebVPN functionality. You must configure at least one authentication server group on the ASA 55X0 Security Appliance before an authentication group to the WebVPN service can be assigned. The **authentication-server-group** *group tag* command is used while in WebVPN mode to assign one or more authentication server groups to the WebVPN service. This command can also be used within the **pop3s, imap4s,** and **smtps** subcommand modes to assign authentication for specific e-mail proxies.

Step 5: Assign a NetBIOS Name Server

Microsoft's Common Internet File System (SMB/CIFS) requires a NetBIOS Name Server (NBNS) for queries to map a NetBIOS name to IP addresses. WebVPN will use NetBIOS to access or allow file sharing through a WebVPN connection. The initial NBNS server configured will be the primary server, and all subsequent servers will be considered redundant backups. The ASA 55X0 supports three NBNS server entries.

NBNS entries are assigned in WebVPN mode nested in global-configuration mode. To assign an NBNS entry, use the following command:

    nbns-server {*ipaddr* or *hostname*} [**master**] [**timeout** *timeout*] [**retry** *retries*]

Table 13-10 describes the parameters for the **nbns-server** command.

Table 13-10 nbns-server *Command Parameters*

Command	Description
hostname	Specifies the hostname for the NBNS server.
ipaddr	Specifies the IP address for the NBNS server.
master	Sets the NBNS server as a master browser, instead of a WINS server.
timeout	Indicates that a timeout value follows.
timeout	Sets the amount of time the ASA 55X0 waits before retrying a query. The default timeout is 2 seconds; the range is 1 to 30 seconds.
retry	Indicates that a retry value follows.
retries	Sets the number of times to retry queries to an NBNS server. The default value is 2; the range is 1 to 10.

Configuring URLs and File Servers

Using the WebVPN home page is useful only if the end user can access resources. Internal websites and Active Directory file servers are some of the more frequently accessed resources in an enterprise network. A security administrator might not want end users to have equal access to internal websites or file servers, especially to confidential documents and information. WebVPN resolves this with the ability to configure access to internal websites and file servers on a per-user or per-group basis. To enable access to the WebVPN service, the user configuration or group-policy configuration mode is entered. The **webvpn** command is then used in either of these modes to enable the WebVPN service for that specific username or group-policy, as demonstrated in Example 13-10.

Example 13-10 *Assigning WebVPN Access to Users and Groups*

```
tgasa(config)# group-policy REMOTE1 attributes
tgasa(config-group-policy)# webvpn
tgasa(config-group-webvpn)#
tgasa(config)# username jsmith attributes
tgasa(config-username)# webvpn
tgasa(config-username-webvpn)#
```

Like the WebVPN mode that is used in the global-configuration mode, WebVPN mode in username-configuration or policy-configuration mode supports commands to define access to files, MAPI proxy, URLs, and TCP applications over WebVPN. Content and ACL filters are also supported in this mode. The commands affect only the user or group in which they are configured, and all globally affecting commands must be done in global-configuration mode.

The ASA 55X0 Security Appliance uses one command to enable access to MAPI Proxy, files, file browsing, and URL entry over WebVPN. The **functions** command can be used in any WebVPN mode to assign file and URL access. These commands can also be combined in one functions statement, granting multiple accesses in one line. The full syntax for the **functions** command is as follows:

```
functions {file-access | file-browsing | file-entry | filter | url-entry | mapi | port-
forwarding | none}
```

Table 13-11 describes the options for the **functions** command.

Table 13-11 functions *Command Options*

Command	Description
file-access	Enables or disables file access.
file-browsing	Enables or disables browsing for file servers and shares.
file-entry	Applies a web-type ACL.
filter	Applies a web-type ACL. When enabled, the Security Appliance applies the web-type ACL defined with the WebVPN **filter** command.
url-entry	Enables or disables user entry of URLs.
mapi	Enables or disables Microsoft Outlook/Exchange port forwarding.
port-forwarding	Enables port forwarding.
none	Sets a null value for all WebVPN **functions**.

A username or group-policy must have file access enabled to access file servers and allow file browsing. The **file-access** command enables the list of file servers to display on the WebVPN home page. The **file-browsing** command is required to allow an end user to access a file server from the displayed list. With these two commands, an end user should have access to any server in the server list. To enable the ability of an end user to connect with a server that is not listed in the application access window, the **file-entry** command must be used. This command enables an end user to fill the network path field on the WebVPN home page and attempt to access a server not on the server list. In Example 13-11, an ASA 5520 is configured to support file browsing access for a group-policy.

Example 13-11 *Configuring an ASA for File Browsing*

```
tgasa(config)# group-policy REMOTE1 attributes
tgasa(config-group-policy)# webvpn
tgasa(config-group-webvpn)# functions file-access file-browsing
tgasa(config-group-webvpn)# exit
```

Access to internal websites, URLs, files, and shared file servers from the WebVPN home page can be achieved through the URL entry field or through the list of preconfigured URLs. A security administrator can create the URL list using the **url-list** command in global configuration mode:

```
url-list {listname displayname url}
```

Table 13-12 describes the arguments for the **url-list** command.

Table 13-12 **url-list** *Global Command Arguments*

Command	Description
listname	Provides the text that will be displayed on the WebVPN home page to identify the URL. Maximum 64 characters.
displayname	Groups the set of URLs that the WebVPN end user can access. Maximum 64 characters. Semicolons (;), ampersands (&), and less-than (<) characters are not allowed.
url	Specifies the URL link. Suports URL types http, https, and cifs.

A URL list can have one or more URL links listed by assigning the URL list a listname. Every list entry for that list must have the same listname:

```
tgasa(config)# url-list URLS "HR Server" http://192.168.1.22
tgasa(config)# url-list URLS "Shared" cifs://192.168.1.210
```

Once the URL lists are created, they must be assigned to a user or group-policy. The **url-list** command can be used in WebVPN mode to assign a URL list to a username or group-policy:

```
url-list {none | value name}
```

The syntax for the **url-list** command differs from the syntax used in global-configuration mode in the following ways:

- **value** *name*—The name of a preconfigured URL list configured using the **url-list** command in global-configuration mode.

- **none**—Sets a null value for URL lists. This prevents inheriting a list from a default group-policy configuration.

Example 13-12 shows the configuration of the URLs list to a group-policy.

Example 13-12 *Assigning a URL List*

```
tgasa(config)# group-policy REMOTE1 attributes
tgasa(config-group-policy)# webvpn
tgasa(config-group-webvpn)# url-list value URLS
tgasa(config-group-webvpn)# exit
```

Configuring Port Forwarding

Some end users will require access to applications outside of e-mail and file access. In a traditional IPSec VPN, this can be done easily, since the end user is directly connected to the enterprise network through the VPN. When using a WebVPN service, the end user has no direct connection to the network, and must redirect all application use through the WebVPN https service. This is done through port forwarding using a Java applet. A security administrator enables port forwarding in two steps:

Step 1   Create port forwarding application maps.

Step 2   Assign a port forward application list to a user or group policy.

NOTE   The Java applet used for modifying the hosts file is sometimes seen as a malicious attack by antivirus and antispyware applications. Disabling checking of the hosts file might be necessary.

Step 1: Create Port Forwarding Application Maps

You must create a port forwarding application map for each application the ASA 55x0 will need to port forward. This mapping information will be used by the ASA 55x0 to modify the host file on the end user's PC with mapping information. An application entry uses a hostname or IP address as a unique identifier for port forwarding. This identifier must be constant; otherwise the end user will be required to modify how these applications are accessed each time the WebVPN service is used. The use of hostnames is recommended, as it streamlines access to the application for the end user.

For the WebVPN service, a hostname can be configured with the IP address of the server the application resides on, as well as the port number from the end user's computer, which is required to access the application. This will give the end user a simpler way to access the application. For example, if the end user needs to telnet to server 10.2.2.12 port 2222, which has been assigned the hostname "Shell" in the Security Appliance, one of the following can be done:

■ **IP address**—The end user must use **telnet 10.2.2.12 2222** to access the specific server on that port.

■ **Hostname**—The end user must use **telnet Shell** to access the server located at 10.2.2.12 on port 2222.

Each application must be entered separately, using the **port-forward** command in global-configuration mode:

```
port-forward {listname localport remoteserver remoteport description}
```

For example:

```
tgasa(config)# port-forward HRApps 2222 10.2.2.12 20351 HR APP
```

To configure multiple applications within a single list group, the same listname is required.

Table 13-13 describes the arguments for the **port-forward** command.

Table 13-13   port-forward *Command Arguments*

Command	Description
listname	Groups the set of applications WebVPN users can access. Maximum 64 characters.
localport	Sets the local port that listens for TCP traffic for an application. This port number must be unique per listname. Recommended TCP ports are from 1024 to 65,535.
remoteserver	Sets the DNS name or IP address of the remote server for an application.
remoteport	Sets the port to connect to for this application on the remote server.
description	Provides the application name or description that displays on the end user port forwarding Java applet. Maximum 64 characters.

Step 2: Assign a Port Forward Application List to a User or Group-Policy

Once you create the application list, you must assign it to a username or group-policy in a fashion similar to URL lists. To assign an application list to a username or group-policy, the WebVPN mode is entered within either configuration mode. The **functions** command is then used to enable port-forwarding for the username or group-policy:

```
tgasa(config-group-webvpn)# functions port-forwarding
```

Once you have enabled port forwarding, you can assign an application list. Use the **port-forwarding** command while in the WebVPN mode of a username or group-policy configuration mode to accomplish this task:

```
port-forwarding {value listname | none}
```

Example 13-13 shows the configuration of an application list on an ASA 5520 Security Appliance.

Example 13-13   *Assigning an Application List*

```
tgasa(config)# group-policy REMOTE1 attributes
tgasa(config-group-policy)# webvpn
tgasa(config-group-webvpn)# functions port-forwarding
tgasa(config-group-webvpn)# port-forwading value HRApps
tgasa(config-group-webvpn)# exit
```

Configuring E-Mail Proxies

The WebVPN service supports four types of e-mail proxies:

- POP3S
- IMAP4S
- STMPS
- MAPI

Of the four types of e-mail proxies, only MAPI is handled through the **functions** command:

```
tgasa(config-group-webvpn)# functions mapi
```

The other three are handled in subcommand mode similar to WebVPN mode, as described previously. Each proxy's subcommand mode can use the commands listed in Table 13-14.

Table 13-14   *Proxy Subcommands*

Command	Description
accounting-server-group	Assigns a preconfigured accounting server group to use with proxy. None are initially configured.
authentication	Assigns an authentication mode for proxy users. The user must always authenticate with the mail host.
authentication-server-group	Assigns a preconfigured authentication server group to use with proxy. None are initially configured.
authorization-server-group	Assigns a preconfigured authorization server group to use with proxy. None are initially configured.

continues

Table 13-14   *Proxy Subcommands (Continued)*

Command	Description
default-group-policy	Assigns a name of the group-policy to use when AAA does not return a CLASSID attribute. If this is not assigned, and no CLASSID has been used with the AAA, the session will be rejected.
port	Assigns the port that the proxy listens to. This defaults to 995.
server address	Assigns the default mail server to be used when the user connects to the mail proxy service and does not specify a mail server.
outstanding number	Sets the number of outstanding, nonauthenticated sessions that are allowed. If the number of connections exceeds this setting, the oldest connection is terminated to help reduce DOS attacks. The default setting is 20; the range is from 1 to 100.
name-separator symbol	This is the separator between the e-mail and VPN usernames and passwords. Choices are "@", "|", ":", "#", "," and ";". The default is ":".
server-separator symbol	This is the separator between the e-mail and server names. Choices are "@", "|", ":", "#", "," and ";". The default is ":".

There are two steps to configure an e-mail proxy:

Step 1   Assign a proxy mail server.

Step 2   Assign an authentication server.

These steps work for POP3S, IMAP4S, and SMTPS. These commands are used in the proxy's subcommand mode.

Step 1: Assign a Proxy Mail Server

To assign an e-mail server, use the following command:

```
server {ipaddr | hostname}
```

This command specifies a default e-mail proxy server to use if an end user does not specify one.

Step 2: Assign an Authentication Server

To assign a preconfigured authentication server group to a proxy e-mail service, use the following command:

```
authentication-server-group group tag
```

The ASA defaults to not having an authentication-group assigned to the proxy e-mail service.

You must set an authentication type for a proxy e-mail service. The ASA 55X0 supports four authentication types (see Table 13-15). The default type used is AAA. Use the **authentication** command to assign the authentication type to the proxy e-mail service:

```
authentication {AAA | certificate | mailhost | piggyback}
```

Table 13-15 *Authentication Types*

Command	Description
AAA	Provides a username and password that the ASA checks against a previously configured AAA server.
certificate	Provides a certificate during SSL negotiations.
mailhost	Authenticates via the remote mail server. POP3S and IMAP4S configure this by default; will not be displayed as a configuration option for those types.
piggyback	Requires that an https WebVPN session already exists.

Example 13-14 shows a proxy e-mail configuration on an ASA 5520.

Example 13-14 *Proxy E-Mail Configuration Example*

```
tgasa(config)# group-policy REMOTE1 attributes
tgasa(config-group-policy)# pop3s
tgasa(config-group-pop3s)# enable outside
tgasa(config-group-pop3s)# enable inside
tgasa(config-group-pop3s)# server 10.2.2.38
tgasa(config-group-pop3s)# authentication-server-group REMOTEGROUP
tgasa(config-group-pop3s)# authentication piggyback
tgasa(config-group-pop3s)# exit
tgasa(config-group)# smtps
tgasa(config-group-smtps)# enable outside
tgasa(config-group-smtps)# enable inside
tgasa(config-group-smtps)# authentication-server-group REMOTEGROUP
tgasa(config-group-pop3s)# authentication mailhost
tgasa(config-group-pop3s)# port 998
```

Setting Up Filters and ACLs

WebVPNs support content filtering and ACL filters. Content filtering is supported only by group-policies. WebVPN content filtering allows the security administrator to block parts of websites that contain malicious or unauthorized content.

The **html-content-filter** command is used to configure these options:

```
html-content-filter {cookies | images | java | none | scripts}
```
The command options are described as follows:

- **cookies**—Removes cookies from images.
- **images**—Removes the <IMG> tags from a website.
- **java**—Removes reference to Java and ActiveX.
- **none**—Disables filtering.
- **scripts**—Removes references to scripting.

You can string multiple attributes onto one **html-content-filter** command. The ASA 55X0 Security Device defaults to no content filtering.

You can assign an ACL to a username or group-policy by using the following command:

```
filter {value ACLname | none}
```
The ACL must use the **access-list web-type** commands to be supported.

Configuring Security Appliances for Scalable VPNs

Earlier in this chapter, you learned about the different methods of negotiating an IPSec connection:

- Manual IPSec, which requires you to configure each peer manually. This method is not recommended by Cisco because it does not allow for key exchanges and, therefore, would be rather easy to decrypt, given enough time and traffic. Obviously, manual IPSec is not a scalable solution.
- IKE, which dynamically negotiates your SA using preshared keys or digital certificates. Preshared keys still require you to enter a preshared key manually into each IPSec peer.
- IKE with digital certificates, which is the most dynamic solution that lets IKE negotiate your IPSec SA and a CA server authenticating each peer. This system is completely dynamic, very secure, and very scalable.

Foundation Summary

The "Foundation Summary" provides a convenient review of many key concepts in this chapter. If you are already comfortable with the topics in this chapter, this summary can help you recall a few details. If you just read this chapter, this review should help solidify some key facts. If you are doing your final preparation before the exam, this summary provides a convenient way to review the day before the exam.

There are four different VPN types:

- Access
- Intranet
- Extranet
- WebVPN

Access VPNs are used for remote users and normally require client software. Intranet and extranet VPNs are configured as site-to-site VPNs. WebVPNs are used for remote users, but they do not require client software.

VPN peers need to authenticate each other and negotiate the IPSec SA. The negotiation is completed automatically using IKE. The authentication is completed using preshared keys, RSA signatures (certificates), or RSA nonces. The Security Appliance does not support RSA nonces. To configure IKE on the PIX, you use the following commands:

- **isakmp policy**

   — Configures the authentication type

   — Configures the message encryption algorithm

   — Configures the message integrity algorithm

   — Configures the key exchange parameters

   — Defines the SA lifetime (reinitiates the Diffie-Hellman key exchange)

- **isakmp enable**—Applies the ISAKMP policy to an interface, allowing that interface to receive UDP 500 traffic

- **isakmp identity**—Identifies the local peer by IP address or host name

- **isakmp key**—If you are using a preshared key, defines the key and the peer (by IP address)

After you configure IKE, you are ready to configure IPSec. Follow these steps:

Step 1   Use the **access-list** command to configure the access list so that the PIX knows which traffic should be encrypted.

Step 2   Use the **transform-set** command to create transform sets to define the encryption and integrity to be used for the session.

Step 3   Use the **ipsec security-association lifetime** command (optional) to define the SA lifetime to reduce the opportunity of others to crack your encryption.

Step 4   Configure the crypto map:

- Define the SA negotiation (manual or IKE)
- Apply the access list to the crypto map
- Apply the transform set to the crypto map
- Identify the SA peer by IP address or host name
- Apply the crypto map to an interface

Three commands (and many options for each) are available to troubleshoot VPN connectivity:

- **show**—Displays the current configuration or current SA status
- **clear**—Removes the current configuration or setting (usually used to regenerate the connection)
- **debug**—Allows you to see ongoing sessions and key negotiations

WebVPNs are a flexible way for end users to access resources on an enterprise network anywhere in the world. WebVPN uses a front-end portal interface to authenticate and give access to end users through a web browser, using an https connection. Services supported by WebVPN are as follow:

- **E-mail proxy**—Support for POP3S, IMAP3S, SMTPS, and MAPI through e-mail proxies.
- **File sharing and browsing**—Support for SMB/CIFS file servers, as well as file access and distribution.
- **Website URL access**—Access to internal and external websites.
- **Port forwarding**—Support for TCP-based port-forwarding through a Java applet.

Security administrators might require content filtering of websites by an end user using WebVPN. This can be done through two means: content filtering and ACLs. Content filtering enables a security administrator to strip unwanted images, scripts, and cookies from unapproved websites. Access restrictions through ACLs can also be applied to WebVPN connections.

Cisco VPN Client is used to connect remote users to internal resources by an encrypted tunnel. The package handles all the negotiation and encryption and can operate using any connection to the Internet.

To develop a scalable VPN solution, you must implement a dynamic means of authentication. The most effective and scalable method today is the use of IKE and certification authorities.

Q&A

As mentioned in the Introduction, the questions in this book are more difficult than what you should experience on the exam. The questions are designed to ensure your understanding of the concepts discussed in this chapter and adequately prepare you to complete the exam. You should take the simulated exams on the CD to practice for the exam.

The answers to these questions can be found in Appendix A:

1. Why is **manual-ipsec** not recommended by Cisco?

2. What is the difference between an access VPN and an intranet VPN?

3. Which hash algorithm is configured by default for phase 1?

4. What are the two methods of identifying SA peers?

5. What happens if you have different ISAKMP policies configured on your potential SA peers, and none of them match?

6. Where do you define your authentication method?

7. What authentication types are supported for e-mail proxy services?

8. What is the default lifetime if not defined in **isakmp policy**?

9. Do your transform sets have to match exactly on each peer?

10. What is the difference between the **isakmp** lifetime and the **crypto map** lifetime?

11. What command do you use to delete any active SAs?

12. What is the command for defining a preshared key?

13. What is the first thing you should check if you are unable to establish a VPN?

14. What commands are required to enable file browsing on a WebVPN connection?

15. What is the command to apply an access list to a crypto map?

16. What is the difference between ESP and AH?

Scenario

This scenario gives you the opportunity to configure three locations (New York, Los Angeles, and Atlanta) for a site-to-site fully meshed VPN. The configurations for the three locations are listed with specific items missing. By reviewing the network layout and each firewall configuration, you will find the items that are missing from the individual firewall configurations.

VPN Configurations

Clearly, the most detail-oriented and time-consuming portion of configuring VPNs is ensuring that both peers have matching configurations. This task usually becomes more complicated because you might have access to only one peer and are relying on someone else to configure the other end. A single discrepancy between the configurations can prevent the key exchange from completing or prevent encryption from occurring. It is best to compare the configurations on both peers before attempting the connection rather than trying to troubleshoot the VPN after an unsuccessful connection.

In this scenario, you are working as a consultant and have been assigned the task of configuring a full-mesh VPN between corporate headquarters and two branch offices. Figure 13-10 shows the layout of each network and how the VPNs are to connect.

Figure 13-10   *VPN Network Layout*

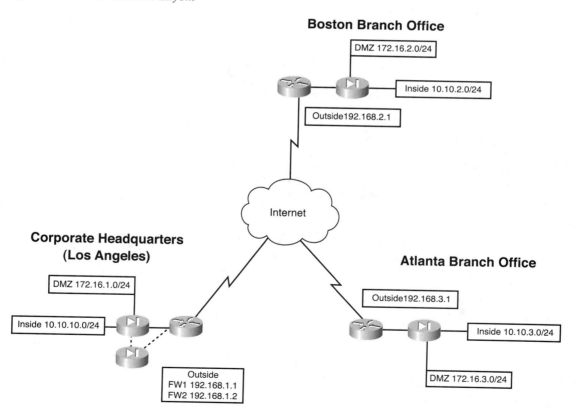

The three locations have all provided their current PIX configurations, but each has a significant amount of information missing. It is your responsibility to complete each of the configurations and ensure that they are correct. Example 13-15 shows the configuration for the corporate headquarters in Los Angeles.

Example 13-15 *PIX Configuration for Los Angeles*

```
1.  : Saved
2.  :
3.  PIX Version 6.3(3)
4.  nameif ethernet0 outside security0
5.  nameif ethernet1 inside security100
6.  nameif ethernet2 DMZ security70
7.  enable password HtmvK15kjhtlyfvcl encrypted
8.  passwd Kkjhlkf1568Hke encrypted
9.  hostname LosAngeles
10. domain-name www.Chapter11.com
11. fixup protocol ftp 21
12. fixup protocol http 80
13. fixup protocol h323 1720
14. fixup protocol rsh 514
15. fixup protocol smtp 25
16. fixup protocol sqlnet 1521
17. fixup protocol sip 5060
18. fixup protocol skinny 2000
19. names
20. access-list inbound permit icmp any host 192.168.1.10
21. access-list inbound permit tcp any host 192.168.1.10  eq www
22. access-list inbound permit tcp any host 192.168.1.10 eq 443
23. access-list inbound permit tcp any host 192.168.1.11  eq www
24. access-list inbound permit tcp any host 192.168.1.11 eq 443
25. access-list inbound permit tcp any host 192.168.1.12  eq www
26. access-list inbound permit tcp any host 192.168.1.12 eq 443
27. access-list inbound permit tcp any host 192.168.1.13  eq ftp
28. access-list inbound permit tcp any host 192.168.1.13 eq 443
29. access-list DMZ permit udp 172.16.1.0 255.255.255.0 host 10.10.10.240 eq ntp
30. access-list VPN permit ip 10.10.10.0 255.255.255.0 10.10.2.0 255.255.255.0
31. _____
32. _____
33. _____
34. pager lines 24
35. logging on
36. logging timestamp
37. interface ethernet0 auto
38. interface ethernet1 auto
39. interface ethernet2 auto
40. mtu outside 1500
41. mtu inside 1500
```

Example 13-15 *PIX Configuration for Los Angeles (Continued)*

```
42. ip address outside 192.168.1.1 255.255.255.0
43. ip address inside 10.10.10.1 255.255.255.0
44. ip address DMZ 172.16.1.1 255.255.255.0
45. failover
46. failover timeout 0:00:00
47. failover poll 15
48. failover ip address outside 192.168.1.2
49. failover ip address inside 10.10.10.2
50. failover ip address DMZ 172.16.1.2
51. arp timeout 14400
52. global (outside) 1 192.168.1.20-250
53. nat (inside) 1 0.0.0.0 0.0.0.0
54. nat (inside) 0 access-list VPN
55. static (inside DMZ) 10.10.10.240 10.10.10.240 netmask 255.255.255.255 0 0
56. static (DMZ outside) 192.168.1.10 172.16.1.10 netmask 255.255.255.255 0 0
57. static (DMZ outside) 192.168.1.11 172.16.1.11 netmask 255.255.255.255 0 0
58. static (DMZ outside) 192.168.1.12 172.16.1.12 netmask 255.255.255.255 0 0
59. static (DMZ outside) 192.168.1.13 172.16.1.13 netmask 255.255.255.255 0 0
60. access-group inbound in interface outside
61. access-group DMZ in interface DMZ
62. route outside 0.0.0.0 0.0.0.0 192.168.1.254 1
63. timeout xlate 3:00:00
64. timeout conn 1:00:00 half-closed 0:10:00 udp 0:02:00 rpc 0:10:00 h323 0:05:00
     sip 0:30:00 sip_media 0:02:00
65. timeout uauth 0:05:00 absolute
66. aaa-server TACACS+ protocol tacacs+
67. aaa-server RADIUS protocol radius
68. no snmp-server location
69. no snmp-server contact
70. snmp-server community public
71. no snmp-server enable traps
72. floodguard enable
73. sysopt connection permit-ipsec
74. no sysopt route dnat
75. crypto ipsec transform-set
76. crypto ipsec transform-set NothingNew esp-3des esp-sha-hmac
77. _____
78. _____
79. _____
80. crypto map Chapter11 10 set transform-set Chapter11
81. crypto map Chapter11 20 ipsec-isakmp
82. _____
83. _____
84. _____
85. crypto map Chapter11 interface outside
86. _____
87. _____
```

continues

Example 13-15 *PIX Configuration for Los Angeles (Continued)*

```
88. _____
89. _____
90. _____
91. _____
92. _____
93. _____
94. _____
95. terminal width 80
96. Cryptochecksum:e0clmj3546549637cbsFds54132d5
```

Example 13-16 shows the configuration for the Boston branch office.

Example 13-16 *PIX Configuration for Boston*

```
1.  : Saved
2.  :
3.  PIX Version 6.3(3)
4.  nameif ethernet0 outside security0
5.  nameif ethernet1 inside security100
6.  nameif ethernet2 DMZ security70
7.  enable password ksjfglkasglc encrypted
8.  passwd kjngczftglkacytiur encrypted
9.  hostname Boston
10. domain-name www.Chapter11.com
11. fixup protocol ftp 21
12. fixup protocol http 80
13. fixup protocol smtp 25
14. fixup protocol skinny 2000
15. names
16. access-list inbound permit icmp any host 192.168.2.10
17. access-list inbound permit tcp any host 192.168.2.10  eq www
18. access-list inbound permit tcp any host 192.168.2.10 eq 443
19. access-list DMZ permit udp 172.16.2.0 255.255.255.0 host 10.10.2.240 eq ntp
20. access-list_____
21. access-list_____
22. access-list_____
23. access-list_____
24. pager lines 24
25. logging on
26. logging timestamp
27. interface ethernet0 auto
28. interface ethernet1 auto
29. interface ethernet2 auto
30. mtu outside 1500
31. mtu inside 1500
32. ip address outside 192.168.2.1 255.255.255.0
33. ip address inside 10.10.2.1 255.255.255.0
```

Example 13-16   *PIX Configuration for Boston (Continued)*

```
34. ip address DMZ 172.16.2.1 255.255.255.0
35. arp timeout 14400
36. global (outside) 1 192.168.2.20-200
37. nat (inside) 1 0.0.0.0 0.0.0.0 0 0
38. nat (inside) 0 access-list VPN
39. static (inside DMZ) 10.10.2.240 10.10.2.240 netmask 255.255.255.255 0 0
40. static (DMZ outside) 192.168.2.10 172.16.2.10 netmask 255.255.255.255 0 0
41. access-group inbound in interface outside
42. access-group DMZ in interface DMZ
43. route outside 0.0.0.0 0.0.0.0 192.168.2.254 1
44. timeout xlate 3:00:00
45. timeout conn 1:00:00 half-closed 0:10:00 udp 0:02:00
46. timeout uauth 0:05:00 absolute
47. aaa-server TACACS+ protocol tacacs+
48. aaa-server RADIUS protocol radius
49. no snmp-server location
50. no snmp-server contact
51. snmp-server community public
52. no snmp-server enable traps
53. floodguard enable
54. _____
55. _____
56. _____
57. crypto map Chapter11 10 ipsec-isakmp
58. crypto map Chapter11 10 match address LosAngeles
59. _____
60. crypto map Chapter11 10 set transform-set Chapter11
61. crypto map Chapter11 20 ipsec-isakmp
62. crypto map Chapter11 20 match address Atlanta
63. crypto map Chapter11 20 set peer 192.168.3.1
64. _____
65. _____
66. isakmp enable outside
67. isakmp key ******** address 192.168.1.1 netmask 255.255.255.255
68. isakmp key ******** address 192.168.3.1 netmask 255.255.255.255
69. isakmp identity address
70. isakmp policy 20 authentication pre-share
71. _____
72. _____
73. _____
74. _____
75. terminal width 80
76. Cryptochecksum:e0c04954fcabd239ae291d58fc618dd5
```

Example 13-17 shows the configuration for the Atlanta branch office.

Example 13-17   *PIX Configuration for Atlanta*

```
1.  : Saved
2.  :
3.  PIX Version 6.3(3)
4.  nameif ethernet0 outside security0
5.  nameif ethernet1 inside security100
6.  nameif ethernet2 DMZ security70
7.  enable password ksjfglkasglc encrypted
8.  passwd kjngczftglkacytiur encrypted
9.  hostname Atlanta
10. domain-name www.Chapter11.com
11. fixup protocol ftp 21
12. fixup protocol http 80
13. fixup protocol smtp 25
14. fixup protocol skinny 2000
15. names
16. access-list inbound permit icmp any host 192.168.3.10
17. access-list inbound permit tcp any host 192.168.3.10   eq www
18. access-list inbound permit tcp any host 192.168.3.10 eq 443
19. access-list DMZ permit udp 172.16.3.0 255.255.255.0 host 10.10.3.240 eq ntp
20. access-list_____
21. access-list_____
22. access-list_____
23. access-list_____
24. pager lines 24
25. logging on
26. logging timestamp
27. interface ethernet0 auto
28. interface ethernet1 auto
29. interface ethernet2 auto
30. mtu outside 1500
31. mtu inside 1500
32. ip address outside 192.168.3.1 255.255.255.0
33. ip address inside 10.10.3.1 255.255.255.0
34. ip address DMZ 172.16.3.1 255.255.255.0
35. arp timeout 14400
36. global (outside) 1 192.168.3.20-200
37. nat (inside) 1 0.0.0.0 0.0.0.0 0 0
38. nat (inside) 0 access-list VPN
39. static (inside DMZ) 10.10.3.240 10.10.3.240 netmask 255.255.255.255 0 0
40. static (DMZ outside) 192.168.3.10 172.16.3.10 netmask 255.255.255.255 0 0
41. access-group inbound in interface outside
42. access-group DMZ in interface DMZ
43. route outside 0.0.0.0 0.0.0.0 192.168.3.254 1
44. timeout xlate 3:00:00
45. timeout conn 1:00:00 half-closed 0:10:00 udp 0:02:00
```

Example 13-17 *PIX Configuration for Atlanta (Continued)*

```
46. timeout uauth 0:05:00 absolute
47. aaa-server TACACS+ protocol tacacs+
48. aaa-server RADIUS protocol radius
49. no snmp-server location
50. no snmp-server contact
51. snmp-server community public
52. no snmp-server enable traps
53. floodguard enable
54. sysopt connection permit-ipsec
55. crypto ipsec transform-set_____
56. crypto ipsec transform-set NothingNew esp-3des esp-sha-hmac
57. crypto map Chapter11 10 ipsec-isakmp
58. crypto map_____
59. crypto map_____
60. crypto map Chapter11 10 set transform-set Chapter11_____
61. crypto map_____
62. crypto map_____
63. crypto map_____
64. crypto map Chapter11 20 set transform-set Chapter11_____
65. crypto map_____
66. isakmp_____
67. isakmp key ********_____
68. isakmp key_____
69. isakmp identity address_____
70. isakmp policy 20_____
71. isakmp policy 20 encryption 3des
72. isakmp policy 20 hash md5
73. isakmp policy 20 group 2
74. isakmp policy 20 lifetime 86400
75. terminal width 80
76. Cryptochecksum:e0c04954fcabd239ae291d58fc618dd5
```

Each line of the configuration is numbered, and certain lines have not been completed. Your job is to complete the lines and verify each configuration against the configuration of the VPN peer. The following sections give the blank lines for each configuration. The completed configurations are listed at the end of the chapter, along with a full description of each element from the configuration in Los Angeles. You will not find all the information needed to complete the configuration on a single firewall. Remember that the configurations must match on each end of the VPN.

Los Angeles Configuration

Fill in the missing lines in Example 13-15:

Line 31: _____

Line 32: _____

Line 33: _____

Line 77: _____

Line 78: _____

Line 79: _____

Line 82: _____

Line 83: _____

Line 84: _____

Line 86: _____

Line 87: _____

Line 88: _____

Line 89: _____

Line 90: _____

Line 91: _____

Line 92: _____

Line 93: _____

Line 94: _____

Boston Configuration

Fill in the missing lines in Example 13-16:

Line 20: _____

Line 21: _____

Line 22: _____

Line 23: _____

Line 54: _____

Line 55: _____

Line 56: _____

Line 59: _____

Line 64: _____

Line 65: _____

Line 71: _____

Line 72: _____

Line 73: _____

Line 74: _____

Atlanta Configuration

Fill in the missing lines in Example 13-17:

Line 20: _____

Line 21: _____

Line 22: _____

Line 23: _____

Line 55: _____

Line 58: _____

Line 59: _____

Line 61: _____

Line 62: _____

Line 63: _____

Line 65: _____

Line 66: _____

Line 67: _____

Line 68: _____

Line 70: _____

Completed PIX Configurations

To reduce confusion, it is a good idea to use a common naming convention when creating access lists, transforms, and crypto maps. Example 13-18 shows the completed configuration for the Los Angeles headquarters.

Example 13-18 *Completed Configuration for Los Angeles*

```
1.  : Saved
2.  :
3.  PIX Version 6.3(3)
4.  nameif ethernet0 outside security0
5.  nameif ethernet1 inside security100
6.  nameif ethernet2 DMZ security70
7.  enable password HtmvK15kjhtlyfvcl encrypted
8.  passwd Kkjhlkf1568Hke encrypted
9.  hostname LosAngeles
10. domain-name www.Chapter11.com
11. fixup protocol ftp 21
12. fixup protocol http 80
13. fixup protocol h323 1720
14. fixup protocol rsh 514
15. fixup protocol smtp 25
16. fixup protocol sqlnet 1521
17. fixup protocol sip 5060
```

continues

Example 13-18 *Completed Configuration for Los Angeles (Continued)*

```
18. fixup protocol skinny 2000
19. names
20. access-list inbound permit icmp any host 192.168.1.10
21. access-list inbound permit tcp any host 192.168.1.10  eq www
22. access-list inbound permit tcp any host 192.168.1.10 eq 443
23. access-list inbound permit tcp any host 192.168.1.11  eq www
24. access-list inbound permit tcp any host 192.168.1.11 eq 443
25. access-list inbound permit tcp any host 192.168.1.12  eq www
26. access-list inbound permit tcp any host 192.168.1.12 eq 443
27. access-list inbound permit tcp any host 192.168.1.13  eq ftp
28. access-list inbound permit tcp any host 192.168.1.10 eq 443
29. access-list DMZ permit udp 172.16.1.0 255.255.255.0 host 10.10.10.240 eq ntp
30. access-list VPN permit ip 10.10.10.0 255.255.255.0 10.10.2.0 255.255.255.0
31. access-list VPN permit ip 10.10.10.0 255.255.255.0 10.10.3.0 255.255.255.0
32. access-list Boston permit ip 10.10.10.0 255.255.255.0 10.10.2.0 255.255.255.0
33. access-list Atlanta permit ip 10.10.10.0 255.255.255.0 10.10.3.0 255.255.255.0
34. pager lines 24
35. logging on
36. logging timestamp
37. interface ethernet0 auto
38. interface ethernet1 auto
39. interface ethernet2 auto
40. mtu outside 1500
41. mtu inside 1500
42. ip address outside 192.168.1.1 255.255.255.0
43. ip address inside 10.10.10.1 255.255.255.0
44. ip address DMZ 172.16.1.1 255.255.255.0
45. failover
46. failover timeout 0:00:00
47. failover poll 15
48. failover ip address outside 192.168.1.2
49. failover ip address inside 10.10.10.2
50. failover ip address DMZ 172.16.1.2
51. arp timeout 14400
52. global (outside) 1 192.168.1.20-192.168.1.250
53. nat (inside) 1 0.0.0.0 0.0.0.0 0 0
54. nat (inside) 0 access-list VPN
55. static (inside DMZ) 10.10.10.240 10.10.10.240 netmask 255.255.255.255 0 0
56. static (DMZ outside) 192.168.1.10 172.16.1.10 netmask 255.255.255.255 0 0
57. static (DMZ outside) 192.168.1.11 172.16.1.11 netmask 255.255.255.255 0 0
58. static (DMZ outside) 192.168.1.12 172.16.1.12 netmask 255.255.255.255 0 0
59. static (DMZ outside) 192.168.1.13 172.16.1.13 netmask 255.255.255.255 0 0
60. access-group inbound in interface outside
61. access-group DMZ in interface DMZ
62. route outside 0.0.0.0 0.0.0.0 192.168.1.254 1
63. timeout xlate 3:00:00
64. timeout conn 1:00:00 half-closed 0:10:00 udp 0:02:00 rpc 0:10:00 h323 0:05:00
```

Example 13-18 *Completed Configuration for Los Angeles (Continued)*

```
      sip 0:30:00 sip_media 0:02:00
65. timeout uauth 0:05:00 absolute
66. aaa-server TACACS+ protocol tacacs+
67. aaa-server RADIUS protocol radius
68. no snmp-server location
69. no snmp-server contact
70. snmp-server community public
71. no snmp-server enable traps
72. floodguard enable
73. sysopt connection permit-ipsec
74. no sysopt route dnat
75. crypto ipsec transform-set Chapter11 esp-3des esp-md5-hmac
76. crypto ipsec transform-set NothingNew esp-3des esp-sha-hmac
77. crypto map Chapter11 10 ipsec-isakmp
78. crypto map Chapter11 10 match address Boston
79. crypto map Chapter11 10 set peer 192.168.2.1
80. crypto map Chapter11 10 set transform-set Chapter11
81. crypto map Chapter11 20 ipsec-isakmp
82. crypto map Chapter11 20 match address Atlanta
83. crypto map Chapter11 20 set peer 192.168.3.1
84. crypto map Chapter11 20 set transform-set Chapter11
85. crypto map Chapter11 interface outside
86. isakmp enable outside
87. isakmp key ******** address 192.168.2.1 netmask 255.255.255.255
88. isakmp key ******** address 192.168.3.1 netmask 255.255.255.255
89. isakmp identity address
90. isakmp policy 20 authentication pre-share
91. isakmp policy 20 encryption 3des
92. isakmp policy 20 hash md5
93. isakmp policy 20 group 2
94. isakmp policy 20 lifetime 86400
95. terminal width 80
96. Cryptochecksum:e0clmj3546549637cbsFds54132d5
```

Example 13-19 shows the completed configuration for the Boston branch office.

Example 13-19 *Completed Configuration for Boston*

```
1.  : Saved
2.  :
3.  PIX Version 6.3(3)
4.  nameif ethernet0 outside security0
5.  nameif ethernet1 inside security100
6.  nameif ethernet2 DMZ security70
7.  enable password ksjfglkasglc encrypted
8.  passwd kjngczftglkacytiur encrypted
9.  hostname Boston
```

continues

Example 13-19 *Completed Configuration for Boston (Continued)*

```
10. domain-name www.Chapter11.com
11. fixup protocol ftp 21
12. fixup protocol http 80
13. fixup protocol smtp 25
14. fixup protocol skinny 2000
15. names
16. access-list inbound permit icmp any host 192.168.2.10
17. access-list inbound permit tcp any host 192.168.2.10  eq www
18. access-list inbound permit tcp any host 192.168.2.10 eq 443
19. access-list DMZ permit udp 172.16.2.0 255.255.255.0 host 10.10.2.240 eq ntp
20. access-list VPN permit ip 10.10.2.0 255.255.255.0 10.10.10.0 255.255.255.0
21. access-list VPN permit ip 10.10.2.0 255.255.255.0 10.10.3.0 255.255.255.0
22. access-list LosAngeles permit ip 10.10.2.0 255.255.255.0 10.10.10.0
       255.255.255.0
23. access-list Atlanta permit ip 10.10.2.0 255.255.255.0 10.10.3.0 255.255.255.0
24. pager lines 24
25. logging on
26. logging timestamp
27. interface ethernet0 auto
28. interface ethernet1 auto
29. interface ethernet2 auto
30. mtu outside 1500
31. mtu inside 1500
32  ip address outside 192.168.2.1 255.255.255.0
33. ip address inside 10.10.2.1 255.255.255.0
34. ip address DMZ 172.16.2.1 255.255.255.0
35. arp timeout 14400
36. global (outside) 1 192.168.2.20-192.168.2.200
37. nat (inside) 1 0.0.0.0 0.0.0.0 0 0
38. nat (inside) 0 access-list VPN
39. static (inside DMZ) 10.10.2.240 10.10.2.240 netmask 255.255.255.255 0 0
40. static (DMZ outside) 192.168.2.10 172.16.2.10 netmask 255.255.255.255 0 0
41. access-group inbound in interface outside
42. access-group DMZ in interface DMZ
43. route outside 0.0.0.0 0.0.0.0 192.168.2.254 1
44. timeout xlate 3:00:00
45. timeout conn 1:00:00 half-closed 0:10:00 udp 0:02:00
46. timeout uauth 0:05:00 absolute
47. aaa-server TACACS+ protocol tacacs+
48. aaa-server RADIUS protocol radius
49. no snmp-server location
50. no snmp-server contact
51. snmp-server community public
52. no snmp-server enable traps
53. floodguard enable
54. sysopt connection permit-ipsec
55. crypto ipsec transform-set Chapter11 esp-3des esp-md5-hmac
```

Example 13-19 *Completed Configuration for Boston (Continued)*

```
56. crypto ipsec transform-set NothingNew esp-3des esp-sha-hmac
57. crypto map Chapter11 10 ipsec-isakmp
58. crypto map Chapter11 10 match address LosAngeles
59. crypto map Chapter11 10 set peer 192.168.1.1
60. crypto map Chapter11 10 set transform-set Chapter11
61. crypto map Chapter11 20 ipsec-isakmp
62. crypto map Chapter11 20 match address Atlanta
63. crypto map Chapter11 20 set peer 192.168.3.1
64. crypto map Chapter11 20 set transform-set Chapter11
65. crypto map Chapter11 interface outside
66. isakmp enable outside
67. isakmp key ******** address 192.168.1.1 netmask 255.255.255.255
68. isakmp key ******** address 192.168.3.1 netmask 255.255.255.255
69. isakmp identity address
70. isakmp policy 20 authentication pre-share
71. isakmp policy 20 encryption 3des
72. isakmp policy 20 hash md5
73. isakmp policy 20 group 2
74. isakmp policy 20 lifetime 86400
75. terminal width 80
76. Cryptochecksum:e0c04954fcabd239ae291d58fc618dd5
```

Example 13-20 shows the completed configuration for the Atlanta branch office.

Example 13-20 *Completed Configuration for Atlanta*

```
1.  : Saved
2.  :
3.  PIX Version 6.3(3)
4.  nameif ethernet0 outside security0
5.  nameif ethernet1 inside security100
6.  nameif ethernet2 DMZ security70
7.  enable password ksjfglkasglc encrypted
8.  passwd kjngczftglkacytiur encrypted
9.  hostname Atlanta
10. domain-name www.Chapter11.com
11. fixup protocol ftp 21
12. fixup protocol http 80
13. fixup protocol smtp 25
14. fixup protocol skinny 2000
15. names
16. access-list inbound permit icmp any host 192.168.3.10
17. access-list inbound permit tcp any host 192.168.3.10   eq www
18. access-list inbound permit tcp any host 192.168.3.10 eq 443
19. access-list DMZ permit udp 172.16.3.0 255.255.255.0 host 10.10.3.240 eq ntp
20. access-list VPN permit ip 10.10.3.0 255.255.255.0 10.10.2.0 255.255.255.0
21. access-list VPN permit ip 10.10.3.0 255.255.255.0 10.10.10.0 255.255.255.0
```

continues

Example 13-20 *Completed Configuration for Atlanta (Continued)*

```
22. access-list LosAngeles permit ip 10.10.3.0 255.255.255.0 10.10.10.0
      255.255.255.0
23. access-list Boston permit ip 10.10.3.0 255.255.255.0 10.10.2.0 255.255.255.0
24. pager lines 24
25. logging on
26. logging timestamp
27. interface ethernet0 auto
28. interface ethernet1 auto
29. interface ethernet2 auto
30. mtu outside 1500
31. mtu inside 1500
32. ip address outside 192.168.3.1 255.255.255.0
33. ip address inside 10.10.3.1 255.255.255.0
34. ip address DMZ 172.16.3.1 255.255.255.0
35. arp timeout 14400
36. global (outside) 1 192.168.3.20-192.168.3.200
37. nat (inside) 1 0.0.0.0 0.0.0.0 0 0
38. nat (inside) 0 access-list VPN
39. static (inside DMZ) 10.10.3.240 10.10.3.240 netmask 255.255.255.255 0 0
40. static (DMZ outside) 192.168.3.10 172.16.3.10 netmask 255.255.255.255 0 0
41. access-group inbound in interface outside
42. access-group DMZ in interface DMZ
43. route outside 0.0.0.0 0.0.0.0 192.168.3.254 1
44. timeout xlate 3:00:00
45. timeout conn 1:00:00 half-closed 0:10:00 udp 0:02:00
46. timeout uauth 0:05:00 absolute
47. aaa-server TACACS+ protocol tacacs+
48. aaa-server RADIUS protocol radius
49. no snmp-server location
50. no snmp-server contact
51. snmp-server community public
52. no snmp-server enable traps
53. floodguard enable
54. sysopt connection permit-ipsec
55. crypto ipsec transform-set Chapter11 esp-3des esp-md5-hmac
56. crypto ipsec transform-set NothingNew esp-3des esp-sha-hmac
57. crypto map Chapter11 10 ipsec-isakmp
58. crypto map Chapter11 10 match address LosAngeles
59. crypto map Chapter11 10 set peer 192.168.1.1
60. crypto map Chapter11 10 set transform-set Chapter11
61. crypto map Chapter11 20 ipsec-isakmp
62. crypto map Chapter11 20 match address Boston
63. crypto map Chapter11 20 set peer 192.168.2.1
64. crypto map Chapter11 20 set transform-set Chapter11
65. crypto map Chapter11 interface outside
66. isakmp enable outside
67. isakmp key ******** address 192.168.1.1 netmask 255.255.255.255
```

Example 13-20   *Completed Configuration for Atlanta (Continued)*

```
68. isakmp key ******** address 192.168.2.1 netmask 255.255.255.255
69. isakmp identity address
70. isakmp policy 20 authentication pre-share
71. isakmp policy 20 encryption 3des
72. isakmp policy 20 hash md5
73. isakmp policy 20 group 2
74. isakmp policy 20 lifetime 86400
75. terminal width 80
76. Cryptochecksum:e0c04954fcabd239ae291d58fc618dd5
```

How the Configuration Lines Interact

Figure 13-11 shows the completed configuration for Los Angeles, with a brief explanation for each entry. Note that each entry is connected to one or more other entries on the right. This diagram depicts how the lines of the configuration are dependent on each other. Keep this in mind when trying to troubleshoot a VPN configuration. It might help you to find which line is missing or incorrectly configured.

Figure 13-11 *LA Configuration with Comments*

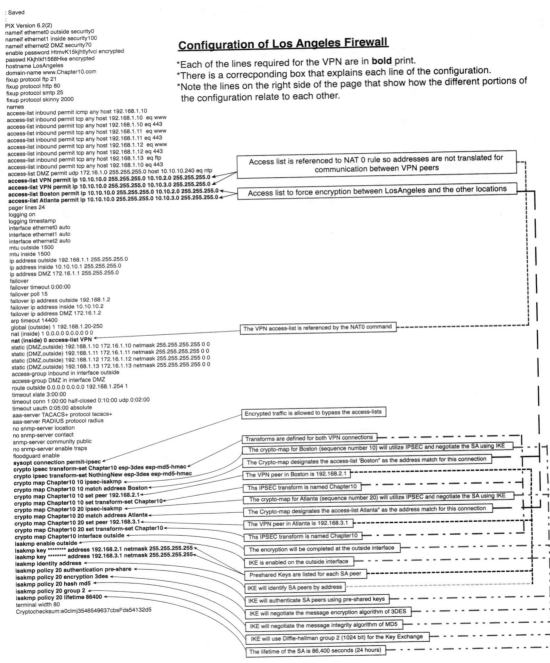

```
: Saved
:
PIX Version 6.2(2)
nameif ethernet0 outside security0
nameif ethernet1 inside security100
nameif ethernet2 DMZ security70
enable password HtmvK15kjhtlyfvcl encrypted
passwd Kkjhlkf1568Hke encrypted
hostname LosAngeles
domain-name www.Chapter10.com
fixup protocol ftp 21
fixup protocol http 80
fixup protocol smtp 25
fixup protocol skinny 2000
names
access-list inbound permit icmp any host 192.168.1.10
access-list inbound permit tcp any host 192.168.1.10  eq www
access-list inbound permit tcp any host 192.168.1.10 eq 443
access-list inbound permit tcp any host 192.168.1.11 eq www
access-list inbound permit tcp any host 192.168.1.11 eq 443
access-list inbound permit tcp any host 192.168.1.12  eq www
access-list inbound permit tcp any host 192.168.1.12 eq 443
access-list inbound permit tcp any host 192.168.1.13  eq ftp
access-list inbound permit tcp any host 192.168.1.12 eq 443
access-list DMZ permit udp 172.16.1.0 255.255.255.0 host 10.10.10.240 eq ntp
access-list VPN permit ip 10.10.10.0 255.255.255.0 10.10.2.0 255.255.255.0
access-list VPN permit ip 10.10.10.0 255.255.255.0 10.10.3.0 255.255.255.0
access-list Boston permit ip 10.10.10.0 255.255.255.0 10.10.2.0 255.255.255.0
access-list Atlanta permit ip 10.10.10.0 255.255.255.0 10.10.3.0 255.255.255.0
pager lines 24
logging on
logging timestamp
interface ethernet0 auto
interface ethernet1 auto
interface ethernet2 auto
mtu outside 1500
mtu inside 1500
ip address outside 192.168.1.1 255.255.255.0
ip address inside 10.10.10.1 255.255.255.0
ip address DMZ 172.16.1.1 255.255.255.0
failover
failover timeout 0:00:00
failover poll 15
failover ip address outside 192.168.1.2
failover ip address inside 10.10.10.2
failover ip address DMZ 172.16.1.2
arp timeout 14400
global (outside) 1 192.168.1.20-250
nat (inside) 1 0.0.0.0.0.0.0.0 0 0
nat (inside) 0 access-list VPN
static (DMZ,outside) 192.168.1.10 172.16.1.10 netmask 255.255.255.255 0 0
static (DMZ,outside) 192.168.1.11 172.16.1.11 netmask 255.255.255.255 0 0
static (DMZ,outside) 192.168.1.12 172.16.1.12 netmask 255.255.255.255 0 0
static (DMZ,outside) 192.168.1.13 172.16.1.13 netmask 255.255.255.255 0 0
access-group inbound in interface outside
access-group DMZ in interface DMZ
route outside 0.0.0.0 0.0.0.0 192.168.1.254 1
timeout xlate 3:00:00
timeout conn 1:00:00 half-closed 0:10:00 udp 0:02:00
timeout uauth 0:05:00 absolute
aaa-server TACACS+ protocol tacacs+
aaa-server RADIUS protocol radius
no snmp-server location
no snmp-server contact
snmp-server community public
no snmp-server enable traps
floodguard enable
sysopt connection permit-ipsec
crypto ipsec transform-set Chapter10 esp-3des esp-md5-hmac
crypto ipsec transform-set NothingNew esp-3des esp-md5-hmac
crypto map Chapter10 10 ipsec-isakmp
crypto map Chapter10 10 match address Boston
crypto map Chapter10 10 set peer 192.168.2.1
crypto map Chapter10 10 set transform-set Chapter10
crypto map Chapter10 20 ipsec-isakmp
crypto map Chapter10 20 match address Atlanta
crypto map Chapter10 20 set peer 192.168.3.1
crypto map Chapter10 20 set transform-set Chapter10
crypto map Chapter10 interface outside
isakmp enable outside
isakmp key ******** address 192.168.2.1 netmask 255.255.255.255
isakmp key ******** address 192.168.3.1 netmask 255.255.255.255
isakmp identity address
isakmp policy 20 authentication pre-share
isakmp policy 20 encryption 3des
isakmp policy 20 hash md5
isakmp policy 20 group 2
isakmp policy 20 lifetime 86400
terminal width 80
Cryptochecksum:e0clmj3546549637cbsFds54132d5
```

Configuration of Los Angeles Firewall

*Each of the lines required for the VPN are in **bold** print.
*There is a correcponding box that explains each line of the configuration.
*Note the lines on the right side of the page that show how the different portions of the configuration relate to each other.

> Access list is referenced to NAT 0 rule so addresses are not translated for communication between VPN peers

> Access list to force encryption between LosAngeles and the other locations

> The VPN access-list is referenced by the NAT0 command

> Encrypted traffic is allowed to bypass the access-lists

> Transforms are defined for both VPN connections

> The crypto-map for Boston (sequence number 10) will utilize IPSEC and negotiate the SA using IKE

> The Crypto-map designates the access-list 'Boston" as the address match for this connection

> The VPN peer in Boston is 192.168.2.1

> This IPSEC transform is named Chapter10

> The crypto-map for Atlanta (sequence number 20) will utilize IPSEC and negotiate the SA using IKE

> The Crypto-map designates the access-list Atlanta" as the address match for this connection

> The VPN peer in Atlanta is 192.168.3.1

> This IPSEC transform is named Chapter10

> The encryption will be completed at the outside interface

> IKE is enabled on the outside interface

> Preshared Keys are listed for each SA peer

> IKE will identify SA peers by address

> IKE will authenticate SA peers using pre-shared keys

> IKE will negotiate the message encryption algorithm of 3DES

> IKE will negotiate the message integrity algorithm of MD5

> IKE will use Diffie-hellman group 2 (1024 bit) for the Key Exchange

> The lifetime of the SA is 86,400 seconds (24 hours)

This chapter covers the following subjects:

- DHCP Server Configuration

- PPPoE and the Security Appliance

- Security Appliance Enables a Secure VPN

  Prepare to Configure VPN Support
- Cisco VPN Client

- Scale Security Appliance VPNs

CHAPTER 14

Configuring Access VPNs

The Cisco Easy VPN, a software enhancement for Cisco Security Appliances and security appliances, greatly simplifies virtual private network (VPN) deployment for remote offices and telecommuters. By centralizing VPN management across all Cisco VPN devices, Cisco Easy VPN reduces the complexity of VPN deployments. Cisco Easy VPN enables you to integrate various remote VPN solutions (Cisco IOS routers, Cisco PIX Firewalls, Cisco ASA 55X0 series firewalls, Cisco VPN 3002 Hardware Clients, and Cisco VPN Software Clients) within a single deployment using a consistent VPN policy and key management method that greatly simplifies administration of the remote clients.

How to Best Use This Chapter

Using VPNs to protect traffic from remote locations is a vital portion of your overall network security solution. Understanding how the Cisco Easy VPN simplifies VPN deployment and management is crucial to securing access from all of your remote locations. Chapter 13, "Virtual Private Networks," explains the technologies and protocols used for creating and maintaining VPNs across public networks. This chapter explains how you can apply those VPNs to secure various remote configurations using the Cisco Easy VPN solution. Test yourself with the "Do I Know This Already?" quiz and see how familiar you are with the Cisco Easy VPN functionality available on Security Appliances.

"Do I Know This Already?" Quiz

The purpose of the "Do I Know This Already?" quiz is to help you decide if you really need to read the entire chapter. If you already intend to read the entire chapter, you do not necessarily need to answer these questions now.

The ten-question quiz, derived from the major sections in the "Foundation and Supplemental Topics" portion of the chapter, helps you determine how to spend your limited study time.

Table 14-1 outlines the major topics discussed in this chapter and the "Do I Know This Already?" quiz questions that correspond to those topics.

Table 14-1 *"Do I Know This Already?" Foundation Topics Section-to-Question Mapping*

Supplemental or Foundation Topics Section	Questions Covered in This Section	Score
Introduction to Cisco Easy VPN		
Overview of the Easy VPN Server	1	
Overview of Easy VPN Remote Feature	2, 3	
Easy VPN Remote Modes of Operation	4, 5	
Overview of Cisco VPN Software Client	6	
PIX Easy VPN Remote Configuration	7	
Point-to-Point Protocol over Ethernet and the Security Appliance	8, 10	
Dynamic Host Configuration Protocol Server Configuration	9	

CAUTION The goal of self assessment is to gauge your mastery of the topics in this chapter. If you do not know the answer to a question or are only partially sure of the answer, you should mark this question wrong for purposes of the self assessment. Giving yourself credit for an answer you correctly guess skews your self-assessment results and might provide you with a false sense of security.

1. What is the Easy VPN Server functionality known as *Initial Contact*?

   a. Ability to cause the Easy VPN Server to delete any existing connections, thus preventing SA synchronization problems

   b. The first connection between an Easy VPN Client and Easy VPN Server

   c. The initial message sent from the Easy VPN Server to the Easy VPN Client

   d. The initial message sent from the Easy VPN Client to the Easy VPN Server

   e. None of theses answers are correct

2. Which of the following platforms does not support the Easy VPN Remote feature functionality?

   a. 800 Series routers

   b. 900 Series routers

   c. 7200 Series routers

   d. 1700 Series routers

   e. None of these answers are correct

3. Which two IKE authentication mechanisms do the Easy VPN Remote Clients support? (Choose two.)

  a. Username/password

  b. Preshared keys

  c. Diffie-Hellman

  d. Digital certificates

  e. XAUTH

4. How many different operation modes does the Easy VPN Remote feature support?

  a. 1

  b. 4

  c. 2

  d. 3

  e. None of these answers are correct

5. In which Easy VPN Remote mode are the IP addresses of the remote systems visible on the Easy VPN Server network?

  a. Client mode.

  b. Network extension mode.

  c. Server mode.

  d. No Easy VPN Remote modes support this functionality.

  e. All Easy VPN Remote modes.

6. The Cisco VPN Software Client supports which key management techniques?

  a. IKE main mode

  b. IKE aggressive mode

  c. IKE active mode

  d. Diffie-Hellman groups 1, 2, 5, and 7

  e. All of these answers are correct

  f. None of these answers are correct

7. What is Secure Unit Authentication (SUA)?

   a. The ability to require the hosts on the remote protected network to be authenticated individually based on the IP address of the inside host

   b. The ability to require one-time passwords, two-factor authentication, and similar authentication schemes before the establishment of a VPN tunnel to the Easy VPN Server

   c. An authentication mechanism between the remote systems and the Easy VPN Remote Client

   d. An authentication mechanism that the Cisco VPN Software Client uses to connect with the Easy VPN Remote feature

   e. None of these answers are correct

8. Which authentication mechanisms are supported with PPPoE?

   a. PAP

   b. CHAP

   c. IKE

   d. MS-CHAP

   e. None of these answers are correct

9. Which command enables the Cisco Security Appliance to pass configuration parameters learned from a DHCP server to its DHCP clients?

   a. dhcpd auto_config

   b. dhcpd option 150

   c. dhcpd address

   d. dhcpd bind

   e. None of these answers are correct

10. Which of the following is false with regard to the Security Appliance?

    a. You can pass configuration parameters learned from the DHCP client to the Security Appliance's DHCP clients.

    b. You can pass configuration parameters learned from the PPPoE client to the Security Appliance's DHCP clients.

    c. You can enable the DHCP client and the DHCP server simultaneously.

    d. You can enable the PPPoE client and the DHCP client on the same interface simultaneously.

    e. All of these statements are true.

The answers to the "Do I Know This Already?" quiz are found in Appendix A, "Answers to the 'Do I Know This Already?' Quizzes and Q&A Sections." The suggested choices for your next step are as follows:

- **8 or less overall score**—Read the entire chapter. This includes the "Foundation and Supplemental Topics," "Foundation Summary," and "Q&A" sections.

- **9 or 10 overall score**—If you want more review of these topics, skip to the "Foundation Summary" section and then go to the "Q&A" section. Otherwise, move to the next chapter.

Foundation and Supplemental Topics

Introduction to Cisco Easy VPN

Cisco Easy VPN greatly simplifies VPN deployment for remote offices and telecommuters. Based on a Cisco Unified Client Framework, Cisco Easy VPN centralizes management across all Cisco VPN devices, thus greatly reducing the complexity in configuring and deploying VPN configurations. The Cisco Easy VPN consists of the following two components (see Figure 14-1):

- Easy VPN Server
- Easy VPN Remote feature

Easy VPN Server

The Easy VPN Server enables Cisco IOS routers, Security Appliances, and Cisco VPN 3000 Series concentrators to serve as VPN headend devices when remote offices are running the Easy VPN Remote feature. The configuration works for both site-to-site and remote access configurations. With Cisco Easy VPN, security policies defined at the headend are pushed to the remote VPN device, ensuring that the connection has up-to-date policies in place before the connection is established.

Mobile workers running the VPN Client software on their PCs can initiate Internet Protocol Security (IPSec) tunnels that are terminated on the Easy VPN Server. This flexibility enables telecommuters and traveling employees to access critical data and applications easily that reside at the headquarter facilities.

Easy VPN Remote Feature

The Easy VPN Remote feature enables Security Appliances, Cisco VPN 3002 Hardware Clients, Cisco VPN Software Clients, and certain Cisco IOS routers to act as remote VPN clients. The Easy VPN Server can push security policies to these clients, thus minimizing VPN configuration requirements at remote locations. This cost-effective solution is ideal for remote offices with little information technology (IT) support as well as large deployments where it is impractical to configure individual remote devices.

Figure 14-1 *Cisco Easy VPN*

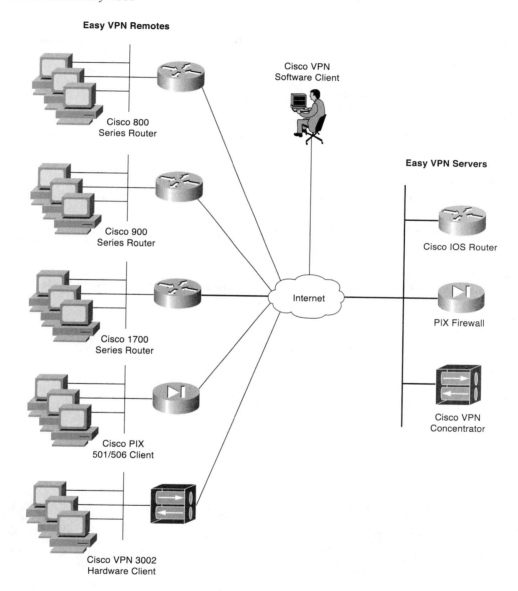

Overview of the Easy VPN Server

The Easy VPN Server serves as the headend for your VPN configuration. To utilize Cisco Easy VPN effectively, you need to understand the following characteristics of the Security Appliance Easy VPN Server:

- Major features
- Server functions
- Supported servers

Major Features

The Security Appliance VPN Server includes the following major features:

- Support for Easy VPN Remote clients
- Ability for remote users to communicate using IPSec with supported Security Appliance gateways
- Central management of IPSec policies that are pushed to the clients by the server

Server Functions

The Security Appliance version 6.3 VPN Server supports the following functionality:

- Mode Configuration version 6
- Extended Authentication (XAUTH) version 6
- Internet Key Exchange (IKE) dead peer detection (DPD)
- Split tunneling control
- Initial contact
- Group-based policy control

Dead Peer Detection

Dead peer detection (DPD) enables two IPSec peers to determine if each other is still "alive" during the lifetime of the VPN connection. This functionality is useful to clean up valuable VPN resources that are allocated to a peer that no longer exists.

A Cisco VPN device can be configured to send and reply to DPD messages. DPD messages are sent when no other traffic is traversing the IPSec tunnel. If a configured amount of time passes without a DPD message, a dead peer can be detected. DPD messages are unidirectional and automatically sent by Cisco VPN Clients. DPD is configured on the server only if the server wishes to send DPD messages to VPN Clients to assess their health.

Initial Contact

If a Cisco VPN Client is suddenly disconnected, the gateway might not immediately detect this, so the current connection information (IKE and IPSec security associations [SA]) will still be valid. Then, if the VPN Client attempts to reestablish a connection, the new connection will be refused because the gateway still has the previous connection marked as valid. To avoid this scenario, *Initial Contact* has been implemented in all Cisco VPN products. Initial Contact enables the VPN Client to send an initial message that instructs the gateway to ignore and delete any existing connections from that client, thus preventing connection problems caused by SA synchronization issues.

The Cisco Easy VPN supports the IPSec options and attributes shown in Table 14-2.

Table 14-2 *IPSec Options and Attributes*

IPSec Option	Attributes
Authentication Algorithms	• Keyed-Hash Message Authentication Code (HMAC) • Message Digest 5 (MD5) • HMAC Secure Hash Algorithm (SHA-1)
Authentication Types	• Preshared keys • Rivest-Shamir-Adleman (RSA) digital signatures (not supported by Cisco Easy VPN Remote phase II)
Diffie-Hellman (DH) Groups	• Group 1 • Group 2 • Group 5
IKE Encryption Algorithms	• Data Encryption Standard (DES) • Triple Data Encryption Standard (3DES) • Advanced Encryption Standard (AES)
IPSec Encryption Algorithms	• DES • 3DES • AES • NULL
IPSec Protocol Identifiers	• Encapsulating Security Payload (ESP) • IP Payload Compression Protocol (IPComp) • STAC-Lempel-Ziv Compression (LZS)
IPSec Protocol Mode	• Tunnel Mode

Supported Servers

The Easy VPN Remote feature requires that the destination peer be a VPN gateway or concentrator that supports the Easy VPN Server. Some of the currently supported Easy VPN Server platforms include the following:

- Cisco 806, 826, 827, and 828 routers (Cisco IOS Software Release 12.2[8]T or later)

- Cisco 1700 Series routers (Cisco IOS Software Release 12.2[8]T or later)

- Cisco 2600 Series routers (Cisco IOS Software Release 12.2[8]T or later)

- Cisco 3620, 3640, and 3660 routers (Cisco IOS Software Release 12.2[8]T or later)

- Cisco 7100 Series VPN routers (Cisco IOS Software Release 12.2[8]T or later)

- Cisco 7200 Series routers (Cisco IOS Software Release 12.2[8]T or later)

- Cisco 7500 Series routers (Cisco IOS Software Release 12.2[8]T or later)

- Cisco uBR905 and uBR925 cable access routers (Cisco IOS Software Release 12.2[8]T or later)

- Cisco VPN 3000 Series (Software Release 3.11 or later)

- Cisco PIX 500 Series (Software Release 6.2 or later)

Overview of Easy VPN Remote Feature

The Cisco Easy VPN Remote feature enables Cisco Security Appliance, Cisco VPN 3002 Hardware Clients, Cisco VPN Software Clients, and certain IOS routers to act as remote Cisco VPN Clients. The Cisco Easy VPN Remote feature provides for automatic management of the following items:

- Negotiating tunnel parameters

- Establishing tunnels according to parameters

- Automatically creating the Network Address Translation (NAT)/Port Address Translation (PAT) and associated access list if necessary

- Authenticating users

- Managing security keys for encryption and decryption

- Authenticating, encrypting, and decrypting data through the VPN tunnel

This section explains the following characteristics of the Easy VPN Remote feature:

- Supported clients

- Easy VPN remote connection process

- XAUTH configuration

Supported Clients

The Easy VPN Remote feature supports the following client platforms:

- Cisco VPN Software Client
- Cisco VPN 3002 Hardware Client
- Cisco PIX 501 and 506/506E VPN Clients
- Cisco Easy VPN Remote router clients

Cisco VPN Software Client

The Cisco Easy VPN Remote feature supports the Cisco VPN Client software (software version 3.*x* and later). Simple to deploy and operate, this client software enables customers to establish secure, end-to-end encrypted tunnels to any Easy VPN Server. The Cisco VPN Software Client is available from the Cisco.com website for any central-site remote access VPN product and is included free of charge with the Cisco VPN 3000 Concentrator.

VPN access policies and configurations are downloaded to the Cisco VPN Software Client from the Easy VPN Server when the client establishes a connection. This configuration simplifies deployment, management, and scalability. By preconfiguring the client software, the initial user login requires little user intervention even in mass deployment scenarios.

The Cisco VPN Software Client operates with the following operating systems:

- Microsoft Windows 95, 98, Me, NT 4.0, 2000, and XP
- Linux
- Solaris (UltraSPARC 32- and 64-bit)
- MAC OS X 10.1

Cisco VPN 3002 Hardware Client

The Cisco VPN Hardware Client has the Cisco VPN Software Client software built into it, enabling it to emulate the Cisco 3000 Series VPN Concentrator Software Client. You simply can connect the remote PCs into the Hardware Client instead of loading the Cisco VPN Software Client software on the remote PCs.

The Hardware Client comes in the following two versions:

- Hardware Client
- Hardware Client 8E

> **NOTE**   Both Hardware Client models have one public Ethernet interface. The difference between the two Hardware Clients is that the 8E has eight private 10/100BASE-T ports instead of only one. These eight ports utilize auto Medium Dependent Interface Crossover (MDIX) technology that eliminates the need for crossover cables when connecting a device to a port.

The Hardware Client operates in one of the following two modes:

- Client mode
- Network extension mode

You can select the modes locally using the command-line interface (CLI) or the graphical user interface (GUI) or remotely using an IPSec tunnel or Secure Shell (SSH).

The Hardware Client is powered by an external power supply and can auto sense either 110V or 220V.

Cisco PIX 501 and 506 VPN Clients

The following two PIX Firewall models are commonly used as VPN clients:

- PIX 501
- PIX 506/506E

The PIX 501 delivers enterprise-class security for small offices and telecommuters. For small offices with always-on broadband connections, the PIX 501 provides security functionality, numerous networking features, and powerful remote management capabilities in a compact single-box solution.

Up to four individual systems can share a single broadband connection, using the integrated four-port auto-sensing, auto MDIX switch for the inside interface. Like the Hardware Client, this switch eliminates the need for crossover cables when connecting a device to a port. The Ethernet ports support 10/100BASE-T (100BASE-T with the 6.3 software release). The PIX 501 also provides a RS-232 console port interface (RJ-45 connector and 9600 baud).

The PIX 506/506E enables companies to utilize the power of the Internet to enable users to work remotely from home securely. It delivers full firewall protection in conjunction with IPSec and VPN functionality. Connecting simultaneously with up to 25 VPN peers, the PIX 506/506E provides a complete implementation of IPSec standards. It comes with two integrated 10/100BASE-T (100BASE-T with the 6.3 software release) ports in a compact platform (8 inches by 12 inches by 1.7 inches). Updates to image files are downloaded using the Trivial File Transfer Protocol (TFTP).

> **NOTE**   Before software release 6.3, the Ethernet ports on the PIX 501 and 506/506E were 10BASE-T. After upgrading to the 6.3 software release on either the PIX 501 or 506/506E, these ports become 10/100BASE-T ports. This speed enhancement is accomplished strictly by a software update (no hardware upgrades are necessary).

Cisco Easy VPN Remote Router Clients

To provide a comprehensive solution, Cisco Easy VPN also supports several router-based clients. You can use the following router platforms as Cisco Easy VPN remote clients:

- Cisco 800 Series routers (806, 826, 827,828)
- Cisco 900 Series routers (uBR905, uBR925)
- Cisco 1700 Series routers (1710, 1720, 1721, 1750, 1751, 1760)

Cable modems, xDSL routers, and other forms of broadband access provide Internet access, but many situations require VPN connections to secure data that traverses the Internet. Establishing a VPN connection between two VPN endpoints, however, can be complicated because it usually requires coordination between administrators to perform the tedious tasks necessary to define the connection parameters.

Cisco Easy VPN Remote eliminates most of the tedious work by implementing the Cisco VPN Client protocol. This protocol allows many of the VPN parameters to be configured on the access server. Once the access server is configured, the additional configuration on the VPN Client is minimal. When the IPSec client initiates the VPN connection, the VPN remote access server pushes the required IPSec policies to the IPSec client and creates the corresponding IPSec tunnel.

Easy VPN Remote Connection Process

When the Easy VPN Remote Client initiates a connection with the Easy VPN Server gateway, the interaction between the peers involves the following major steps:

Step 1   VPN Client initiates the IKE phase 1 process.

Step 2   VPN Client negotiates an IKE SA.

Step 3   Easy VPN Server accepts the SA proposal.

Step 4   Easy VPN Server initiates a username/password challenge.

Step 5   Mode configuration process is initiated.

Step 6   IKE quick mode completes the connection.

Step 1: VPN Client Initiates IKE Phase 1 Process

When initiating the VPN connection, the client can use one of the following two IKE authentication mechanisms:

- Preshared keys
- Digital certificates

When using preshared keys, the client initiates IKE aggressive mode negotiation. The group name entered in the configuration GUI (ID-KEY-ID) is used to identify the group profile associated with the VPN Client.

Using digital certificates requires the client to initiate IKE main mode negotiation. The Organizational Unit (OU) field of the distinguished name (DN) is used to identify the group profile associated with the VPN Client.

Step 2: VPN Client Negotiates an IKE Security Association

The client attempts to establish an SA between the client and server peer Internet Protocol (IP) addresses by sending multiple IKE proposals to the Easy VPN Server. To reduce manual configuration on the VPN Client, these IKE proposals include several combinations of the following parameters:

- Encryption and hash algorithms
- Authentication methods
- Diffie-Hellman (DH) group sizes

Proposing multiple IKE proposals with various parameters means that one combination is likely to match one of the options configured on the server.

Step 3: Easy VPN Server Accepts the SA Proposal

After receiving the various proposals from the VPN Client, the Easy VPN Server searches for a valid match in its configuration. The first proposal to match is accepted. To ensure that the most secure proposal is always accepted, you should store the valid proposals on the server in order from the most secure option to the least secure option.

Step 4: Easy VPN Server Initiates a Username/Password Challenge

If the Easy VPN Server is configured for XAUTH, the VPN Client waits for a username/password challenge once the proposal is accepted. The username and password entered by the user are checked against the data stored in an authentication, authorization, and accounting (AAA) server.

> **NOTE**   VPN devices that handle remote Cisco VPN Clients should always be configured to enforce user authentication.

Step 5: Mode Configuration Process Is Initiated

After successfully authenticating with the Easy VPN Server, the VPN Client requests the remaining configuration parameters from the Easy VPN Server such as the following:

- IP address
- Domain Name System (DNS) information
- Split tunneling configuration

> **NOTE**   The IP address is the only required parameter in the group profile. All other parameters are optional.

Step 6: IKE Quick Mode Completes the Connection

After the VPN Client receives the various configuration parameters from the Easy VPN Server, IKE quick mode is initiated to negotiate the IPSec SA establishment.

Extended Authentication Configuration

XAUTH enables the Easy VPN Server to require username/password authentication in order to establish the VPN connection. This authentication is performed by an AAA server. To configure the Easy VPN Server to use XAUTH for remote VPN clients, you must set up the Easy VPN Server and configure it to perform XAUTH. The complete configuration process involves performing the following tasks:

- Create an Internet Security Association and Key Management Protocol (ISAKMP) policy for remote Cisco VPN Client access
- Create an IP address pool
- Define a group policy for mode configuration push
- Create a transform set
- Create a dynamic crypto map
- Assign the dynamic crypto map to a static crypto map
- Apply the static crypto map to an interface
- Configure XAUTH
- Configure NAT and NAT 0
- Enable IKE DPD

Create an ISAKMP Policy

To create the ISAKMP policy, you must use the standard ISAKMP configuration commands to define the following parameters:

- Authentication type
- Encryption algorithm
- Hash algorithm
- Diffie-Hellman group ID
- SA lifetime

The syntax for these commands is as follows:

```
isakmp policy priority authentication {pre-share Irsa-sig}
isakmp policy priority encryption {aes I aes-192 I aes-256 I des I 3des}
isakmp policy priority group {1 I 2 I 5}
isakmp policy priority hash {md5 I sha}
isakmp policy priority lifetime seconds
```

Table 14-3 outlines the parameters for the **isakmp policy** command.

Table 14-3 isakmp policy *Parameters*

Parameter	Description
aes	Specifies AES with a 128-bit key to be the encryption algorithm used by the IKE policy.
aes-192	Specifies AES with a 192-bit key to be the encryption algorithm used by the IKE policy.
aes-256	Specifies AES with a 256-bit key to be the encryption algorithm used by the IKE policy.
des	Specifies DES with a 56-bit key to be the encryption algorithm used by the IKE policy.
3des	Specifies 3DES to be the encryption algorithm used by the IKE policy.
encryption	Keyword indicating that the next parameter specifies the encryption algorithm for the IKE policy
group	Keyword indicating that the next parameter is a Diffie-Hellman group. You can specify 1, 2, or 5 (1 is the default).
hash	Keyword indicating that the next parameter specifies the hash algorithm to be used by the IKE policy.

Table 14-3 isakmp policy *Parameters (Continued)*

Parameter	Description
lifetime	Keyword indicating that the next parameter specifies the lifetime for the IKE policy.
md5	Specifies that the MD5 hash algorithm will be used by the IKE policy.
pre-share	Specifies that the IKE policy will use preshared keys for initial authentication.
priority	An integer (1 to 65,534) uniquely identifying the IKE policy and assigning it a priority (1 is the highest priority, and 65,534 is the lowest priority).
rsa-sig	Specifies that the IKE policy will use RSA signatures for initial authentication.
sha	Specifies that the SHA-1 hash algorithm will be used by the IKE policy. This is the default hash algorithm.

For instance, suppose that you want to configure an ISAKMP policy based on the following criteria:

- Preshare key initial authentication
- AES encryption algorithm (128-bit)
- SHA hash algorithm
- Diffie-Hellman group 5

The commands to define this ISAKMP policy are as follows:

```
Pix(config)# isakmp enable outside
Pix(config)# isakmp policy 30 authentication pre-share
Pix(config)# isakmp policy 30 encryption aes
Pix(config)# isakmp policy 30 hash sha
Pix(config)# isakmp policy 30 group 5
```

Create an IP Address Pool

If the remote client is using the Easy VPN Server to obtain its IP address, you must define a local address pool using the **ip local pool** command. The syntax for this command is as follows:

```
ip local pool {pool_name low_ip_address [-high_ip_address]}
```

For instance, suppose that you want to assign the remote clients addresses in the range from 10.20.100.1 through 10.20.100.254. Using a pool name of *vpn-pool*, then the command line would be as follows:

```
Pix(config)# ip local pool vpn_pool 10.20.100.1-10.20.100.254
```

Define Group Policy for Mode Configuration Push

Several parameters are pushed to the VPN Client from the Easy VPN Server. These parameters are specified by the group policy assigned to a set of remote VPN Clients. The major group policy parameters are as follows:

- IKE preshared key
- DNS servers
- Windows Internet Naming Service (WINS) servers
- DNS domain
- Local IP address pool
- Idle timeout

> **NOTE** Each remote VPN user belongs to a specific VPN group. As users establish VPN tunnels to the Easy VPN Server, they identify to which group they belong.

You configure these parameters using the **vpngroup** command. The syntax for these commands is as follows:

```
vpngroup group_name password preshared_key
vpngroup group_name dns-server primary-server [secondary-server]
vpngroup group_name wins-server primary-server [secondary-server]
vpngroup group_name default-domain domain_name
vpngroup group_name address-pool pool_name
vpngroup group_name idle-time seconds
```

Create Transform Set

A transform identifies an encryption algorithm and hash algorithm pair. A group of transforms defines a transform set. For each group policy, you can define one or more transforms to indicate which pairs of algorithms are acceptable for new IPSec connections. You specify the transform information for your group policy using the **crypto ipsec transform-set** command. The syntax for this command is as follows:

```
crypto ipsec transform-set transform-set-name transform1 [transform2 [transform3]]
```

You can assign up to three different transforms to a specific transform set name. The order in which the transforms are listed indicates the order in which the transforms will be checked. Therefore, you must place the highest-priority (most secure) transforms first so that they will be matched before less-secure transforms. A remote client, however, can end up using any of the transforms that you specify in the list.

> **NOTE** For an IPSec-manual crypto map, you can specify only a single transform. When using IPSec-ISAKMP or dynamic crypto map entries, however, you can specify up to six transform sets.

The transform sets that you can use are as follows:

- ah-md5-hmac
- ah-sha-hmac
- esp-aes
- esp-aes-192
- esp-aes-256
- esp-des
- esp-3des
- esp-null
- esp-md5-hmac
- esp-sha-hmac

Each transform defines either **ah** or **esp** (indicating either Authentication Header [AH] or Encapsulating Security Payload [ESP]). The keyword used in the transform is an algorithm abbreviation (see Table 14-4).

Table 14-4 *Encryption and Hash Algorithms*

Keyword	Algorithm
aes	Advanced Encryption Standard
des	Data Encryption Standard
3des	Triple Data Encryption Standard
md5	MD5 message digest algorithm
sha	SHA message digest algorithm

Create a Dynamic Crypto Map

When your VPN Clients connect to the Easy VPN Server, they will negotiate the parameters of the IPSec session. Creating a dynamic crypto map enables you to define a crypto map that does not have all of the parameters configured. It acts as a sort of policy template in which the missing parameters get configured to match the remote peer's requirements (as part of the IPSec negotiation). By using dynamic crypto maps, your Easy VPN Servers do not have to be preconfigured for all of the requirements of your remote peers, thus making the configuration process more flexible.

> **NOTE**   Dynamic crypto maps are not used to initiate IPSec SAs with remote peers. They are used only when remote peers initiate IPSec SAs and during the evaluation of traffic coming to the server.

You create dynamic crypto maps using the **crypto dynamic-map** command. The syntax for this command is as follows:

```
crypto dynamic-map dynamic-map-name dynamic-map-seqnum
```

Assign a Dynamic Crypto Map to a Static Crypto Map

After creating a dynamic crypto map, you need to assign the dynamic crypto map to a static crypto map using the **crypto map** command. The syntax for this command is as follows:

```
crypto map map-name seq-num {ipsec-isakmp|ipsec-manual} [dynamic dynamic-map-name]
```

Apply the Static Crypto Map to an Interface

Once the static crypto map has been created, you need to identify to which interface the map needs to be applied by using another variation of the **crypto map** command. The syntax for this command is as follows:

```
crypto map map-name interface interface-name
```

Configure Extended Authentication

Configuring XAUTH on the Easy VPN Server for your remote VPN Clients involves the following three steps:

Step 1   Enable AAA login authentication.

Step 2   Define AAA server IP address and encryption key.

Step 3   Enable IKE XAUTH for the crypto map.

To enable AAA login authentication, you use the **aaa-server** command. The syntax for this command is as follows:

```
aaa-server server-tag protocol {tacacs+|radius}
```

Besides enabling AAA login authentication, you need to configure the location of the AAA server by specifying its IP address. The syntax for this variation of the **aaa-server** command is as follows:

```
aaa-server server-tag [(if_name)] host server-ip [key][timeout seconds]
```

Finally, you need to enable IKE XAUTH for the crypto map that you defined using another variation of the **crypto map** command. This syntax for this command is as follows:

```
crypto map map-name client [token] authentication aaa-server-name
```

> **NOTE** The optional keyword **token** when specified informs the Security Appliance that the AAA server uses a token-card system and to thus prompt the user for a username and password during the IKE authentication.

An example configuration for XAUTH that utilizes Terminal Access Controller Access Control System Plus (TACACS+) is as follows:

```
pix515a(config)# aaa-server MYSERVER protocol tacacs+
pix515a(config)# aaa-server MYSERVER (inside) host 192.168.1.15 S3cr3TK3y!
pix515a(config)# crypto map MYMAP client authentication MYSERVER
```

Configure NAT and NAT 0

The traffic traversing the IPSec tunnel is encrypted. Some traffic originating from the Easy VPN Server network, however, simply must be translated using NAT and then sent without being encrypted. Figure 14-2 shows a situation in which a remote VPN Client is connecting across the Internet to the PIX VPN Server.

Figure 14-2 *Configuring NAT and NAT 0*

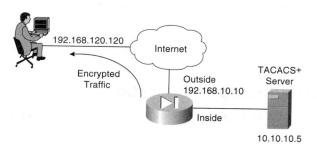

Traffic from the TACACS+ server destined for 192.168.120.120 needs to be encrypted and sent through the IPSec tunnel without translation. Traffic to the Internet (from the TACACS+

server), however, needs to be translated (by NAT) but not encrypted. The commands to perform this configuration are as follows:

```
pix515a(config)# access-list 101 permit ip 10.10.10.0 255.255.255.0 192.168.120.120
   255.255.255.255
pix515a(config)# nat (inside) 0 access-list 101
pix515a(config)# nat (inside) 1 0.0.0.0 0.0.0.0
pix515a(config)# global (outside) 1 interface
```

Traffic that matches **access-list 101** is encrypted and sent through the IPSec tunnel to the remote system. Other traffic is translated (by NAT) and transmitted without encryption out the same interface.

Enable IKE DPD

DPD allows two IPSec peers to determine that the other is still "alive" during the lifetime of the VPN connection. In many situations, the one peer may reboot or the link may be unexpectedly disconnected for some other reason. The other peer may not quickly detect that the connection has been terminated. DPD enables an IPSec peer to send notification of the disconnection to the user, attempt to switch to another IPSec host, or clean up valuable resources that were allocated to a peer that is no longer connected.

A Cisco VPN device can be configured to send and reply to DPD messages. DPD messages are sent when no other traffic is traversing the IPSec tunnel. If a configured amount of time passes without a reply to a DPD message, a dead peer can be detected. DPD messages are unidirectional and are automatically sent by Cisco VPN Clients. DPD is configured on the server only if the server wishes to send DPD messages to VPN Clients to assess their health.

You use the **isakmp keepalive** command to enable the Security Appliance gateway to send IKE DPD messages. You need to specify the number of seconds between DPD messages and the number of seconds between retries (if a DPD message does not receive a response). The syntax for this command is as follows:

```
isakmp keepalive seconds [retry_seconds]
```

Easy VPN Remote Modes of Operation

The Easy VPN Remote supports the following two modes of operation:

- Client mode
- Network extension mode

In client mode, the Easy VPN Server automatically creates NAT/PAT associations that allow the PCs and other hosts on the client side of the VPN connection to form a private network that does not use any IP addresses in the address space of the Easy VPN Server.

> **NOTE**   The NAT/PAT translations and access control list (ACL) configurations created by the Easy VPN Remote feature are not written to either the startup configuration or the running configuration. You can view these configurations, however, using the **show ip nat statistics** and **show access-list** commands (or the **show vpnclient detail** on the Security Appliance) when the configuration is active.

In network extension mode, the PCs and other hosts at the client end of the IPSec tunnel are assigned fully routable IP addresses that are reachable from the server network (by the IPSec tunnel session), forming one logical network. In this mode, PAT is not used so that client systems have direct access to the PCs and hosts on the destination network.

Client Mode

Client mode enables you to deploy a VPN quickly and easily in a small office/home office (SOHO) environment. In situations where there is no need to access the devices behind the VPN client directly and ease of use and quick installation are important, the client mode is the ideal solution.

In client mode, the Easy VPN Remote device uses PAT to isolate the private network from the public network. PAT causes all of the traffic from the SOHO network to appear on the private network as a single source IP address. Figure 14-3 illustrates the Easy VPN Remote client mode of operation. The remote clients are on the 192.168.10.0 network. Traffic from these clients is converted (by PAT) to a single address (10.20.10.2).

Figure 14-3   *Easy VPN Remote Client Mode*

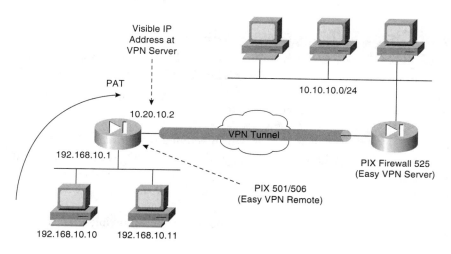

Network Extension Mode

In network extension mode, all SOHO PCs connected to the Easy VPN Remote device are uniquely addressable by the VPN tunnel. This allows devices to connect directly to PCs behind the Easy VPN Remote device. Figure 14-4 illustrates the Easy VPN Remote network extension mode. The remote client hosts are assigned IP addresses that are fully routable by the destination network through the tunnel.

Figure 14-4 *Easy VPN Remote Network Extension Mode*

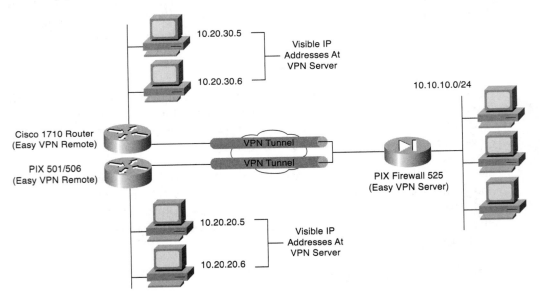

Overview of Cisco VPN Software Client

The Cisco VPN Software Client is software that enables you to establish secure end-to-end encrypted tunnels to any Easy VPN Server. The Cisco VPN Software Client is IPSec compliant and available from Cisco.com for customers with SMARTnet support and is included free of charge with the concentrator.

The Cisco VPN Software Client can easily be preconfigured for mass deployment situations. Initial logins require very little user intervention because VPN access policies and configurations are downloaded from the Easy VPN Server and pushed to the Cisco VPN Client when a connection is established, enabling simple deployment and management.

The Cisco VPN Software Client provides support for the following operating systems:

■ Windows 95, 98, Me, NT 4.0, 2000, and XP

■ Linux

- Solaris (UltraSPARC 32- and 64-bit)
- MAC OS X 10.1

Features

The Cisco VPN Software Client provides numerous features and benefits. Some of the major benefits of the Cisco VPN Software Client include the following:

- Intelligent peer availability detection
- Simple Certificate Enrollment Protocol (SCEP)
- Data compression (LZS)
- Command-line options for connecting, disconnecting, and monitoring connection status
- Configuration file with option locking
- Support for Microsoft network login (all Windows platforms)
- DNS, WINS, and IP address assignment
- Load balancing and backup server support
- Centrally controlled policies
- Integrated personal firewall (stateful firewall): Zone Labs technology (Windows only)
- Personal firewall enforcement: Zone Alarm, BlackICE (Windows only)

NOTE   The Cisco VPN Software Client supports more features than the Easy VPN Server platforms. You should always compare the Cisco VPN Software Client specifications against the Easy VPN Server supported and unsupported feature list. For instance, although the Cisco VPN Client supports Zone Labs and BlackICE firewall features, the Easy VPN Server does not. The features supported on the Easy VPN Server determine which policies and configurations can be pushed from the Easy VPN Server to the VPN Client.

Specifications

Effectively utilizing the Cisco VPN Software Client on your network requires an understanding of its major functional specifications. The specifications for the Cisco VPN Software Client fall into the following major categories:

- Tunneling protocols
- Encryption and authentication
- Key management techniques

- Data compression
- Digital certificates
- Authentication methodologies
- Policy and profile management

Tunneling Protocols

The Cisco VPN Software Client supports the following tunneling options:

- IPSec Encapsulating Security Payload (ESP)
- IPSec over TCP: NAT or PAT
- IPSec over UDP: NAT, PAT, or firewall

NOTE   IPSec over TCP and IPSec over UDP refer to the VPN Client encapsulating the IPSec traffic inside of either TCP or UDP packets. By encapsulating the complete IPSec packets inside of another transport protocol (such as UDP), the integrity checks on the IPSec packets remain valid even when a NAT device changes the IP addresses on the outer transport protocol.

Encryption and Authentication

The Cisco VPN Software Client supports the following encryption algorithms:

- DES
- 3DES
- AES (128- and 256-bit)

It also supports the following cryptographic hash algorithms:

- MD5
- SHA-1

Key Management Techniques

The Cisco VPN Client supports the following key management techniques:

- IKE main mode
- IKE aggressive mode
- Diffie-Hellman (DH) groups 1, 2, 5, and 7

Data Compression

The only supported data compression technique is LZS. LZS provides an algorithm for compressing Point-to-Point Protocol (PPP)–encapsulated packets (see RFC 1974).

Digital Certificates

Digital certificates help to verify the identity of the peers in an IPSec session. The digital certificate functionality provided by the Cisco VPN Software Client falls into the following categories:

- Enrollment mechanisms
- Certificate authorities
- Smart cards

Enrollment mechanisms define the means by which digital certificates are securely issued. *Certificate authorities* (CAs) actually issue the certificates by signing them with their own private key. The Cisco VPN Software Client supports the following CAs:

- Entrust
- GTE Cybertrust
- Netscape
- Baltimore
- RSA Keon
- VeriSign
- Microsoft

Using smart cards also can help secure the login process by verifying the identification of the user. The Cisco VPN Software Client supports various smart cards by using the Microsoft crypto application programming interface (API) CRYPT-NOHASHOID, including the following:

- ActivCard (Schlumberger cards)
- eToken from Aladdin
- Gemplus
- Datakey

Authentication Methodologies

Authentication is crucial for providing secure remote access through VPN tunnels. The Cisco VPN Software Client supports XAUTH and Remote Authentication Dial-In User Service (RADIUS) with support for the following:

- State (token cards)
- Security Dynamics (RSA SecurID ready)
- Microsoft Windows NT domain authentication
- Microsoft Challenge Handshake Authentication Protocol version 2 (MS-CHAPv2)— Windows NT password authentication
- X.509 version 3 digital certificates

Policy and Profile Management

You can easily distribute Cisco VPN Software Clients with preconfigured Profile Configuration Files (PCFs) that regulate the operation of the client software. You can also centrally control policies such as the following:

- DNS information
- WINS information
- IP address
- Default domain name

Cisco VPN Client Manual Configuration Tasks

When using the Cisco VPN Software Client, the Easy VPN Server can push the VPN policy to help facilitate the management of the client systems. Initially, however, you still need to install the Cisco VPN Software Client on the remote system. This manual process involves the following tasks:

- Installing the Cisco VPN Software Client
- Creating a new connection entry
- Modifying VPN Client options (optional)

Installing the Cisco VPN Software Client

Installation of the Cisco VPN Software Client varies slightly between the different supported operating systems. The best source of detailed installation information is the release notes that accompany the Cisco VPN Software Client that you are installing. Installing the Cisco VPN Software Client on a Windows-based system follows the usual software installation process. The on-screen instructions ensure the installation is quick and not very complicated.

After the software is installed, the following new options are added to your Programs menu (see Figure 14-5):

- **Help**—Accesses the Cisco VPN Client Help text
- **Set MTU**—Enables you to set the maximum transmission unit (MTU) for a specific interface
- **VPN Client**—Launches the Cisco VPN Client so that you can choose a connection and establish a VPN session

Figure 14-5 *Cisco VPN Software Client Program Menu*

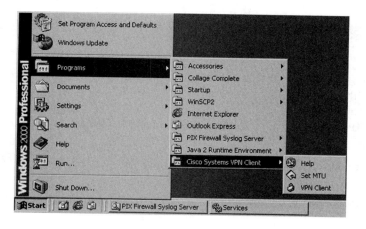

If you try to launch the Cisco VPN Client when you already have a session established, it displays the same window you see when you launch the Cisco VPN Client Software (see Figure 14-6).

Figure 14-6 *VPN Client Window*

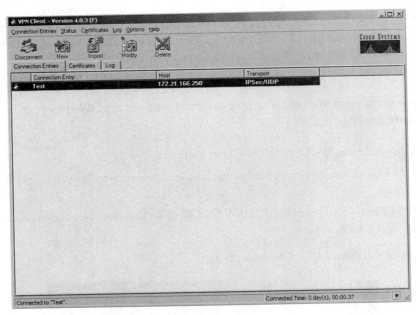

Either typing **Ctrl-S** or selecting **Statistics** from the **Status** drop-down menu displays the following information about your connection (see Figure 14-7):

- **Client IP address**—The IP address assigned to the Cisco VPN Client for the current session.

- **Server IP address**—The IP address of the Easy VPN Server to which the client is currently connected.

- **Bytes Received**—The total number of bytes received by the client software.

- **Bytes Sent**—The total number of bytes sent by the client software.

- **Packets Encrypted**—The total number of data packets transmitted.

- **Packets Decrypted**—The total number of data packets received.

- **Packets Discarded**—The total number of packets rejected because they did not come from the Easy VPN Server.

- **Packets Bypassed**— The total number of packets that were not processed (such as Address Resolution Protocol [ARP] and Dynamic Host Configuration Protocol [DHCP] packets).

- **Encryption**—The data encryption method in use for traffic in the tunnel.

- **Authentication**—The data or packet authentication method used for traffic through the tunnel.

- **Transparent Tunneling**—The status of transparent tunneling (either active or inactive).

- **Local LAN Access**—Indicates whether local local area network (LAN) access is enabled or disabled.

- **Compression**—Indicates whether data compression is in effect and identifies the compression being used (currently, only LZS compression is supported).

Transparent Tunneling

Transparent tunneling enables a secure transmission between the VPN Client and a secure VPN Server when the traffic passes through an intermediary device that is performing NAT (such as a firewall). Transparent tunneling encapsulates Internet Protocol 50 (ESP) traffic within either UDP or TCP packets to prevent the IPSec traffic from being changed by the NAT/PAT device. Transparent tunneling is commonly used with VPN Client deployments that are behind a home router that is performing NAT/PAT.

Figure 14-7 *VPN Client Statistics Window*

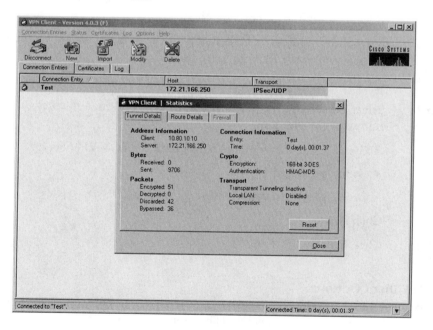

Creating a New Connection Entry

After installing the Cisco VPN Software Client on your system, you need to create a connection entry that will define the properties of your VPN connection, such as the following:

- IP address of Easy VPN Remote server
- Group name
- Group password

Creating a new connection entry involves the following steps on a Windows 2000 system:

Step 1   Choose **Start > Programs > Cisco Systems VPN Client > VPN Client**. The Cisco VPN Client window is displayed.

Step 2   Click **New** to launch the new connection wizard.

Step 3   Enter a name for the new connection in the Name of the new connection entry field. Optionally, you can also provide a description for this connection in the Description of the new connection entry.

Step 4   After entering the name, click **Next**.

Step 5   Enter the IP address or DNS name for the public interface on the Easy VPN Server in the Remote Server field.

Step 6   Click **Next**.

Step 7   Select the **Group Access Information** radio button, and enter the following information:

- Group name that matches a group on the Easy VPN Server
- Group password
- Group password confirmation

Step 8   Click **Next**.

Step 9   Click **Finish**.

Modifying VPN Client Options

Besides creating a new connection entry, you can also optionally define various characteristics of the connection entry. These options are accessible by using the **Options** drop-down menu on the main Cisco VPN Software Client screen (see Figure 14-8).

Figure 14-8   *Cisco VPN Software Client Options*

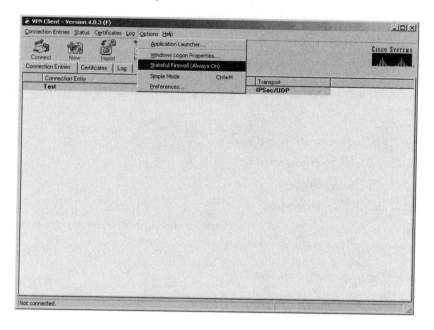

From the **Options** drop-down menu, you can configure the characteristics of the current connection entry as listed in Table 14-5.

Table 14-5   *Cisco VPN Software Client Options*

Option	Description
Application Launcher	Defines an application that you want to launch before establishing the VPN connection. This is used in conjunction with the Windows Login Properties option.
Windows Login Properties	Enables the Cisco VPN Client to make a connection to the concentrator before the user logs in.
Stateful Firewall (Always On)	Blocks all inbound traffic to the Cisco VPN Client that is not related to the outbound session when set to Always On.
Simple Mode	Changes the VPN Client window to a smaller compressed version. You then use the Advanced Mode option to return to the original window.
Preferences	Enables you to configure basic VPN Client preferences such as whether the VPN Client window automatically hides itself upon establishing a successful VPN connection.

> **NOTE**   If you want to know the version of the Cisco VPN Software Client installed on your PC, you can right-click the **Cisco VPN Dialer** icon in the system tray. This will also indicate if the stateful firewall functionality is always on because Stateful Firewall (Always On) will have a check mark next to it if enabled.

Clicking the **Modify** icon enables you to configure the following characteristics of the Cisco VPN Client:

- VPN Client authentication properties
- VPN Client transport properties
- VPN Client backup servers
- VPN Client dialup properties

Although these properties vary slightly between the supported operating systems, the major general properties that you can configure are as follows:

- Enabling transparent tunneling
- Allowing IPSec over UDP
- Allowing IPSec over TCP
- Allowing local LAN access
- Configuring peer response timeout

> **NOTE**   Allowing IPSec over TCP (or UDP) enables you to use the VPN Client in an environment where your traffic must go though a firewall or router that is using NAT or PAT. This option must also be configured on the Easy VPN Server for it to operate correctly.

The Authentication tab of the VPN Client Properties window enables you to configure the VPN Client to use either a group name and password or digital certificates for authentication (see Figure 14-9).

Figure 14-9 *Authentication Tab of the VPN Client Properties Window*

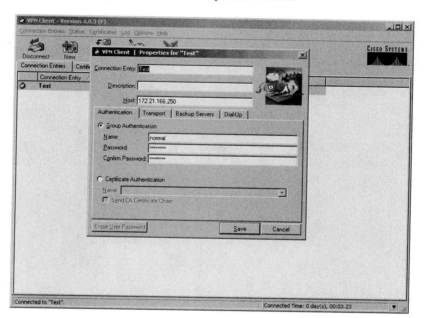

The Transport tab in the VPN Client Properties window enables you to configure the transparent tunneling properties for the VPN connection (see Figure 14-10). Transparent tunneling enables your VPN connection to travel across devices that are performing NAT or PAT on the traffic. Without transparent tunneling, the traffic would be considered invalid because the integrity checks on the packets would fail.

The Backup Servers tab of the VPN Client Properties window defines backup Easy VPN Servers (see Figure 14-11), and the Dial-Up tab of the VPN Client Properties window defines whether the connection to the Internet using dialup networking is enabled (see Figure 14-12).

An enterprise network may have multiple Easy VPN Servers. Backup servers for the connections enable your Cisco VPN Clients to utilize these alternate Easy VPN Servers if the primary Easy VPN Server is unavailable. When establishing a VPN connection, clients attempt to connect to the primary Easy VPN Server first. If that device is unavailable, one of the backup servers will be used.

NOTE   You also can configure the backup servers on the Easy VPN Server and have them pushed to the VPN Client after a successful connection. Then, on subsequent connections, the VPN Client can use these backup servers if the primary server is unavailable.

Figure 14-10 *Transport Tab of the VPN Client Properties Window*

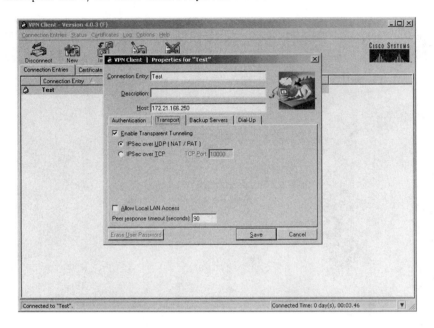

Figure 14-11 *Backup Servers Tab of the VPN Client Properties Windows*

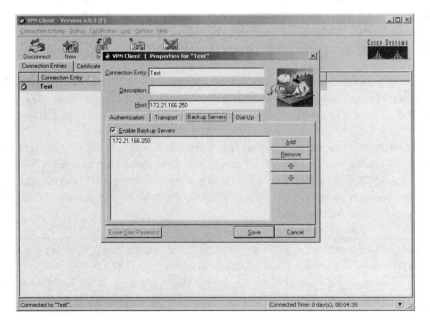

Figure 14-12 *Dial-Up Tab of the VPN Client Properties Window*

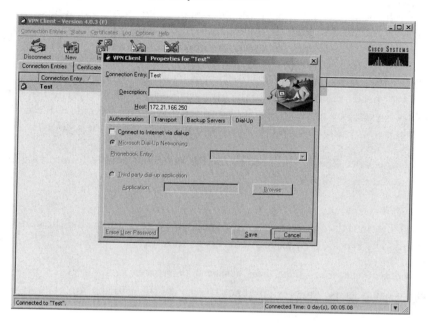

Security Appliance Easy VPN Remote Configuration

The Easy VPN Server controls the policy enforced on the Security Appliance Easy VPN Remote device. To establish the initial connection to the Easy VPN Server, you must complete some configuration locally on the remote client device. You can perform this configuration using the Cisco Adaptive Security Device Manager (ASDM) or by using the command-line interface. These configuration tasks fall into the following categories:

- Basic configuration
- Client device mode
- SUA
- Individual User Authentication (IUA)

Basic Configuration

To enable the Security Appliance Easy VPN Remote client to communicate with the Easy VPN Server, you need to identify the location of the Easy VPN Server using the **vpnclient server** command. The syntax for this command is as follows:

```
vpnclient server {Primary_IP} [Secondary_IPs]
```

You need to specify the IP address of the primary Easy VPN Server. In addition to the primary Easy VPN Server, you also can specify up to ten additional secondary Easy VPN Servers. If the primary server is not accessible, the client will use one of the secondary servers.

To enable the VPN Client, you need to use the **vpnclient enable** command. The syntax for this command is as follows:

```
vpnclient enable
```

If you use preshared keys, you also must specify this key value using the **vpnclient vpngroup** command. The syntax for this command is as follows:

```
vpnclient vpngroup {groupname} password {preshared_key}
```

The client needs to use the preshared key to encrypt the information being transmitted to the server.

One other basic configuration task involves XAUTH. If you use XAUTH, you need to specify the username and password for the VPN Client using AAA or the **vpnclient username** command. The syntax for this command is as follows:

```
vpnclient username {xuath_username} password {xauth_password}
```

Client Device Mode

The Cisco VPN Client operates in the following two modes (see the "Easy VPN Remote Modes of Operation" section earlier in the chapter for more information):

- Client mode
- Network extension mode

To configure the client device mode, you use the **vpnclient mode** command. The syntax for this command is as follows:

```
vpnclient mode {client-mode|network-extension-mode}
```

Client mode applies NAT/PAT to all IP addresses of the clients connected to the higher-security (inside) interface. Network extension mode, on the other hand, does not apply NAT/PAT to any IP addresses of clients on the higher-security interface.

Secure Unit Authentication

Secure Unit Authentication (SUA) is a feature introduced in Security Appliance software version 6.3 to improve security when using a Security Appliance as an Easy VPN Remote device. With SUA, the Easy VPN Remote Server can require one-time passwords, two-factor authentication, and similar authentication schemes before the establishment of a VPN tunnel to the Easy VPN Server.

SUA is configured as part of the VPN policy on the Easy VPN Server and cannot be configured directly on the VPN Remote device. The Easy VPN Remote device downloads the VPN policy (after connecting to the Easy VPN Server), which enables or disables SUA.

Client Operation with Secure Unit Authentication Disabled

When SUA is disabled and the Easy VPN Remote device is operating in network extension mode, a connection is automatically initiated by the Security Appliance VPN Remote device for the remote protected hosts. In client mode, the connection is initiated whenever traffic from the remote protected network is sent through the Security Appliance to the network protected by the Easy VPN Server.

Client Operation with Secure Unit Authentication Enabled

When SUA is enabled, static credentials included in the local configuration of the Easy VPN Remote device are ignored. A connection request is initiated as soon as any Hypertext Transfer Protocol (HTTP) request is sent from the remote network to the network protected by the Easy VPN Remote Server. All other traffic to the network protected by the Easy VPN Server is dropped until a VPN tunnel is established.

NOTE You also can initiate a connection request from the command-line interface (CLI) of the Easy VPN Remote device.

Before a VPN tunnel is established, any HTTP request to the network protected by the Easy VPN Server is redirected to a Uniform Resource Locator (URL) in the following format:

```
https://<inside-ip-address>/vpnclient/connstatus.html
```

inside-ip-address is the inside (protected) interface of the Easy VPN Remote device. For instance, if the inside interface of the Easy VPN Remote device is 10.10.10.1, the requests will be redirected to the following URL:

```
https://10.10.10.1/vpnclient/connstatus.html
```

You can check the status of the VPN tunnel by manually entering this URL into your browser (from one of the remote protected hosts). This URL displays a page containing a *Connect* link that displays an authentication page. If authentication is successful, the VPN tunnel has been established.

> **NOTE**   You can also activate the connection by manually entering this URL into your browser (on a remote protected host).

To enable SUA, you use the following command on the Easy VPN Server:

        vpngroup *groupname* `secure-unit-authentication`

groupname is the alphanumeric identifier for the VPN group for which you want to enable SUA.

After the tunnel is established, other users on the remote network (protected by the Easy VPN Remote device) can access the network protected by the Easy VPN Server without further authentication. If you want to control access by individual users, you need to implement Individual User Authentication (IUA). IUA is explained in the next section.

Individual User Authentication

IUA causes the hosts on the remote protected network (behind the Easy VPN Remote device) to be authenticated individually based on the IP address of the inside host. IUA supports authentication based on both static and dynamic password mechanisms.

Similar to SUA, IUA is enabled by the VPN policy downloaded from the Easy VPN Server and cannot be configured locally. When IUA is enabled, each user on the remote protected network is prompted for a username and password when trying to initiate a connection to the network protected by the Easy VPN Server. Unlike SUA, which requires an HTTP connection to initiate the authentication request, when IUA is enabled the user will automatically be prompted for authentication (to establish the tunnel) whenever any traffic is sent across the tunnel.

A Security Appliance (serving as an Easy VPN Server) downloads the contact information for the AAA server to the Easy VPN Remote device. The Easy VPN Remote device then sends authentication requests directly to the AAA server.

> **NOTE** A Cisco 3000 Series VPN Concentrator used as an Easy VPN Server performs proxy authentication to the AAA server. The Easy VPN Remote device sends each authentication request to the Cisco 3000 Series VPN Concentrator instead of directly to the AAA server.

To enable IUA, you use the following command on the Easy VPN Server:

```
vpngroup groupname user-authentication
```

groupname is the alphanumeric identifier for the VPN group for which you want to enable IUA.

You also must use the following command on the Easy VPN Server to specify the AAA server to use for authentication:

```
vpngroup groupname authentication-server server-tag
```

The *server-tag* identifies the AAA server to use for the specified VPN group.

To specify the length of time that the VPN tunnel will remain open without any user activity, you use the following command on the Easy VPN Server:

```
vpngroup groupname user-idle-timeout seconds
```

You specify the idle time for the specified VPN group in seconds.

Point-to-Point Protocol over Ethernet and the Security Appliance

Many Internet service providers (ISPs) deploy PPPoE because it provides high-speed broadband access using their existing remote access infrastructure. PPPoE is also easy for customers to use.

Figure 14-13 depicts a typical PPPoE network configuration that uses a Security Appliance to secure a low-cost always-on Internet connection. The Security Appliance can secure various broadband connections including the following:

- Digital Subscriber Line (DSL)
- Cable modem
- Fixed wireless

Figure 14-13   *PIX Firewall PPPoE Client Configuration*

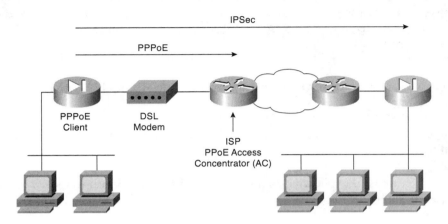

PPPoE (see RFC 2516) provides an authenticated method for assigning IP addresses to client systems by combining the following two widely accepted standards:

■   Point-to-Point Protocol (PPP)

■   Ethernet

PPP

Point-to-Point Protocol (PPP) provides a secure and reliable mechanism to transport multiprotocol datagrams over point-to-point links. It has been reliably used for many years to transmit data from dialup clients across modem-based connections.

PPPoE is composed of the following two main phases:

■   Active discovery phase

■   PPP session phase

PPPoE connects a network of systems over a simple bridging access device to a remote access concentrator (AC). In the active discovery phase, the PPPoE client locates the AC (or PPPoE server). After locating an AC, the PPPoE client establishes a PPP session.

When establishing a session, PPP options are negotiated and authentication is performed. Once the session is completely established, the information from the client is sent across the Ethernet network by encapsulating the PPP messages in unicast Ethernet packets. The session ID enables the AC to determine to which client the PPP messages belong.

After configuration, the Security Appliance automatically connects to a service provider's AC without user intervention. By setting the MTU to 1492 bytes, the Security Appliance can encapsulate PPPoE messages inside regular Ethernet frames by attaching PPPoE/PPP headers.

The Security Appliance PPPoE Client can operate in environments that are using other firewall features such as the following:

- NAT to or from the outside interface (or over a VPN)
- URL content filtering before transmission (to or from outside interface)
- Firewall rules on traffic before transmission to or from the outside interface (or over a VPN)

If your ISP distributes certain configuration parameters, such as DNS and WINS, the Security Appliance's PPPoE Client can retrieve these parameters and automatically pass these parameters to its Dynamic Host Configuration Protocol (DHCP) clients. You need to use the **dhcpd auto-config** command on the Security Appliance to enable your DHCP clients to receive the configuration parameters automatically from the PPPoE client.

NOTE   Although the Security Appliance DHCP server operates with the PPPoE client, the PPPoE client and the DHCP clients are mutually exclusive. Therefore, if you configure the PPPoE client on the outside interface, the DHCP client functionality is automatically disabled on that interface. Similarly, if you enable the DHCP client on the outside interface, the PPPoE client is automatically disabled on the outside interface.

NOTE   The Security Appliance's PPPoE Client is not interoperable with failover, Layer Two Tunneling Protocol (L2TP), or Point-to-Point Tunneling Protocol (PPTP).

Configuring the PPPoE client on the Security Appliance involves the following tasks:

- Configuring the Virtual Private Dial-Up Networking (VPDN) group
- Configuring VPDN group authentication
- Assigning the VPDN group username
- Configuring the VPDN username and password
- Enabling the PPPoE client

Configuring the VPDN Group

The first task in configuring the Security Appliance PPPoE Client is to define the VPDN group using the following command:

```
vpdn group group-name request dialout pppoe
```

Configuring VPDN Group Authentication

Your ISP may require you to use authentication with PPPoE. The Security Appliance PPPoE Client supports the following authentication protocols:

■   Password Authentication Protocol (PAP)

■   Challenge Handshake Authentication Protocol (CHAP)

■   Microsoft Challenge Handshake Authentication Protocol (MS-CHAP)

To define the authentication protocol for the PPPoE client, you use the following command:

```
vpdn group group-name ppp authentication pap | chap | mschap
```

NOTE   ISPs that use CHAP or MS-CHAP may refer to the username as the remote system name and the password as the CHAP secret.

Assigning the VPDN Group Username

To assign the username provided by your ISP to the VPDN group, you use the following command:

```
vpdn group group-name localname username
```

Configuring the VPDN Username and Password

The Security Appliance uses a username and password pair to authenticate to the AC. To assign a username and password pair for PPPoE authentication, you use the following command:

```
vpdn username username password password
```

NOTE   The username specified must be the username that has already been associated with the VPDN group specified for PPPoE (using the **vpdn group** command).

Enabling the Point-to-Point over Ethernet Client

By default, the PPPoE client on the Security Appliance is disabled. Use the following command to enable the PPPoE client:

```
ip address interface-name pppoe [setroute]
```

You also can enable PPPoE by manually entering the IP address using the following command:

```
ip address interface-name ip-address netmask pppoe [setroute]
```

This command causes the Security Appliance to use the specified IP address instead of negotiating with the PPPoE server to assign an address dynamically.

The parameters for the **ip address** command are shown in Table 14-6.

Table 14-6   ip address *Command Parameters*

Parameter	Description
interface-name	The name of the outside interface on the Security Appliance
ip-address	The IP address assigned to the Security Appliance's outside interface
netmask	The subnet mask assigned to the Security Appliance's outside interface
setroute	Configures the Security Appliance to use the default gateway parameter that the DHCP or PPPoE server returns as the default route

The **setroute** keyword causes a default route to be created based on the default gateway parameter returned by either the DHCP or PPPoE server. This keyword, however, cannot override an existing default route. If you use the **setroute** keyword when a default route already exists, the Security Appliance will be unable to override the existing default route with the information learned from PPPoE. Therefore, if you already have an existing default route configured on the Security Appliance, you must delete the default route before using the **setroute** keyword.

Monitoring the Point-to-Point over Ethernet Client

The **show vpdn** command displays information about the PPPoE traffic on the Security Appliance. Without any other keywords, this command displays information about the PPPoE tunnels and sessions, such as in the following:

```
pix515a# show vpdn
```

```
%No active L2TP tunnels

PPPoE Tunnel and Session Information (Total tunnels=1 sessions=1)

Tunnel id 0, 1 active sessions
  time since change 4294967 secs
  Remote MAC Address 00:02:3B:02:32:2E
  9005625 packets sent, 11376588 received, 1755681415 bytes sent, -407696198 received
Remote MAC is 00:02:3B:02:32:2E
  Session state is SESSION_UP
    Time since event change 4294967 secs, interface outside
    PPP interface id is 1
    9005625 packets sent, 1265856 received, 1755681415 bytes sent, 865125131 received
pix515a#
```

To view the information only on your VPDN sessions, you can add the **session** keyword to the **show vpdn** command, as in the following:

```
pix515a# show vpdn session

%No active L2TP tunnels

PPPoE Tunnel and Session Information (Total tunnels=1 sessions=1)

Remote MAC is 00:02:3B:02:32:2E
  Session state is SESSION_UP
    Time since event change 4294967 secs, interface outside
    PPP interface id is 1
    9005664 packets sent, 1265894 received, 1755684373 bytes sent, 865127247 received
pix515a#
```

To view the information only on your VPDN tunnels, you can add the **tunnel** keyword to the **show vpdn** command, as in the following:

```
pix515a# show vpdn tunnel

%No active L2TP tunnels

PPPoE Tunnel and Session Information (Total tunnels=1 sessions=1)

Tunnel id 0, 1 active sessions
  time since change 4294967 secs
  Remote MAC Address 00:02:3B:02:32:2E
  9005704 packets sent, 11376666 received, 1755687225 bytes sent, -407691806 received
pix515a#
```

You can use the **show vpdn pppinterface** command when a PPPoE connection is established to view the address of the AC. If the Security Appliance cannot locate the AC, the address displayed is 0.0.0.0. The syntax for this command is as follows:

```
show vpdn pppinterface [id interface_name]
```

The output of the **show vpdn pppinterface** command is similar to the following:

```
pix515a# show vpdn pppinterface

PPP virtual interface id = 1
PPP authentication protocol is PAP
Server ip address is 214.8.252.151
Our ip address is 88.235.123.14
Transmitted Pkts: 1002469, Received Pkts: 1265984, Error Pkts: 0
MPPE key strength is None
  MPPE_Encrypt_Pkts: 0,  MPPE_Encrypt_Bytes: 0
  MPPE_Decrypt_Pkts: 0,  MPPE_Decrypt_Bytes: 0
  Rcvd_Out_Of_Seq_MPPE_Pkts: 0

pix515a#
```

To view the local usernames, you use the **show vpdn username** command, and the **show vpdn group** command displays the configured VPDN groups. The syntax for these commands is as follows:

```
show vpdn username [specific-name]
show vpdn group [specific-group-name]
```

To view the IP address assigned by the PPPoE server on an established PPPoE session, you use the **show ip address** command using the interface on which PPPoE is enabled. The syntax for this command is as follows:

```
show ip address interface-name pppoe
```

Finally, you can debug the PPPoE packets processed by the Security Appliance with the **debug pppoe** command. The syntax for this command is as follows:

```
debug pppoe {event | error | packet}
```

Dynamic Host Configuration Protocol Server Configuration

DHCP provides automatic allocation of reusable network addresses on a Transmission Control Protocol/Internet Protocol (TCP/IP) network. Without DHCP, IP addresses must be manually entered on each computer or device that is connected to the network. Automatic allocation dramatically reduces administration and user error.

DHCP can also distribute other configuration parameters such as DNS and WINS server addresses and domain names. The system requesting an IP address and configuration parameters is known as the *DHCP client*. The system that automatically allocates the IP addresses is known as the *DHCP server*.

> **NOTE** Because the DHCP client does not know the IP address of the DHCP server, the initial DHCP requests are broadcast to every host on the network segment. Instead of deploying a DHCP server on every network segment, you can configure your IOS router to forward the DHCP requests to a single DHCP server by using the **ip helper-address** command.

Any Security Appliance (version 5.2 or later) provides both DHCP server and DHCP client functionality. As a DHCP server, the Security Appliance provides hosts protected by the firewall with the network parameters necessary for them to access the enterprise or corporate network. As a DHCP client, the Security Appliance can obtain its own IP address and network mask and optionally a default route from the DHCP server.

DHCP Overview

DHCP communications consist of several messages sent between the DHCP client and DHCP server by broadcast messages. This exchange of messages consists of the following events:

Step 1 The client broadcasts a DHCPDISCOVER message on its local subnet to locate available DHCP servers that can provide it an IP address.

Step 2 Any DHCP servers that receive the DHCPDISCOVER message can respond with a DHCPOFFER message that includes an available IP address and other configuration parameters.

Step 3 Based on the DHCPOFFER messages received, the client chooses one of the offers. It then broadcasts a DHCPREQUEST message requesting the offered parameters from the chosen DHCP server and implicitly declining all of the other offers received.

Step 4 The DHCP server selected in the DHCPREQUEST message responds with a DHCPACK message containing the configuration parameters for the requesting client.

> **NOTE** If the selected DHCP server cannot satisfy the DHCPREQUEST (for instance, the requested address has already been assigned to another system), it sends a DHCPNAK message to the DHCP client.

Configuring the Security Appliance DHCP Server

Configuring the Security Appliance to operate as a DHCP server involves the following tasks:

- Configuring the address pool
- Specifying WINS, DNS, and the domain name
- Configuring the DHCP options
- Configuring the DHCP lease length
- Enabling the DHCP server

NOTE   Configuring the Security Appliance to serve as a DHCP server also requires you to assign a static IP address to the inside interface. This is one of the basic configuration tasks when setting up your Security Appliance.

Configuring the Address Pool

A DHCP server needs to know which addresses it can assign to DHCP clients. It must also keep track of the IP addresses that it has already given out. The **dhcpd address** command specifies the range of IP addresses for the Security Appliance DHCP server to distribute. The syntax for this command is as follows:

```
dhcpd address ipaddress1 [-ipaddress2] [interface]
```

NOTE   To remove an existing DHCP address pool, use the **no dhcpd address** command.

Table 14-7 shows the parameters for the **dhcpd address** command.

Table 14-7   dhcpd address *Command Parameters*

Parameter	Description
ipaddress1	The low IP address of the IP address pool.
ipaddress2	The high IP address of the IP address pool.
interface	Name of the Security Appliance interface (the default is the inside interface).

NOTE   The DHCP address pool is limited to 32 addresses for the PIX Firewall 501 with a 10-user license. With the 50-user license, 128 addresses are supported. The maximum size of the address pool is 256 addresses for the unlimited license and for all other Security Appliance models.

Specifying WINS, DNS, and the Domain Name

Besides providing IP addresses to DHCP clients, a DHCP server can also provide other configuration parameters, such as the following:

- WINS servers
- DNS servers
- Domain name

To configure the DNS servers that the Security Appliance DHCP server provides in its DHCPOFFER messages, you use the **dhcpd dns** command. The syntax for this command is as follows:

```
dhcpd dns dns-server1 [dns-server2]
```

To configure the WINS servers that the Security Appliance DHCP server provides in its DHCPOFFER messages, you use the **dhcpd wins** command. The syntax for this command is as follows:

```
dhcpd wins wins-server1 [wins-server2]
```

Finally, you also can specify the domain name that will be provided to the DHCP clients using the **dhcpd domain** command. The syntax for this command is as follows:

```
dhcpd domain domain_name
```

Configuring DHCP Options

Because Cisco IP Phones use TFTP to load phone images, the Security Appliance supports the **dhcpd option** command to define the TFTP servers that will be identified to the client by DHCP. The syntax for this command is as follows:

```
dhcpd option 66 ascii {server-name|server-ip-str}
dhcpd option 150 ip server-ip1 [server-ip2]
```

NOTE The difference between these two commands is that the **option 150** enables you to specify a list of TFTP servers to be used by the DHCP client.

Configuring DHCP Lease Length

The **dhcpd lease** command specifies the amount of time (in seconds) that the DHCP clients can use the assigned IP address received from the DHCP server. The syntax for this command is as follows:

```
dhcpd lease lease_length
```

NOTE The default lease length is 3600 seconds. The minimum lease length that you can specify is 300 seconds, and the maximum lease length that you can specify is 2,147,483,647 seconds.

Enabling the DHCP Server

You enable DHCP on the PIX Firewall on a per-interface basis. The command to enable the DHCP daemon on an interface is **dhcpd enable**. The syntax for this command is as follows:

```
dhcpd enable [interface-name]
```

For instance, to enable DHCP on the inside interface, you would use the following command:

```
dhcpd enable inside
```

DHCP Server Auto Configuration

The Security Appliance can serve as a DHCP server, DHCP client, or a DHCP server and DHCP client simultaneously. When the Security Appliance is operating as a DHCP client, it can pass the configuration parameters learned (such as DNS, WINS, and the domain name) automatically to the clients that its DHCP server services. To enable the Security Appliance to pass the learned DHCP configuration parameters to its DHCP clients automatically, you use the **dhcpd auto-config** command. The syntax for this command is as follows:

```
dhcpd auto-config [client_interface_name]
```

> **NOTE**   The **dhcpd auto-config** command also enables the Security Appliance to pass information learned from its PPPoE interface to its DHCP clients.

The *client_interface_name* represents the interface on which you have enabled the Security Appliance to operate as a DHCP client using the **ip address** *interface* **dhcp** command.

DHCP Debugging Commands

To help debug the operation of your Security Appliance DHCP server and Security Appliance DHCP client, you can use the following two commands:

```
debug dhcpd {event | packet}
debug dhcpc {detail | error | packet}
```

The **debug dhcpd** command displays information associated with the DHCP server running on the Security Appliance. The **event** keyword displays information about the events related to the DHCP server, and the **packet** keyword displays information about the packets received for the DHCP server.

The **debug dhcpc** command displays information about the Security Appliance DHCP client running on the Security Appliance. The **packet** keyword specifies information about the packets received for the DHCP client. The **detail** keyword provides detailed information on the packets received by the DHCP client. The **error** keyword enables you to view information on the error messages associated with the DHCP client running on the Security Appliance.

To show or clear the IP address bindings that the PIX DHCP server has issued, you use the following two commands:

```
show dhcpd [binding | statistics]
clear dhcpd [binding | statistics]
```

Both of these commands accept the same two keywords. The **binding** keyword causes the command to operate only on the DHCP leases (binding of an IP address to a specific Layer 2 Ethernet address). The **statistics** keyword operates on the statistics that are tracked on the DHCP server. The following information illustrates the output from the **show dhcpd** commands:

```
pix515a# show dhcpd
dhcpd address 10.10.10.129-10.10.10.254 inside
dhcpd lease 84400
dhcpd ping timeout 750
dhcpd dns 10.200.10.32 10.100.20.40
dhcpd enable inside
pix515a# show dhcpd statistics

Address pools       1
Automatic bindings  1
Expired bindings    1
Malformed messages  0

Message             Received
BOOTREQUEST         0
DHCPDISCOVER        1
DHCPREQUEST         2
DHCPDECLINE         0
DHCPRELEASE         0
DHCPINFORM          0

Message             Sent
BOOTREPLY           0
DHCPOFFER           1
DHCPACK             1
DHCPNAK             0

pix515a(config)# show dhcpd bindings

IP address      Hardware address    Lease expiration    Type
10.10.10.129    00A0.CC5C.8163      46500 seconds       automatic
10.10.10.130    00E0.B605.43B2      32503 seconds       automatic
pix515a#
```

Foundation Summary

The "Foundation Summary" provides a convenient review of many key concepts in this chapter. If you are already comfortable with the topics in this chapter, this summary can help you recall a few details. If you just read this chapter, this review should help solidify some key facts. If you are doing your final preparation before the exam, this summary provides a convenient way to review the day before the exam.

Cisco Easy VPN greatly simplifies VPN deployment for remote offices and telecommuters. The Cisco Easy VPN centralizes management across all Cisco VPN devices, thus greatly reducing the complexity in configuring and deploying VPN configurations. It comprises the following two components:

- Easy VPN Server
- Easy VPN Remote feature

The Security Appliance VPN Server supports the following major features:

- Support for Easy VPN Remote Clients
- Ability for remote users to communicate using IPSec with supported Security Appliance gateways
- Central management of IPSec policies that are pushed to the clients by the server

The Security Appliance VPN Server supports the following functionality:

- Mode configuration version 6
- XAUTH version 6
- IKE DPD
- Split tunneling control
- Initial contact
- Group-based policy control

The Cisco Easy VPN Remote feature enables certain IOS routers, Cisco Security Appliances, Cisco VPN 3002 Hardware Clients, and Cisco VPN Software Clients to act as remote Cisco VPN Clients. The Cisco Easy VPN Remote feature provides for automatic management of the following items:

- Negotiating tunnel parameters
- Establishing tunnels according to parameters

- Automatically creating the NAT/PAT and associated access list if necessary
- Authenticating users
- Managing security keys for encryption and decryption
- Authenticating, encrypting, and decrypting data through the tunnel

The Easy VPN Remote feature supports the following client platforms:

- Cisco VPN Software Client
- Cisco VPN 3002 Hardware Client
- Cisco PIX 501 and 506/506E VPN Clients
- Cisco Easy VPN Remote router clients

When the Easy VPN Remote Client initiates a connection with the Easy VPN Server gateway, the interaction between the peers involves the following major steps:

Step 1   VPN Client initiates the IKE phase 1 process.

Step 2   VPN Client negotiates an IKE SA.

Step 3   Easy VPN Server accepts the SA proposal.

Step 4   The Easy VPN Server initiates a username/password challenge.

Step 5   Mode configuration process is initiated.

Step 6   IKE quick mode completes the connection.

XAUTH enables the Easy VPN Server to require username/password authentication to establish the VPN connection. This authentication is performed by a AAA server. To configure the Easy VPN Server to use XAUTH for remote VPN Clients, you need to perform the following tasks:

- Create an ISAKMP policy for remote Cisco VPN Client access
- Create an IP address pool
- Define a group policy for mode configuration push
- Create a transform set
- Create a dynamic crypto map
- Assign the dynamic crypto map to a static crypto map
- Apply the static crypto map to an interface
- Configure XAUTH
- Configure NAT and NAT 0
- Enable IKE DPD

The Easy VPN Remote feature supports the following two modes of operation:

- Client mode
- Network extension mode

The Cisco VPN Software Client is software that enables you to establish secure end-to-end encrypted tunnels to any Easy VPN Server. Some of the major benefits of the Cisco VPN Software Client are the following:

- Intelligent peer availability detection
- SCEP
- Data compression (LZS)
- Command-line options for connecting, disconnecting, and monitoring connection status
- Configuration file with option locking
- Support for Microsoft network login (all platforms)
- DNS, WINS, and IP address assignment
- Load balancing and backup server support
- Centrally controlled policies
- Integrated personal firewall (stateful firewall): Zone Labs technology (Windows only)
- Personal firewall enforcement: Zone Alarm, BlackICE (Windows only)

The Easy VPN Server controls the policy enforced on the PIX Firewall Easy VPN Remote device. To establish the initial connection to the Easy VPN Server, you must complete some configuration locally on the client end such as configuring the client device mode. You also can enable the following two features on the Easy VPN Server:

- SUA
- IUA

Beginning with software version 6.2, you can configure the Security Appliance as a PPPoE client. Using PPPoE, the Security Appliance can secure various broadband connections including the following:

- DSL
- Cable modem
- Fixed wireless

PPPoE is composed of the following two main phases:

- Active discovery phase
- PPP session phase

The Security Appliance PPPoE Client can operate in environments that are using other firewall features such as the following:

- NAT to or from the outside interface (or over a VPN)
- URL content before transmission (to or from outside interface)
- Firewall rules on traffic before transmission to or from the outside interface (or over a VPN)
- Configuring the PPPoE client on the Security Appliance involves the following tasks:
- Configuring the VPDN group
- Configuring VPDN group authentication
- Assigning the VPDN group username
- Configuring the VPDN username and password
- Enabling the PPPoE client

Any Security Appliance provides both DHCP server and DHCP client functionality. As a DHCP server, the Security Appliance provides hosts protected by the firewall with the network parameters necessary for them to access the enterprise or corporate network. As a DHCP client, the Security Appliance can obtain its own IP address and network mask and optionally a default route from the DHCP server.

Configuring the Security Appliance to operate as a DHCP server involves the following tasks:

- Configuring the address pool
- Specifying WINS, DNS, and the domain name
- Configuring DHCP options
- Configuring the DHCP lease length
- Enabling the DHCP server

Q&A

As mentioned in the Introduction, the questions in this book are more difficult than what you should experience on the exam. The questions are designed to ensure your understanding of the concepts discussed in this chapter and adequately prepare you to complete the exam. You should use the simulated exams on the CD to practice for the exam.

The answers to these questions can be found in Appendix A:

1. Which two major components comprise the Easy VPN solution?

2. Which three types of devices can serve as Easy VPN Servers?

3. What is DPD?

4. What is Initial Contact?

5. Which client platforms support the Easy VPN Remote feature?

6. Which router platforms can be used as Cisco Easy VPN Clients?

7. What are the six major steps that occur when the Easy VPN Remote client initiates a connection with the Easy VPN Server gateway?

8. When initiating the VPN connection, the client can use which two IKE authentication mechanisms?

9. What is XAUTH?

10. Which two modes of operation does the Easy VPN Remote support?

11. In which Easy VPN Remote mode are the addresses of the remote system visible on the Easy VPN Server network?

12. What feature enables the Cisco VPN Software Client to be simple to deploy and manage?

13. Which encryption algorithms are supported by the Cisco VPN Software Client?

14. What is SUA?

15. What is IUA?

16. What is PPPoE?

17. What type of DHCP functionality does the Security Appliance provide?

18. Which command enables you to configure the Security Appliance to pass configuration parameters learned by using either PPPoE or DHCP to its DHCP clients?

This chapter covers the following subjects:

- ASDM Overview

- ASDM Operating requirements

- Preparing for ASDM

- Using ASDM to Configure the Security Appliance

- Using ASDM to Create a Site-to-Site VPN

- Using ASDM to Create a Remote-Access VPN

CHAPTER 15

Adaptive Security Device Manager

Cisco Adaptive Security Device Manager (ASDM) is a secure, graphical configuration tool that is designed to help you configure and monitor your Cisco Security Appliance graphically, without requiring you to have extensive knowledge of the Cisco Security Appliance command-line interface (CLI). The Cisco ASDM can be implemented by either a browser or a standalone application installed on the host.

This chapter begins with an overview of ASDM and the workstation requirements needed to run ASDM, followed by ASDM installation instructions. All of these tasks are necessary to get ASDM operational on your Security Appliance. Besides initially setting up ASDM, this chapter also outlines how you can use ASDM to perform various Security Appliance configuration tasks such as the following:

- Defining system properties
- Defining hosts and networks
- Configuring translation rules
- Configuring access rules
- Creating a site-to-site virtual private network (VPN)
- Creating a remote-access VPN

How to Best Use This Chapter

Effectively managing the configuration on your Security Appliance is a very important step in protecting your network from attack. The Cisco ASDM provides a graphical interface that enables you to easily perform common configuration tasks on your Security Appliance. Compared to manually entering commands on the command line, using ASDM also reduces configuration errors. Test yourself with the "Do I Know This Already?" quiz and see how familiar you are with the functionality provided by Cisco Adaptive Security Device Manager (ASDM).

"Do I Know This Already?" Quiz

The purpose of the "Do I Know This Already?" quiz is to help you decide if you really need to read the entire chapter. If you already intend to read the entire chapter, you do not necessarily need to answer these questions now.

The ten-question quiz, derived from the major sections in the "Foundation Topics" portion of the chapter, helps you determine how to spend your limited study time.

Table 15-1 outlines the major topics discussed in this chapter, and the "Do I Know This Already?" questions correspond to those topics.

Table 15-1 *"Do I Know This Already?" Foundation Topics Section-to-Question Mapping*

Foundations Topics Section	Questions Covered in This Section	Score
ASDM Overview	1, 3 to 5, 9	
Prepare ASDM	2	
Using ASDM to Configure the Security Appliance	6 to 10	

CAUTION   The goal of selfassessment is to gauge your mastery of the topics in this chapter. If you do not know the answer to a question or are only partially sure of the answer, you should mark this question "wrong" for purposes of the selfassessment. Giving yourself credit for an answer you correctly guess skews your self-assessment results and might provide you with a false sense of security.

1. How many tabs does ASDM have under its Configuration button?

   a. Three

   b. Five

   c. Nine

   d. Six

2. How do you connect to ASDM?

   a. By accessing the Security Appliance through Telnet and entering ASDM

   b. By entering **http://***inside_interface_ip* in your browser

   c. By entering **https://***inside_interface_ip* in your browser

   d. By entering **https://PIX_ASDM** in your browser

   e. By a downloadable installer application

   f. By entering **https://***inside_interface_ip* in your browser and by a downloadable installer application

3. What version of Security Appliance software is required for ASDM 5.0 to run?

   a. 6.1

   b. 5.2

   c. 6.3

   d. 7.0

4. Which model of the Security Appliance does ASDM not support?

   a. 515

   b. 525

   c. 5520

   d. 506E

   e. All of these answers are correct

5. Where does ASDM reside?

   a. On a Windows NT/2000 server

   b. On a Red Hat Linux 7.0 server

   c. On a Solaris server

   d. In the Security Appliance Flash memory

6. What default security mechanism does ASDM employ for browsers to connect to it?

   a. RSA

   b. Biometrics

   c. MD5

   d. SSL

7. Which of the following is a prerequisite for access rules to be created?

   a. Hosts or networks must be defined before access rule creation.

   b. A dynamic or static translation rule must be defined before access rule creation.

   c. There are no prerequisites.

   d. Hosts or networks must be defined before access rule creation, and a dynamic or static translation rule must be defined before access rule creation.

8. What is a translation exemption rule?

   a. A rule that exempts addresses from being encrypted or translated

   b. A rule that denies access to addresses

   c. A rule that increases security on selected addresses

   d. None of these answers are correct

9. What is the largest recommended configuration file size to use with ASDM?

    a. 500 KB

    b. 1500 KB

    c. 110 MB

    d. 25 KB

10. Which of the following is required to access ASDM?

    a. Cisco Secure access control server

    b. Transport Layer Security (TLS) enabled

    c. JavaScript and Java enabled on the browser

    d. A VPN connection to the Security Appliance

    e. Transport Layer Security (TLS) enabled and JavaScript and Java enabled on the browser.

The answers to the "Do I Know This Already?" quiz are found in Appendix A, "Answers to the 'Do I Know This Already?' Quizzes and Q&A Sections." The suggested choices for your next step are as follow:

■ **8 or less overall score**—Read the entire chapter. This includes the "Foundation Topics," "Foundation Summary," and "Q&A" sections.

■ **9 or 10 overall score**—If you want more review on these topics, skip to the "Foundation Summary" section and then go to the "Q&A" section. Otherwise, move to the next chapter.

Foundation Topics

ASDM Overview

ASDM is a graphical configuration tool that is designed to help you set up, configure, and monitor your Cisco Security Appliance. It is installed as a separate software image on the Security Appliance and resides in the Flash memory of all firewall units running software version 7.0 and higher. A standalone or browser-based Java applet can be used as a client to access the ASDM graphical user interface (GUI) for configuration. ASDM uses tables, drop-down menus, and task-oriented selection menus to assist you in administering your Security Appliance. Additionally, ASDM maintains compatibility with the Security Appliance CLI and includes a tool for using the standard CLI commands within the ASDM application. ASDM also lets you print or export graphs of traffic through the Security Appliance and system activity.

NOTE   ASDM is a signed Java applet that downloads from the Security Appliance to your web browser or a standalone installer.

Figure 15-1 shows the ASDM GUI with the three main buttons: Home, Configuration, and Monitoring.

Figure 15-1 *Security Appliance Adaptive Security Device Manager GUI*

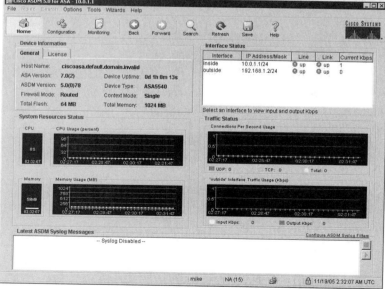

If your Cisco Security Appliance unit is new and came with software version 7.0, the software is already loaded in Flash memory. If you are upgrading from a previous version of Cisco Security Appliance, you must use Trivial File Transfer Protocol (TFTP) from the Security Appliance unit's inside interface to copy the ASDM image to your Security Appliance. ASDM works with software version 7.0 and later, and it can operate on the Security Appliance 515, 515E, 525, 535, 5510, 5520, and 5540 units as soon as they are upgraded to version 7.0 or later.

ASDM is designed to assist you in managing your network security in these ways:

■ Letting you visually monitor your Cisco Security Appliance system, connections, Intrusion Detection System (IDS), and traffic on the interfaces.

■ Creating new Security Appliance configurations or modifying existing configurations that were originally implemented using the Security Appliance.

■ Using visual tools such as task-oriented selections and drop-down menus to configure your Cisco Security Appliance.

■ Using Secure Sockets Layer (SSL) to secure communication between ASDM and the Security Appliance.

■ Monitoring and configuring Security Appliance units individually.

Multiple Cisco Security Appliances can be monitored and configured from a single workstation via the web browser. It is also possible to have up to five administrators accessing a given Security Appliance unit or context via ASDM at the same time. A maximum of 32 total sessions can be active on a unit running multiple mode.

For the SNPA exam, this chapter focuses on ASDM version 5.0 running on software version 7.0.

Security Appliance Requirements to Run ASDM

Like all software, ASDM 5.0 has minimum hardware and software requirements for it to work. ASDM 5.0 is available on all PIX 515/515E, PIX 525, PIX 535, ASA 5510, ASA 5520, and ASA 5540 platforms running software version 7.0. Depending on the type of model on which ASDM will be running, it must have at least 256 MB of RAM and the Flash memory sizes listed in Table 15-2.

Table 15-2 *Flash Memory Requirements for each PIX and ASA Model to Support ASDM 5.0*

PIX Firewall Model	Flash Memory Required
PIX 515/515E	16 MB
PIX 520	16 MB
PIX 525	16 MB

Table 15-2   *Flash Memory Requirements for each PIX and ASA Model to Support ASDM 5.0 (Continued)*

PIX Firewall Model	Flash Memory Required
PIX 535	16 MB
ASA 5510	256 MB
ASA 5520	256 MB
ASA 5540	256 MB

To use ASDM version 5.0 to manage your Security Appliance, you must meet the following minimum requirements:

- You must have an activation (license) key that enables Data Encryption Standard (DES) or the more secure 3DES, which PDM requires for support of the SSL protocol.

- You must have Cisco Security Appliance software version 7.0 or higher.

- You must have a minimum of 16 MB of Flash memory on the Security Appliance unit.

ASDM Workstation Requirement

ASDM, as mentioned previously, is accessed via a browser interface. The following sections provide an overview of ASDM requirements for these:

- Browser

- Windows-based workstation

- Sun Solaris–based workstation

- Linux-based workstation

ASDM 5.0 does not support Windows 3.1, Windows 95, Windows 98, Windows Me, or Windows NT operating systems.

Browser Requirements

The following are the requirements to access ASDM from a browser:

- **JavaScript and Java must be enabled**—If these are not enabled, ASDM helps the administrator enable them. When using your browser, Java Plug-in version 1.4.2 or 1.5.0 is supported. To check which version the administrator has, launch ASDM. In the main ASDM menu, click **Help > About Cisco ASDM 5.0 for PIX**. When the About Cisco ASDM 5.0 for PIX window opens, it displays the browser specifications in a table, including the Java version. If the administrator has an older Java version, the administrator can download the supported Java plug-in version from Microsoft.

- **Browser support for SSL must be enabled**—The supported versions of Internet Explorer and Netscape Navigator support SSL without requiring additional configuration.

- **Pop-up blockers may prevent ASDM from starting**—If ASDM does not start, it is advisable to disable pop-up blocking.

Windows Requirements

The following are required to access ASDM from a Windows 2000/XP operating system:

- Windows 2000 (Service Pack 4) or Windows XP.

- Supported browsers—Internet Explorer 6.0 with the Java Plug-in version 1.4.2 or 1.5.0, Netscape Communicator 7.2 with the Java Plug-in version 1.4.2 or 1.5.0 or higher (4.76 recommended).

- Any Pentium or Pentium-compatible processor running at 450 MHz or higher.

- At least 256 MB of RAM.

- A 1024 x 768-pixel display and at least 256 colors are recommended.

Sun Solaris Requirements

The following requirements apply to the use of ASDM with Sun Scalable Processor ARChitecture (SPARC):

- Sun Solaris 2.8 or later running CDE or OpenWindows window manager.

- SPARC microprocessor.

- Supported browser—Mozilla 1.7.3 with Java Plug-in version 1.4.2 or 1.5.0.

- At least 256 MB of RAM.

- A 1024 x 768-pixel display and 256 colors are recommended.

NOTE ASDM does not support Solaris on IBM PCs.

Linux Requirements

The following requirements apply to the use of ASDM with Linux:

- Any Pentium or Pentium-compatible processor running at 450 MHz or higher.

- Red Hat Linux 9.0 or Red Hat Linux WS version 3 running the GNOME or KDE 2.0 desktop environment.

- Supported browser—Mozilla 1.7.3 with Java Plug-in version 1.4.2 or 1.5.0.

- At least 256 MB of RAM.

- A 1024 x 768-pixel display and 256 colors.

ASDM Installation

Before installing ASDM, follow these steps:

Step 1   Save or print your Security Appliance configuration and write down your activation key.

Step 2   If you are upgrading from a previous version of Security Appliance software, you must obtain the ASDM software from Cisco in the same way you download the Security Appliance software. Then, use TFTP to download the image to your Security Appliance unit.

Step 3   If you upgrade your Cisco Security Appliance Software to version 7.0 and you plan to use ASDM, both the Security Appliance image and the ASDM image must be installed on your failover units.

Step 4   You must configure the Security Appliance with some information before ASDM will be available to a web browser:

- **Time**—Set the Security Appliance clock to Universal Coordinated Time (UTC, also known as Greenwich Mean Time, or GMT). Use the **clock set** command to set the time on the Security Appliance:

`clock set` `hh:mm:ss day month year`

- **Inside IP address**—Specify the IP address of the Security Appliance's inside interface. Use the **ip address** command to set the inside interface on the Security Appliance:

`ip address` `ip_address [netmask]`

- **Hostname**—Specify up to 16 characters as a name for the Security Appliance. Use the **hostname** command to set the host name on the Security Appliance:

`hostname` `newname`

- **Domain name**—Specify the domain name for the Security Appliance. Use the **domain-name** command to set the domain name on the Security Appliance:

`domain-name` `name`

- **IP address of the host running ASDM**—Specify the IP address of the workstation that will access ASDM from its browser. Use the **http** command to set the IP address for the workstation:

`http` `ip_address [netmask] [if_name]`

- **HTTP server**—Enable the HTTP server on the Security Appliance. Use the **http server enable** command to set the IP address for the workstation.

> **NOTE**   Cisco PIX Firewalls have a smaller Flash drive than the ASA Security Appliances.
> This restricts the amount of images that can coexist with the ASDM image, and usually it
> restricts it to a single operating system (OS) image and a single ASDM image. Generally,
> you will be required to erase both the OS and ASDM images before any future code
> upgrades.

The install procedure is similar to that of the Cisco Security Appliance image upgrade.
Example 15-1 shows the procedures for ASDM installation.

Example 15-1   *ASDM Installation Procedures*

```
PIXFIREWALL(config)# copy tftp flash:pdm
Address or name of remote host [127.0.0.1]   192.168.1.2
Source file name [cdisk] asdm-500.bin
copying tftp://192.168.1.2/  asdm-500.bin to flash:asdm
[yes I no I again]y
```

After you successfully install your ASDM, you are ready to access it using your web browser.
On a browser running on a workstation that has a network connection to the Security
Appliance unit, enter the following:

https://*Security Appliance_Inside_Interface_IP_Address*

This will bring you to the ASDM launch page shown in Figure 15-2. This page gives you the
option of launching the Java applet or downloading a stub installer to run ASDM as a local
application.

Figure 15-2   *ASDM Launch Page*

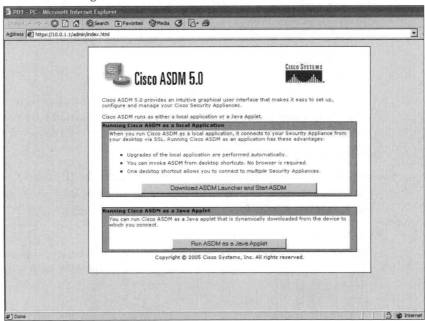

If you use the Java Applet button, the page launches the ASDM applet, as shown in Figure 15-3. If this is the first time you have used the Java applet on this PC, you will get a browser warning that indicates the certificate used by ASDM is from an organization currently untrusted by your browser. Use the install certificate option to download the certificate and stop this notice from appearing again. After you have chosen how you will run ASDM from your workstation, use your enable password and leave the username blank to access the PDM interface when prompted to provide a username and password.

NOTE   When you access ASDM, the Security Appliance prompts you for login credentials. You can restrict access via the enable password, which is encrypted and stored locally on the Security Appliance. You can also use an external authentication server to store username and password information, which you will be asked by ASDM to provide when you request access (see Figure 15-3).

Figure 15-3   *Launching the ASDM Applet*

NOTE   It is common that the first time ASDM is installed and used, there will be problems connecting through the applet. Remember: You have to use HTTPS, not HTTP, when accessing ASDM; otherwise, the browser cannot connect. If problems still persist, turn on console logging and check for any errors that may occur during login. Additionally, make sure that ASDM is turned on for the right interface and that WebVPN has not been enabled on that same interface.

Using ASDM to Configure the Cisco Security Appliance

The Cisco Security Appliance ASDM Startup Wizard, shown in Figure 15-4, walks you through the initial configuration of your Cisco Security Appliance. You are prompted to enter information about your Security Appliance. The Startup Wizard applies these settings, so you should be able to start using your Security Appliance right away.

Figure 15-4 *Cisco Security Appliance Adaptive Security Device Manager Startup Wizard*

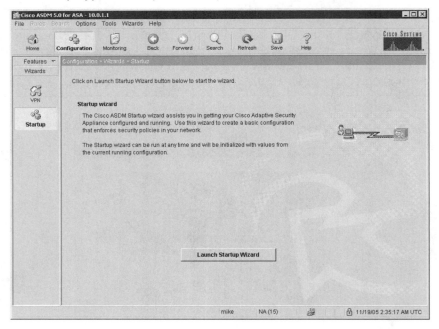

The Startup Wizard configures the following attributes on your Cisco Security Appliance:

- A host name for your Security Appliance.

- A domain name for your Security Appliance.

- A default gateway for your Security Appliance.

- An enable password that is required to access ASDM or the Security Appliance's CLI.

- The speed and IP address information of the outside interface on the Security Appliance.

- Your Security Appliance's other interfaces, such as the inside or demilitarized zone (DMZ) interfaces, can be configured from the Startup Wizard.

- Network Address Translation (NAT) or Port Address Translation (PAT) rules for your Security Appliance.

■ Dynamic Host Configuration Protocol (DHCP) settings for the inside interface, as a DHCP server.

The Startup Wizard helps you set up a *shell configuration*—a basic configuration for your Cisco Security Appliance, as the initial "setup" program does for the CLI. To customize and modify your Security Appliance configuration, ASDM provides the Configuration button. After you click the **Configuration** button on ASDM, you see nine main tabs for configuring and modifying the Security Appliance configuration:

■ Interfaces

■ Security Policies

■ NAT

■ VPN

■ IPS (Optional)

■ Routing

■ Building Blocks

■ Device Administration

■ Properties

> **NOTE** The layout of ASDM will change slightly based on the Security Appliance being used. The PIX Firewalls do not have all of the features, such as the IPS features, that the ASA Security Appliance supports.

The sections that follow examine in more detail the Interfaces, Security Policies, NAT, VPN, IPS, Routing, Building Blocks, Device Administration, and Properties tabs. The section "Using ASDM to Create a Site-to-Site and Remote-Access VPNs," later in this chapter, describes all actions associated with the VPN tab.

Interfaces Tab

The Interfaces tab, shown in Figure 15-5, lets you view configured interfaces and subinterfaces. Each configured interface will have a separate line with all configuration details, including security level and name.

Figure 15-5 *Interfaces Tab on ASDM*

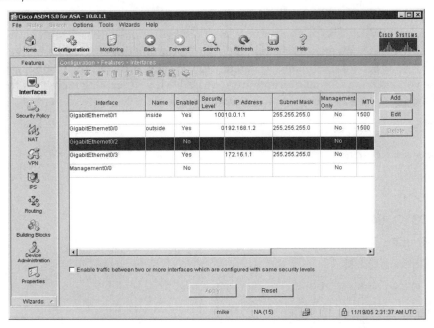

An administrator can add, edit, or remove interfaces from the Security Appliance through this tab. If there is a requirement for two or more interfaces to communicate with each other within the same security level, you can check this feature at the bottom of the tab to enable. An interface can be reset using the Reset button at the bottom of the tab. This will force the interface to shut down and re-enable, causing all traffic to halt over that interface until the rest is complete.

Using the Add or Edit button will create a new window in which all of the interface setting can be configured. Shown in Figure 15-6, an interface can be assigned all of the same configurations that are available through the CLI.

Figure 15-6 *Edit Interface Window on ASDM*

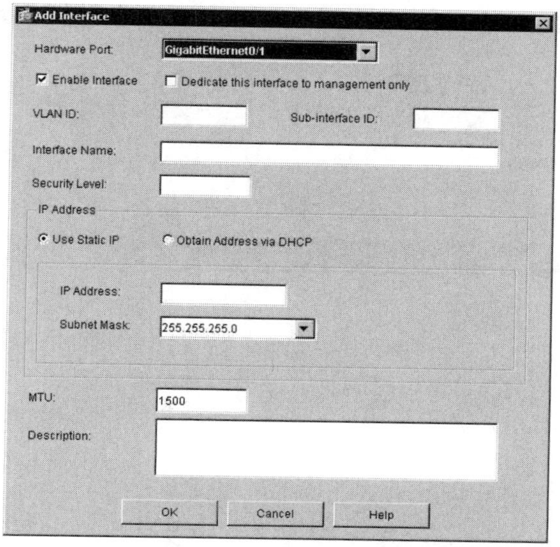

Security Policies Tab

The Security Policies tab, shown in Figure 15-7, lets you view and configure all of the security rules and policies for the Security Appliance. The available rules, located at the top of the tab, are as follow:

- **Access Rules**—Displays your entire network security policy expressed in rules. This window enables the security administrator to define access control lists (ACL).

- **AAA Rules**—Displays your AAA configuration. The security administrator can define and modify AAA rules.

- **Filter Rules**—Displays the filter rules that are currently configured on the Security Appliance. It also provides buttons that the security administrator can use to add or modify the filter rule.

- **Service Policy Rules**—Define how specific types of application inspection are applied to different types of traffic received by the Security Appliance. The security administrator can apply a rule specifically to an interface or globally to every interface.

Figure 15-7 *Security Policies Tab on ASDM*

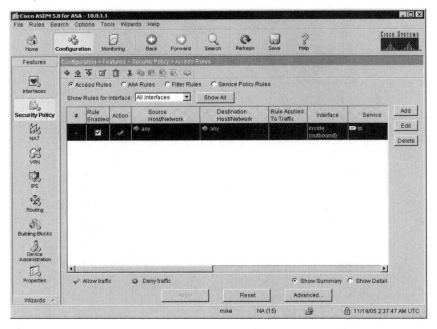

Access Rules

The Access Rules window, shown in Figure 15-8, gives the security administrator a place to add or modify an access-list rule for the Security Appliance. This window combines the concepts of access lists, outbound lists, and conduits to describe how a specific host or network interacts with another host or network to permit or deny a specific service and/or protocol. Clicking the Add or Edit button will open a new window, shown in Figure 15-8, which will allow you to configure or modify an access rule. The options available in this window are the same as if you are configuring an access-list rules statement from the CLI, including source and destination classifications, as well as source and destination ports.

Access rules are listed in sequential order and are applied in the order in which they appear on the Access Rules tab. This is the order in which the PIX Firewall evaluates them. An implicit, unwritten rule denies all traffic that is not permitted. If traffic is not explicitly permitted by an access rule, it is denied. Additionally, the window displays a diagram that helps the security administrator understand how the new rule will be applied on the Security Appliance.

Figure 15-8 *Add Access Rule Window on ASDM*

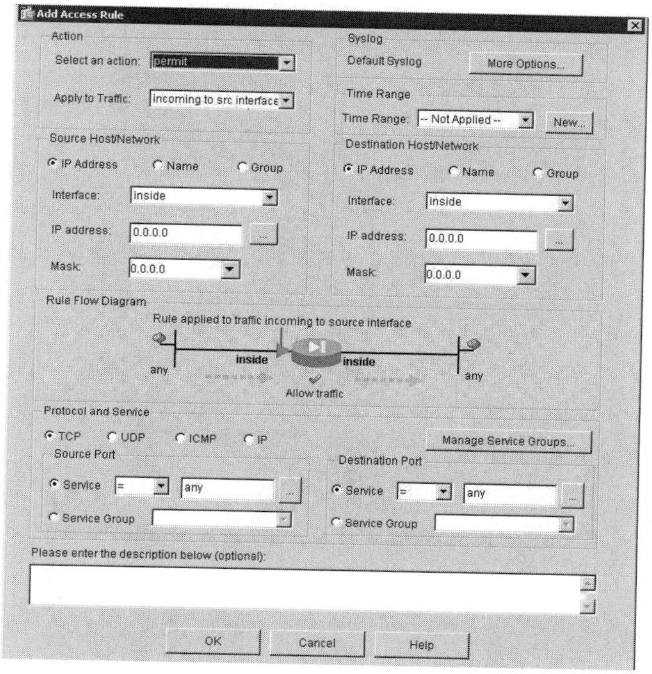

AAA Rules

Complicated configurations such as AAA have been made significantly more intuitive and easier with the AAA Rules window. The AAA Rules window, shown in Figure 15-9, allows you to define the authentication, authorization, and accounting rules for the Security Appliance.

AAA systems are designed to maintain which user can access the Security Appliance, what permissions the user is granted, and what that user did while connected to the Security Appliance. A rule can be added through the Add button or edited through the Edit button. These buttons open up a new window, as shown in Figure 15-9, where you input the configurations.

Filter Rules

The Filter Rules window, shown in Figure 15-10, gives the security administrator a place to add or modify URL filter rules for the Security Appliance.

Figure 15-9 *Add AAA Rule Window on ASDM*

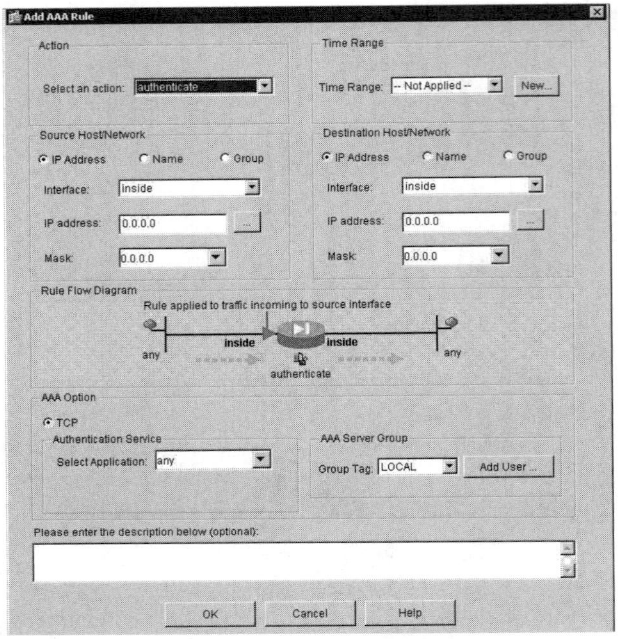

Figure 15-10 *Filter Rules Window on ASDM*

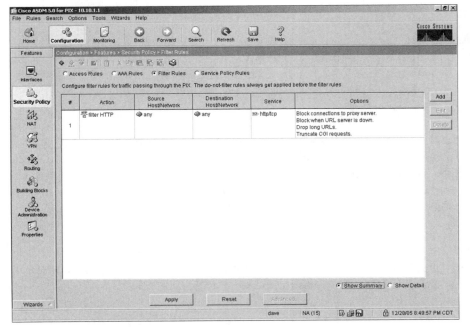

The Filter Rules window lets you prevent internal users from accessing external URLs that you designate using the Websense filtering server. Additionally, the Filter Rules window can set Java and ActiveX policies for the Security Appliance.

NOTE   You can configure a total of 16 URL servers.

You can configure the Security Appliance to use either N2H2 or Websense, but not both. For example, if the Security Appliance unit is configured to use two Websense servers, when N2H2 is selected, a warning appears after you add the first N2H2 server and click Apply. All the previously configured Websense servers are dropped, and the new N2H2 server is added. This also takes place when you switch from N2H2 to Websense. Content filtering is discussed further in Chapter 16, "Content Filtering on the Cisco Security Appliance."

Service Policy Rules

The Service Policy Rules window, shown in Figure 15-11, gives the security administrator a place to add or modify QoS rules for the Security Appliance.

Figure 15-11   *Service Policy Rules Window on ASDM*

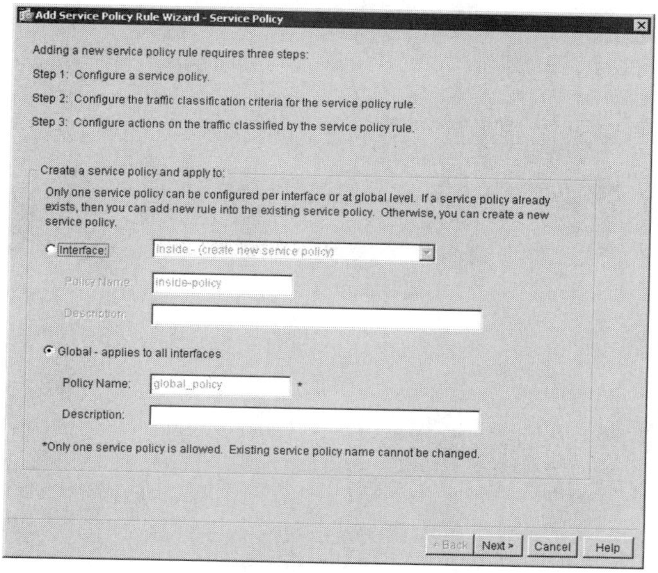

The ASA uses a menu-driven wizard to configure a service policy through this window. When you press the Add button, a new window opens and starts the wizard. The wizard takes you through three steps to configure a Service Policy Rule:

Step 1   Configure a service policy.

Step 2   Configure the traffic classification criteria for the service policy rule.

Step 3   Configure actions on the traffic classification by the service policy rule.

With version 7.0, the Service Policy Rules window can be used to configure the Modular Policy Framework settings for the Security Appliance. This is covered in more detail in Chapter 8, "Modular Policy Framework."

NAT Tab

The NAT tab, shown in Figure 15-12, lets you view all the address translation rules or NAT exemption rules applied to your network.

Figure 15-12 *NAT Tab on ASDM*

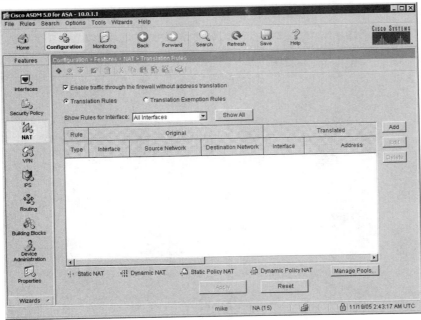

The Cisco Security Appliance supports both NAT, which provides a globally unique address for each outbound host session, and PAT, which provides a single, unique global address for more than 64,000 simultaneous outbound or inbound host sessions. The global addresses used for NAT come from a pool of addresses to be used specifically for address translation. The unique global address that is used for PAT can be either one global address or the IP address of a given interface.

From the NAT tab, you also can create a translation exemption rule, which lets you specify traffic that is exempt from being translated. The exemption rules are grouped by interface in the table, and then by direction. If you have a group of IP addresses that will be translated, you can exempt certain addresses from being translated by using the exemption rules. If you have a previously configured access list, you can use that to define your exemption rule. ASDM writes the exemption to the Security Appliance using a **nat** 0 command through the CLI. You can re-sort your exemption's view by clicking the column heading.

It is important to note that the order in which you apply translation rules can affect how the rules operate. ASDM lists the static translations first and then the dynamic translations. Each rule type will be examined in order, with the Security Appliance handling the packet based on the first rule the packet qualifies for in each set. The Security Appliance will first look at NAT 0, the static translations, NAT, and lastly PAT rules. If a packet arrives at the Security Appliance and is destined for a web server using PAT, the packet must pass all of the previous rules defined in NAT 0, static, and NAT before PAT translation even happens. When processing NAT, the Cisco Security Appliance first translates the static translations in the order they are configured. The packet will be handled based on the first match in the translation rule set. You can use the **Insert Before** or **Insert After** commands to determine the order in which static translations are processed. Because dynamically translated rules are processed on a best-match basis, the option to insert a rule before or after a dynamic translation is disabled. Use the Manage Pools button to create global address pools to be used by NAT. You can view or delete existing global pools through the global address pools window.

VPN Tab

The Security Appliance can create three different types of secure connections:

- Remote-access VPNs
- Site-to-site VPNs
- WebVPNs

The ASDM uses a VPN wizard to create remote-access and site-to-site VPNs. After the wizard has completed the VPN configurations, the administrator will be able to add, delete, or modify VPN-specific features. The wizard is described in more detail later in this chapter.

The VPN tab, shown in Figure 15-13, allows a security administrator to configure group policies and individual VPN tunnels.

Figure 15-13 *VPN Tab on ASDM*

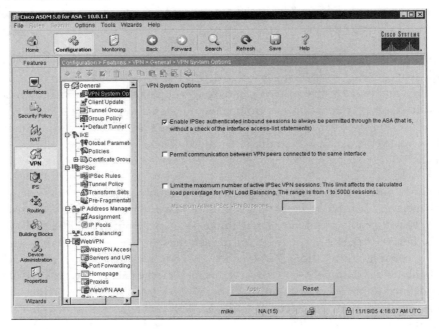

IPS Tab

The IPS tab is optional and will only be displayed if the Security Appliance has enabled IPS sensors through the CLI. You can use the IPS tab to manage network settings and signatures for intrusion prevention (see Figure 15-14). The IPS can configure the sensor to control blocking devices, as well as configure several SNMP features. Additionally, you can configure a sensor to automatically restore the sensor to factory defaults, reboot, update the software, or shut down.

Routing Tab

The Routing tab, shown in Figure 15-15, is where a security administrator can configure the different routing protocols for the Security Appliance. The Routing window is subdivided into each supported routing protocol: static routes, RIP, OSPF, IGMP, and PIM. Each of these routing protocols has the same features as can be found through the CLI configuration.

Figure 15-14 *IPS Tab on ASDM*

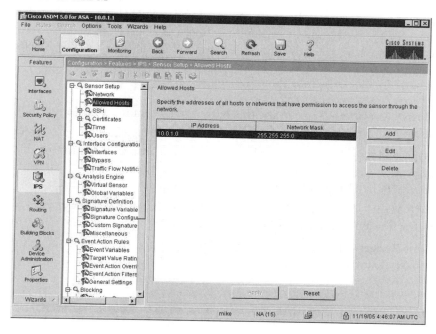

Figure 15-15 *Routing Tab on ASDM*

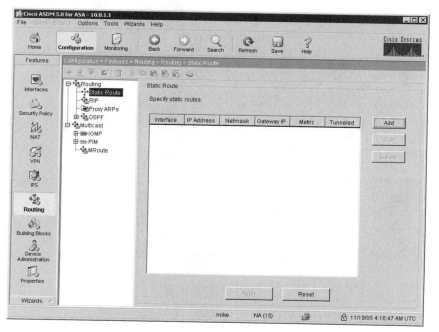

Building Blocks Tab

The ASDM uses the name "building blocks" for the reusable components that must be implemented for your policy. The Building Blocks tab, shown in Figure 15-16, provides a single location where you can configure, view, and modify the building blocks.

These building blocks include the following:

- **Hosts/Networks**—You can use this option to add, modify, or remove hosts and networks from specific interfaces.

- **Inspect Maps**—You can use this option to create inspect maps for specific protocol inspection engines. The inspect map can then be applied to a type of traffic through the Service Policy Rules tab using Modular Policy Framework features.

- **TCP Maps**—You can use this option to assign TCP connection settings for different traffic flows using Modular Policy Framework features.

- **Time Ranges**—You can use this option to assign a start and end time range to various security features and policies.

Figure 15-16 *Building Blocks Tab on ASDM*

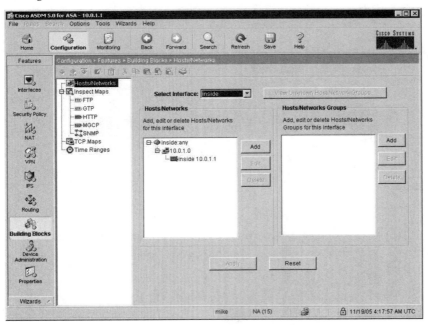

Device Administration Tab

The ASDM gives you a single location where you can manage the basic parameters of the Security Appliance. The Device Administration tab, shown in Figure 15-17, can set the basic parameters for the Security Appliance, such as passwords, user accounts, banners, system access, and so on. While in this tab, the administrator can also generate and manage certificates.

Figure 15-17 *Device Administration Tab on ASDM*

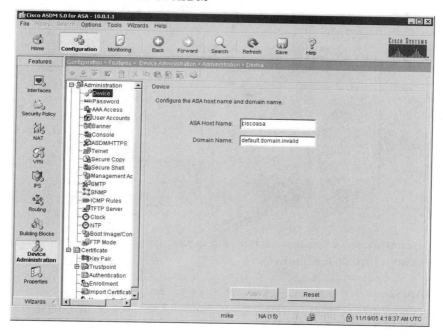

Properties Tab

Security Appliance features and configurations, such as AAA servers, failover, and logging, are placed in a single configuration tab called Properties. The Properties tab, shown in Figure 15-18, gives the security administrator the option to customize the Security Appliance with advanced and optional features.

Figure 15-18 *Properties Tab on ASDM*

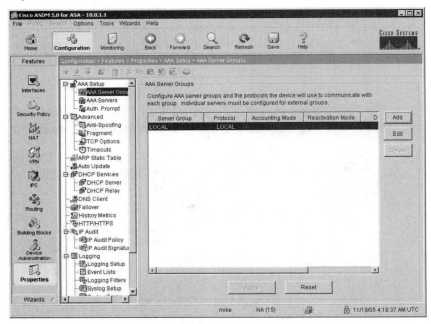

The tab consists of 14 sections, each with a specific feature that can be configured. Some of these sections include the following:

- **AAA Setup**—Configures AAA server groups. The Security Appliance can provide AAA servers and the authentication prompt. Each AAA server group directs different types of traffic to the authentication servers in its group. If the first authentication server listed in the group fails, the Security Appliance seeks authentication from the next server in the group. You can have up to 14 groups, and each group can have up to 14 AAA servers, for a total of up to 196 AAA servers.

- **Advanced**—Configures advanced protection features including antispoofing, fragment options, and connection settings through the Advances window.

- **ARP Static Table**—Normally, MAC addresses as learned dynamically over the inside-out outside interfaces. The ARP Static Table gives the security administrator the option of adding static MAC address entries on the Security Appliance.

- **Auto Update**—Enables the Auto Update server to push configuration information and send requests for information to the Security Appliance. Additionally, by causing the Security Appliance to periodically poll the Auto Update server, the Auto Updater can pull configuration information.

- **DHCP Server**—Provides network configuration parameters, such as IP addresses, to DHCP clients. DHCP server or DHCP proxy relay services are provided by the Security Appliance to DHCP clients attached to Security Appliance interfaces.

- **DNS Client**—Specifies one or more DNS servers for the Security Appliance so it can resolve server names to IP addresses.

- **Failover**—The settings for configuring failover on the Security Appliance.

- **History Metrics**—The ASDM can display history graphs and tables to allow the security administrator a means to track various statistics. This window allows you to configure the Security Appliance to keep a history of various statistics. Statistics can only be monitored in real time if this feature is not enabled.

- **HTTP/HTTPS**—Displays information on HTTP redirection and HTTPS user certificate requirements for each interface on the Security Appliance.

- **IP Audit**—Provides basic IPS functionality.

- **Logging**—Enables or disables sending informational messages to the console, to a syslog server, or to an Simple Network Management Protocol (SNMP) management station.

- **priority-queue**—Priority queuing features enable QoS options on packet flows passing through the Security Appliance. To create a priority queue for an interface, use this window. All administrator-created priority queues will be enabled before priority queuing takes effect.

Monitoring

The Monitoring tab, shown in Figure 15-19, is one of the most useful tools to help you make sense of the different statistics that the Cisco Security Appliance can generate. The different sections on the Monitoring tab help you to analyze your Security Appliance's performance using colorful graphs.

The Monitoring tab enables you to examine the operation of the Security Appliance. When monitoring the operation of the Security Appliance, you can directly view the settings or statistics for many features and parameters. For other features, you have the option of displaying a graph that represents the usage of the features over time. The left column in Figure 15-19 shows the different categories of information that you can monitor on your Security Appliance.

Figure 15-19 *Monitoring Button on the ASDM Menu Bar*

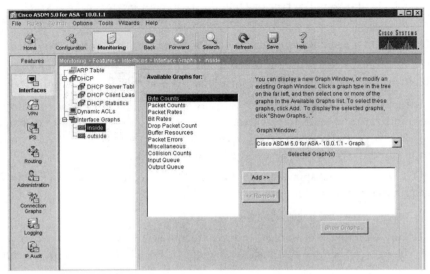

NOTE After specifying the information to be graphed, the graphical information is displayed in a separate window (New Graph window) when you click the **Show Graphs** button (see Figure 15-19). The graphical information displayed in the New Graph window can be printed or bookmarked in your browser for later recall. The data may also be exported for use by other applications.

Selecting any of the following options in the Categories list provides a corresponding pane of monitoring statistics for the Cisco Security Appliance:

■ **ASDM Log**—Displays the Syslog messages currently in the PDM Log buffer on the Security Appliance. A snapshot of the ASDM Log buffer contents on the Security Appliance can be displayed.

■ **ASDM/HTTPS**—Enables you to monitor connections made to the Security Appliance using ASDM. A snapshot of the current ASDM user sessions to the Security Appliance is displayed.

■ **Telnet Sessions**—Enables you to monitor connections made to the Security Appliance using Telnet. A snapshot of current Telnet sessions to the Security Appliance is displayed.

■ **Secure Shell Sessions**—Enables you to monitor connections made to the Security Appliance using Secure Shell (SSH). When the Secure Shell pane is displayed, a snapshot of the current SSH sessions to the Security Appliance is available.

- **User Licenses**—Displays the number of current users, which is subtracted from the maximum number of users for your Security Appliance licensing agreement.

- **DHCP Client**—Displays DHCP-assigned interface parameters when DHCP addressing is configured on the outside interface of the Security Appliance. A snapshot of the current DHCP lease information is displayed.

- **VPN Statistics**—Lets you graphically monitor the following functions:

    — Number of active IPSec tunnels

    — Detailed IPSec information (similar to the CLI command **show ipsec sa detail**)

- **System Graphs**—Enables you to build the New Graph window, which monitors the Security Appliance's system resources, including block utilization, CPU utilization, failover statistics, and memory utilization.

- **Connection Graphs**—Enables you to monitor a wide variety of performance statistics for Security Appliance features, including statistics for xlates, connections, AAA, inspect, URL filtering, and TCP intercept.

- **IPS (located under Miscellaneous Graphs)**—Enables you to monitor intrusion detection statistics, including packet counts for each IPS signature supported by the Security Appliance.

- **Interface Graphs**—Enables you to monitor per-interface statistics, such as packet counts and bit rates, for each enabled interface on the Security Appliance.

NOTE   If an interface is not enabled using the Interfaces tab, no graphs are available for that interface.

Using ASDM for VPN Configuration

Chapter 13, "Virtual Private Networks," explained how to configure VPN on the Cisco Security Appliance via the CLI. One of the difficult configuration and troubleshooting issues occurs with VPNs. Quite often, typos occur when you create a VPN configuration via the CLI. For novice administrators of the Cisco Security Appliance, remembering the commands and their sequence can sometimes be difficult. ASDM presents a user-friendly VPN Wizard that creates both site-to-site and remote-access VPNs for the Cisco Security Appliance (accessible via the Wizards menu on ASDM). Administrators are prompted for unique parameters such as IP addresses, and they use drop-down menus to configure their VPN. The following sections discuss the steps involved in creating a site-to-site VPN and a remote-access VPN using the VPN Wizard on ASDM.

Using ASDM to Create a Site-to-Site VPN

The following steps and corresponding figures show a sample site-to-site VPN configuration using the VPN Wizard on ASDM:

Step 1   Select the VPN Wizard from the Wizard's drop-down menu, as shown in Figure 15-20, to start the VPN Wizard.

Figure 15-20   *ASDM with VPN Wizard Selected*

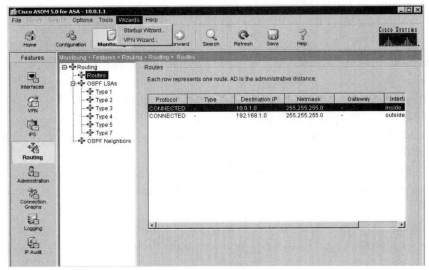

Step 2   Select the site-to-site radial buttons, as shown in Figure 15-21, to create a site-to-site VPN configuration. This configuration is used between two IPSec security gateways, which can include Cisco PIX Firewalls, VPN concentrators, or other devices that support site-to-site IPSec connectivity. Use this window to also select the type of VPN tunnel you are defining and to identify the interface on which the tunnel will be enabled. In Figure 15-21, the outside interface is selected as the VPN termination point.

Step 3   In the Remote Site Peer window, shown in Figure 15-22, you specify the IP address of the remote IPSec peer that will terminate the VPN tunnel you are configuring. Also, you use this window to identify which of the following methods of authentication you want to use:

- Preshared keys
- Certificates

Figure 15-22 shows the Remote Site Peer window configured with the remote IPSec peer and the preshared authentication keys.

Figure 15-21 *VPN Wizard with Site-to-Site VPN Selected*

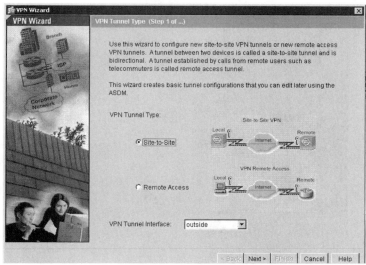

Figure 15-22 *Remote Site Peer Window*

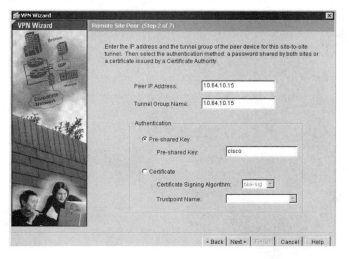

Step 4 Configure the encryption and authentication algorithms for IKE
Phase I in the IKE Policy window, as shown in Figure 15-23.

Figure 15-23 *IKE Policy Window*

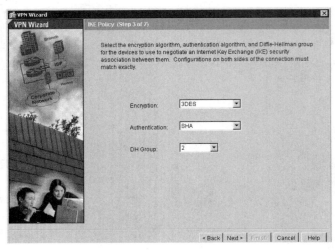

Step 5 Configure the transform set to specify the encryption and authentication algorithms used by IPSec, as shown in Figure 15-24. IPSec provides secure communication over an insecure network, such as the public Internet, by encrypting traffic between two IPSec peers, such as your local Security Appliance and a remote Security Appliance or VPN concentrator.

Figure 15-24 *Transform Set Window (IPSec Encryption and Authentication)*

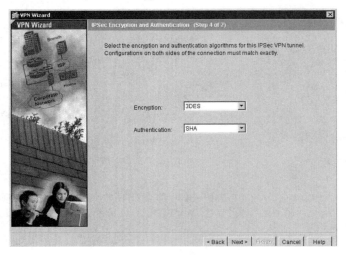

Step 6   Identify the traffic you want to protect using the current IPSec tunnel, as shown in Figure 15-25. The current IPSec tunnel protects packets that are sent to or received from the hosts or networks you select in this window. Use this window to identify the hosts and networks protected by your local Cisco Security Appliance. In Figure 15-25, packets that are sent to and received from the 192.168.4.0/24 network are protected.

Figure 15-25   *IPSec Traffic Selector Window: On Local Site*

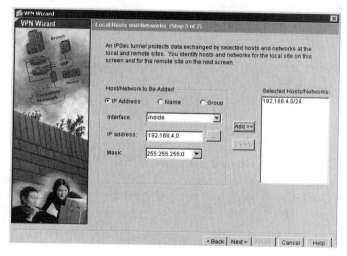

Step 7   Identify the hosts and networks protected by the remote IPSec peer, as shown in Figure 15-26.

Step 8   At this point, the site-to-site VPN configuration has been completed.

Figure 15-26 *IPSec Traffic Selector Window: On Remote Site*

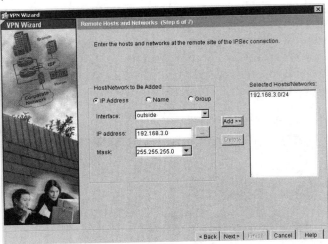

Using ASDM to Create a Remote-Access VPN

With a remote-access VPN, your local Cisco Security Appliance provides secure connectivity between individual remote users and the LAN resources protected by your local Security Appliance. To start the VPN Wizard, go to the wizard's menu on ASDM and select the VPN Wizard option:

Step 1 From the opening window of the ASDM VPN Wizard, shown in Figure 15-27, select the Remote Access VPN radio button to create a remote-access VPN configuration. This configuration enables secure remote access for VPN clients, such as mobile users. A remote-access VPN allows remote users to securely access centralized network resources. When you select this option, the system displays a series of panels that let you enter the configuration required for this type of VPN. In Figure 15-27, the outside interface is selected as the interface on which the current VPN tunnel will be enabled.

Figure 15-27 *VPN Wizard with Remote-Access VPN Selected*

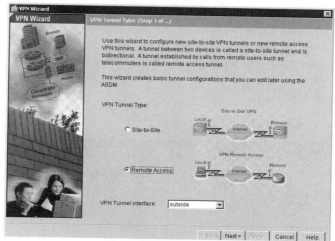

Step 2   In the Remote Access Client window, shown in Figure 15-28, identify the type of remote-access client that will use the current VPN tunnel to connect to your local Cisco PIX Firewall. The options are as follow:

- **Cisco VPN Client**—Select to support remote-access clients using Cisco VPN Client v3.*x* or higher (Cisco Unified VPN Client Framework).

- **Cisco VPN 3000 Client**—Select to support remote-access clients using Cisco VPN 3000 Client, Release 3.0 or higher.

Figure 15-28 *Remote Access Client Window*

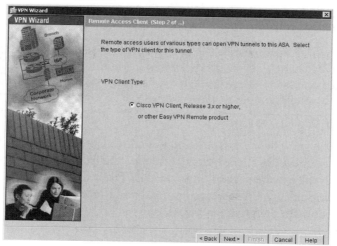

Step 3   Create a VPN client group to group remote-access users who are using
the Cisco VPN client. The attributes associated with a group are applied
and downloaded to the clients that are part of a given group. The
Group Password is a preshared key to be used for IKE authentication.
Figure 15-29 shows the VPN Client Group window with Cisco ASA as
a group name and the Pre-shared Key radio button selected for IKE
authentication.

Figure 15-29   *VPN Client Group Window*

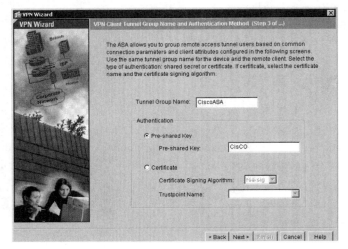

A preshared key is a quick and easy way to set up communications with
a limited number of remote peers. To use this method of authentication,
exchange the preshared key with the remote access user through a
secure and convenient method, such as an encrypted e-mail message.

NOTE   Preshared keys must be exchanged between each pair of IPSec peers that needs to
establish secure tunnels. This authentication method is appropriate for a stable network
with a limited number of IPSec peers. It might cause scalability problems in a network with
a large or increasing number of IPSec peers.

Step 4   Use the Client Authentication window, shown in Figure 15-30, to
require VPN client users to authenticate from a AAA server for access
to the private network on your PIX Firewall. Client authentication
through a AAA server is optional and is not required for VPN client
access to the private network.

Figure 15-30   *Client Authentication Window*

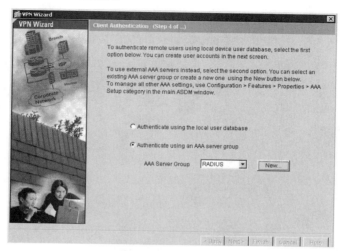

Extended Authentication (XAuth) is a feature within the IKE protocol. XAuth lets you deploy IPSec VPNs using TACACS+ or RADIUS as your user authentication method. This feature, which is designed for VPN clients, provides user authentication by prompting users for a username and password and verifies them with the information stored in your TACACS+ or RADIUS database. XAuth is negotiated between IKE Phase 1 (the IKE device authentication phase) and IKE Phase 2 (the IPSec SA negotiation phase). If XAuth fails, the IPSec security association is not established, and the IKE security association is deleted. The AAA server must be defined before XAuth will work on the Cisco Security Appliance. You can define the AAA server using the New button. This opens the AAA Server Group window, where you can define the location of the AAA server, the group name, and the protocol used for AAA.

Step 5   Define the location of the AAA server, the group name, and the protocol used for AAA, as shown in Figure 15-31.

Figure 15-31 *AAA Server Group Window*

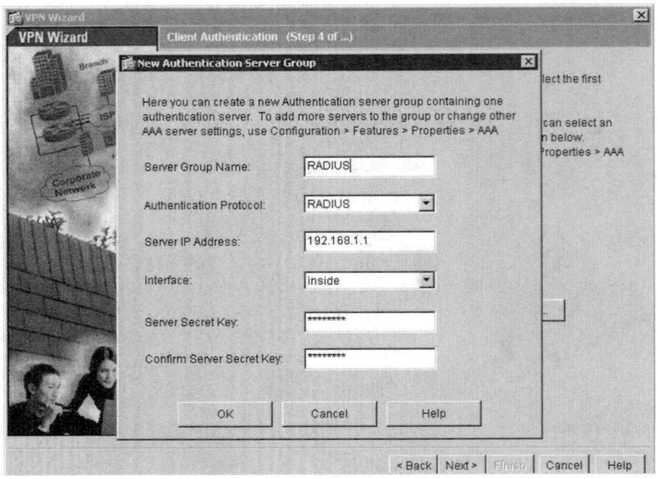

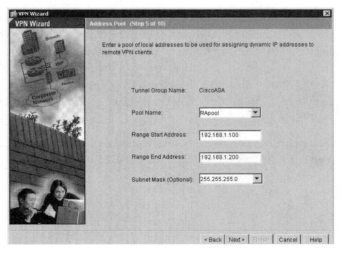

Step 6 Create a pool of local addresses that can be used to assign dynamic addresses to remote-access VPN clients. Enter a descriptive identifier for the address pool. Figure 15-32 shows a sample configuration for the remote sales group in the Address Pool window.

Figure 15-32 *Address Pool Window*

Step 7 (Optional) Configure the DNS and WINS addresses that can be pushed down to the remote client, as shown in Figure 15-33.

Figure 15-33 *Attributes Pushed to Client Window*

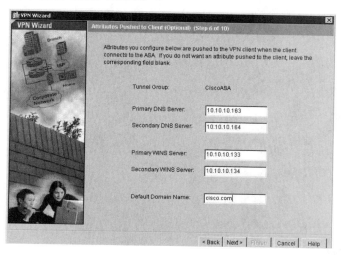

Step 8   Specify the encryption and authentication algorithms used by IKE (Phase 1), as shown in Figure 15-34.

Figure 15-34 *IKE Policy Window*

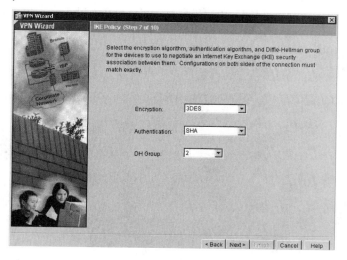

Step 9   Specify the encryption and authentication algorithms used by the IPSec VPN tunnel, as shown in Figure 15-35.

Figure 15-35 *Transform Set Window (IPSec Encryption and Authentication)*

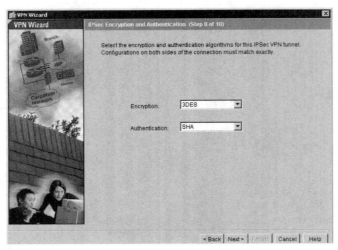

Step 10   (Optional) The Address Translation Exemption window, shown in Figure 15-36, identifies local hosts/networks that are to be exempted from address translation. By default, the Security Appliance hides the real IP address of internal networks from outside hosts through dynamic or static NAT. The security provided by NAT helps to minimize the risk of being attacked by untrusted outside hosts, but it is inappropriate for those who have been authenticated and protected by VPN.

Figure 15-36 *Address Translation Exemption Window*

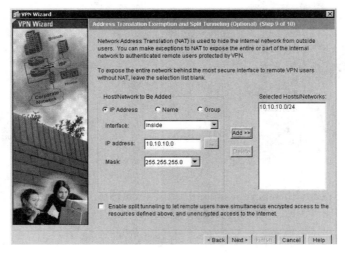

As shown at the bottom of Figure 15-36, a checkbox option is available to enable split tunneling. A split tunnel allows the VPN client to access the networks protected by the VPN headend via the VPN tunnel and the Internet in clear data (outside the VPN tunnel) simultaneously.

NOTE Split tunneling is scalable and reduces the drain on institutional computing and network resources. A dangerous and very insecure drawback is that this VPN client could be a relay agent if someone on the clear-data side compromised the client's workstation and used that workstation to get information from the VPN-protected networks.

Step 11   At this point, the remote-access VPN configuration is complete.

Foundation Summary

The "Foundation Summary" provides a convenient review of many key concepts in this chapter. If you are already comfortable with the topics in this chapter, this summary can help you recall a few details. If you just read this chapter, this review should help solidify some key facts. If you are doing your final preparation before the exam, this summary provides a convenient way to review the day before the exam.

ASDM is a browser-based configuration tool designed to help you set up, configure, and monitor your Cisco Security Appliance graphically. It is installed as a separate software image on the Cisco Security Appliance and resides in the Flash memory of all Security Appliance units running Secure Firewall software version 7.0 and higher. Multiple Security Appliance units can be monitored and configured using ASDM from a single workstation via the web browser. ASDM can be permanently installed on workstations that frequently manage Security Appliances.

ASDM uses tables, drop-down menus, and task-oriented selection menus to assist you in administering your Cisco Security Appliance. To provide secure management access to your Security Appliance, ASDM allows access only via HTTPS. Nine main tabs are used for configuring and modifying the Security Appliance configuration:

- Interfaces
- Security Policies
- NAT
- VPN
- IPS (Optional)
- Routing
- Building Blocks
- Device Administration
- Properties

The optimal configuration file size to use with ASDM is less than 500 KB. Cisco Security Appliance configuration files larger than 500 KB might interfere with ASDM's performance on your workstation.

Q&A

The questions in this book are more difficult than what you should experience on the exam. The questions are designed to ensure your understanding of the concepts discussed in this chapter and to adequately prepare you to complete the exam. Use the simulated exams on the CD to practice for the exam.

The answers to these questions can be found in Appendix A:

1. What is a translation exemption rule?

2. What are the nine main configuration buttons on the ASDM?

3. How do you access ASDM?

4. What version of Cisco Security Appliance software is required to run ASDM version 5.0?

5. Which models of Cisco Security Appliance are supported by ASDM?

6. What versions of Windows does ASDM support?

7. Where does ASDM reside?

8. What is the quickest method to configure site-to-site VPN using ASDM?

9. What is the command to install or upgrade ASDM on the Security Appliance?

This chapter covers the following subject:

- URL Filtering

- ActiveX Object Filtering

- Java Applet Filtering

CHAPTER 16

Content Filtering on the Cisco Security Appliance

Up to now, you focused on how to configure the Security Appliance and how to protect against unwanted traffic from outside in. This chapter focuses specifically on outbound traffic and content filtering—traffic moving from inside out.

More and more companies today have some form of network policy in place. Websites that are not related to their business or that are otherwise considered inappropriate are prohibited for use by their employees. This chapter discusses how the Cisco Security Appliance mitigates some of the threats posed by Java applets and ActiveX objects and how the Cisco Security Appliance enforces URL filtering.

How to Best Use This Chapter

Users on your network frequently surf the Internet looking for information. Some websites contain content that is not appropriate for a business environment. Besides inappropriate content, many attacks also originate from traffic brought into your network by internal users surfing the Internet via ActiveX objects and Java applets. Filtering ActiveX objects and Java applets along with restricting access to specific URLs is an important aspect in your overall network security policy. Test yourself with the "Do I Know This Already?" quiz and see how familiar you are with the content filtering functionality available on Security Appliances.

"Do I Know This Already?" Quiz

The purpose of the "Do I Know This Already?" quiz is to help you decide if you really need to read the entire chapter. If you already intend to read the entire chapter, you do not necessarily need to answer these questions now.

The ten-question quiz, derived from the major sections in the "Foundation Topics" portion of the chapter, helps you determine how to spend your limited study time.

Table 16-1 outlines the major topics discussed in this chapter and the "Do I Know This Already?" quiz questions that correspond to those topics.

Table 16-1 *"Do I Know This Already?" Foundation Topics Section-to-Question Mapping*

Foundations Topics Section	Questions Covered in This Section	Score
URL Filtering	2 to 10	
Configuring Java and ActiveX Filtering	1	

> **CAUTION** The goal of self assessment is to gauge your mastery of the topics in this chapter. If you do not know the answer to a question or are only partially sure of the answer, you should mark this question wrong for purposes of the self assessment. Giving yourself credit for an answer you correctly guess skews your self-assessment results and might provide you with a false sense of security.

1. How does the Security Appliance filter Java applets and ActiveX objects?

   a. By commenting out the <OBJECT> </OBJECT> tags or the <APPLET> </APPLET> tags in the HTML page.

   b. By deleting the <OBJECT CLASSID> </OBJECT> tags or the <APPLET> </APPLET> tags in the HTML page.

   c. It notifies the content-filtering server, which in turn disables the ActiveX objects and Java applets.

   d. The Security Appliance does not filter ActiveX objects or Java applets.

2. What is the command to designate or identify the URL-filtering server?

   a. filter url-server

   b. url-server

   c. filtering server

   d. server url

3. What is the longest URL length supported by a Cisco Security Appliance with Websense Enterprise URL-filtering software?

    a. 12 KB

    b. 15 KB

    c. 4 KB

    d. 6 KB

4. What is the command to filter URLs?

    a. **filter url**

    b. **url-filter**

    c. **url-server**

    d. **filter web page**

5. What happens when the only URL-filtering server is unavailable?

    a. If the **allow** option is set, the Security Appliance forwards HTTP traffic without filtering.

    b. SMTP traffic is dropped because the URL-filtering server is unavailable.

    c. HTTP requests are queued until the URL-filtering server is available.

    d. The Security Appliance reverts to the onboard URL-filtering engine to filter HTTP traffic.

6. What is the default port used by the N2H2 server to communicate with the Cisco Security Appliance?

    a. TCP/UDP 1272

    b. TCP 5004 only

    c. TCP/UDP 4005

    d. UDP 5004 only

7. What command identifies N2H2 servers on a Cisco Security Appliance?

    a. **websense url filter** *server-ip*

    b. **filter url** *server-ip* **vendor n2h2**

    c. **url-server** (*if-name*) **vendor n2h2 host** *local-ip*

    d. All of these answers are correct

8. How many URL servers can be configured on a single Cisco Security Appliance?

   a. 5

   b. 12

   c. 3

   d. 16

9. What command disables URL caching on the Cisco Security Appliance?

   a. no url-cache

   b. caching-url

   c. disable url-cache

   d. None of these answers are correct

10. Which of the following URL-filtering servers supports FTP and HTTPS filtering?

   a. N2H2

   b. Cisco Works

   c. Websense

   d. CSACS

The answers to the "Do I Know This Already?" quiz are found in Appendix A, "Answers to the 'Do I Know This Already?' Quizzes and Q&A Sections." The suggested choices for your next step are as follows:

■ **8 or less overall score**—Read the entire chapter. This includes the "Foundation Topics," "Foundation Summary," and "Q&A" sections.

■ **9 or 10 overall score**—If you want more review on these topics, skip to the "Foundation Summary" section and then go to the "Q&A" section. Otherwise, move to the next chapter.

Foundation Topics

Filtering ActiveX Objects and Java Applets

ActiveX objects and Java applets are designed to make the browsing experience more interactive. Based on the Component Object Model (COM), ActiveX objects are written for a specific platform of Microsoft Windows. When the user displays a page containing ActiveX or Java, the browser downloads the control dynamically. ActiveX objects are native programs, so they can do all the things that local programs can do. For example, they can read and write to the hard drive, execute programs, perform network administration tasks, and determine which system configuration they are running on. While ActiveX objects and Java applets can perform powerful tasks, they can also be used maliciously to damage systems.

One way to prevent the threats posed by ActiveX objects and Java applets is to disallow ActiveX objects and Java applets at the browser or user level. Users can configure their web browsers not to run ActiveX objects or Java applets. Although you can disable ActiveX objects and Java applets within the browser, this requires a great deal of effort for a large enterprise network. In these cases, it is easier to prevent the ActiveX objects and Java applets from reaching the browser.

When configured for filtering, the Cisco PIX Firewall filters ActiveX objects and Java applets from HTML web pages before those pages reach the browser. Java applet and ActiveX object filtering of HTML files is performed by selectively replacing the <APPLET> and </APPLET> tags and the <OBJECT> and </OBJECT> tags with comments.

Filtering Java Applets

The **filter java** command filters out Java applets that return to the Cisco Security Appliance from an outbound connection. The user still receives the HTML page, but the web page source for the applet is commented out so that the applet cannot execute. The syntax for **filter java** is

```
filter java port[-port] local-ip mask foreign-ip-mask
```

The following example specifies that Java applet blocking applies to web traffic on port 80 from local subnet 10.10.10.0 and for connections to any foreign host:

```
filter java http 10.10.10.0 255.255.255.0 0 0
```

Table 16-2 describes the different parameters for the **filter** command.

Table 16-2 **filter** *Command Parameters*

Parameter	Description
activex	Blocks inbound ActiveX objects, Java applets, and other HTML <OBJECT> tags from outbound packets.
allow	Filters URL only. When the server is unavailable, lets outbound connections pass through the Cisco Security Appliance without filtering. If you omit this option, and if the N2H2 or Websense server goes offline, Cisco Security Appliance stops outbound port 80 (web) traffic until the N2H2 or Websense server is back online.
cgi-truncate	Sends a CGI script as an URL.
except	Filters URL only. Creates an exception to a previous filter condition.
foreign-ip	The IP address of the lowest security level interface to which access is sought. You can use 0.0.0.0 (or, in shortened form, 0) to specify all hosts.
java	Filters out Java applets returning from an outbound connection.
local-ip	The IP address of the highest security level interface from which access is sought. You can set this address to 0.0.0.0 (or, in shortened form, 0) to specify all hosts.
local-mask	Network mask of *local-ip*. You can use 0.0.0.0 (or, in shortened form, 0) to specify all hosts.
longurl-deny	Denies the URL request if the URL is over the URL buffer size limit or if the URL buffer is unavailable.
longurl-truncate	Sends only the originating host name or IP address to the Websense server if the URL is over the URL buffer limit.
mask	Subnet mask.
port	The port that receives Internet traffic on the Cisco Security Appliance. Typically, this is port 80, but other values are accepted. The **http** or **www** literal can be used for port 80.
proxy-block	Prevents users from connecting to an HTTP proxy server.
url	Filters URLs from data moving through the Cisco Security Appliance.
interact-block	Prevents users from connecting to the FTP server through an interactive program.

NOTE   Table 16-2 lists the parameters for the **filter** command that appear in this chapter.

Filtering ActiveX Objects

The **filter activex** command filters out ActiveX objects and other HTML <OBJECT> usages from inbound packets. These controls include custom forms, calendars, and extensive third-party forms for gathering or displaying information. The syntax for filtering ActiveX objects is as follows:

```
filter activex port local-ip local-mask foreign-ip foreign-mask
```

Note that if the <OBJECT> and </OBJECT> HTML tags split across network packets or if the code in the tags is longer than the number of bytes in the maximum transmission unit (MTU), Cisco Security Appliance cannot block the tag.

Filtering URLs

Most organizations today have human resources policies that specify indecent materials cannot be brought into the workplace. Similarly, most organizations have network security policies that prohibit users from visiting websites that are categorized as indecent or inappropriate to the business mission of the organization.

Using other content-filtering vendor products, the Cisco Security Appliance enforces network security policy as it relates to URL filtering. When a user issues an HTTP request to a website, the Cisco Security Appliance sends the request to the web server and to the URL-filtering server at the same time. If the policy on the URL-filtering server permits the connection, the Cisco Security Appliance allows the reply from the website to reach the user who issued the original request. If the policy on the URL-filtering server denies the connection, the Cisco Security Appliance redirects the user to a block page, indicating that access was denied.

The PIX Firewall works in conjunction with two types of URL-filtering application servers:

- **Websense Enterprise**—Supported by Cisco Security Appliance Version 5.3 and later
- **N2H2 Sentian**—Supported by Cisco Security Appliance Version 6.2

Identifying the URL-Filtering Server

The **url-server** command designates the server that is running the N2H2 or Websense URL-filtering application. The Security Appliance allows you to configure a maximum of 16 URL servers (with the first one entered being the primary URL server), and you can use only one URL-filtering server at a time, either N2H2 or Websense. Configuration is performed both on the Security Appliance and the URL-filtering server. You can identify more than one URL-filtering server by entering the **url-server** command multiple times. The primary URL-filtering server is the first server that you identify. The syntax for identifying an N2H2 URL-filtering server is as follows:

```
url-server [(if-name)] vendor n2h2 host local-ip [port number]
     [timeout seconds] [protocol {TCP | UDP}]
```

The default protocol is TCP. The **timeout** parameter in the **url-server** command is the maximum idle time permitted before the Security Appliance switches to the next URL-filtering server you specified. The default time is 5 seconds.

The following example identifies an N2H2 URL-filtering server with an IP address of 10.10.10.13:

```
pixfw(config)#url-server (inside) vendor n2h2 host 10.10.10.13
```

The default port used by the N2H2 server to communicate with the Cisco Security Appliance via TCP or UDP is 4005.

The syntax for identifying a Websense URL-filtering server is as follows:

```
url-server [(if-name)] vendor websense host local-ip [timeout seconds]
     [protocol {TCP | UDP} version{1 | 4}]
```

The following example identifies a Websense URL-filtering server with an IP address of 10.10.10.14:

```
pixfw(config)# url-server (inside) vendor websense host 10.10.10.14
```

To view the URL-filtering server, use the **show url-server** command, as shown in Example 16-1.

Example 16-1 *Displaying the URL-Filtering Server Information*

```
pixfw# show url-server
url-server (inside) vendor n2h2 host 10.10.10.13 port 4005 timeout 5 protocol TCP
```

Configuring URL-Filtering Policy

You must identify and enable the URL-filtering server before you use the following filtering commands. If all URL-filtering servers are removed, any associated filtering commands are also removed. The **filter url** command enables you to prevent outbound users from accessing URLs that you designate as inadmissible. The syntax for filtering URLs is as follows:

```
filter url port [except] local-ip local-mask foreign-ip foreign-mask [allow]
     [proxy-block] [longurl-truncate | longurl-deny] [cgi-truncate]
```

With URL filtering enabled, the Cisco Security Appliance stops outbound HTTP, HTTPS, and FTP traffic until a URL-filtering server permits the connection. If the primary URL-filtering server and the secondary server do not respond, then outbound web traffic (port 80) stops until the URL-filtering server comes back online. However, the **allow** option causes the Cisco Security Appliance to forward HTTP traffic without filtering when the URL-filtering server(s) is unavailable.

> **NOTE**   Security Appliance supports filtering of HTTPS and FTP sites for Websense servers. HTTPS and FTP filtering are not supported for the N2H2 URL-filtering server.

The following example filters all HTTP traffic:

```
filter url http 0 0
```

You can make an exception to URL-filtering policies by using the **except** parameter in the **filter url** command. For example:

```
pixfw(config)#filter url http 0 0 0 0
pixfw(config)#filter url except 10.10.10.20 255.255.255.255 0 0
```

This policy filters all HTTP traffic with the exception of HTTP traffic that originates from host 10.10.10.20.

Websense database version 4 contains the following enhancements:

- URL filtering allows the Cisco Security Appliance to check outgoing URL requests against the policy defined on the Websense server.

- Username logging tracks the username, group, and domain name on the Websense server.

- Username lookup lets the Cisco Security Appliance use the user authentication table to map the host's IP address to the username.

There are instances in which the web server replies to a user HTTP request faster than the URL-filtering servers. In these instances, the **url-cache** command provides a configuration option to buffer the response from a web server if its response is faster than that from the N2H2 or Websense URL-filtering server. This prevents the web server's response from being loaded twice, improving throughput. The syntax of the **url-cache** command is as follows:

```
url-cache {dst | src-dst} size kbytes
```

Table 16-3 describes the parameters for the **url-cache** command.

Table 16-3 **url-cache** *Command Parameters*

Parameter	Description
dst	Caches entries based on the URL destination address. Select this mode if all users share the same URL-filtering policy on the N2H2 or Websense server.
src-dst	Caches entries based on the source address initiating the URL request and the URL destination address. Select this mode if users do not share the same URL-filtering policy on the N2H2 or Websense server.
size *kbytes*	Specifies a value for the cache size within the range 1 to 128 KB.

Use the **url-cache** command to enable URL caching, set the size of the cache, and display cache statistics.

Caching also stores URL access privileges in memory on the Cisco Security Appliance. When a host requests a connection, the Cisco Security Appliance first looks in the URL cache for matching access privileges before it forwards the request to the N2H2 or Websense server.

The **clear url-cache** command removes **url-cache** command statements from the configuration, and the **no url-cache** command disables caching.

Filtering HTTPS and FTP

As mentioned in the previous section, HTTPS and FTP filtering can be configured on the Security Appliance using Websense servers. These new features provide a convenient mechanism of enforcing access policy in your environment. Just as it does with HTTP filtering, the Security Appliance sends FTP requests to both the destination and the Websense server when a user makes an FTP request. If the Websense server denies the connection, the Security Appliance alters the FTP return code to show that the connection was denied. If the Websense server permits the connection, the Security Appliance allows the successful FTP return code to reach the user unchanged.

HTTPS filtering, on the other hand, works by preventing the completion of SSL connection negotiation if the site is not allowed. The browser displays an error message such as "The Page or the content cannot be displayed." The command syntax to enable FTP and HTTPS filtering is as follows:

```
filter ftp dest-port localIP local-mask foreign-IP foreign-mask
    [allow] [interact-block]
filter https dest-port localIP local-mask foreign-IP foreign-mask [allow]
```

Filtering Long URLs

Cisco Security Appliance supports filtering URLs up to 6000 bytes for the Websense URL-filtering server. The default is 2000 bytes. In addition, Cisco Security Appliance supports the **longurl-truncate** and **cgi-truncate** parameters to allow handling of URL requests longer than the maximum permitted size. The format for these options is as follows:

```
filter url [http | port[-port]] local-ip local-mask foreign-ip foreign-mask] [allow]
       [proxy-block] [longurl-truncate | longurl-deny | cgi-truncate]
```

Table 16-4 identifies the major parameters for the **filter url** command.

Table 16-4   **filter url** *Command Parameters*

Parameter	Description
http	Specifies that the filtering be applied to port 80
port	Specifies that the filtering be applied to whatever port (or port range) is specified by either *port* or *port-port*
local-ip	Specifies the source IP addresses for which filtering will be applied
local-mask	Specifies the network mask for *local-ip* (note: using **0.0.0.0** specifies all hosts)
foreign-ip	Specifies the destination IP addresses for which filtering will be applied
foreign-mask	Specifies the network mask for *foreign-ip* (note: using **0.0.0.0** specifies all hosts)
allow	Allows the connection to pass through the firewall without filtering if the filtering server is unavailable
proxy-block	Prevents users from connecting to an HTTP proxy server
longurl-truncate	Causes the Cisco Security Appliance to send only the host name or IP address portion of the URL for evaluation to the URL-filtering server, when the URL is longer than the maximum length permitted
longurl-deny	Denies outbound traffic if the URL is longer than the maximum permitted
cgi-truncate	Sends a CGI script as the URL

Cisco Security Appliance supports a maximum URL length of 1159 bytes for the N2H2 URL-filtering server. To increase the maximum length of a single URL (for Websense only), enter the following command:

```
url-block url-size size
```

The value of the *size* variable is 2 to 6 KB.

Viewing Filtering Statistics and Configuration

The **show url-cache** command with the **stat** option displays the URL caching statistics. Example 16-2 demonstrates sample output from this command.

Example 16-2 show url-cache *Command Output*

```
PIX# show url-cache stat
URL Filter Cache Stats
--------------------
    Size:         128KB
 Entries:         1415
  In Use:            1
 Lookups:            0
    Hits:            0
```

The significant fields in this output are as follows:

■ **Size**—The size of the cache in kilobytes, set with the **url-cache** *size* option

■ **Entries**—The maximum number of cache entries based on the cache size

■ **In Use**—The current number of entries in the cache

■ **Lookups**—The number of times the Cisco Security Appliance has looked for a cache entry

■ **Hits**—The number of times the Cisco Security Appliance has found an entry in the cache

You can view more statistics about URL filtering and performance with the **show url-server stats** and **show perfmon** commands. Example 16-3 shows output from **show url-server stats**.

Example 16-3 show url-server stats *Command Output*

```
PIX(config)# show url-server stats
URL Server Statistics:
--------------------
Vendor                    Websense
URLs total/allowed/denied 2370/1958/412
URL Server Status:
----------------
10.10.10.13      UP
```

Example 16-4 shows output from the **show perfmon** command.

Example 16-4   show perfmon *Command Output*

```
PIX# show perfmon
PERFMON STATS:     Current       Average
Xlates             0/s           0/s
Connections        0/s           2/s
TCP Conns          0/s           2/s
UDP Conns          0/s           0/s
URL Access         0/s           2/s
URL Server Req     0/s           3/s
TCP Fixup          0/s           0/s
TCPIntercept       0/s           0/s
HTTP Fixup         0/s           3/s
FTP Fixup          0/s           0/s
AAA Authen         0/s           0/s
AAA Author         0/s           0/s
AAA Account        0/s           0/s
```

Foundation Summary

The "Foundation Summary" provides a convenient review of many key concepts in this chapter. If you are already comfortable with the topics in this chapter, this summary can help you recall a few details. If you just read this chapter, this review should help solidify some key facts. If you are doing your final preparation before the exam, this summary provides a convenient way to review the day before the exam.

The **filter java** command lets you filter Java applets out of HTTP traffic before it reaches a user's web browser. The Java applets are commented out in the HTML information that the user's web browser receives so that it will not attempt to process them. Similarly, the **filter activex** command enables you to filter ActiveX objects and other HTML <OBJECT> usages from inbound HTTP packets.

The **filter url** command lets you prevent outbound users from accessing World Wide Web URLs that you designate using one of the following URL-filtering server applications:

- **Websense Enterprise**—Supported by the Cisco Security Appliance Version 5.3 and later
- **N2H2 Sentian**—Supported by the Cisco Security Appliance Version 6.2

When a user issues an HTTP request to a website, the Security Appliance sends the request to the web server and to the URL-filtering server at the same time. If the URL-filtering server permits the connection, the Security Appliance allows the reply from the website to reach the user who issued the original request. If the URL-filtering server denies the connection, the Security Appliance redirects the user to a block page, indicating that access was denied.

Q&A

As mentioned in the Introduction, the questions in this book are more difficult than what you should experience on the exam. The questions are designed to ensure your understanding of the concepts discussed in this chapter and adequately prepare you to complete the exam. You should use the simulated exams on the CD to practice for the exam.

The answers to these questions can be found in Appendix A:

1. With what two URL-filtering servers does the Security Appliance work?

2. What command filters out Java applets from HTML pages?

3. Why are Java applets and ActiveX objects considered a threat?

4. How does the Cisco Security Appliance filter Java applets and ActiveX objects?

5. What is the command to designate or identify the URL-filtering server?

6. Which Security Appliance version supports the Websense URL-filtering server?

7. What is the longest URL filter that is supported by Cisco Security Appliances?

8. What is the command to filter URLs?

9. How would you configure the Security Appliance to buffer the response from a web server if its response is faster than that from the N2H2 or Websense URL-filtering server on the Security Appliance?

This chapter covers the following subjects:

- Overview of AAA
- Installation of Cisco Secure ACS for Windows NT/2000
- Authentication Configuration

CHAPTER 17

Overview of AAA and the Cisco Security Appliance

This chapter presents authentication, authorization, and accounting, more commonly known as AAA. It discusses how the Cisco Security Appliance is incorporated with AAA servers and the relationship between the Cisco Security Appliance and the AAA servers. This chapter also introduces Cisco Secure Access Control Server (ACS), an AAA server product offered by Cisco.

How to Best Use This Chapter

If you are very familiar with AAA but are not very familiar with Cisco Secure ACS, you should skim the first half of this chapter to reinforce your knowledge of AAA and to focus on the installation of Cisco Secure ACS. The AAA process is relatively simple to understand, although there are quite a few different configuration options. This chapter explains the AAA process, discusses how the Cisco Security Appliance fits into this process, and covers the installation of Cisco Secure ACS.

"Do I Know This Already?" Quiz

The purpose of the "Do I Know This Already?" quiz is to help you decide if you really need to read the entire chapter. If you already intend to read the entire chapter, you do not necessarily need to answer these questions now.

The nine-question quiz, derived from the major sections in the "Foundation Topics" portion of the chapter, helps you determine how to spend your limited study time.

Table 17-1 outlines the major topics discussed in this chapter and the "Do I Know This Already?" quiz questions that correspond to those topics.

Table 17-1 *"Do I Know This Already?" Foundation Topics Section-to-Question Mapping*

Foundations Topics Section	Questions Covered in This Section	Score
Overview of AAA	1, 4	
Installation of Cisco Secure ACS for Windows NT/2000	2, 3, 5, 8, 9	
Authentication Configuration	6, 7	

CAUTION The goal of self assessment is to gauge your mastery of the topics in this chapter. If you do not know the answer to a question or are only partially sure of the answer, you should mark this question wrong for purposes of the self assessment. Giving yourself credit for an answer you correctly guess skews your self-assessment results and might provide you with a false sense of security.

1. Which platform does Cisco Secure ACS for Windows version 3.3 currently support?

   a. Windows XP Professional

   b. Windows 2000 Server

   c. Windows NT Workstation

   d. Windows 2000 Professional

2. What is a new feature of Cisco Secure ACS for Windows version 3.3?

   a. A password generator

   b. A password database

   c. Additional configuration steps for your Cisco IOS Network Access Server

   d. New graphics and tables

3. If you are installing Cisco Secure ACS 3.2 for Windows and do not understand a configuration option, what should you do?

   a. Check the explanation page.

   b. Push F7 for help.

   c. Select the About Cisco Secure ACS drop-down option.

   d. Open a case with Cisco TAC.

4. Which of the following are *not* connection types for authenticating to a Security Appliance? (Select all that apply.)

   a. Telnet

   b. SSH

   c. FTP

   d. HTTPS

5. When installing Cisco Secure ACS version 3.3 for Windows, you have the option to authenticate users against an existing user database. Which database can you check?

   a. A currently configured Cisco Secure ACS

   b. Any RADIUS server on the network

   c. The primary domain controller (PDC)

   d. The Windows user database

6. What access does cut-through proxy allow a user after they have successfully authenticated?

   a. Access to anything on the network

   b. Access only to web servers

   c. Access based on the user profile (authorization)

   d. Access only to the Cisco Secure ACS

7. What options are available to authenticate users on a Security Appliance?

   a. Local user database

   b. Remote RADIUS server

   c. Remote TACACS+ server

   d. All of the above

   e. None of these answers are correct

8. What technologies does the Cisco Secure ACS use to communicate with the NAS? (Choose two.)

    a. TACACS

    b. RADIUS

    c. TACACS+

    d. RADIUS+

    e. Virtual Telnet

9. What does the Cisco Secure ACS consider the Security Appliance to be (i.e., what is it referred to as during configuration of the Cisco Secure ACS)?

    a. A perimeter security device.

    b. A Network Access Server.

    c. Cisco Secure ACS does not work with the Security Appliance.

    d. None of these answers are correct.

The answers to the "Do I Know This Already?" quiz are found in Appendix A, "Answers to the 'Do I Know This Already?' Quizzes and Q&A Sections." The suggested choices for your next step are as follows:

■ **7 or less overall score**—Read the entire chapter. This includes the "Foundation Topics," "Foundation Summary," and "Q&A" sections.

■ **8 or 9 overall score**—If you want more review of these topics, skip to the "Foundation Summary" section and then go to the "Q&A" section. Otherwise, move to the next chapter.

Foundation Topics

Overview of AAA and the Cisco Security Appliance

Authentication, authorization, and accounting (AAA) has become an extremely important component in any network infrastructure. AAA is used in our everyday lives not only for network security but also for physical security, or any other function that requires access control. This chapter discusses the AAA process, its components, the responsibilities of each component, and how the Cisco Security Appliance fits into the equation.

Definition of AAA

The best way to understand AAA is to look at the three components individually. Each is distinct and has its own responsibility. AAA is now integrated into nearly every situation that requires access control. Access control can be applied to users, hosts on a network (such as servers and workstations), networking components (such as routers, switches, VPN appliances, and firewalls), and other automated devices that require access and that perform a function. This chapter discusses AAA as it pertains to a user, but you will see how the principles can apply to many automated functions. The three components of AAA are as follows:

- **Authentication**—The process of validating an identity. The identity that is being validated could be a user, a computer, a networking component, and so on. Authentication is by far the most important step. No access is granted until the requestor has been authenticated. There are three layers of user authentication:

  — **What the user knows**—This normally is a user password or passphrase.

  — **What a user has**—This normally is a user token or badge issued to the user by whomever has authority over what the user is attempting to access.

  — **What a user is**—This area includes biometrics, such as checking the user's fingerprint or retinal scan against a stored image in the database.

  Many organizations do not incorporate all three layers of authentication; however, it is very common to use a minimum of two layers at one time.

- **Authorization**—After the user has been authenticated, he or she is granted access rights to perform specific functions.

- **Accounting**—After the user is granted access, the accounting function tracks what tasks the user performs and saves that information in a log that can be reviewed later. Accountability of users and their actions is an issue that is becoming increasingly important in the security of enterprise networks.

The three functions of AAA can be performed by a single server or can be divided among several servers. Most large enterprise networks create a hierarchy of AAA servers, with the lower-level servers tending to user functions and the upper-level servers working as a central point for updating and distributing user information.

AAA and the Cisco Security Appliance

So how does the Security Appliance factor into the AAA equation? Any user who requests access or a service that is configured for authentication and who goes through the Security Appliance is prompted by the firewall for a username and password. If the Security Appliance has a local database configured for user authentication, it matches this user information against that database and permits or denies access.

In a Security Appliance, the local database can be used only for console authorization and command authorization. If the Security Appliance is configured to use a separate AAA server, it forwards the user information to that server for authentication and authorization. In this case, the Security Appliance and the AAA server act in a client/server mode, with the Security Appliance being the client. The Security Appliance acts as a network access server (NAS) but operates as a client to the AAA server. It is a common practice to configure redundant AAA servers. It is also possible to configure a local database on the Security Appliance for use when no other AAA servers can be contacted.

> **NOTE**   The local user database on a Cisco Security Appliance can be processor-intensive and should be used only for small organizations with a limited number of users.

Remember that the AAA server not only authenticates the user but also tells the firewall what the user is authorized to do. If a user is authorized to access websites via HTTP and attempts to connect to the same servers over FTP, that connection is dropped at the firewall even though that user has been authenticated. Additionally, the AAA server should log the fact that the user attempted to make a connection that was outside the user's authority. The use of specific authorization and accounting functions is not a prerequisite for the use of authentication. It is possible to configure only authentication, which by default authorizes access to authenticated users.

Cut-Through Proxy

Cut-through proxy is a feature on the Cisco Security Appliance that allows transparent AAA services and a seamless connection through the firewall to the destination. It provides significantly better performance than application-proxy firewalls because it completes user authentication at the application layer, verifies authorization against the security policy, and then opens the connection as authorized by the security policy. In other words, the connection request needs to go up to the application layer only once to be authorized. After that, all authorized traffic is passed at the lower layers, dramatically increasing the rate at which it can pass through the firewall.

There are four ways to connect to the Cisco PIX Firewall and activate the cut-through proxy:

- HTTP

- FTP

- Telnet

- SSH

The firewall responds to each of these connections with a username and password prompt. Figure 17-1 shows the Telnet user authentication prompt. The user information is either authenticated against a local database on the PIX Firewall or forwarded to an AAA server for authentication. After the user is authenticated, the firewall completes the connection that is requested (if authorized).

Figure 17-1 *Telnet Logon Prompt*

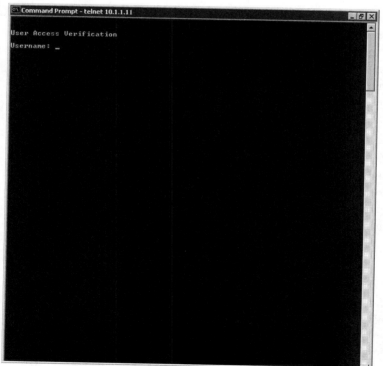

Figure 17-2 shows the steps for cut-through proxy on a Cisco Security Appliance.

Figure 17-2 *Cut-Through Proxy Steps*

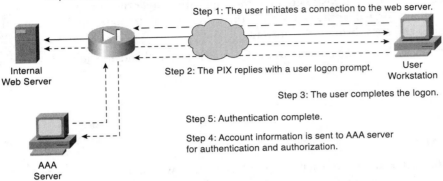

Step 7: Communication is established between source and destination and ASA process begins.

Step 6: Connection completed with web server.

Step 1: The user initiates a connection to the web server.

Internal
Web Server

Step 2: The PIX replies with a user logon prompt.

User
Workstation

Step 3: The user completes the logon.

Step 5: Authentication complete.

Step 4: Account information is sent to AAA server
for authentication and authorization.

AAA
Server

Supported AAA Server Technologies

The Cisco Security Appliance supports six AAA server authentication protocols:

- **Remote Authentication Dial-In User Service (RADIUS)**—RADIUS was developed by Livingston Enterprises as an AAA server. It uses a UDP connection between the client (NAS) and the server (AAA). RADIUS combines the authentication and authorization into a single response to a query from the NAS. By default, RADIUS authentication is performed on TCP port 1645.

NOTE The Cisco ACS server uses nonstandard ports for RADIUS authentication and accounting services. The standard RADIUS ports are 1812/1813.

- **Terminal Access Controller Access Control System Plus (TACACS+)**—TACACS+ was developed by Cisco Systems as an alternative to RADIUS. TACACS+ uses a TCP connection between the client and server and divides the authentication and authorization into separate transmissions. The default port for TACACS+ is TCP port 49.

- **SDI**—RSA SecureID uses a username and one-time password to authenticate an end user or application. This authentication type is used for VPN authentication to the Security Appliance VPN server.

- **NT**—Supports Microsoft Windows NTLM version 1 authentication for VPN authentication.

- **kerberos**—Supports Kerberos authentication for VPN end-user access; 3DES, DES, and RC4 encryption types are supported through kerberos.

- **Lightweight Directory Access Protocol (LDAP)**—Supports LDAP through *tunnel-groups* for VPN authentication.

Cisco Secure Access Control Server

Cisco Secure ACS is an AAA server product developed by Cisco that can run on Windows NT/2000 Server and UNIX, although Cisco has discontinued support for the Windows NT and UNIX platforms. It supports a number of NASs, including the Cisco Security Appliance. Cisco Secure ACS supports both RADIUS and TACACS+.

Cisco has replaced the UNIX platform with the Cisco Secure ACS Solution Engine Server. The server is a standalone 1U server with Cisco Secure ACS 3.3 preinstalled.

With the release of Cisco Secure ACS 3.3, several new features have been added to strengthen an already powerful AAA server platform:

- **Network Admission Control**—Using the Network Admission Control (NAC) feature, the Cisco Secure ACS will acts as a policy decisions point within NAC deployments. Policies are created to evaluate the host on several different levels before assigning AAA-client ACS appropriate for the host's security state. Through these policies, the ACS can evaluate the host's credentials using Cisco Trust Agents. Additionally, policies can be created to determine the state of the host based on such details as the host's operating systems patch level and the antivirus DAT file version.

- **Machine Access Restrictions**—The Cisco Secure ACS can help control authorization of EAP-TLS and Microsoft PEAP users using Machine Access Restrictions (MAR). Users who authenticate with a Windows external user database that does not pass machine authentication within a configured length of time can be given authorizations of a user group, limited authorization, or denial of network access.

- **Network Access Filters**—Cisco has added a new shared profile component with ACS 3.3 called Network Access Filters (NAF). NAFs can apply network access restrictions and can allow ACLs to be downloaded using specific AAA client names, IP addresses, or specific devices.

Minimum Hardware and Operating System Requirements for Cisco Secure ACS

Table 17-2 documents the minimum requirements needed by a system to run Cisco Secure ACS version 3.3.

Table 17-2 *Cisco Secure ACS Version 3.3 System Requirements*

System Requirement Type	Requirements
Hardware	Pentium III Processor, 550 MHz or greater. 256 MB of RAM. 250 MB of available drive space. Additional space is required if you intend to run the Cisco Secure ACS database on this system. Screen resolution of 800×600 pixels and 256-color display.
Operating system	Microsoft Windows 2000 Server with Service Pack 4. Microsoft Windows 2000 Advanced Server with Service Pack 4, without Microsoft Clustering Services installed and without any other Windows 2000 Advanced Server features enabled. Microsoft Windows Server 2003, Enterprise Edition. Microsoft Windows Server 2003, Standard Edition.
Browser	Microsoft Internet Explorer 6.0 Service Pack 1 with Microsoft Java Virtual Machine. Netscape Communicator 7.1 for Windows. With Sun Java Plug-In 1.4.2 04 or later.

Table 17-3 documents the configuration specifications of the Cisco Secure ACS Solution Engine Server.

Table 17-3 *Cisco Secure ACS Solution Engine Server*

System	Specification
CPU	3.2-GHz Pentium 4
Memory	1 GB RAM
Hard drive	80 GB free disk space
Interfaces	2 built-in 100/100 Mbps Ethernet controllers and 1 floppy drive

Installing Cisco Secure ACS Version 3.3 on Windows Server

You can download a 90-day trial version of Cisco Secure ACS from the Cisco Software Center at Cisco.com. You must register as a user to receive your CCO *login*. You must have the CCO login to download software from the software center. The installation of Cisco Secure ACS is an easy, step-by-step process. It is a good idea to verify that your Windows server is up to the current patch level. When you are ready to begin the installation, just run setup.exe. Figure 17-3 shows the initial Cisco Secure ACS installation window.

Figure 17-3 *Cisco Secure ACS Setup Welcome Window*

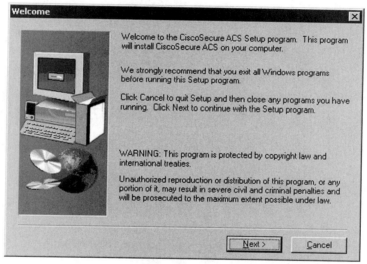

The second window, shown in Figure 17-4, prompts you to verify that your system is ready for this installation. Before this installation, you should verify that your Windows server is up to date, including Internet Explorer, and that you have connectivity with the NAS. In this case, the Security Appliance functions as the NAS.

You are prompted to specify the installation directory, as shown in Figure 17-5. You can use the default directory, C:\Program Files\CiscoSecure ACS v3.2, or select another directory for the installation.

Figure 17-4 *Preinstallation Window*

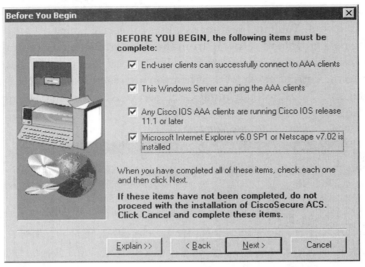

Figure 17-5 *Installation Directory (Default)*

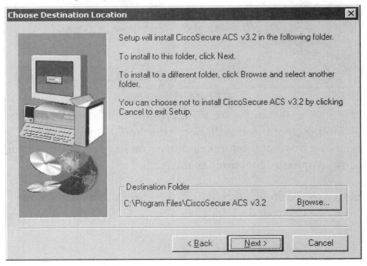

In the next window, shown in Figure 17-6, you select whether to authenticate against only the Cisco Secure ACS user database or the combination of the Cisco Secure ACS database and the Windows user database. The latter selection lets you use Windows username/password management and integrate Windows performance monitoring, which provides you with real-time login statistics.

For the purpose of this installation, the Cisco Secure ACS database only is used.

Figure 17-6   *User Database Window*

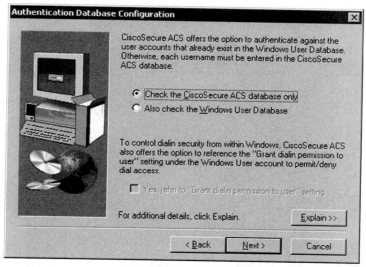

In the next window, shown in Figure 17-7, you are prompted to select any of ten possible choices for the connection type to the NAS. Remember that the Cisco Security Appliance is acting as the NAS. For this configuration, TACACS+ (Cisco IOS) is selected.

Figure 17-7   *NAS Technology (TACACS+ Selected)*

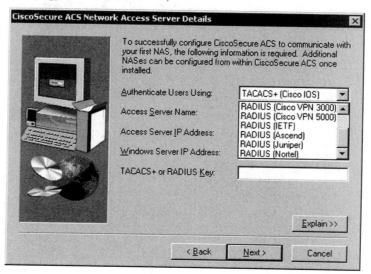

Next, you need to finish the NAS information to complete the connection between the AAA server and the NAS. Figure 17-8 shows the NAS Details window. Note the Explain button in the lower-right corner. Click this button to get an explanation of each of the settings, as shown in Figure 17-9.

Figure 17-8 *NAS Information (RADIUS Selected)*

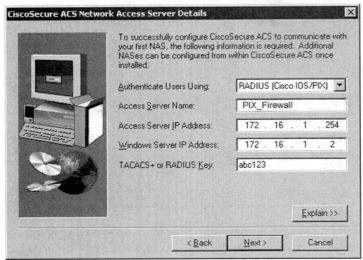

Figure 17-9 *Explanation of Settings*

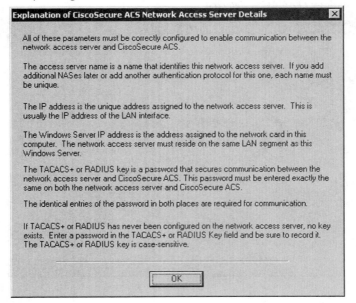

After you click **Next** in the NAS Details window, you are prompted to select the advanced features that you want to appear in the user interface, as shown in Figure 17-10. This allows you to determine how much (or how little) detail you want to see when working in the user interface. If you click the **Explain** button, you see the explanation window shown in Figure 17-11, which describes each of the available options. These settings can be configured during the initial configuration (installation), or you can skip this step and change the settings after Cisco Secure ACS is installed.

Figure 17-10 *Available Options in the User Interface*

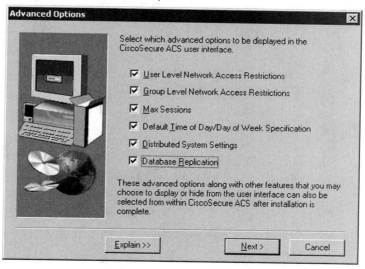

Figure 17-11 *Explanation of Advanced Options*

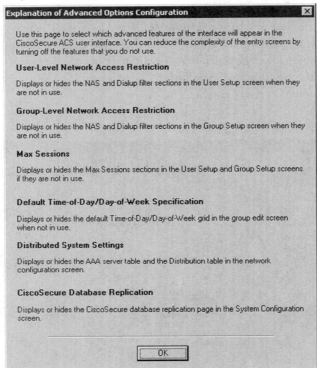

Next, you select from three actions (Restart All, Restart RADIUS/TACACS+, Reboot) for the AAA server to initiate if a communications failure occurs between the Cisco Secure ACS and the NAS. These settings also include SMTP settings and the user account for the Cisco Secure ACS to send an alert to if a failure occurs. Figures 17-12 and 17-13 show the settings window and the settings explanation window, respectively.

Figure 17-12 *Alert Action and Notification Settings*

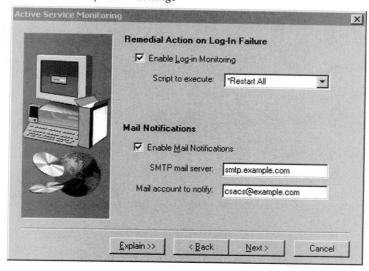

Figure 17-13 *Explanations for Alert Action and Notification Settings*

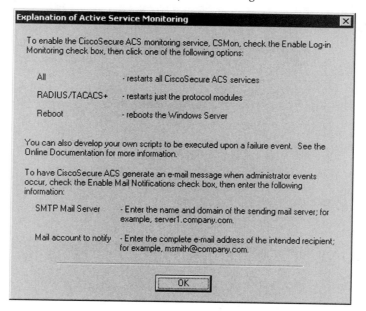

Cisco Secure ACS version 3.3 includes an optional NAS Configuration window, shown in Figure 17-14, to assist you with the initial configuration of the Cisco IOS Software. If you need further explanation, click the **Explain** button to review the window shown in Figure 17-15. This option works only when you are using a Cisco IOS router as your NAS. This option should not be selected when using the Security Appliance as the NAS.

Figure 17-14 *Cisco IOS Configuration Options*

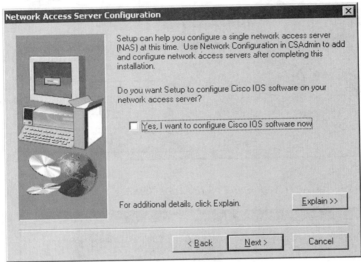

Figure 17-15 *Cisco IOS Configuration Explanation*

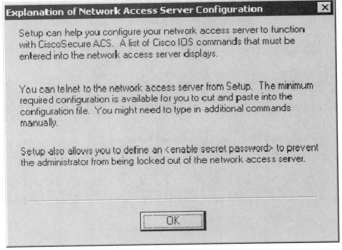

The installation/configuration of Cisco Secure ACS skips several steps if you do not elect to configure the Cisco IOS components. Figure 17-16 depicts the window that appears when the Cisco Secure ACS configuration is nearly complete. This window includes options for starting the Cisco Secure ACS Service, launching the Cisco Secure ACS Administrator from your browser, and viewing the Cisco Secure ACS Readme file.

Figure 17-16 *Cisco Secure ACS Startup Options*

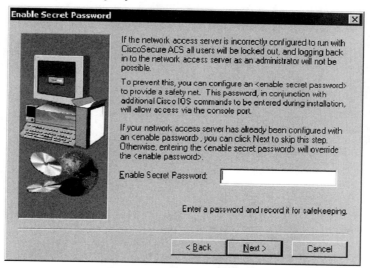

Cisco Secure ACS displays an activity bar as the Cisco Secure ACS Service is started (see Figure 17-17). Figure 17-18 shows the final configuration window that appears when the installation is complete.

Figure 17-17 *Service Start Flash Window*

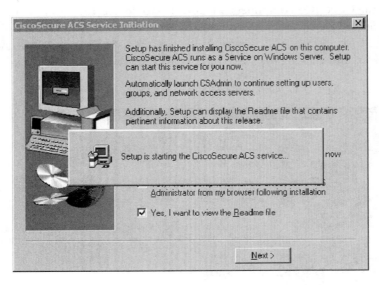

Figure 17-18 *Cisco Secure ACS Installation Complete*

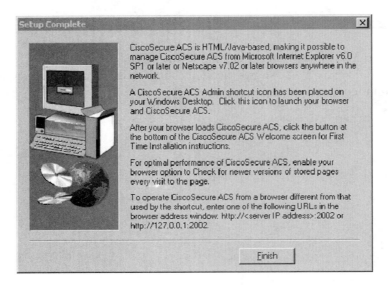

If you select the option to launch the Cisco Secure ACS administration browser window, the system launches a window that is similar to Figure 17-19.

Figure 17-19   *Cisco Secure ACS Administration Window*

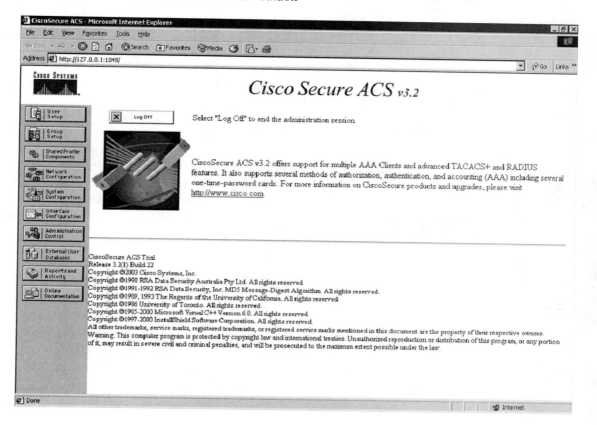

Congratulations! You have completed the installation of Cisco Secure ACS on a Windows server. Chapter 18, "Configuration of AAA on the Cisco Security Appliance," shows you how to configure Cisco Secure ACS.

Foundation Summary

The "Foundation Summary" provides a convenient review of many key concepts in this chapter. If you are already comfortable with the topics in this chapter, this summary can help you recall a few details. If you just read this chapter, this review should help solidify some key facts. If you are doing your final preparation before the exam, this summary provides a convenient way to review the day before the exam.

Authentication, authorization, and accounting are three separate functions performed by AAA servers to allow access to resources. Each of these functions has a specific goal. If you are using AAA, then authenticating the user is key. No access is granted if the requestor is not authenticated. The use of authorization and accounting are dependant on authentication, but it is not necessary to configure either authorization or accounting to make authentication function properly. This list defines each of the components of AAA:

- **Authentication**—Identifies the entity (user)
- **Authorization**—Gives the user access based on his or her profile
- **Accounting**—Maintains a record of user access

Cisco Security Appliance version 6.2 can maintain an internal user database for console authentication and command authorization or connect to an external AAA server. The Security Appliance supports RADIUS, TACACS+, SDI, NT, Kerberos, and LDAP authentication technologies. Figure 17-20 shows the steps that the AAA server takes during the entire AAA process.

Figure 17-20   *AAA Server Steps*

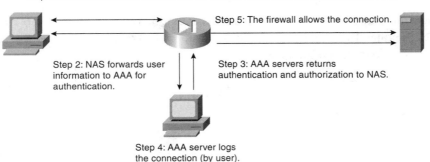

Step 1: User initiates connection to web server and is prompted for username/password.

Step 5: The firewall allows the connection.

Step 2: NAS forwards user information to AAA for authentication.

Step 3: AAA servers returns authentication and authorization to NAS.

Step 4: AAA server logs the connection (by user).

Cisco Secure ACS is available for Windows Server and can be configured for TACACS+ and RADIUS. The Cisco Secure ACS installation on Windows is an easy, step-by-step wizard installation.

Q&A

As mentioned in the Introduction, the questions in this book are more difficult than what you should experience on the exam. The questions are designed to ensure your understanding of the concepts discussed in this chapter and adequately prepare you to complete the exam. You should use the simulated exams on the CD to practice for the exam.

The answers to these questions can be found in Appendix A:

1. What is the relationship between the Cisco Security Appliance and the AAA server?

2. Name three methods that are used to authenticate to the Cisco Security Appliance.

3. How does the Cisco Security Appliance process cut-through proxy?

4. What are the main differences between RADIUS and TACACS+?

5. What patch level must you have Windows 2000 Professional configured to before you install Cisco Secure ACS?

6. Why is it important to authenticate a user before you complete authorization?

7. What are the three layers of authentication?

8. What is the purpose of the Explain button during the Cisco Secure ACS installation?

9. What do you need to verify before installing Cisco Secure ACS?

10. Why is it important to have Internet Explorer up to date on your Cisco Secure ACS?

11. True or false: With authorization configured, cut-through proxy authenticates users and then allows them to connect to anything.

12. True or false: The Cisco Secure ACS installation on Windows Server is a relatively simple, wizard-based installation.

This chapter covers the following subjects:

- Examining the Cisco Security Appliance Status

- Overview of AAA

- Installation of Cisco Secure ACS for Windows NT/2000

- Authentication Configuration

- Downloadable ACLs

C H A P T E R **18**

Configuration of AAA on the Cisco Security Appliance

This chapter addresses the commands necessary to configure authentication, authorization, and accounting (AAA) on the Cisco Security Appliance. As mentioned in the Introduction, remembering the Security Appliance commands is important. In the real world, it is possible to navigate your way around the Security Appliance and figure out the correct syntax for a command. This is not possible in the testing environment. You will be asked to select a command that performs a certain function from a list of very similar commands. It is *very* important that you understand the correct syntax for each Security Appliance command.

How to Best Use This Chapter

This chapter covers the communications between the Cisco Security Appliance and the Cisco Secure Access Control Server (ACS). You will learn how to configure the Security Appliance to work with an AAA server and how to configure the Cisco Secure ACS to work with the Security Appliance. The configurations for AAA are very similar and should be relatively simple to remember. Quite a few commands and options are available for configuring each AAA component, but each command and option is used for nearly every component. Cisco Secure ACS is a simple GUI package that includes online help. You need to become familiar with the tabs on the navigation bar and how the different configurations interact.

"Do I Know This Already?" Quiz

The purpose of the "Do I Know This Already?" quiz is to help you decide if you really need to read the entire chapter. If you already intend to read the entire chapter, you do not necessarily need to answer these questions now.

The 11-question quiz, derived from the major sections in the "Foundation Topics" portion of the chapter, helps you determine how to spend your limited study time.

Table 18-1 outlines the major topics discussed in this chapter and the "Do I Know This Already?" quiz questions that correspond to those topics.

Table 18-1 *"Do I Know This Already?" Foundation Topics Section-to-Question Mapping*

Foundations Topics Section	Questions Covered in This Section	Score
Examining the Security Appliance Status	1	
Overview of AAA	2	
Installation of Cisco Secure ACS for Windows NT/2000	4, 5, 7, 8	
Authentication Configuration	3, 9, 11	
Downloadable ACLs	6	

CAUTION   The goal of self assessment is to gauge your mastery of the topics in this chapter. If you do not know the answer to a question or are only partially sure of the answer, you should mark this question wrong for purposes of the self assessment. Giving yourself credit for an answer you correctly guess skews your self-assessment results and might provide you with a false sense of security.

1. What is the best way to authenticate an H.323 connection?

    a. Authenticate to the H.323 server

    b. Telnet to the H.323 server

    c. Virtual Telnet to the PIX Firewall for authentication

    d. Virtual HTTP to the Cisco Secure ACS for authentication

2. What three services are used to authenticate by default in the Cisco Security Appliance?

    a. FTP, HTTP, HTTPS

    b. FTP, Telnet, SSH

    c. Auth-proxy, Local-auth, console

    d. FTP, HTTPS, Telnet

    e. None of these answers are correct

3. Which options are mandatory in every **aaa authentication** command on the PIX Firewall? (Select all that apply.)

    a. include/exclude

    b. inbound/outbound

    c. local-ip/mask

    d. group-tag

    e. acl-name

4. How do you configure client IP address assignment on the Cisco Secure ACS when using the Security Appliance as the AAA client?

  a. Edit the AAA-client IP address in the System Configuration window.

  b. Edit the AAA-client information in the Network Configuration window.

  c. Edit the AAA Server information in the Interface Configuration window.

  d. Edit the Security Appliance information in the Network Configuration window.

  e. None of these answers are correct.

5. Why is it a good idea to rename your groups in Cisco Secure ACS?

  a. To get the groups into a hierarchical format.

  b. To increase the performance of the Cisco Secure ACS.

  c. To simplify administration of users and groups.

  d. You cannot rename groups after they have been created.

  e. None of these answers are correct.

6. You are trying to create downloadable IP ACLs in Cisco Secure ACS, but the option is not available. What are two possible reasons?

  a. You are running an older version of Cisco Secure ACS that does not support downloadable ACLs.

  b. The Security Appliance cannot connect to the Cisco Secure ACS.

  c. Your authentication protocol is not RADIUS.

  d. You do not have User-Level or Group-Level Downloadable ACLs selected in the Interface Configuration window, Advanced Options pane.

7. Where do you see the logs on the Cisco Secure ACS?

  a. Interface Configuration window

  b. Reports and Activity window

  c. Network Configuration window

  d. System Configuration window

8. You are installing Cisco Secure ACS on your new Windows 2000 Professional, but you cannot get it to load correctly. What is most likely the problem?

   a. Cisco Secure ACS requires server software.

   b. Your patch level is not up to date.

   c. You are running a personal firewall or host-based IDS that is blocking the installation.

   d. You do not have administrative privileges on that system.

   e. All of these answers are correct.

9. Cisco Secure ACS comes with its own online documentation.

   a. True

   b. False

10. The **show aaa** command shows you everything that has to do with your AAA server in its configuration.

    a. True

    b. False

11. What happens to virtual HTTP if you disable **timeout uauth absolute**?

    a. The user cannot authenticate.

    b. The user authenticates and never has to reauthenticate because the connection stays open.

    c. The user can authenticate but cannot connect to the server.

    d. None of these answers are correct.

The answers to the "Do I Know This Already?" quiz are found in Appendix A, "Answers to the 'Do I Know This Already?' Quizzes and Q&A Sections." The suggested choices for your next step are as follows:

■ **9 or less overall score**—Read the entire chapter. This includes the "Foundation Topics," "Foundation Summary," and "Q&A" sections.

■ **10 or 11 overall score**—If you want more review of these topics, skip to the "Foundation Summary" section and then go to the "Q&A" section. Otherwise, move to the next chapter.

Foundation Topics

Chapter 17, "Overview of AAA and the Cisco Security Appliance," provided a good overview of the AAA process and the Cisco Secure ACS for Windows 2000. This chapter addresses the configuration of the Cisco Security Appliance and the Cisco Secure ACS required to build an operational AAA solution. The Security Appliance must be configured to communicate with the Cisco Secure ACS, and the Cisco Secure ACS must be configured to control the Security Appliance. Although the Security Appliance configuration is completed using the command-line interface, the commands required are rather simple and fairly intuitive. The Cisco Secure ACS is completely web-based, with instructions on every page, and it is very simple to configure. After completing this chapter, you should be intimately familiar with the configurations of both the Security Appliance and the Cisco Secure ACS combined as a functional AAA solution.

Specifying Your AAA Servers

Only two components are required to build an AAA solution:

- AAA server

- Network access server (NAS)

It is possible to divide the AAA functions among multiple devices to reduce the processing required by any single server. It is also possible for a single AAA server to support multiple NASs. The point is that there is no single solution. The number of AAA servers and NASs should be tailored to support the size and scope of the network being accessed. Configuring the Security Appliance to connect to an AAA server requires only a few commands. Of course, quite a few options are available with each command. In this exercise, a Security Appliance, in this case a PIX Firewall, is configured to connect to a Cisco Secure ACS located on the DMZ segment. Figure 18-1 depicts the network configuration used for the examples in this chapter. Note that the Cisco Secure ACS is located on a DMZ segment rather than on the inside or outside segments. This allows you to restrict access to the Cisco Secure ACS from either segment, making the system more secure.

Figure 18-1 *Cisco PIX Firewall and Cisco Secure ACS Topology for Chapter*

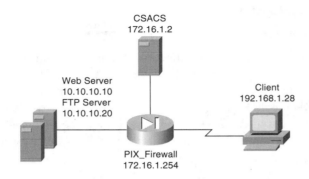

Configuring AAA on the Cisco Security Appliance

Four steps are required to configure AAA on the Security Appliance:

Step 1   Identify the AAA server and the NAS.

Step 2   Configure authentication.

Step 3   Configure authorization.

Step 4   Configure accounting.

Each of these steps can be completed for the Security Appliance to communicate with the AAA servers; however, it is possible to configure authentication without authorization or accounting. Each step is discussed in detail in the following sections.

Step 1: Identifying the AAA Server and NAS

You must be sure to have the correct information about your AAA server before you attempt to configure your Security Appliance. You use the **aaa-server** command (from configuration mode on the Security Appliance) to specify the AAA server. Remember that you are dealing with at least two devices: the Security Appliance and the Cisco Secure ACS.

You must configure the Security Appliance to recognize the Cisco Secure ACS as its AAA server for authentication. You also must configure the Cisco Secure ACS to communicate with the Security Appliance with the necessary account information so that the Cisco Secure ACS can validate authentication requests from the Security Appliance. To accomplish both tasks, you need to use the following commands:

```
aaa-server server-tag protocol auth-protocol
aaa-server server-tag [if-name] host server-ip key [timeout seconds]
```

You must define the following command options and parameters for the configuration to be successful:

- **aaa-server**—Designates the AAA server or server group. A group can have as many as 16 servers, and the PIX Firewall can handle up to 15 single-mode groups of AAA servers, for a total of 240 AAA servers. This enables you to tailor which AAA servers handle certain services and lets you configure your AAA servers for redundancy. When a user logs in, the NAS contacts the first server in the group (see the *group-tag* description). If it does not receive a response within the designated timeout period, it moves to the next server in the group.

- *server-tag*—The name used for the AAA server group. The *server-tag* is also used in the **aaa authentication, aaa authorization**, and **aaa accounting** commands.

- **protocol** *auth-protocol*—The type of AAA server used (kerberos, ldap, NT, SDI, TACACS+, or RADIUS).

- *if-name*—The interface name for the interface on which the AAA server resides. This designates how the firewall connects to the AAA server.

- **host** *server-ip*—The AAA server's IP address.

- *key*—A shared secret between the Cisco Secure ACS (server) and the Security Appliance (client). It is an alphanumeric password that can be as many as 127 characters.

- **timeout** *seconds*—How long the Security Appliance waits between transmission attempts to the AAA server. The Security Appliance makes four attempts to connect with the AAA server before trying to connect to the next AAA server in the group. The default timeout is 5 seconds; the maximum timeout is 30 seconds. Using the default timeout of 5 seconds, the Security Appliance attempts four transmissions, waiting 5 seconds between each attempt, for a total of 20 seconds.

For the network example in this chapter, you would enter the syntax shown in Example 18-1.

Example 18-1 *Identifying AAA Servers on the PIX Firewall*

```
PIXFirewall(config)# aaa-server TACACS+ protocol tacacs+
PIXFirewall(config)# aaa-server TACACS+ (DMZ) host 172.16.1.2 abc123 timeout 20
PIXFirewall(config-aaa-server)#
```

The **aaa-server** subcommand attributes will vary based upon the authentication protocol you assigned to the AAA server group. For smaller networks with a limited number of users, you can authenticate to a database configured locally on the Security Appliance. This is not a recommended configuration for medium-size to large networks because the processing required to maintain and authenticate against a local database reduces the firewall's performance. The AAA server group "local" is predefined for console authentication and command authorization. The command to configure authentication to a local database is **aaa-server local**.

> **NOTE** To remove the **AAA server** from the configuration, enter **no aaa-server**. This disables the AAA server function, but the configuration for that server remains on the Security Appliance.

You finish configuring the Cisco Secure ACS to connect to the Security Appliance by selecting the Security Appliance during the Cisco Secure ACS installation, as shown in Figure 17-2.

Figure 18-2 *Selecting the Network Access Server*

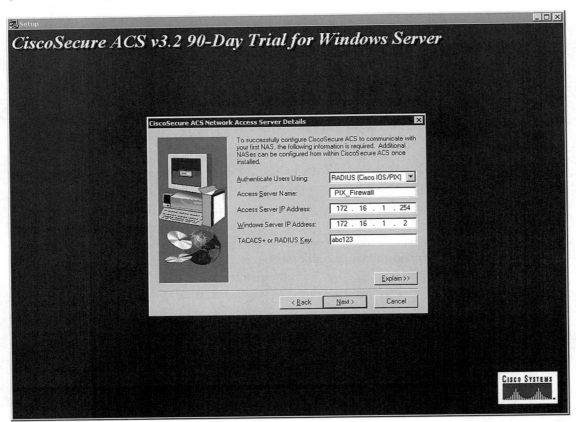

You also can create additional NASs or edit the current NAS settings in Cisco Secure ACS by clicking the **Network Configuration** button in the Cisco Secure ACS main window. Remember that the Cisco Secure ACS calls the NAS the "AAA client." Figure 18-3 shows the settings for the Security Appliance in the Cisco Secure ACS. Notice that the authentication protocol has been changed from RADIUS to TACACS+.

Figure 18-3 *Configuring NAS in Cisco Secure ACS*

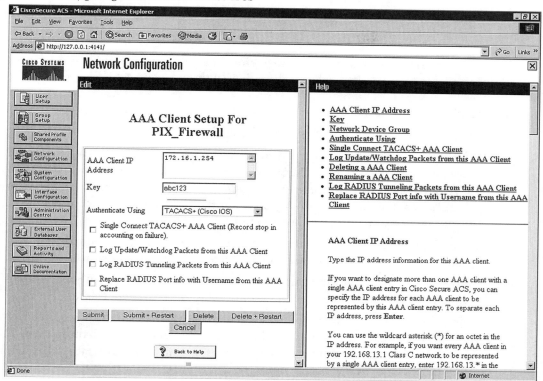

> **NOTE** The TACACS+ or RADIUS key specified on Cisco Secure ACS must exactly match the key specified in the **aaa-server** command for communication between the Cisco Secure ACS server and the NAS to be established.

Step 2: Configuring Authentication

Now that you have the AAA server and the NAS configured to communicate with each other, you need to configure both for user authentication. First, you need to configure the authentication parameters on the Security Appliance Cisco Secure ACS. Seven types of authentication are supported on the PIX Firewall:

- TACACS+
- RADIUS
- LDAP
- NT
- SDI
- Kerberos
- LOCAL

Both TACACS+, LDAP, and RADIUS support numerous vendor-specific attributes (VSAs) or attribute value (AV) pairs. For a list of the specific VSAs or AV pairs and their definitions, see the *User Guide for Cisco Secure ACS for Windows Version 3.3.*

The **aaa authentication** command has three different types. The following list describes the options and variables you find collectively within all three:

- **include**—Creates a rule with a specified service.
- **exclude**—Creates an exception to a previously defined rule.
- *authen-service*—The service that is included or excluded. It is the application with which the user accesses the network. The Security Appliance can authenticate only via FTP, HTTP, and Telnet. You can configure the *authen-service* as "any" to allow the Security Appliance to authenticate any of the three, but this does not allow your users to authenticate using any protocol other than FTP, HTTP, or Telnet.
- **inbound**—Specifies that the Security Appliance is to authenticate inbound traffic (originates on the outside interface and is directed to the inside interface).
- **outbound**—Specifies that the Security Appliance is to authenticate outbound traffic (originates on the inside interface and is directed to the outside interface).
- *if-name*—The interface name from which the users should be authenticated. This is optional. By default, the user must authenticate before being allowed through the PIX Firewall. Therefore, outbound traffic authenticates at the inside interface, and inbound traffic authenticates at the outside interface.
- *local-ip*—The host address or network segment with the highest security level. As with the other address definitions on the Security Appliance, 0 is used to define "any."
- *local-mask*—The subnet mask that applies to the *local-ip*; 0 is used to define "any."
- *foreign-ip*—Defines the address space with the lowest security level. The use of 0 defines "any."
- *foreign-mask*—The subnet mask that applies to the *foreign-ip*; 0 is used to define "any."
- *group-tag*—The name used for the AAA server group. The *group-tag* is also used in the **aaa-server, aaa authorization**, and **aaa accounting** commands.

The following sections describe the three different formats and functions of the **aaa authentication** command in greater detail.

Manually Designating AAA Authentication Parameters

The first command enables you to manually designate the authentication parameters using the items in the preceding list. The syntax for this command is as follows:

```
aaa authentication include | exclude authen-service inbound | outbound if-name local-ip
    local-mask foreign-ip foreign-mask group-tag
```

Example 18-2 shows the syntax for requiring all inbound traffic to authenticate except for traffic connecting from host 192.168.1.28 based on the network shown in Figure 18-1.

Example 18-2 *Configuring AAA Authentication on the PIX Firewall*

```
PIXFirewall(config)# aaa authentication include any outside 0 0 0 0 TACACS+
PIXFirewall(config)# aaa authentication exclude http outside 0 0 192.168.1.28
  255.255.255.255 TACACS+
```

The *local-ip* must be the actual IP address configured on a system without Network Address Translation (NAT). To configure this authentication, you must ensure that you have a static address translation or NAT configured for your *local-ip* but you must list the original IP address as the *local-ip*.

Designating AAA Authentication Parameters Via Access Lists

It is also possible to configure your AAA authentication to reference access lists using the **match** command. This configuration removes the requirement of manually defining the local and foreign addresses. The syntax for AAA authentication using access lists is as follows:

```
aaa authentication match acl-name if-name server-tag
```

Example 18-3 is an example of the **aaa authentication** command, including the referenced access list.

Example 18-3 *Configuring* aaa authentication match

```
PIXFirewall(config)# static (inside,outside) 192.168.200.1 10.10.10.10 netmask
  255.255.255.255
PIXFirewall(config)# access-list PIXTEST permit tcp any host  192.168.200.1 eq 80
PIXFirewall(config)# access-group PIXTEST in interface outside
PIXFirewall(config)# aaa authentication match PIXTEST outside TACACS+
```

The static translation and access group are also included in this example because each is required to have the correct public address and to apply the access list.

NOTE   Chapter 7, "Configuring Access," discusses access lists in greater detail.

One additional command you should use when configuring authentication is **sysopt uauth allow-http-cache**. This command allows the system to cache user authentication for HTTP requests, which relieves the user from having to reauthenticate when navigating the Internet when HTTP authentication is required. This could be a security concern in certain situations and, thus, you should carefully consider it before you add it to the PIX Firewall configuration.

Console Access Authentication

The final type of AAA authentication is for direct connections to the Cisco Security Appliance. It is very important to restrict access to the firewall as much as possible. One way to increase your firewall's security is to require all access to the firewall to be authenticated by an AAA server. Console access is traditionally password protected; however, the **aaa authentication console** command prompts the user to authenticate differently, depending on the method used to access the Security Appliance:

- **serial**—Causes the user to be prompted before the first command of the command-line prompt when connecting directly to the firewall via a serial cable. Users are continually prompted until they successfully log in.

- **telnet**—Causes the user to be prompted before the first command-line prompt when attempting a Telnet session to the CLI. Users are continually prompted until they successfully log in.

- **ssh**—Causes the user to be prompted before the first command-line prompt when attempting a Secure Shell (SSH) session to the CLI. If users are unable to successfully authenticate within three attempts, they are disconnected and receive the message "Rejected by Server."

- **http**—This option is selected when you use the Adaptive Security Device Manager (ASDM) to manage your Security Appliance. ASDM users see a pop-up window in their browser (PIX Device Manager). Users are continually prompted until they successfully log in.

- **enable**—With this option, the Security Appliance requires AAA server authentication to enter privileged mode. The **enable** option prompts the user for a username and password before entering privileged mode for serial, Telnet, and SSH connections. If users are unable to successfully authenticate after three attempts, they see the "Access Denied" message.

NOTE By default, the ASDM can access the Security Appliance with no username and the enable password unless the **aaa authentication http console** *group-tag* command is set.

The Security Appliance supports usernames that are up to 127 characters and passwords that are up to 63 characters. Usernames and passwords cannot contain the @ character. The PDM is limited to a maximum of 30 characters for the username and 15 characters for the password.

> **NOTE**   To remove the **aaa authentication** from the configuration, enter **no aaa authentication**.

Authentication of Services

The Cisco Security Appliance is designed to authenticate users via FTP, HTTP, HTTPS, and Telnet. Many other services that pass through the Security Appliance require authentication. To fulfill this requirement, the Security Appliance supports *virtual services*. The Security Appliance can perform functions for servers that do not exist and configures the Security Appliance to authenticate users who want to connect to services other than FTP, HTTP, HTTPS, and Telnet. After a user has been authenticated, that user can access whatever authorized services they are requesting.

If your company uses Microsoft NetMeeting to communicate among its many different branch offices, NetMeeting runs on the H.323 protocol, which uses a number of different ports. To allow this access, users must authenticate via FTP, HTTP, or Telnet. If you do not have a server available to accept the FTP, HTTP, or Telnet connections, you can configure the Security Appliance to accept the connections via a virtual service.

Virtual Telnet

Virtual Telnet enables the user to authenticate using Telnet and use a service that does not support authentication. The Security Appliance accepts the user's connection and challenges the user for a username and password. The username and password are verified by the TACACS+ or RADIUS server. If the user successfully authenticates, the connection to the user's requested service is completed. An additional server is not required to accept the connection, because the Security Appliance creates a virtual server to handle the authentication requests. Virtual Telnet sessions can be inbound or outbound on the Security Appliance.

To configure virtual Telnet on the Security Appliance, you must first create the virtual server on a segment that can be reached via the Security Appliance. Normally, this is an address on the firewall's outside interface. In Figure 18-4, the virtual IP address is 192.168.1.4. This public IP address can be accessed from both inside networks and public networks (such as the Internet). The syntax of the **virtual telnet** command is as follows:

```
virtual telnet ip-address
```

Figure 18-4   *Assigning the IP Address for Virtual Services for Outbound Traffic*

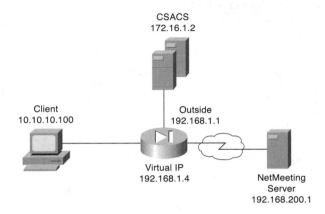

Example 18-4 shows the virtual Telnet configuration that authenticates host 10.10.10.100 when you make an outbound connection to a NetMeeting server located on the Internet.

Example 18-4   *Configuring Virtual Telnet Outbound Connections*

```
PIXFirewall(config)# ip address outside 192.168.1.1 255.255.255.0
PIXFirewall(config)# ip address inside 10.10.10.1 255.255.255.0
PIXFirewall(config)# global (outside) 1 192.168.1.20-192.168.1.40 netmask
  255.255.255.0
PIXFirewall(config)# nat (inside) 1 0 0 0 0
PIXFirewall(config)# aaa-server TACACS+ protocol tacacs+
PIXFirewall(config)# aaa-server TACACS+ (DMZ) host 172.16.1.2 abc123 timeout 20
PIXFirewall(config)# aaa authentication include any inside 0 0 0 0 TACACS+
PIXFirewall(config)# virtual telnet 192.168.1.4
```

Now let us change the positions of the client and server. This time, the NetMeeting server is behind the Security Appliance, and the client is on the Internet. Figure 18-5 depicts the configuration with the NetMeeting server on the internal network and the client on the Internet.

Figure 18-5   *Assigning the IP address for Virtual Services for Inbound Traffic*

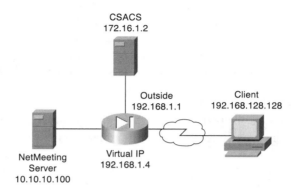

The Security Appliance configuration must change to allow the inbound traffic to connect to the NetMeeting server. First, the NetMeeting server needs to have a public IP address, which means that you need to perform static translation. Second, you need to configure the access lists to allow the inbound traffic. Example 18-5 shows the configuration required to allow inbound connections to a destination on the protected network.

Example 18-5   *Configuring Virtual Telnet Inbound Connections*

```
PIXFirewall(config)# ip address outside 192.168.1.1 255.255.255.0
PIXFirewall(config)# ip address inside 10.10.10.1 255.255.255.0
PIXFirewall(config)# global (outside) 1 192.168.1.20-192.168.1.40 netmask 255.255.255.0
PIXFirewall(config)# nat (inside) 1 0 0 0 0
PIXFirewall(config)# aaa-server TACACS+ protocol tacacs+
PIXFirewall(config)# aaa-server TACACS+ (DMZ) host 172.16.1.2 abc123 timeout 20
PIXFirewall(config)# aaa authentication include any outside 0 0 0 0 TACACS+
PIXFirewall(config)# virtual telnet 192.168.1.4
PIXFirewall(config)# static (inside, outside) 192.168.1.4 10.10.10.100 netmask
  255.255.255.255 0 0
PIXFirewall(config)# access-list NetMeeting permit tcp any host 192.168.1.4 eq 23
PIXFirewall(config)# access-list NetMeeting permit tcp 192.168.128.128
  255.255.255.255 192.168.1.4 255.255.255.255 eq H323
PIXFirewall(config)# access-group NetMeeting in interface outside
```

NOTE   To remove the virtual Telnet from the configuration, enter **no virtual telnet**.

Virtual HTTP

Virtual HTTP functions similarly to virtual Telnet in that the PIX Firewall acts as the HTTP server via an additional IP address assigned to the firewall. Users might believe that they are accessing the web server, but they are actually accessing the virtual server for the authentication prompt, being authenticated by an AAA server, and being redirected to their destination after successful authentication. The syntax for **virtual http** is

```
virtual http ip-address [warn]
```

The *warn* option is used for text-based browsers that cannot automatically be redirected. The option adds a link that would be used to redirect to the virtual HTTP server.

Normally, the *ip-address* should be an address that the inside network routes to the Security Appliance. This way, the internal users access it directly, and the external users connect to it via static address translation at the firewall. Of course, the inbound users require authentication and also must be permitted by an access list or conduit. Example 18-6 depicts the configuration for virtual HTTP on the Security Appliance. This is the configuration shown in Figure 18-5.

Example 18-6 *Configuring Virtual HTTP Inbound Connections*

```
PIXFirewall(config)# ip address outside 192.168.1.1 255.255.255.0
PIXFirewall(config)# ip address inside 10.10.10.1 255.255.255.0
PIXFirewall(config)# global (outside) 1 192.168.1.20-192.168.1.40 netmask 255.255.255.0
PIXFirewall(config)# nat (inside) 1 0 0 0 0
PIXFirewall(config)# aaa-server TACACS+ protocol tacacs+
PIXFirewall(config)# aaa-server TACACS+ (DMZ) host 172.16.1.2 abc123 timeout 20
PIXFirewall(config)# static (inside, outside) 192.168.1.5 10.10.10.5 netmask
  255.255.255.255 0 0
PIXFirewall(config)# aaa authentication include any outside 192.168.1.5 255.255.255.255
  0 0 TACACS+
PIXFirewall(config)# access-list WebTest permit tcp any host 192.168.1.5 eq www
PIXFirewall(config)# access-group WebTest in interface outside
PIXFirewall(config)# virtual http 192.168.1.5
```

> **NOTE** To remove the virtual HTTP from the configuration, enter **no virtual http**.

Authentication Prompts

The **auth-prompt** command is used to configure the exact text used when the user is challenged to authenticate, successfully authenticates, or does not authenticate. This command sets the text for FTP, HTTP, and Telnet session authentication. The syntax of this command is

```
auth-prompt [prompt | accept | reject] string
```

The *string* is the text that is displayed. It can be up to 235 characters in length for FTP and Telnet connections. It is limited to 120 characters for HTTP connections using Netscape Navigator, and it is limited to 37 characters for HTTP connections using Microsoft Internet Explorer. The *string* should not include any special characters. It ends either by typing a question mark (?) or by pressing the **Enter** key.

The **auth-prompt** command has three options:

- **prompt**—Configures the text that is displayed when the user is prompted to authenticate: "Access to this location is restricted, please provide username and password."

- **accept**—Configures the text that is displayed if the user successfully authenticates using a Telnet session: "User Authentication complete, please continue." No text is displayed for authentication using FTP or HTTP.

- **reject**—Configures the text that is displayed if the user is unable to successfully authenticate using a Telnet session: "Authentication unsuccessful; if you feel that you have received this message in error, please contact your systems administrator." The text for FTP and HTTP authentication sessions cannot be configured on the Security Appliance.

Authentication Timeout

After a user is successfully authenticated, their user information is saved in cache for a predetermined amount of time. You set this time by configuring the **timeout uauth** command. It is specified in hours, minutes, and seconds. If the user session idle time exceeds the timeout, the session is terminated and the user is prompted to authenticate during the next connection. To disable caching of users, use the **timeout uauth 0** command. Be sure not to use **timeout uauth 0** when using **virtual http**. This setting prevents any connections to the real web server after successful authentication at the Security Appliance.

> **NOTE**   If the firewall is performing NAT, the **timeout uauth** value must be less than the **timeout xlate** value to ensure that the user authentication times out before the address translation.

Two command options or settings are associated with the **timeout uauth** command:

- **absolute**—The default setting for the **uauth** timer. This setting sets the timer to prompt the user to reauthenticate after the timer elapses only when the user starts a new connection. If the user leaves the session open and the timer elapses, and the user closes the browser without clicking another link, the user is not prompted to reauthenticate. Setting the **uauth** timer to 0 disables caching of user authentication and therefore disables the **absolute** option.

- inactivity—The inactivity timer starts after the connection becomes idle. If the user establishes a new connection before the duration of the inactivity timer, the user is not required to reauthenticate. If a user establishes a new connection after the inactivity timer expires, the user must reauthenticate.

Example 18-7 depicts the **timeout** command with the **absolute** and **inactivity** settings. The first command sets the timer to 4 hours and tells the system not to prompt the user after the session times out unless the user initiates another session. The second command defines a 30-minute period of inactivity as an idle session and tells the system to start the timer at that point.

Example 18-7 *Configuring Timeout on the PIX Firewall*

```
PIXFirewall(config)# timeout uauth 4:00:00 absolute
PIXFirewall(config)# timeout uauth 0:30:00 inactivity
```

The final command associated with timeouts is **clear uauth**. This command forces the system to delete the authorization cache for all users. This makes the system reauthenticate every user when they initiate their next connection.

Step 3: Configuring Authorization

When discussing authorization, you should first understand the difference between authentication and authorization:

- Authentication identifies who the user is.

- Authorization determines what the user can do.

- Authentication can be implemented without authorization.

- Authorization cannot be used unless the user has successfully authenticated.

Authorization is not a requirement but rather a method of allowing you to become more granular in what access you give specific users. After users have successfully authenticated, they can be given the access they have requested. This access is configured using the **aaa authorization** command, the syntax for which is very similar to the **aaa authentication** command, except for the service. The Security Appliance does not permit or deny any traffic based solely on the **aaa authorization** commands. This configuration merely tells the firewall which services it needs to reference the AAA server for authorization before allowing or denying the connection. A TACACS+ server performs AAA authorization. The server is configured using the following syntax:

```
aaa authorization include | exclude svc if-name local-ip
    local-mask foreign-ip foreign-mask
```

tacacs-server-tag specifies the TACACS+ server to be used for authorization.

author-service is the service defined for **aaa authorization**. The *author-service* parameter defines any service that requires authorization by listing them as **include** or **exclude** and the interface that the traffic is passing through. Services not listed are implicitly authorized. *author-service* can be **any, ftp, http, telnet,** or *protocol/port*. Authorization of services is configured using the following syntax:

```
aaa authorization include | exclude service if-name local-ip
    local-mask foreign-ip foreign-mask
```

Example 18-8 shows the commands used to authorize outbound DNS requests and all inbound services except HTTP requests from 192.168.1.28 to any destination.

Example 18-8   *Configuring Authorization on the PIX Firewall*

```
PIXFirewall(config)# aaa authorization include any outside 0 0 0 0 TACACS+
PIXFirewall(config)# aaa authorization exclude http outside 0 0 192.168.1.28
  255.255.255.255 TACACS+
PIXFirewall(config)# aaa authorization include udp/53 inside 0 0 0 0 TACACS+
```

> **NOTE**   To remove the AAA authorization from the configuration, enter **no aaa authorization.**

Cisco Secure ACS and Authorization

After the Cisco Security Appliances is configured correctly, you must configure authorization on your Cisco Secure ACS. If your Cisco Secure ACS is already configured with the Security Appliances as the NAS, a few steps remain to configure authorization:

Step 1   Configure user accounts within the Cisco Secure ACS.

Step 2   Assign users to a group.

Step 3   Apply authorization rules to the group.

Steps 1 and 2: Configuring User Accounts Within the Cisco Secure ACS and Assigning Users to a Group

To configure new users in Cisco Secure ACS, click the **User Setup** button on the left navigation bar. When the User Setup window appears, shown in Figure 18-6, enter the username in the User box and then click **Add/Edit.**

Figure 18-6 *Creating User Accounts on the Cisco Secure ACS*

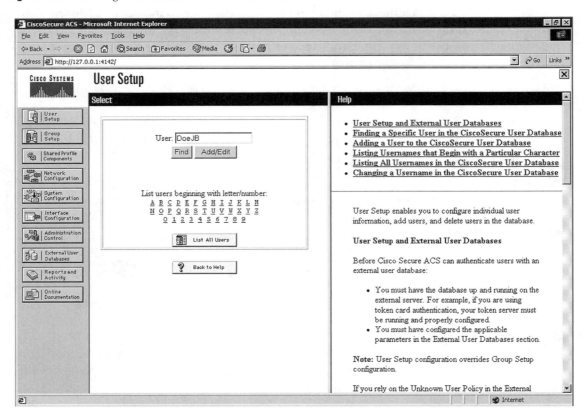

In the Edit pane of the User Setup window, shown in Figure 18-7, you can configure many options pertaining to the user account as described in the following list.

Figure 18-7 *Configuring User Accounts on the Cisco Secure ACS*

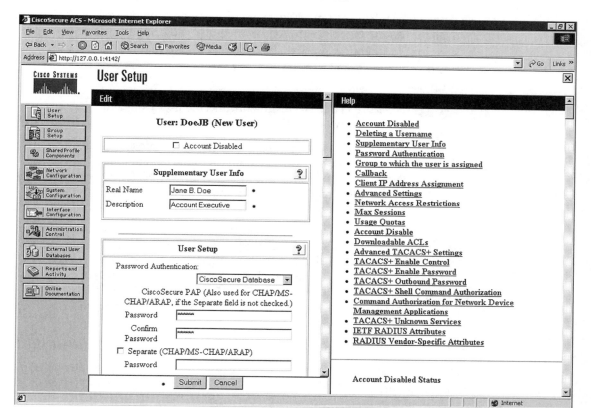

- **Account Disabled**—Checking this box lets you create accounts for users who are not yet ready to begin using the system. For example, suppose you are told that the company has hired a new employee who is scheduled to begin working in three weeks. You can configure the user account and then turn it on by deselecting the check box when the new employee starts work.

- **Supplementary User Info**—An optional field for entering user information. It is a very good idea to complete these fields because they help you keep track of your user accounts as your user base grows:

  — **Real Name**—The user's name, not the user account name.

  — **Description**—A description of the user. Normally, this field describes the user's position within the company.

■ **User Setup**—Select the type of authentication database, and enter the user password:

— **Password Authentication**—Two types of password authentication are available on the Cisco Secure ACS by default. You can add a number of additional authentication types by clicking the **External User Databases** button on the left navigation bar. Select the authentication type from the drop-down menu:

CiscoSecure Database—Authenticates the user from a database installed locally on the Cisco Secure ACS.

Windows NT/2000—Authenticates the user against a Windows NT/2000 Server that is located on the same system that is running the Cisco Secure ACS or any Windows NT/2000 system that has a trust relationship with the domain that the Cisco Secure ACS is part of.

External User Database—You can add multiple configurations for each of the following authentication services: Vasco Token Server, RSA SecurID Token Server, RADIUS Token Server, External ODBC Database, Windows NT/2000, Novell NDS, Leap Proxy RADIUS Server, Generis LDAP, SafeWord Token Server, CryptoCard Token Server, AXENT Token Server, and ActivCard Token Server.

— **Password and Confirm Password**—Enter and confirm the user's password.

— **Separate (CHAP/MS-CHAP/ARAP) Password**—This feature is not used on the Security Appliance.

— **Group**—Select a user group from the drop-down box. All users are assigned to the default group unless they are specifically assigned to another group. Grouping the users and applying rules to groups enables you to efficiently administer the authentication services.

— **Callback**—This feature is not used on the Security Appliance.

— **Client IP Address Assignment**—This feature is not used on the Security Appliance.

■ **Network Access Restrictions**—Defines per-user network access restrictions.

- Max Sessions—Contains three radio buttons that define the maximum number of concurrent sessions the user can have:

    — Unlimited—The user can maintain an unlimited number of concurrent sessions through the firewall.

    — Fill in the Box—Defines the maximum number of concurrent sessions.

    — Use Group Settings—The default setting. The maximum number is defined at the group level.

- Account Disable—Configures the parameters for disabling a user account based on the date or a number of failed logon attempts. Do not confuse this option with the Account Disabled option at the top of the User Setup window:

    — Never—The default setting. It allows the user unlimited attempts to log on.

    — Disable Account If:

        Date Exceeds—Select the date from the drop-down boxes. The default setting is 30 days after the account is created.

        Failed Attempts Exceed—Add the number of allowed failed attempts to the box.

        An indicator shows the number of failed attempts since the last successful logon.

        There is a check box for you to reset the failed attempts count. If this box is checked, the reset will occur when you click the **Submit** button.

Step 3: Applying Authorization Rules to the Group

Now that you have created the user account and assigned the user to a group, it is time to apply authorization rules to the group. Click the **Group Setup** button on the navigation bar on the left.

Figure 18-8 shows the available selections in the initial Group Setup window.

Figure 18-8   *Configuring a Group Setup on the Cisco Secure ACS*

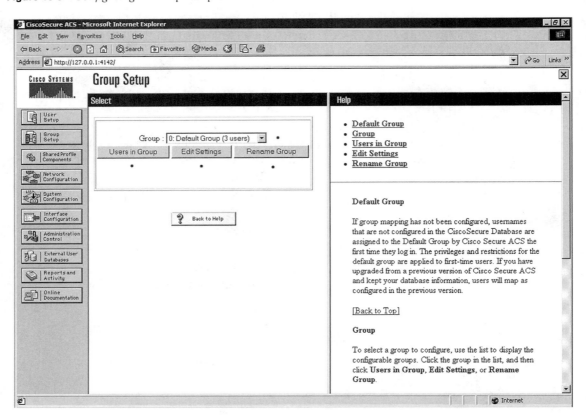

You can select the group from the drop-down box and select any of the following three options for that group:

■ **Users in Group**—Replaces the Help pane on the right side of the window with a list of the users assigned to the selected group, as shown in Figure 18-9. Each username is a link to that user's configuration in the User Setup window.

■ **Edit Settings**—Allows you to edit the specific settings for the selected group. This is where the authorization rules are applied to the group.

■ **Rename Group**—Enables you to rename groups to simplify administration. You can add users to groups based on like positions or job functions (such as marketing, sales, infrastructure, and security).

Figure 18-9 *Users in Group*

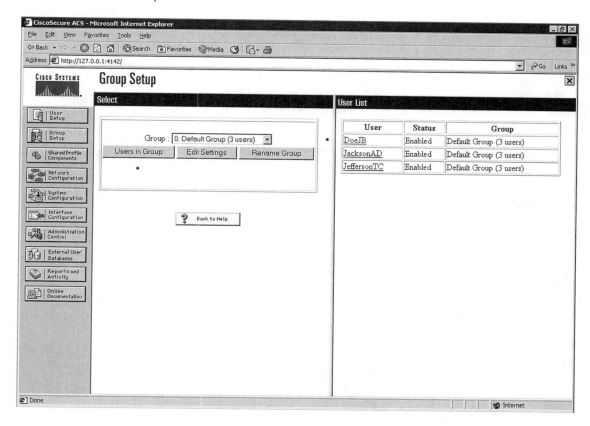

You configure commands by editing the settings for a specific group. Select **Group Setup** from the navigation bar, click **Edit Settings**, and scroll down to the Shell Command Authorization Set. You see radio buttons and a Command box that is a subset of the Command Authorization Set, as shown in Figure 18-10.

To configure shell command authorization for AAA clients using TACACS+, set the options in this section as applicable:

■ **None**—If you do not want to apply TACACS+ shell command authorization for users who belong to this group, select this option (selected in Figure 18-10).

■ **Assign a Shell Command Authorization Set for Any Network Device**—To apply a shell command authorization set to all TACACS+ AAA clients, select this option and then select the set you want from the corresponding list.

Figure 18-10   *Command Authorization Sets*

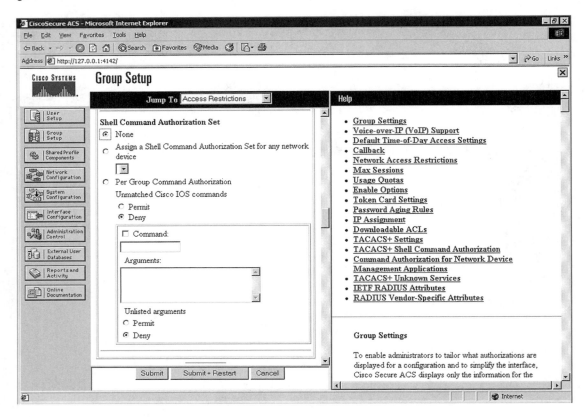

- **Assign a Shell Command Authorization Set on a Per Network Device Group Basis**—In ACS version 3.1 and later, to apply a shell command authorization set to the TACACS+ AAA clients who belong to a particular Network Device Group (NDG), select this option, and then use the following options:

    — **Device Group**—From the list, select the NDG to which you want to assign a shell command authorization set.

    — **Command Set**—From the list, select the shell command authorization set you want to apply to the NDG.

    — **Add Association**—Click to add the NDG and command set selected to the Device Group/Command Set list.

    — **Remove Association**—To remove an NDG/command set association, select the NDG/command set association you want to remove from the Device Group/Privilege list, and then click **Remove Association**.

Shell command authorization sets are created and configured in the Shared Profile Components window.

■ **Per Group Command Authorization**—To set TACACS+ shell command authorization on a command-by-command basis, select this option, and then use the following options:

— **Unmatched Cisco IOS Commands**—To determine how Cisco Secure ACS handles commands that you do not specify in this section, select either Permit or Deny as applicable.

— **Command**—Select this check box, and then enter the command in the corresponding box. The command can be listed by name for well-known commands such as **telnet**, **ftp**, or **http**; otherwise, the command should be listed by protocol/port number (i.e., tcp/23).

— **Arguments**—In this case, the term "argument" refers to the target address. This box lists to which target host you should allow (or deny) access via the previously listed command. These should be entered in the format **permit** *argument* or **deny** *argument*. This allows you to specify which commands are permitted or denied.

— **Unlisted Arguments**—To permit only the arguments listed, select **Deny**. To allow users to issue all arguments not specifically listed, select **Permit**. This setting allows you to permit or deny all commands and arguments not listed previously.

Figure 18-11 shows the configuration that would allow Telnet access to hosts at 172.16.1.5 and 172.16.1.7.

Figure 18-11 *Configuring Per User Command Authorization*

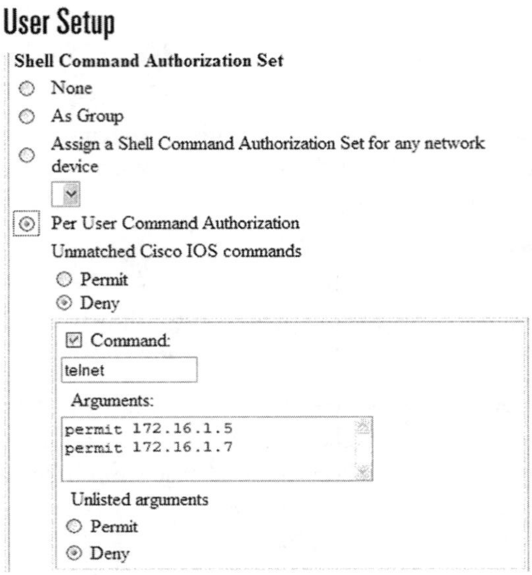

This excerpt of a PIX Firewall configuration corresponds the Figure 18-11:

```
nameif ethernet0 outside security0
nameif ethernet1 inside security100
nameif ethernet2 dmz1 security50

ip address inside 192.168.1.231 255.255.255.0
ip address dmz1 10.10.1.1 255.255.255.0

access-list from-inside-to-dmz permit tcp 192.168.1.0 255.255.255.0 host 10.10.1.3 eq
5631
access-list from-inside-to-dmz permit udp 192.168.1.0 255.255.255.0 host 10.10.1.3 eq
5632
access-list from-inside-to-dmz permit tcp 192.168.1.0 255.255.255.0 host 10.10.1.5 eq
telnet
access-list from-inside-to-dmz deny ip any host 10.10.1.3

access-list 121 permit tcp any host 10.10.1.3
access-list 121 permit udp any host 10.10.1.3
access-list 121 permit tcp any host 10.10.1.5 eq telnet

access-list 101 permit ip 192.168.1.0 255.255.255.0 host 10.10.1.3

nat (inside) 0 access-list 101

static (inside,dmz1) 192.168.1.1 192.168.1.1 netmask 255.255.255.255 0 0

access-group from-inside-to-dmz in interface inside
```

```
aaa-server AuthOutbound protocol tacacs+
aaa-server AuthOutbound (inside) host 192.168.1.4 xxxxxxxx timeout 10

aaa authentication match 121 inside AuthOutbound
aaa authorization match 121 inside AuthOutbound

virtual telnet 10.10.1.5
```

This Security Appliance will not allow any connections from its inside hosts (192.168.1.0) to host 10.10.1.3 on DMZ1 except PCAnywhere (TCP/5631 and UDP/5632) application. But to allow this connection, it asks authentication as well as authorization using a Cisco Secure ACS. A user on the 192.168.1.1 host would telnet to virtual telnet address at 10.10.1.5, authenticate, and afterwards will run his PCAnywhere application with the target host as 10.10.1.3. The Cisco Secure ACS will authorize this user if in its database for this user has the following, shown in Figure 18-12.

Figure 18-12   *Configuring Shell Command Authorization Sets*

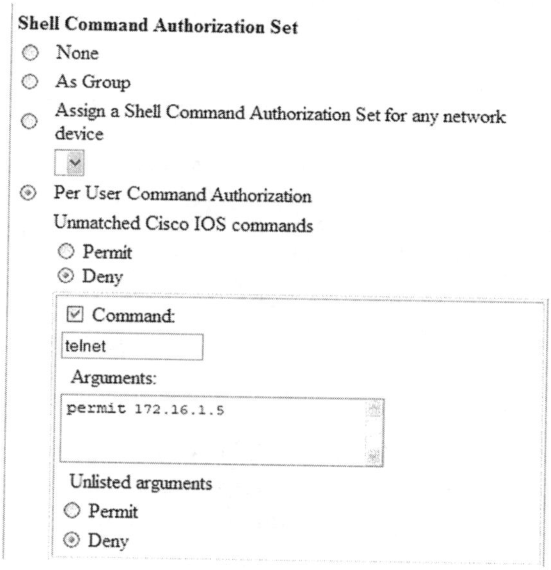

Refer to the network map in Figure 18-13 for the following exercise. The configuration of the Security Appliance and the Cisco Secure ACS controls access to the host 172.16.1.3.

In the Security Appliance configuration in Example 17-9, hosts on the internal network are not allowed to make connections to 172.16.1.3 on the DMZ segment except for the PCAnywhere (TCP/5631 and UDP/5632) application. But to allow this connection, the Firewall will ask authentication as well as authorization using a Cisco Secure ACS.

Example 18-9   *Configuring AAA Authorization on the PIX Firewall*

```
nameif ethernet0 outside security0
nameif ethernet1 inside security100
nameif ethernet2 dmz1 security50
ip address outside 192.168.0.1 255.255.255.0
ip address inside 10.10.10.254 255.255.255.0
ip address dmz1 172.16.1.254 255.255.255.0
access-list from-inside-to-dmz permit tcp 10.10.10.0 255.255.255.0 host 172.16.1.3 eq 5631
access-list from-inside-to-dmz permit udp 10.10.10.0 255.255.255.0 host 172.16.1.3 eq 5632
access-list from-inside-to-dmz permit tcp 10.10.10.0 255.255.255.0 host 172.16.1.5 eq telnet
access-list from-inside-to-dmz deny ip any host 172.16.1.3
access-list 121 permit tcp any host 172.16.1.3
access-list 121 permit udp any host 172.16.1.3
access-list 121 permit tcp any host 172.16.1.5 eq telnet
access-list 101 permit ip 10.10.10.0 255.255.255.0 host 172.16.1.3
nat (inside) 0 access-list 101
static (inside,dmz1) 10.10.10.1 10.10.10.1 netmask 255.255.255.255 0 0
access-group from-inside-to-dmz in interface inside
aaa-server AuthOutbound protocol tacacs+
aaa-server AuthOutbound (inside) host 10.10.10.4 xxxxxxxx timeout 10
aaa authentication match 121 inside AuthOutbound
aaa authorization match 121 inside AuthOutbound
virtual telnet 172.16.1.5
```

A user on the 10.10.10.1 host would telnet to virtual telnet address at 172.16.1.5, authenticate, and afterwards will run his PCAnywhere application with the target host as 172.16.1.3. The Cisco Secure ACS authorizes this user if in its database for this user the Command Authorization configuration of the Cisco Secure ACS is similar to Figure 18-13.

Figure 18-13 *Configuring Shell Commands*

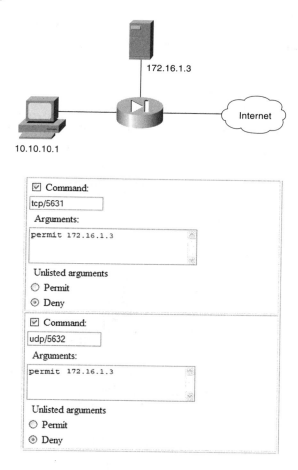

Step 4: Configuring Accounting

You have successfully configured both your Cisco Security Appliance and your Cisco Secure ACS for authentication and authorization. The final portion is to configure accounting. Accounting is used to track specific traffic passing through the firewall. It also ensures that users are performing functions in keeping with company policies. Log data is commonly stored and can be used to investigate employees who are using their Internet connections for activities not authorized by the employer. The general syntax for the command that accomplishes accounting is as follows:

```
aaa accounting include | exclude acctg-service | if-name local-ip
    local-mask foreign-ip foreign-mask server tag
```

The following items are defined within the **aaa accounting** command:

- **include**—Creates a rule with a specified service.

- **exclude**—Creates an exception to a previously defined rule.

- *acctg-service*—The service that is included or excluded. It is the service that the user is requesting access to via the network. You can configure *acctg-service* as **any, ftp, http, telnet,** or *protocol/port*. When you configure *protocol/port*, the *protocol* is listed as a number:

  — **ICMP**—1

  — **TCP**—6

  — **UDP**—17

- *if-name*—The interface name from which the users should be authenticated and accounting should be performed.

- *local-ip*—The host address or network segment with the highest security level. As with the other address definitions on the Security Appliance, 0 is used to define "any."

- *local-mask*—The subnet mask that applies to the *local-ip*; 0 is used to define "any."

- *foreign-ip*—Defines the address space with the lowest security level. The use of 0 defines "any."

- *foreign-mask*—The subnet mask that applies to the *foreign-ip*; 0 is used to define "any."

- *server-tag*—The name used for the AAA server group. The *server-tag* is also used in the **aaa-server, aaa authorization,** and **aaa accounting** commands.

Example 18-10 shows how to configure AAA accounting on the PIX Firewall.

Example 18-10 *Configuring AAA Accounting on the PIX Firewall*

```
PIXFirewall(config)# aaa accounting include any inbound 0 0 0 0 TACACS+
PIXFirewall(config)# aaa accounting include any outbound 0 0 0 0 TACACS+
```

As with authentication and authorization, it is possible to configure the Security Appliance to match an access list, as demonstrated in Example 18-11.

Example 18-11 *Configuring AAA Accounting to Match an ACL*

```
PIXFirewall(config)# access-list PIXTEST permit tcp any host 65.197.254.5 eq 80
PIXFirewall(config)# access-group PIXTEST in interface outside
PIXFirewall(config)# aaa accounting match PIXTEST inbound TACACS+
```

> **NOTE** To remove AAA accounting from the configuration, enter **no aaa accounting**.

Viewing Accounting Information in Cisco Secure

Now that the Cisco Security Appliance is configured to perform accounting, you need to ensure that the Cisco Secure ACS is properly configured to log the events. Select **System Configuration** in the navigation panel to open the System Configuration window, shown in Figure 18-14; then, click the **Logging** link in the Select pane, and check off the log format and the items you want to log (see Figure 18-15). Logs can be saved in a CSV (flat file) or ODBC (database) format.

Figure 18-14 *Cisco Secure ACS System Configuration Window*

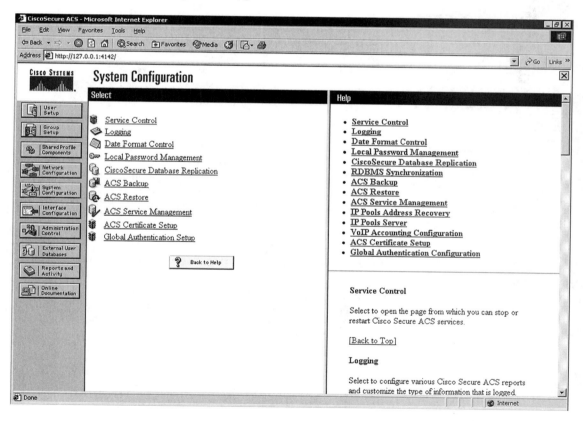

Figure 18-15 *Cisco Secure ACS Logging Targets and Options*

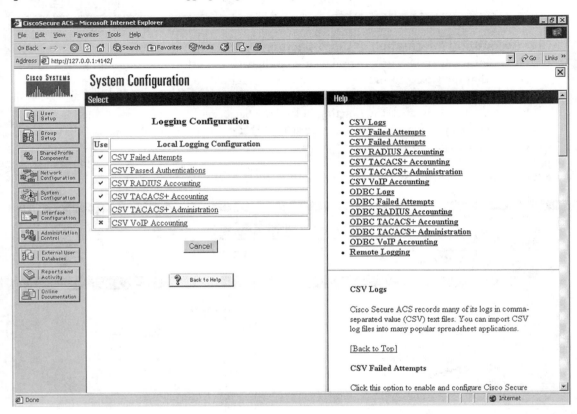

You can view several reports from the Cisco Secure ACS browser interface. Select **Reports and Activity** from the navigation bar to open the Reports and Activity window, shown in Figure 18-16. Then, choose the report you want by clicking the applicable button in the Reports list. Reports are available for TACACS+ and/or RADIUS only if an AAA client has been configured to use that protocol.

Figure 18-16   *Cisco Secure ACS Reports and Activity Window*

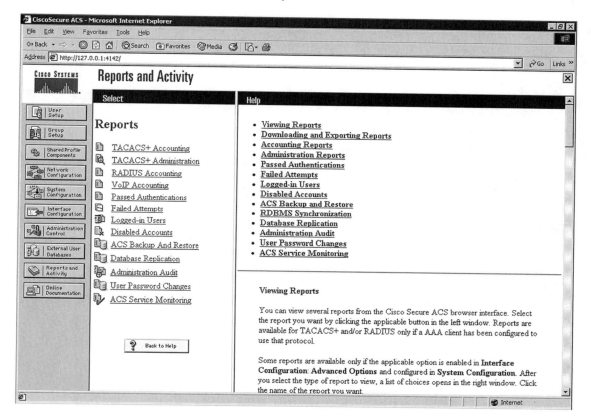

Reports are generated daily and can be viewed or downloaded in comma-separated value (CSV) format. Figure 18-17 lists the titles of the TACACS+ reports that are available. Notice that there are gaps in the dates of available reports. This is because this particular Cisco Secure ACS is not in production, and the system generates logs and, therefore, reports only when it is running.

Figure 18-17 *Available TACACS+ Reports*

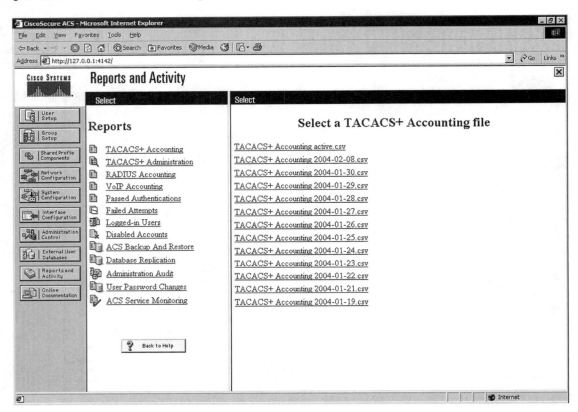

Some reports are available only if the applicable option is enabled in the Interface Configuration window, Advanced Options pane (see Figure 18-18) and configured in the System Configuration window. After you select the type of report to view, a list of choices appears in the right window. Click the name of the report you want.

Figure 18-18 *Interface Configuration Options for Cisco Secure ACS Reports*

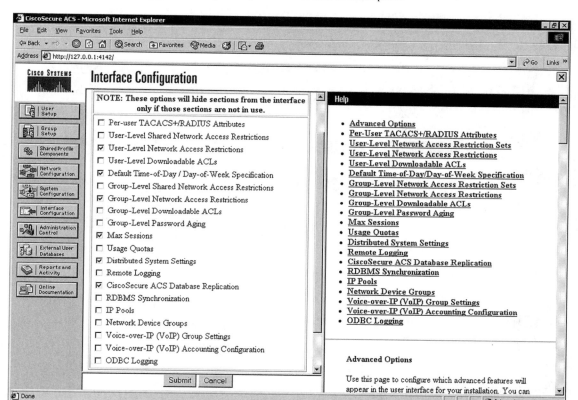

Cisco Secure and Cut-Through Configuration

Cut-through proxy is a feature of the Cisco Security Appliance that enables it to open connections after authenticating and authorizing a user with the AAA server. This feature was discussed in Chapters 1 and 2. The user initiates a connection to their destination and is prompted for a username and password by the Security Appliance. The user-provided information is verified by the AAA server, and the connection is allowed by the firewall.

Configuring Downloadable Security Appliance ACLs

Version 3.0 and later of Cisco Secure ACS allows you to create a "downloadable ACL" using the shared profile component. The downloadable ACL configuration is supported only for RADIUS servers. To verify that your configuration is for a RADIUS server, select **Network**

Configuration from the navigation bar and click **AAA Client**. Verify that RADIUS (Cisco IOS/Security Appliance) is selected, as shown in Figure 18-19.

Figure 18-19   *RADIUS (Cisco IOS/PIX) Configuration*

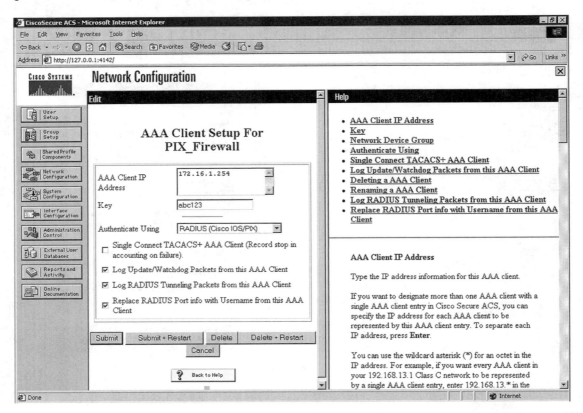

Select **Shared Profile Components** from the navigation bar, click the link for **Downloadable Security Appliance ACL,** and select **Add**.

> **NOTE**   If you are not configured for a RADIUS server, the Downloadable Security Appliance ACL link is unavailable.

If the Cisco Secure ACS is configured as a RADIUS server, but you still do not have the Downloadable Security Appliance ACL option available, you must select either **User-Level** or **Group-Level Downloadable ACLs** in the Advanced Options menu of the Interface Configuration window, shown in Figure 18-20.

Figure 18-20 *Advanced Options Menu*

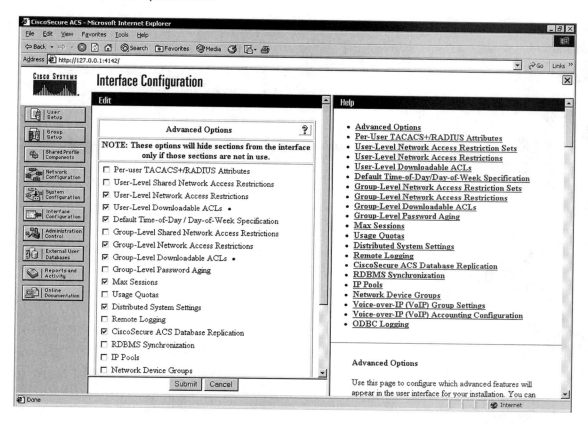

Add the following information in the Downloadable PIX ACLs configuration box, and click **Submit**:

- **Name**—The access list name.

- **Description**—A description of the access list.

- **ACL Definitions**—A test of the command. This should use the same format as the command used on the Security Appliance Firewall, except for the access list name and the fact that there is no requirement for the keyword "access-list." It also is not necessary to add the access list to an access group. This is done automatically when the ACL is downloaded to the Security Appliance Firewall.

Figure 18-21 shows a downloadable ACL configured to allow outbound access to www.cisco.com.

Figure 18-21 *Creating a Downloadable ACL*

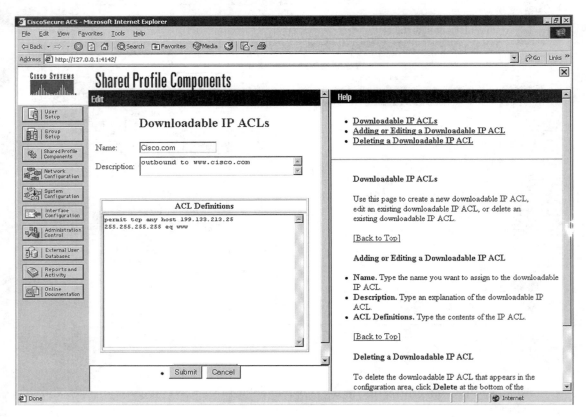

After you configure the downloadable ACL in the Shared Profile Components window, you can add it to either an individual user setup or a group setup. Figure 18-22 shows the Downloadable ACLs box in the Group Setup window. To add the downloadable ACL to the group, simply check the **Assign IP ACL** box and select the ACL name from the drop-down box.

Figure 18-22 *Selecting a Downloadable ACL*

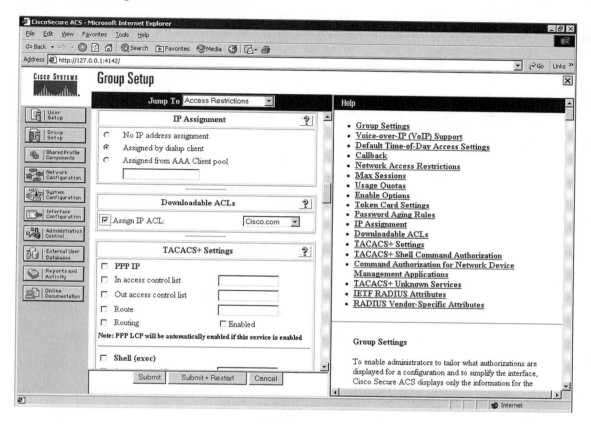

Troubleshooting Your AAA Setup

Troubleshooting your AAA configuration can be a simple function or a difficult process, depending on how complicated the configuration is and how well you documented it. It is always in your best interest to document any configuration and to be as detailed as possible when doing so. It is also recommended that you use best practices such as adding users to groups and applying rules to groups rather than to users, using a *standardized* naming convention, and completing the description fields and comment blocks when creating elements, rules, components, and so on. Neglecting these basic steps can turn a relatively simple issue into an extremely difficult troubleshooting event. It also is a good idea to remember the basic troubleshooting method of "divide and conquer." In other words, do not start checking the Security Appliance or the Cisco Secure ACS configuration until you have verified connectivity between the two devices.

Checking the Security Appliance

The most effective command for troubleshooting the Security Appliance is **show**. The **show** command is run in configuration mode and can be used to show the configuration for all the AAA components on the Security Appliance. The following is a list of the **show** commands pertaining to the AAA configuration:

- **show aaa-server**—Shows you the different *group-tag*s, which protocol is used for each *group-tag*, and the *ip-address*, *key*, and *timeout* for each AAA server.

- **show aaa**—Provides you with the output of the following commands:

  — **show aaa authentication**—Shows you all AAA authentication rules

  — **show aaa authorization**—Shows you all AAA authorization rules

  — **show aaa accounting**—Shows you all AAA accounting rules

  — **show timeout**—Shows the maximum idle time for a session

  — **show timeout uauth**—Shows the duration in hours, minutes, and seconds before the authentication and authorization cache times out

  — **show auth prompt**—Shows the prompt, accept, and reject text messages when a user attempts to authenticate via a Telnet session

  — **Show uauth**—Shows the number of authenticated users and the number of authentications in progress

Troubleshooting Authentication

If you encounter issues with your AAA authentication, you can use the **debug aaa authentication** command to display the communication between the Cisco Security Appliance and the AAA server. This command lets you determine the method of authentication and verify successful communication between the Security Appliance and the AAA server. Example 18-12 shows where a login causes the Security Appliance to initiate a connection to the AAA server at 17.16.1.2, requesting a login using TACACS+ and generating an eight-digit session ID. The session ID is used to distinguish between multiple concurrent authentication requests.

Example 18-12 debug aaa authentication *Command Output (Continued)*

```
PIX-Firewall# debug aaa authentication
10:15:01: AAA/AUTHEN: create-user user='' ruser='' port='tty19'
  rem-addr='172.16.1.2' authen-type=1 service=1 priv=1
10:15:01: AAA/AUTHEN/START (0): port='tty19' list='' action=LOGIN service=LOGIN
10:15:01: AAA/AUTHEN/START (0): using "default" list
10:15:01: AAA/AUTHEN/START (12345678): Method=TACACS+
10:15:01: TAC+ (12345678): received authen response status = GETUSER
10:15:02: AAA/AUTHEN (12345678): status = GETUSER
10:15:02: AAA/AUTHEN/CONT (12345678): continue-login
```

Example 18-12 debug aaa authentication *Command Output (Continued)*

```
10:15:02: AAA/AUTHEN (12345678): status = GETUSER
10:15:02: AAA/AUTHEN (12345678): Method=TACACS+
10:15:02: TAC+: send AUTHEN/CONT packet
10:15:03: TAC+ (12345678): received authen response status = GETPASS
10:15:03: AAA/AUTHEN (12345678): status = GETPASS
10:15:03: AAA/AUTHEN/CONT (12345678): continue-login
10:15:03: AAA/AUTHEN (12345678): status = GETPASS
10:15:03: AAA/AUTHEN (12345678): Method=TACACS+
10:15:03: TAC+: send AUTHEN/CONT packet
10:15:03: TAC+ (12345678): received authen response status = PASS
10:15:03: AAA/AUTHEN (12345678): status = PASS
```

Troubleshooting Authorization

If you encounter issues with your AAA authorization, you can use the **debug aaa authorization** command to display the communication between the Security Appliance and the AAA server, as demonstrated in Example 18-13.

Example 18-13 debug aaa authorization *Command Output*

```
PIX-Firewall# debug aaa authorization
10:15:01: AAA/AUTHOR (0): user='jdoe'
10:15:01: AAA/AUTHOR (0): send AV service=shell
10:15:01: AAA/AUTHOR (0): send AV cmd*
10:15:01: AAA/AUTHOR (123456789): Method=TACACS+
10:15:01: AAA/AUTHOR/TAC+ (123456789): user=jdoe
10:15:01: AAA/AUTHOR/TAC+ (123456789): send AV service=shell
10:15:01: AAA/AUTHOR/TAC+ (123456789): send AV cmd*
10:15:01: AAA/AUTHOR (123456789): Post authorization status = FAIL
```

Troubleshooting Accounting

If you encounter issues with your AAA accounting, you can use the **show accounting** command to step through the sessions and, if necessary, print records of actively accounted sessions. The **debug aaa accounting** command is used to display the output of AAA accounting and is independent of the protocol used to transfer records to the log server, as demonstrated in Example 18-14.

Example 18-14 debug aaa accounting *Command Output*

```
PIX-Firewall# debug aaa accounting
10:15:01: AAA/ACCT: EXEC acct start, line 10
10:15:01: AAA/ACCT: Connect start, line 10, glare
10:15:01: AAA/ACCT: Connection acct stop:
task-id=70 service=exec port=10 protocol=telnet address=172.16.1.13 cmd=glare
bytes-in=308 bytes-out=76 paks-in=45 paks-out=54 elapsed-time=14
```

If you believe you have encountered a protocol-specific problem, you can view the individual protocols using the following commands:

- **debug tacacs**—Displays the packet information for communication between the Security Appliance and the AAA server. Example 18-15 demonstrates typical output from this command.

- **debug radius**—Displays the output of the RADIUS communication. This is more difficult to read, except for the obvious "Access-Accept" or "Access-Reject" message. Example 18-16 demonstrates typical output from this command.

Example 18-15 debug tacacs *Command Output*

```
PIX-Firewall# debug tacacs
10:15:01: TAC+: Opening TCP/IP connection to 172.16.1.2 using source 172.16.1.1
10:15:01: TAC+: Sending TCP packet number 123456789-1 to 172.16.1.2 (AUTHEN/START)
10:15:01: TAC+: Receiving TCP packet number 123456789-2 from 172.16.1.2
10:15:01: TAC+ (123456789): received authen response status = GETUSER
10:15:01: TAC+: send AUTHEN/CONT packet
10:15:02: TAC+: Sending TCP packet number 123456789-3 to 172.16.1.2 (AUTHEN/CONT)
10:15:02: TAC+: Receiving TCP packet number 123456789-4 from 172.16.1.2
10:15:02: TAC+ (123456789): received authen response status = GETPASS
10:15:02: TAC+: send AUTHEN/CONT packet
10:15:03: TAC+: Sending TCP packet number 123456789-5 to 172.16.1.2 (AUTHEN/CONT)
10:15:03: TAC+: Receiving TCP packet number 123456789-6 from 172.16.1.2
10:15:03: TAC+ (123456789): received authen response status = PASS
10:15:03: TAC+: Closing TCP connection to 172.16.1.2
```

Example 18-16 debug radius *Command Output*

```
PIX-Firewall# debug radius
10:15:01: Radius: IPC Send 0.0.0.0:1645, Access-Request, id 0xE len 12
10:15:01:        Attribute 5 5 CDA14568
10:15:01:        Attribute 7 9 B475B47A
10:15:01:        Attribute 6 2 45C4E78A
10:15:01:        Attribute 4 1 14568521
10:15:01: Radius: Received from 172.16.1.2:1645, Access-Accept, id 0xE len 33
10:15:01:        Attribute 2 2 0000000F
```

NOTE It is important that you not run the **debug** command continuously because these commands can generate a significant amount of output.

The command to terminate the debug is **no debug** *insert your command here.*

Checking the Cisco Secure ACS

After you verify your settings on the Cisco Security Appliance, you should double-check the settings on the Cisco Secure ACS to ensure that they match the Security Appliance. You also can use the extensive logging information available in the Cisco Secure ACS Reports and Activity window. You can find a list of troubleshooting information for the Cisco Secure ACS in the Cisco Secure ACS online documentation. Simply enter **Troubleshooting Information for Cisco Secure ACS** in the Search box at Cisco.com to find this documentation.

Foundation Summary

The "Foundation Summary" provides a convenient review of many key concepts in this chapter. If you are already comfortable with the topics in this chapter, this summary can help you recall a few details. If you just read this chapter, this review should help solidify some key facts. If you are doing your final preparation before the exam, this summary provides a convenient way to review the day before the exam.

The Cisco Security Appliance and the Cisco Secure ACS combine to make an effective AAA solution. The **aaa-server** command configures the Security Appliance to communicate with the AAA server. This command determines the authentication protocol used between the Security Appliance and the AAA server, the IP address of the AAA server, and the *group-tag* or the name of the group the AAA server is in.

The Security Appliance can group up to 14 servers and handle up to 14 server groups. The Cisco Secure ACS is installed on either a Windows NT server or Windows 2000 server. It considers itself an AAA server and the Security Appliance the AAA client. Command-line entries are put on the Security Appliance to configure authentication, authorization, and accounting. User accounts, groups, logging, and downloadable Security Appliance ACLs are all configured on the Cisco Secure ACS. Although you can assign authorization to individual users, it is recommended that you assign users to groups and assign authorization rules to the groups.

There are three main steps for troubleshooting AAA issues:

- Verify connectivity between the Security Appliance and the Cisco Secure ACS.
- Verify the configuration of the Security Appliance.
- Verify the configuration of the Cisco Secure ACS.

Table 18-2 outlines the commands and syntax necessary to configure the Security Appliance as a NAS.

Table 18-2 *Commands to Configure the Security Appliance as a NAS*

Command	Description
aaa authentication include | **exclude** *authen-service if-name local-ip local-mask foreign-ip foreign-mask group-tag*	Implements AAA authentication to include or exclude a specific service that is inbound or outbound in a specific interface for a specific source and destination address assigned to a specific AAA server group as assigned by the group tag.

Table 18-2 *Commands to Configure the Security Appliance as a NAS (Continued)*

Command	Description
aaa authentication match *acl-name if-name server-tag*	Matches the requirement for AAA authentication with a specific ACL.
show aaa	Displays your AAA configuration.
debug aaa authentication	Displays the authentication communication between the NAS and the AAA server.
aaa authorization include | exclude *author-service if-name local-ip local-mask foreign-ip foreign-mask server-tag*	Implements AAA authorization to include or exclude a specific service that is inbound or outbound in a specific interface for a specific source and destination address assigned to a specific AAA server group as assigned by the group tag.
aaa authorization match *acl-name* inbound | outbound *if-name group-tag*	Matches the requirement for AAA authorization with a specific ACL.
debug aaa authorization	Displays the authorization communication between the NAS and the AAA server.
aaa accounting include | exclude *author-service if-name local-ip local-mask foreign-ip foreign-mask server-tag*	Implements AAA accounting to include or exclude a specific service that is inbound or outbound in a specific interface for a specific source and destination address assigned to a specific AAA server group as assigned by the group tag.
aaa accounting match *acl-name if-name server-tag*	Matches the requirement for AAA accounting with a specific ACL.
show aaa accounting	Steps through individual recorded logs.
debug aaa accounting	Displays the accounting communication between the NAS and the AAA server.

The commands listed in Table 18-3 let you display protocol-specific communication between the NAS (Security Appliance) and the AAA server.

Table 18-3 *Commands to Display Communication Between the Security Appliance and the AAA Server*

Command	Description
debug tacacs	Debugs TACACS communications between the Security Appliance and the AAA server.
debug radius	Debugs RADIUS communications between the Security Appliance and the AAA server.

Q&A

As mentioned in the Introduction, the questions in this book are more difficult than what you should experience on the exam. The questions are designed to ensure your understanding of the concepts discussed in this chapter and adequately prepare you to complete the exam. You should use the simulated exams on the CD to practice for the exam.

The answers to these questions can be found in Appendix A:

1. Both your Cisco Security Appliance and your Cisco Secure ACS are configured for TACACS+, but you cannot configure the downloadable Security Appliance ACLs. What is the problem?

2. What is the command to get authorization to work with access lists?

3. What Cisco Secure ACS window is used to configure the Security Appliance, and what is the firewall considered?

4. How do you put text messages into the logon prompt for a Telnet session?

5. What three messages can you change with the **auth-prompt** command?

6. If your **timeout uauth** is set to 0:58:00, when is the user prompted to reauthenticate after the session times out?

7. What two formats can logs be written to using the Cisco Secure ACS?

8. You have added a new RSA SecurID Token Server to the network. In which two places do you configure the Cisco Secure ACS to use it?

9. What commands are most commonly used to check your AAA configuration on the Security Appliance?

10. What is the total number of AAA servers to which the Security Appliance can connect?

11. How do you disable caching of user authentication?

This chapter covers the following subjects:

- Multimedia Support

- Application Inspection

- Intrusion Prevention

CHAPTER 19

IPS and Advanced Protocol Handling

The primary function of the Cisco Security Appliance is to prevent and to protect internal hosts from malicious attacks from the outside network. Some hackers try to gain access to the internal network, but others attack network resources to disrupt network services. This chapter describes some of the features of the Cisco Security Appliance that are used to mitigate known attacks against network resources. This chapter also discusses how the Security Appliance handles multimedia application protocols.

How To Best Use This Chapter

The Security Appliance provides various attack guards that protect your network by actually decoding traffic received for various protocols. Test yourself with the "Do I Know This Already?" quiz and see how familiar you are with the attack guard and multimedia functionality available on Security Appliances.

"Do I Know This Already?" Quiz

The purpose of the "Do I Know This Already?" quiz is to help you decide if you really need to read the entire chapter. If you already intend to read the entire chapter, you do not necessarily need to answer these questions now.

The nine-question quiz, derived from the major sections in the "Foundation Topics" portion of the chapter, helps you determine how to spend your limited study time.

Table 19-1 outlines the major topics discussed in this chapter and the "Do I Know This Already?" quiz questions that correspond to those topics.

Table 19-1 *"Do I Know This Already?" Foundation Topics Section-to-Question Mapping*

Foundations Topics Section	Questions Covered in This Section	Score
Multimedia Support	3, 4	
Application Inspection	1, 2, 5 to 7	
Intrusion Prevention	8 to 9	

> **CAUTION** The goal of self assessment is to gauge your mastery of the topics in this chapter. If you do not know the answer to a question or are only partially sure of the answer, you should mark this question wrong for purposes of the self assessment. Giving yourself credit for an answer you correctly guess skews your self-assessment results and might provide you with a false sense of security.

1. What does the ICMP inspection feature on the Security Appliance do?

    a. It prevents the Security Appliance from being flooded with water.

    b. It protects the inside network from being engulfed by rain.

    c. It protects against SYN flood attacks.

    d. It protects against AAA attacks.

2. Which Security Appliance feature mitigates a DoS attack that uses port 53?

    a. Floodguard

    b. Incomplete guard

    c. Fragguard

    d. DNS inspection

3. Which of the following multimedia application(s) is(are) supported by Security Appliance?

    a. MGCP

    b. RTSP

    c. H323

    d. All of these answers are correct

4. Which is the default port that Security Appliance inspects for H.323 traffic?

    a. 1628

    b. 1722

    c. 1720

    d. 1408

5. Which of the following describes how the mail inspection works on the Security Appliance?

   a. It lets all mail in except for mail described by an access list.

   b. It restricts SMTP requests to seven commands and eight ESTMP commands, as well as concealing the SMTP banner.

   c. It revokes mail messages that contain attacks.

   d. It performs virus checks on each mail message.

6. Which of the following statements about DNS inspection is true?

   a. It is disabled by default.

   b. It allows only a single DNS response for outgoing requests.

   c. It monitors the DNS servers for suspicious activities.

   d. It is enabled by default.

7. Which of the following are Security Appliance attack mitigation features?

   a. DNS inspection

   b. ICMP inspection

   c. Remote guard

   d. Mail inspection

   e. Webguard

8. Which command installs the Security Appliance IPS Software?

   a. copy tftp flash

   b. upgrade AIP-SSM software

   c. hw-module 1 recover boot

   d. hw-module 1 upgrade system

9. What does the reset action do in the Security Appliance IPS configuration?

   a. Warns the source of the offending packet before it drops the packet

   b. Drops the offending packet and closes the connection if it is part of an active connection with a TCP RST

   c. Waits 2000 offending packets, and then permanently bans the connection to the source host

   d. Reports the incident to the syslog server and waits for more offending packets from the same source to arrive

The answers to the "Do I Know This Already?" quiz are found in Appendix A, "Answers to the 'Do I Know This Already?' Quizzes and Q&A Sections." The suggested choices for your next step are as follows:

- **7 or less overall score**—Read the entire chapter. This includes the "Foundation Topics," "Foundation Summary," and "Q&A" sections.

- **8 or 9 overall score**—If you want more review on these topics, skip to the "Foundation Summary" section and then go to the "Q&A" section. Otherwise, move to the next chapter.

Foundation Topics

Multimedia Support on the Cisco Security Appliance

Chapter 7, "Configuring Access," begins a discussion of some applications that require special handling by the Cisco Security Appliance. Multimedia applications have special behaviors that require special handling by the Security Appliance inspection feature.

During normal mode of operation, multimedia application protocols open more than one communication channel and several data channels. For example, a client might transmit a request on Transmission Control Protocol (TCP), get responses on User Datagram Protocol (UDP), or use dynamic ports. The **inspect** command, formerly the **fixup protocol** command, helps the Security Appliance identify such protocols so that it can perform inspections.

The Security Appliance dynamically opens and closes UDP ports for secure multimedia connections. There is no need to open a range of ports, which creates a security risk, or to reconfigure any application clients.

The Security Appliance supports multimedia with or without Network Address Translation (NAT). Many firewalls that cannot support multimedia with NAT limit multimedia usage to only registered users or require exposure of inside Internet Protocol (IP) addresses to the Internet.

Many popular multimedia applications use Real-Time Streaming Protocol (RTSP) or the H.323 suite protocol standard.

RTSP

RTSP, described in RFC 2326, controls the delivery of real-time data, such as audio and video. It is used for large-scale broadcasts and audio- or video-on-demand streaming. It supports applications such as Cisco IP/TV, RealNetworks RealAudio G2 Player, and Apple QuickTime 4 software.

RTSP applications use port 554 with TCP (and rarely UDP) as a control channel. The TCP control channel is used to negotiate the two UDP data channels that are used to transmit audio/video traffic. RTSP does not typically deliver continuous data streams over the control channel, usually relying on a UDP-based data transport protocol such as standard Real-Time Transport Protocol (RTP) to open separate channels for data and for RTP Control Protocol

(RTCP) messages. RTCP carries status and control information, and RTP carries the actual data.

The **inspect** command is used for RTSP connections to let the Cisco Security Appliance do inspection. The **inspect rtsp** command lets the Security Appliance dynamically create conduits for RTSP UDP channels. For example, the standard RTSP port 554 is enabled by the following command:

```
inspect  rtsp
```

Application Inspection Support for Voice over IP

The steady growth of voice over IP (VoIP) technology has also seen the development of new standards. IP phones and devices, unlike their regular phone counterparts, are not fixed to a specific switch device, so they must contain processors that enable them to function and be intelligent on their own, independent from a central switching location. Regular phones are relatively inexpensive because they do not need to be complex; they are fixed to a specific switch at a central switching location. Why is this important to you? Well, you might be running a network that supports VoIP and would want a firewall that supports the different protocols that are involved with it. Security Appliance support application inspection of the major protocols and applications that provide VoIP services including the following, each of which is discussed in the following sections:

■ Computer Telephony Interface Quick Buffer Encoding (CTIQBE)

■ H.323

■ Media Gateway Control Protocol (MGCP)

■ Skinny Client Control Protocol (SCCP)

■ Session Initiation Protocol (SIP)

CTIQBE

The Telephony Application Programming Interface (TAPI) and Java Telephony Application Programming Interface (JTAPI) are used by many Cisco VoIP applications. Cisco TAPI Service Provider (TSP) uses CTIQBE to communicate with Cisco CallManager. CTIQBE protocol is disabled by default. The **inspect ctiqbe** command enables CTIQBE protocol inspection that supports NAT, PAT, and bidirectional NAT. This enables Cisco IP SoftPhone and other Cisco TAPI/JTAPI applications to work successfully with Cisco CallManager for call setup across the firewall. Additionally, CTIQBE is used as a signaling protocol by older Cisco IP phones and the newer Cisco IP Communicator to perform call setup with the Cisco CallManager.

There are, however, instances when CTIQBE application inspection has limits or does not support some configuration types. CTIQBE application inspection does not support the following:

- Stateful failover of CTIQBE calls

- CTIQBE messages fragmented in multiple TCP packets

- Configurations that use the **alias** command

The following summarizes special considerations when using CTIQBE application inspection in specific scenarios:

- If two Cisco IP SoftPhones are registered with different Cisco CallManagers, which are connected to different interfaces of a Security Appliance, calls between these two phones will fail.

- When Cisco CallManager is located on the higher-security interface compared to Cisco IP SoftPhones, if NAT or outside NAT is required for the Cisco CallManager IP address, the mapping must be static because Cisco IP SoftPhone requires the Cisco CallManager IP address to be specified explicitly in its Cisco TSP configuration on the PC.

- When using PAT or outside PAT, if the Cisco CallManager IP address is to be translated, its TCP port 2748 must be statically mapped to the same port of the PAT (interface) address for Cisco IP SoftPhone registrations to succeed. The CTIQBE listening port (TCP 2748) is fixed and is not user-configurable on Cisco CallManager, Cisco IP SoftPhone, or Cisco TSP.

H.323

The H.323 collection of protocols collectively uses up to two TCP connections and four to six UDP connections. Most of the ports, with the exception of one TCP port, are negotiated just for that particular session. Figure 19-1 shows the H.323 protocols in relation to the Open System Interconnection (OSI) reference model.

Figure 19-1 *H.323 Protocols Mapped to the OSI Reference Model*

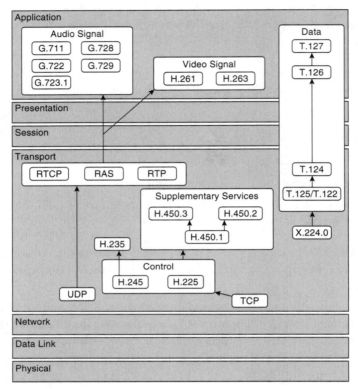

As shown in Figure 19-1:

- H.225 Registration, Admission, and Status (RAS) messages define communications between endpoints and gatekeepers.
- H.225 administers security and authentication.
- H.245 negotiates channel usage.

The content of the streams in H.323 is far more difficult for firewalls to understand than existing protocols because H.323 encodes packets using Abstract Syntax Notation (ASN.1).

The H.323 control channel handles H.225 and H.245 and H.323 RAS. H.323 inspection uses the following ports:

- **1718**—Gatekeeper discovery UDP port
- **1719**—RAS UDP port
- **1720**—TCP control port

> **NOTE**   PAT support for H.323 is available in Security software version 6.2 software.

inspect h323 Command

The Cisco Security Appliance inspects port 1720 (default) connections for H.323 traffic. If you must change port 1720 because you have applications using H.323 on other ports, use the **class-map** command to identify these other traffic flows with their different port numbers.

Example 19-1 demonstrates how to assign a new port for H.323 inspection.

Example 19-1 *Assigning a New Port for H.323 Inspection*

```
Pixfirewall(config)# class-map h323_port
Pixfirewall(config-cmap)# match port tcp eq 1721
Pixfirewall(config-cmap)# exit
Pixfirewall(config)# policy-map voip_map
Pixfirewall(config-pmap)# class h323_port
Pixfirewall(config-pmap-c)# inspect h323
Pixfirewall(config-pmap-c)# exit
```

Use the **no** form of this command to disable the inspection of traffic on the indicated port. An H.323 client might initially establish a TCP connection to an H.323 server using TCP port 1720 to request Q.931 call setup. The H.323 terminal supplies a port number to the client to use for an H.245 TCP connection.

The two major functions of H.323 inspection are as follows:

■ Performs NAT on the embedded IP addresses in the H.225 and H.245 messages. In other words, it translates the H.323 payload to a NAT address. (PIX Firewall uses an ASN.1 decoder to decode the H.323 messages.)

■ Dynamically creates conduits for TCP and UDP channels to allocate the negotiated H.245 and RTP/RTCP connections.

Each UDP connection with a packet going through H.323 inspection is marked as an H.323 connection and times out with the H.323 timeout as configured by the administrator using the **timeout** command. The syntax for the **inspect h323** command is as follows:

```
inspect h323 [h225 | ras]
```

Table 19-2 inspect h323 *Command Syntax*

Parameter	Description
h225	Specifies the use of H.225, which is the ITU standard that governs H.225.0 session establishment and packetization with H.323.
ras	Specifies the use of RAS with H.323 to enable the dissimilar communication devices to communicate with each other.

MGCP

MGCP is a voice protocol that runs in conjunction with Signaling System 7 (SS7), an interoffice signaling protocol for circuit-switched services, and an IP protocol, such as H.323 or SIP, to bridge circuit-switched and packet networks. MGCP separates the signaling and call control from the media gateway. A media gateway is typically a network element that provides conversion between the audio signals carried on telephone circuits and the data packets carried over the Internet or over other packet networks, such as trunking gateways, residential gateways, and business gateways.

Application inspection for MGCP is disabled by default. To use MGCP, you typically need to configure at least two ports: one on which the gateway receives commands and one for the ort on which the call agent receives commands. Normally, a call agent will send commands to port 2427, whereas a gateway will send commands to port 2727.

To enable MGCP application inspection for call agents and gateways using the default ports, use the following command in global-configuration mode:

```
mgcp-map [map_name]
```

This map will then be applied to a policy-map to enable inspection using the **inspect mgcp** command.

MGCP messages are transmitted over UDP. A response is sent back to the source address (IP address and UDP port number) of the command, but the response may not be sent from the same address to which the command was sent. Multiple MGCP call agents can be supported by the Security Appliance.

The **call-agent** command specifies a group of call agents that can manage one or more gateways. Assigning several call agents to a group for a specific gateway will allow any of the assigned call agents to send a response. The **gateway** command is used to specify which group of call agents is managing a particular gateway. These commands are applied in the mgcp-map configuration mode:

```
call-agent ip-address group-id
gateway ip-address group-id
```

Example 19-2 allows call agents 10.1.1.30 and 10.1.1.35 to control gateway 10.1.2.20, and allows call agents 10.1.1.12 and 10.1.1.14 to control gateway 10.1.2.21.

Example 19-2 *Sample MGCP Configuration*

```
PIXfirewall(config)# mgcp-map mgcp1
PIXfirewall(config-mgcp-map)# call-agent 10.1.1.30 101
PIXfirewall(config-mgcp-map)# call-agent 10.1.1.35 101
PIXfirewall(config-mgcp-map)# call-agent 10.1.1.12 102
PIXfirewall(config-mgcp-map)# call-agent 10.1.1.14 102
PIXfirewall(config-mgcp-map)# gateway 10.1.2.20 101
PIXfirewall(config-mgcp-map)# gateway 10.1.2.21 102
PIXfirewall(config-mgcp-map)# exit
PIXfirewall(config)# policy-map global_policy
PIXfirewall(config-pmap)# class inspection_default
PIXfirewall(config-pmap-c)# inspect mgcp mgcp1
PIXfirewall(config-pmap-c)# exit
```

SCCP

Cisco IP Phones using SCCP can coexist in an H.323 environment. When used with Cisco CallManager, the SCCP client can interoperate with H.323-compliant terminals. Application layer functions in the Security Appliance recognize SCCP version 3.3. The functionality of the application layer software ensures that all SCCP signaling and media packets can traverse the firewall by providing NAT of the SCCP signaling packets.

Application inspection for SCCP is enabled by default using the **inspect sccp** command. You can use the **class-map** command to change the default port assignment for SCCP, as shown in Example 19-3.

Example 19-3 *Assigning a New Port for SCCP Inspection*

```
Pixfirewall(config)# class-map sccp_port
Pixfirewall(config-cmap)# match port tcp eq 2435
Pixfirewall(config-cmap)# exit
Pixfirewall(config)# policy-map voip_map
Pixfirewall(config-pmap)# class sccp_port
Pixfirewall(config-pmap-c)# inspect sccp
Pixfirewall(config-pmap-c)# exit
```

Although the Security Appliance does support PAT and NAT for SCCP, it does have limitations, including the following:

- PAT will not work with configurations using the **alias** command.
- Stateful failover of SCCP calls is not supported.

- Using the **debug skinny** command may delay sending messages, which can have a performance impact in a real-time environment.

- No support for fragmented SCCP messages is provided.

- Outside NAT or PAT is not supported.

Security Appliance does not support NAT or PAT of the file content transferred using Trivial File Transfer Protocol (TFTP), if the address of a Cisco CallManager server is configured for NAT or PAT to a different address or port and outside phones register to it using TFTP. Even though Security Appliance does support NAT of TFTP messages and opens holes for the TFTP file to pass through the firewall, Security Appliance cannot translate the Cisco CallManager IP address and port embedded in the Cisco IP Phone's configuration files that are transferred using TFTP during phone registration.

> **NOTE** Cisco IP Phones need to reregister with the Cisco CallManager to establish calls through the Security Appliance if the **clear xlate** command is entered. This is because the xlates for the Cisco CallManager are permanently deleted.

SIP

SIP, RFC 2543, is a signaling protocol for Internet conferencing, telephony, presence, events notification, and instant messaging. SIP was developed in the mid-1990s by the Internet Engineering Task Force (IETF) as a real-time communication protocol for IP voice, and it has expanded into video and instant-messaging applications. SIP works with Session Description Protocol (SDP), RFC 2327, for call signaling. SDP specifies the ports for the media stream. Using SIP, the Security Appliance can support any SIP VoIP gateways and VoIP proxy servers.

To support SIP calls through the Security Appliance, signaling messages for the media connection addresses, media ports, and embryonic connections for the media must be inspected, because although the signaling is sent over a well-known destination port (UDP/ TCP 5060), the media streams are dynamically allocated. Also, SIP embeds IP addresses in the user data portion of the IP packet. SIP inspection applies NAT for these embedded IP addresses.

Application inspection for SIP is enabled by default, using the **inspect sip** command. You can use the **class-map** command to change the default TCP port assignment for SIP. You can use the **show conn state sip** command to view all active SIP connections.

Application Inspection

Hackers use several methods to cause network service disruption. Denial of service (DoS) is a popular way of causing network disruption. Cisco Security Appliance has some attack mitigation features to combat against some of the following attacks:

- File Transfer Protocol (FTP) attacks
- Hypertext Transfer Protocol (HTTP) attacks
- Domain Name System (DNS) attacks
- Simple Mail Transfer Protocol (SMTP)–based attacks
- Internet Control Message Protocol (ICMP) flooding and spoofing attacks
- Remote shell connection hijacking
- SQL*Net connection hijacking and attacks

The Security Appliance supports application inspection through the Adaptive Security Algorithm (ASA) function. Through the stateful application inspection used by the ASA, the Security Appliance tracks each connection traversing the firewall and ensures that they are valid. The firewall, through stateful inspection, also monitors the state of the connection to compile information to place in a state table. Using the state table in addition to administrator-defined rules, filtering decisions are based on context that has been established by packets previously passed through the firewall. Some applications require additional handling that goes beyond the ASA's stateful inspection feature. These applications embed IP addressing information in the user data packet or require a second communications channel to be dynamically opened, causing the additional handling through specific inspect commands. Application inspection and the inspect command will work with NAT enabled to help identify the location of embedded addressing information.

By default, protocol inspection is enabled on the Security Appliance. Through the *inspection_default* class-map, the Security Appliance monitors, by default, the following protocols:

- ctiqbe
- dns
- ftp
- gtp
- h323-h225
- h323-ras
- http
- icmp
- ils
- mgcp
- netbios
- rpc

- rsh
- rtsp
- sip
- skinny
- smtp
- sqlnet
- tftp
- xdmcp

NOTE   It is recommended that any inspection engines assigned in the *inspection_default* class-map but that are not required be disabled. This will reduce any possible security-policy violations by denying unused inspection engines that may allow a malicious user to circumvent the security policy. This ideal is referred to as the *principle of least privilege.*

The default *inspection_default* class-map is applied to the *global_policy* policy-map, affecting all TCP and UDP traffic through the Security Appliance. Remember that the *global_policy* policy-map is applied to the global interface. At times, common applications must be run over a nonstandard port. This can be the case for specialized applications or to hide the port from malicious users. The **inspect** command uses the standard ports for each of the assigned applications it will inspect, such as TCP port 80 for HTTP. To change the port in which the inspect command will monitor, you must assign a specific class map to direct the traffic flow, as shown in Example 19-4. Unless you deny port 80 traffic to the class map, the inspect HTTP will inspect port 80 traffic in addition to the new port assigned in Example 19-4. You will then assign the class map to a policy and configure the appropriate **inspect** command to the traffic class.

Example 19-4   *Changing the Port for HTTP*

```
PIXfirewall(config)# class-map http-2010
PIXfirewall(config-cmap)# match port tcp eq 2010
PIXfirewall(config-cmap)# exit
PIXfirewall(config)# policy-map global_policy
PIXfirewall(config-pmap)# class-map http-2010
PIXfirewall(config-pmap-c)# inspect http
PIXfirewall(config-pmap-c)# exit
PIXfirewall(config-pmap)# exit
PIXfirewall(config)#
```

FTP Inspection

The FTP protocol requires some special handling due to its use of two ports per FTP session. The FTP protocol uses two ports when activated for transferring data: a control channel and a data channel using ports 21 and 20, respectively. The user, who initiates the FTP session over the control channel, makes all data requests through that channel. The FTP server will then initiate a request to open a port from server port 20 to the user's computer. FTP will always use port 20 for data channel communications. If FTP inspection has not been enabled on the Security Appliance, this request will be discarded and the FTP session will not transmit any requested data. If FTP inspection is enabled on the Security Appliance, the Security Appliance will monitor the control channel, trying to recognize a request to open the data channel. The FTP protocol embeds the data-channel port specifications in the control-channel traffic, requiring the Security Appliance to inspect the control channel for data-port changes. If the Security Appliance recognizes a request, it temporarily creates an opening for the data-channel traffic that lasts for the life of the session. In this way, the FTP inspection function monitors the control channel, identifies a data-port assignment, and allows data to be exchanged on the data port for the length of the session.

The Security Appliance inspects port 21 connections for FTP traffic by default through the global-inspection class-map. The Security Appliance will also recognize the difference between an active and a passive FTP session. If the FTP session supports passive FTP data transfer, the Security Appliance, through the **inspect ftp** command, will recognize the data port request from the user and open the new data port greater than 1023. The FTP inspection inspects the FTP sessions and performs four tasks:

- Prepares dynamic secondary data connections
- Tracks **ftp** command-response sequence
- Generates an audit trail
- NATs embedded IP addresses

The **inspect ftp strict** option can be enabled, which will cause the Security Appliance to track each **ftp** command and response sequence for anomalous activity.

FTP inspection also supports FTP deep packet inspection. This will allow a security administrator greater control over what a user can do through an FTP session by restricting specific FTP request commands. An FTP session is closed if a user attempts to use a blocked FTP request command, such as the command to remove a file. The following commands can be blocked through FTP deep packet inspection:

- **appe**—Append to a file
- **cdup**—Change to parent of current directory
- **dele**—Delete a file

- **get**—Retrieve a file

- **help**—Remote help information from server

- **mkd**—Create a directory

- **put**—Store a file

- **rmd**—Remove a directory

- **rnfr**—Rename from

- **rnto**—Rename to

- **site**—Specify server specific command

- **stou**—Store a file with a unique name

Filtering FTP commands must be done through a special **ftp-map** command in the global-configuration mode. Once created, you must assign the **ftp-map** to a **class-map** to identify the proper FTP traffic flows. When configuring the actions in an **ftp-map,** use the **request-cmd deny** command to restrict specific FTP request commands. Multiple FTP request commands can be restricted with a single **request-cmd deny** command:

```
ftp-map [map_name]
request-cmd deny { appe | cdup | dele | get | help | mkd | put | rmd | rnfr | rnto | site | stou}
```

Example 19-5 *Configuring FTP Request Command Inspection*

```
PIXfirewall(config)# ftp-map in_ftp1
PIXfirewall(config-ftp-map)# request-cmd deny dele rnfr rnto appe put rmd
PIXfirewall(config-ftp-map)# exit
PIXfirewall(config)# class-map ftp_port
PIXfirewall(config-cmap)# match port 1024
PIXfirewall(config-cmap)# exit
PIXfirewall(config)# policy-map inbound
PIXfirewall(config-pmap)# class ftp_port
PIXfirewall(config-pmap-c)# inspect ftp strict in_ftp1
PIXfirewall(config-pmap-c)# exit
PIXfirewall(config-pmap)# exit
```

HTTP Inspection

Many known exploits have used HTTP as the transport. Many of these exploits relied on embedded applications or scripting languages, such as Java or ActiveX, to take control of a user's system. Additionally, exploits have been known to take advantage of web browsers or computers that do not fully comply with RFC 2616 standards. With HTTP inspections, the Security Appliance can help control these exploits by filtering out specific attacks and threats that are known to associate with HTTP traffic flows. HTTP inspection is enabled by default through the *inspection_default* class-map. HTTP inspections can perform the following services through the **inspect http** command:

- URL screening through N2H2 or Websense.

- Java and ActiveX filtering.

- **HTTP inspection**—Check whether an HTTP message is compliant to the RFC.

- **Enhanced HTTP inspection**—Verify that HTTP messages conform to RFC 2616, use RFC-defined methods or supported extension methods, and comply with various other configurable message criteria.

To use the enhanced HTTP inspection features, you must use an **http-map** command, similar to the **ftp-map** command for FTP request command filters. The **http-map** command supports several options to control HTTP traffic flow. You can verify that the HTTP traffic flow conforms to the RFC 2616 standard, uses RFC-defined methods of access, or uses supported extension methods by using the **request-method** command in the **http-map** configuration mode:

```
request-method { ext ext_methods I rfc rfc_methods } action I allow I drop I reset I [log]
```

Table 19-3 describes the request-method command options and arguments.

Table 19-3 request-method *Command Syntax*

Parameter	Description
ext	Specifies the extension methods.
ext_methods	Identifies one of the extended methods that will be allowed to pass through the Security Appliance.
rfc	Specifies RFC 2616 supported methods.
rfc_method	Identifies one of the RFC methods that will be allowed to pass through the Security Appliance.
action	Identifies the action taken when a message fails this command inspection.
allow	Allows the message.
drop	Closes the connection.
reset	Sends a TCP reset message to the client and server.
log	(Optional) Generates a syslog.

In addition to HTTP request filtering, you can inspect the HTTP message content through the **http-map** command, as shown in Example 19-6. The following HTTP content criteria can be inspected:

- **Content-length**—Content length range inspection

- **Content-type-verification**—Content type inspection

- Max-header-length—Maximum header size inspection
- Max-uri-length—maximum URI size inspection

Example 19-6   *Configuring* **http-map** *Inspection*

```
PIXfirewall(config)# http-map http_office
PIXfirewall(config-http-map)# request-method rfc post action reset log
PIXfirewall(config-http-map)# request-method rfc-put action reset log
PIXfirewall(config-http-map)# port-misuse p2p action reset log
PIXfirewall(config-http-map)# exit
PIXfirewall(config)# policy-map inbound
PIXfirewall(config-pmap)# class inbound_http_traffic
PIXfirewall(config-pmap-c)# inspect http http_office
PIXfirewall(config-pmap-c)# exit
PIXfirewall(config-pmap)# exit
```

In Example 19-6, port 80 traffic is inspected for HTTP RFC compliance using the **request-method** command. Each **request-method** command has been assigned a reset action if any part of the HTTP traffic flow fails to comply with RFC standards. The **reset** action will cause the HTTP connection to reset if the request-method fails. Additional actions that can be used are **allow** and **drop**.

To inspect the content length of an HTTP message, you must use the content-length command in http-map configuration mode. You can set the minimum and maximum length of the complete HTTP message and assign actions that react to noncompliance to these settings:

> content-length { min *bytes* | max *bytes* } action | allow | drop | reset | [log]

The **content-type-verification** command checks the content-type field in the HTTP response to verify that it matches the accept field in the corresponding HTTP request message:

> content-type-verification [match-re-rsp] action {allow | reset | drop} [log]

Several exploits using popular web servers have exploited HTTP header sizes. You can control the allowed HTTP message header size using the **max-header-length** command in the http-map configuration mode. All messages that do not exceed the maximum header size will be allowed through the Security Appliance. You can assign a maximum header size of no more than 65,635 bytes:

> max-header-length {request *bytes* | response *bytes*} action | allow | drop | reset | [log]

In addition to limiting the length of HTTP message headers, you can limit the length of Uniform Resource Identifiers (URI). Using the **max-uri-length** command in http-map configuration mode, you can set the maximum length to no more than 65,535 bytes:

> max-uri-length *bytes* action | allow | drop | reset | [log]

port-misuse Command

In an office environment, it is common practice to restrict Internet activities to work-related content. With the popularity of P2P programs and instant messaging services, this can be hard to manage. The Security Appliance, through the **http-map** command, can limit or even block the use of these programs and services through the use of the **port-misuse** command. The **port-misuse** command can restrict instant messaging, P2P programs, and unauthorized tunneling to and from the network:

```
port-misuse {im | p2p | tunneling} action | allow | deny | drop | reset | [log]
```

New worms and viruses come in many forms, usually through an e-mail message. Many of these messages are compressed to avoid antivirus programs. Once uncompressed, these messages are free to attack a system or network. You can restrict the use of compressed files that pass through the Security Appliance, from e-mail or other means, by using the **transfer-encoding** command in http-map configuration mode:

```
transfer-encoding {chunked | compress | deflate | gzip | identity | default} action | allow
    | drop | reset | [log]
```

Domain Name Inspection

To understand the DNS attack protection provided by Cisco Security Appliance, it helps to understand how DNS can be exploited to cause a DoS attack. DNS queries are sent from the attacker to each of the DNS servers. These queries contain the target's spoofed address. The DNS servers respond to the small query with a large response. These responses are routed to the target, causing link congestion and possible denial of Internet connectivity.

The port assignment for DNS cannot be configured on the Cisco Security Appliance. DNS requires application inspection so that DNS queries will not be subject to generic UDP handling based on activity timeouts. The Security Appliance allows only a single DNS response for outgoing DNS requests. Additionally, if an inside host queries multiple independent name server, the Security Appliance will only allow on response to return to the inside host. The UDP connections associated with DNS queries and responses are torn down as soon as a reply to a DNS query is received, dropping all other responses and averting a DoS attack. This functionality is called *DNS inspection*. DNS inspection is enabled by default.

DNS inspection performs two tasks:

- It monitors the message exchange to ensure that the ID of the DNS reply matches the ID of the DNS query.
- It translates the DNS A record on behalf of the **alias** command.

Only forward lookups are translated using NAT, so pointer (PTR) records are not touched. DNS zone transfers can also trigger built-in intrusion detection signatures on the Security Appliance.

> **NOTE** A pointer record is also called a reverse record. A PTR record associates an IP address with a canonical name.

Cisco Security Appliances fully support NAT and PAT of DNS messages originating from either inside (more-secure) or outside (less-secure) interfaces. This means that if a client on an inside network requests DNS resolution of an inside address from a DNS server on an outside interface, the DNS A record is translated correctly. This also means that the use of the **alias** command is now unnecessary.

To enable DNS inspection, use the **inspect dns** command within a class-map. This command is on by default in the *inspection_default* class-map:

```
inspect dns [maximum-length max_pkt_length]
```

> **NOTE** If the Security Appliance is protecting hosts that connect to Microsoft Windows 2003 DNS servers, the following inspect DNS command must be used:
>
> ```
> inspect dns maximum-length 1280
> ```
>
> Microsoft uses EDNS as the DNS server software on Windows 2003 servers. EDNS violates the previous max-length attribute of 512, requiring the **inspect dns maximum-length 1280** command to override.

Mail Inspection

An SMTP or ESMTP server responds to client requests with numeric reply codes and optional human-readable strings. SMTP application inspection controls and reduces the commands that the user can use, as well as the messages the server returns. SMTP inspection performs three primary tasks:

- It restricts SMTP requests to seven commands: **HELO, MAIL, RCPT, DATA, RSET, NOOP,** and **QUIT.**

- It restricts SMTP requests to eight extended SMTP commands: **AUTH, DATA, EHLO, ETRN, SAML, SEND, SOML, and VRFY.**

- It monitors the SMTP command-response sequence.

- It generates an audit trail–audit record 108002 when an invalid character embedded in the mail address is replaced. For more information, see RFC 821.

By default, the Cisco Security Appliance inspects port 25 connections for SMTP and ESMTP traffic. ESMTP inspection monitors the command-response sequence for the following anomalous signatures:

- Truncated commands.

- Incorrect command termination (those not terminated with <CR><LF>).

- Unallowed characters. The **MAIL** and **RCPT** commands specify the sender and recipient of the mail. Mail addresses are scanned for strange characters. The pipe character (|) is deleted (changed to a blank space), and < and > are allowed only if they are used to define a mail address (> must be preceded by <).

- An unexpected transition by the SMTP server.

- Unknown commands, for which the Security Appliance changes all the characters in the packet to X. In this case, the server generates an error code to the client. Because of the change in the packet, the TCP checksum has to be recalculated or adjusted.

The **inspect smtp** command enables the Mail inspection feature. This restricts mail servers to receiving only the seven commands defined in RFC 821 section 4.5.1 (**HELO, MAIL, RCPT, DATA, RSET, NOOP,** and **QUIT**). Additional support for eight extended SMTP commands can be enabled through these commands: **AUTH, DATA, EHLO, ETRN, SAML, SEND, SOML, and VRFY.** All other commands are rejected.

NOTE   The **inspect smtp** command has been superseded by the **inspect esmtp** command in version 7.0 of the software, which supports all 13 SMTP command restrictions. If **inspect smtp** is used, it will automatically be changed to **inspect esmtp** in the running-config.

The strict implementation of RFC 821 section 4.5.1 sometimes causes problems for mail servers that do not adhere to the standard. For example, Microsoft Exchange Server does not strictly comply with RFC 821 section 4.5.1 and uses extended SMTP commands such as **EHLO.** The Cisco Security Appliance converts any such commands into **NOOP** commands, which, as specified by the RFC, forces SMTP servers to fall back to using minimal SMTP commands only. This might cause Microsoft Outlook clients and Exchange servers to function unpredictably when their connection passes through the Security Appliance.

Mail inspection, however, is not the magic bullet for all mail server–related attacks. It protects your mail server only from known attacks.

ICMP Inspection

ICMP has been used in many different exploits and DoS attacks. One such exploit that has been termed a "smurf attack" is a command attack used throughout the Internet. A malicious host sends a stream of ICMP echo request packets to a network broadcast address. The source of the packets is spoofed to appear as though the packets originate from the intended target. Because the broadcast segment may have several hundred hosts, the replies to the echo request overwhelm the target of the attack with echo replies that were never requested. Using ICMP stateful inspection, the Security Appliance can restrict these attacks. ICMP inspection enables the Security Appliance to track ICMP traffic and inspect each packet like TCP and UDP traffic. The Security Appliance will only send a single replay to any one ICMP request received, using this **inspect icmp** command. ICMP inspection allows replies only when the ICMP reply session information matches a request by scanning the ICMP payload for pertinent information, specifically the source IP address, destination IP address, protocol, identification number, and sequence number. It will then attempt to match the information with each ICMP request and response pair. The **inspect icmp** command is enabled by default in the *inspection_default* **class-map**.

Remote Shell Inspections

Using a remote shell (rsh) application allows an administrator to run commands on a remote computer running either an rsh service or an rsh daemon. Rsh uses two channels when connected, with the first channel operating as the communications channel and the second channel operating as an output for standard error. When a client first starts an rsh connection, it opens a TCP channel from one of its high-order ports to port 514 on the server. This works in the same way as the **inspect ftp** command.

To manage rsh traffic, you must enable the **inspect rsh** command in a class-map. When a standard error message is received from the rsh server, the **inspect rsh** command will open a temporary inbound opening through the Security Appliance for the standard error channel. Once the rsh session is complete, the opening will be torn down.

SNMP Inspection

SNMP inspection can restrict the version of SNMP that can pass through the Security Appliance. Using the **snmp-map** command in global-configuration mode, you can limit the SNMP version to 1, 2, 2c, or 3. You can also allow multiple versions and just strict one version. Once the **snmp-map** is configured, you will apply it to an inspection class using the **inspect snmp** command, similar to the mgcp inspection configuration.

SQL*Net Inspection

Oracle is one of the most common database systems deployed today. Like most popular network applications, Oracle relies on specific ports for communication with clients and servers, specifically 1521, 1810, 2481, and 7778. Oracle's use of port 1521 for SQL*Net services is well-known and a focus for hackers and malicious users attempting to exploit known flaws and security holes. SQL*Net only requires one channel to communicate between the client and server. Communication between client and server initiates through port 1521 on the server side and an assigned port above 1023 on the client's side. Once the connection has been established, the SQL*Net server will request a redirect to a new port on the server, usually an unused port above 1023. Once communication has been established between the client and the new port, the SQL*Net server will tear down the old connection. This behavior must be tracked and managed by the Security Appliance to verify that the redirection of the ports was not done by a hacker attempting to hijack the connection.

To manage SQL*Net traffic, you must enable the **inspect sqlnet** command in a class map. The **inspect sqlnet** command will monitor outbound TCP traffic for SQL*Net traffic, and if the Security Appliance does not implicitly allow TCP traffic through, the command will open an access control list (ACL) for the redirected SQL*Net channel between the client and the server. For inbound TCP connections, the Security Appliance opens an inbound opening for the redirected channel if an ACL exists, allowing inbound connections to an SQL*Net server.

Example 19-7   *Managing SQL*Net Traffic via a Class Map*

```
Pixfirewall(config)# class-map sqlnet_port
Pixfirewall(config-cmap)# match port tcp eq 1521
Pixfirewall(config-cmap)# exit
Pixfirewall(config)# policy-map dmz_map
Pixfirewall(config-pmap)# class sqlnet_port
Pixfirewall(config-pmap-c)# inspect sqlnet
Pixfirewall(config-pmap-c)# exit
```

NOTE   If you are running an IANA-compliant SQL*Net database, you must inspect port 66 instead of port 1521.

Security Appliance Intrusion Protection Feature

Cisco Security Appliance includes an IP-only intrusion protection feature through the AIP-SSM module for the ASA Security Appliance series. It provides visibility at network perimeters or for locations where additional security between network segments is required.

After it is configured, the IPS module watches packets and sessions as they flow through the firewall, scanning each for a match with any of the IPS configured filters. When suspicious activity is detected, the Security Appliance responds immediately and can be configured to do the following:

1. Send an alarm to a syslog server.

2. Drop the packet.

3. Reset the TCP connection.

AIP-SSM Module

The Cisco ASA Security Appliance series supports the Advanced Inspection and Protection Security Service Module (AIP-SSM). The AIP-SSM comes in two modules: the AIP-SSM-10 and the AIP-SSM-20. Both modules function the same way, support the same features, and look identical. The only difference between the two modules is the processor speed and memory size of the AIP-SSM-20, which is faster and larger than that of the AIP-SSM-10. The AIP-SSM uses two physical channels to communicate with the Security Appliance. All Intrusion Protection System (IPS) packets transmit through a Gigabit Ethernet interface that connects the AIP-SSM to the Security Appliance. A second connection that handles the control traffic between the module and the Security Appliance transmits through an internal 10/100 Ethernet interface. The AIP-SSM module also contains an external 10/100/1000 Ethernet management port that is primarily used for software upgrades and Cisco Adaptive Security Device Manager (ASDM) management access. The AIP-SSM can analyze the traffic flow through the packet content by opening the packet envelope as well as the payload, allowing it to inspect Layers 3 to 7.

The AIP-SSM can monitor the traffic flow in two ways. In promiscuous mode, the AIP-SSM takes a copy of the traffic flow and inspects the copy of the traffic instead of the live traffic flow. This eliminates the chance that the inspection will affect the actual flow of traffic on the Security Appliance, as it is never actually touched. This will reduce the effectiveness of the IPS services, since the AIP-SSM will not be able to react to the traffic flow instantly and may allow malicious packets through before the AIP-SSM intervenes with the assigned action for the attack. To directly prevent attacks through the AIP-SSM, the in-line mode must be enabled.

Inline mode directly monitors and inspects the live traffic flows through the Security Appliance. If an attack is detected, the packets that the inspection found as malicious, as well as all other packets in that traffic flow, are "stopped" by the AIP-SSM before they enter the network.

Like the Security Appliance, the AIP-SSM supports a failover configuration that handles how the Security Appliance permits traffic. In a failed-open mode, the Security Appliance will continue to transmit traffic flows without IPS inspection and possibly will allow malicious packets through unhindered. The AIP-SSM can also fail-closed, which will drop all traffic flows that have been configured to use the AIP-SSM IPS service. This means that all traffic that must pass through the AIP-SSM will stop at the Security Appliance until the AIP-SSM is enabled again.

Installing the AIP-SSM Module

After the AIP-SSM module has been installed into the Security Appliance, you must verify that the software used by the AIP-SSM for IPS services is functional. You can do this by using the **show module 1 detail** command in privileged mode on the Security Appliance. The output of the command, shown in Example 19-8, displays the status of the modules, firmware version, and software version. If the IPS software is missing or corrupt, the software version will not be displayed.

Example 19-8   show module 1 detail *Output*

```
Getting details from the Service Module, please wait...
Unable to read details from slot 1
ASA 5500 Series Security Services Module-10
Model:              ASA-SSM-10
Hardware version:    1.0
Serial Number:       12345678
Firmware version:    1.0(7)2
Software version:
Status:             Init
```

The Status field displays the current status of the module and can have the following states:

- **Initializing**—The module has been recognized and is in the process of being initialized with the system.
- **Up**—The module is online and functioning properly.
- **Unresponsive**—The Security Appliance cannot communicate with the module.
- **Reloading**—The module is reloading.
- **Shutting**—The module is in the process of shutting down.
- **ShuttingDown**—The module has completed the shutdown procedures and is offline.
- **Recover**—The module is attempting to download a recovery image.

In Example 19-8, you will notice that the software version is not displayed. The reason is that the AIP-SSM cannot read the IPS image due to corruption or nonexistence. To resolve this, the AIP-SSM module requires a new IPS image from which to initialize. The Security Appliance uses the **hw-module module 1 recover** command to define where to download an IPS image file from a TFTP server. To manually specify the TFTP server, filename, and network configurations, you can add the **configure** keyword to the preceding command, as shown in Example 19-9.

Example 19-9 *TFTP an IPS Image*

```
PIXfirewall(config)# hw-module module 1 recover configure
Image URL [tftp://0.0.0.0/]: tftp://192.168.10.3/AIP-SSM-K9-sys-1.1-a-5.0-0.22.img
Port IP Address [0.0.0.0]:
VLAN ID [0]:
Gateway IP Address [0.0.0]:
```

Once you have defined the TFTP server and IPS image, you must download and load the new image onto the AIP-SSM and reboot the module. Use the **hw-module 1 recover boot** command to start this process. This will download the image from the defined TFTP server and then attempt to boot and initialize the AIP-SSM module with the new image. You can view the process in detail by using the **module-boot debug** command preceding the **hw-module 1 recover boot** command, as shown in Example 19-10.

Example 19-10 module-boot debug *Output*

```
PIXfirewall (config)# module-boot debug
debug module-boot enabled at level 1
PIXfirewall (config)# hw module 1 recover boot
The module in slot 1 will be recovered. This may
erase all configuration and all data on that device and
attempt to download a new image for it.
Recover module in slot 1? [confirm]
Recover issued for module in slot 1
PIXfirewall (config)# %The module in slot 1 is unresponsive.
%The module in slot 1 is recovering.
Slot-1 8> tftp AIP-SSM-K9-sys-1.1-a-5.0-0.22.img@10.0.31.10
Slot-1 9> !!!!!!!!!!!!!!!!!!!!!!!!!!!!!!!!!!!!!!!!!!!!!!!!!!!!!!!!!!!!!!!!!!!!!!!!
!!!!!!!!!!!
%The module in slot 1 is recovering.
Slot-1 10>
!!!!!!!!!!!!!!!!!!!!!!!!!!!!!!!!!!!!!!!!!!!!!!!!!!!!!!!!!!!!!!!!!!!!!!!!!!!!!!
!!!!!!!!!!!
........
Slot-1 79> !!!!!!!!!!!!!!!!!!!!!!!!!!!!!!!!!!!!!!!!!!!!!!!!!!!!!
Slot-1 80> Received 23140374 bytes
Slot-1 81> Launching TFTP Image...
%The module in slot 1 is recovering.
%The module in slot 1 is recovering.
%The module in slot 1 is recovering.
%The module in slot 1 is recovering.
Slot-1 82> Launching BootLoader...
%The module in slot 1 is recovering.
%The module in slot 1 is recovering.
```

After this is complete, use the **show module 1** command again to verify that the module initialized correctly, as shown in Example 19-11.

Example 19-11 *AIP-SSM Module Correctly Initialized*

```
PIXfirewall(config)# show module 1
Mod Card Type                                           Model           Serial No.
--- ------------------------------------------------    --------------  ----------
  1 ASA 5500 Series Security Services Module-10    ASA-SSM-10         12345678
Mod MAC Address Range                       Hw Version  Fw Version   Sw Version
--- ------------------------------------    ----------  -----------  -----------
  1 000b.fcf8.0170 to 000b.fcf8.0170  1.0         1.0(7)2      5.0(0.22)S129.0
Mod Status
--- ---------------------
  1 Up
```

Setting Up the AIP-SSM Module

Now that you have a working IPS image on the AIP-SSM, you must perform an initial configuration setup on the module. The setup process can be done through the command-line interface (CLI) of the AIP-SSM module. To access the module's CLI, telnet to the module using the **session 1** command in privileged mode on the Security Appliance. When you use this command, you will telnet to the module and be prompted for a username and password to gain access to the CLI. Since this will be the first time you have accessed the module, you must use the default username and password, which are *cisco* and *cisco,* respectively. Immediately after you enter the password, the module will prompt you to enter a new password for the username *cisco*. This will replace the default password for the module.

You can now run the **setup** command, which will allow the administrator to configure the basic AIP-SSM settings, including the hostname, IP interfaces, Telnet server, web server port, access control lists (ACL), and time settings. The module will initially display the current configuration of the module, which should be the default settings. The next section will allow you to modify each attribute that you may need changed, such as the IP address or ACLs, as shown in Example 19-12.

Example 19-12 *Configuring Basic AIP-SSM Settings*

```
sensor# setup
--- System Configuration Dialog ---
Current Configuration:
service host
network-settings
host-ip 10.1.9.201/24,10.1.9.1
host-name sensor
telnet-option disabled
ftp-timeout 300
```

continues

Example 19-12 *Configuring Basic AIP-SSM Settings (Continued)*

```
login-banner-text
exit
time-zone-settings
offset 0
standard-time-zone-name UTC
exit
summertime-option disabled
ntp-option disabled
exit
service web-server
port 443
exit
............
Continue with configuration dialog?[yes]: <yes>
Enter host name[sensor]: sensor1
Enter IP interface[192.168.10.31/24,192.168.10.1]: 192.168.10.41/24,198.168.10.1
Enter telnet-server status[disabled]:
Enter web-server port[443]:
Modify current access list?[no]: yes
Current access list entries:
No entries
Permit: 192.168.10.0/24
Permit:
............
[0] Go to the command prompt without saving this config.
[1] Return back to the setup without saving this config.
[2] Save this configuration and exit setup.
Enter your selection[2]: 2
Warning: Reboot is required before the configuration change will take effect
Configuration Saved.
Warning: The node must be rebooted for the changes to go into effect.
Continue with reboot? [yes]: yes
```

The attributes that you can change are these:

- **Hostname**—You can use this attribute to change the hostname of the module. The hostname can be no longer than 64 characters.

- **IP Interface**—You can use this attribute to set the IP address of the external 10/100/100 Ethernet port.

- **Telnet Server**—You can enable this attribute if you wish to allow a remote user Telnet access to the module. Since Telnet is not a secure terminal application, it is recommended that this attribute be disabled at all times.

- **Web Server**—You can use this attribute to set the TCP port for the internal web server. The default is 443 (HTTPS).

- **Modify Current Access List**—You can use this attribute list to input hosts or networks that can have access to the module through remote ASDM or Telnet connections.

Configuring IPS Through ASDM

The AIP-SSM module can be configured for IPS features through the CLI or on an ASDM window. It is recommended that the administrator configure the IPS features through the ASDM as it removes most of the user error that can come from direct CLI configurations, like typos. To use the ASDM for configuration, the module will require an HTTPS web server to be enabled, as shown in Example 19-8 in the preceding section, as well as for the HTTPS web server to have an IP address that is accessible on the network. Once you have completed the **setup** command, you will be able to access the IPS configuration options from ASDM. Once you bring up an ASDM window for the Security Appliance, you will see the IPS button on the left side of the window, as shown in Figure 19-2.

Figure 19-2 *ASDM Home Panel with IPS Enabled*

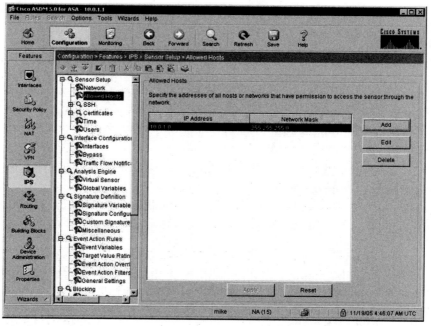

To access the IPS configuration window, click the **IPS** button. This will bring up an IPS popup window that will request which interface you will use to connect to the module, as shown in Figure 19-3. If the management interface IP address has been configured through the **setup** command, choose the **Management IP address** checkbox and press **continue**.

Figure 19-3 *IPS Connection Popup Window*

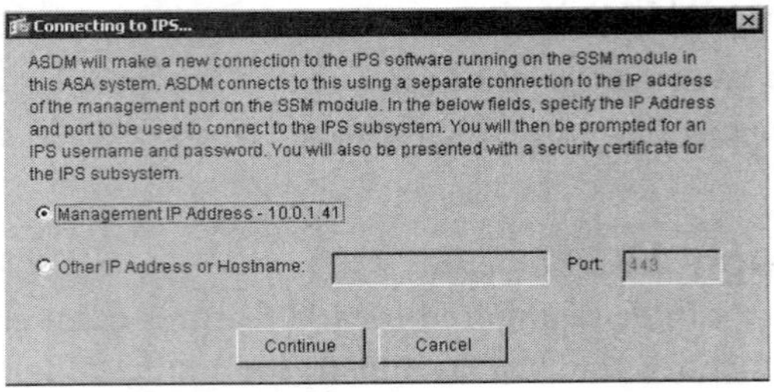

You will then be brought to a session login prompt similar to what you used when you initially telneted into the module from the Security Appliance, shown in Figure 19-4. Use the same username and the new password you set earlier to create the session with the IPS.

Figure 19-4 *IPS Session Login Popup Window*

Once you have connected to the IPS through the ASDM, you will be placed in the IPS window, shown in Figure 19-5. From here, you can control access to the module by allowing or disallowing hosts or networks through the Allow Hosts window. Additionally, you can add new users with limited access to the module through the Users window. The AIP-SSM will only allow a single user to connect to the module at any one time, even if multiple users have been configured on the module.

Configuring Security Policies for IPS

You must redirect traffic flows to the AIP-SSM module through security policies, be it a copy or live traffic. This can be done through service-policies on the Security Appliance. The ASDM can use a service-policy wizard, or you can use the CLI to configure a service-policy. You can also use an already configured service-policy. Using the Service-Policy button, you can access an existing service-policy, or through the wizard you can enable an IPS-policy on that service-policy. Figure 19-6 shows the window that you will use to enable the IPS policy and which access mode, promiscuous or inline, you will use for the service-policy. You almost must define which failure state you would like the service-policy to use for the AIP-SSM. You have now applied an IPS policy to the Security Appliance and can monitor it through the **Monitor** tab in ASDM.

Figure 19-5 *ASDM IPS Configuration Panel*

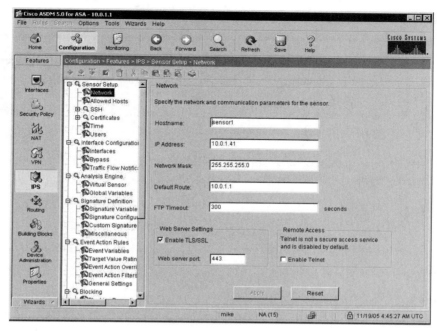

Figure 19-6 *ASDM IPS Add Service Policy Rule Window*

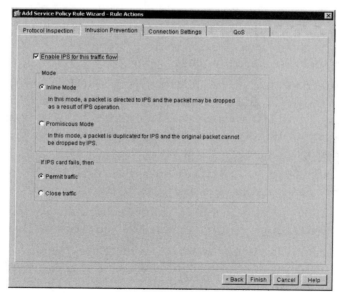

Foundation Summary

The "Foundation Summary" provides a convenient review of many key concepts in this chapter. If you are already comfortable with the topics in this chapter, this summary can help you recall a few details. If you just read this chapter, this review should help solidify some key facts. If you are doing your final preparation before the exam, this summary provides a convenient way to review the day before the exam.

PIX Firewall version 6.3 and later support application inspection of the major protocols and applications that provide VoIP services, including the following:

- CTIQBE
- H.323
- MGCP
- SCCP
- SIP

Cisco Security Appliance has preconfigured application inspection commands that help it mitigate most known attacks:

- **FTP Inspection**—Protects the inside systems for hijacked connections and allows dynamic port assignments when using FTP passive transfer mode. Using FTP-maps will allow greater control over what can be done through the inspected FTP session, restricting specific commands from being run.

- **HTTP Inspection**—Protects the inside systems from HTTP messages that fail to meet RFC 2616 standards. Additionally, with the use of an http-map, HTTP inspection can restrict the allowed HTTP commands that can be accessed through the connection. HTTP inspection can also control port misuse, such as peer-to-peer applications and instant messaging.

- **rsh Inspections**—Protects the inside systems from hijacked rsh connections and allows for dynamic port assignments for the Standard Error Channel.

- **DNS Inspection**—DNS queries and responses are torn down as soon as a reply to a DNS query is received, dropping all other responses and averting a DoS attack.

- **Mail Inspection**—The **inspect esmtp** command enables the Mail Guard feature, which restricts mail servers to receiving only the seven commands defined in RFC 821 section 4.5.1 (**HELO, MAIL, RCPT, DATA, RSET, NOOP,** and **QUIT**). Additionally, mail inspection supports eight ESMTP commands (**AUTH, DATA, EHLO, ETRN, SAML, SEND, SOML,** and **VRFY**). All other commands are rejected.

- **ICMP Inspection**—Protects inside systems from DoS attacks that flood the network broadcast with SYN packets or modified ICMP packets.

- **SQL*Net Inspection**—Protects the inside systems from hijacked SQL*Net connections and allows for dynamic port assignments for the reassigned communications channel.

The Cisco Security Appliance also includes an intrusion protection feature. The Security Appliance supports both inbound and outbound auditing through the AIP-SSM module. The AIP-SSM module can work in promiscuous mode or inline mode when analyzing traffic flows. The AIP-SSM can also be set to fail-open or fail-closed when the AIP-SSM goes offline. Through the use of a service-policy, the Security Appliance can redirect traffic flows to the AIP-SSM and allow auditing through the IPS feature. When an attack is detected, the AIP-SSM can send an alarm, drop the packet, or reset the TCP connection.

Q&A

As mentioned in the Introduction, the questions in this book are more difficult than what you should experience on the exam. The questions are designed to ensure your understanding of the concepts discussed in this chapter and adequately prepare you to complete the exam. You should use the simulated exams on the CD to practice for the exam.

The answers to these questions can be found in Appendix A:

1. Which PIX feature mitigates a DoS attack using an rewritten ICMP datagram?

2. On which port does the Security Appliance inspect for H.323 traffic by default?

3. How do you enable the Security Appliance Mail inspection feature?

4. What are some of the Security Appliance limitations on CTIQBE application inspection?

5. How do you install a new IPS image on a AIP-SSM module?

6. Which policies are available in the Cisco Security Appliance IPS configuration?

7. How does DNS inspection on the Cisco Security Appliance prevent DoS attacks that exploit DNS?

8. What basic configurations are required to fully enable IPS features on a Security Appliance?

9. How does the mail inspection feature prevent SMTP-related attacks?

10. How do you enable MGCP application inspection for call agents and gateways using the default ports?

CHAPTER 20

Case Study and Sample Configuration

The DUKEM consulting firm is a medium-size company with 700 employees. It has three offices across the continental United States. Twenty percent of DUKEM's employees are mobile or telecommute. Figure 20-1 shows the current DUKEM network infrastructure.

Figure 20-1 *DUKEM Network Infrastructure*

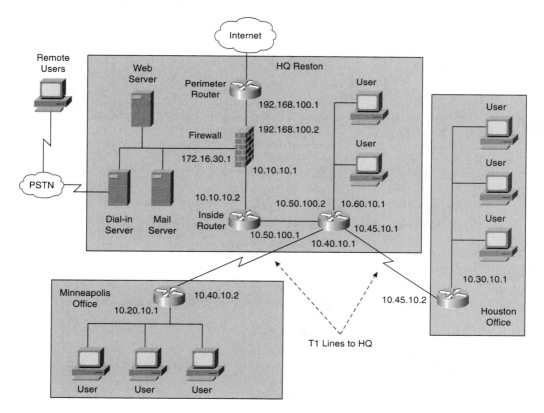

Remote Offices

The branch offices are connected to headquarters (Reston) by T1 connections. All Internet-bound traffic goes out through Reston. Telecommuting and mobile users call an 800 number that connects to a pool of modems at Reston.

Firewall

A server-based application firewall is used at headquarters (HQ). The firewall cannot be configured for Internet Protocol Security (IPSec) or generic routing encapsulation (GRE). The firewall has a history of irregular behavior, which has created network disruptions.

Growth Expectation

DUKEM has grown by 13 percent during each of the past two years and expects to have an average growth rate of 15 percent over the next few years. It also has experienced an increase in the number of employees who telecommute.

DUKEM's CIO has put forth the following requirements:

■ A highly available firewall solution

■ Secure communication channels between branch offices and HQ, telecommuters and HQ, and possible business partners

An information technology (IT) consulting firm hired by DUKEM has recommended that Cisco Security Appliance replace the existing firewall system. You have been selected to do the Cisco Security Appliance configuration for DUKEM.

Figure 20-2 shows the Cisco Security Appliance solution in the new network design.

Use the information in Figure 20-2 to configure your firewalls by completing the following tasks:

> Task 1—Basic configuration for the Cisco Security Appliance
> Task 2—Configuring access rules on HQ
> Task 3—Configuring authentication
> Task 4—Configuring logging
> Task 5—Configuring a virtual private network (VPN) between HQ and remote sites
> Task 6—Configuring a remote-access VPN to HQ
> Task 7—Configuring failover

Good luck!

Figure 20-2   *Proposed Network Design with PIX Firewall*

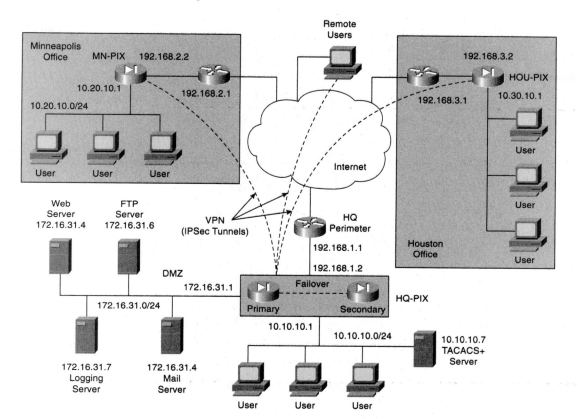

Task 1: Basic Configuration for the Cisco Security Appliance

Tables 20-1 through 20-5 list the information required for you to configure the Cisco Security Appliance at the Reston headquarters. Use the information from the tables to configure your Cisco Security Appliance according to the network diagram shown in Figure 20-2.

Basic Configuration Information for HQ-PIX

Table 20-1 lists the physical interfaces of the Cisco PIX Firewall that is installed in the Reston headquarters. This table includes the interface name, physical interface ID, assigned address, and speed/duplex.

Table 20-1 *PIX Interface Information for HQ*

Interface Name	Hardware ID	Interface IP Address	Interface Speed
Outside	Ethernet0	192.168.1.2	100full
Inside	Ethernet1	10.10.10.1	100full
DMZ	Ethernet2	172.16.31.1	100full
Failover	Ethernet3	1.1.1.1	100full

Table 20-2 shows what routing information needs to be configured on the PIX. Note that the only route required is the default route. No specific routes are defined on the firewall.

Table 20-2 *PIX Routing Information for HQ*

Interface Name	Destination Network IP Address	Network Mask	Gateway (Router) IP Address
Outside	0.0.0.0	0.0.0.0	192.168.1.1

Table 20-3 shows which outside addresses or address ranges are available for the global address pool. Remember that the global addresses are used in conjunction with the **nat** command to assign the addresses to which the PIX is translating (this is not the original source but the translated source).

Table 20-3 *Recording Global IP Information for HQ*

Interface Name	NAT ID Number	Beginning of IP Address Range	End of IP Address Range
Outside	1	192.168.1.12	192.168.1.150
Outside	1	192.168.1.152	
DMZ	1	172.16.31.12	172.16.31.100

Table 20-4 shows which Internet Protocol (IP) addresses or network segments are to be translated (into the global addresses) as they pass through the firewall.

Table 20-4 *NAT IP Information for HQ*

Interface Name	NAT ID Number	Network Address	Network Mask for This Address
Inside	1	10.10.10.0	255.255.255.0
DMZ	1	172.16.31.0	255.255.255.0

Table 20-5 shows static IP address mapping for resources that are accessed from the outside (public) network. The static IP address is the address that is configured on the individual server, and the host IP address is the IP address that the PIX uses when answering for the server.

Table 20-5 *Static IP Address Mapping Information for HQ*

Interface on Which the Host Resides	Interface Name Where the Global Address Resides	Static IP Address	Host IP Address	Description
DMZ	Outside	192.168.1.4	172.16.31.4	Mail server
DMZ	Outside	192.168.1.5	172.16.31.5	Web server
DMZ	Outside	192.168.1.6	172.16.31.6	FTP server

Example 20-1 shows the individual configuration commands for all the items documented in Tables 20-1 through 20-5.

Example 20-1 *Firewall Configuration for the Reston Headquarters*

```
interface Ethernet 0
   nameif outside
   security-level 0
   ip address 192.168.1.2 255.255.255.0
   speed 100
   duplex full
interface Ethernet 1
   nameif inside
   security-level 100
   ip address 10.10.10.1 255.255.255.0
   speed 100
   duplex full
interface Ethernet 2
   nameif DMZ
   security-level 80
   ip address 172.16.31.1 255.255.255.0
   speed 100
   duplex full
```

continues

Example 20-1 *Firewall Configuration for the Reston Headquarters (Continued)*

```
interface Ethernet 3
  nameif failover
  security-level 90
  ip address 1.1.1.1 255.255.255.0
  speed 100  duplex full



hostname HQ-PIX
nat (inside) 1 10.10.10.0 255.255.255.0
global (outside) 1 192.168.1.12-192.168.1.150 netmask 255.255.255.0
global (outside) 1 192.168.1.152 netmask 255.255.255.0
global (DMZ) 1 172.16.31.12-172.16.31.100 netmask 255.255.255.0
static (DMZ,outside) 192.168.1.4  172.16.31.4 netmask 255.255.255.255 0 0
static (DMZ,outside) 192.168.1.5  172.16.31.5 netmask 255.255.255.255 0 0
static (DMZ,outside) 192.168.1.6  172.16.31.6 netmask 255.255.255.255 0 0

route outside 0.0.0.0 0.0.0.0 192.168.1.1
```

Basic Configuration Information for MN-PIX

Tables 20-6 through 20-9 provide the information needed to configure the PIX Firewall at the Minneapolis office.

Table 20-6 shows information about the physical interfaces on the PIX Firewall.

Table 20-6 *PIX Interface Information for Minneapolis*

Interface Name	Hardware ID	Interface IP Address	Interface Speed
Outside	Ethernet0	192.168.2.2	100full
Inside	Ethernet1	10.20.10.1	100full

Table 20-7 depicts which routes need to be configured on the PIX Firewall in the Minneapolis office.

Table 20-7 *Routing Information for the Minneapolis PIX*

Interface Name	Destination Network IP Address	Network Mask	Gateway (Router) IP Address
Outside	0.0.0.0	0.0.0.0	192.168.2.1

Table 20-8 lists the global IP addresses or address ranges that are used in conjunction with Network Address Translation (NAT) for translation purposes.

Table 20-8 *Global IP Address Information for the Minneapolis PIX*

Interface Name	NAT ID Number	Beginning of IP Address Range	End of IP Address Range
Outside	1	192.168.2.12	192.168.2.250
Outside	1	192.168.2.252	

Table 20-9 lists which addresses are dynamically translated on the PIX Firewall.

Table 20-9 *NAT IP Address Information for the Minneapolis PIX*

Interface Name	NAT ID Number	Network Address	Network Mask for This Address
Inside	1	10.20.10.0	255.255.255.0

Example 20-2 depicts the individual configuration commands for each of the items listed in Tables 20-6 through 20-9.

Example 20-2 *Firewall Configuration for the Minneapolis Office*

```
interface Ethernet 0
   nameif outside
   security-level 0
   ip address 192.168.2.2 255.255.255.0
   speed 100   duplex full
interface Ethernet 1
   nameif inside
   security-level 100
   ip address 10.20.10.1 255.255.255.0
   speed 100
   duplex full


hostname MN-PIX

nat (inside) 1 10.20.10.0 255.255.255.0
global (outside) 1 192.168.2.12-192.168.2.250 netmask 255.255.255.0
global (outside) 1 192.168.2.252 netmask 255.255.255.0

route outside 0.0.0.0 0.0.0.0 192.168.2.1
```

Basic Configuration Information for HOU-PIX

Tables 20-10 through 20-13 provide the information needed to configure the PIX Firewall in the Houston office.

Table 20-10 shows information about the physical interfaces of the Cisco PIX Firewall.

Table 20-10 *Interface Information for the Houston PIX*

Interface Name	Hardware ID	Interface IP Address	Interface Speed
Outside	Ethernet0	192.168.3.2	100full
Inside	Ethernet1	10.30.10.1	100full

Table 20-11 depicts which routes need to be configured on the PIX Firewall in the Houston office.

Table 20-11 *Routing Information for the Houston PIX*

Interface Name	Destination Network IP Address	Network Mask	Gateway (Router) IP Address
Outside	0.0.0.0	0.0.0.0	192.168.3.1

Table 20-12 lists the global IP addresses or address ranges that are used in conjunction with NAT for translation purposes.

Table 20-12 *Global IP Address Information for the Houston PIX*

Interface Name	NAT ID Number	Beginning of IP Address Range	End of IP Address Range
Outside	1	192.168.3.12	192.168.3.250
Outside	1	192.168.3.252	

Table 20-13 lists which addresses are dynamically translated on the PIX Firewall.

Table 20-13 *NAT IP Address Information for the Houston PIX*

Interface Name	NAT ID Number	Network Address	Network Mask for This Address
Inside	1	10.30.10.0	255.255.255.0

Example 20-3 depicts the individual configuration commands for each of the items listed in Tables 20-10 through 20-13.

Example 20-3 *Firewall Configuration for the Houston Office*

```
interface Ethernet 0
  nameif outside
  security-level 0
  ip address 192.168.3.2 255.255.255.0
  speed 100
  duplex full
  interface Ethernet 1
  nameif inside
  security100
  ip address 10.30.10.1 255.255.255.0
  speed 100
  duplex full




hostname HOU-PIX

nat (inside) 1 10.30.10.0 255.255.255.0
global (outside) 1 192.168.3.12-192.168.3.250 netmask 255.255.255.0
global (outside) 1 192.168.3.252 netmask 255.255.255.0

route outside 0.0.0.0 0.0.0.0 192.168.3.1
```

Task 2: Configuring Access Rules on HQ

After configuring the basic PIX Firewall parameters, you must create the access rules for the PIX Firewall at the Reston site (HQ-PIX). The access rules are necessary to enable the remote sites to connect to the Reston location while limiting access from unauthorized locations. The following steps define the access rules needed on HQ-PIX:

Step 1   To allow users on the outside interface access to the mail server on the demilitarized zone (DMZ) interface, enter the following commands:

```
access-list acl-out permit tcp any host 192.168.1.4 eq smtp
access-group acl-out in interface outside
```

The **access-group** command binds the **acl-out** access list command statement group to the outside interface.

Step 2   To allow users on the outside interface to access the web server on the DMZ interface, use the following command:

```
access-list acl-out permit tcp any host 192.168.1.5 eq www
```

Step 3   To allow users on the outside interface to access the File Transfer Protocol (FTP) server on the DMZ interface, use the following command:

```
access-list acl-out permit tcp any host 192.168.1.6 eq ftp
```

Example 20-4 shows the access list configured on the HQ PIX.

Example 20-4 *Access List on the HQ PIX*

```
access-list acl-out permit tcp any host 192.168.1.4 eq smtp
access-list acl-out permit tcp any host 192.168.1.5 eq www
access-list acl-out permit tcp any host 192.168.1.6 eq ftp
access-list acl-out permit udp any host 192.168.1.8 eq 514
access-group acl-out in interface outside
```

Task 3: Configuring Authentication

Incoming FTP connections to HQ-PIX are authenticated using the Terminal Access Controller Access Control System Plus (TACACS+) server located on the internal network. To use a TACACS+ server for authentication, you must first identify the IP address of the TACACS+ server and then indicate which connections will use the TACACS+ server. This configuration requires the following two steps:

Step 1   Configure the TACACS+ server:

   `aaa-server TACACS+ (inside) host 10.10.10.7 tacpass`

Step 2   Configure authentication, authorization, and accounting (AAA) authentication for FTP access:

   `aaa authentication include ftp inside 0.0.0.0 0.0.0.0 TACACS+`

Example 20-5 shows the TACACS+ configuration.

Example 20-5 *TACACS+ Configuration*

```
aaa-server TACACS+ (inside) host 10.10.10.7 tacpass
aaa authentication include ftp inside 0.0.0.0 0.0.0.0 TACACS+
```

Task 4: Configuring Logging

To help protect your network configuration, it is important to log events that are happening on the network. This log information provides valuable insight into what is happening on the network, especially when the network is being attacked or proved. The following steps outline the commands necessary to enable logging at the three locations:

Step 1   Enable logging on HQ-PIX to the logging server:

```
logging  on
logging  trap  informational
logging  host  DMZ  172.16.31.7
```

Step 2   Enable logging on HOU-PIX:

```
logging  on
logging  trap  informational
logging  host  outside  172.16.31.7
```

Step 3   Enable logging on MN-PIX:

```
logging  on
logging  trap  informational
logging  host  outside  172.16.31.7
```

NOTE   Sending logging information from Houston and Minneapolis to the actual logging server IP address (172.16.31.7) prevents the logging traffic from traversing the Internet in the clear. Sending the logging traffic through the VPN tunnel prevents the logging information from being observed on the Internet, but the real IP address (172.16.31.7) is reachable only when the VPN tunnel is active.

Task 5: Configuring a VPN Between HQ and Remote Sites

The two remote sites communicate with the Reston location (HQ-PIX) using VPN connections that traverse the Internet. To enable these VPNs, you must define the VPN characteristics at the headquarters location, as well as at the remote sites. Configuring the VPN connections between HQ-PIX and the two remote sites (MN-PIX and HOU-PIX) involves the following tasks:

- Configuring the central PIX Firewall, HQ-PIX, for VPN tunneling

- Configuring the Houston PIX Firewall, HOU-PIX, for VPN tunneling

- Configuring the Minneapolis PIX Firewall, MN-PIX, for VPN tunneling

NOTE   The VPN tunnels shown in this example enable the two remote sites (Houston and Minneapolis) to communicate with the main location at Reston. If the two remote sites also must be able to communicate with each other, you would also need to establish a VPN tunnel from HOU-PIX to MN-PIX. This example assumes that the two remote sites need to communicate only with the main location and not with each other.

Configuring the Central PIX Firewall, HQ-PIX, for VPN Tunneling

Both remote sites connect to the Reston location using VPN tunneling. The VPN protects the traffic coming from the remote sites. The following steps define the VPN characteristics on HQ-PIX:

Step 1   Configure an Internet Security Association and Key Management Protocol (ISAKMP) policy:

```
isakmp  enable  outside
isakmp  policy  10  authentication  pre-share
isakmp  policy  10  encryption  des
isakmp  policy  10  hash  md5
isakmp  policy  10  group  1
isakmp  policy  10  lifetime  1000
```

Step 2   Configure a preshared key and associate it with the peers (Houston and Minneapolis):

```
isakmp key C2I#ghi address 192.168.3.2
isakmp key B2I#def address 192.168.2.2
```

Step 3   Configure the supported IPSec transforms:

```
crypto ipsec transform-set myset esp-des esp-md5-hmac
```

Step 4   Create an access list:

```
access-list 130 permit ip 10.10.10.0 255.255.255.0 10.30.10.0
   255.255.255.0
access-list 130 permit ip 172.16.31.0 255.255.255.0 10.30.10.0
   255.255.255.0
access-list 120 permit ip 10.10.10.0 255.255.255.0 10.20.10.0
   255.255.255.0
access-list 120 permit ip 172.16.31.0 255.255.255.0 10.20.10.0
   255.255.255.0
```

Step 5   Define a crypto map for both Houston and Minneapolis:

```
crypto map Dukem-Map 20 ipsec-isakmp
crypto map Dukem-Map 20 match address 120
crypto map Dukem-Map 20 set peer 192.168.2.2
crypto map Dukem-Map 20 set transform-set myset

crypto map Dukem-Map 30 ipsec-isakmp
crypto map Dukem-Map 30 match address 130
crypto map Dukem-Map 30 set peer 192.168.3.2
crypto map Dukem-Map 30 set transform-set myset
```

Step 6   Apply the crypto map to the outside interface:

```
crypto map Dukem-Map interface outside
```

Step 7   Specify that IPSec traffic is implicitly trusted (permitted):

```
sysopt connection permit-ipsec
```

Step 8   Configure a NAT 0 policy so that traffic between the offices is excluded from NAT:

```
access-list VPN permit ip 10.10.10.0 255.255.255.0 10.30.10.0
   255.255.255.0
access-list VPN permit ip 172.16.31.0 255.255.255.0 10.30.10.0
   255.255.255.0
access-list VPN permit ip 10.10.10.0 255.255.255.0 10.20.10.0
   255.255.255.0
access-list VPN permit ip 172.16.31.0 255.255.255.0 10.20.10.0
   255.255.255.0
nat (inside) 0 access-list VPN
```

Example 20-6 shows the complete configuration for the HQ-PIX.

Example 20-6   *HQ PIX Firewall Configuration (Continued)*

```
interface Ethernet 0
   nameif outside
   security-level 0
   ip address 192.168.1.2 255.255.255.0
   speed 100
   duplex full
interface Ethernet 1
   nameif inside
   security-level 100
   ip address 10.10.10.1 255.255.255.0
   speed 100
   duplex full
interface Ethernet 2
   nameif DMZ
   security-level 80
   ip address 172.16.31.1 255.255.255.0
   speed 100
   duplex full
interface Ethernet 3
   nameif failover
   security-level 90
   ip address 1.1.1.1 255.255.255.0
   speed 100
   duplex full
enable password 8Ry2YjIyt7RRXU24 encrypted
passwd 2KFQnbNIdI.2KPPU encrypted
hostname HQ-PIX
access-list IPS permit ip any any
access-list acl-out permit tcp any host 192.168.1.4 eq smtp
access-list acl-out permit tcp any host 192.168.1.5 eq www
access-list acl-out permit tcp any host 192.168.1.6 eq ftp
!--- Traffic to HOU-PIX:
access-list 130 permit ip 10.10.10.0 255.255.255.0 10.30.10.0 255.255.255.0
access-list 130 permit ip 172.16.31.0 255.255.255.0 10.30.10.0 255.255.255.0
!--- Traffic to MN-PIX:
access-list 120 permit ip 10.10.10.0 255.255.255.0 10.20.10.0 255.255.255.0
access-list 120 permit ip 172.16.31.0 255.255.255.0 10.20.10.0 255.255.255.0
!--- Do not Network Address Translate (NAT) traffic to other branches:
access-list VPN permit ip 10.10.10.0 255.255.255.0 10.30.10.0 255.255.255.0
access-list VPN permit ip 10.10.10.0 255.255.255.0 10.20.10.0 255.255.255.0
access-list VPN permit ip 172.16.31.0 255.255.255.0 10.30.10.0 255.255.255.0
access-list VPN permit ip 172.16.31.0 255.255.255.0 10.20.10.0 255.255.255.0
pager lines 24
logging on
no logging timestamp
no logging standby
```

continues

Example 20-6 *HQ PIX Firewall Configuration (Continued)*

```
no logging console
no logging monitor
no logging buffered
logging trap
no logging history
logging facility 20
logging queue 512
logging host DMZ 172.16.31.7




ip audit info action alarm
ip audit attack action alarm no failover
failover timeout 0:00:00
failover poll 15
class-map ips_class
   match access-list IPS
class-map inspection_default
   match default-inspection-traffic
policy-map global_policy
   class inspection_default
       inspect dns maximum length 512
       inspect ftp
       inspect h323 h225
       inspect h323 ras
       inspect netbios
       inspect sunrpc
       inspect rsh
       inspect rtsp
       inspect sip
       inspect skinny
       inspect esmtp
       inspect sqlnet
       inspect tftp
       inspect xdmcp
       inspect icmp
   class ips-class
       ips promiscuous fail-close
service-policy global_policy global

failover ip address outside 192.168.1.3
failover ip address inside 10.10.10.2
failover ip address DMZ 172.16.31.2
arp timeout 14400
```

Example 20-6 *HQ PIX Firewall Configuration (Continued)*

```
global (outside) 1 192.168.1.12-192.168.1.150 netmask 255.255.255.0
global (outside) 1 192.168.1.152 netmask 255.255.255.0
nat (inside) 1 10.10.10.0 255.255.255.0
!--- Do not NAT traffic to other PIXes:
nat (inside) 0 access-list VPN

static (DMZ,outside) 192.168.1.4  172.16.31.4 netmask 255.255.255.255 0 0
static (DMZ,outside) 192.168.1.5  172.16.31.5 netmask 255.255.255.255 0 0
static (DMZ,outside) 192.168.1.6  172.16.31.6 netmask 255.255.255.255 0 0
access-group acl-out in interface outside
route outside 0.0.0.0 0.0.0.0 192.168.1.1
timeout xlate 3:00:00
timeout conn 1:00:00 half-closed 0:10:00 udp 0:02:00 rpc 0:10:00 h323 0:05:00 sip 0:30:00
sip-media 0:02:00
timeout uauth 0:05:00 absolute

aaa-server TACACS+ protocol tacacs+
aaa-server RADIUS protocol radius
aaa-server TACACS+ (inside) host 10.10.10.7 tacpass

aaa authentication include ftp inside 0.0.0.0 0.0.0.0 TACACS+
aaa authentication include telnet inside 0.0.0.0 0 0.0.0.0 TACACS+
no snmp-server location

no snmp-server contact
snmp-server community public
snmp-server enable traps

sysopt connection permit-ipsec
no sysopt route dnat
crypto ipsec transform-set myset esp-des esp-md5-hmac

!--- Traffic to HOU-PIX:
crypto map Dukem-Map  20 ipsec-isakmp
crypto map Dukem-Map  20 match address 120
crypto map Dukem-Map  20 set peer 192.168.3.2
crypto map Dukem-Map 20 set transform-set myset

!--- Traffic to MN-PIX:
crypto map Dukem-Map 30 ipsec-isakmp
crypto map Dukem-Map  30 match address 130
crypto map Dukem-Map  30 set peer 192.168.2.2
crypto map Dukem-Map  30 set transform-set myset
crypto map Dukem-Map  interface outside

isakmp enable outside
isakmp key ******** address 192.168.3.2 netmask 255.255.255.255
isakmp key ******** address 192.168.2.2 netmask 255.255.255.255
```

continues

Example 20-6   *HQ PIX Firewall Configuration (Continued)*

```
isakmp identity address
isakmp policy 10 authentication pre-share
isakmp policy 10 encryption des
isakmp policy 10 hash md5
isakmp policy 10 group 1
isakmp policy 10 lifetime 1000
telnet timeout 5 ssh timeout 5 terminal width 80
Cryptochecksum:fb446986bcad922ec40de6346e9e2729
: end
```

Configuring the Houston PIX Firewall, HOU-PIX, for VPN Tunneling

Similar to configuring the VPN characteristics on HQ-PIX, you also must define the VPN characteristics at each of the remote sites. The following steps outline the commands necessary to define the VPN characteristics on HOU-PIX at the Houston remote site:

Step 1   Configure an ISAKMP policy:

```
isakmp  enable  outside
isakmp  policy  10  authentication  pre-share
isakmp  policy  10  encryption  des
isakmp  policy  10  hash  md5
isakmp  policy  10  group  1
isakmp  policy  10  lifetime  1000
```

Step 2   Configure a preshared key and associate it with the peer (HQ-PIX):

```
isakmp key A1!#abc address 192.168.1.2
```

Step 3   Configure the supported IPSec transforms:

```
crypto ipsec transform-set myset esp-des esp-md5-hmac
```

Step 4   Create an access list:

```
access-list 110 permit ip 10.30.10.0 255.255.255.0 10.10.10.0
   255.255.255.0
access-list 110 permit ip 10.30.10.0 255.255.255.0 172.16.31.0
   255.255.255.0
```

Step 5   Define a crypto map for HQ-PIX:

```
crypto  map  Dukem-Map  20  ipsec-isakmp
crypto  map  Dukem-Map  20  match  address  110
crypto  map  Dukem-Map  20  set  peer  192.168.1.2
crypto  map  Dukem-Map  20  set  transform-set  myset
```

Step 6   Apply the crypto map to the outside interface:

```
crypto map Dukem-Map interface outside
```

Step 7   Specify that IPSec traffic is implicitly trusted (permitted):

```
sysopt connection permit-ipsec
```

Step 8   Configure a NAT 0 policy so that traffic between the offices is excluded from NAT:

```
access-list VPN permit ip 10.30.10.0 255.255.255.0 10.10.10.0
   255.255.255.0
access-list VPN permit ip 10.30.10.0 255.255.255.0 172.16.31.0
   255.255.255.0
nat (inside) 0 access-list VPN
```

Example 20-7 shows the Houston PIX configuration.

Example 20-7   *Houston PIX Firewall Configuration*

```
interface Ethernet 0
   nameif outside
   security-level 0
   ip address 192.168.3.2 255.255.255.0
   speed 100
   duplex full
interface Ethernet 1
   nameif inside
   security-level 100
   ip address 10.30.10.1 255.255.255.0
   speed 100
   duplex full
enable password 8Ry2YjIyt7RRXU24 encrypted
passwd 2KFQnbNIdI.2KPPU encrypted
hostname HOU-PIX
class-map ips_class
   match access-list IPS
class-map inspection_default
   match default-inspection-traffic
policy-map global_policy
   class inspection_default
      inspect dns maximum length 512
      inspect ftp
      inspect h323 h225
      inspect h323 ras
      inspect netbios
      inspect sunrpc
      inspect rsh
      inspect rtsp
      inspect sip
      inspect skinny
      inspect esmtp
      inspect sqlnet
```

continues

Example 20-7 *Houston PIX Firewall Configuration (Continued)*

```
        inspect tftp
        inspect xdmcp
        inspect icmp
   class ips-class
        ips promiscuous fail-close
service-policy global_policy global

access-list IPS permit ip any any
!--- Traffic to Reston HQ:
access-list 110 permit ip 10.30.10.0 255.255.255.0 10.10.10.0 255.255.255.0
access-list 110 permit ip 10.30.10.0 255.255.255.0 172.16.31.0 255.255.255.0
!--- Do not NAT traffic to Reston HQ:
access-list VPN permit ip 10.30.10.0 255.255.255.0 10.10.10.0 255.255.255.0
access-list VPN permit ip 10.30.10.0 255.255.255.0 172.16.31.0 255.255.255.0
pager lines 24
logging on
no logging timestamp
no logging standby
no logging console
no logging monitor
no logging buffered
logging trap 6
no logging history
logging facility 20
logging queue 512
logging host 192.168.1.8


ip audit info action alarm
ip audit attack action alarm no failover
failover timeout 0:00:00
failover poll 15
failover ip address outside 0.0.0.0
failover ip address inside 0.0.0.0
arp timeout 14400

global (outside) 1 192.168.3.12-192.168.3.250 netmask 255.255.255.0
global (outside) 1 192.168.3.252 netmask 255.255.255.0
nat (inside) 1 10.30.10.0 255.255.255.0
!--- Do not NAT traffic to Reston HQ:
nat (inside) 0 access-list VPN
route outside 0.0.0.0 0.0.0.0 192.168.3.1 1

timeout xlate 3:00:00
timeout conn 1:00:00 half-closed 0:10:00 udp 0:02:00 rpc 0:10:00
h323 0:05:00 sip 0:30:00 sip-media 0:02:00
timeout uauth 0:05:00 absolute
aaa-server TACACS+ protocol tacacs+
```

Example 20-7 *Houston PIX Firewall Configuration (Continued)*

```
aaa-server RADIUS protocol radius
no snmp-server location
no snmp-server contact

snmp-server community public
no snmp-server enable traps
sysopt connection permit-ipsec no sysopt route dnat
crypto ipsec transform-set myset esp-des esp-md5-hmac
!--- Traffic to Reston HQ:
crypto map Dukem-Map  10 ipsec-isakmp
crypto map Dukem-Map  10 match address 110
crypto map Dukem-Map  10 set peer 192.168.1.2
crypto map Dukem-Map  10 set transform-set myset
crypto map Dukem-Map  interface outside
isakmp enable outside
isakmp key ******** address 192.168.1.2 netmask 255.255.255.255
  no-xauth no-config-mode
isakmp identity address
isakmp policy 10 authentication pre-share
isakmp policy 10 encryption des
isakmp policy 10 hash md5
isakmp policy 10 group 1
isakmp policy 10 lifetime 1000 telnet timeout 5
ssh timeout 5
terminal width 80
Cryptochecksum:b23cc9772a79ea76d711ea747f182a5f
```

Configuring the Minneapolis PIX Firewall, MN-PIX, for VPN Tunneling

Similar to configuring the VPN characteristics on HQ-PIX, you also must define the VPN characteristics at each of the remote sites. The following steps outline the commands necessary to define the VPN characteristics on MN-PIX at the Minneapolis remote site:

Step 1   Configure an ISAKMP policy:

```
isakmp  enable  outside
isakmp  policy  10  authentication  pre-share
isakmp  policy  10  encryption  des
isakmp  policy  10  hash  md5
isakmp  policy  10  group  1
isakmp  policy  10  lifetime  1000
```

Step 2   Configure a preshared key and associate it with the peer (HQ-PIX):

```
isakmp key A1!#abc address 192.168.1.2
```

Step 3   Configure the supported IPSec transforms:

```
crypto ipsec transform-set myset esp-des esp-md5-hmac
```

Step 4   Create an access list:

```
access-list 110 permit ip 10.20.10.0 255.255.255.0 10.10.10.0
  255.255.255.0
access-list 110 permit ip 10.20.10.0 255.255.255.0 172.16.31.0
  255.255.255.0
```

Step 5   Define a crypto map for HQ-PIX:

```
crypto map Dukem-Map 20 ipsec-isakmp
crypto map Dukem-Map 20 match address 110
crypto map Dukem-Map 20 set peer 192.168.1.2
crypto map Dukem-Map 20 set transform-set myset
```

Step 6   Apply the crypto map to the outside interface:

```
crypto map Dukem-Map interface outside
```

Step 7   Specify that IPSec traffic be implicitly trusted (permitted):

```
sysopt connection permit-ipsec
```

Step 8   Configure a NAT 0 policy so that traffic between the offices is excluded from NAT:

```
access-list VPN permit ip 10.20.10.0 255.255.255.0 10.10.10.0
  255.255.255.0
access-list VPN permit ip 10.20.10.0 255.255.255.0 172.16.31.0
  255.255.255.0
nat (inside) 0 access-list VPN
```

Example 20-8 shows the configuration for the Minneapolis PIX Firewall.

Example 20-8 *Minneapolis PIX Firewall Configuration*

```
interface Ethernet 0
  nameif outside
  security-level 0
  ip address 192.168.2.2 255.255.255.0
  speed 100
  duplex full
interface Ethernet 1
  nameif inside
  security-level 100
  ip address 10.20.10.1 255.255.255.0
  speed 100
  duplex full
enable password 8Ry2YjIyt7RRXU24 encrypted
passwd 2KFQnbNIdI.2KPPU encrypted
hostname MN-PIX
class-map ips_class
  match access-list IPS
class-map inspection_default
  match default-inspection-traffic
```

Example 20-8   *Minneapolis PIX Firewall Configuration (Continued)*

```
policy-map global_policy
   class inspection_default
      inspect dns maximum length 512
      inspect ftp
      inspect h323 h225
      inspect h323 ras
      inspect netbios
      inspect sunrpc
      inspect rsh
      inspect rtsp
      inspect sip
      inspect skinny
      inspect esmtp
      inspect sqlnet
      inspect tftp
      inspect xdmcp
      inspect icmp
   class ips-class
      ips promiscuous fail-close
service-policy global_policy global

access-list IPS permit ip any any
!--- Traffic to Reston HQ:
access-list 110 permit ip 10.20.10.0 255.255.255.0 10.10.10.0 255.255.255.0
access-list 110 permit ip 10.20.10.0 255.255.255.0 172.16.31.0 255.255.255.0
!--- Do not NAT traffic to Reston HQ:
access-list VPN permit ip 10.20.10.0 255.255.255.0 10.10.10.0 255.255.255.0
access-list VPN permit ip 10.20.10.0 255.255.255.0 172.16.31.0 255.255.255.0
pager lines 24
logging on
no logging timestamp
no logging standby
no logging console
no logging monitor
no logging buffered
logging trap 6
no logging history
logging facility 20
logging queue 512
logging host outside 192.168.1.8


ip audit info action alarm
ip audit attack action alarm no failover
failover timeout 0:00:00
failover poll 15
failover ip address outside 0.0.0.0
```

continues

Example 20-8 *Minneapolis PIX Firewall Configuration (Continued)*

```
failover ip address inside 0.0.0.0
arp timeout 14400

global (outside) 1 192.168.2.12-192.168.2.250 netmask 255.255.255.0
global (outside) 1 192.168.2.252 netmask 255.255.255.0
nat (inside) 1 10.20.10.0 255.255.255.0
!--- Do not NAT traffic to Reston HQ:
nat (inside) 0 access-list VPN
route outside 0.0.0.0 0.0.0.0 192.168.2.1 1

timeout xlate 3:00:00
timeout conn 1:00:00 half-closed 0:10:00 udp 0:02:00 rpc 0:10:00
h323 0:05:00 sip 0:30:00 sip-media 0:02:00
timeout uauth 0:05:00 absolute
aaa-server TACACS+ protocol tacacs+
aaa-server RADIUS protocol radius
no snmp-server location
no snmp-server contact
snmp-server community public no
snmp-server enable traps
sysopt connection permit-ipsec
no sysopt route dnat
crypto ipsec transform-set myset esp-des esp-md5-hmac
!--- Traffic to Reston HQ:
crypto map Dukem-Map 10 ipsec-isakmp
crypto map Dukem-Map 10 match address 110
crypto map Dukem-Map 10 set peer 192.168.1.2
crypto map Dukem-Map 10 set transform-set myset
crypto map Dukem-Map interface outside
isakmp enable outside
isakmp key ******** address 192.168.1.2 netmask 255.255.255.255 no-xauth
  no-config-mode
isakmp identity address
isakmp policy 10 authentication pre-share
isakmp policy 10 encryption des
isakmp policy 10 hash md5
isakmp policy 10 group 1
isakmp policy 10 lifetime 1000
telnet timeout 5 ssh timeout 5 terminal width 80
Cryptochecksum:d962d33d245ad89fb7c9b4f0db3c2dc0
```

Verifying and Troubleshooting

After you configure the PIX for VPNs, the next step is to verify the configuration. The **show, clear,** and **debug** commands are used to verify and troubleshoot your configuration.

show Commands

- **show crypto ipsec sa**—Displays the current status of the IPSec security associations. This is useful in determining whether traffic is being encrypted.

- **show crypto isakmp sa**—Displays the current state of the Internet Key Exchange (IKE) security associations (SA).

Debug Commands

If you have problems establishing any of the VPN tunnels, use the following commands for troubleshooting:

Step 1   If you are connected to the PIX by the console port, enable debugging on the console using this command:

```
logging console debugging
```

If you are connected to the PIX by Telnet, enable debugging using this command:

```
logging monitor debugging
```

Step 2   To view debug information related to the VPN configuration, use the following commands:

- **debug crypto ipsec**—Used to debug IPSec processing

- **debug crypto isakmp**—Used to debug ISAKMP processing

- **debug crypto engine**—Used to display debug messages about crypto engines, which perform encryption and decryption

Step 3   To clear SAs, use the following commands in the PIX configuration mode:

- **clear [crypto] ipsec sa**—Deletes the active IPSec SAs. The keyword **crypto** is optional.

- **clear [crypto] isakmp sa**—Deletes the active IKE SAs. The keyword **crypto** is optional.

Task 6: Configuring a Remote-Access VPN to HQ

Similar to the remote sites, the remote users must also have a secure mechanism to connect to the Reston location. The remote users, however, do not use fixed VPN tunnels. Instead, the remote users use Easy VPN remote to connect to the HQ location and dynamically establish a VPN tunnel. The configuration process involves performing the following tasks:

- Create an IP address pool
- Define a group policy for mode configuration push
- Enable IKE dead peer detection (DPD)

Create an IP Address Pool

For instance, suppose that you want to assign the remote clients addresses in the range from 10.20.100.1 through 10.20.100.254. Using a pool name of *vpn-pool*, the command line would be as follows:

```
ip local pool vpn-pool 10.10.10.154-10.10.10.200
```

Define a Group Policy for Mode Configuration Push

When remote VPN clients connect to HQ-PIX, the firewall must push certain configuration information to them. You configure these parameters using the **vpngroup** command:

```
vpngroup  remote-users  password  B#!42Dd
vpngroup  remote-users  dns-server  10.200.10.35
vpngroup  remote-users  wins-server  10.100.10.25
vpngroup  remote-users  default-domain  dukem.com
vpngroup  remote-users  address-pool  vpn-pool
vpngroup  remote-users  idle-time  10
```

> **NOTE**   You also need to configure the VPN client software on the remote user PCs. This configuration involves identifying the IP address of HQ-PIX and indicating the VPN group name (remote-users) and group password (B#!42Dd).

Enable IKE Dead Peer Detection

You need to specify the number of seconds between DPD messages and the number of seconds between retries (if a DPD message does not receive a response). The syntax for this command is as follows:

```
isakmp keepalive seconds [retry-seconds]
```

Task 7: Configuring Failover

Failover is configured on the PIX only at the Reston site (HQ-PIX). When configuring failover, you first configure the failover parameters on the primary PIX Firewall (leaving the secondary PIX Firewall powered off). Then, you configure the failover parameters on the secondary PIX Firewall. The steps to configure failover are as follows:

Step 1   Make sure that failover is enabled on the primary PIX Firewall using the following command:

```
failover
```

Failover is not enabled by default.

Step 2   Configure Ethernet 3 for LAN-based failover through the following commands:

```
failover lan interface LANFAIL ethernet3
failover interface ip LANFAIL 1.1.1.1 255.255.255.0 standby 1.1.1.2
failover lan unit primary
failover key 1234567
failover
```

Step 3   Configure **failover ip address** for all interfaces that have an IP address configured on them:

```
failover  ip  address  inside  10.10.10.2
failover  ip  address  outside  192.168.1.3
failover  ip  address  DMZ  172.16.31.2
```

Step 4   Check the status of your failover configuration:

```
show  failover

Failover On
Cable status: Normal
Failover unit Primary
Failover LAN Interface: N/A - Serial-based failover enabled
Unit Poll frequency 15 seconds, holdtime 45 seconds
Interface Poll frequency 15 seconds
Interface Policy 1
Monitored Interfaces 3 of 250 maximum
Last Failover at: 13:21:38 UTC Dec 10 2004
        This host: Primary - Active
                Active time: 300 (sec)
                Interface outside (192.168.1.2): Normal
                Interface inside (10.10.10.1): Normal
                Interface dmz (172.16.31.1): Normal
        Other host: Secondary - Standby Ready
                Active time: 0 (sec)
                Interface outside (192.168.1.3): Normal
                Interface inside (10.10.10.2): Normal
                Interface dmz (172.16.31.2): Normal
```

Step 5   Enable stateful failover:

```
failover link lanfail
```

Step 6   Connect the failover cable between the two PIX Firewalls if you have not already connected it.

Step 7   Power on the secondary unit.

Step 8   Check the status of your failover configuration:

```
HQ-PIX# show failover
Failover On
Cable status: Normal
Failover unit Primary
Failover LAN Interface: lanfail Ethernet 3 (up)
Unit Poll frequency 15 seconds, holdtime 45 seconds
Interface Poll frequency 15 seconds
Interface Policy 1
Monitored Interfaces 3 of 250 maximum
Last Failover at: 13:21:38 UTC Dec 10 2004
        This host: Primary - Active
                    Active time: 300 (sec)
                    Interface outside (192.168.1.2): Normal
                    Interface inside (10.10.10.1): Normal
                    Interface dmz (172.16.31.1): Normal
        Other host: Secondary - Standby Ready
                    Active time: 0 (sec)
                    Interface outside (192.168.1.3): Normal
                    Interface inside (10.10.10.2): Normal
                    Interface dmz (172.16.31.2): Normal
Stateful Failover Logical Update Statistics
        Link : failover
        Stateful Obj    xmit        xerr        rcv         rerr
        General         435         0           0           0
        sys cmd         415         0           0           0
        up time         0           0           0           0
        xlate           27          0           0           0
        tcp conn        203         0           0           0
        udp conn        0           0           0           0
        ARP tbl         0           0           0           0
        RIP Tbl         0           0           0           0

        Logical Update Queue Information
                        Cur     Max     Total
        Recv Q:         0       0       0
        Xmit Q:         0       1       614
```

What Is Wrong with This Picture?

Now that you have successfully gone through the configuration scenarios in the previous sections, this section focuses on problem solving after or during an implementation of Cisco PIX Firewall. Examples 20-9 through 20-11 show the configuration of three PIX Firewalls for this exercise.

Example 20-9 *Atlanta PIX Firewall Configuration*

```
1.   : Saved
2.   :
3.   PIX Version 7.0(2)
4.   interface Ethernet 0
5.    nameif outside
6.    security-level 0
7.    speed 100
8.    duplex aito
9.    ip address 10.10.3.1 255.255.255.0
10.  interface Ethernet 1
11.   nameif outside
12.   security-level 100
13.   speed 100
14.   duplex auto
15.   ip address 192.168.3.1 255.255.255.0
16.  interface Ethernet 2
17.   nameif outside
18.   security-level 70
19.   speed 100
20.   duplex auto
21.   ip address 172.16.3.1 255.255.255.0
22.  enable password ksjfglkasglc encrypted
23.  passwd kjngczftglkacytiur encrypted
24.  hostname Atlanta
25. domain-name www.BranchVPN.com
26.   class-map inspection_default
27.     match default-inspection-traffic
28.   policy-map global_policy
29.    class inspection_default
30.      inspect dns maximum length 512
31.      inspect ftp
32.      inspect h323 h225
33.      inspect h323 ras
34.      inspect netbios
35.      inspect sunrpc
36.      inspect rsh
37.      inspect rtsp
38.      inspect sip
39.      inspect skinny
40.      inspect esmtp
```

continues

Example 20-9 *Atlanta PIX Firewall Configuration (Continued)*

```
41.      inspect sqlnet
42.      inspect tftp
43.      inspect xdmcp
44.      inspect icmp
45.   service-policy global_policy global
46.  access-list inbound permit icmp any host 192.168.3.10
47.  access-list inbound permit tcp any host 192.168.3.10   eq www
48.  access-list inbound permit tcp any host 192.168.3.10 eq 443
49.  access-list DMZ permit udp 172.16.3.0 255.255.255.0 host 10.10.3.240 eq ntp
50.  access-list VPN permit ip 10.10.3.0 255.255.255.0 10.10.2.0 255.255.255.0
51.  access-list VPN permit ip 10.10.3.0 255.255.255.0 10.10.10.0 255.255.255.0
52.  access-list LosAngeles permit ip 10.10.3.0 255.255.255.0 10.10.10.0
     255.255.255.0
53.  access-list Boston permit ip 10.10.3.0 255.255.255.0 10.10.2.0 255.255.255.0
54.  pager lines 24
55.  logging on
56.  logging timestamp


57.  arp timeout 14400
58.  global (outside) 1 192.168.3.20-200
59.  nat (inside) 1 0.0.0.0 0.0.0.0 0 0
60.  nat (inside) 0 access-list VPN
61.  static (DMZ,outside) 192.168.3.10 172.16.3.10 netmask 255.255.255.255 0 0
62.  access-group inbound in interface outside
63.  access-group DMZ in interface DMZ
64.  route outside 0.0.0.0 0.0.0.0 192.168.3.254 1
65.  timeout xlate 3:00:00
66.  timeout conn 1:00:00 half-closed 0:10:00 udp 0:02:00
67.  timeout uauth 0:05:00 absolute
68.  aaa-server TACACS+ protocol tacacs+
69.  aaa-server RADIUS protocol radius
70.  no snmp-server location
71.  no snmp-server contact
72.  snmp-server community public
73.  no snmp-server enable traps
74.  sysopt connection permit-ipsec
75.  crypto ipsec transform-set BranchVPN esp-3des esp-md5-hmac
76.  crypto ipsec transform-set NothingNew esp-3des esp-sha-hmac
77.  crypto map BranchVPN 10 ipsec-isakmp
78.  crypto map BranchVPN 10 match address LosAngeles
79.  crypto map BranchVPN 10 set peer 192.168.1.1
80.  crypto map BranchVPN 10 set transform-set BranchVPN
81.  crypto map BranchVPN 20 ipsec-isakmp
82.  crypto map BranchVPN 20 match address Boston
83.  crypto map BranchVPN 20 set peer 192.168.2.1
84.  crypto map BranchVPN 20 set transform-set BranchVPN
```

Example 20-9 *Atlanta PIX Firewall Configuration (Continued)*

```
85.  crypto map BranchVPN interface DMZ
86.  isakmp enable outside
87.  isakmp key ******** address 192.168.1.1 netmask 255.255.255.255
88.  isakmp key ******** address 192.168.2.1 netmask 255.255.255.255
89.  isakmp identity address
90.  isakmp policy 20 authentication pre-share
91.  isakmp policy 20 encryption 3des
92.  isakmp policy 20 hash md5
93.  isakmp policy 20 group 2
94.  isakmp policy 20 lifetime 86400
95.  terminal width 80
96.  Cryptochecksum:e0c04954fcabd239ae291d58fc618dd5
```

Example 20-10 *Boston PIX Firewall Configuration*

```
1.   : Saved
2.   :
3.   PIX Version 7.0(2)
4.   interface Ethernet 0
5.    nameif outside
6.    security-level 0
7.    speed 100
8.    duplex auto
9.    ip address 192.168.2.1 255.255.255.0
10.  interface Ethernet 1
11.   nameif inside
12.   security-level 100
13.   speed 100
14.   duplex auto
15.   ip address 10.10.2.1 255.255.255.0
16.  interface Ethernet 2
17.   nameif dmz
18.   security-level 70
19.   speed 100
20.   duplex auto
21.   ip address 172.16.2.1 255.255.255.0
22.  enable password ksjfglkasglc encrypted
23.  passwd kjngczftglkacytiur encrypted
24.  hostname Boston
25. domain-name www.BranchVPN.com
26.   class-map inspection_default
27.     match default-inspection-traffic
28.   policy-map global_policy
29.    class inspection_default
30.     inspect dns maximum length 512
31.     inspect ftp
32.     inspect h323 h225
```

continues

Example 20-10 *Boston PIX Firewall Configuration (Continued)*

```
33.        inspect h323 ras
34.        inspect netbios
35.        inspect sunrpc
36.        inspect rsh
37.        inspect rtsp
38.        inspect sip
39.        inspect skinny
40.        inspect esmtp
41.        inspect sqlnet
42.        inspect tftp
43.        inspect xdmcp
44.        inspect icmp
45.    service-policy global_policy global
46.  access-list inbound permit icmp any host 192.168.2.10
47.  access-list inbound permit tcp any host 192.168.2.10   eq www
48.  access-list inbound permit tcp any host 192.168.2.10 eq 443
     access-list DMZ permit tcp 192.168.1.13 255.255.255.255 192.168.2.11 eq 1521
49.  access-list DMZ permit udp 172.16.2.0 255.255.255.0 host 10.10.2.240 eq ntp
50.  access-list VPN permit ip 10.10.2.0 255.255.255.0 10.10.10.0 255.255.255.0
51.  access-list VPN permit ip 10.10.2.0 255.255.255.0 10.10.3.0 255.255.255.0
52.  access-list LosAngeles permit ip 10.10.2.0 255.255.255.0 10.10.10.0
     255.255.255.0
53.  access-list Atlanta permit ip 10.10.2.0 255.255.255.0 10.10.3.0 255.255.255.0
54.  pager lines 24
55.  logging on
56.  logging timestamp


57.  arp timeout 14400
58.  global (outside) 1 192.168.2.20-200
59.  nat (inside) 1 0.0.0.0 0.0.0.0 0 0
60.  nat (inside) 0 access-list VPN
61.  static (DMZ,outside) 192.168.2.10 172.16.2.10 netmask 255.255.255.255 0 0
     static (DMZ,outside) 192.168.2.11 172.16.2.11 netmask 255.255.255.255 0 0
62.  access-group inbound in interface outside
63.  access-group DMZ in interface DMZ
64.  route outside 0.0.0.0 0.0.0.0 192.168.2.254 1
65.  timeout xlate 3:00:00
66.  timeout conn 1:00:00 half-closed 0:10:00 udp 0:02:00
67.  timeout uauth 0:05:00 absolute
68.  aaa-server TACACS+ protocol tacacs+
69.  aaa-server RADIUS protocol radius
70.  no snmp-server location
71.  no snmp-server contact
72.  snmp-server community public
73.  no snmp-server enable traps
```

Example 20-10 *Boston PIX Firewall Configuration (Continued)*

```
74.  crypto ipsec transform-set BranchVPN esp-3des esp-md5-hmac
75.  crypto ipsec transform-set NothingNew esp-3des esp-sha-hmac
76.  crypto map BranchVPN 10 ipsec-isakmp
77.  crypto map BranchVPN 10 match address LosAngeles
78.  crypto map BranchVPN 10 set peer 192.168.1.1
79.  crypto map BranchVPN 10 set transform-set BranchVPN
80.  crypto map BranchVPN 20 ipsec-isakmp
81.  crypto map BranchVPN 20 match address Atlanta
82.  crypto map BranchVPN 20 set peer 192.168.3.1
83.  crypto map BranchVPN 20 set transform-set BranchVPN
84.  crypto map BranchVPN interface outside
85.  isakmp enable outside
86.  isakmp key ******** address 192.168.1.1 netmask 255.255.255.255
87.  isakmp key ******** address 192.168.3.1 netmask 255.255.255.255
88.  isakmp identity address
89.  isakmp policy 20 authentication pre-share
90.  isakmp policy 20 encryption 3des
91.  isakmp policy 20 hash md5
92.  isakmp policy 20 group 2
93.  isakmp policy 20 lifetime 86400
94.  terminal width 80
95.  Cryptochecksum:e0c04954fcabd239ae291d58fc618dd5
```

Example 20-11 *Los Angeles PIX Firewall Configuration*

```
1.   : Saved
2.   :
3.   PIX Version 7.0(2)
4.   interface Ethernet 0
5.    nameif outside
6.    security-level 0
7.    speed 100
8.    duplex auto
9.    ip address 192.168.1.1 255.255.255.0
10.  interface Ethernet 1
11.   nameif inside
12.   security-level 100
13.   speed 100
14.   duplex auto
15.   ip address 10.10.10.1 255.255.255.0
16.  interface Ethernet 2
17.   nameif dmz
18.   security-level 70
19.   speed 100
20.   duplex auto
21.   ip address 172.16.1.1 255.255.255.0
22.  enable password HtmvK15kjhtlyfvcl encrypted
23.  passwd Kkjhlkf1568Hke encrypted
```

continues

Example 20-11 *Los Angeles PIX Firewall Configuration (Continued)*

```
24.    hostname LosAngeles
25.  domain-name www.BranchVPN.com
26.    class-map inspection_default
27.     match default-inspection-traffic
28.    policy-map global_policy
29.     class inspection_default
30.      inspect dns maximum length 512
31.      inspect ftp
32.      inspect h323 h225
33.      inspect h323 ras
34.      inspect netbios
35.      inspect sunrpc
36.      inspect rsh
37.      inspect rtsp
38.      inspect sip
39.      inspect skinny
40.      inspect esmtp
41.      inspect sqlnet
42.      inspect tftp
43.      inspect xdmcp
44.      inspect icmp
45.    service-policy global_policy global
       access-list inbound permit tcp any host 192.168.1.9 eq ftp
46.    access-list inbound permit icmp any host 192.168.1.10
47.    access-list inbound permit tcp any host 192.168.1.10  eq www
48.    access-list inbound permit tcp any host 192.168.1.10 eq 443
49.    access-list inbound permit tcp any host 192.168.1.11  eq www
50.    access-list inbound permit tcp any host 192.168.1.11 eq 443
51.    access-list inbound permit tcp any host 192.168.1.12  eq www
52.    access-list inbound permit tcp any host 192.168.1.12 eq 443
53.    access-list inbound permit tcp any host 192.168.1.13  eq ftp
54.    access-list Exchange permit tcp any host 192.168.1.14 eq 25
       access-list Exchange permit tcp any host 192.168.1.14 eq 443
       access-list DMZ permit tcp 172.16.1.13 255.255.255.255 10.10.11.221 eq 1521
55.    access-list DMZ permit udp 172.16.1.0 255.255.255.0 host 10.10.10.240 eq ntp
56.    access-list VPN permit ip 10.10.10.0 255.255.255.0 10.10.2.0 255.255.255.0
57.    access-list VPN permit ip 10.10.10.0 255.255.255.0 10.10.3.0 255.255.255.0
58.    access-list Boston permit ip 10.10.10.0 255.255.255.0 10.10.2.0 255.255.255.0
59.    access-list Atlanta permit ip 10.10.10.0 255.255.255.0 10.10.3.0 255.255.255.0
60.    pager lines 24
61.    logging on
62.    logging timestamp
63.    failover
64.    failover timeout 0:00:00
65.    failover poll 15
66.    failover ip address outside 192.168.1.2
67.    failover ip address inside 10.10.10.2
```

Example 20-11 *Los Angeles PIX Firewall Configuration (Continued)*

```
68.  failover ip address DMZ 172.16.1.2
69.  arp timeout 14400
70.  global (outside) 1 192.168.1.20-250
71.  nat (inside) 1 0.0.0.0 0.0.0.0 0 0
72.  nat (inside) 0 access-list VPN
73.  static (DMZ,outside) 192.168.1.10 172.16.1.10 netmask 255.255.255.255 0 0
74.  static (DMZ,outside) 192.168.1.11 172.16.1.11 netmask 255.255.255.255 0 0
75.  static (DMZ,outside) 192.168.1.12 172.16.1.12 netmask 255.255.255.255 0 0
76.  static (DMZ,outside) 192.168.1.13 172.16.1.13 netmask 255.255.255.255 0 0
     static (DMZ,outside) 192.168.1.14 172.16.1.14 netmask 255.255.255.255 0 0
77.  access-group inbound in interface outside
     access-group Exchange in interface outside
78.  access-group DMZ in interface DMZ
79.  route outside 0.0.0.0 0.0.0.0 192.168.1.254 1
80.  timeout xlate 3:00:00
81.  timeout conn 1:00:00 half-closed 0:10:00 udp 0:02:00 rpc 0:10:00 h323 0:05:00
     sip 0:30:00 sip-media 0:02:00
82.  timeout uauth 0:05:00 absolute
83.  aaa-server TACACS+ protocol tacacs+
84.  aaa-server RADIUS protocol radius
85.  no snmp-server location
86.  no snmp-server contact
87.  snmp-server community public
88.  no snmp-server enable traps
89.  sysopt connection permit-ipsec
90.  no sysopt route dnat
91.  crypto ipsec transform-set BranchVPN esp-3des esp-md5-hmac
92.  crypto ipsec transform-set NothingNew esp-3des esp-sha-hmac
93.  crypto map BranchVPN 10 ipsec-isakmp
94.  crypto map BranchVPN 10 match address Boston
95.  crypto map BranchVPN 10 set peer 192.168.2.1
96.  crypto map BranchVPN 10 set transform-set BranchVPN
97.  crypto map BranchVPN 20 ipsec-isakmp
98.  crypto map BranchVPN 20 set peer 192.168.3.1
99.  crypto map BranchVPN 20 set transform-set BranchVPN
100. crypto map BranchVPN interface outside
101. isakmp enable outside
102. isakmp key ******** address 192.168.2.1 netmask 255.255.255.255
103. isakmp key ******** address 192.168.3.1 netmask 255.255.255.255
104. isakmp identity address
105. isakmp policy 20 authentication pre-share
106. isakmp policy 20 encryption 3des
107. isakmp policy 20 hash md5
108. isakmp policy 20 group 2
109. isakmp policy 20 lifetime 86400
110. terminal width 80
111. Cryptochecksum:e0clmj3546549637cbsFds54132d5
```

After you have reviewed the configuration files for the three PIX Firewalls, answer the following questions. (The answers appear in Appendix A, "Answers to the 'Do I Know This Already?' Quizzes and Q&A Sections.")

> **NOTE** The questions should be answered in order, and the later questions assume that the configuration changes needed to correct previous problems have already been applied. For instance, question 4 assumes that the configuration changes needed to resolve questions 1 though 3 have been applied to the configurations listed in the chapter when considering the answer to question 4.

1. The VPN session is established, but no traffic, or just one-way traffic, is passing between the Boston firewall and Los Angeles firewall. Ellen starts debugging the problem using **debug icmp trace**. She pings the other end of the VPN node and gets the following results:

   ```
   LOCAL-PIX(config)#
   609001: Built local-host inside:10.10.2.21
   106014: Deny inbound icmp src outside:10.10.10.31 dst
   inside:10.10.2.21 (type 8, code 0)106014: Deny inbound icmp src
   outside:10.10.10.31 dst
   inside:10.10.2.21 (type 8, code 0)
   106014: Deny inbound icmp src outside:10.10.10.31 dst
   inside:10.10.2.21 (type 8, code 0)
   106014: Deny inbound icmp src outside:10.10.10.31 dst
   inside:10.10.2.21 (type 8., code 0)
   106014: Deny inbound icmp src outside:10.10.10.31 dst
   inside:10.10.2.21 (type 8, code 0)
   609002: Teardown local-host inside:10.10.2.21duration 0:00:15
   ```

   What do these results indicate and what could be causing this problem? How would you help Ellen resolve this issue?

2. Eric cannot get the VPN tunnel to work from HQ to the Atlanta branch office. He starts a debug and gets the following results:

   ```
   crypto-isakmp-process-block: src 10.10.10.40, dest 10.10.3.34
   VPN Peer: ISAKMP: Added new peer: ip:10.10.10.40 Total VPN Peers:1
   VPN Peer: ISAKMP: Peer ip:10.10.10.40 Ref cnt incremented to:1
     Total VPN Peers:1
   OAK-MM exchange
   ISAKMP (0): processing SA payload. message ID = 0

   ISAKMP (0): Checking ISAKMP transform 1 against priority 10 policy
   ISAKMP:      encryption DES-CBC
   ISAKMP:      hash MD5
   ISAKMP:      default group 1
   ISAKMP:      auth pre-share
   ISAKMP:      life type in seconds
   ISAKMP:      life duration (basic) of 2400
   ISAKMP (0): atts are acceptable. Next payload is 0
   ISAKMP (0): SA is doing pre-shared key authentication using id type ID-IPV4
    -ADDR
   ```

```
return status is IKMP-NO-ERROR
crypto-isakmp-process-block: src 10.10.10.40, dest 10.10.3.34
OAK-MM exchange

ISAKMP (0): processing KE payload. message ID = 0
ISAKMP (0): processing NONCE payload. message ID = 0
ISAKMP (0): processing vendor id payload
ISAKMP (0): processing vendor id payload
ISAKMP (0): remote peer supports dead peer detection
ISAKMP (0): processing vendor id payload
ISAKMP (0): speaking to another IOS box!

return status is IKMP-NO-ERROR
crypto-isakmp-process-block: src 10.10.10.40, dest 10.10.3.34
OAK-MM exchange
ISAKMP (0): processing ID payload. message ID = 0
ISAKMP (0): processing HASH payload. message ID = 0
ISAKMP (0): SA has been authenticated

ISAKMP (0): ID payload
        next-payload : 8
        type         : 1
        protocol     : 17
        port         : 500
        length       : 8
ISAKMP (0): Total payload length: 12
return status is IKMP-NO-ERROR
crypto-isakmp-process-block: src 10.10.10.40, dest 10.10.3.34
ISAKMP (0): processing NOTIFY payload 24578 protocol 1
        spi 0, message ID = 2457631438
ISAKMP (0): processing notify INITIAL-CONTACTIPSEC(key-engine): got a queue
  event...
IPSEC(key-engine-delete-sas): rec'd delete notify from ISAKMP
IPSEC(key-engine-delete-sas): delete all SAs shared with   10.10.10.40

return status is IKMP-NO-ERR-NO-TRANS
crypto-isakmp-process-block: src 10.10.10.40, dest 10.10.3.34
OAK-QM exchange
oakley-process-quick-mode:
OAK-QM-IDLE
ISAKMP (0): processing SA payload. message ID = 133935992
ISAKMP : Checking IPSec proposal 1
ISAKMP: transform 1, ESP-DES
ISAKMP:    attributes in transform:
ISAKMP:       encaps is 1
ISAKMP:       SA life type in seconds
ISAKMP:       SA life duration (basic) of 28800
ISAKMP:       SA life type in kilobytes
ISAKMP:       SA life duration (VPI) of  0x0 0x46 0x50 0x0
ISAKMP:       authenticator is HMAC-MD5
IPSEC(validate-proposal): invalid local address 10.10.3.34
ISAKMP (0): atts not acceptable. Next payload is 0
ISAKMP (0): SA not acceptable!
ISAKMP (0): sending NOTIFY message 14 protocol 0
return status is IKMP-ERR-NO-RETRANS
crypto-isakmp-process-block: src 10.10.10.40, dest 10.10.3.34
ISAKMP (0:0): phase 2 packet is a duplicate of a previous packet.
```

What could be the cause of this problem?

3. Bruce is having problems establishing a VPN session to the Atlanta office. He gets the following debug results:

    ```
    IPSEC(crypto-map-check): crypto map BranchVPN 20 incomplete. No peer or
        access-list specified. Packet discarded
    ```

    What is causing this problem, and how would you help Bruce successfully establish a VPN tunnel to the Atlanta office?

4. The web administrator in Los Angeles needs to maintain the web servers in the DMZ from the internal network using Terminal Services (Transmission Control Protocol [TCP] port 3389). Is the firewall in Los Angeles configured to allow this access? Explain your answer.

5. The web administrator in Los Angeles also needs to administer the web servers in Boston and Atlanta. Are the three firewalls configured to allow this access? Explain your answer.

6. The web server 172.16.1.13 needs to access an Oracle database server that sits on a segment connected to the internal network at 10.10.11.221. The web server initiates the connection on TCP port 1521 and retrieves inventory data. Can this connection be completed? Explain your answer.

7. The web server 172.16.1.13 needs to access an Oracle database server on the DMZ in Boston using the address 172.16.2.11. The web server initiates the connection on TCP port 1521 to retrieve financial data. Can this connection be completed? Explain your answer.

8. Is the configuration solution to question 7 a good idea? Explain your answer.

9. The company has installed an FTP server on the DMZ segment in Los Angeles that customers can access to download updates. The FTP server address is 172.16.1.9. Can all external users access this FTP server? Explain your answer.

10. The exchange server is installed on the DMZ segment in Los Angeles using the address 172.16.1.14. The firewall is configured to allow Simple Mail Transfer Protocol (SMTP) access for inbound mail and Secure Sockets Layer (SSL) access for users who want to connect using Outlook Web Access over an HTTP over SSL (HTTPS) connection. Will any users be able to receive their mail with this configuration? Explain your answer.

11. What needs to be done in Los Angeles to allow access to the mail server?

Answers to the "Do I Know This Already?" Quizzes and Q&A Sections

Chapter 1

"Do I Know This Already?" Quiz

1. e
2. b, c, and e
3. a
4. c
5. d
6. b
7. e
8. c
9. b
10. b

Q&A

1. What is the difference between the network security policy and the network security process?

   Answer: The network security process is an ongoing process that ensures the constant improvement of security in accordance with the security policy.

2. For unstructured threats, what is the normal anatomy of an attack?

   Answer: The attacker first gains information about the network by launching a reconnaissance attack against specific targets and then attempts to exploit vulnerabilities discovered during the reconnaissance.

3. What information can you gain from a ping sweep?

    Answer: Replies from ICMP requests will tell you which addresses on the network are assigned to running systems.

4. What is the single most important component when implementing defense in depth?

    Answer: There is no single most important component. Defense in depth is a combination of products, processes, and architecture used to identify and mitigate attacks.

5. Why could an organization be legally responsible if its systems are compromised during an attack?

    Answer: Organizations are expected to exercise "reasonable care" to secure their networks and resources.

Chapter 2

"Do I Know This Already?" Quiz

1. a
2. c
3. b
4. b
5. b
6. b
7. b
8. d
9. c
10. b

Q&A

1. What items does a packet filter look at to determine whether to allow the traffic?

    Answer: Source address/port, destination address/port, and protocol.

2. What are the advantages of the Cisco Security Appliance family of firewalls over competing firewall products?

Answer: The Cisco Security Appliance has a single embedded operating system, the Adaptive Security Algorithm, cut-through proxy, and redundancy.

3. How many Security Appliances can you operate in a high-availability cluster?

    Answer: The Security Appliance can be configured in a failover configuration consisting of two firewalls.

4. What is the ASA, and how does the Cisco Security Appliance use it?

    Answer: The Adaptive Security Algorithm is what the Security Appliance uses to perform stateful inspection. The ASA not only tracks the session information in the state table but also randomly generates TCP sequence numbers to ensure that a session cannot be hijacked.

5. Why is cut-through proxy more efficient than traditional proxy?

    Answer: Cut-through proxy is a feature that the Cisco Security Appliance uses to authenticate and authorize a user during the initial creation of the session. Cut-through proxy uses the ASA to track session information but does not perform any proxy services. This greatly increases the firewall's performance compared to traditional proxy firewalls.

6. What are the advantages of a real-time embedded system?

    Answer: The advantages are improved security, functionality, and performance.

Chapter 3

"Do I Know This Already?" Quiz

1. b
2. a
3. b
4. d
5. b
6. e
7. b
8. e
9. d
10. c

Q&A

1. What is the ASA, and how does Cisco PIX Firewall use it?

    Answer: The ASA is an algorithm used by the PIX Firewall to provide better security than packet filters and better performance than application proxies.

2. Why does the ASA generate random TCP sequence numbers?

    Answer: The initial TCP sequence numbers for outbound connections are randomly generated by the Security Appliance to greatly reduce the chances of an inbound TCP session being hijacked.

3. What components of a TCP session does the ASA write to the state table to create a session object?

    Answer:

    — Source IP and port

    — Destination IP and port

    — TCP sequencing information

    — Additional TCP and UDP flags

    — A new random TCP sequence number

4. What can cause a session object to be deleted from the state table?

    Answer: The session is not authorized by the security policy, the session has ended, or the session has timed out.

5. What are the three ways to initiate a cut-through proxy session?

    Answer: Initiate an HTTP, FTP, or Telnet session.

6. What X.509 certificates do SCEP and the Security Appliance support?

    Answer:

    — Entrust Technologies, Inc.—Entrust/PKI 4.0

    — Microsoft Corp.—Windows 2000 Certificate Server 5.0

    — VeriSign—Onsite 4.5

    — Baltimore Technologies—UniCERT 3.05

7. How many physical interfaces does the PIX 515E support?

Answer: PIX 515E supports up to six 10/100 interfaces.

8. What is the lowest model number of the PIX Firewall family to support failover?

Answer: The PIX 515E is the lowest model to support failover.

9. What are two methods of managing a Cisco ASA Security Appliance?

Answer:

— Command-line interface (CLI)

— Cisco Adaptive Security Device Manager (ASDM)

10. List four advantages of the ASA.

Answer:

— It is more secure than packet filtering.

— It has greater performance than application proxy.

— It can guard against session hijacking.

— It is part of the embedded PIX operating system.

11. List the three parts to a Modular Policy.

Answer:

— A *class-map* identifies the type of traffic flow that the MPF will use. The flow type is packet specific and can be any packet type, such as a VPN tunnel, voice traffic, or basic IP traffic.

— The *policy-map* assigns one or more actions to traffic flows specified by a class-map. For example, all basic IP traffic entering a site would be packet inspected and rate limited through a policy-map.

— The *service policy* assigns one or more policy-maps to an interface.

Chapter 4

"Do I Know This Already?" Quiz

1. d
2. a
3. b
4. d
5. b
6. d
7. c
8. c
9. a, d
10. d

Q&A

1. How many ways can you access the PIX Firewall?

   Answer: You can access the PIX Firewall through Telnet, SSH, PDM, and the console port.

2. What is the command to change the Telnet password?

   Answer: passwd or Password

3. Which command would you use to view the privilege level assigned to the **access-list** command?

   Answer: show running-config privilege command access-list

4. Which version of SSH does PIX Firewall support?

   Answer: The ASA Security Appliance supports SSH version 1.

5. What is the activation key?

   Answer: The activation key is the license key or number for the ASA Security Appliance.

6. Give one reason why you would need to change the activation key on your Security Appliance.

   Answer:

   — Your Cisco ASA 5100 does not have failover activated.

   — Your PIX Firewall does not currently have VPN-DES or VPN-3DES encryption enabled.

   — You are upgrading from a connection-based license to a feature-based license.

7. How many privilege levels are available on the PIX Firewall?

   Answer: 16

8. How do you determine which version of the Security Appliance operating system is installed?

   Answer: The **show version** command displays the version information on your PIX Firewall.

9. Which command would you use to create locally a user called mason with a password of Fr33 on the PIX Firewall?

   Answer: username mason password Fr33

10. How do you find out what your activation key is?

    Answer: Use the **show activation-key** command for versions earlier than 6.2, and use the **show version** command for Version 6.2 and later.

Chapter 5

"Do I Know This Already?" Quiz

1. d
2. c
3. b
4. b
5. d

6. b

7. a

8. a

9. b

10. e

Q&A

1. What is the difference between TCP and UDP?

Answer: TCP is a connection-oriented protocol, and UDP is a connectionless protocol.

2. What is the default security for traffic origination on the inside network segment going to the outside network?

Answer: By default, traffic is permitted from the inside (higher security level) to the outside (lower security level) network as long as the appropriate **nat/global/static** command has been configured.

3. True or false: You can have multiple translations in a single connection.

Answer: False. Multiple connections can take place in a single translation.

4. What commands are required to configure NAT on a Cisco Security Appliance?

Answer: **nat** and **global** are required to configure NAT on a Cisco Security Appliance.

5. How many nodes can you hide behind a single IP address when configuring PAT?

Answer: You can hide approximately 64,000 nodes. This is determined by subtracting the 1024 previously assigned ports from the 65,535 available ports. It is also estimated that that number could be significantly lower because there might be multiple connections occurring behind a single translation.

6. What is an embryonic connection?

Answer: An embryonic connection is a half-open TCP session.

7. What is the best type of translation to use to allow connections to web servers from the Internet?

Answer: Static translations provide a one-to-one translation from external to internal/DMZ addresses.

8. How does the Cisco Security Appliance handle outbound DNS requests?

   Answer: A Cisco Security Appliance allows multiple outbound queries but allows only a single query response. All responses after the first are dropped.

9. True or false: The quickest way to clear the translation table is to reboot the Cisco Security Appliance.

   Answer: False. The command **clear xlate** is the fastest method of clearing the translation table.

10. True or false: If you configure a static translation for your web server, everyone can connect to it.

    Answer: False. You also need to configure an ACL or conduit allowing the connection.

11. What does a Security Appliance, such as a PIX Firewall, normally change when allowing a TCP handshake between nodes on different interfaces and performing NAT?

    Answer: The Cisco Security Appliance translates the local address to a global address and randomly generates a new initial TCP sequence number.

12. What does the Cisco Security Appliance normally change when allowing a TCP handshake between nodes on different interfaces and performing PAT?

    Answer: The Cisco Security Appliance changes the local address and source port to a global address and random port and generates a random initial TCP sequence number.

13. True or false: TCP is a much better protocol than UDP because it does handshakes and randomly generates TCP sequence numbers.

    Answer: False. Each transport protocol has its strengths and weaknesses. UDP is connectionless and has much less overhead than TCP; however, TCP is more reliable.

14. What are the two commands (syntax) to perform NAT of all internal addresses?

    Answer:

    - LabCSA(config)# **nat (inside) 1 0.0.0.0 0.0.0.0**
    - LabCSA(config)# **nat (inside) 1 0 0**

15. When would you want to configure NAT and PAT for the same inside segment?

Answer: You would want to configure NAT and PAT for the same inside segment when you have more internal users than addresses in the global pool. If you use only PAT, you limit all of your local addresses to a single global address.

16. What is RFC 1918?

Answer: RFC 1918 defines specific address ranges that are not routable across the Internet. These addresses are reserved for private networks.

17. Why is there an *id* field in the **nat** command?

Answer: The **nat** command has an *id* field so that the Cisco Security Appliance can map a specific NAT statement to a global statement.

Chapter 6

"Do I Know This Already?" Quiz

1. a
2. c
3. c
4. c
5. c
6. b
7. a
8. a
9. b
10. b

Q&A

1. How do you access privileged mode?

Answer: Enter the **enable** command and the enable password to access the privileged mode.

2. What is the function of the **nameif** command?

    Answer: The **nameif** command is used to name a PIX Firewall interface.

3. Which seven commands produce a basic working configuration for a Cisco Security Appliance?

    Answer: The seven commands that are used to create a very basic PIX configuration are **nameif, security-level, interface, ip address, nat, global,** and **route**.

4. Why is the **route** command important?

    Answer: The **route** command is important because it instructs the PIX Firewall where to send a packet that arrives at its interfaces.

5. What is the command to flush out the Address Resolution Protocol (ARP) cache on a Cisco PIX Firewall?

    Answer: clear arp

6. What is the syntax to configure a MOTD banner that says, "System shall not be available on 18:00 Monday January 19th for 2 hours due to system maintenance?"

    Answer: First, enter the configuration mode on the PIX Firewall. Then, enter the following command: **banner motd System shall not be available on 18:00 Monday January 19th for 2 hours due to system maintenance.**

7. What is the command used to configure PAT on a Cisco Security Appliance?

    Answer: The NAT command, **nat** (*if-name*) *nat-id local-ip* [**netmask**], is used to configure PAT on the Cisco PIX Firewall.

8. Which command releases and renews an IP address on the PIX?

    Answer: ip address dhcp

9. Give at least one reason why it is beneficial to use NTP on the Cisco PIX Firewall.

    Answer: You can use NTP on the PIX Firewall (1) for certificate revocation lists (CRL) because it is time stamp sensitive; and (2) because it makes troubleshooting events easier.

10. Why would you want to secure the NTP messages between the Cisco PIX Firewall and the NTP server?

    Answer: To prevent the Cisco PIX Firewall from synchronizing with unauthorized NTP servers.

11. What is the difference between a Security Appliance in transparent mode and a Security Appliance in routed mode?

    Answer: Transparent firewalls act like Layer 2 filtering bridges when handling traffic, while standard firewalls act like a Layer 3 routed device.

Chapter 7

"Do I Know This Already?" Quiz

1. c, d
2. c
3. a
4. b
5. c
6. a
7. e

Q&A

1. What do static NAT settings do?

    Answer: Static NAT creates a one-to-one mapping between a host/network on both the interfaces.

2. What is the difference between regular NAT and policy-based network translation?

    Answer: The policy NAT feature lets you identify traffic for address translation by specifying the source and destination addresses (or ports) in an access list, whereas regular NAT uses only source addresses/ports.

3. True or false: The following commands constitute the correct way to set up NAT on a ASA 5520?

```
pixfw(config)#access-list 120 permit ip 10.10.100.0 255.255.255.0
  172.16.1.10 255.255.255.255
pixfw(config)#access-list 130 deny ip 10.10.100.0 255.255.255.0
  172.16.22.67 255.255.255.255
pixfw(config)#nat (inside) 1 access-list 120
pixfw(config)#global (outside) 1 192.168.100.62 255.255.255.255
pixfw(config)#nat (inside) 2 access-list 130
pixfw(config)#global (outside) 2 192.168.100.25 255.255.255.255
```

    Answer: False. Deny statements are not supported in policy NAT.

4. Which command would you use to create a description/remark "Linda's group extranet server access" for access list 112?

Answer: access-list 112 remark Linda's group extranet server access

5. How would you change the default port assignment for FTP?

Answer: To change the port for FTP inspection or any form of inspection, you must create a class map that directs traffic from that specific port into a traffic class for inspection.

6. What is the function of object groups?

Answer: Object groups are used to group hosts/networks, services, protocols, and icmp-types. Object grouping provides a way to reduce the number of access rules required to describe complex security policies.

7. What are the four object type options available when you are creating object groups?

Answer: network, protocol, service, and icmp-type

8. How would you specify the maximum number of concurrent deny flows that can be created with an access list?

Answer: With the **access-list deny-flow-max** *num-of-flows* command.

9. What are the seven SMTP commands allowed by SMTP inspection?

Answer: HELO, MAIL, RCPT, DATA, RSET, NOOP, and QUIT

Chapter 8

Do I Know This Already?

1. 1.c

2. e

3. b, c, d, f, and g

4. c

5. e

6. a

7. d

8. f

Q&A

1. What differentiates Modular Policy Framework from classic policy maps?

Answer: A Modular Policy Framework (MPF) gives the security administrator the tools to segment traffic flows into traffic classes and to assign one or more actions to each traffic class. Traditional policy maps only allowed actions to be assigned to the total traffic flow on the Security Appliance, whereas with an MPF, HTTP traffic can have a policy separate from H.323 or ICMP.

2. What are the three parts to an MPF and what do they do?

Answer:

- A class map to create traffic classes.
- A policy map to assign one or more actions to the traffic classes.
- A service policy to assign the policy to an interface.

3. How many matches are allowed in a class map?

Answer: Multiple. Though the standard class map allows for only a single match, class maps that support tunnel groups and default-inspection statements allow multiple match criteria.

4. What is an embryonic connection?

Answer: An embryonic connection is a half-open TCP connection.

5. Which actions are available in the IPS policy configuration?

Answer: You can set how the traffic flows to the AIP-SSM sensor through two different modes: promiscuous mode and inline mode.

6. What are the feature domains and what do they do?

Answer:

- The inspect domain inspects traffic flow assigned to it.
- The IPS domain sends traffic to the AIP-SSM sensor for deep packet inspection.
- The priority domain assigns traffic flows to the low-latency queue for prioritization.
- The police domain sets rate limits and burst limits on assigned traffic flows.

- The TCP normalization domain allows the limiting of TCP and UDP connections, as well as embryonic connections.

7. How does the IPS policy handle hardware failure?

Answer: The IPS policy can handle failure in two ways. You can set the IPS to allow all traffic through the firewall that would normally be assigned to the IPS sensor through the **fail-open** command. You can also drop all traffic assigned to the IPS sensor through the **fail-close** command.

8. How many policy maps can be assigned to an interface?

Answer: There is no limit to the amount of policy maps that can be assigned to a single service map. Only one service map may be assigned to an interface.

9. Are policy maps directional, and if so, what feature groups access which directions?

Answer: Yes, and the directions for each group are as follows.

Policy Type	Single Interface Direction	Global Direction
IPS	Bidirectional	Ingress
TCP normalization; connection limits and timeouts (set-connection)	Bidirectional	Ingress
QoS policing	Egress	Egress
QoS priority queue	Egress	Egress
Application inspection	Bidirectional	Ingress

10. What does the default policy map do, and how is it applied?

Answer: The default policy map applies the default class map to predefined inspection actions:

```
policy-map global_policy
  class inspection_default
   inspect dns maximum length 512
   inspect ftp
   inspect h323 h225
   inspect h323 ras
   inspect netbios
   inspect sunrpc
   inspect rsh
   inspect rtsp
   inspect sip
   inspect skinny
   inspect esmtp
   inspect sqlnet
   inspect tftp
     inspect xdmcp
```

Chapter 9

Do I Know This Already?

1. d
2. e
3. c
4. e
5. e
6. c
7. b
8. b

Q&A

1. What are the two methods used to direct traffic flows to a security context?

   Answer: Source interface (VLAN) and Destination address

2. Using Figure 9-2, configure the security contexts for PIXFX1. Assume that Context1 to Context3 store their configuration files on the web server configs.cisco.com in the directory/configlets using the username PIXCONFIG and password CISCO123. Context 2 stores its configuration on the Flash drive. All nonadministrative contexts use the naming scheme context[x].cfg.

Figure 9-2 *Sample Security Context Network*

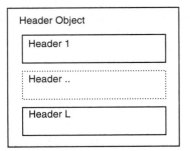

Answer:

```
pixfw1(config)# admin-context administrator
pixfw1(config)# context administrator
pixfw1(config-ctx)# allocate-interface gigabitethernet0/0
pixfw1(config-ctx)# config-url flash:/admin.cfg

pixfw1(config-ctx)# context context1
pixfw1(config-ctx)# allocate-interface gigabitethernet0/1 int1
pixfw1(config-ctx)# config-url http://PIXCONFIG:CISCO123@configs.cisco.com/configlets/
context1.cfg

pixfw1(config-ctx)# context context2
pixfw1(config-ctx)# allocate-interface gigabitethernet1/0.1int1
pixfw1(config-ctx)# allocate-interface gigabitethernet1/0.2 int2
pixfw1(config-ctx)# config-url flash:/context2.cfg

pixfw1(config-ctx)# context context3
pixfw1(config-ctx)# allocate-interface gigabitethernet1/0.2int1
pixfw1(config-ctx)# allocate-interface gigabitethernet2/0 int2
   pixfw1(config-ctx)# config-url http://PIXCONFIG:CISCO123@configs.cisco.com/
   configlets/context3.cfg
```

3. How do you enable multiple security contexts?

    Answer: To enable multiple security contexts, you must use the **mode multiple**
    [**noconfirm**] command.

4. What are the interface limitations of a security context when the firewall is in transparent
    mode?

    Answer: If a Security Appliance is configured to be a transparent firewall, each context
    can only be assigned two interfaces, with the exception of the management port, which
    can be assigned as the third interface.

5. What happens to the configuration files when multiple context mode is enabled?

    Answer: The configuration files are split into two new configuration files: the system
    configuration and the admin context configuration. Additionally, the running-config is
    saved to old_*running.cfg* in the root of Flash.

6. What are the potential problems when you change the **config-url** setting for a context
    that is live?

    Answer: If you change the **config-url** command for a context while the context is active,
    the Security Appliance will attempt to merge the new and old configurations into a single
    new configuration.

7. What are the limitations of the **allocate-interface** command?

   Answer: The mapped name configured by the **allocate-interface** command must consist of an alphabetic portion followed by a numeric portion. If a range of interfaces is specified, the alphabetic portion of the mapped name must be consistent throughout the assigned range of interfaces.

   The numeric portion of the mapped name must include the same quantity of numbers as the subinterface range.

8. What does **clear configure context** do?

   Answer: It removes all currently configured contexts on a Security Appliance.

Chapter 10

"Do I Know This Already?" Quiz

1. b
2. a
3. c
4. c
5. b
6. d
7. c
8. c
9. b

Q&A

1. What command would you use to view logs that are in memory?

   Answer: show logging buffered

2. On which port does syslogd listen by default?

   Answer: Syslogd listens on UDP port 514 by default.

3. What is the total number of logging facilities available for Cisco Security Appliance syslog configuration?

    Answer: Eight logging facilities are commonly used for syslog—facilities 16 to 23.

4. What is the command for sending syslog messages to Telnet sessions?

    Answer: logging monitor

5. For what is the **logging trap** command used?

    Answer: The **logging trap** command determines which levels of syslog messages are sent to the syslog server.

6. What is the command used to enable logging on the failover Cisco Security Appliance unit?

    Answer: logging standby

7. Why would you use the *timestamp* command parameter?

    Answer: The *timestamp* command parameter specifies timestamp values on the syslog messages sent to the syslog server for later analysis of the logs.

8. What is PFSS?

    Answer: The PIX Firewall Syslog Server (PFSS) is a Windows NT–based syslog server designed for use with the PIX Firewall.

Chapter 11

"Do I Know This Already?" Quiz

1. e
2. c
3. d
4. c
5. d
6. d
7. a
8. e

9. d

10. b

Q&A

1. What type of Ethernet tagging does the Cisco Security Appliance support?

Answer: The PIX Firewall supports 802.1Q tagging.

2. Which command do you use to configure logical interfaces?

Answer: You use the **interface** command to define one or more logical interfaces on a single physical interface.

3. What three basic configuration parameters do you need to define for each logical interface?

Answer: For each logical interface, you need to define an interface name, a VLAN ID, a security level, and an IP address.

4. What command do you use to define static routes on a PIX Firewall?

Answer: The **route** command enables you to define static routes on the PIX Firewall or any Security Appliance.

5. What is the default route, and what values do you use for the IP address and netmask when creating the default route?

Answer: The default route is a static route that is used when no other route matches the specified destination address. When configuring the default route, you use 0.0.0.0 for both the destination IP address and the network mask.

6. The ASA Security Appliance provides functionality for which two routing protocols?

Answer: The Security Appliance provides functionality for both RIP and OSPF. This is true for any Security Appliance.

7. Can a Security Appliance propagate RIP routes?

Answer: The Security Appliance only passively listens to RIP routing updates. It cannot propagate this information to other devices. It can, however, advertise a default route for one of its interfaces.

8. Which LSAs can the Security Appliance filter, and why is this important?

    Answer: OSPF routes are advertised to all the interfaces configured for OSPF. This can send information about private networks to public interfaces. Therefore, you can filter Type 3 LSAs to prevent the public interfaces from receiving information on private networks.

9. Which two commands enable you to configure LSA filtering?

    Answer: The **prefix-list** command defines which advertisements are permitted and which advertisements are not permitted (denied). The **area** command then applies this prefix list to a specific OSPF area.

10. What are the steps involved in setting up OSPF on your Security Appliance?

    Answer: To set up OSPF, you must first enable OSPF. Next, you define the Security Appliance interfaces that will run OSPF. Finally, you define the OSPF areas. Optionally, you may need to configure LSA filtering to protect private addresses.

11. Can a Security Appliance operate as a fully functional multicast router?

    Answer: The PIX Firewall, or any Security Appliance, cannot operate as a fully functional multicast router, but it can operate as a Stub Multicast Router (SMR), in which case, it proxies all IGMP requests to the actual multicast router.

12. If you have clients that cannot send IGMP messages, which command do you use to statically configure the Security Appliance to receive messages from a multicast group?

    Answer: To statically configure the Security Appliance to join a multicast group, you use the **igmp join-group** command that is available as a subcommand to the **multicast interface** command.

13. What is the range of addresses for multicast traffic?

    Answer: Multicast traffic uses Class D addresses in the range of 224.0.0.0 through 239.255.255.255.

14. If the multicast transmission source is protected by the Security Appliance, which command do you use to configure the Security Appliance to allow clients to access it?

    Answer: When the multicast traffic is coming from a protected network behind the Security Appliance, you need to use the **mroute** command to statically configure routes for the multicast traffic to the next hop.

15. Which two commands can you use to view the multicast configuration on a PIX 535 Firewall?

    Answer: To view the multicast configuration on the PIX Firewall, or any other Security Appliance, you can use the **show multicast** command to display multicast settings for one or more interfaces. The **show igmp** command displays information about one or more IGMP groups, and the **show mroute** command shows the current multicast routes.

16. Which command enables you to view the routes currently in use on the Security Appliance?

    Answer: The **show route** command enables you to view the routes currently being used by the Security Appliance.

17. Which command enables you to pass OSPF routing information between multiple OSPF domains or processes?

    Answer: The **redistribute ospf** command enables you to pass OSPF routes between multiple OSPF processes on your PIX Firewall.

18. Why would you run multiple OSPF processes on your Security Appliance?

    Answer: When you are using your Security Appliance as an ASBR OSPF router using multiple interfaces, you need to use two OSPF processes if you want to perform address filtering.

Chapter 12

"Do I Know This Already?" Quiz

1. a

2. a

3. e

4. e

5. a

6. c

7. b

8. c

9. b

10. b

11. b

Q&A

1. What are some things that trigger a failover event?

Answer: A failover event may be triggered by a loss of power, cable error, memory exhaustion, or an administrator forcing the standby.

2. What command assigns an IP address to the standby PIX Firewall?

Answer: The **failover ip address** *if-name ip-address* command assigns an IP address to the standby PIX Firewall.

3. How many PIX Firewall devices can be configured in a failover configuration?

Answer: Two PIX Firewall devices can be configured in a failover configuration.

4. What are the disadvantages of LAN-based failover?

Answer: The following are the disadvantages of LAN-based failover:

— The PIX Firewall takes longer to fail because it cannot immediately detect the loss of power of the standby unit.

— The switch between the two units can be another point of hardware failure.

— A separate interface is required for the failover link, which otherwise could have been used for normal traffic.

5. What is some of the information that is updated to the standby unit in a stateful failover configuration?

Answer: The following is some information that is updated to the standby unit in a stateful failover configuration: TCP connection table; translation table (xlate); negotiated H.323 UDP ports; port allocation table bitmap for PAT; SIP; HTTP sessions; and MGCP UDP media connections.

6. What command forces replication to the standby unit?

Answer: The **write standby** command forces replication to the standby unit.

7. What command configures a LAN-based failover?

   Answer: The **failover lan interface** *interface-name* command configures a LAN-based failover.

8. What is the default failover poll, in seconds?

   Answer: The default failover poll is 15 seconds.

9. Does configuration replication save the running configuration to Flash memory on the standby unit during normal operations?

   Answer: No, the running configuration is only stored in memory on the active unit. When a **write memory** command issued on the active unit, configuration replication causes the changes to the current configuration to be saved on the standby unit.

10. How long does it take to detect a failure?

    Answer: Network and failover communication errors are detected within two consecutive polling intervals (by default, 15-second intervals).

11. How many failover groups are allowed per Security Appliance?

    Answer: Each Security Appliance can support two failover groups.

Chapter 13

"Do I Know This Already?" Quiz

1. d
2. c
3. e
4. d
5. c
6. b
7. e
8. c
9. d
10. b
11. a, b, and c

Q&A

1. Why is **manual-ipsec** not recommended by Cisco?

   Answer: The session keys are manually coded and never change.

2. What is the difference between an access VPN and an intranet VPN?

   Answer: Access VPNs require VPN client software on the remote machine and intranet VPNs do not.

3. Which hash algorithm is configured by default for phase 1?

   Answer: SHA-1

4. What are the two methods of identifying SA peers?

   Answer: By IP address or host name

5. What happens if you have different ISAKMP policies configured on your potential SA peers, and none of them match?

   Answer: They will not be able to negotiate the connection.

6. Where do you define your authentication method?

   Answer: isakmp policy

7. What authentication types are supported for e-mail proxy services?

   Answer:
   AAA
   certificate
   mailhost
   piggyback

8. What is the default lifetime if not defined in **isakmp policy**?

   Answer: 86,400 seconds

9. Do your transform sets have to match exactly on each peer?

   Answer: No, the peers will continue to go through the transforms until they find a match. If there is no match, they will be unable to negotiate the connection.

10. What is the difference between the **isakmp** lifetime and the **crypto map** lifetime?

Answer: isakmp lifetime initiates a renegotiation of IKE based on time only; the crypto map lifetime initiates a renegotiation of the IPSec SA based on time or the amount of traffic the passes through the connection (in kilobytes).

11. What command do you use to delete any active SAs?

Answer: clear crypto isakmp sa

12. What is the command for defining a preshared key?

Answer: isakmp key string **address** peer-address **netmask** peer netmask

13. What is the first thing you should check if you are unable to establish a VPN?

Answer: You should verify connectivity prior to attempting to establish the VPN. If you have connectivity but cannot establish the VPN, you should verify that the configuration of the peers matches.

14. What commands are required to enable file browsing on a WebVPN connection?

Answer: functions file-browsing

15. What is the command to apply an access list to a crypto map?

Answer: crypto map map-name seq-num **match address** acl-name

16. What is the difference between ESP and AH?

Answer: AH does only header authentication; ESP can perform authentication of the header and the data as well as encryption.

Chapter 14

"Do I Know This Already?" Quiz

1. a

2. c

3. b

4. c

5. b

6. a, b, d

7. b

8. a, b, d

9. a

10. d

Q&A

1. Which two major components comprise the Easy VPN solution?

   Answer: The Easy VPN comprises Easy VPN Server and Easy VPN Remote feature.

2. Which three types of devices can serve as Easy VPN Servers?

   Answer: You can use Cisco Security Appliances, Cisco VPN 3000 Series Concentrators, and Cisco IOS routers as Easy VPN Servers.

3. What is DPD?

   Answer: DPD enables two IPSec peers to determine if the other is still "alive" during the lifetime of the VPN connection.

4. What is Initial Contact?

   Answer: Initial Contact enables the VPN Client to send an initial message that informs the gateway to ignore and delete any existing connections from that client, thus preventing connection problems caused by SA synchronization issues.

5. Which client platforms support the Easy VPN Remote feature?

   Answer: The Easy VPN Remote feature is supported on the Cisco VPN Software Client, Cisco VPN 3002 Hardware Client, Cisco PIX 501 and 506/506E VPN Clients, and Cisco Easy VPN Remote router clients.

6. Which router platforms can be used as Cisco Easy VPN Clients?

   Answer: The 800 Series routers, 900 Series routers, and 1700 Series routers can serve as Cisco Easy VPN Remote clients.

7. What are the six major steps that occur when the Easy VPN Remote client initiates a connection with the Easy VPN Server gateway?

   Answer: When the Easy VPN Remote client initiates a connection with the Easy VPN Server, it goes through the following six steps: (1) VPN Client initiates the IKE phase 1 process; (2) VPN Client negotiates an IKE SA; (3) Easy VPN Server accepts the SA proposal; (4) the Easy VPN Server initiates a username/password challenge; (5) mode configuration process is initiated; and (6) IKE quick mode completes the connection.

8. When initiating the VPN connection, the client can use which two IKE authentication mechanisms?

   Answer: When initiating the VPN connection, the client can use preshared keys and digital certificates for IKE authentication.

9. What is XAUTH?

   Answer: Extended authentication (XAUTH) enables the Easy VPN Server to require username/password authentication (performed by a AAA server) in order to establish the VPN connection.

10. Which two modes of operation does the Easy VPN Remote support?

    Answer: The Easy VPN Remote supports client mode and network extension mode.

11. In which Easy VPN Remote mode are the addresses of the remote system visible on the Easy VPN Server network?

    Answer: When operating in network extension mode, the remote system addresses are visible on the Easy VPN Server network. In client mode, PAT is used on the Easy VPN Remote client so the remote system addresses are not visible.

12. What feature enables the Cisco VPN Software Client to be simple to deploy and manage?

    Answer: The ability to push VPN access policies automatically from the Easy VPN Server to the Cisco VPN Software Client simplifies deployment and management.

13. Which encryption algorithms are supported by the Cisco VPN Software Client?

    Answer: The Cisco VPN Software Client supports DES, 3DES, and AES (128- and 256-bit) encryption algorithms.

14. What is SUA?

    Answer: Secure Unit Authentication (SUA) enables the Easy VPN Remote server to require one-time passwords, two-factor authentication, and similar authentication schemes before the establishment of a VPN tunnel to the Easy VPN Server.

15. What is IUA?

    Answer: Individual User Authentication (IUA) causes the hosts on the remote protected network to be individually authenticated based on the IP address of the inside host.

16. What is PPPoE?

    Answer: Point-to-Point Protocol over Ethernet (PPPoE) provides an authenticated method for assigning IP addresses to client systems over broadband connections by combining PPP and Ethernet.

17. What type of DHCP functionality does the Security Appliance provide?

    Answer: Any Cisco Security Appliance provides both DHCP server and DHCP client functionality. As a DHCP server, the Security Appliance provides hosts protected by the firewall with the network parameters necessary for them to access the enterprise or corporate network. As a DHCP client, the Security Appliance can obtain its own IP address and network mask and, optionally, a default route from the DHCP server.

18. Which command enables you to configure the Security Appliance to pass configuration parameters learned by using either PPPoE or DHCP to its DHCP clients?

    Answer: To enable the Security Appliance to pass the learned DHCP configuration parameters automatically to its DHCP clients, you use the **dhcpd auto_config** command.

Chapter 15

Do I Know This Already?

1. c
2. f
3. d
4. d
5. d
6. d
7. a, b, d
8. a
9. a
10. e

Q&A

1. What is a translation exemption rule?

    Answer: A translation exemption rule specifies traffic that is exempt from being translated.

2. What are the nine main configuration buttons on the ASDM?

   Answer: The nine main ASDM button are Interfaces, Security Policies, NAT, VPN, IPS, Routing, Building Blocks, Device Administration, and Properties.

3. How do you access ASDM?

   Answer: ASDM is accessed via a web browser using SSL or through the standalone ASDM Application installer. (For instance, https://interface IP, where interface IP represents the IP address of a Security Appliance interface that has been configured to allow HTTP access using the http *local_ip [mask] [interface]* command.)

4. What version of Cisco Security Appliance software is required to run ASDM version 5.0?

   Answer: Cisco Security Appliance version 7.0 or later is required to run ASDM 5.0.

5. Which models of Cisco Security Appliance are supported by ASDM?

   Answer: PIX 515/515E, 525, and 535 are supported by ASDM. ASA 5510, 5520, and 5540 are also supported.

6. What versions of Windows does ASDM support?

   Answer: Windows XP and Windows 2000 are supported by ASDM.

7. Where does ASDM reside?

   Answer: ASDM resides in the Security Appliance Flash memory or can be installed locally on workstations that are frequently used to manage Security Appliances.

8. What is the quickest method to configure site-to-site VPN using ASDM?

   Answer: The quickest method to configure site-to-site VPN using ASDM is to use the VPN Wizard.

9. What is the command to install or upgrade ASDM on the Security Appliance?

   Answer: There are two steps that are required to install or upgrade the ASDM image on a Security Appliance. First, the **copy tftp flash:asdm** command is used to install or upgrade ASDM on the Security Appliance. After the new image has been downloaded and saved in Flash memory, you must tell the Security Appliance that it should use this new image for ASDM. Use the **asdm image flash:** command to set this.

Chapter 16

"Do I Know This Already?" Quiz

1. a
2. b
3. d
4. a
5. a
6. c
7. c
8. d
9. a
10. c

Q&A

1. With what two URL-filtering servers does the Security Appliance work?

   Answer: The Security Appliance works with the Websense Enterprise and N2H2 Sentian servers.

2. What command filters out Java applets from HTML pages?

   Answer: The filter java port *local-ip local-mask foreign-ip foreign-mask* command filters out Java applets form HTML pages.

3. Why are Java applets and ActiveX objects considered a threat?

   Answer: Java applets and ActiveX objects are considered a threat because they can be used to execute malicious tasks on the network and the local machine.

4. How does the Cisco Security Appliance filter Java applets and ActiveX objects?

   Answer: Java and ActiveX filtering of HTML files is performed by selectively replacing the <APPLET> </APPLET> tags and the <OBJECT CLASSID> </OBJECT CLASSID> tags with comments.

5. What is the command to designate or identify the URL-filtering server?

   Answer: The command to designate or identify the URL-filtering server is url-server.

6. Which Security Appliance version supports the Websense URL-filtering server?

   Answer: Cisco PIX Firewall Version 5.3 and later support the Websense URL-filtering server.

7. What is the longest URL filter that is supported by Cisco Security Appliance?

   Answer: The longest URL filter supported by Cisco Security Appliance is 6 KB.

8. What is the command to filter URLs?

   Answer: The command to filter URLs is **filter url**.

9. How would you configure the Security Appliance to buffer the response from a web server if its response is faster than that from the N2H2 or Websense URL-filtering server on the Security Appliance?

   The **url-cache** command provides a configuration option to buffer the response from web servers that respond faster than the available URL-filtering servers.

Chapter 17

"Do I Know This Already?" Quiz

1. b
2. c
3. a
4. b, d
5. d
6. c
7. d
8. b, c
9. b

Q&A

1. What is the relationship between the Cisco Security Appliance and the AAA server?

    Answer: The Cisco Security Appliance acts as the AAA client to the Cisco Secure ACS (AAA Server). Although the Security Appliance acts as the AAA client, it is referred to as the network access server (NAS) when configuring the Cisco Secure ACS.

2. Name three methods used to authenticate to the Cisco Security Appliance.

    Answer: HTTP, Telnet, and FTP are the three methods used to authenticate to the Cisco Security Appliance.

3. How does the Cisco Security Appliance process cut-through proxy?

    Answer: The user connects to the Security Appliance using HTTP, FTP, or Telnet, and the Security Appliance either authenticates to a local database or forwards the authentication request to the AAA server. After the authentication is completed, the Security Appliance allows whatever connection is authorized by the rulebase for that user.

4. What are the main differences between RADIUS and TACACS+?

    Answer: RADIUS is connectionless and combines the authentication components. TACACS+ is connection-oriented and sends the authentication and authorization separately.

5. What patch level must you have Windows 2000 Professional configured to before you install Cisco Secure ACS?

    Answer: Trick question . . . Cisco Secure ACS must be installed on Windows 2000 Server.

6. Why is it important to authenticate a user before you complete authorization?

    Answer: Permissions can be assigned only after the user account has been authenticated.

7. What are the three layers of authentication?

    Answer: The three layers of authentication are something you know (password), something you have (token), and something you are (biometrics).

8. What is the purpose of the Explain button during the Cisco Secure ACS installation?

    Answer: Clicking the **Explain** button opens a window that explains the possible configuration options for the window in which the button appears.

9. What do you need to verify before installing Cisco Secure ACS?

   Answer: You need to verify that the systems are up to date, meet the minimum hardware/browser requirements, and have connectivity with the Cisco Security Appliance (NAS).

10. Why is it important to have Internet Explorer up to date on your Cisco Secure ACS?

    Answer: Cisco Secure ACS is managed via a browser-based web interface and has specific minimum browser requirements.

11. True or false: With authorization configured, cut-through proxy authenticates users and then allows them to connect to anything.

    Answer: False. Cut-through proxy allows users to access only resources to which they have been authorized access.

12. True or false: The Cisco Secure ACS installation on Windows Server is a relatively simple, wizard-based installation.

    Answer: True. The Cisco Secure ACS installation uses an installation wizard.

Chapter 18

"Do I Know This Already?" Quiz

1. c
2. e
3. a, b, d
4. b
5. c
6. c, d
7. b
8. a
9. a
10. b
11. c

Q&A

1. Both your Cisco Security Appliance and your Cisco Secure ACS are configured for TACACS+, but you cannot configure the downloadable Security Appliance ACLs. What is the problem?

   Answer: Downloadable ACLs are supported only by RADIUS.

2. What is the command to get authorization to work with access lists?

   Answer: The command to get authorization to work with access lists is **aaa authorization match** *acl-name if-name server-tag.*

3. What Cisco Secure ACS window is used to configure the Security Appliance, and what is the firewall considered?

   Answer: The Security Appliance is configured as an AAA client in the Network Configuration window.

4. How do you put text messages into the logon prompt for a Telnet session?

   Answer: You use the **auth-prompt** command put text messages into the logon prompt for a Telnet session.

5. What three messages can you change with the **auth-prompt** command?

   Answer: You can change the prompt, accept, and reject messages with the **auth-prompt** command.

6. If your **timeout uauth** is set to 0:58:00, when is the user prompted to reauthenticate after the session times out?

   Answer: By default, **timeout uauth absolute** does not prompt the user to reauthenticate until they start a new connection after the uauth timer has expired.

7. What two formats can logs be written to using the Cisco Secure ACS?

   Answer: Logs are written to either the CSV or ODBC formats.

8. You have added a new RSA SecurID Token Server to the network. In which two places do you configure the Cisco Secure ACS to use it?

   Answer: The RSA SecurID Token Server must be configured as an external user database, and you must select it for password authentication in the User Setup window.

9. What commands are most commonly used to check your AAA configuration on the Security Appliance?

   Answer: The **show aaa** or **show aaa-server** commands are most commonly used to check the AAA configuration on the Security Appliance.

10. What is the total number of AAA servers to which the Security Appliance can connect?

    Answer: The total number of AAA servers that the Security Appliance can connect to is 196 (14 groups, each group containing a maximum of 14 servers).

11. How do you disable caching of user authentication?

    Answer: You use the **timeout uauth** 0 command to disable caching of user authentication.

Chapter 19

"Do I Know This Already?" Quiz

1. d
2. c
3. d
4. c
5. b
6. d
7. c
8. b
9. c
10. b

Q&A

1. Which PIX feature mitigates a DoS attack using a rewritten ICMP datagram?

   Answer: ICMP inspection mitigates ally ICMP-based SYN and spoofed broadcast attacks.

2. On which port does the Security Appliance inspect for H.323 traffic by default?

   Answer: Port 1720

3. How do you enable the Security Appliance Mail inspection feature?

   Answer: The Mail inspection feature is enabled by default. If it is disabled, it can be enabled by using the **fixup protocol smtp** command in class-map configuration mode within a policy map.

4. What are some of the Security Appliance limitations on CTIQBE application inspection?

   Answer: Some of the limitations of the application inspection for CTIQBE include 1) stateful failover of CTIQBE calls is not supported; 2) CTIQBE messages that are fragmented across multiple TCP packets are not supported.

5. How do you install a new IPS image on an AIP-SSM module?

   Answer: There are two steps to installing a new IPS image on an AIP-SSM module. First, you need to run the **hw-module module 1 recover configure** command. Use this command to define where the IPS image is located and all the network settings associated with getting to that location. Then, use the **hw-module module 1 recover boot** command to install and reset the AIP-SSM module with the new image.

6. Which policies are available in the Cisco Security IPS configuration?

   Answer: alarm, drop, reset

7. How does DNS inspection on the Cisco Security Appliance prevent DoS attacks that exploit DNS?

   Answer: The Security Appliance allows only a single DNS response for outgoing DNS requests. Any other responses are dropped.

8. What basic configurations are required to fully enable IPS features on a Security Appliance?

   Answer: The hostname must be set for the module, an IP address must be assigned to the external 10/100/1000 Ethernet port, the Telnet server must be enabled, the HTTP server must be enabled, and the main ACL must allow you into the module.

9. How does the Mail inspection feature prevent SMTP-related attacks?

   Answer: Mail inspection allows only a restricted set of SMTP commands, namely, **HELO, MAIL, RCPT, DATA, RSET, NOOP,** and **QUIT.** It can also allow a limited set of **ESMTP** commands through **AUTH, DATA, EHLO, ETRN, SAML, SEND, SOML,** and **VRFY.**

10. How do you enable MGCP application inspection for call agents and gateways using the default ports?

Answer: Use the **fixup protocol mgcp 2427** and **fixup protocol mgcp 2727** commands.

Chapter 20

1. The VPN session is established, but no traffic, or just one-way traffic, is passing between the Boston firewall and Los Angeles firewall. Ellen starts debugging the problem using **debug icmp trace**. She pings the other end of the VPN node and gets the following results:

```
LOCAL-PIX(config)#
609001: Built local-host inside:10.10.2.21
106014: Deny inbound icmp src outside:10.10.10.31 dst
inside:10.10.2.21 (type 8, code 0)106014: Deny inbound icmp src
outside:10.10.10.31 dst
inside:10.10.2.21 (type 8, code 0)
106014: Deny inbound icmp src outside:10.10.10.31 dst
inside:10.10.2.21 (type 8, code 0)
106014: Deny inbound icmp src outside:10.10.10.31 dst
inside:10.10.2.21 (type 8., code 0)
106014: Deny inbound icmp src outside:10.10.10.31 dst
inside:10.10.2.21 (type 8, code 0)
609002: Teardown local-host inside:10.10.2.21duration 0:00:15
```

What do these results indicate and what could be causing this problem? How would you help Ellen resolve this issue?

Answer: The sysopt connection IPSec statement is missing from the configuration on the local PIX (Boston) and needs to be added. By default on the PIX Firewall, any inbound session must be explicitly permitted by a conduit or access list statement. With IPSec-protected traffic, the secondary access list check could be redundant. To ensure that IPSec-authenticated inbound sessions are always permitted, make sure that the configuration contains the following command:

```
sysopt connection permit-ipsec
```

2. Eric cannot get the VPN tunnel to work from HQ to the Atlanta branch office. He starts a debug and gets the following results:

```
crypto-isakmp-process-block: src 10.10.10.40, dest 10.10.3.34
VPN Peer: ISAKMP: Added new peer: ip:10.10.10.40 Total VPN Peers:1
VPN Peer: ISAKMP: Peer ip:10.10.10.40 Ref cnt incremented to:1
  Total VPN Peers:1
OAK-MM exchange
ISAKMP (0): processing SA payload. message ID = 0

ISAKMP (0): Checking ISAKMP transform 1 against priority 10 policy
ISAKMP:      encryption DES-CBC
ISAKMP:      hash MD5
ISAKMP:      default group 1
ISAKMP:      auth pre-share
ISAKMP:      life type in seconds
```

```
ISAKMP:      life duration (basic) of 2400
ISAKMP (0): atts are acceptable. Next payload is 0
ISAKMP (0): SA is doing pre-shared key authentication using id type ID-IPV4
 -ADDR
return status is IKMP-NO-ERROR
crypto-isakmp-process-block: src 10.10.10.40, dest 10.10.3.34
OAK-MM exchange

ISAKMP (0): processing KE payload. message ID = 0
ISAKMP (0): processing NONCE payload. message ID = 0
ISAKMP (0): processing vendor id payload
ISAKMP (0): processing vendor id payload
ISAKMP (0): remote peer supports dead peer detection
ISAKMP (0): processing vendor id payload
ISAKMP (0): speaking to another IOS box!

return status is IKMP-NO-ERROR
crypto-isakmp-process-block: src 10.10.10.40, dest 10.10.3.34
OAK-MM exchange
ISAKMP (0): processing ID payload. message ID = 0
ISAKMP (0): processing HASH payload. message ID = 0
ISAKMP (0): SA has been authenticated

ISAKMP (0): ID payload
        next-payload : 8
        type         : 1
        protocol     : 17
        port         : 500
        length       : 8
ISAKMP (0): Total payload length: 12
return status is IKMP-NO-ERROR
crypto-isakmp-process-block: src 10.10.10.40, dest 10.10.3.34
ISAKMP (0): processing NOTIFY payload 24578 protocol 1
        spi 0, message ID = 2457631438
ISAKMP (0): processing notify INITIAL-CONTACTIPSEC(key-engine): got a queue
  event...
IPSEC(key-engine-delete-sas): rec'd delete notify from ISAKMP
IPSEC(key-engine-delete-sas): delete all SAs shared with   10.10.10.40

return status is IKMP-NO-ERR-NO-TRANS
crypto-isakmp-process-block: src 10.10.10.40, dest 10.10.3.34
OAK-QM exchange
oakley-process-quick-mode:
OAK-QM-IDLE
ISAKMP (0): processing SA payload. message ID = 133935992
ISAKMP : Checking IPSec proposal 1
ISAKMP: transform 1, ESP-DES
ISAKMP:    attributes in transform:
ISAKMP:       encaps is 1
ISAKMP:       SA life type in seconds
ISAKMP:       SA life duration (basic) of 28800
ISAKMP:       SA life type in kilobytes
ISAKMP:       SA life duration (VPI) of  0x0 0x46 0x50 0x0
ISAKMP:       authenticator is HMAC-MD5
IPSEC(validate-proposal): invalid local address 10.10.3.34
ISAKMP (0): atts not acceptable. Next payload is 0
```

```
ISAKMP (0): SA not acceptable!
ISAKMP (0): sending NOTIFY message 14 protocol 0
return status is IKMP-ERR-NO-RETRANS
crypto-isakmp-process-block: src 10.10.10.40, dest 10.10.3.34
ISAKMP (0:0): phase 2 packet is a duplicate of a previous packet.
```

What could be the cause of this problem?

Answer: The crypto map has not been applied to the correct interface. This is a common problem. Examining the Atlanta configuration, you notice that the crypto map has been applied to the DMZ instead of the outside interface. To fix the problem, apply the crypto map to the outside interface using the following command:

```
crypto map BranchVPN interface outside
```

3. Bruce is having problems establishing a VPN session to the Atlanta office. He gets the following debug results:

```
IPSEC(crypto-map-check): crypto map BranchVPN 20 incomplete. No peer or
    access-list specified. Packet discarded
```

What is causing this problem, and how would you help Bruce successfully establish a VPN tunnel to the Atlanta office?

Answer: The crypto map statements on both peers must match each other. Examining the configuration reveals that the match address statement (for Atlanta) is missing from the HQ-PIX crypto map. The following command needs to be added to the HQ-PIX configuration:

```
crypto map BranchVPN 20 match address Atlanta
```

4. The web administrator in Los Angeles needs to maintain the web servers in the DMZ from the internal network using Terminal Services (Transmission Control Protocol [TCP] port 3389). Is the firewall in Los Angeles configured to allow this access? Explain your answer.

Answer: Yes. Since the web administrator is coming from the inside interface, which has a security level of 100, and is going to the DMZ interface, which has a security level of 70, the traffic is allowed without a specific access list. Traffic from a higher-security-level interface is automatically allowed to traverse to a lower-security-level interface without a conduit or access list.

5. The web administrator in Los Angeles also needs to administer the web servers in Boston and Atlanta. Are the three firewalls configured to allow this access? Explain your answer.

Answer: No. Although VPNs are configured between Los Angeles and the other two locations (and the sysopt connection permit IPSec line is in the configuration), the VPNs permit traffic only between each location's internal network segments. To access the web servers, you need to configure a VPN connection from the internal network in Los Angeles to the DMZ segments of Boston and Atlanta.

6. The web server 172.16.1.13 needs to access an Oracle database server that sits on a segment connected to the internal network at 10.10.11.221. The web server initiates the connection on TCP port 1521 and retrieves inventory data. Can this connection be completed? Explain your answer.

    Answer: No. Although an access list allows traffic between the web server and the database server on port 1521, there is no route to the 10.10.11.X network segment. Therefore, traffic for the 10.10.11.X network is routed to the default route (192.168.1.254) instead of going to the internal web server.

7. The web server 172.16.1.13 needs to access an Oracle database server on the DMZ in Boston using the address 172.16.2.11. The web server initiates the connection on TCP port 1521 to retrieve financial data. Can this connection be completed? Explain your answer.

    Answer: Yes. An access list on the Boston firewall allows the inbound connection, and static IP address translations are configured on both firewalls. An access list is not required for the web server in Los Angeles to initiate outbound connections.

8. Is the configuration solution to question 7 a good idea? Explain your answer.

    Answer: No. With the current configuration, the financial data retrieved from the database would traverse the Internet in the clear (without being encrypted). An attacker could watch this traffic and observe sensitive financial information.

9. The company has installed an FTP server on the DMZ segment in Los Angeles that customers can access to download updates. The FTP server address is 172.16.1.9. Can all external users access this FTP server? Explain your answer.

    Answer: No. The configured inbound access lists allow incoming FTP traffic to hosts 192.168.1.9 and 192.168.1.13. A static translation exists for 172.16.1.13, but there is no static translation for 172.16.1.9.

10. The exchange server is installed on the DMZ segment in Los Angeles using the address 172.16.1.14. The firewall is configured to allow Simple Mail Transfer Protocol (SMTP) access for inbound mail and Secure Sockets Layer (SSL) access for users who want to connect using Outlook Web Access over an HTTP over SSL (HTTPS) connection. Will any users be able to receive their mail with this configuration? Explain your answer.

    Answer: No. It appears that the access list named "Exchange" permits the users to access port 25 (SMTP) because it is applied to the outside interface. Unfortunately, only one access group can be applied to a specific interface for a specific traffic direction. The "inbound" access list has already been applied to the outside interface for incoming traffic.

11. What needs to be done in Los Angeles to allow access to the mail server?

Answer: By changing the access list statements labeled "Exchange" to "inbound," the statements become part of the existing access group that is already applied to the outside interface.

Index

W

X-Y-Z

CISCO SYSTEMS

Cisco Press

3 STEPS TO LEARNING

STEP 1

First-Step

STEP 2

Fundamentals

STEP 3

Networking
Technology Guides

STEP 1 **First-Step**—Benefit from easy-to-grasp explanations.
No experience required!

STEP 2 **Fundamentals**—Understand the purpose, application,
and management of technology.

STEP 3 **Networking Technology Guides**—Gain the knowledge
to master the challenge of the network.

NETWORK BUSINESS SERIES

The Network Business series helps professionals tackle the
business issues surrounding the network. Whether you are a
seasoned IT professional or a business manager with minimal
technical expertise, this series will help you understand the
business case for technologies.

Justify Your Network Investment.

Look for Cisco Press titles at your favorite bookseller today.

Visit **www.ciscopress.com/series** for details on each of these book series.

Cisco Press

NETWORKING TECHNOLOGY GUIDES

MASTER THE NETWORK

Turn to Networking Technology Guides whenever you need **in-depth knowledge of complex networking technologies.** Written by leading networking authorities, these guides offer theoretical and practical knowledge for **real-world networking applications and solutions.**

Look for Networking Technology Guides at your favorite bookseller

Cisco CallManager Best Practices:
A Cisco AVVID Solution
ISBN: 1-58705-139-7

Cisco IP Telephony: Planning, Design,
Implementation, Operation, and Optimization
ISBN: 1-58705-157-5

Cisco PIX Firewall and ASA Handbook
ISBN: 1-58705-158-3

Cisco Wireless LAN Security
ISBN: 1-58705-154-0

End-to-End QoS Network Design:
Quality of Service in LANs, WANs, and VPNs
ISBN: 1-58705-176-1

Network Security Architectures
ISBN: 1-58705-115-X

Optimal Routing Design
ISBN: 1-58705-187-7

Top-Down Network Design, Second Edition
ISBN: 1-58705-152-4

Visit **www.ciscopress.com/series** for details about Networking Technology Guides and a complete list of titles.

Learning is serious business.
Invest wisely.

CISCO SYSTEMS

 **Cisco Press**

CISCO CERTIFICATION SELF-STUDY
#1 BEST-SELLING TITLES FROM CCNA® TO CCIE®

Look for Cisco Press Certification Self-Study resources at your favorite bookseller

Learn the test topics with **Self-Study Guides**

CCNA Self-Study:
Interconnecting Cisco Network Devices (ICND)
Second Edition

Cisco authorized self-study book for CCNA® 640-801
and ICND 640-811 foundation learning

Edited by:
Steve McQuerry, CCIE® No. 6108

1-58705-142-7

Gain hands-on experience with **Practical Studies** books

CCNA® Practical Studies

Practice for CCNA exam #640-607 with
hands-on networking lab scenarios

Gary Heap, CCIE®
Lynn Maynes, CCIE

1-58720-046-5

Prepare for the exam with **Exam Certification Guides**

CCNA® Self-Study
CCNA ICND
Exam Certification Guide

The official self-study test preparation guide
for the Cisco CCNA ICND exam 640-811

Wendell Odom, CCIE® No. 1624

1-58720-083-X

Practice testing skills and build confidence with **Flash Cards and Exam Practice Packs**

CCNA® Self-Study
CCNA Flash Cards
and Exam Practice Pack
Second Edition

More than 1100 flash cards, practice questions,
and quick reference sheets for the CCNA 640-801,
INTRO 640-821, and ICND 640-811 exams

Eric Rivard
Jim Doherty

1-58720-079-1

Visit **www.ciscopress.com/series** to learn more about the Certification Self-Study product family and associated series.

Learning is serious business.
Invest wisely.

THIS BOOK IS SAFARI ENABLED

INCLUDES FREE 45-DAY ACCESS TO THE ONLINE EDITION

The Safari® Enabled icon on the cover of your favorite technology book means the book is available through Safari Bookshelf. When you buy this book, you get free access to the online edition for 45 days.

Safari Bookshelf is an electronic reference library that lets you easily search thousands of technical books, find code samples, download chapters, and access technical information whenever and wherever you need it.

TO GAIN 45-DAY SAFARI ENABLED ACCESS TO THIS BOOK:

- Go to **http://www.ciscopress.com/safarienabled**
- Complete the brief registration form
- Enter the coupon code found in the front of this book before the "Contents at a Glance" page

If you have difficulty registering on Safari Bookshelf or accessing the online edition, please e-mail customer-service@safaribooksonline.com.